RE-MAPPING THE AMERICAS

T0348102

The International Political Economy of New Regionalisms Series

The International Political Economy of New Regionalisms Series presents innovative analyses of a range of novel regional relations and institutions. Going beyond established, formal, interstate economic organizations, this essential series provides informed interdisciplinary and international research and debate about myriad heterogeneous intermediate-level interactions.

Reflective of its cosmopolitan and creative orientation, this series is developed by an international editorial team of established and emerging scholars in both the South and North. It reinforces ongoing networks of analysts in both academia and think-tanks as well as international agencies concerned with micro-, meso- and macro-level regionalisms.

Re-mapping the Americas
Trends in Region-making

Edited by

W. ANDY KNIGHT
*The University of the West Indies, St Augustine, Trinidad and Tobago
on secondment from the University of Alberta*

JULIÁN CASTRO-REA
University of Alberta, Canada

HAMID GHANY
The University of the West Indies, St Augustine, Trinidad and Tobago

Routledge
Taylor & Francis Group

LONDON AND NEW YORK

First published 2014 by Ashgate Publishing

Published 2016 by Routledge
2 Park Square, Milton Park, Abingdon, Oxfordshire OX14 4RN
711 Third Avenue, New York, NY 10017, USA

First issued in paperback 2016

Routledge is an imprint of the Taylor & Francis Group, an informa business

British Library Cataloguing in Publication Data
A catalogue record for this book is available from the British Library

The Library of Congress has cataloged the printed edition as follows:
Re-mapping the Americas : trends in region-making / edited by W. Andy Knight, Julián Castro-Rea and Hamid Ghany.
   p. cm.
 Includes bibliographical references and index.
 ISBN 978-1-4094-6402-0 (hardback)
1. Latin America—Economic conditions—21st century.
2. Latin America—Economic integration. 3. Caribbean Area—Economic conditions—21st century. 4. Caribbean Area—Economic integration. 5. Economic development—Latin America. 6. Economic development—Caribbean Area. 7. Free Trade Area of the Americas (Organization) 8. Caribbean Community. 9. Comunidad de Estados Latinoamericanos y Caribeqos. I. Knight, W. Andy, author, editor of compilation. II. Castro-Rea, Julián, author, editor of compilation. III. Ghany, Hamid A., author, editor of compilation. IV. Title: Re-mapping the Americas.
 HC125.R38 2014
 382.098—dc23

2013041420

ISBN 13: 978-1-138-26982-8 (pbk)
ISBN 13: 978-1-4094-6402-0 (hbk)

Contents

List of Tables

List of Contributors

Obijiofor Aginam is Academic Officer and Chief of Section, International Cooperation and Development in the Institute for Sustainability and Peace, United Nations University headquarters, Tokyo and concurrently Adjunct Research Professor of Law at Carleton University, Ottawa.

Greg Anderson is Associate Professor in the Department of Political Science at the University of Alberta. He holds a PhD from John Hopkins University (SAIS) in Washington, DC and teaches and researches in the areas of International Political Economy, Canada–US Relations, International Trade and Finance and US Foreign Economic Policy.

Matthew Louis Bishop is Lecturer in International Relations at The University of the West Indies, Trinidad and Tobago. He also holds an Honorary Research Fellowship from the Sheffield Political Economy Research Institute (SPERI) and a Senior Visiting Fellowship from the Royal Netherlands Institute of Southeast Asian and Caribbean Studies (KITLV).

Julián Castro-Rea (PhD, Université de Montréal) is Associate Professor of Political Science at the University of Alberta. His main area of research interest is North American politics, both from comparative and trilateral perspectives.

Joseph Y.S. Cheng is Chair and Professor of Political Science and Coordinator of the Contemporary China Research Project, City University of Hong Kong. He is the founding editor of the *Hong Kong Journal of Social Sciences* and the *Journal of Comparative Asian Development*.

Kalowatie Deonandan is Professor of Political Studies and received her BA (Hons) and MA in Political Science from York University, and her PhD from Queen's University. Her teaching and research interests include comparative politics of LAC, IR, US Foreign Policy and International Organizations.

Gaspare M. Genna is an Associate Professor of Political Science at the University of Texas at El Paso. He is an Associate Editor of *Politics & Policy*, Senior Research Fellow at the TransResearch Institute and Associate Research Fellow at the Institute on Comparative Regional Integration Studies, United Nations University.

Hamid Ghany is the former Dean of the Faculty of Social Sciences at The University of the West Indies (UWI), St Augustine Campus and a Senior Lecturer in Government. In March 2013 he was appointed a Commissioner on a new Constitution Review Commission of Trinidad and Tobago.

Norman Girvan is Professor Emeritus of The University of the West Indies. Until recently he was Professorial Research Fellow at the UWI Graduate Institute of International Relations. In 2010 he was appointed as the United Nations Secretary General's Personal Representative on the Guyana-Venezuela Border Controversy.

Fred Judson is Professor Emeritus in the Department of Political Science at the University of Alberta. He served as Department Chair from 2003 to 2006. From 1979 to 2010, he taught a variety of courses in International Relations at various universities, at both graduate and undergraduate levels.

Mark Kirton is a Senior Lecturer at the Institute of International Relations, University of the West Indies, St Augustine Campus, where he teaches graduate courses in the Global Studies programme. His current research interests include foreign policy making in LAC, citizen security in the hemisphere and contemporary regional integration initiatives.

W. Andy Knight is Director of the Institute of International Relations (IIR) at The University of the West Indies and Professor and former Chair of the Department of Political Science at the University of Alberta. Professor Knight is a Fellow of the Royal Society of Canada and former Governor of the International Development Research Centre (IDRC).

Patsy Lewis is a Senior Fellow at the Sir Arthur Lewis Institute for Social and Economic Studies (SALISES), University of the West Indies, Mona, Jamaica. Her research focuses on the developmental challenges of small states with special emphasis on international trade, regional integration movements and regionalism and international trade.

Vaughan A. Lewis is a former Prime Minister of St Lucia and a past Professor of International Relations of the Caribbean at the Institute of International Relations, The University of the West Indies, St Augustine Campus. He has held various academic positions such as Temporary Assistant Lecturer and Lecturer at different universities.

Annita Montoute has been a Lecturer at the Institute of International Relations at The University of the West Indies since July 2010. She lectures in the areas of international organizations, global governance and multilateralism at the Post Graduate Diploma and MSc levels.

Albert R. Ramdin has served as Assistant Secretary General of the Organization of American States since July 2005. The Surinamese diplomat has had a distinguished career in public service at the national and international level.

Foreword

Re-mapping the Americas:
The Western Hemisphere in the
Global Economy

The world today is characterized by change. Within the past 25 years we have seen fundamental shifts: old paradigms have lost their potency; traditional centres of power have shifted; state-to-state relationships are evolving in unexpected ways; trading systems are being transformed; national borders are increasingly porous; national and global security are now interlinked; technology has democratized access to information and upended traditional notions of competitiveness and productivity; the contemporary world is viewed by some as flat, because of globalization and technological innovations; for some people politics are still the driver of economic dynamics in the world.

In the Americas there have been specific changes as well: democracy is now an established precept in the Americas, even though it has not always delivered on its expectations and promises; the countries of this hemisphere have been exposed to new opportunities and economic gains; in the face of the global economic downturn, countries in the Americas have still made progress in poverty reduction; while points of contention remain between individual member-states of the Organization of American States (OAS), there is also a forging of new relationships; regional security issues have been brought to the fore and have demonstrated the impact of development and the potential for contagion; environmental awareness has increased and protection policies are being actively reviewed; issues of corruption and crime have become more complex, challenging our policy-makers to seek more efficient and effective solutions; traditional barriers of language and distance are gradually being torn down, giving way to new cooperation opportunities in the Americas; the lines which routinely separated national from regional and global have become blurred; and countries which traditionally pursued individual agendas are now accepting the need for a convergence of interests.

It is against this background that I believe the time is right to consider charting a new course in the Americas; a new path which takes into consideration the analysis of yesterday and the projections for today, tomorrow and the future. As old perceptions shift and are challenged, the time has come to facilitate a re-mapping of the Americas.

The OAS Agenda

The boldness of the objective inherent in the notion of '*Re-Mapping the Americas*' suggests a need to break from the traditional and a willingness to forge new paths. It is in this context that the OAS as the world's oldest hemispheric multilateral institution has been adapting to change. The Organization has actively charted a new course to facilitate a reinvigorated, pragmatic approach to the hemispheric agenda, emphasizing *strategic partnership*, *constructive action* and *measurable results*. As a crucial platform for political dialogue and consensus building with singular convening power, the OAS brings together all 34 Member States of this hemisphere on a regular basis to dialogue on a range of issues. Together with 68 Permanent Observers from Europe, the Middle East, Asia and Africa as well as international organizations and specialized agencies, the OAS continues to monitor critical issues of democracy, development, human rights and security.

The OAS recognizes that these four pillars are interdependent, complementary and mutually reinforcing; the strength of each is critical to the integrity of the whole. Playing a key role as a political facilitator and strategic partner, the Organization has become, in essence, a western hemisphere of nations where advancing the national interest is a priority and promoting the hemispheric good is the norm.

Integral Development, Governance and the Battle against Poverty

Economic integration and trade liberalization hold great promise for the nations and peoples of the Americas. However, the evidence is clear that growth without distribution is not sustainable. The needs of citizens of the Americas continue to evolve; requiring a review of traditional development agendas and a re-mapping of priorities and policies.

Recent surveys in Latin America reveal that almost half of the population is disappointed with young democracies that have failed to deliver results based on the expected relationship between democracy and development. When we examine crime and its impact on development in Central America and the Caribbean, for example, we encounter a high level of frustration and public scepticism with the link between democracy, development and positive change. Experience shows that development starts with solid policy and adequate opportunity. It is executed through pointed action and results-driven institutions. Integrated development which combines state policies, economic realities, and cultural and environmental factors, requires careful thought and regular review.

At the Sixth Summit of the Americas in Cartagena, Colombia, Heads of State and Government of this hemisphere mandated the OAS to prepare a report on the illegal drug challenge in the Americas. 'The Drug Problem in the Americas' report, launched in the first half of 2013, immediately stimulated frank and open dialogue on drug policies in the Americas, at almost every level of governance. The report and subsequent policy discussions have offered an unprecedented opportunity for government policy-makers to rethink aspects of the traditional approach to this challenge.[1] Such windows of opportunity offer a mechanism for rethinking conventional approaches to problems we face in our hemisphere. Clearly, if we fail to adapt our operating models in a changing environment, we run the risk of becoming obsolete and irrelevant.

Progress has become both necessary and urgent in the western hemisphere. In the context of the global economy, trade agreements, economic reforms and business initiatives must provide increased benefits that are accessible to everyone, particularly those in rural areas. Seventy per cent of the world's extremely poor live in rural areas. In the Americas, this population includes indigenous peoples, youth and women. While strides have been made in the right direction as a result of the Millennium Development Goals (MDGs) initiative, with extreme poverty being cut in half in the developing world in 2010, 167 million people (or 27.8 per cent of the population) of Latin America and the Caribbean combined are still living in poverty and surviving on US$2 a day or less.[2]

If we are to continue the trend of moving people out of poverty, reducing income inequality and providing opportunity in the Americas, then economic growth and social equality must be matched at the domestic policy level in our countries. The disparity is too great when one considers that on average the richest 10 per cent of Latin Americans receive 32 per cent of total income, while the poorest 40 per cent receive only 15 per cent.[3] The imbalances in our region are much too great, and sincere political commitment and dedicated action are required to address this jarring reality.

Rethinking the Concepts of 'Free and Fair'

Facilitating a democratic and developed environment is no longer solely the responsibility of the state. The private sector in the hemisphere must be prepared to work, through more active participation, with governments in pursuit of economic development by promoting the concepts of free and fair trade.

---

1 For example note the 'Seminar on the OAS Report: The Drug Problem in the Americas', jointly sponsored by the National Drug Council of the Ministry of National Security of the Government of Trinidad and Tobago, the Organization of American States, and the Institute of International Relations, held at St Augustine Campus, The University of the West Indies on 22 July 2013.

2 World Bank, Poverty Analysis, http://web.worldbank.org/WBSITE/EXTERNAL/ TOPICS/EXTPOVERTY/EXTPA/0,contentMDK:20040961~menuPK:435040~pagePK:1 48956~piPK:216618~theSitePK:430367~isCURL:Y,00.html, accessed 16 July 2013.

3 Social panorama of Latin America 2012, ECLAC, http://www.eclac.cl/cgi-bin/ getProd.asp?xml=/prensa/noticias/comunicados/9/48459/P48459.xml&xsl=/prensa/tpl-i/ p6f.xsl&base=/washington/tpl-i/top-bottom.xsl, accessed 16 July 2013.

Private sector integration is now ahead of government-led drives. The focus on doing business with traditional partners through conservative, risk-averse operating models is changing as more open economies are beginning to shift their outlooks. Yet, the most effective path toward economic development is not necessarily through globalization, regionalization or free trade agreements alone. Society demands, now more than ever, that growth be more equitable. At the national level, therefore, there must be a deliberate effort to ensure the benefits of global integration reach and create opportunities for the most disadvantaged populations.

At the time of writing, there are over 70 trade agreements in existence in the hemisphere; not counting the ones currently under negotiation. North America and Europe, the traditional partners of Latin America and the Caribbean, represent around 60 per cent of all signed agreements; while non-traditional partners, Asia and Oceania, account for roughly 30 per cent of the trade arrangements. Fundamentally, in this plethora of economic integration movements across regions and continents, we are witnessing a realignment – *an almost organic re-mapping of alliances, partnerships and strategic interests.*

The strengthening of relations between the Caribbean and Latin America, a key aspect for integrating the Americas, is on the rise. The insertion of two CARICOM member states (Guyana and Suriname) in the Community of South American Nations adds an encouraging dynamic to CARICOM's integration. With 21 countries and 69 million people, Central America and the Caribbean have yet to take full advantage of untapped business opportunities, investment and trade, which only reached $754 million in 2010. CARICOM exports to Central America and the Dominican Republic amount to only 3.4 per cent of total exports. Belize's membership in both CARICOM and the Central American Integration System (SICA) realizes the same dynamic in the Spanish sub-regional integration process, while the Dominican Republic, which is seeking membership in CARICOM, aspires to a bridging role between CARICOM and Central America.

As the re-mapping of the Americas evolves through increasing partnerships and shifting markets, countries from both sub-regions must seek to offer new incentives to facilitate successful interconnection. The potential results would be evidenced in greater efficiency, economies of scale, opportunities for innovation, and more modern business processes.

New Challenges: Peace, Security and Development

Security issues continue to be at the forefront of challenges to economic development, foreign direct investment and the successful integration of parts of the hemisphere into the global economy. With this in mind, I believe it has become imperative to review and assess conventional security and development models in the Americas through a multi-dimensional approach which encompasses new and non-traditional security threats and challenges to political, economic, social, health and environmental stability.

Multi-dimensional security threats include the three-way dynamic of inter-state, intra-state and transnational conflict; ranging from violent armed conflict, threats and acts of terror, to territorial disputes, and socio-political insecurity stemming from corruption and organized crime, drug trafficking, trafficking in persons, cyber-crime, money laundering, gang violence, and natural disasters. The creation and implementation of an effective and inclusive framework to address the above and to promote peace, enhance security and advance sustainable development can be seen from two perspectives.

The first perspective is the impact that instability and insecurity have on development and economic growth. Much of the funds that should be used in development are instead funnelled into attempts to deal with conflicts. The combined military spending of Africa, Asia, the Middle East and Latin America was more than $520 billion in 2012. That expenditure dwarfs the resources needed to achieve development goals.

The second perspective views the impact that inequity and lack of economic opportunities have on the poor, on political stability, and on crime and violence. This is of particular concern in the Americas where organized crime is sometimes viewed as an attractive alternative for honest employment. As we saw in the 'Arab Spring' of 2012, the uprising was fuelled largely by poverty, unemployment and lack of economic opportunity. In re-mapping the Americas we must, therefore, factor in global experience which has proven that public trust and confidence in the State is challenged when there is a failure to provide opportunity.

Another major challenge to development in the Americas is the management of natural disasters. Preparedness, mitigation and risk management are crucial issues which are directly linked to economic growth and sustainable development. The prognosis from disaster experts suggests that the frequency, scope and impact of these occurrences are likely to increase. Therefore, it is imperative that sectoral, national, regional and multilateral stakeholders incorporate disaster preparedness and risk reduction into the development agenda from the earliest stages. Since disasters are rarely limited to one border, and given the shared impact on multiple economies through aid, I believe the time is right to put in place a concrete hemispheric disaster relief fund to finance short-term emergency relief, as well as economic reconstruction in the longer term.

New Economic Pragmatism

Countries in Latin America and the Caribbean must work together to secure their position in the global economy through the conscious pursuit of strategic integration. In light of the failed hemispheric-wide Free Trade Area of the Americas (FTAA), countries filled the gap with bilateral trade agreements signed with their main trading partners. The FTAA, which sought to join 34 heterogeneous economies with very different sizes and levels of development into a comprehensive FTA, has been replaced by economic pragmatism. Not as optimal, and certainly more costly to businesses than a hemispheric agreement, the alternative approach has allowed countries to continue accessing markets in the hemisphere and beyond. The challenge is the harmonization and convergence of the different trade arrangements in the Americas, as the editors of this volume point out.

The Pacific Alliance, a regional bloc launched in June 2012, is an example of this pragmatism, seeking innovative approaches to increasing trade and investment and deepening integration. The Alliance seeks to supplement the existing bilateral trade agreements between Chile, Colombia, Mexico and Peru, and create an economic common market to negotiate and trade, as a unified group, with other economies. The bloc is to increase competitiveness by integrating its economies and allowing for the free flow of capital, goods, people, and services among its members, in addition to seeking expanded trans-regional trade with Asia-Pacific countries.

With four of the most dynamic economies in Latin America, averaging 7 per cent annual growth, and a consumer market of 207 million people, the Pacific Alliance accounts for more than one-third of Latin America's GDP and 55 per cent of the region's exports. The four Latin American members of the alliance exported goods worth about $71 billion to Asia in 2011. Costa Rica, Guatemala, Panama, and Uruguay are official observers to the Pacific Alliance and are candidates for future membership. Paraguay requested observer status and a number of countries outside of Latin America are also observers: Australia, Canada, Japan, New Zealand, and Spain. Portugal is expected to become an observer and China has formally requested observer status. The Alliance also invited the Association of Southeast Asian Nations (ASEAN) to join as an official observer.

The Pacific Alliance's relations with Asia-Pacific will offer an opportunity for Latin America to rethink strategically the composition of its trade. Does Latin America want its trade relations with Asia to be dominated by the exports of unrefined natural resources? Can Latin America become a provider of value added goods to Asia and become part of integrated value chains and content supply chains to make products more competitive vis-à-vis other parts of the world? It should be noted that while the Pacific Alliance is set to become the most important trading bloc in Latin America with an Asia-Pacific focus, the United States is pursuing a bold and ambitious commercial agenda seeking to sustain its leadership in international trade.

After signing agreements with major economies in the western hemisphere, the United States has turned its attention to its major partners from the Atlantic and Pacific. The Trans-Atlantic and Trans-Pacific Partnerships have the United States' innovative growth, employment and competitiveness interests at the centre. The Trans-Atlantic Trade and Investment Partnership (T-TIP) agreement between the United States and the European Union, which will start negotiations in July 2013, seeks to establish a free trade agreement with a market of 800 million consumers.

The other bold trade goal for the US, the Trans-Pacific Partnership, will soon be joined by Japan. Comprised of Australia, Brunei, Malaysia, New Zealand, Singapore, the United States, Vietnam, Canada, Chile, Mexico, and Peru, the

Trans-Pacific Partnership represents the largest potential growth area in the world in a decade, but excludes the large economies of the BRICS – Brazil, Russia, India, China, and South Africa.

Anticipating a United States-EU FTA, Brazil is revising long-stalled efforts to negotiate a trade agreement with the European Union and to offset a growing dependency on China. MERCOSUR has failed to negotiate trade agreements with countries outside the hemisphere. The eighth largest goods trading partners, the United States and Brazil, do not have a trade arrangement. A first step in deepening dialogue and cooperation between the two largest economies in the Americas is the Agreement on Trade and Economic Cooperation to enhance cooperation on trade and investment, signed by Presidents Obama and Rousseff in 2011.

Economic pragmatism has been at the centre of the hemispheric relations with China, which has become a key trading partner for the region. China is the first target market for Brazilian and Chilean exports, and the second market for Peru and Costa Rica. China is the third-largest source of imports in Latin America and the Caribbean, representing 13 per cent of total imports. Latin America and the Caribbean have become one of the most popular destinations of Chinese FDI. Latin American and Caribbean countries need to have a coordinated approach to respond to the broad cooperation agenda with China.

Determining Factors

Though the Americas is undoubtedly one of the most democratic regions of the world, it does not enjoy the full range of benefits enjoyed by other advanced democracies, in particular in terms of productivity, competitiveness and income equality. Even though Latin America has experienced strong growth rates and important gains in the fight against poverty, our productivity performance has not been able to regain the levels seen before 1975. In addition, the inhospitable business climate, low investment in human capital and infrastructure, and inequality continue to be key impediments to accelerating inclusive growth in Latin America and the Caribbean.

Institutions also matter significantly for growth and sustainable development to take hold, and they are particularly important for the region's future. Yet, year after year, the region scores negatively in the World Competitiveness Report in the area of institutions and the culprits continue to be excessive bureaucracy and red tape, overregulation, lack of transparency, uncertainty in dealing with public contracts, and the lack of independence of the judicial system. The legal and administrative framework within which individuals, firms, and governments interact to generate wealth remains weak in our continent. They all impose significant economic costs to businesses and slow the process of economic development.

Countries have made some improvements in business climate but not enough has been done. Entrepreneurs in the region face a regulatory environment that is on average less business friendly than in OECD countries. They face costlier and more bureaucratic procedures to start a business, deal with construction permits, register property, trade across borders and pay taxes.

Another serious deficit is in the area of innovation and education. Investments in research and development (R&D) in the Latin American and Caribbean region average 0.66 per cent as a percentage of GDP. In contrast, OECD countries invest on average 2.47 per cent of their GDP in R&D. While 90 per cent of R&D investments in developed countries come from the private sector, in our region the private sector only invests 10 per cent of total research and development investments.

In 2007, the number of researchers in the labour force in 27 countries surveyed in the region was only one researcher per 1,000 workers. This is seven times lower than the OECD average. There is scant integration of researchers in the industry sector, partly due to the lack of academic-industry partnerships and the use of research purely for academic purposes.

Latin American countries must take advantage of the commodity price boom to create synergies between human capital, technology and research and development and natural resources. Over the last 15 years, commodity price increases due to China's demand have been an important driver of economic growth in South America. With the risk of commodity price fluctuations in the future, the region must administer the gains well and invest in education and innovation, and in infrastructure for production to ensure long-term sustainable economic growth.

If these areas are not prioritized, the challenge for the region is the middle-income country trap, risking not leaping forward to higher income growth and continuing instead to compete for low-skill labour. The only way forward is through a qualitative jump in productivity, more value-added and diversified exports and skilled labour for a competitive workforce. This has to be accompanied by a modern infrastructure and energy agenda with a regional integration focus.

Similarly, I am of the view that the time is right to rethink the reach of trade agreements. Development must be at the core of trade negotiations and key to the formulation of the economic agenda. Poverty reduction, social responsibility and access to opportunity cannot be divorced from the trade and economic agendas. With this in mind, the OAS Member States adopted by acclamation the Social Charter of the Americas in June 2012 to address extreme poverty, inequity and social injustice, among other topics as integral areas in the pursuit of hemispheric development. The gap between the economically advantaged and the economically marginalized, the haves and have-nots, remains the main challenge for Latin American and Caribbean countries. The reasons for this phenomenon and prescriptions for remedying this unwanted outcome should be on the agenda at negotiating tables, and addressed in the programmes of multilateral institutions and lending agencies.

Along with an active trade agenda in the Americas, and the need to prioritize the impact of trade on poverty reduction, I believe member states should consider convening a dialogue of trade and social development authorities to discuss collaboration and promote the inclusion of poor and marginalized groups in the benefits of trade and investment. I believe that the OAS is well placed to create the space for policy dialogue in this area.

Change is inevitable. The ability to respond to and manage change will be determining factors for success. The trading regimes of the last century will not return. Business as usual is no longer an option.

High levels of public debt, coupled with low growth and insufficient competitiveness in the Caribbean, difficult economic management decisions challenging social ramifications. CARICOM has recognized this reality. CARICOM's move toward the establishment of a Caribbean Single Market and Economy (CSME) is a pragmatic strategy to mitigate the constraints of size and capitalize on combined strengths and capacities. But the ability of Latin American and Caribbean economies to grow in the face of competition from China, India and other areas with low-cost production will be a challenging and complex proposition.

An Agenda for Change

The world and our hemisphere have indeed changed. These dynamics have added new challenges to existing ones but have also opened up opportunities. We live in a hemisphere that is far from homogeneous: what is relevant to Central America may be different from the interest of the Andean Community, and their objectives may be quite different from what the Caribbean Community wants. These are the realities we have to accept and translate into our policy-making. At the same time countries and sub-regions continue to compete for political opportunity, funding, negotiating power, expertise and economic opportunities and market access, and these dynamics take place in an increasingly inter-dependent Americas. So how do countries and sub-regions take advantage of these dynamics and use them to strengthen their democracies and economies?

New Forms of Multilateralism

The answer, in my opinion, is for countries in the region to continue to cooperate multilaterally on addressing shared problems and pursuing common goals. Multilateralism is and continues to be an important vehicle for working collectively toward a common agenda. Greater regional cooperation and closer collaboration between and within the sub-regions is no longer merely a major political objective, but an economic imperative, if the region is to integrate into a global economy that is increasingly structured around regional or sub-regional value chains.

Thus, new forms of development and cooperation in areas such as infrastructure, energy, connectivity and trade and transport facilitation will be crucial for competitiveness and growth.[4] Small, vulnerable economies, Caribbean states must focus on the future of their economies promoting stronger diplomatic relations and partnerships in vital issues and trade and investment with Central America and South America. Central America shares many challenges with the Caribbean and by working together and advocating their cause with one voice the sub-regions can enhance economic growth. Central America and the Caribbean make up 75 per cent of the OAS membership. Central America and the Caribbean have not taken full advantage of opportunities stemming from complementarities and geographic location to insert themselves more successfully in the global economy.

The high dependency on the US and European markets for exports and investments has had an adverse effect in the SICA and CARICOM economies during the global economic crisis. While CARICOM and Central American countries are differentiated by language, by the size of population (17 million people in CARICOM and over 50 million in Central America and the Dominican Republic) and by Gross Domestic Product (in 2010, $64 billion in the CARICOM countries and $198.6 billion in the SICA countries), GDP per capita is similar in both sub-regions: $3,798 in the Caribbean and $3,813 in Central America and the Dominican Republic. This implies a similarity in purchasing power and a potential for trade and investment.[5]

Today new and competing asymmetries and emerging counterweights in flux throughout the Americas are manifest in an array of regional groupings.[6] Some are a product of divergent national interests and strategic priorities and as such reflect conflicting economic agendas and geographical positions. From the Latin American Bolivarian Alternative (ALBA) that Venezuela started in 2004 to the 12-member Union of South American Nations (UNASUR)[7] created by Brazil in 2008, to the Community of Latin American and Caribbean Nations (CELAC), these crosscutting and often overlapping mechanisms have developed little institutional backing. They have become forums for strategic South-South dialogue and cooperation. Given the diverse political interests in these new institutional

---

4   http://www.eclac.org/publicaciones/xml/5/38525/Opportunities_convergence_regional_cooperation_proposals.pdf, accessed 18 July 2013.

5   http://www.eclac.org/cgi-bin/getProd.asp?xml=/publicaciones/xml/2/46722/P46722.xml&xsl=/mexico/tpl/p9f.xsl&base=/mexico/tpl/top-bottom.xslt, accessed 18 July 2013.

6   ALBA, Andean Community, UNASUR, MERCOSUR, CELAC, Rio Group, Pacific Alliance, SEGIB, the Transpacific Partnership, and Tuxtla.

7   So far, UNASUR has served mainly as a public forum for leaders from member states. South American leaders signed an agreement in 2009 to create the Bank of the South, a development bank advocated by Venezuelan President Hugo Chávez. The bank, which would be based in Caracas, could eventually finance economic development projects in UNASUR member states. Some UNASUR countries, led by Ecuador have called for the creation of an alternate arbitration centre in response to dissatisfaction with the International Centre for Settlement of Investment Disputes (ICSID), the World Bank institution for arbitrating disputes between foreign investors and host states.

arrangements, it is important for member states to go with clear priorities and objectives that result in greater socio-economic development.

Finally, allow me to draw your attention to some items for an agenda for hemispheric and regional change:

1. In the Americas of the twenty-first century, there will likely be increased competition for influence in the western hemisphere. We recognize that international relations and diplomacy have changed in nature, conduct and objectives, and this process will continue to evolve. For countries and groups of countries it is of critical importance to demonstrate an in-depth analysis and understanding of the driving forces and interests behind these dynamics. I believe that universities and think-tanks can facilitate this process and provide the necessary policy guidance to governments. Governments actively engage the private sector and go hand-in-hand to identify the most competitive and effective insertion in the global markets.

2. This understanding and the domestic opportunities and strengths should translate into a strategic foreign policy, using every opportunity to insert the identified political and economic agenda in hemispheric and global negotiating processes.

3. In isolation no country can strengthen its economic and political systems, so building strategic political, commercial and social partnerships is of critical importance and an important tool in the foreign policy strategy.

4. Promoting communication and understanding between the peoples of the hemisphere should be enhanced. Promoting knowledge and respect for each other builds understanding, reduces conflict, bolsters stability and helps promote greater integration.

5. We should reform legislation to strengthen the institutions that safeguard democracy, human rights, and the rule of law, ensure transparency, accountability and good governance.

6. We should also seek to strengthen the inter-American system to make multilateralism work more effectively by defining a specific and clear mandate for organizations in developmental and political processes in the hemisphere. The OAS is ready to be a full partner in this regard and is already working to strengthen cooperation and consultation with global and other regional organizations for the benefit of the hemisphere.

7. Governments must invest significantly more in education and human capital development and make it a stronger priority. The private sector must be willing partners in this regard, providing internships, assisting with training, and supporting entrepreneurship and investing in innovation. Instruction offered by institutions of learning must be responsive to market needs, providing the training, skills and values for the upcoming generations to realize their full human potential and to prepare them to become entrepreneurs and skilled and knowledge workers. The importance of education cannot be overstated when you consider that approximately

35 per cent of the population in Latin America and the Caribbean is under 30 years of age. These are the workers and leaders of the twenty-first century. Educating this and future generations, and equipping them with the tools for a changing world, is our ultimate responsibility.

8. Partnerships at regional, state and community levels will be essential. The practice of statecraft will undergo a sea change. The Caribbean Single Market and Economy (CSME) is a bold step on this new path, as are other efforts towards integration. In this new environment, governments must work with the private sector and civil society to advance a comprehensive development agenda.

9. Inter-sectoral linkages (for example, between agriculture and tourism) should be strengthened to take full advantage of productive capacity, inherent synergies and expanded market potential.

10. And finally, keeping current with innovations in technology is essential for productivity and competitiveness and reducing the digital divide. In addition, technology is a growth area that offers opportunities for entrepreneurs and smaller economies.

Once again, business as usual cannot be an option. Creativity and a mentality of thinking outside of the box will be required and governments will have to be more alert in seizing opportunities. I firmly believe that regardless of the region of the world, for peace to be sustainable, governments, regional organizations and civil society need to centre their efforts on people, on creating a positive climate for social peace and economic growth and development.

By developing a proactive and coordinated approach, an integrated strategy that draws together different actors at the community, state and multilateral levels and using the power of partnership, we can build long-term capacity and expertise; ensuring quicker and more effective responses.

H.E. Ambassador Albert R. Ramdin
Assistant Secretary General
Secretario General Adjunto
Organization of American States

Acknowledgements

The idea for this book emerged from a joint research project between researchers from the University of Alberta and The University of the West Indies. Professor W. Andy Knight initiated the project after receiving some seed funding from the University of Alberta's Office of the Vice President Research. The money was used to pull together scholars at the University of Alberta whose research interests related to the Caribbean and Latin America. Further seed funding was provided to Professor Knight from the University of Alberta's Faculty of Arts Endowment Fund for the Future Support for the Advancement of Scholarship (SAS) Research, and the University of Alberta's International Office Fund for the Support of International Development Assistance (FSIDA) in order to embark on collaborative research dealing with 'Re-mapping the Americas: Globalization, Regionalisation and the FTAA'.

In March 2006, Professor Knight was the recipient of a Strategic Research Clusters Development Grant from the Social Sciences and Humanities Research Council (SSHRC) of Canada to develop a Re-mapping the Americas Knowledge Network. It was through the development of this knowledge network, using joomla software, that scholars at both The University of the West Indies and the University of Alberta began to think about the publication of a book that would address what we saw as a fertile and evolving remaking of the regions within our hemisphere. Bhoendradatt Tewarie, currently the Minister of Planning and Sustainable Development in the Government of the Republic of Trinidad and Tobago and who was at the time the St Augustine campus Principal of The University of the West Indies in Trinidad, worked closely with Professor Andy Knight to cement the relationship between the two institutions which led to the signing of a Memorandum of Understanding that would produce joint conferences, exchange of students and faculty, joint research projects, joint academic papers and joint books. That MOU provided the foundation for the partnership which resulted in the publication of this volume. Professor Knight brought on board Julián Castro-Rea (the University of Alberta) and Hamid Ghany (The University of the West Indies) as co-editors of this volume.

As editors, we reached out to specific scholars across the hemisphere who have been following with close attention the redrawing of regional entities in response to local, regional, trans-regional and global pressures. We asked them to submit chapters that reflected the essence of this re-mapping. We thank them for their patience during the long gestation period it took to get this volume out on the shelves. Their efforts were certainly worth it. Including the chapter contributors to this work, we would sincerely like to thank the following individuals for their involvement in the research project that eventually led to the publication of this volume: Katie Bibbs, Keshan Latchman, Janine Brodie, Makere Stewart-Harawira, Renny Khan, Rolf Mirus, Linda Rief, Steffi Peuckert, Renee Vaugeois, Hamid Ghany, Bhoendradatt Tewarie, Kenneth Valley, Ruben Silie, Ralph Carnegie, Edmund Dillion, Trevor Farrow, Julián Castro-Rea, Donna Coombs-Montrose, Joseph Yu-Shek Cheng, Jay Mandle, Christopher Sands, Mark Kirton, Kelowatie Deonandan, Anthony Bryan, Lancelot Cowie, Kelvin Singh, Esteban Perez Caldentey, Anesa Ali, Gaspare Genna, Patrick Watson, Varune Ramlal, Sahadeo Basdeo, Krissy Lake, Kevin Ramnarine, Barbara Kotschwar, Agustin Cornejo, Ramesh Chaitoo, Kirk Meighoo, Raghunath Mahabir, Ria Tony, Acolla Lewis-Cameron, Roche Mahon, Kumar Mahabir, Chris Mahadeo, Patricia Mohammed, Philomina Okeke, Dave Ramsaran, Wendy Theodore, Kameel Mungrue, Derrick Raphael, Vaughan Lewis, Christopher Brown, Jay Johnson, Adrian Smith, Fred Judson, Roger Hosein, Obijiofor Aginam, Jonelle Watson, Ian Bethell Bennett, Norman Girvan, Lisa Samuel, Patsy Lewis, Taimoon Stewart, Brinsley Samaroo, Fazal Ali, Matthew Bishop, Annita Montoute, Lynelle Clarke, Raeisa Perreira, Riyad Insanally, Winston Dookeran and Ambassador Albert Ramdin.

This work would not have been possible without input from the above individuals as well as the support of some senior administrators at the University of Alberta and The University of the West Indies, especially in the Office of the Vice President Research, the Office of the Provost, the Office of the Dean of the Faculty of Arts, and the Department of Political Science at the University of Alberta; and the Office of the Principal, the Faculty of Social Sciences, and the Institute of International Relations at The University of the West Indies. So we acknowledge the guidance and substantive support provided by Indira Samarasekera, Carl Amrhein, Andrew Greenshaw, Britta Baron, Colleen Skidmore, David Rampersad, Anthony Gonzales, and Timothy Shaw. At the end of the day, we, the editors, are solely responsible for any errors or omissions in this volume. But we recognize that it took many dedicated individuals to ensure the successful publication of this work, including the personnel at Ashgate Publishing in the UK such as Carolyn Court, Margaret Younger, Kirstin Howgate, Brenda Sharp and Sadie Copley-May, without whom this book may never have seen the light of day. For their patience and hard work, we thank them all profusely and sincerely.

W. Andy Knight, Julián Castro-Rea and Hamid Ghany

List of Abbreviations

ACP	African, Caribbean and Pacific Group of States
ACS	Association of Caribbean States
AGOA	African Growth and Opportunity Act
ALADI	Latin American Integration Association
ALBA	Bolivarian Alliance of the Peoples of Our Americas
AOSIS	Alliance of Small Island States
APD	Air Passenger Duty
APEC	Asia-Pacific Economic Co-operation
ASEAN	Association of Southeast Asian Nations
BIS	Bank of International Settlements
BRICS	Association of emerging national economies: Brazil, Russia, India, China and South Africa
C-TPAT	Customs Trade Partnership Against Terrorism
CACM	Central American Common Market
CAFRA	Caribbean Association for Feminist Research and Action
CAFTA	Central America Free Trade Agreement
CAFTA-DR	Free Trade Agreement with Central America and the Dominican Republic
CALC	Latin America-Caribbean Summit on Development and Integration
CARIBCAN	Caribbean-Canada Trade Agreement
CARICOM	Caribbean Community
CARIFORUM	The Caribbean Forum
CARIFTA	Caribbean Free Trade Association
CBD	Convention on Biological Diversity
CBERA	Caribbean Basin Economic Recovery Act
CBI	Caribbean Basin Initiative
CBTPA	Caribbean Basin Trade and Production Act
CCJ	Caribbean Court of Justice
CCL	Caribbean Congress of Labour
CCP	Common Commercial Policy
CDCC	Caribbean Development and Cooperation Committee
CELAC/CLACS	Community of Latin American and Caribbean States
CEMAC	Economic and Monetary Community of Central Africa
CET	Common External Tariff

CGR	Comptroller General of the Republic (Contralor General de la República)
COHA	Council of Hemispheric Affairs
COMESA	Common Market of East and Southern Africa
COP	Congress of the People (Trinidad and Tobago)
COTED	Council for Trade and Economic Development
CPC	Communist Party of China
CPDC	Caribbean Policy Development Centre
CPI	Corruption Perception Index
CSI	Container Security Initiative
CSJ	Court of Justice (Corte Suprema de Justicia)
CSME	Caribbean Single Market and Economy
CSO	Civil Society Organizations
CUSFTA	Canada-US Free Trade Agreement
DHS	Department of Homeland Security
EAAI	The International Airports Management Company (Empreza Administradora de Aeropuertos Internacionales)
EAI	Enterprise for the Americas Initiative
EBA	EU's Everything but Arms
EC	European Commission
ECLAC	Economic Commission for Latin America and the Caribbean
ECOWAS	Economic Community of Western African States
EDF	Environmental Defence Fund
EEC	European Economic Community
EESC	European Economic and Social Committee
EPA	Economic Partnership Agreements
ESAF	Enhanced Structural Adjustment Facility
EU	European Union
FAST	Free and Secure Trade
FDA	US Food and Drug Administration
FDI	Foreign Direct Investment
FITUN	Federation of Independent Trade Unions and NGOs (Trinidad and Tobago)
FSLN	Sandinista National Liberation Front (Frente Sandinista Liberación Naciónal)
FTA	Free Trade Agreement
FTAA	Free Trade Area of the Americas
G-20	Group of Twenty (20) Finance Ministers and Central Bank Governors from Twenty (20) Major Economies
GAO	US Government Accountability Office
GATS	General Agreement on Trade in Services
GATT	General Agreement on Tariffs and Trade

GDP	Gross Domestic Product
GRPA	Guyana Rice Producers' Association
GSP	Generalised Scheme of Preferences
HCP	Hemispheric Cooperation Program
ICDF	International Co-operation and Development Fund
IDB	Inter-American Development Bank
IFIs	International Financial Institutions
IIRSA	The Initiative for the Integration of the Regional Infrastructure of South America
ILO	International Labour Organization
IMF	International Monetary Fund
IMPACS	CARICOM's Implementation Agency for Crime and Security
INTUR	Institute of Tourism
JPA	Joint Parliamentary Assembly
LAFTA	Latin American Free Trade Association
LDCs	Least Developed Countries
MAS	Market Access Strategy
MCCA	Mercado Común Centroamericano (Central American Common Market)
MERCOSUR	Southern Common Market (economic and political agreement among Argentina, Brazil, Paraguay, Uruguay, Venezuela and Bolivia)
MFN	Most Favoured Nation
NAFTA	North American Free Trade Agreement
NEI	National Export Initiative
NGO	Non-Governmental Organization
NICs	Newly Industrializing Countries
NPC	National People's Congress
NUPW	National Union of Public Workers (Barbados)
OAS	Organization of American States
OECD	The Organization for Economic Co-operation and Development
OECS	Organisation of Eastern Caribbean States
OTN (formerly CRNM)	CARICOM Office of Trade Negotiations (formerly Caribbean Regional Negotiating Machinery)
PAHO	Pan-American Health Organization
PAPDA	Haitian Platform for Alternative Development
PLC	Constitutionalist Liberal Party (Partido Liberal Constitucionalista – Nicaragua)
PNM	People's National Movement (Trinidad and Tobago)
PPPs	Public-Private Partnerships
PRC	People's Republic of China
PRGF	Poverty Reduction and Growth Facility

PRSPs	Poverty Reduction Strategies
PTAs	Preferential Trade Agreements
RMB	Renminbi (Official Currency of China)
ROOS	Rules Of Origins
RPTF	Regional Preparatory Task Force
RTAs	Regional Trade Agreements
SAC	South American Community
SADC	Southern African Development Community
SDT	Special and Differential Treatment
SIA	Sustainability Impact Assessment
SICA	Central American Integration System
SOE	State-Owned Enterprise
SPP	North American Security and Prosperity Partnership
TI	Transparency International
TNC	Transnational Corporation
TPA	Trade Promotion Authority
TPP	Trans-Pacific Partnership
TRIMS	Trade Related Investment Measures
TRIPS	Trade Related aspects of Intellectual Property Rights
UN	United Nations
UNASUR	Union of South American Nations
UNC	United National Congress (Trinidad and Tobago)
UNCTAD	UN Conference on Trade and Development
UNDP	United Nations Development Programme
UNFCCC	United Nations Framework Convention on Climate Change
UNO	National Opposition Union (Unión Nacional Opositora – Nicaragua)
US	United States of America
US-VISIT	US Visitor and Immigrant Status Indicator Technology program
USTR	US Trade Representative
WB	World Bank
WHO	World Health Organization
WINFA	Windward Islands Farmers' Association
WOLA	Washington Office on Latin America
WTO	World Trade Organization

In Memory of Henry Gill

Henry Gill was the typical Caribbean Renaissance man. He acquired what the French call 'une culture generale' and could talk comfortably about sport, the humanities, the arts and the social sciences. He pursued knowledge with relentless vigour, and with his acquaintance of languages and cultures along with his travels, he could sit and talk about societies in almost any part of this globe. He was a true global citizen. Academically, he was devoted to rigorous scholarship and concerned about the region making the correct foreign policy choices. His writings on these subjects are still relevant today and the task falls on those of us who understood his work to make it available to this and coming generations.

Quote from the Eulogy delivered by Anthony Peter Gonzales

PART I
Backdrop

Chapter 1
Re-mapping the Americas

W. Andy Knight, Julián Castro-Rea and Hamid Ghany

Introduction

This book is about re-mapping. Maps are graphic representations of the land, human records of the geography where populations of our species live. Maps are not fixed. Over time, they change as the size of the population that lives on the land expands, contracts or simply changes their perceptions of space. In using the term re-mapping, we want to convey this idea of constantly changing maps, while offering snapshots of maps at conjunctural moments – i.e., different, or specific, points in time.[1] Re-mapping has little regard for political or legal jurisdictional boundaries. It may lead to the emergence of overlapping regions. Regions include geographical areas that span more than one country, and over time their boundaries have been remarkably dynamic. The concept of re-mapping, in our minds, conveys the idea of the organic growth of regions, expanding and shrinking in response to the perceptions and actions of social actors living in them.

Re-mapping and the Re-emergence of Regions

Since the end of the Cold War, there has been a revitalization of regions around the world, promoted by a new desire on the part of most states to 'merge' into regional entities. We have of course seen these trends developing in Europe, with the deepening and widening of the European Union (EU), emerging from the former European Economic Community (EEC). But they can also be observed in the creation of new regional projects such as *Mercado Común del Sur* (Southern Common Market, or MERCOSUR), the Caribbean Community (CARICOM) and the North American Free Trade Agreement (NAFTA). Moreover, some existing regional schemes have been revitalized and updated; among them the Latin American Integration Association (LAIA), the Central American Common Market, the Andean Pact – which became the Andean Community of Nations (CAN), the Organization of African Unity that was transformed into the African Union

---

1 Anthony Payne entitled a review essay published in 1999 'The Remapping of the Americas'. He did not elaborate, however, neither on the meaning of the term re-mapping nor on its theoretical implications. See Anthony Payne, 'The Remapping of the Americas', review essay, *Review of International Studies*, 25 (3) (July 1999), 507–514.

(AU), the Southern African Development Community (SADC), the Economic Community of West African States (ECOWAS), the Association of Southeast Asian States (ASEAN), the South Asian Association for Regional Cooperation (SAARC), and the Arab League. This long list, while not exhaustive, underscores the global reach of the region-making momentum.

An attempt at regional revitalization was particularly evident in the western hemisphere, where an omnibus regional trading arrangement called the Free Trade Area of the Americas (FTAA) was expected to be operating by 2005. However, the member states of this potential regional re-mapping became entangled in a negotiation process that finally stalled during the Fourth Summit of the Americas held in November 2005 at Mar del Plata, Argentina.[2] We believe it is important to understand the reasons why some regional re-mapping is successful while others fail to come to fruition. The following chapters in this book will hopefully help the reader to gain that understanding. When applying the concept of re-mapping to the Americas, we discovered that in this part of the world, particularly since the nineteenth century, there has been an ongoing transformation of regions, animated by different ideas about regionalism and by different processes of regionalization. It is important at the outset to define the precise way in which we will use these concepts throughout this volume.

Conceptualizing Region, Regionalism, Regionalization

Region is a notion commonly used in political analysis. However, it may adopt many different meanings, and the exact sense of the word is rarely made explicit even in academic literature. Because this concept is so central to this book, it is necessary to be clear about what is meant by region, as well as its derivative concepts – regionalism and regionalization. Generally, a region is considered the projection of a social, political or economic concept over a given geographical area or territory. In other words, it is the application of human perception to make sense of the physical environment. Defining a region is a way to making discreet an otherwise continuous, undifferentiated land mass; a strategy to make human sense of it.

This definition espouses a constructivist approach, taking distance from rationalist perspectives.[3] Constructivism understands the emergence of regions as a result of the redefinition of norms and identities associated with a territory by governments, business and other civil society groups. Rationalism, in contrast, uses data on economic and institutional ties among states to define regions, as for instance most economists studying international trade do, only looking at formalized country groupings. We wish to go beyond the rationalist, institutional

---

2   Elisabeth Bumiller and Larry Rohter, 'Bush's Troubles Follow Him to Summit in Argentina', *The New York Times*, 4 November 2005.

3   Raimo Väyrynen, 'Regionalism: Old and New', *International Studies Review*, 5 (2003), 26.

approach, assuming that regions are not only government-sanctioned territorial demarcations but also social constructs, shaped by collective perceptions of their meaning, with constantly changing boundaries.[4]

According to S. Hoelscher, regions as social constructs are shaped by tradition, cultural memory and heritage.[5] While we accept that culturalist focus as valid, we want to go beyond it. In our opinion, regions are also instruments designed to achieve specific political and economic goals, which are never intrinsic but assigned depending on the interests of the actors involved. Any region may be placed somewhere along a continuum between small and proximate geographical areas (the land over which a human community is reproduced, which they collectively consider to be the place where their everyday lives are created) and large and symbolically-united areas (such as national states or continents). Furthermore, a region may be defined by environmental features, such as river banks or mountain ranges, or abstract attributes, such as the degree of development (e.g. the Global North or the Global South) or spoken language (e.g. La Francophonie or The Commonwealth).

An important distinction is to be made between physical and functional regions. Physical regions encompass contiguous spaces controlled by more than one state, articulated by a military, political or economic rationale. In contrast, functional regions are defined by non-territorial factors such as migration, identities, markets, and ideologies; they encompass areas that may not necessarily be contiguous but whose claims are usually upheld by non-state actors (e.g. Aztlán, the area of the Southern United States that the Chicano movement claims as its homeland).[6] These two kinds of regions correspond respectively to what Manuel Castells calls 'spaces of places' and 'spaces of flows'.[7] Spaces of places are generally created by sovereign states. They are contained within defined borders and their form, use and meaning are historically rooted within a confined territory. Spaces of flows, in contrast, are usually defined by networks created through social practices, and organized independently of physical contiguity. These social practices can be economic or cultural, and are seldom directed, or even acknowledged, by states.

Other authors have made further distinctions between different kinds of regions. For example, R. Ostergren[8] presents three classifications of regions: instituted, objectively denoted and naïvely perceived. M. Frey and G. Friesen conceive of regions as either sub-systems of larger entities, as conglomerates

---

4   Väyrynen, 'Regionalism … ', 27.

5   Cited in Elena Shadrina, 'Regionalization and Regionalism: Featuring Northeast Asia', *Gendai Shakai Bunka Kenkyu*, 37 (December 2006), 405.

6   Väyrynen, 'Regionalism …', 27.

7   Manuel Castells, *The Rise of the Network Society, Vol. I: The Information Age: Economy, Society, and Culture* (Oxford: Blackwell, 1996), 423.

8   In Lothar Honnighausen, et al. (eds), *Regionalism in the Age of Globalism. Vol. 1: Concepts of Regionalism*, 2005. Ostergren also conceives regions as structures of dialectic interactions.

of states, or as subdivisions of the global order.[9] A. Witt, embracing a rationalist approach, sees a region only when a transnational space has been formalized by a given authority.[10] Elena Shadrina's definition is more demanding, as she views regions as geographically-based entities with a sense of distinct community and collective identity, which may also have some degree of homogeneity, similar political behaviour within and outside it, common political institutions, economic interdependence, and similar norms.[11] She also writes that regions encompassing more than one state are an intermediate form of community, between the sovereign state and the global order. However, these distinctions do not necessarily add further analytical power to the concept as we have defined it earlier. The terms regionalism and regionalization are also understood in very different ways in the academic literature and in common parlance.

In this book, we understand regionalism as a normative term, expressing an intention – either explicit or implicit – usually spelled out by a government, of creating a region encompassing territories under more than one sovereign authority. According to this perspective, regionalism is a plan aimed at enhancing a state's military, socio-cultural, economic or political influence by pooling its resources with a set of territories under different authorities. Regionalization, in contrast, is a descriptive term that refers to the actual practice of linking geographical areas under diverse jurisdictions to achieve military, cultural, social, political or economic purposes. In other words, regionalization is a process that results in the creation of a region. This process may or may not have a master plan. In other words, regionalization may or may not be the result of regionalism. Whatever occurs in the regionalization process may not necessarily be what was foreseen in any given regionalism plan.

As previously stated, there are in the existing literature contrasting interpretations of regionalism and regionalization. According to Ann Capling and Kim Richard Nossal, for instance, regionalism refers to '... state-led efforts to deepen regional integration through the fostering of other formal mechanisms to support institutionalised cooperation and collective action', whereas regionalization is '... the process of economic integration that is driven from the bottom-up by private actors such as firms in response to the opportunities created by the liberalisation of investment and trade'. In other words, whereas for these authors regionalism is formal, *de jure* cooperation among governments, regionalization refers to informal, *de facto* intensified interaction among private actors in different countries.[12] Along the same lines, Samuel Kim, while also assuming that regionalism is a normative

---

9   M. Frey and G. Friesen, cit. in Lothar Honnighausen et al. (eds), *Regionalism in the Age of Globalism. Vol. I Concepts of Regionalism* (2005), 16–17.

10   A. Witt, cit. in Lothar Honnighausen et al. (eds), *Regionalism ...*, 48.

11   Elena Shadrina, 'Regionalization and Regionalism: Featuring Northeast Asia', *Gendai Shakai Bunka Kenkyu*, 37 (December 2006), 12.

12   Ann Capling and Kim Richard Nossal, 'The contradictions of regionalism in North America', *Review of International Studies*, 35 (February 2009), 148.

concept, adds to it that it is based on shared norms, values, identity and aspirations. For him, regionalism is therefore about 'state-led projects of cooperation that emerge from intergovernmental dialogues and agreements'.[13] It refers largely to market-driven processes of integration.

We contest, here, these distinctions. We are convinced that they do little more than simplify a more complex reality. Indeed, regionalism can be conceived by both state and non-state actors, while regionalization can be practised by national states as well as by private non-state actors. Although, in most instances, states and governments may be the main actors in regionalism, and private actors (corporations, NGOs, criminal organizations, etc.) in regionalization, this is certainly not always the case. Non-state actors engage in regionalism whenever they plan strategically the expansion of their activities across borders, when they create master plans to take advantage of the assets that different territories offer to enhance the reach of the goals they pursue. Conversely, states may, and do, practice regionalization whenever they reach across their borders to achieve specific objectives, without necessarily having a larger normative scheme in mind. Quite often, states find piecemeal solutions to pressing issues that develop both within and outside their territories, which aim at finding short-term fixes to those issues without assessing the long-term impacts. Moreover, states may also engage in practices that divert from regionalism plans, either because they are applying tactical adaptations of broader strategies or because regionalism is not delivering the expected results.

Other authors have also theorized about regionalism and regionalization in different, indeed contrasting ways. Arie Kacowicz defines regionalism as '… the proneness of the governments and peoples of states to establish voluntary associations and to pool together resources in order to create common functional and institutional arrangements'.[14] In contrast, regionalization would be the growth of societal integration within a given region, including the undirected process of social and economic interaction among the units, according to Kacowicz. Gilbert Rozman suggests that regionalism includes five dimensions: economic integration, institutional integration, social integration, formation of a regional identity, and security.[15] For Andrew Hurrell regionalism is an ideology or slogan, the mental and/or physical disposition toward forming a regional identity, which leads in turn to further regionalization viz., the creation of a regional identity, closer cooperation and/or integration. Regionalization is, according to the latter

---

13   Samuel Kim, 'Regionalisation and Regionalism in East Asia', *Journal of East Asian Studies*, 4 (2004), 39–67.

14   Arie M. Kacowicz, *Regionalisation, Globalisation and Nationalism: Converging, Diverging or Overlapping?* (Notre Dame: The Helen Kellogg Institute for International Studies, 1998).

15   Gilbert Rozman, 'Korea at the Center: The Growing Quest for Regionalism in Northeast Asia', in Charles Armstrong et al. (eds), *Korea at the Center: The Search for Regionalism in Northeast Asia* (New York: M.E. Sharpe, 2005).

author, the set of moves primarily directed by market forces which shape closer international regional integration. Additionally, for this author regionalism comprises overall five dimensions: regionalization, regional awareness and identity, regional interstate cooperation, state-promoted regional integration and regional cohesion.[16]

Michael Schulz, in turn, defines regionalism as the '… general phenomenon, denoting formal projects as well as process in the broadest possible sense and represents the body of ideas, values and concrete objectives that are aimed at creating, maintaining or modifying the provision of security and wealth, peace and development within a region'.[17] Regionalization is thus the change, within a given geographical space, from relative heterogeneity and lack of cooperation to increased cooperation, integration, convergence, coherence and identity in the realms of culture, security, economic development and politics. Finally, Elena Shadrina, explicitly following S. Kim, conceives of regionalization as '… the process of integration through which regional agendas and identity are formed …', mainly thanks to the action of market and grassroots agents, while regionalism, pursued by governments and other official agents, is the end result of that process.[18] However, these contributions add little clarity or useful insights to the definitions that we proffer in this chapter. A further distinction among different variants of regionalism is nonetheless still required in order to fully understand this trend. Schulz, Söderbaum and Öjendal[19] state that the 'return' of regionalism by the end of the twentieth century 'is undoubtedly one important trend in international relations'. Drawing on Hettne and Inotai, Schulz et al. refer to this trend as 'the new regionalism'.[20] It is a regionalism characterized by a widening of its scope and diversity and an increase in its fluidity and non-conformity.[21] Above all, it is a regionalism that accepts the global market as a given and encourages states to open themselves to competition following the rules of capitalism. Regions become the pieces that conform to the global order, a new form of transnational governance, spaces of competition, investment and trade flows where national states get involved in order not to be marginalized by globalization.[22]

Schulz et al. further assert that this regionalism is 'a qualitatively *new* phenomenon' (their italics) that began in the mid-1980s in Europe and gradually

---

16   Andrew Hurrell and Louise Fawcett, *Regionalism in World Politics: Regional Organization and International Order* (New York: Oxford University Press, 1995).

17   Michael Schulz et al., *Regionalization in a Globalizing World* (London: Zed Books, 2001).

18   Elena Shadrina, 'Regionalization and Regionalism featuring Northeast Asia', *Gendai Shakai Bunka Kenkyu*, 37 (December 2006), 403–436.

19   Schulz et al., *Regionalization* … .

20   Björn Hettne and Andras Inotai, *The New Regionalism: Implications for Global Development and International Security* (Helsinki: UNU/WIDER, 1994).

21   Schulz et al., *Regionalization* …, 1.

22   Wendy Larner and William Walters, 'The Political Rationality of "New Regionalism": Toward a Genealogy of Region', *Theory and Society*, 31 (2002), 408.

blossomed 'into a truly worldwide phenomenon'.[23] While we agree that this wave of regionalism is clearly distinguishable from the older one because of its neo-liberal, globalized character, we do not believe it is particularly 'new', as it has been present in global politics for over 20 years now. Instead, from now on, we will refer to this post-Cold War regionalism as *open regionalism*, thus drawing a contrast to the *closed regionalism* practiced before. Whereas open regionalism embraces global competition as the main engine of economic growth, closed regionalism makes use of protectionism as the main policy tool to achieve development.

Closed regionalism was practiced, for example, in Latin America under the inspiration of dependency theory in the 1960s. In that instance, Latin American regional arrangements were developed with the distinct goal of setting up barriers against foreign products, supporting regional industrialization, and seeking local markets for goods manufactured in the region. It became evident in the 1980s that this approach had failed, and that the more open regional approach in Asia seemed to be providing better results. Open regionalism is congenial with the neo-liberal free trade policies of what John Williamson aptly called the 'Washington consensus', that is, the combination of economic policies preferred both by the international financial institutions (IMF, World Bank, IDB) and the US federal government; all of which are headquartered in Washington, DC.[24] It allowed for the insertion of markets in Latin America and the Caribbean into the global arena through the elimination of barriers to trade. But it also allowed for countries in the region to explore strategic partnerships and commercial relations with countries that traditionally did not have a strong connection to this region.

That being said, there is in fact a 'newer' version of regionalism currently emerging in the world. It is developing amidst what seems to be a relative decline in US hegemony and a relative movement up the ladder of the international hierarchy by other states, such as the so-called BRICs (Brazil, Russia, India and China). This newer regionalism is taking place within the broader context of what appears to be a shift away from the Washington consensus. In this book, we refer to this post-neo-liberal regionalism as *managed hybrid regionalism*, to convey the idea that it contains a combination of policy tools that neither fully embrace market competition nor totally shield domestic markets from that competition. In a way, managed hybrid regionalism expresses a more mature economic policy-making, as states have learned through experience what works and what doesn't when it comes to linking their economies to the rest of the world.

---

23   Schulz et al., *Regionalization* ..., 3.

24   John Williamson, 'What Washington Means by Policy Reform', in John Williamson (ed.), *Latin American Readjustment: How Much has Happened* (Washington: Institute for International Economics, 1989).

Towards a Theory of Regionalism

Developing a theory of regionalism requires one to stand outside the prevailing focus on governance at the international and national/local political levels. Regionalism studies, in fact, force us to conceptualize the middle layer of governance, i.e., that layer between the state and the global. Robert Cox, in his studies of world orders and historical change, provides us with an excellent framework for developing a theory of regionalism. Cox utilizes history, philosophy, economics and geopolitics to show that politics cannot be separated from economics, that theory cannot be separated from practice, and that material elements cannot be divorced from ideas and institutional practices. Ideas, institutions and material capabilities, according to Cox, combine in an interactive way to co-produce world orders.[25]

Cox's dialectical approach to understanding shifts in world orders is a useful starting point for our discussion of the re-mapping of the Americas. The emergence of regionalism and regionalization can be linked to the ideological and processional shifts that are occurring in the historical structure of the prevailing world order. These shifts are producing a dialectical tension between dominant/extant and alternative/emergent social forces. Cox envisions two future scenarios as the outcome of these global shifts. One is the relative decline of US hegemony, thus giving way 'to a more plural world with several centers of world power that would be in continuous negotiation for a constantly adjustable *modus vivendi*, much akin to the European 19th-century balance of power system'. The other scenario is an ongoing struggle for global domination (full spectrum dominance), that pits US-led forces against a 'potential consolidation of Eurasian power'.[26] In either scenario, there would be a role for regional arrangements. If US hegemony is in fact on the decline, regional arrangements might in fact be a rational alternative to the centralization of power that characterized US hegemony. If the US continues its struggle for global domination, the emergence of regional arrangements could be one geopolitical way of countering that trend.

Certainly, countries that live immediately under the shadow of the US giant have more at stake than others as the geopolitical tectonic plates begin to shift. The biggest challenge for those countries is to adjust to whatever the outcome of those shifts might be. As shown in this book, the re-mapping that is occurring in our region reflects the decisions made by leaders to find ways of adjusting to the new realities of the twenty-first century and of buffering their national units, via regional and sub-regional arrangements, against the onslaught of globalization and against the US's quest to sustain geopolitical dominance. Re-mapping has also been the result of the newfound activism of non-state actors whose influence

---

25   Theory Talk #37, 'Robert Cox on World Orders, Historical Change, and the Purpose of Theory in International Relations', found at www.theory-talks.org/2010/03/theory-talk-37.html, posted 12 March 2010, accessed 16 August 2010.

26   Ibid., 1.

in a globalized world is growing and certainly much stronger than it has been in the past.

Another way of conceptualizing the emergence of regionalism and regionalization is through the lens provided by the late James Rosenau. Rosenau argued that the shifts in world order we are currently witnessing are really an outcome of tensions between 'globalizing and localizing forces'. Rosenau labels this dialectical phenomenon as 'fragmegration' – a 'composite designation which connotes the interaction of fragmentation and integration'.[27] In other words, fragmegration dynamics can be described as oscillation between centralizing and decentralizing tendencies. One can conclude that these dialectical and oscillating forces are contributing to the re-mapping we are currently witnessing in the western hemisphere. Rosenau would describe this re-mapping as a shifting in the 'boundaries of communities'.[28] These boundaries are certainly in flux as states within our hemisphere adopt the ideology of regionalism or engage in processes of regionalization.

Linked to Rosenau's concept of fragmegration and Cox's dialectical approach to shifts in world order is Robertson's concept of 'glocalization'.[29] The term glocalization describes a mutual interpenetration of the global and the local, or the universal and the particular. Thus, the local is not created in a vacuum, but is created in reference to the global and vice-versa.

The evolution of regional arrangements can also be generally viewed as a means of easing the burden placed on global governance mechanisms. The UN Charter, in Chapter VIII, recommends the development of such subsidiarity arrangements and burden-sharing agencies as a means of contributing to the global role of the UN system.[30] This Chapter of the Charter became increasingly important at the end of the Cold War when the UN became overburdened and overstretched as it went through a period of assertive multilateralism.[31] There is a tendency, in the increasingly globalized world, to utilize regional arrangements to deal with transnational issues that cannot be handled properly either by national governments or by global institutions. Some scholars claim that regionalism is one way for some vulnerable states to deal with the onslaught of globalization. Thus, regionalism can be a reaction against globalization but also, paradoxically, a force for enhancing global governance over the long run.

---

27   See James N. Rosenau, 'New Dimensions of Security: the interaction of globalizing and localizing dynamics,' *Security Dialogue*, 25 (3) (1994), 256.

28   James Rosenau, 'New Dimensions of Security', 258.

29   Roland Robertson, 'Globalisation or Glocalisation?', *The Journal of International Communication*, 1 (1), 33–52.

30   W. Andy Knight, 'Towards a Subsidiarity Model for Peacemaking and Preventive Diplomacy: Making Chapter VIII of the UN Charter Operational,' *Third World Quarterly*, 17 (1) (March 1996), 31–52.

31   See Stanley Meisler, 'From Hope to Scapegoat', *The Washington Monthly* (July–August 1996), 36.

The Origins of Regionalism in the Americas

The idea that countries in the Americas have an advantage in transcending the limits of the national state in order to achieve economic, political and social objectives is not new. Indeed, some of its earlier formulations date back to the early nineteenth century when former European colonies in the region achieved independence. Illustrations of this movement can be found in the creation of the Republic of Central America (encompassing present day Guatemala, Honduras, El Salvador, Nicaragua and Costa Rica) in 1823, and the Gran Colombia in 1819 (encompassing present day Panama, Colombia, Venezuela and Ecuador). These experiences of full-fledged political integration were, however, short-lived and gave way to more complex mechanisms of mutual cooperation within formalized legal frameworks.

But before describing these regional and sub-regional arrangements, it is important to note here that two distinct kinds of hemispheric regionalisms emerged during the post-war period. The first were those that included the United States, and the second were those that restricted membership to Latin American countries. The difference between these two approaches is crucial for analytical purposes: the first kind attempted to build alliances under US leadership; the second type was concerned with building alternatives to, or even confronting, US hegemony in the hemisphere. These two contrasting models of regionalism have been present and competing with each other in the Americas for almost 200 years. Both types are still manifest in the newest hemispheric alliances being built in the twenty-first century, as we shall see later in this introductory chapter.

Regional and Sub-regional Arrangements

We begin here by examining 13 regional and sub-regional arrangements which can be viewed as early experimentations with hemispheric economic and political collaboration. These are: the International American Conference; the Pan American Union; the Organization of American States; the Latin American Economic System; the Inter-American Development Bank; the Economic Commission for Latin America; the Latin American Free Trade Agreement; the Latin American Integration Association; the Andean Pact; the Central American Common Market; the Caribbean Common Market; the Caribbean Free Trade Area; and the Caribbean Community and Common Market.

The International American Conference

The first ever International American[32] Conference (IAC) was held in Havana in 1889–90, in an effort to create a hemispheric community of states. In contrast to

---

32   It matters to recall here that the noun 'America' (in singular) and its adjective 'American' originally refer to the whole western hemisphere, not just to the United States.

previous integration experiences, this initiative was aimed at being comprehensive, with invitations to all countries in the hemisphere to join in.[33] The United States not only eagerly participated; it became the leader and promoter of the whole process. This conference was not about political integration *per se*, but mostly about cooperation around ambitious functional economic objectives such as establishing a monetary union, creating a hemispheric development bank, and adopting common customs and transportation norms. Trade liberalization, however, was excluded from the agenda mostly due to the reluctance on the part of the US to give up its protectionist policies of the time, fearing it could not stand competition from other countries in the hemisphere. As Knight notes in the next chapter, this may also have to do with the reluctance by the US to take on the mantle of responsibility of 'the global hegemon' after Great Britain had more or less relinquished that role. This approach would stand in stark contrast to the official position of the US government 100 years later,[34] as will be discussed later in this introduction.

The Pan American Union

The Havana Conference (1890) resulted in a call for the creation of a Pan American Union that would be headquartered in Washington. At the second gathering of the International American Conference held in Washington, DC in 1901 and convened by US Secretary of State, James Blaine, 18 nations resolved to establish an International Union of American Republics, which would be served by a permanent secretariat called the Commercial Bureau of the American Republics (later renamed the 'International Commercial Bureau' in 1901–02). By the Fourth International Conference of American States (held in Buenos Aires in 1910), the name of the organization was officially changed to the 'Union of American

---

This original meaning, which is still in common use in most countries in the hemisphere, was used in naming the first hemisphere-wide international organizations. Gradually, the United States imperialistically appropriated to itself the terms 'America' and 'American', as explained in James W. Russell, *Class and Race Formation in North America* (Toronto: University of Toronto Press, 2009), 6. As a result, hemispheric organizations resorted to alternative names, such as 'pan American', 'inter-American', or, more recently, the plural 'Americas'.

33   Canada was an exception to this open invitation. At the time, this country's foreign relations were still dictated from London, and it was thus viewed with suspicion by most countries in the hemisphere, as an outpost of the British Empire. Even after Canada gained foreign policy autonomy in the 1920s, this country embraced gradually and slowly its hemispheric belonging. As a revealing indication, it became a member of the OAS only in 1990.

34   Julián Castro-Rea, 'Du pessimisme chronique à l'optimisme téméraire. L'intégration latino-américaine et l'Initiative pour les Amériques', in *Continentalisation*, 93–3, Montreal: UQAM, May 1993, 42–43. Discussion on the origins of regionalization in this introduction draws heavily from this work.

Republics' and the Bureau to service that organization became the 'Pan American Union' (PAU).

The Pan American Union Building was constructed in 1910 on Constitution Avenue, Northwest, Washington, DC. The primary mandate of the PAU was to promote peace through cooperation between Latin American countries and the US. It was also supposed to address a number of areas of common commercial and juridical problems that had cropped up among the countries of the Americas. However, the Union fell short of the Conference's ambitious economic objectives, becoming rather a facilitating mechanism for diplomatic relations, and especially a tool for the exercise of US diplomacy in the hemisphere. In the mid-1930s, US President Franklin Delano Roosevelt organized an inter-American conference in Buenos Aires at which one of the items placed on the agenda was the establishment of a 'League of Nations of the Americas' – an idea first proposed by Colombia, Guatemala and the Dominican Republic.[35] At the subsequent Inter-American Conference for the Maintenance of Peace, 21 nations came together and pledged to remain neutral in the event of a conflict between any two members.[36]

By World War II the member governments of this inter-American body were convinced that unilateral action would not ensure the territorial integrity of nations in the hemisphere in the event of extra-continental aggression. This is why they decided that in order to meet the challenges of future global conflict, like World War II, and to contain any conflicts within the hemisphere, they would embrace a system of collective security – the Inter-American Treaty of Reciprocal Assistance (or the Rio Treaty). That Treaty was signed in 1947 in Rio de Janeiro.

The Organization of American States (OAS)

The Pan American Union was replaced in 1948 by the Organization of American States (OAS), the first international institution created in the Americas in the postwar era. In contrast to its predecessor, the OAS was, above all, primarily a political organization with limited economic objectives. Moreover, it was soon perceived as a tool of US hegemony in the hemisphere, something that became even more evident when Cuba was expelled from the organization in 1962. Nonetheless, the OAS provided a space for some independent action by member countries, such as the creation of the Latin American Economic System (*Sistema económico Latinoamericano*, SELA) in 1975 – a mechanism designed to promote cooperation in the areas of development and 'economic security' among 25 Latin American countries, through joint ventures and industrial and technological exchanges. On the political front, SELA aimed to coordinate the strategies of member countries vis-à-vis other states and also to coordinate member governments' voting behaviour in multilateral organizations.

---

35   Special to *The New York Times*, 'League of Nations in Americas urged by 3 Latin states,' *The New York Times* (13 April 1936), 1.

36   'Americas adopt neutrality pact', *The New York Times* (20 December 1936).

The Inter-American Development Bank

Other regional institutions that were created during the early post-war years, in response to the hemisphere's goal of promoting industrial development and economic modernization, were the Inter-American Development Bank (IDB) and the Economic Commission for Latin America and the Caribbean (ECLAC). The IDB was founded in 1959 as the hemispheric-specific branch of the World Bank. ECLAC was a UN offspring established in February 1948, which aimed to explore and suggest policies for development of the region. During the decade of the 1960s, inspired by the European example, regionalism witnessed a revival in the Americas. These sub-regional and regional integration experiments systematically excluded the United States to the extent that they had a strong autonomous development thrust. Inspired by dependency theory, largely elaborated and promoted by influential Argentinian economist Raul Prebisch within ECLAC, these hemispheric integration efforts were driven largely by the goal of supporting the quest of member countries to expand their markets, thus reversing the deterioration of the terms of international trade by implementing import substitution industrialization (ISI) policies to encourage national industrialization. Among the various regional integration experiments of this kind we highlight the following.

The Latin American Free Trade Agreement

The Latin American Free Trade Agreement (*Asociación Latinoamericana de Libre Comercio*, LAFTA/ALALC) was created by Argentina, Brazil, Chile, Mexico, Paraguay, Peru and Uruguay through the Treaty of Montevideo in 1960. The intent of the signatories to this Treaty 'was to create a common market in Latin America' and to offer tariff rebates among member states. LAFTA was brought into effect on 2 January 1962 with the above seven members. Its primary goal was to eliminate all duties and restrictions on the majority of trade among member governments within 12 years. By the late 1960s, the LAFTA area comprised 220 million people, the area was producing roughly $90 billion of goods and services each year and its per capita gross national product averaged $440.[37]

The LAFTA agreement did not bring about the kind of political and economic integration that was manifested in the European Union. But by 1970, LAFTA had expanded to include Bolivia, Colombia, Ecuador and Venezuela, bringing the total membership to 11 states. In LAFTA, high barriers to external trade into member countries were maintained, despite the GATT Kennedy and Tokyo Round's efforts to push in the opposite direction. LAFTA justified this by appealing to GATT's article 24, which allowed member countries to team up in regional clusters provided they created new trade rather than divert within the region existing exchanges with the rest of the world. LAFTA's objective was to create a full-fledged common

---

37 *Latin American Integration Association (Aladi) Handbook* (International Business Publications, 2007), 33.

market within 12 years, through gradual trade liberalization among its member countries. Foreign investment was welcome but strictly regulated with quotas and performance requirements, and soft attempts were made to divide commercial and governmental functions between members. Within LAFTA, the reduction of tariffs and other barriers were negotiated on the basis of product lists, which limited the extent of cross-sector trade-offs. Other subjects were likewise addressed on a piecemeal rather than on a comprehensive basis; the members sought to regulate economic specialization by agreement rather than via the market. Relative differences in development levels and market power were acknowledged, allowing weaker economies to claim special treatment.

Member countries were initially enthusiastic about exchanging preferences within LAFTA, but the game was up once all of the easy items – usually goods that were not produced domestically – were liberalized. The process stalled when difficult sectors – e.g. automobiles, other consumer durables, agriculture and textiles – came up for discussion. Only about 25 per cent of intra-regional trade ended up being liberalized. In other words, the theory of industrial rationalization behind LAFTA broke down in practice – the victim of domestic pressure from business which benefited from protectionism and the member states' reluctance to give up significant amounts of sovereignty over foreign transactions. On the whole, LAFTA served political rather than economic purposes.

Latin American Integration Association

By 1980, LAFTA was replaced by the less ambitious Latin American Integration Association (*Asociación Latinoamericana de Integración*, LAIA/ALADI). Based in Montevideo, Uruguay, the LAIA's main objective was to establish a common market and pursue economic and social development of the region. The Montevideo Treaty, which was signed on 12 August 1960, provided the international legal framework that established and governed the Latin American Integration Association. It laid out a set of principles under which this regional integration body would operate, e.g. pluralism, convergence, flexibility, differential treatment and multiplicity, which was largely structured around bilateral and sectoral trade preferences and was much more modest on the wholesale trade liberalization front.

LAFTA brought many new positive changes to Latin America, including the utilization of productive capacity more fully to supply regional needs; the reduction of costs to industries as a result of potential economies through expanded output and regional specialization, and attracting new investment as a result of the regional market area. While LAFTA brought many constructive results, like other FTAs it has also brought problems to individual nations and to Latin America as a whole. Some of the problems which individual countries faced were the way they were grouped together by their economic strengths according to LAFTA. The groupings placed Argentina, Brazil and Chile in one group, Colombia, Chile, Peru, Uruguay and Venezuela in the second group, and Bolivia, Ecuador and Paraguay in the final group. The problem with this classification is that it ignores the great economic and other differences between the countries. One of the other problems which Latin America faced as a whole had to do with many of the nations in the continent being underdeveloped. However, the Free Trade Agreement was seen as a way for these countries to have greater economic interactions with each other and thus improve the economic state of the poorer nations.

Andean Pact

Partly due to the limited progress on LAFTA's goals, and partly due to a feeling that Argentina and Brazil were grabbing all of LAFTA's gains, in 1969 six of the 11 LAFTA members established their own new arrangement – the Andean Pact. The original membership in this new agreement included Bolivia, Colombia, Ecuador, Peru and Chile (which left the Pact in 1976). Earlier, in 1973, Venezuela had joined the Pact. The Andean Pact gave priority to mutual support for industrial development rather than to trade in itself. Production-sharing arrangements between the Andean countries were a major focus of negotiation, buttressed by a highly restrictive investment regime. Moreover, the Pact established a development bank, the Andean Development Corporation, and an emergency financial pool, the Andean Reserve Fund. This highly institutionalized structure was modelled after the European Economic Community (EEC), and embraced the ambitious goal of becoming a customs union before ALALC became a full-fledged free trade zone.

However, unlike the EEC, the Pact did little to liberalize trade between its members. In fact, severe external barriers were maintained by all members with the exception of Colombia. Political instability in Chile and Peru further hindered the achievement of the ambitious regional objectives. Eventually, in 1985, the Pact members re-launched the project, this time abandoning their contribution to the achievement of ALADI's goals.

Central American Common Market (CACM)

Another early sub-regional trade arrangement was the Central American Common Market (CACM) comprising five Central American countries.[38] It was created in 1960 as a sub-regional alternative to ALALC, similar to the Andean Pact. CACM built on the political coordination achieved by the Organization of Central-American States (ODECA), a multilateral institution parallel to the OAS that was inspired by the historical commonalities of the region. Early liberalization measures produced trade growth among the members, and common external tariffs and trade policy were achieved. However, common industrial policy including efforts at production and investment sharing led to acrimonious debate among CACM members. Achievement of integration objectives was further compromised by border conflicts, revolutionary movements and civil war. By the 1980s, the

---

38   Guatemala, El Salvador, Honduras, Nicaragua and Costa Rica.

CACM sub-regional arrangement was totally overshadowed by political and military conflicts within the region and by economic instability.

CARIFTA and CARICOM

Immediately after gaining independence from the British Empire, several Caribbean states attempted to merge into a single political entity in 1958 – the West Indies Federation. The Federation, however, proved short lived, collapsing in 1962 and thus following the path that Central and South America had taken almost a century and a half earlier. Although political integration proved unsuccessful at that time, attempts at economic integration had a better record. In 1968 several Caribbean countries[39] launched the Caribbean Free Trade Area (CARIFTA). From the outset, CARIFTA took the trade liberalization goal seriously; the historical tariffs to intra-regional trade were abolished from the moment the treaty took effect, with the exception of some products that were considered 'sensitive'. In 1973 CARIFTA was replaced by the Caribbean Community and Common Market (CARICOM), to reflect the adoption of more ambitious objectives, such as common external tariffs, policy coordination in transportation, financing, industrial development and joint gathering of statistics. CARICOM member countries also adopted common positions on foreign policy issues, thus making CARICOM a sub-regional political arrangement as well. On the downside, trade between member states was extremely limited, thus contrasting with other integration schemes in the Americas where intra-regional trade flourished, although at the expense of exchanges with the rest of the world.

The Move from Import Substitution to Open Regionalism

By the mid-1980s, as a complement to the macroeconomic policies adopted in the wake of the international debt crisis, Latin American and Caribbean countries moved decisively away from protectionist policies, thus discontinuing the import substitution approach. They opened up their economies by reducing trade barriers and putting in practice export promotion strategies. Unilateral trade liberalization was carried out by simplifying tariff structures and reducing their rates from astronomical to merely high levels, and eliminating many non-tariff barriers, such as quotas or stringent sanitary regulations, except on agriculture. Furthermore, foreign investment was welcomed with fiscal and other enticements, instead of being restricted, conditioned to performance, or licensed. In the late 1980s and 1990s, a series of new agreements was negotiated throughout the Americas in the spirit of this new approach called 'open regionalism', designed to be

---

39   Anguilla, Antigua and Barbuda, Barbados, Belize, Dominica, Grenada, Guyana, Jamaica, Montserrat, Saint Vincent and the Grenadines, Saint Lucia and Trinidad and Tobago.

complementary with, and a prod to, GATT/WTO negotiations for freer trade on a multilateral basis.

Open regionalism essentially represented a neoliberal approach to inserting countries in the region into the world economy via regionalization. In one sense, it demonstrated a shift away from the Keynesian approach to economic integration through import substitution industrialization (ISI). Open regionalism focuses on industrialization on an intra-regional scale rather than on national industrialization and it attempted to liberalize and deregulate the economies of Latin American and Caribbean countries whilst drawing these economies more fully into the globalization process in an attempt to make the regional economies more competitive on the international and multilateral level.[40] In effect, open regionalism is an attempt to ensure that regional arrangements are in practice building blocks towards further global liberalization rather than stumbling blocks in the path of such liberalization.[41] Open regionalism was linked to the phenomenon of 'porous regions' during the decades of the 1980s and 1990s.[42] It was aided by the problems associated with 'uneven' globalization.

Understanding the Shift

It would be misleading to understand the shift from ISI to open regionalism as purely motivated by domestic actors and factors. In fact, this period of hemispheric relations was remarkable not only for the dramatic reorientation of the Latin American approach towards regional integration, but also for the intensive participation of multilateral organizations, the United States and Canada in hemispheric trade matters. We now turn to these developments.

The abandonment of import substitution and the opening up of hemispheric economies was promoted and carried out under the supervision of the International Monetary Fund (IMF), the World Bank (IBRD), the Inter-American Development Bank (IDB) and other money lenders. In most instances, credits were actually conditioned to the shift in the neo-liberal macroeconomic policies just described. Therefore, it is not coincidental those countries which found themselves in financial trouble ended up implementing similar policies: policies that were, in fact, the result of purposeful directives emanating from global financial institutions,

---

40   See Nicola Phillips, 'The rise and fall of open regionalism? Comparative reflections on regional governance in the Southern Cone of Latin America', *Third World Quarterly*, 24 (2) (2003), 217–234.

41   C. Fred Bergsten, 'Open Regionalism', Working Paper 97–3, Peterson Institute for International Economics (1997).

42   Timothy Shaw, 'New Regionalisms at the Start of the Second Decade of 21st Century: Lessons from/for the South?', paper presented at the Institute of International Relations, The University of the West Indies, St Augustine, Trinidad; and Peter J. Katzenstein, *A World of Regions: Asia & Europe in the American Imperium* (Ithaca: Cornell University Press, 2005).

aimed at promoting the participation of countries in the Americas into the global economy, within specific parameters.

Ironically, even ECLAC, the institution that created and promoted import substitution, eventually became the major exponent of open regionalism, encouraging countries to simultaneously participate in two or more trade and integration arrangements as long as each participatory step was driven by liberalization, both among the member countries and with the rest of the world. As Eduardo Gudynas points out, the concept of open regionalism as practiced in Latin America actually originated in ECLAC's proposal of the early 1990s aimed at generating new concepts about development.[43]

It is instructive that the US government was an eager promoter of this macroeconomic shift. The role the US has played, and the extent of its influence, in the shaping of inter-American relations can hardly be overstated. Ever since most countries in the hemisphere reached independence in the early nineteenth century, the US has tried to play a leadership role in the region. The infamous 1823 Monroe Doctrine and Theodore Roosevelt's militaristic, interventionist policies of the early twentieth century are dramatic illustrations of a continuous pattern of Washington's meddling in the Americas. As discussed above, the very creation of the Pan American Union, and its successor organization the OAS, reflected US hegemonic ambitions in the region.

During the Cold War, US policies in the Americas focused on bilateral aid; John F. Kennedy's 'Alliance for Progress' programme was its most representative example.[44] However, the aid strategy enjoyed limited success for a number of reasons. First, funding was transferred from government to government, leaving to the beneficiary country's discretion the use of the funds. Secondly, no significant effort was made to use the funds to alleviate poverty. Finally, most countries were not receptive to the implicit message about improving economic relations with the United States, being instead committed to inward-looking import substitution and domestically generated development. A change of approach came with the launching of the Caribbean Basin Initiative (CBI) in 1984 and the Enterprise for the Americas Initiative (EAI) in 1990.

The CBI targeted 22 Caribbean countries, whereas EAI was in principle open to all countries in the Americas, and it proposed the creation of a hemisphere-wide free trade area.[45] This time, the primary means for enhancing US hegemonic influence in the hemisphere was not military intervention, diplomacy or aid, but rather trade liberalization. In other words, as an enticement for cooperation, Washington offered states within the region the prospect of unrestricted business

---

43   Eduardo Gudynas, '"Open Regionalism" or Alternative Regional Integration?', *Hemispheric Watch* (26 October 2005).

44   See L. Ronald Scheman (ed.), *The Alliance for Progress: A Retrospective* (New York: Praeger, 1988).

45   For a more detailed description of these two initiatives, see J. Castro-Rea, 'Du pessimisme ...', 31–38.

with partner countries, opening up the huge US market to partner countries' exports and floating the potential for increased US investment in those countries. The main actors in the realizations of these promises would not be governments anymore, but rather private corporations that were given fiscal or regulatory incentives to expand their businesses internationally. Needless to say, this cooperation was conditioned upon adherence to principles of open regionalism. It also implied that partner governments would acquiesce to US leadership and support the hegemon's liberal economic agenda.

As domestic policies in Latin America and the Caribbean turned decidedly pro-market, the countries in that region embarked on a new generation of regional agreements. Pro-market approaches translated into lower external tariffs (unilaterally as well as within the WTO regime), privatization, disciplined macroeconomic policies (such as elimination of budget deficits and the maintenance of low inflation) coupled with harder currencies and democratic elections. While pro-market analysts praise the new approach of trade agreements in the hemisphere, there are those who are troubled by their proliferation – and have described the hemisphere as resembling a spaghetti bowl. A kinder term would be network – and the networking continues. A summary explanation of the various plurilateral and bilateral agreements in force today follows.

NAFTA   The Canada-US Free Trade Agreement (CUSFTA), implemented in 1989, turned out to be the forerunner of the 1994 North American Free Trade Agreement (NAFTA) and of other pacts within the hemisphere. These FTAs were consciously viewed as a template for the Uruguay Round of GATT negotiations – and were in fact used as such. NAFTA served as a welcome mat for Mexico's entrance into the world trading system, and marked a sharp turn from historical US-Mexican political and commercial antagonism.

As a consequence of the bilateral agreements negotiated by Canada and Mexico, NAFTA's principles, rules and disciplines have been indirectly 'exported' to other Latin American countries. From this perspective, NAFTA became a trailblazer for open regionalism in the Americas. All of Mexico's post-NAFTA agreements are built upon NAFTA disciplines. The G-3 agreement between Mexico, Colombia and Venezuela as well as Mexico's bilateral agreements with Bolivia and Costa Rica incorporate NAFTA-type principles and rules. The Canada-Chile free trade agreement even goes beyond the NAFTA in certain areas (notably, it rules out antidumping proceedings between the parties). Mexico and Chile are currently renegotiating their 1992 free trade agreement, in keeping with this trend.

Within the western hemisphere, in addition to the three NAFTA countries, Bolivia, Chile, Colombia, Costa Rica and Venezuela have also accepted NAFTA-type principles, rules and disciplines in important areas. For example, these five countries will grant foreign investors national treatment and accept international arbitration for the resolution of investment-related disputes. This is a far cry from the old Calvo Clause which asserted that investor disputes had to be adjudicated by local courts. In the service sector, these countries have agreed to undertake liberalizing measures which exceed those called for in the WTO, using a 'top-down' approach to free trade in all services. They have also agreed to national treatment-based rules in government procurement and have updated their intellectual property rights regimes. Finally and importantly, these agreements have adopted NAFTA-type dispute settlement mechanisms to resolve trade disagreements.

Increasing commonality in bilateral and plurilateral agreements bodes well for trade and investment relations within the Americas, particularly from a business vantage point. Common principles, rules and procedures and a strengthened legal framework are expected to smooth the way in future negotiations. NAFTA did not serve as the direct path to the FTAA, but it certainly played, and likely will continue to play, a significant role in structuring the framework for trade and investment liberalization (i.e. open regionalism) in the Americas.

MERCOSUR   The most important of this new generation of open regionalism arrangements is the Southern Common Market (MERCOSUR). In force since October 1991, this agreement initially included Brazil, the largest and wealthiest South American country, Argentina, Uruguay and Paraguay. Like the original European Common Market, the MERCOSUR served an important political purpose, namely to defuse tensions between Argentina and Brazil. Unlike earlier Latin American regional agreements, the MERCOSUR countries drastically decreased intra-regional tariffs – by 47 per cent immediately upon the implementation of the agreement, and completely since 1995, reduced their external barriers, liberalized investment, and tackled difficult sectors. This arrangement proved extremely successful at stimulating trade: intra-MERCOSUR exports grew by an average of 30 per cent per year during its first five years of existence. MERCOSUR has not visibly restricted its trade and investment with the rest of the world – both EU and US exports to countries that are parties to this agreement have grown at respectable rates.

Challenges remain to be tackled within the MERCOSUR, on the monetary as well as on the trade front. Argentina is highly vulnerable to a possible Brazilian devaluation and both countries depend on the credibility of each other to sustain their economic stability. Overall, intra-regional trade has increased. However, the Argentinian trade balance with Brazil has deteriorated, whereas Uruguay and Paraguay, the two minor partners, have increased their dependence on business with Brazil.

Andean Community of Nations (Comunidad Andina de Naciones, CAN)
Created in 1991, the Andean Community of Nations[46] is the Andean Pact in modern packaging. Formally called the Andean Common Market (CAN), this sub-regional grouping was intended as a corrective of the Andean Pact's modest

---

46   Current member countries are Bolivia, Ecuador, Peru and Colombia. Chile withdrew in 1976, Venezuela in 2006. Both countries are nonetheless considering joining CAN again.

achievements. Still highly institutionalized, the new Andean grouping discarded the more trade-discouraging measures and adopted a more investor-friendly regime, supplemented with economic policy coordination among member countries. The result has been genuine investment liberalization and free trade in some sectors, less bureaucracy overall, and an approach that is half FTA, half customs union. Trade among members has grown considerably as the member countries liberalized their trade regimes and as the Andean Community was reformed. A common Andean passport was created in 2001, and the movement of people among member countries was eased since 2005. In 2003, the Andean Community concluded a trade liberalization agreement with MERCOSUR, thus linking two major sub-regional re-mapping initiatives. If these two regional blocs granted full membership to each other, a true South American Free Trade Area – or SAFTA – would materialize.

Yet many puzzles remain. Trade is free from tariffs and non-tariff barriers among only three of the four country members, Peru standing apart. Three share a common external tariff – although there are exceptions even among these three; with Colombia tending to be more protectionist than the remaining member countries. Meanwhile, Bolivia and Peru are outside the common external tariff. Bolivia is now in the process of joining MERCOSUR, and has been allowed by the Andean Community to maintain its flat external tariff rate. Political hurdles also stand in the way of the Andean Community's successful achievement of its integration goals. Peru's membership came into question in 1992 when the other Andean countries condemned President Alberto Fujimori's 1992 closing of Congress and suspension of Constitutional rights. Venezuela broke off relations with Peru, and Peru's membership in the Andean group was suspended. Although Peru has since been reinstated, and in fact houses the Secretariat, its continued membership remains open to question. It should be noted that Peru also maintains its own bi-level tariff schedule and has parallel bilateral free trade agreements with each of the Andean countries.

Venezuela announced its intention to withdraw from CAN in April 2006 over charges that the trade agreements concluded between the US and Colombia and Peru made the Andean Community's objectives irrelevant. However, the withdrawal is not yet formalized, which leads to speculation that Venezuela may indeed re-join CAN in the future. Meanwhile, Venezuela is negotiating full membership into MERCOSUR. Despite its growing pains, the Andean Community is nevertheless moving forward with its integration goals and its expansion of trade relations with other countries. The Andean Community members spoke with one voice during the FTAA negotiations – and are in the process of negotiating as a unit with a number of other Latin American partners. However, one crucial question remains: will CAN eventually be gutted or even swallowed up by MERCOSUR?

CACM　　There has been a new burst of energy for sub-regional development in Central America, particularly after the countries in the region decided to resolve their civil wars. From the early 1990s on, the core Central American countries were actively engaged in developing liberalization agreements with Mexico and the United States. In 1991, a General Co-operation Agreement between Mexico-Central America was adopted. In August 2004, a Dominican Republic-Central America-United States Free Trade Agreement (CAFTA-DR) was drafted, partnering the US with Costa Rica, El Salvador, Guatemala, Honduras, Nicaragua and the Dominican Republic, and taking effect in January 2009. After February 1993, the CACM was merged into the Central American Integration System (SICA), the overarching economic, cultural and political organization of the six Central American states plus the Dominican Republic. Four member countries – Guatemala, El Salvador, Honduras and Nicaragua – are pursuing further political, cultural and migratory integration and have formed the CA4 (the Central America Four) union. Costa Rica is part of the CA4, but only in regards to matters dealing with economic integration and regional solidarity.

Central American integration, however, is far from a successful achievement. On the trade liberalization front, members have been negotiating together but signing and implementing agreements separately. Costa Rica has been especially active in reaching preferential agreements with Mexico, Venezuela, Chile and the US without any regard to the other Central American states. Similarly, Panama concluded a separate Trade Promotion Agreement with the US in July 2007, without taking into consideration how this might affect the other countries in the sub-region.

CARICOM   The Caribbean countries' integration process has kept pace with other sub-regional integration efforts, and has expanded to include the Bahamas in 1983, Suriname in 1995 and Haiti in 2002 (the latter became the fifteenth member state of the Caribbean Community). Note that since 1989 the Dominican Republic expressed a desire to be part of CARICOM. At the 2013 celebration of the 40th anniversary of signing of the Treaty of Chaguaramas in Trinidad, it looked like the Dominican Republic would get its wish, if a few issues raised by some of the heads of CARICOM could be clarified.[47] However, by November 2013, CARICOM, at the urging of Prime Minister Ralph Gonsalves of St Vincent and the Grenadines, suspended consideration of the Dominican Republic's request for full membership in the regional body.[48] This about face was in response to an outrageous ruling made by the Constitutional Court of the Dominican Republic which would deny

---

47   See Peter Richards, 'Venezuela and Dominican Republic come calling at CARICOM', *Inter Press Service News Agency* (8 July 2013), http://www.ipsnews.net/2013 /07/venezuela-and-dominican-republic-come-calling-at-caricom/, accessed 29 December 2013.

48   'CARICOM to Suspend Consideration of Dominican Republic's Bid For Membership', *Caribbean Journal* (26 November 2013), http://www.caribjournal.com/ 2013/11/26/caricom-to-suspend-consideration-of-dominican-republics-bid-for-member ship/, accessed 29 December 2013.

citizenship in that country to individuals of Haitian descent and therefore render these people stateless.[49]

Note that in Grenada, in 1989, the CARICOM Common Market was transformed into a single market and economy in which factors of production – including labour – were expected to move freely as a basis for enhancing internationally competitive production of goods and provision of services. As a result, CARICOM has been renamed the 'CARICOM Single Market and Economy' (CSME). The intent here was to provide people of the region with better opportunities to produce and sell their products and services and to attract investment. The CARICOM CSME has some lofty integration goals which are yet to be fully attained: e.g., the free movement of goods and services; the right to establish businesses in any member state of CARICOM without restriction; the imposition of a common external tariff; the free movement of goods imported from extra-regional sources and the sharing of collected customs revenue among member states; a common trade policy; the free movement of labour across the region and the harmonization of social services; the harmonization of intellectual property rights and other laws; and the coordination of macro-economic policies and the harmonization of foreign investment policy for the region.[50]

Despite the appearance of moving towards a single integrated sub-region, paradoxically Caribbean states have placed far more value on their dealings with the European Union (EU) and the United States than on the creation of any free trade area between the islands. In fact, they continue to focus on negotiations with the EU, based on the 1975 Lomé Treaty that created a preferential trade regime for former European colonies (see later in this introduction). Indeed, most Caribbean countries seemed to be waiting for an invitation to join NAFTA, or for more US unilateral liberalization via the extension of the 1984 Caribbean Basin Initiative (CBI). Many Caribbean states were cautiously enthusiastic about the prospects of a FTAA. Indeed, Trinidad and Tobago actively promoted its capital, Port of Spain, as the site for the FTAA's secretariat. Expectations of more substantial economic gains go a long way towards explaining this attitude of CARICOM.

Agreements Involving Chile, Mexico and Canada   Since the early 1970s, as a result of the early adoption of market-oriented macroeconomic policies during Pinochet's dictatorship, Chile has had a head start over most Latin American economies in regards to trade liberalization. Not surprisingly, this country actively put open regionalism into practice. In the early 1990s, Chile sought membership in NAFTA. However, Washington's politics proved too much of a hurdle and Chile negotiated, instead, a series of bilateral FTAs with Mexico (1998), MERCOSUR

---

49   Ralph Gonsalves, 'An Outrageous Ruling', *Trinidad Express* (21 October 2013), http://www.trinidadexpress.com/commentaries/An-outrageous-ruling-228702751.html, accessed 29 December 2013.

50   See Caribbean Community Secretariat, http://www.caricom.org/jsp/single_market/single_market_index.jsp?menu=csme, accessed 29 December 2013.

(1996), Canada (1996) and Central America (1999). Eventually, a United States-Chile Free Trade Agreement was concluded in 2003, and it was made effective the following year. This agreement was soon followed by agreements with Colombia, Panama and Peru in 2006.[51] In addition, Chile has negotiated preferential agreements (involving only specific industrial sectors) with all South American countries except Brazil. Mexico and Canada have also been particularly active in promoting bilateral FTAs within the western hemisphere, sometimes one-on-one arrangements (e.g. Chile-Mexico, 1998), sometimes one-on-one-plus. Usually these bilateral deals are designed to be NAFTA and/or MERCOSUR consistent (e.g. Mexico with Colombia and Venezuela in the Group of Three Agreement, G-3; an agreement that has been in place since 1994). Besides the FTAs already mentioned, Mexico also reached trade liberalization agreements with Uruguay (2003), El Salvador, Honduras and Guatemala (2000), Nicaragua (1997), Bolivia (1994) and Costa Rica (1994). Additionally, Mexico reached a framework agreement with MERCOSUR (2002) and preferential agreements with six South American countries plus Panama. We should also note that Canada has reached agreements with the US, Mexico and Chile and has formed FTAs with Costa Rica (2001) and Peru (2008). Similar agreements that were reached with Colombia and Panama are awaiting implementation.

Agreements Involving Cuba   Cuba is a regional player that has been side-lined in many of the hemispheric re-mapping endeavours. It was, for example, excluded from the OAS in 1962 due to United States pressure on all OAS member countries to ostracize Cuba. While the US continues its embargo on the island, Cuba trades substantially with the countries of the Caribbean as well as with Mexico and Venezuela. Canada and Mexico invest in the Cuban economy, especially in the tourism and mining sectors. The Association of Caribbean States (ACS), which includes Cuba in its membership, is considering a proposal for a wider Caribbean Free Trade Area. When Cuba once again joins the inter-American system, the implications will be significant. A large island with rich natural resources and a talented workforce, Cuba has the potential to be a frontrunner in the Caribbean. It has potential in mining, pharmaceuticals, sugar, rum and bananas. Added to this, there is a pent-up desire of many people in the US to spend their tourist dollars in Cuba – a factor that will undoubtedly boost Cuba's tourism sector – most likely at the expense of its Caribbean neighbours. President Obama's new strategy of seeking a rapprochement with Cuba might change the stalled US–Cuban relations, possibly making it easier for Cuba to

---

51   Full information about existing trade liberalization agreements is provided by the OAS at http://www.sice.oas.org/agreements_e.asp, accessed 20 July 2010.

become part of certain sub-regional and hemispheric relations. This in itself would be an interesting case of re-mapping.[52]

In sum, open regionalism in the Americas is progressing by the day, with all 34 countries in the hemisphere somehow involved in one way or another. It has, in effect, facilitated a re-mapping of the hemisphere as actors in the region try to take advantage of an environment of intensified globalization, or protect themselves from the onslaught of the negative impacts of globalization, by strengthening regional and sub-regional arrangements. The authors in this book accept the assumption that regionalism and regionalization are dynamic, multidimensional and pluralistic ideas and processes that are helping to re-map the Americas in ways that are still unfolding. These ideas and processes can be tracked down, described and analysed at conjectural moments, but their ultimate result cannot be definitely defined at the present moment.

Framework of Analysis

The chapters that follow this introduction will provide the reader with a snapshot of the regional re-mapping that is ongoing within the hemisphere. The chapters are divided into four sections: 1) the Backdrop; 2) Hegemony, Regionalization and the Changing Hemisphere; 3) Regional Security, Governance and Multilateralism; and 4) Conclusions.

This chapter, which is a lead-in to the Backdrop, introduces the reader to the subject of re-mapping the Americas and provides a brief history of the mapping and re-mapping that have taken place in the hemisphere so far. We provide the conceptual framework used by the chapter contributors to understand the making and remaking of regional and sub-regional groups in the hemisphere. Re-mapping implies a constantly changing and dynamic scenario. Thus, the best that can be offered in a volume such as this is a snapshot of a conjunctural moment in which the hemisphere seems to be undergoing a revitalization of regions, regionalism and regionalization. An effort is made to define these three terms so that readers will be 'singing from the same song sheet' as the chapter contributors, as they plough through this volume. As editors of the volume, we offer our own take on a theory of regionalism to guide the analyses throughout the book and we flag, here in the framework of analysis, some of the key issues taken up by the various authors in the subsequent chapters.

Vaughan A. Lewis, a former Prime Minister of St Lucia, extends the backdrop section of this volume with his contribution – in Chapter 2, titled 'Regional and Global Governance: Theory and Practice in the Caribbean'. Vaughan A. Lewis argues that the relatively common rules and procedures of national governance

---

52 See Celestino del Arenal, 'Relations between the EU and Latin America: Abandoning Regionalism in Favour of a New Bilateral Strategy?', working paper 36/2009 (Madrid: Real Instituto Elcano, 2009), 30 pp.

regimes in the CARICOM area have allowed for the growth in regional institutions. However, the move towards regionalisms in this hemisphere is also triggered by reactions to changes in the international political economy, to changes in the LOMEÉ arrangement, to the US push for liberalization of economies in the region and omnibus trade arrangements, to rapid technological advances, and to the rise of the BRICs and, in particular, to China's increasing engagement in the region. Clearly, for Lewis, regionalism in the Caribbean and Latin American areas is a reaction to the negative onslaught of certain globalization processes. In such cases, it is in the self-interest of small states like those in the Caribbean to 'adopt a stance of self-assertion as a collectivity in the international system'. Small states in the CARICOM area have no choice but to plug into larger global governance entities such as the Commonwealth and the United Nations for their survival, and it is best that they do so, according to Lewis, as regional collectivities rather than singly.

The author uses the case study of climate change to illustrate his point that the interests of small island developing states (SIDS) are best served when those states are able to be cohesive in advancing their positions in regional and global multilateral fora. Lewis notes that the widening of options available to SIDS in the Caribbean and Latin America, is due, in large part, to the proliferation of hemispheric and sub-regional governance bodies such as UNASUR, CARIFORUM, CELAC, PETROCARIBE, ALBA, etc. He asks a critical question: 'to what extent within that complex of simultaneous activities does the CARICOM cum Caribbean find space for a self-defined spectrum of geo-economic negotiations', given the fact that the Latin America countries in the hemisphere are finding ways to plug into the wider, global political economy? Where does this leave the Caribbean? Lewis concludes that for small states in the Caribbean, regional arrangements and regional diplomacy should be the route to engagement with larger countries, particularly those within this hemisphere.

In the next section of the volume, labelled 'Hegemony, Regionalization and the Changing Hemisphere', there are seven chapters. W. Andy Knight in Chapter 3 examines 'The FTAA and its Untimely Demise'. He explains that if the FTAA negotiations were successful, the hemisphere could have been 're-mapped' in a way that most people would not have foreseen when the negotiations began. This proposed omnibus free trade area, involving 34 states, could have supplanted sub-regional integration efforts and actually helped to consolidate the US's neo-liberal global hegemonic position and strengthen the US's hand in global trade negotiations in the World Trade Organization. Knight's description of the framework and structure used in the negotiations of the FTAA provides useful insight into the unfolding of the process of liberalization first embodied in the Enterprise for the Americas Initiative and the North American Free Trade Agreement (NAFTA) and carried over into the attempt to introduce this new hemispheric trade arrangement – 'NAFTA on steroids'. The FTAA was conceived by the US as a hub-and-spoke regional order that would foster economic progress and democratization across the 34 member states and create the largest trading bloc in history.

Underpinning the FTAA negotiation structure and process was the ideology behind what some have called 'the Washington Consensus'. In the end, this ideology might have been responsible for the untimely demise of the FTAA, according to Knight. Certainly, there was a counter-hegemonic ground swell of resistance to this creeping neo-liberal free trade ideology by 2005 – the year that FTAA was supposed to become a reality – that came not only from leaders such as Brazil's President Luiz Inacio 'Lula' da Silva but also from labour unions, non-governmental organizations and other societal groups across the region. Knight offers a number of reasons why the FTAA failed and concludes that, along with the fact that there was little support for the neo-liberal project from the increasing left-leaning governments in the region, the FTAA petered out after the 9-11 terrorist attacks on US soil as the US government diverted its attention to address the new security imperatives.

In Chapter 4, titled 'Free Trade: A Tool for US Hegemony in the Americas', Julián Castro-Rea picks up where Knight leaves off. After explaining that the roots of the FTAA are to be found in NAFTA, Castro-Rea argues that trade liberalization under the FTAA would have promoted US hegemony throughout the Americas by aligning trade practices with US 'corporate behaviour and negotiations'. The free trade agreement between Mexico, Canada and the United States is used by this author to illustrate the detrimental effects of economic liberalization: viz., both Canadian and Mexican economies have become incredibly dependent on their US counterpart, while the best interests of their environments and citizens have come second to corporate profits. As Castro-Rea points out, essentially NAFTA has certainly demonstrated that its goals are not to promote fair and equal trade relations, but rather to promote what is in the best interests of multinational corporations.

For these reasons, Castro-Rea suggests that the proposed FTAA should not be considered an instrument for development. Rather, it must be seen as a mechanism that would enable corporate power and increased political influence of the US over the hemisphere. Liberalization of the market benefits corporations, and the standardization of trade policy promotes conformity along other dimensions of public policy. In so doing, it creates a dependency on the US, and therefore increases US influence and power over other states' policy decisions – for example, the increased Canadian and Mexican border security harmonization in the aftermath of 9-11.

Chapter 5, 'Re-mapping Trade Relations in the Americas: The Influence of Shifting Power', is written by Gaspare M. Genna, who explains why the EU, the US and MERCOSUR are better able to form FTAs with individual countries in the western hemisphere than with each other. He states that two interacting variables that influence the success of a FTA are the economic size of the actors, and their respective preferences. Preferences are based on the actors' comparative advantage; therefore developing actors desire a trade agreement that protects their infant industries while developed actors seek to protect their agricultural sectors and make the most of their capital-intensive exports. The main argument, according to Genna, is that 'successful development of regional integration depends on economic asymmetries and compatible preferences'.

According to Genna, the strategy for both the EU and US is one of competitive liberalization – the US is explicit in its intention, whereas the EU follows an implicit strategy under its Common Commercial Policy. This approach motivates non-members to join based on their concern about being excluded from the FTA, and makes expansion of the economic blocs depend on the preferences of the dominant economic power. This can only work, however, if there is a single dominant economy – if mid-size economies fail to comply, a stalemate will result. As Genna points out, this was exemplified by the MERCOSUR relations with the EU and the US. Brazil has essentially '[re-mapped] the conditions in the formation of MERCOSUR, for while MERCOSUR is more dependent on trade with both the EU and the US, both economic powers in turn rely significantly on MERCOSUR'. This relative balance of power contributed, according to Genna, to the stalemates faced in both relationships with regards to proposed FTAs.

Gaspare M. Genna's chapter convincingly shows how stronger global trade actors – the EU and US in particular – are unwilling to use their power capabilities to reduce the frustration of relatively weaker (MERCOSUR) actors when negotiating international agreements. In contrast, newly emergent economies, such as China's, are much more amenable to compromises with subaltern states. This finding goes a long way in explaining why a more balanced global trade regime may not be a reality at this juncture, and it underscores the contradictions of trade leaders at the time of negotiating. Genna also explains that one significant reason why the FTAA project collapsed is that the major partner in the agreement was not flexible enough to accommodate to the needs of minor partners. The way ahead, in his opinion, is a much needed opening of the agricultural, services and government procurement markets of stronger economies in order to make room for competition from smaller economies; as well as the strengthening of trans-Pacific trade links among emergent economies.

Mark Kirton in Chapter 6, titled 'CARICOM's Engagement with Latin America: The Community of Latin American and Caribbean States (CELAC), its Promise and Challenges', argues that in spite of the disappointments with regional integration efforts in Latin America and the Caribbean, the region has continued to witness its share of political and economic reconfigurations. For instance, in Latin America we have seen the establishment of the Latin American Free Trade Association (LAFTA), the Central American Common Market (CACM), the Andean Group, and the Latin American Integration Association (ALADI) over three decades since the 1960s. Similarly, in the Caribbean, since the 1950s, we have witnessed the rise and fall of the West Indies Federation and then the establishment of The Caribbean Free Trade Area (CARIFTA), the Caribbean Community (CARICOM), the Organization of Eastern Caribbean States (OECS), and the Association of Caribbean States (ACS).

In many respects, as Kirton notes, the regional integration efforts in Latin America and in the Caribbean were being developed on parallel tracks or in isolation of each other until recently. Now, it would appear that there is a greater perception of the shared economic and political space that both sub-regions occupy and there is a sense of converging interests between Latin American and Caribbean states. CARICOM, for instance, is beginning to build institutional ties with Latin America. This trend can be further seen with the establishment of the Bolivarian Alliance of the Peoples of our Americas (ALBA), the PETROCARIBE arrangement by Venezuela, the fact that Guyana and Suriname are now members of the Union of South American Nations (UNASUR), and the recent acceptance of Belize's engagement with the Central American Integration System (SICA). For Kirton, the apogee of this new intersection of Latin American and Caribbean integration efforts is best seen in the establishment of the Community of Latin American and Caribbean States (CELAC) in 2010. The author places this new integration effort under the umbrella of 'new regionalism', drawing on Hettne. It is a post-liberal, post-hegemonic regionalism that goes beyond merely trade and economic activity and encompasses as well social and cultural relations and reflects a convergence of interests and agendas on the part of Latin American and Caribbean states and peoples.

Kirton lays out the potential prospects and challenges for CELAC in the future. Clearly, one of the biggest challenges will be how to make sense of the overlapping and sometimes confusing nature of the myriad of regional and sub-regional bodies and processes that cut across Latin America and the Caribbean. Membership in regional and sub-regional organizations requires some material commitment. Small Caribbean states may have difficulty in meeting such commitments if they are members of so many organizations. Kirton points out that another challenge is the leadership question. With the death of Venezuelan President Hugo Chavez, the region has lost one of the main driving forces behind this new regionalism. Finally, questions remain about whether or not CELAC can co-exist with the Organization of American States and whether it will eventually subsume the other regional integration efforts.

Joseph Y.S. Cheng in Chapter 7, 'Latin America in China's Peaceful Rise', places his analysis in the context of the strategy that is orienting China's foreign policy in the Americas. Latin America is considered to be integral to the success of China's industrialization and growth, and the numerous agreements and commissions on economic and technological cooperation with various Latin American countries reflect the importance of this relationship. Cheng discusses the history of China–Latin America diplomatic relations, including trade, investment and the competition with Taiwan. This history is quite young, as close ties between China and Latin America only began to form in the 1990s after several decades of minimal interaction. In the 1980s, China had diplomatic relations with every country in the region but Paraguay, but had yet to make great use of those ties. However, China currently shares 'strategic partnerships with Brazil, Argentina, Venezuela and Mexico'. A history of the trade relationship between China and Latin America is discussed, and Cheng argues that the region has been, and will continue to be, a significant factor in the expansion of China's heavy industries.

China identifies with the struggle Latin America has faced trying to rise out of Third World status, and recognizes its potential to expand its trade partnerships (both for export and import relationships) while securing access to Latin American natural resources. It also opposes the threat of 'Americanization' in Latin America, and sees the importance of solidarity between itself and the states in Latin America (South-South cooperation).

Cheng also discusses the FTAA, as it was of great concern to China, threatening to create 'keen competition' between many Latin American countries and China, a situation that at some point Beijing deemed 'inevitable'. However, the country's exports are becoming focused on higher tech products, which will reduce the competition. Furthermore, while investment in Latin America remains rather small, it has increased with China's interest in securing access to the continent's natural resources. Cheng also addresses the issue of Taiwan's relationship with the region, stating that while Taiwan has garnered US$1.87 billion (China $3.8 billion) in trade surplus from its trade with Mexico and Panama, its 'investment ... has been much exaggerated by its investment in the British Territories ... [and therefore] such investment ultimately goes to China'. The emphasis Chinese leadership has placed on a multipolar world for the twenty-first century is part of a strategy that would allow China to increase its global influence in a peaceful way, and allow the Sino-Latin American relationship to flourish.

Patsy Lewis, in Chapter 8 – 'Assessing the Developmental Potential of the FTAA and EPA for Small Developing States' – compares the FTAA-style trade liberalization schemes to the EU-sponsored Economic Partnership Agreements (EPAs) from the perspective of small Caribbean states. Although both models share important components, including the fact that they were intended as 'WTO plus' and that their primary goal was the full integration of developing economies into global markets as a way of enhancing their prosperity, EPAs seem to offer better prospects for the developmental needs of weaker countries. As Patsy Lewis puts it: 'developmental concerns were always at the centre of these arrangements', with aid and trade twin pillars for addressing the developmental issues of the ACP countries. However, recent changes in the way EPAs are framed pose important challenges to those states when they try to engage in trade liberalization talks with economic powers. The key, in Lewis' estimation, is not to treat trade liberalization as separate and distinct from developmental objectives. Trade must serve development. Furthermore, in Latin America and the Caribbean, states are becoming wary of the homogenizing tendencies in the globalization and liberalization models proposed by developed countries in both the FTAA and EPA arrangements.

In Chapter 9, Matthew Louis Bishop takes a critical look at the progress, or lack thereof, made by the Caribbean Community over the years with respect to regional integration. His chapter, 'Whither CARICOM?', poses a question that many have asked in the past, and are asking today, about the state of permanent crisis that seems to prevail within CARICOM. There is a clear sense in Bishop's analysis that CARICOM is more or less spinning its wheels. The impasse with respect to regional integration in the Caribbean has become so embedded that one is tempted to call into question the very notion of integration. At the same time, Bishop notes that observers in this region do care about CARICOM and realize that unless something drastically changes in the way in which the Caribbean Community operates, then CARICOM itself will have a very bleak future.

But the author is also careful to situate CARICOM within what he calls 'the complex processes of structural re-mapping' that have taken hold within the hemisphere and within the Caribbean region. He provides a story of attempts at Caribbean regional integration that begins with the failed West Indies Federation (1958 to 1962) and continues with the emergence of CARIFTA in 1968 and its merging into CARICOM in 1973 with promises of deepening the integration process. This history also includes the announcement of the CSME process in 1989 which really did not materialize until 2006. That process was supposed to result in both deepening and widening of integration in the region and the expansion of trade with non-traditional partners outside the region. Yet, as Bishop points out, very little has actually been accomplished in any of those areas. The idea of a 'Single Domestic Space' may have worked during the 2007 Cricket World Cup, but since then we have seen almost a reversal from that forward movement towards true integration of the region.

Part of the problem, of course, lies in what Bishop calls the 'structural' impediments facing CARICOM. One cannot divorce CARICOM's problems from the economic downturn in Europe, the dramatic rise of the BRICs, the challenges to embedded liberalism, the attempts at entrenching the Washington Consensus and the accompanying neo-liberal order, the end of preferences and the shift to reciprocal trade arrangements, the graduation of some of the Caribbean states from donor aid and finance, and the 'spaghetti bowl' of overlapping regional and sub-regional institutions that have sprung up as alternatives to the FTAA. If Bishop's conclusion that the commitment to regional integration is dwindling, then the answer for vulnerable states in the Caribbean region might lie outside in trans-regional relationships (e.g. the EPA, which seems to have superseded the CSME process, and others like CELAC, ALBA, Petrocaribe, and the Trans-Pacific Alliance). Following on the Trinidad and Tobago Foreign Minister Winston Dookeran's vision of 'Caribbean Convergence', Bishop hints that there might be some hope for CARICOM, now in its fortieth year, to realize its promise. However, the answer to 'Whither CARICOM' may in the end be resolved by structural forces external to the region unless the leadership in CARICOM takes the bull by the horns and ushers in the kind of deepening and widening of the Caribbean integration process which is absolutely essential for the small, vulnerable states in this region to survive and thrive.

The next section of the book, 'Regional Security, Governance and Multilateralism', is comprised of seven chapters. It leads off with Chapter 10, by Greg Anderson, titled 'The Political Economy of Post-9/11 US Security in Latin America: Has Anything Really Changed?' In this chapter, Anderson focuses on three elements relating to US influence on Latin America in the aftermath of 9/11:

the pre-9/11 environment, the new realities after 9/11, and a discussion of the actual changes that have taken place in Latin America since 9/11. He begins by stating that, while Latin America and the Caribbean have historically been considered by the US as its 'backyard', the degree to which its power/influence has been exerted has waxed and waned over the last century. Anderson refers to this as 'sporadic attention' that was followed by 'inattention and neglect'. But by the end of the Cold War, US interest in the region was renewed and seemingly sustained with a focus on economic openness and the encouragement of democratic governance.

The initiatives pursued in the region by the US, such as the Enterprise for the Americas, NAFTA and the Summit of the Americas, all seem to reflect that underlying ideology of open markets and democratic governance. The ultimate reflection of that ideological goal for the US was the Free Trade Area of the Americas (FTAA). Anderson sees the FTAA as an attempt to spread the market benefits of open regionalism while at the same time supersede 'the inefficient patchwork of economic arrangements' that existed in the hemisphere. But the FTAA hit a snag with the competition from MERCOSUR and with the ideological conflicts that emerged between Brazil and the US during the process of the FTAA negotiations. Furthermore, as Anderson points out, the US's attention to the region shifted with the 9/11 terrorist attacks on American soil. The US's global 'War on Terror' was soon coupled with the 'War on Drugs' as the link between narco-terrorism and terrorist finance became increasingly evident. Further links between terrorism, drug trafficking and the trafficking in illicit arms led to the introduction of the Merida Initiative. According to Anderson, the impact of 9/11 on Latin America can be seen in the following:

- Attention shifted to the War on Terror, with enhanced 'scrutiny to a range of transactions between Latin America and the United States';
- Immigration and even travel has become more restrictive;
- The US has continued to pursue regionalization through economic interdependence with the western hemisphere;
- Due to the nature of their shipments, proximity, and a history that does not include terrorists, security measures imposed by the US on its trading partners have not been as severe on Latin America as they have been on other regions.

What has really changed with respect to US relations with Latin America? According to Anderson, not much! The Bush administration still pursued the guest-worker program, the FTAA process faced barriers unrelated to 9/11, yet trade agreements and trade liberalization have flourished, including under the Obama Presidency with its National Export Initiative. Immigration reform and border control have had the most impact, but for many Latin Americans this has not meant much change (Canadians were arguably more affected). In fact, the Obama regime has pushed a series of immigration reforms which could ease tensions between Latin American countries and the US.

Chapter 11 by Hamid Ghany raises the issue of the strategic culture that can affect a country's politics. Titled 'The Constitutional and Political Aspects of Strategic Culture in Trinidad and Tobago', this chapter, while focused on Trinidad and Tobago, is insightful for helping us understand the constitutional and political tensions that exist because of the British and American influences in the Caribbean. While the Westminster-Whitehall political system is still dominant in much of the Caribbean, the fact that Trinidad and Tobago – a leader in the region – has embraced elements of the American electoral system speaks volumes about the possibilities of shifts in the strategic culture of individual states in the Caribbean. If the experimentation with constitutional hybridization takes off in Trinidad and Tobago, is it possible that such a political system could be tried in other parts of the Caribbean? And will this have an impact on the nature and direction of regional re-mapping?

In Chapter 12, 'From Engagement to Influence: Civil Society Participation in the EPA Trade Negotiations and Regional Integration Processes', Annita Montoute argues that the attempt by Caribbean leaders to make the transition from CARICOM to the Caribbean Single Market Economy (CSME) was in large part a reflection of the global shift from 'closed regionalism' to 'open regionalism'. In that context, the author examines the CARIFORUM-EU Economic Partnership Agreement from the perspective of civil society and its attempt to influence the direction of the process leading to the agreement as well as the direction of Caribbean regionalism more broadly. She comes to the conclusion that while civil society did play a role in terms of engagement in the process, in the end, civil society failed to influence the outcome of the negotiations and in so doing lost the opportunity to influence the direction of regional integration in the Caribbean.

Norman Girvan, in Chapter 13, provides a different take on the ways in which Caribbean integration can be realized. Beginning with the assumption that the things that unite Caribbean people are far more powerful than the things that divide this people, Girvan takes the reader on a personal tour of cultural festivities, like the Festival del Caribe, to demonstrate how culture can in fact overcome the linguistic and political barriers to integration. The title of his chapter says it all: 'Caribbean Integration: Can Cultural Production Succeed where Politics and Economics have Failed? (Confessions of a Wayward Economist)'. As Girvan notes, if one looks at the Caribbean strictly through a political-economic lens, one would conclude that the region is one of 'extreme political fragmentation, linguistic diversity and disconnected economies'. That top-down view, he argues, is out of sync with the 'bottom-up view' seen through the lens of culture – music, dance, festivals, carnivals, literature, poetry, drama, film, food, art and sport. While the political leaders in the region have had dubious success with their various economic integration plans, there seems to be another process evolving – i.e. the building of a 'community of identities' – the result of a 'process of mutual self-discovery of ourselves as a Caribbean people ...'

Girvan finds examples of 'trans-Caribbeanity', cultural intercourse, cultural creativity that transcend the barriers of language, economics and polity. In fact, this evidence of regional integration via culture leads the author to ask: 'can cultural production succeed in driving integration, where economics and politics have failed?'

Obijiofor Aginam recognizes that globalization can be a double-edged sword when it comes to regional integration. In Chapter 14, titled 'Liberalization of Fair Trade or Globalization of Human (In)security? Protecting Public Goods in the Emerging Economic Integration of the Americas', Aginam highlights the challenges of globalization within the context of the Americas, and questions to what extent trade liberalization has had a positive or detrimental impact on human development in certain states. The question acknowledged by Aginam is whether trade liberalization will 'genuinely liberalize "fair trade" or accelerate vulnerability to human insecurity'. With the creation of the WTO in 1995, globalization evolved from strictly traded goods to trade in services, in addition to regulations imposed on governments and significant influence over state policy-making. Aginam points out that within the WTO, 'trade takes precedence over national public health measures' and he includes two case studies within his chapter to bolster the argument that the WTO has to a certain extent stripped states of their sovereignty, and capacity to perhaps look out for the best interests of their citizens.

Aginam warns that there is a chance that economic globalization could become predatory in nature and that free trade will end up trampling public goods in national jurisdictions. To avoid this, the author recommends that 'a policy space' should be created that will enable weaker states, especially those within the developing world, 'to strengthen their institutional capacity to generate and promote public goods' in accordance with the specific country's social and economic conditions.

Fred Judson in Chapter 15, titled 'The Dynamics, Limits and Potential of Formal Liberal Democracy in Latin America', discusses the ways in which the evolution of Latin American political systems has been interpreted, and he advances the perceived limits and possibilities for democracy there. Judson organizes the bulk of his discourse around three interconnected 'matrices': globalization, the hegemonizing regime of global security and the hegemonizing ideology of liberal democracy. Applying this outline, Judson explains through the lens of various political philosophers the path Latin America has taken during and since the Cold War.

In Chapter 16, 'Why Democracy and the Free Market are Good for *Caudillos*: The Nicaragua Case', Kalowatie Deonandan recognizes the road blocks to 're-mapping the Americas', such as corruption, which impedes foreign investment and therefore the economic growth of developing nations. The bulk of her chapter seeks to explain that liberalization and corruption are indeed linked, because opening up the economy provides an opportunity for the elite classes to exploit their positions of power for personal economic and political gain.

Corruption is defined in several ways, and then both individual and organizational aspects of corruption are used to analyse the case of Nicaragua, a developing state that has suffered multiple times first hand the negative effects of trade liberalization, including hyperinflation, dramatic dives in GDP and rampant government corruption. Corruption, according to Deonandan, 'is facilitated not only by calls for political pluralism but also by demands for economic liberalization'; therefore, IFIs and SAPs have actually created environments within developing states for corruption to thrive. She warns that the re-mapping of the Americas, by implementing neo-liberal free trade mechanisms and debt reduction initiatives such as SAPs, will only serve to increase the problem of corruption.

In the Conclusions, the editors reiterate the trends in regionalism in the Americas, explaining the hegemonic and counter-hegemonic tensions in those trends. They tease out the role of non-state actors in the process of region-making in the hemisphere, noting that the top-down approach to regionalism may not always be the most fruitful strategy, as the FTAA attests. The editors then explore the possible options for Latin American and Caribbean states as they welcome extra-regional trade and economic relations, including the overtures of emerging powers like China and India. They conclude that the re-mapping of the Americas is dynamic and on-going.

Chapter 2

Regional and Global Governance: Theory and Practice in the Caribbean

Vaughan A. Lewis

Introduction

What is immediately visible in the CARICOM area is a large similarity in rules and procedures of national governance regimes that has permitted, before and into the period of national independence, a growth of regional institutions common to the member states. This, as is well known, derives from the previous existence of a common colonial authority, and in the interests of economy and parsimony of institutions, collective systems of governance. The Windward and Leeward islands, for example, have long shared common judicial arrangements – where these have served, inter alia, as arbitrators of governance procedures; and for similar reasons of commonality of colonial rules, the assumption of an easy extension of judicial arrangements to other English-speaking countries in the region has been partially institutionalized in the Caribbean Court of Justice.

But the concept of global governance, more recently introduced into the literature of political science, has introduced another dimension, going beyond our understanding of commonality of governance institutions in neighbouring jurisdictional spaces largely for reasons of economy, to a concern with self or national preservation in the face of phenomena negative to national well-being. This relates to two kinds of situations or cases; the first being that in which the behaviour of a particular state, or institutions or actors in that state has, through action or inaction, negative effects on populations in other states. The resolution of the difficulties experienced in such a situation is then deemed to require, secondly, collective activity on the part of neighbouring states, as well as states in areas not necessarily in geographical proximity, on the basis of rules of procedure and behaviour that have to be negotiated, given differences in objectives, or in juridical approaches and systems, or in terms of the mere lack of interest of effects on others.

Where such differences exist, the process, or processes, of collective activity cannot necessarily be based on commonality of assumptions regarding appropriate behaviour, but rather on perceptions or beliefs that, over the medium to long run, self-interest requires voluntary or opportunistic adherence to specific rules of conduct, *in recognition of the possibility that default on the part of one state will negatively affect others, regardless of whether these others have themselves been adhering to the agreed rules.*

This latter preoccupation, as it relates to small states like those of the Caribbean, has induced them to adopt a stance of self-assertion as a collectivity in the international system, in order to alert larger powers involved, in particular, with varied types of industrialization, as to the latter's responsibilities in making accommodation for the inadequacies of the small states in coping with damage caused by their actions.

The interest of the states of the Caribbean Community (CARICOM) in active participation in discussions, and then on arrangements, for institutionalizing the concern of small states on the effects of climate change, and for engaging the wider international community to that end has been illustrative of their concern that only through organizational efforts that encompass rules of cooperation and governance can they come to terms with issues incapable of being solved otherwise.

In that regard their diplomatic orientation was to ensure active participation in international arrangements and institutions in which there was a sufficiency of states whose predicament in respect of climate change was similar to their own, this leading to their activities and coalition building in at least two substantial international organizations, the Commonwealth and the United Nations.

The interest of CARICOM states, along with other small island states in the Pacific and the Indian Ocean, in pursuing such courses of action is evident in the persistent treatment of the matter within the Commonwealth forum, as evidenced in the Lengkawi Declaration on the Environment at that institution's Heads of Government meeting in 1989, through the establishment in 1990 of the Association of Small Island States and leading to the UN Global Conference on the Sustainable Development of Small Island States in Barbados in 1994; and then to the Port of Spain Climate Change Consensus in the Commonwealth Climate Change Declaration of 2009, where the issue of climate change is described as 'the predominant global challenge'.

The methodology of pursuing sustained regional and international concordance on the issues involved has been, first, to forge bases for coalitions of sufficient size and commonality of concerns among the states likely to be affected, so as to be in a position to influence international organizations of which they have been a part – whether, for example, the Commonwealth or the United Nations; and secondly, through this coalition mechanism, to persuade larger and more influential states to treat the issue as one of major long-term international concerns. Then a third task has been to ensure that the rules for cooperation and governance of country conduct and country support for climate change resolutions and work schedules is sufficiently institutionalized in regional and international organizations – and particularly in the United Nations instruments.

These continuing preoccupations with effective coalitions among states likely to be affected are recognizable in a recent declaration of the Commonwealth, where small states emphasize that they 'represent a third of the world's population in all continents and oceans and more than one quarter of the Parties to the United

Nations Framework Convention on Climate change. We have the global reach and diversity to help forge the inclusive global solutions to combat climate change'.[1]

This orientation has continued to be pursued particularly in respect of the effects of climate change especially by the Pacific low-lying small island states concerned as they are with the effects of, among other things, not only hurricanes but sea-level rise.[2] And the issues involved have been recently surveyed at the recent United Nations Framework Convention on Climate Change (UNFCCC) in Doha in December 2012. And the small states' preoccupation with these issues was well summed up by the St Lucian Minister for Sustainable Development in his assertion that 'for the vast majority of the people who live in Small Island Developing States like mine, climate change is an inseparable part of life'.[3]

As is well known, however, the resolution of such issues is, more often than not, a function of the intertwining of a variety of larger states' preoccupations – economic and otherwise – which are often traded off at various times not in relation to particular aspects of the small states' preoccupations but as parts of larger bargains within the sphere of big power geopolitics.

In such a context, almost dominating the processes of negotiation, small countries have indicated, through their establishment of AOSIS, that it is an instrument designed to ensure the cohesion of their own coalition. Then they use that cohesion to advance their positions by seeking to influence larger entities – e.g. middle level states and coalitions of the like-minded – who have more direct access to the manoeuvrings of the dominant powers. And in that regard, CARICOM states have found the Commonwealth, with its diversity of countries and a common language of legal arrangements as well as diplomatic intercourse, a useful medium.

Changing Determinants of Multi-state Relations

Accommodation to issues relating to climate change, however, as a relatively new preoccupation of the major powers, is in part a function of their wider fixation with adjustment to technological and economic change that has begun to re-arrange the relations of nations, and to change the nature of competition between them. The phenomenon can be summed up in the concept of 'globalization' that has, first, induced a process of dissolution of old state and multi-state formations as in the case of the collapse of the Soviet Union and its sphere of economic and geopolitical dominance; or secondly, as in the case of the Commonwealth itself

1   Port of Spain Climate Change consensus: The Commonwealth Climate Change Declaration (November 2009), www.thecommonwealth.org/document/181889.34293/216780/climatechange_consensus.htm.

2   See for some discussion Malia Talakai, 'Climate conversations – small island states need action on climate loss and damage', *Alert Net*, 15 January 2013.

3   Minister of Sustainable Development, Government of St Lucia, 5 December 2012.

which has, over time, found itself needing to respond to a changing sphere, not only of international political relationships, but of economic organization, as evidenced in the longevity, and then virtual collapse, of the Imperial and then Commonwealth Preference systems which partly induced the United Kingdom to initiate the search for a wider sphere of global influence through adherence to the then European Community (EC).[4]

Further, as is now well recognized, as a response to the economic globalization process, China has been making a relatively successful transition from a closed economic system as it has sought alternative modes of economic development and, in effect, global economic viability through integration with the wider capitalist system.

Complementary to this has come China's engagement with the western sphere of global geopolitics, most evidenced in its now strategic role in the United Nations system; as well as the beginning of an intense competition for sale of goods and purchase of commodities that is drawing the country into the institutional readjustment of wider international economic relations. In turn, this has meant a Chinese commitment to what in the Western world has come to be known as 'global governance', with fixed rules of engagement now evolving, first through the current, though slow, movement of the Doha Round of international trade negotiation, and second, through China's increasing concern that it will need to be able to exercise an influence in the international monetary arrangements so far dominated by the Western powers.

In effect, the traditional one-power, or few-powers, dominant mode of determining the rules of international trade and production evidenced in, for example, the Commonwealth system and then the GATT, has gradually been giving way to balance of power type-negotiations for new terms of global economic governance. In that connection, what might be termed 'new middle economic powers', now described as emerging powers, are sought as weights and counterweights, with countries like China seeking alliances with states such as those in Latin America but also increasingly in Africa and Asia, in the process of the continuing, prolonged global institutional negotiations. The objective is the establishment of a new balance of economic power, sanctified by common acceptance of new international rules for trade and production engagement.

The perspective of new major entrants is indicated in a statement recently emanating from China itself to the effect that that country now 'has the need to enhance its capacity of in-depth involvement in global governance'; and that

---

4   In that regard, it can be said that Britain came to quickly recognize that the modes of governance that made the Commonwealth its operative instrument of international cooperation, had to give way to a wider European instrument, as indicated in the establishment of the ACP-EU relationship. This relationship itself has been partially giving way to Western Europe's preoccupation with the terms of arrangements to be established in wider Europe in the face of the dissolution of the Soviet Union and the entry into the EU of non-Western European members.

China's in-depth involvement in global governance is conducive to the adjustment of the new international order toward the direction of fairness and reasonableness. Since the international financial crisis, emerging market countries have increasingly become the stabilizer and even the engine for the world economy. Neglect of their demands in the discussion of 'global governance', or simply distribution of responsibilities according to powers will restrain the effectiveness of 'global governance'.[5]

But at the same time, stress, indicating a certain scepticism, is placed on the nature of the country's intervention or participation in global governing:

By adhering to the principle of 'common but differentiated responsibilities' in the field of international environmental protection, China's involvement in 'global governance' is increasingly intensified and more attention is paid to in depth involvement from the level of system and basic principles.[6]

The import of this is that globalization requires being managed collectively rather than by a few countries which have traditionally sat at the apex of the international production and trading system. But some emerging powers would want to argue that the traditionally dominant powers in international economic negotiations still wish to pursue contemporary negotiations as if the hierarchy of power remains the same – hence the blocks continually occurring in international trade negotiations of the last decade or so.

CARICOM Responses

From the perspective of some critics from CARICOM countries, the style of the traditional European Union mode of negotiation would appear to have been neglected by the European Union in the last round of ACP-EU negotiations for Economic Partnership Agreements, where a sense developed that the approach and basic assumptions relating to development, which had defined the establishment of the Lomé Convention of 1975 was no longer feasible as a model.

The result was a virtual split among CARICOM countries and between negotiating technocrats and academics as to the extent to which the conclusions of these negotiations would satisfy the requirements for adjustment to the emerging system of international economic relations dominated by the attributes of globalization. Recent articles by Norman Girvan and others have reviewed the

---

5   'Unleash "China energy" in global governance', *People's Daily Online* (14 January 2013).

6   Ibid.

issue, indicating the views and preferred approaches of some of the academics observing the EPA negotiations.[7]

Similarly, the effects of a counter-posing of positions between some governments and the European Union are also reflected in the relatively long period taken for the EU to conclude negotiations with some of the African state-partners in proposed EPAs. And it would therefore appear that the relatively different weightings between Caribbean and African states in these negotiations have not allowed the EU to as easily dismiss the contentions of some African states as it was possible to do in the case of the CARICOM states.

Yet as far as responses and adjustments to the globalization process and its consequences for production and trade go, from within the wider Caribbean we see a perhaps less inflexible position. The CARICOM was initially ahead in coming to terms with changing the United States' perceptions of the need to reformulate trade and production agreements in the globalization context. This was indicated in acceptance of the Caribbean Basin Initiative (CBI), as eventually reflected in the Caribbean Basin Trade and Production Act (CBTPA), which seemed to indicate a general American concern (albeit originally within the context of the Cold War) for encouraging the adjustment of CARICOM economies to spheres of the international economy beyond the disappearing Commonwealth regime.

But the CARICOM states themselves appear to have been less keen to pursue the American offer of a US-Caribbean free trade area regime in the context of the US's wider, post-Cold War perspective of its own rearrangement of economic relations on the North American continent (NAFTA). What is noticeable in this regard is the comparison between the rapid conclusion of a US Central America FTA, and a still to be pursued similar offer to CARICOM. To some extent the same, in terms of the prolonged character of the evolution of a new trade regime, may be said of CARICOM–Canada relations.

The result is a multiplicity of regimes, some more advanced than others, within the relatively small space of the Caribbean. This in turn leads to an overlapping of regimes among countries. Specifically, the alacrity with which a US-CAFTA proposal was accepted by the Central American states (in spite of rigid domestic approval requirements including referenda – which are not required in the CARICOM zone) must have some impact on wider international perceptions of the differences in capacities for institutional adjustments between the two parts of the Caribbean. And those perceptions must include the relative consideration of the fact that the Dominican Republic, which is part of the CARIFORUM-EU agreement, has had no hesitation in adhering to the US-CAFTA agreement. In that specific context, whether the terms of an eventual CARICOM-US FTA will be largely determined by this agreement, closing the space, in any negotiation with the CARICOM, for any meaningful differentiation or specific consideration

---

7   See Norman Girvan, 'The Cariforum-ECEPA – A Critical Evaluation' (2008); and Joyce Van Genderen-Naar, 'The Cariforum-EUEPA- Five Years After', Presentation to the ACP-EU Joint Parliamentary Assembly (JPA), Paramaribo, Suriname (27 November 2012).

of the characters of Caribbean economies, must be a matter for consideration as time elapses.

So at the level of regional economic governance regimes – if we consider the first region of relevance to the Caribbean, in the post-colonial order, to be, now, that of the North-South American zone, we can perceive a relative reluctance of the CARICOM section to come to terms, with any real sense of urgency, with the adjustments being made in the hemisphere to the challenges of economic globalization. In some measure, Guyana and Belize are probably likely to stand out as partial exceptions to this generalization, given their specific location in the South and Central American regions. But the general conclusion must be that, while other states define the rules of engagement in this arena, the CARICOM may well be left in a position which suggests that, at some future time, it will find at its disposal what is in effect a geopolitical/geo-economic fait accompli.

The first ideological counter-argument to such a conclusion may be posed by saying that the character of CARICOM states' historical integration into the international system has been somewhat different from other small-country counterparts in the rest of the hemisphere. Yet, as we have seen, it is becoming reasonably clear that the terms of engagement which have tied the CARICOM to the wider European sphere are themselves changing, particularly as policy positions of the United Kingdom deviate from CARICOM expectations particularly in respect of possibilities for remaining areas of economic preferentialism, as has been indicated in the British Government's decision to impose an Air Passenger Duty issue on CARICOM states' passengers travelling to and from the UK.[8]

A second ideological counter-argument may be that there is an evolution in hemispheric economic and diplomatic options and relations that may provide a wider space for the CARICOM to engage with – the reference being to the institutional innovations emanating from within Latin America – whether in the case of the Union of South American Nations (UNASUR), or Community of Latin American and Caribbean States (CELAC), or the reformulations of aid and trade arrangements that are indicated in the PETROCARIBE and ALBA aid, trade and development initiatives (see Mark Kirton's chapter later in this volume). The argument suggests a widening of options to the small states of the hemisphere that are perhaps likely to be less constraining than those emanating from the northern part of the hemisphere.

---

8   The Air Passenger Duty (APD) has been deemed by CARICOM governments to have been disproportionately prejudicial to their states, when compared with similar arrangements vis-à-vis the United States for example. See Caribbean Tourist Organization, *Caribbean Response to the UK Government's Consultation on Reform of the air Passenger Duty* (June 2011), www.onecaribbean.org/content/files/CaribbeanResponseAPDBriefing DocJune 2011.pdf.

The Latin American Environment: Its Relevance

Yet this perspective must be required to take into account that what has been occurring in the southern hemisphere is largely a two-pronged initiative in response to the changes in the wider global environment, involving a simultaneous effort of renegotiating the terms of trade engagements between some of the larger states there and the United States, and seeking to come to terms with the significance of China's new participation in the entire global economic system, including the South American continent. And that this is taking place in the context of the old regime of developed states now being induced to, simultaneously, renegotiate the wider international terms of the WTO regime in the context of a perhaps stronger South American presence and influence than during the period of the original negotiation of that regime.

On the other hand, it will be observed that, particularly in the case of Mexico, there is less of a discrepancy perceived between its favoured terms in NAFTA, and a longer-term arrangement that includes both itself and the South American countries now pursuing CELAC; or pursuing spatial integration arrangements as suggested in the case of UNASUR. Yet, it may be that, for some of the larger South American states, discrepancies between the terms of production and trade agreements or orientations, are to be worked out not in what might be perceived as privileged regional agreements, but at the level of the WTO where juridical and conciliation arrangements are more diverse, consequently less susceptible to pressure from the North Atlantic states, and allies can be sought who are not originally committed to the dominant partner in the hemispheric agreements, the United States.

The issue arising, then, is to what extent within that complex of simultaneous activities does the CARICOM *cum* Caribbean find space for a self-defined spectrum of geo-economic negotiations that have to take into account what would appear to be a variety of economic diplomacy initiatives on the part of the Latin American states towards the wider, emerging world.

Where Does this Leave the Caribbean?

It may be an understatement to observe that the contemporary history of CARICOM relationships with global or regional regimes cannot be said to be entirely satisfactory, and this, in itself, may create ground for scepticism vis-à-vis on-time, successful negotiations for full adherence to wider schemes. There seems no real recourse to adjudication as far as the APD is concerned, and Antigua and Barbuda's experience in respect of internet gambling might well lead to the conclusion that the old belief in one law for the rich and another for the poor has hardly lost its salience, particularly where capabilities for urgent implementation of juridical decisions are so diverse among states. And that from this perspective, CARICOM states can find little space for leverage in international economic institutions for responding to adverse conclusions vis-à-vis the spaces open to them in international trade in particular. The old regimes are passing away without, as yet, adequate replacements that can have equitable results for some smaller states.

In one regard it could be argued that as the old regimes disappear, or lose their significance (because senior partners have lost either sentimental or philosophical or economic policy commitment), it is up to the CARICOM states to seek to find new diplomatic allies who can be of assistance in negotiating fora, or in simply fortifying the positions of the CARICOM states. There was, indeed, a time when Canada, for example, could be seen as a useful ally in various fora, as in some measure it still is, for the CARICOM in the IMF-World Bank arenas. But perhaps what might be considered a certain slowness in negotiating an FTA agreement between CARICOM and that country,[9] is unlikely to encourage additional experiments of that kind or is not based on a sufficiently continuous diplomatic engagement at the CARICOM level that would induce thinking about innovative ways of making assistance possible in various negotiating fora. The point is not really that CARICOM would necessarily need narrow technical help, but diplomatic and organizational capability assistance from allies, like Canada, which have other allies who can be helpful to one or other of CARICOM's international causes.

So the argument here is not so much for formal agreements, apart, in the first instance for a Canada-CARICOM FTA, but for means of persistent diplomacy that has a recognized coherence at the CARICOM level which can, over time, persuade such a country that there is a definitive, long-term consistency of positions collectively taken by regional governments which reflects the coherent wider positioning of the region as a whole, as distinct from periodic initiatives of specific member states. For individual member state initiatives would be seen, more often than not, as leading to an unsatisfactory situation of perceptions of differences among CARICOM member states, however subtle.

What can apply in the case of Canada could well apply in respect of specific larger states in Latin America, including those, like Brazil which, as we have observed, are in proximity to particular CARICOM states. The objective there, too, would be to develop, at the CARICOM level, specific positions not only on international issues, but also on issues that are (CARICOM) regional in nature for which CARICOM seeks specific support in one or other international forum, and

---

9   As a recent government of Canada Fact sheet indicates, negotiations for a CARICOM-FTA were first announced in January 2001, and formal negotiations began in July 2007. A summary of the state of negotiations is given as follows: 'Canada and CARICOM have held four rounds of negotiations to date. The first and second rounds took place in ... November 2009 and March 2010. A third round of negotiations was held ... during the week of July 16, 2012. Progress was made during the fourth round, including on goods, market access, services, investments and development support. This progress included an exchange of views and information that assisted both sides in better understanding each other's interest and concerns'. www.international/gc/trade-agrements-accords-commerciaux/agro-acc/caricom/index.aspx?viewcd, accessed 26 December 2013.

which the region, as a unity, would wish to systematically maintain and assert at the international level. To the extent that central to CARICOM country concerns, in this period, would be their objectives in the pursuit of economic development in the new global economic context, and regional integration, defined as both among CARICOM states, and between them and Latin American states, it would seem that a diplomacy supporting these objectives needs to be devised and consistently held, as a regional initiative.

The point here is that, for small states such as our own, regional arrangements and regional diplomacy, formally organized and with continuity – not only when specific meetings are due, or specific issues are emerging – should be the route to engagement with larger countries, particularly those in the hemisphere, as also to what we might call 'critical' states in their own geopolitical spheres. The emphasis here is on continuity of engagement, as distinct from contacts vis-à-vis particular issues at points of crisis. That continuity would have to be properly institutionalized at the regional level – as distinct from being ad hoc.

This suggests a greater attention to collective location or positioning of the region in significant areas on a continuous basis. But it has to be taken into account that it is an even more difficult enterprise than the efforts that we have previously made at specific times – for example, the negotiation of the Lomé Conventions. Part of the reason is that what we today call CARICOM is, in fact, more complex as the CARIFORUM which, in turn, is likely to be – difficult as it might be – the appropriate geographical/regional geopolitical arena for international engagement, particularly towards the hemisphere, in the future.

What we draw from this is that regional building blocs, recognized as such by the international community, and constructed on institutionalized arrangements of governance – including the appropriate juridical mechanisms – are the appropriate basis for CARICOM states' international engagement in an increasingly globalized world, but one which, apart from the major states of the globe, is redefining regionalisms away from their original colonial inspirations and formulations. I emphasize here, too, the importance of having regional juridical institutions properly and consistently supported. For confidence in juridical reasoning constitutes an important part of international negotiation, particularly in what used to be called the Western world, which, in large measure, still tends to dominate many international institutions.

The fact, however, is that CARICOM's own experience with commitment to regional juridical regimes, seen as the foundations of wider international agreements, has not been itself entirely persuasive. The failure to permit the Caribbean Court of Justice to establish itself vis-à-vis all jurisdictions has not helped, since it gives an impression of countries not willing to definitively commit to regional regimes.[10] Yet, regional regimes must be seen, for small states, as

---

10   The reference here is to the difficulties which two of the largest CARICOM countries, Jamaica and Trinidad and Tobago, have had in fulfilling their commitments to adhere to the Caribbean Court of Justice.

stepping stones to international regimes, capable of locally fortifying decisions of the states. Otherwise we may find, as in the case of the Antigua Internet gambling issue, a lack of credibility, in terms of capacity for effective implementation of decisions handed down by the international juridical regimes, given the discrepancy in weight among the contenders.

Further Re-arranging the Regional Arena

To some degree it was assumed that the establishment of the CARIFORUM-EU Economic Partnership Agreement would have strengthened formal arrangements between the Anglophone jurisdictions and the remaining colonial presences in the region – particularly in the Southern Caribbean. One of the objectives which the EU has always supported has been a focus on regional integration – which we take to mean substantially regional economic integration. For small countries of different political jurisdictions, spatial reorganization and physical or structural integration are significant avenues for effecting economic integration. To take only one contemporary example, it is becoming obvious, and particularly in the Eastern and Southern Caribbean, that with regard to air transportation, for example, a variety of jurisdictional distinctions can reduce the possibilities for cost-effective activities; and there are indications that the same may well apply to the effective use of energy resources as bases for economic development, in the region.

As the example of the European Union itself has demonstrated, differences in legal and constitutional arrangements are not necessarily to be taken as impediments to effective economic integration. And in their case too, the establishment of governance arrangements were not impeded by differing legal or language regimes.

It is perhaps unfortunate that in the negotiations towards the EPA, the issue of economic policy-based spatial reconfiguration in the Eastern Caribbean was not given appropriate recognition. And as is increasingly recognized in Latin America, regimes (naturally involving governance arrangements) of so-called infrastructural integration are being advanced as a prime path to economic integration – a policy line that will come increasingly to influence the relationship between the South American states and the South American CARICOM countries.

From this perspective, the countries of the Eastern Caribbean need to be thinking through the modalities of infrastructural integration between themselves and the French Departments there, a perspective that should therefore be supported by the wider CARICOM in governments' dealings with the European Union. This is obviously an initiative in effecting sub-regional governance mechanisms that would be somewhat different from, and somewhat more complex than, the integration process between CARICOM and Haiti – a situation in which the latter has more or less accepted the institutional and governance arrangements of the former.

There is, however, perhaps for obvious reasons, an area where efforts have been made to institutionalize forms of regional governance between the CARICOM states and other larger jurisdictions, and that is the area of regional security, though mainly as it pertains to the movement of narcotics throughout the region. Yet even here, there are indications, taking an example from the hemispheric sphere, of a certain imbalance in objectives, which is leading to concerns on the part of some Latin American and Caribbean countries that the machinery of regional surveillance has become insufficient to cope with the problem.

A forceful indication of this was given at the Sixth Summit of the Americas in April 2012, in Cartagena, Colombia, where a number of countries found that the military pursuit of persons and organized groups involved in narcotics may only be half of the solution to the problem. From that perspective, a search for consensus on deliberate efforts of decriminalization of certain activities within states relating to the movement of narcotics was initiated, though not supported by the United Sates, and in this plea some CARICOM countries joined.

The implication of this must be that there should be arrangements for a more balanced and diverse approach to this subject, even while there is a broad consensus on the dangers posed by it. Obviously institutional arrangements, initiated at the hemispheric level, would need to be put in place for this, but as with other arenas of global governance, a level of normative consensus would be a pre-requirement. The issue is, obviously of particular significance to small countries in the hemisphere plagued by narcotics movement, to the extent that the search for resources is essentially externally based and is likely to be influenced by the strategic positions of the donors.

In Conclusion: Where is CARICOM's Place in Dealing with the Effects of the Globalization Process?

The first systematic Caribbean attempt at dealing with the institutional effects of the globalization process was that introduced by the need to come to terms with the United Kingdom's integration into the European Union. In retrospect, the first Lomé Convention can be seen as a holding operation, largely favourable to the CARICOM states, especially as it permitted the maintenance of the key lines of (agricultural) trade based on Caribbean production. In addition the effort of agreement induced a degree of organization of institutionalized cohesion in coming to terms with the need to participate autonomously in the reconfiguration of external trade agreements. At that time, too, the European leadership – in particular that of France and Germany, were perceived as, in some measure, *interlocuteurs valable*, in respect of legitimating the Convention on our behalf, along with the United Kingdom.

Subsequent to that, with the push by the United States towards persistent liberalization of production arrangement, reflecting the rapidity of technological innovation in international production processes, the EU states were placed somewhat on the defensive in legitimating and protecting the Lomé arrangements, this implying a certain diplomatic isolation, over time, of the ACP countries as a kind of privileged, exclusive grouping divorced from the concerns of other developing countries.

While the regimes established for subsequent Conventions gave clear indications of the EU's inability to defend their protectionist nature persistently, it also meant that, unlike the situation in the original Lomé Agreement, there was less normative consensus between the EU countries and their ACP interlocutors. And, in turn, the relative consensus of 1973–75 among the ACP states themselves was subject to a certain diffusion, as preoccupation with the interests of specific regional/sub-regional groupings became increasingly intense. For the Caribbean this means a need to find new mechanisms for diplomatic interaction with the other ACP states, and in particular with the African sector, itself increasingly diverse. It can be said that in the international context, the role of Australia still has a certain salience in advocacy for the small Pacific states, in a context in which, in response to China's participation in the globalization process, Australia has made a significant effort of diplomatic and economic engagement with that country.

We conclude that what exists is an institutional arrangement of CARICOM regional diplomacy, without external handmaidens as in the case of the Australia-Pacific case; without increasing attraction as locations of investment and raw material exploitation as is the case of certain countries on the African continent; and without a coherent regional approach to development diplomacy that might exploit the current specific interest of a China willing to involve itself, today, in all aspects of economic intercourse over the globe as a whole.[11] In the case of the CARICOM, the regional coherence of the grouping would appear still too limited to present an institutional diplomatic face to the wider international community. As we have intimated, the CARIFORUM (in any case, a partly exogenous creation of one section of the industrialized world) is, at this time, insufficiently coherent for this. And a deliberate CARICOM path to diplomatic engagement with the Latin American sphere remains somewhat inchoate and reactive, if we contrast it with the positions/initiatives of various states in the wider hemispheric arena.

---

11   The Government of the People's Republic of China has initiated a development cooperation and aid arrangement for the countries of the Caribbean. But there is no indication that the CARICOM countries themselves see the initiative as potentially supporting regional infrastructural integration. In addition there is, of course, diversity in the CARICOM area in the context of recognition of the Peoples Republic vis-à-vis Taiwan, which requires that it be referred to as the Republic of China.

PART II
Hegemony, Regionalization and the Changing Hemisphere

Chapter 3

The FTAA and its Untimely Demise

W. Andy Knight

Introduction

The negotiations to create what could have become the largest free trade area on the face of this planet, the Free Trade Area of the Americas (FTAA), were stymied. But if those negotiations were successful, the Americas would have been reconfigured or 're-mapped' in ways that we may not have been able to foresee at the start of the negotiations. Certainly, based on the projected goals of the proposed project, the FTAA would have created a new trade architecture for the entire western hemisphere that would have had major implications not only for the sub-regional trade arrangements in place throughout the region but also for the global neo-liberal project spearheaded by US capitalism.[1]

The impact of such a monumental trade arrangement on the global economy would have been difficult to ignore given the fact that the Free Trade Area of the Americas (FTAA) would have created a market place of 854 million people from Alaska to Patagonia – a population twice the size of that of the European Union (EU), and the free trade area itself would have comprised of 34 democratic countries with a combined gross domestic product (GDP) in excess of US$13 trillion, and total exports of more than US$1 trillion annually. Before the negotiations collapsed, one author notes that in 'an increasingly regionalized world economy, the FTAA would become a very powerful regional grouping'.[2]

Origin of the FTAA

While the formal plans for an FTAA were launched publicly at the first Summit of the Americas in Miami, Florida in 1994 and endorsed openly by the then-US President, Bill Clinton, the roots of the idea for a free trade area in our hemisphere can be traced back to a much earlier time when organizations controlled largely by the Rockefeller family, like David Rockefeller's Council for the Americas, developed strategies for building a network through a common market of 'insider

---

1   See Mario E. Carranza, 'Mercosur and the end game of the FTAA negotiations: challenges and prospects after the Argentine crisis', *Third World Quarterly*, 25 (2) (2004), 319–337.

2   Mario E. Carranza, 'Mercosur and the end game of the FTAA negotiations', 319.

allies' in Latin America.[3] But one can go even further back to find an earlier example of the seed of the idea of an FTAA.

According to right wing American journalist, William Jasper, this idea can be traced to a proposal by Fidel Castro in 1959 at a conference in Buenos Aires which called for a regional common market. Of course, this was before Castro had publicly acknowledged his Communist ties, according to the journalist. Less than two years later, members of US President Kennedy's administration advanced a similar proposal labelled 'The Alliance for Progress', which aimed to meld the countries of the region into a common market through free trade and infusions of aid/investment.[4]

In essence, the immediate forerunner of the FTAA was George H.W. Bush's Enterprise for the Americas Initiative (EAI), while the foundation of the proposed FTAA was built on the neo-liberal ideology that underpinned the 'Washington Consensus'. Some see the FTAA process as a deliberate attempt by the US to consolidate its hegemony in the western hemisphere through peaceful economic integration while at the same time strengthening the US hand in global trade negotiations taking place at the level of the World Trade Organization (WTO).[5]

Goal of this Chapter

While there is a tremendous amount of interest in the issue of whether or not the proposed FTAA would have strengthened or weakened existing regional and sub-regional integration efforts in Central America, Latin America and the Caribbean,[6] this chapter focuses instead not on the substance but on the structure of the FTAA negotiation process itself, including the principles that were behind it, the institutional mechanism created to sustain it, and the main events and outcomes that resulted from it. It must be borne in mind that the FTAA negotiation process did not take place in a vacuum but rather against the backdrop of a series of multiple and simultaneous trade liberalization negotiation processes taking place at the global level (World Trade Organization rounds), at the level of regions, and at the

---

3   Other organizations credited with conceiving and nurturing the idea included: the Americas Society (David Rockefeller, chairman), the Forum of the Americas (David Rockefeller, founder), the US Council of the Mexico-US Business Committee (Rodman C. Rockefeller, chairman), the Council on Foreign Relations (David Rockefeller, former chairman), the Trilateral Commission (David Rockefeller, founder and honorary chairman), the Chase Manhattan Bank (David Rockefeller, former chairman), and the Institute for International Economics (David Rockefeller, financial backer and board member).

4   William F. Jasper, 'Welcome Mat for Terrorists', *The New America* (29 December 2003), at http://www.stoptheftaa.org/artman/publish/article_89.shtml, accessed 16 October 2005.

5   See for example the argument made by Peter J. Katzenstein, *A World of Regions: Asia and Europe in the American Imperium* (Ithaca: Cornell University Press, 2005), 233.

6   For a good discussion of this issue see Nicola Phillips, 'Hemispheric integration and subregionalism in the Americas', *International Affairs*, 79 (2) (2003), 327–349.

sub-regional level. As the reader will see below, the FTAA negotiation process was a dynamic one involving multiple actors – state and non-state, sovereignty-bound and sovereignty-free. The chapter also deals with some of the reasons for the failure of the FTAA and argues that its untimely demise was due in large part to the withdrawal of support for the idea by some of the key players in Latin America and the Caribbean – at the level of governments, the corporate sector and civil society. But there was also another important reason for the failure of the FTAA. After 9-11-2001 the US administration's attention was diverted away from these trade issues as it concentrated on the so-called 'war on terror'.

FTAA Negotiation: Principles, Structure and Process

When George H.W. Bush was President of the United States of America, he established an 'Enterprise for the Americas Initiative' (EAI) in June 1990 that aimed to support economic reform in the countries of the western hemisphere and to contribute to sustained economic growth in the region. This Initiative was based on three distinct pillars: trade, investment and debt relief. But it was at the first Summit of the Americas in Miami (December 1994) that the proposal for a FTAA was launched by 34 democracies of the western hemisphere with the view to building a trade architecture for the entire hemisphere. It was agreed that 2005 would be set as the target date for the adoption of this agreement and that there would be a progressive regional elimination of barriers to trade and investment as a result of this FTAA.

In effect, the intent of the FTAA was to broaden and deepen the economic integration experienced in the tri-national North American Free Trade Agreement (NAFTA) and harmonize policies throughout the entire western hemisphere on, *inter alia*, agriculture, business, criminal justice, defence, education, environment, immigration, industry, labour, taxation, trade, transportation and health. To this end, it was implied that the FTAA's end game would be to shore up US hegemony in an area considered the 'sphere of influence' of the hegemon and to overlay, or eventually supplant, sub-regional integration efforts throughout the region. This would be accomplished by getting Central, Latin American and South American countries to buy into the neo-liberal strategy advocated by the American government on the promise that these countries would benefit economically and socially in the long run.

The basic principles upon which the FTAA idea was built can be summarized as follows:

1. *Economic growth* within the western hemisphere was to be fostered by the elimination of impediments to trade in goods and services;
2. *Domestic prosperity* in the western hemisphere would have been enhanced as each country became more fully integrated into the global economy;

3. *Free trade and progressive economic integration* were to be the keys to raising living standards, improving working conditions, and better protecting the environment in the countries of the western hemisphere.

The basic initial structure within which the FTAA negotiation process was conducted was the Summits, attended by Heads of Governments, and Ministerial meetings. The first Summit of the Americas was held in Miami, Florida in 1994. This was followed by an unofficial Summit on Sustainable Development in 1996. The second Summit occurred in Santiago, Chile in 1998, followed by the third one in Quebec City, Canada (2001) and an unofficial special Summit in Monterrey, Mexico in 2004. The fourth Summit was held from 4–5 November 2005 in Mar del Plata, Argentina and the fifth Summit took place in Port-of-Spain in Trinidad and Tobago in 2009.[7]

At the first Summit, Heads of Governments agreed on a *Declaration of Principles* that would guide the FTAA negotiations.[8] The first set of principles revolved around partnership for development and prosperity and was linked to goals of democracy, free trade and sustainable development in the Americas. The Heads of Governments committed themselves to advance prosperity throughout the region and to promote and sustain democratic values and institutions. To enhance the possibility for prosperity in the hemisphere, they concluded that the countries would have to develop closer bonds of cooperation, open up their markets and adhere to the rule of law. It was also recognized that the building of such a partnership would have to be based on respect for heterogeneity and diversity of resources and cultures in the region while at the same time forging shared interests and values.

The second set of principles dealt with preserving and strengthening the community of democracies in the Americas. The Heads of Government agreed that representative democracy is essential for stability, peace and development of the region. Their view was that democracies guarantee respect for human rights and the rule of law and usually safeguard cultural diversity, pluralism and respect for minorities. These basic elements were deemed necessary for building sustained peace among nations as well as within nations. Thus, free and transparent elections, as well as the right of all citizens to participate in government, were considered keys to the maintenance of a democratic tradition and would reinforce economic development and vice versa.

The Heads of Government of the 34 countries made a commitment to work through the Organization of American States (OAS), the United Nations (UN) and

---

7   Note that there has been one other Summit of the Americas since 2009 – the Sixth Summit of the Americas in Cartagena, Colombia (17–19 April 2012). The Seventh Summit of the Americas is scheduled for Panama in 2015 and the Eighth Summit has been carded for 2018 in Suriname.

8   http://www.ftaa-alca.org/Summits/Miami/declara_e.asp, accessed 26 December 2013.

other multilateral bodies to strengthen democratic institutions throughout the hemisphere and to promote and defend constitutional democratic rule. To accomplish this would mean modernizing the state, making its institutions more transparent and accountable, and ensuring that justice was accessible to all in society, including women, the aged, indigenous people, the disabled, children and minorities. It also meant attacking corruption, since this was seen as the cause of much social disintegration and it can distort domestic economic systems while corroding the legitimacy of governments.

The third set of principles dealt with the promotion of prosperity through economic integration and free trade. Emphasis was placed here on the importance of a vital private sector, the development of sound economic policies, and the advancement of trade without barriers, subsidies and unfair practices. The Heads of Governments agreed to work together to eliminate impediments to market access for goods and services in the hopes that this would foster strong economic growth in the countries of the hemisphere. In essence, this move would also support the growing world economy, thus enhancing prosperity for all in the region. It was assumed by these leaders that free trade and the broadening and deepening of economic integration would lead to improvements of living standards and working conditions, and that the enhanced collaboration among such a large bloc could only help to improve the economic environment in the region. This set of principles also included the notion that the FTAA could build on existing sub-regional and bilateral/trilateral arrangements in promoting the development and progressive integration of capital markets.

To ensure the above, there would have to be cooperative ventures with International Financial Institutions (IFIs) and the private sector. There would also have to be cooperative ventures in such fields as telecommunication, energy and transportation in order to promote the efficient movement of goods, services, capital, information, technology and people. Additionally, the countries in the hemisphere would have to draw on their resources, ingenuity and individual capacities if they were to achieve these goals.

The fourth set of principles addressed during the FTAA negotiations was the issue of eradicating poverty and eliminating discrimination. The focus here was on ensuring greater justice for all people in the hemisphere, improving access to quality education and primary health care, and eradicating extremes of poverty and illiteracy. As the Heads of Government put it, all must share in the prosperity expected to come from free trade, regardless of gender, race, national origin and religious affiliation. Emphasis was placed on strengthening the role of women in political, social and economic life, since this was considered to be essential for reducing poverty, eliminating social inequalities and enhancing the level of democracy and sustainable development.

The fifth and final set of principles that undergirded the FTAA negotiation process revolved around the guarantee of sustainable development and the conservation of the natural environment for future generations. It was concluded that all people and countries in the hemisphere required a healthy environment as they prospered economically and progressed socially. The region's ecosystems and natural resources would therefore have to be managed carefully and responsibly. To do so, creative cooperative partnerships would be required that would strengthen the countries' capacity to prevent pollution, protect ecosystems, use biological resources on a sustainable basis, and encourage clean and efficient use of energy. At the base of these sets of principles was the notion of being cognizant of peoples' impact on their environment as they try to advance materially.

Accompanying the *Declaration of Principles* was an Action Plan which was subdivided into 18 steps.[9] A vice-ministerial level Trade Negotiations Committee (TNC) was created to oversee the negotiations. In addition, nine negotiating groups were created to facilitate the negotiations, as well as three non-negotiating entities.[10] There have been eight Ministerial meetings so far.

1. Denver, USA (June 1995)
2. Cartagena, Colombia (March 1996)
3. Belo Horizonte, Brazil (May 1997)
4. San Jose, Costa Rica (March 1998)
5. Toronto, Canada (November 1999)
6. Buenos Aires, Argentina (April 2001)
7. Quito, Ecuador (November 2002)
8. Miami, USA (November 2003)

At each Ministerial meeting, preparatory work was conducted for active negotiations and the delegates tried to find ways of implementing commitments made at the Heads of Government Summits. Working groups were established for specific issue areas. Each group identified and examined existing trade-related measures in each of the subject areas with the view to establishing possible approaches to the negotiations. Timetables were established to move the work along and guidance was provided to assist the negotiations of the working groups.

A Tripartite Committee comprising of members of the OAS, the IDB and ECLAC provided analytical reports, technical assistance, and relevant studies that helped working groups in the process of their negotiations. Coordinators were

---

9 The main headings for these steps are as follows: 1. make democracy work; 2. strengthen the human rights system; 3. promote justice, the rule of law and security of the individual; 4. hemispheric security; 5. strengthen civil society; 6. trade, investment and financial stability; 7. infrastructure and regulatory environment; 8. disaster management; 9. environmental foundation for sustainable development; 10. agricultural management and rural development; 11. labour and employment; 12. growth with equity; 13. education; 14. health; 15. gender equality; 16. indigenous people; 17. cultural diversity; 18. children and youth.

10 The areas covered were agriculture, market access, government procurement, investment, competition policy, intellectual property rights, dispute settlement, smaller economies, civil society, institutional issues, subsidies/anti-dumping and countervailing duties, and electronic commerce.

generally provided for each working group and progress reports expected from each. The 34 countries of the hemisphere engaged in the FTAA negotiations agreed that the following guiding principles would be used during their negotiations:

1. Consensus decision making;
2. A single undertaking will be concluded by a set date (no later than 2005);
3. The FTAA agreement must comply with WTO agreements (particularly GATT Article XXIV and GATS Article V (re. free trade areas and common markets);
4. FTAA to coexist with existing bilateral/trilateral/multilateral sub-regional arrangements in the western hemisphere;
5. Permit the countries in the Americas to negotiate the FTAA either individually or as a bloc of member countries from sub-regional trading groups (like CARICOM, MERCOSUR, etc.);
6. Technical assistance to be provided to facilitate those countries that require help in their negotiations;
7. Take into consideration the variations in levels of development and the size of economies of the countries involved;
8. The FTAA negotiations should be a transparent process that involves groups from civil society – including NGOs and business organizations.

There were three added principles as the negotiations went on. These were:

1. The FTAA agreement should improve on WTO rules and disciplines wherever possible;
2. The delegates should aim to produce a balanced and comprehensive result;
3. Take into consideration the views of environmental groups and labour movements, but reject protectionism.

Since it was expected that this agreement would have major impacts on every level of society within the 34 countries, the Heads of Government decided to invite groups from civil society to take part in a formal dialogue with the negotiation teams. To demonstrate transparency, FTAA negotiators made public a draft text of the future agreement in four languages after the third Summit in Quebec City in April 2001. It should be pointed out that this occurred only after much protest from civil society over the absence of transparency. The second draft (about 434 pages) was later released by the non-negotiating groups after the Quito Ministerial meeting in Ecuador in November 2002. Included in the negotiation procedures were a number of innovative practices, such as:

1. Enhancement of custom procedures to facilitate the commercial exchange among the 34 countries;
2. Allowance of participation, during negotiations, of the Joint Government-Private Sector Committee of Experts on electronic commerce;

3. Solicitation of technical, analytical and financial support from a Tripartite Committee that comprised of the Inter-American Development Bank (IADB), the OAS, and the UN Economic Commission for Latin America and the Caribbean (ECLAC);

4. Creation of the Hemispheric Cooperation Programme (HCP) to provide central support to the 34 countries for capacity building, development, negotiation strategies, and the actual implementation of the FTAA.

Note that Canada chaired the TNC, Ministerial and the FTAA process for the first 18-month period that ended with the Toronto Ministerial in November, 1999 and Argentina chaired the negotiations during the second round through the April 2001 Ministerial in Buenos Aires. Ecuador served as chair during the third round of negotiations which concluded with a Ministerial in Quito on 1 November 2002. The US and Brazil co-chaired the final phase of meetings before the idea of the FTAA was more or less abandoned.

The Demise of the Idea of the Free Trade Area of the Americas

As discussed in the introductory chapter, after the failures of import substitution industrialization (ISI) strategies (of the 1960s and 70s) in many of the developing countries of the Americas, the leaders of those states were ready to experiment with other approaches to development. The financial collapse, in the wake of the Latin American debt crisis of the 1980s, gave international financial institutions (IFIs) the upper hand in determining the neo-liberal macroeconomic policies these countries were to adopt. These policies were coupled with the building of competitive pressures due to globalization and NAFTA throughout the 1990s. State leaders therefore sought the expansion of trade and economic relations with their giant neighbour and regional and global hegemon, the United States of America.

The Free Trade Area of the Americas (FTAA) was expected to be the culmination of this new approach, which, as we have discussed, had prompted the proliferation of a web of trade liberalization agreements.[11] When the FTAA was first floated in 1994 at the Summit of the Americas in Miami, following on US President George H.W. Bush's announcement of the 'Enterprise for the Americas Initiative',[12] Cuba was noticeably absent from the discussion. The FTAA was hailed as an attempt to expand the North American Free Trade Agreement (NAFTA) beyond Canada, the US and Mexico to include every country in Central America, South America and the Caribbean, with the exception of Cuba. This proposed hemispheric trade arrangement was conceived by the US as a hub-and-

---

11   Kellogg, Paul, 'Regional Integration in Latin America: Dawn of an Alternative to Neoliberalism?', in *New Political Science*, 19 (2) (June 2007), 188.

12   See Gary Clyde Hufbauer and Jeffrey J. Schott, *North American Free Trade: Issues and Recommendations* (Washington: Institute for International Economics, 2002).

spoke regional order, based on principles of trade and investment liberalization[13] that would foster economic progress throughout the hemisphere by eliminating trade and investment obstacles between the 34 nations involved. If the FTAA had proven to be successful, it would have led to a deep pan American integration approach to trade liberalization and deregulation in the region, which would have, according to proponents, resulted in spurring economic growth and modernization across the hemisphere.[14] According to critics, the FTAA was also a strategy for the US to implement a new and revised Monroe Doctrine. At any rate, it would have certainly become the largest trading bloc in global history and it was the most ambitious attempt at developing a free trade area that the world has ever seen.

This notion of free trade-driven economic growth for an entire region stemmed from the apparent experience of the European Union and, more specifically, of NAFTA. As E. Timothy Smith puts it, NAFTA seemed to have established free trade as a 'scientifically established principle of economics' that enhanced free market economics and economic efficiency on a regional scale.[15] In effect, the NAFTA experiment proved that the corporate-driven free market economic system, which emerged under the US administration of President Reagan, could be very successful when working in an alliance between multinational enterprises (MNEs) and the US government to promote the principles of the Washington Consensus – principles that were certainly pushed, not all that subtly, during the negotiations around the FTAA.

However, some critics of the FTAA saw these negotiations as a clever trap by liberal internationalists to undermine the authority of states in Latin America and the Caribbean through the building of new hemispheric governance arrangements that would be controlled behind the scenes by Washington. Such a view held that this omnibus arrangement would only serve to keep the developing states of the region entangled, both economically and politically, in a governance web that would limit the political and economic decision making of most of the countries involved. In other words, the FTAA had the potential to become an 'enormously effective power grab' – to quote one of the groups that tried to stop the FTAA in its tracks.[16]

Moreover, supporters of the FTAA were oblivious to one of NAFTA's more galling shortcomings: i.e., while trade and investment increased and GDP kept growing in the three NAFTA countries, newly created wealth did not benefit everyone and inequality persisted and even grew during specific periods of

---

13   Jean Grugel, 'Regionalist governance and transnational collective action in Latin America', *Economy and Society*, 35 (2) (2006), 209–231, 210, 214–215.

14   See Jose Briceno Ruiz, 'Strategic regionalism and regional social policy in the FTAA process', *Global Social Policy*, 7 (3) (2007), 294–315, 297.

15   E. Timothy Smith, 'From Miami to Quebec and beyond: Opposition to the Free Trade Area of the Americas', *Peace & Change*, 29 (2) (April 2004), 221–249, 228.

16   Stop the FTAA, http://www.stoptheftaa.org/faq/faq1.html#answer, accessed 21 August 2010.

time. This was the 'dirty little secret' of NAFTA-inspired trade liberalization agreements. While deregulation and competitiveness are good for large MNEs, they are not necessarily positive for smaller business, workers and depressed regions within each country. The market is usually not concerned with those who are not 'competitive' enough; big business managers care much more about increasing their companies' profits than attending to social needs. The freer trade is, the more it is used to increase businesses' bottom-lines.

Negotiations to initiate this omnibus trade arrangement, labelled by some as 'NAFTA on steroids' began right after the Santiago summit in 1998. US leaders' party affiliations did not seem to matter much on this issue. Both US Presidents William Clinton (a Democrat) and his successor George W. Bush (a Republican) were enthusiastically in favour of this new hemispheric trade arrangement. It was President Clinton who revived Ronald Reagan's vision of a hemispheric free trade area and announced the timetable for completion of the FTAA negotiations. But it was President George W. Bush who promised to fast-track the FTAA through Congress, for it to become a reality by 1 January 2005. However, on the first day of 2005, the FTAA agreement was still not signed. The trade arrangement was in fact derailed by a combination of opposition from strong social movements across the entire hemisphere and from the governments of countries like Venezuela, Argentina, Bolivia and Brazil. In the end, these countries rejected this model of US-dominated hemispheric integration and began, instead, to search for a better model of regional integration. Social movements, in turn, highlighted the shortcomings of business-oriented trade liberalization that the FTAA was proposing. In brief, the central reason for the death of the FTAA can be found in the regional/state/ civil society counter-hegemonic resistance to the further spread of neo-liberal free trade ideology that was driven by the US government and by the principles of the Washington Consensus.

Brazil, which had been tactically named co-chair of the negotiations when the talks were in their final phase (2003–04), in fact led the counter-hegemonic initiative that eventually killed the FTAA. But Argentina, Venezuela and Bolivia also played a major role in derailing the negotiations. And it is hard to dismiss the part that a variety of non-state actors such as labour unions, non-governmental organizations and civil society grass roots protest movements played in that derailment. The fate of the FTAA was sealed with the 2002 election of Luiz Inácio 'Lula' da Silva as the thirty-fifth President of Brazil. The election of Lula, as he is popularly called in Brazil, and that of his Workers' Party (PT – *Partido dos Trabalhadores*), was considered a major defeat for neo-liberalism not just in Brazil but throughout Latin America. Lula's rise heralded the genesis of a new era in Brazil, an era in which the people would be put before the dictates of international capital. Lula had always referred to the FTAA as a 'policy of annexation of Latin America by the United States'.[17] But Brazil has had a history of resisting the US –

17	Luiz Alberto Bandeira, 'Brazil as a regional power and its relations with the United States', *Latin American Perspectives*, 33 (3) (2006), 12–27, 25.

a history that dates back to the mid-twentieth century. In fact, President Lula did not stray far from the economic and foreign policy position of his predecessor, President Fernando Henrique Cardoso.

Lula took a central role in developing alternative regional arrangements to the one being pushed heavily by the US. His leadership in MERCOSUR can be seen as an attempt to re-map the Americas in a manner that would build a distinctly 'Latin' alternative to the US-sponsored FTAA.[18] Grugel contends that MERCOSUR represents a regional arrangement that is undergirded by the desirability of having some degree of autonomy from the US. He states, 'Mercosur is usually regarded as an alternative project of integration, based on inter-governmentalism, common cultural values ("Latin-ness") and a view that South America – which Mercosur aspires to represent – is best served by a degree of distance and autonomy from the US'.[19] In effect, the FTAA was seen by Brazil and Argentina as a threat to the viability of MERCOSUR. By resisting the implementation of the FTAA that threat was ostensibly removed.

Another reason why the FTAA failed had to do with the fact that there were divisions among the Latin American states over the merits of entrenching this omnibus trade arrangement. For instance, during the Fourth Summit of the Americas, held in Argentina in 2005, a strong dispute erupted between countries that, under Mexican leadership, tried to put forward a final declaration in support of the US-led Free Trade Area of the Americas (FTAA) and countries that, led by Brazil and Venezuela, fiercely opposed that initiative. This division demonstrated a marked ideological difference between the political leadership of the two groups of countries. This situation was exacerbated in 2006 when some countries in the hemisphere had elections resulting, in the case of Mexico and Colombia, in a reaffirmation of right-wing political leadership. During that same year, elections in Ecuador and Bolivia returned left of centre governments that immediately joined that group of states in the region that were in opposition to the FTAA.

Furthermore, in some of the latter countries, such as Brazil, there was really never a strong constituency for this agreement. Even the Brazilian business community that might have been expected to support the FTAA was divided over the initiative. The Brazilian private sector, for instance, was very much concerned that a FTAA would make it very difficult for that country's industrial sector to compete with North America, particularly in those industries that produce electronic parts, chemicals and pharmaceuticals.[20] Brazilian agro-exporters also felt that the huge subsidies the US gives to its farmers, along with that country's

---

18   See Paulo Roberto Almeida, 'Lula's Foreign Policy: Regional and Global Strategies', in Joseph Love and Werner Baer (eds), *Brazil under Lula: Economy, Politics, and Society under the Worker-President* (New York: Palgrave-Macmillan, 2009), 178.

19   Jean Grugel, 'Regionalist Governance and Transnational Collective Action in Latin America', *Economy and Society*, 35 (2), 210.

20   Jose Briceno Ruiz, 'Strategic regionalism and regional social policy in the FTAA process', *Global Social Policy*, 7 (3) (2007), 301.

anti-dumping and countervailing duty policies, effectively erect crippling barriers to Brazilian exports.[21]

But the business and farming communities in Brazil were not the only ones in Latin America and the Caribbean that harboured doubts about the FTAA. Anti-globalization civil society groups' agitation against the World Trade Organization (WTO) provided important lessons to civil society organizations throughout the western hemisphere on how to mobilize effectively against the dominant neo-liberal agenda. For instance, the global federation of farmers' organization had galvanized opposition to the WTO in Cancún in 2003. The G-21 coalition of developing countries, which also emerged as a powerful alliance again the WTO in Cancún, included representation from 13 Latin American countries. Increasingly, the FTAA was viewed by many NGOs in the region as undemocratic and lacking in transparency for society as a whole; for the business sector; for workers; for indigenous, cultural, and environmental groups; for political parties; for parliament; and for the media.

The chief concern of many of these constituencies was the apparent disconnect between the economic policy embedded in the FTAA negotiations and social policy of the developing countries in the region. For many of them, the FTAA represented a hegemonic, neo-liberal agenda that would strengthen US control in the region and entrench the economic power of MNEs.[22] This was the view shared by such civil society groups as the Continental Social Alliance (CSA), the Hemispheric Social Alliance (HSA), and the Citizens Trade Campaign (CTC) whose own goal became one of seeking out and promoting an alternative vision to the neo-liberal one embodied in the FTAA. The latter was a coalition of labour, environmental, religious, family farm and consumer organizations that represented constituencies across the United States. In a nutshell, this is what these civil society groups had to say about the FTAA:

> We believe that increased cooperation between nations of the western hemisphere can be a powerful tool to increase prosperity, democracy, sustainable development, and stability within the region. However, by subjugating crucial social concerns such as public health, equity, environmental protection, and human and worker rights to the goal of increased international investment and trade, the FTAA as currently constructed, promises to bring about the opposite results for the people of North, Central, and South America.[23]

---

21   Peter Hakim, 'The reluctant partner', *Foreign Affairs*, 83 (1) (2004), 114–123, 117.

22   Gary Prevost, 'Contesting free trade: The development of the anti-FTAA movement in the streets and in the corridors of state power', *Journal of Developing Societies*, 21 (3–4) (2005), 369–387, 370.

23   Campaign for Labour Rights, 'Civil Society Comments on FTAA', 1 May 2003, found at www.iadb.org/intal/intalcdi/PE/2007/00394.pdf, accessed 19 May 2013.

As Saguier put it, initially, the general aim of these civil society groups was to 'make the FTAA project a means of advancing equitable, democratic and sustainable development in the region rather than strictly trade liberalization'. This civil society moment's broad base of support included social organizations working on such issues as labour, human rights, the environment, indigenous rights, gender issues, rural concerns and religion.[24] But as it became clear that the FTAA would not necessarily embrace the goals of these groups, opposition to it increased exponentially.

Conclusion

As more and more Latin Americans began to reject the corporate globalization agenda promoted by elites, they began to elect governments whose policies more closely represented the interests of the majority – the poor people in those countries. These governments were increasingly left-leaning, populous ones with a distinct and sometime explicit anti-neoliberal bias[25] and they began to voice concerns with the FTAA, particularly including their concerns with foreign investment regulation, the deregulation of capital controls, privatization and liberalization strategies, the limitation of the ability of governments in the region to put conditions or performance requirements on foreign investment, investor-to-state dispute resolution proposals, expanded rules on regulatory takings, regulations related to intellectual property rights, and the promotion of genetically modified organisms (GMOs) and biotechnology deregulation.[26] It certainly took states to derail the FTAA process. But these states would not have defeated the FTAA without the support of NGO alliances and the agitation of grass roots civil society organization.

In sum, the FTAA failed largely because it had little support from some of the key players in Latin America and the Caribbean. Over the course of the negotiation, support for the FTAA crumbled in administrative and domestic levels of governments, at the corporate level, and among civil society. In addition, due to the asymmetrical development of the region, there was considerable concern that the FTAA could in fact exacerbate those inequities by promoting income disparity. After all, this is precisely what NAFTA had done through its existence. All in all, one can view the opposition to the FTAA as the emergence of a counter-

24   Marcelo Saguier, 'The hemispheric social alliance and the Free Trade Area of the Americas process: The challenges and opportunities of transnational coalitions against neo-liberalism', *Globalizations*, 4 (2) (2007), 251–265, 252.

25   Paul Kellogg, 'Regional integration in Latin America: Dawn of an alternative to neoliberalism?', *New Political Science*, 29 (2) (June 2007), 187–209, 188–189.

26   Gary Prevost, 'Contesting free trade: the development of the anti-FTAA movement in the streets and in the corridors of state power', *Journal of Developing Societies*, 21 (3–4) (2005), 373–376.

hegemonic alternative vision to the dominant Washington Consensus of the time, and as a signal that the western hemisphere would no longer be mapped solely by the dictates of the regional and global hegemon.

Finally, the FTAA failed in large part because the US administration's centre of attention was diverted after the 11 September 2001 terrorist attack on US soil. The new security imperatives of the US, post 9-11, has meant a refocusing of the attention of US foreign policy away from the hemisphere to Afghanistan and Iraq. As argued later in this volume, this diversion in the US's attention opened a window of opportunity for the emerging trading juggernaut, China, to penetrate into the US backyard. It has also reminded countries in the region that US attention to the area has waxed and waned over the decades and that developing an alternative to the FTAA might not be a bad idea after all. Certainly, it seems as though most political leaders in the developing countries of the western hemisphere began to heed the voices of their people who, in large demonstrations, were chanting 'No to the FTAA, another world is possible'.[27]

---

27   Jean Grugel, 'Regionalist governance and transnational collective action in Latin America', *Economy and Society*, 35 (2) (May 2006), 219.

Chapter 4

Free Trade: A Tool for US Hegemony in the Americas

Julián Castro-Rea

The Cow, the Goat and the patient Lamb once made an association with the Lion so they could enjoy a quiet life once and for all, since the predatory activities of the monster (as they called him behind his back) kept them in a constant state of anguish and desperation that they could only escape by treating him nicely.

Making use of the well-known hunting abilities of these four animals, one afternoon they hunted an agile Elk (whose meat of course disgusted the Cow, the Goat and the Lamb, used to feed from pasture they grazed), and according to their agreement they divided the large carcass among equal parts.

At this point, expressing at once all kinds of complaints and arguing their defencelessness and extreme weakness, the three started yelling loudly, having previously secretly agreed to keep the Lion's share because, as the Ant taught them, they wanted to put aside something for hard winter days.

This time, however, the Lion did not even bother to list the well known reasons why the Elk belonged to him alone, he instead ate all of his partners at one sitting, in the midst of long and loud complaints in which one could hear expressions such as social contract, Constitution, human rights and others equally strong and overriding.

Augusto Monterroso, 'The Lion's Share'[1]

Introduction

The FTAA project, originally planned to be put into practice by January 2005, clearly experienced a major setback. Nonetheless, the free trade agenda it represented is well and alive, so some revamped form of the FTAA project will arguably be revived in the near future, although perhaps under a different name. The project in particular, and free trade in general, have consistently been portrayed by governments, business representatives and international agencies alike as a unique opportunity offered to most countries in the Americas to benefit from the unlimited wealth created by unrestrained markets across the hemisphere. Moreover, from the outset, and notably since its predecessor project – the Enterprise for the Americas

---

1   Augusto Monterroso, *La oveja negra y demás fábulas* (Mexico City: Joaquín Mortiz, 1969), 78–80. Author's translation.

Initiative – was launched in 1990, trade liberalization has equally garnered strong support from the United States.

In this chapter, I argue that this support is not casually offered. It rather represents the first step in a strategy adopted in Washington to affirm US hegemony in the Americas. Countries that do not realize this real meaning of free trade promotion and still believe that free trade is only about opening up markets are deluding themselves, the same way that the Lion's partners did in Monterroso's story. Moreover, they risk having the same fate.

Indeed, away from state-centred aid programmes and dependence theory-inspired integration schemes of yesteryears,[2] the FTAA aimed at creating an international environment that increases the competitive edge of US-based corporations, and is favourable to US corporate behaviour and regulations. On this, the FTAA followed the guidelines set up originally in the North American Free Trade Agreement (NAFTA). Such environment ensures US corporations will cross borders smoothly, without facing unexpected regulatory red tape and political uncertainties, and will have access to legal resources similar to the ones the US domestic legal system offers. Coupled with their economic strength and political clout, this 'tamed' environment provides clear advantages to these corporations, both from market and managerial perspectives.

Moreover, market liberalization also bears political consequences. First, induced and formalized standardization of trade and economic policies across borders also means reforms will be 'locked in', committing future governments in each country to abide by the accepted rules. Secondly, a common trade regime encourages harmonization in other fields of public policy. Thirdly, intensification of trade and investment, to the extent that it increases asymmetrical interdependence, enhances the leverage of the US government over partner countries on specific policy areas, ranging from minor bilateral issues to major foreign policy actions and long-term domestic reforms.

Mexico and Canada have experienced the processes just described. Eighteen years into NAFTA, these countries provide case studies to test the consequences of market liberalization agreements with the United States.

In order to substantiate the statements above, this chapter provides some evidence on the following issues:

- What is the origin of the hemispheric trade liberalization agenda;
- Sources of US support to the FTAA project. How US officials have rationalized that support;
- Some examples of compatibility between the FTAA proposed regime and US domestic corporate regulations;
- How the FTAA intended to implement market liberalization along NAFTA's guidelines;

---

2 See the origins of regionalization in the Americas as explained in Chapter 1 in this volume.

- Advantages obtained by US corporations within an open market environment;
- Instances in which changes in regulations affecting NAFTA rules have been challenged and rolled back by US actors;
- Areas of public policy in which harmonization has occurred;
- Some cases where the US has made use of asymmetrical interdependence to demand from partner countries behaviours compatible with its interests.

The Origins: Where Did the FTAA Idea Come From?

The very term 'free trade' is easy to sell to the general public because it conveys a positive image. Indeed, who does not like freedom? Put otherwise, how can you say no to something that is free? Applying the adjective to trade, there is an implication that it also means unrestricted exchanges, less hurdles to action and lighter costs to consumers thanks to intensified competition among suppliers of goods and services. But in fact all the so-called free trade agreements that have been concluded among sovereign countries are, with no exception, much more about *regulated* trade than unrestricted exchanges. The FTAA project was no exception either, since rules about what was permitted and what was not were carefully built into the agreement's preliminary drafts.[3]

Moreover, the FTAA was not a project originally conceived and jointly promoted by all governments in the western hemisphere in a consensual way. It rather resulted from various plans the US government had conceived through the post-Cold War era, aimed at promoting a hemispheric regime increasingly compatible with its country's interests, regulations and values.

The first such plan was the Enterprise for the Americas Initiative (EAI), introduced by President George Bush Sr. in June 1990; that is, within months of the fall of the Berlin Wall. As its name suggests, the main goal of this initiative was to promote the adoption and development of private enterprise values and practices throughout the Americas, with the support of US private investment.

EAI was reframed by the Clinton administration as a summitry process, gathering all heads of state and government of the Americas, except for Cuba's, on a periodical basis (every three to four years). Starting in Miami in 1994, six official Summits of the Americas have been convened, where amid numerous photo-ops and calls for a renewed Inter-American dialogue talks about trade liberalization have developed. The summits have been the following:

Second summit – Santiago, Chile, 1998
Third summit – Quebec City, Canada, 2001
Fourth summit – Mar del Plata, Argentina, 2005

---

3   As confirmed in the FTAA's last draft made public, available at http://www.ftaa-alca.org/FTAADraft03/Index_e.asp, accessed 26 December 2013.

Fifth summit – Port of Spain, Trinidad and Tobago, 2009
Sixth summit – Cartagena, Colombia, 2012.[4]

The summitry process was drastically challenged from the third, 2001 summit on. Civil society stakeholders and parliamentarians across the Americas felt they had been unduly excluded from the talks, monopolized by government executive branches and representatives of transnational corporations, and publicly demonstrated for the right to be heard and see their concerns and priorities reflected in intergovernmental agreements negotiated in the summits. From then on, clashes between thousands of demonstrators and riot police discredited the summitry process. The fourth, 2005 summit is also important for the purposes of this chapter, because that is when the FTAA project was definitely killed.

The FTAA project was developed within that controversial process. The fact that it was always led by successive US governments should not be surprising, as the goals pursued would serve well US hegemonic interests, as we will see below.

The FTAA, NAFTA, and US Domestic Corporate Regulations

Another important precedent to the FTAA project is the North American Free Trade Agreement (NAFTA), linking the Canadian, Mexican and US economies together since January 1994. In fact, the FTAA project adopted NAFTA's regulations as its template. Ever since the NAFTA text was completed, after intensive negotiations running from June 1991 to August 1992, the US government has used this agreement as the model to follow for subsequent trade deals it has concluded around the world. NAFTA in turn incorporated, and improved, the main components of its predecessor, the Canada-US Free Trade Agreement (CUSFTA).

The fact CUSFTA was the template for NAFTA meant that Mexico, a developing economy, was considered as a partner endowed with the same rights and the same obligations Canada and the United States assumed. During the negotiations, some special concessions were granted to Mexico, such as longer time frames for full liberalization of selected agricultural products and exemption of energy industries from the disciplines of state deregulation and open investment. However, these measures were seen as mere exceptions to the general rule of national treatment, the same way Canada retained its ability to subsidize its cultural industries or the US its heavy state supports to agriculture. The general rule was the assumption that the three member states should be treated equally, in order to benefit from market access that would allegedly allow for fair competition to thrive. The market – the rationale of the argument pursued – would be the only mechanism that will eventually make existing socio-economic disparities disappear, by promoting shared prosperity.

---

4   For a description of the main events during each summit, consult http://www. summit-americas.org/previous_summits.html, accessed 26 December 2013.

Moreover, NAFTA included policy areas whose consideration as trade-related was until then controversial within multilateral trade fora, such as investment, intellectual property, and trade in services. It created a new horizon, a yardstick against which future economic integration schemes would be measured.

The FTAA project was no exception to the trends described above. It inherited from all the assumptions and biases NAFTA contains. NAFTA is not a neutral common ground resulting from a consensual agreement among equals. It is rather a negotiated agreement, resulting from asymmetrical power struggles, and thus bears the imprint that the stronger party in that negotiation left in it. Many institutional assumptions, mechanisms and legal definitions in NAFTA are inspired in US corporate culture, practices and legal regulations.

A case in point is the concept of expropriation, as incorporated in NAFTA's chapter 11. In that chapter, NAFTA grants to foreign corporations the ability to sue governments whenever they consider public policy decisions affect their business prospects. In some high profile cases, the Mexican and Canadian governments were forced to pay millions of dollars in compensation to US corporations, simply because those governments decided to act and legislate with the public interest in mind.

The first such high profile case was filed by Metalclad corporation against the government of Mexico in January 1997. The corporation had obtained permission to build a waste disposal facility, but the adjacent community of Guadalcázar found out that toxic residues were to be buried in that facility. Concerned about the impacts over the water table, the municipality successfully lobbied the San Luis Potosí state government, who decided to reverse the permit and declare the area an environmentally protected zone. Metalclad's claim included not only the cost of the equipment bought and works already performed, but also the alleged 'lost revenue' that the cancellation of the permit provoked. This abstract calculation, alien to Mexican legislation, invokes the broad definition of expropriation as understood under US law. In the end, once the litigation ended, Mexico's federal government was ordered to pay US$16.7 million to Metalclad as compensation for having implemented measures 'tantamount to expropriation'.

The second notable case was filed by Abitibi Bowater Inc. against the Canadian government in April 2009; in reaction to the decision of the provincial government of Newfoundland and Labrador to return the company's water use and timber rights to the Crown and to expropriate certain Abitibi Bowater lands and assets. It is important to note that water and timber did not legally belong to the corporation, but to the provincial government, who had only granted a license for their private exploitation. Under Canadian constitutional law, the withdrawal of rights over Crown lands is not considered compensable. Nonetheless, Abititbi Bowater claimed US$467.5 million in compensation, invoking NAFTA's chapter 11 powerful mechanisms and expansive definitions. The Canadian federal government decided to settle the claim without waiting for the arbitration process to be completed, paying Abitibi Bowater CA$130 million in compensation.[5]

Until October 2010, a total of 28 chapter 11 lawsuits had been filed against Canada, 19 against Mexico and also 19 against the United States. As a result, the Canadian government had paid CA$157 million while its Mexican counterpart paid US$187, not including undisclosed legal fees and interests also reimbursed. Interestingly, though, during the same period of time the US government lost no case and made no payment whatsoever, a fact that is in itself testimony to the slanted nature of NAFTA's legal dispute resolution regime.[6] By slanted I mean that while US corporations and their lawyers have had the leisure of acting within a familiar legal environment, their Mexican and Canadian counterparts have been forced to lose millions of dollars in the process of learning how those rules and institutions work.

This way, foreign investors' rights are prevailing above the ones of their domestic counterparts, let alone those of ordinary citizens and the common good. US-based corporations have especially benefited from this regime. Thanks to NAFTA's chapter 11 business interests are also entitled to legally limit the outputs of the political process, as failure to yield to foreign corporate interests may force governments to pay hefty compensations. This clearly means an erosion of accountability, sovereignty and democracy.

From the institutional side, NAFTA is a quite loose agreement with very limited common governance bodies. A notorious absence is a permanent tribunal to deal with trade disputes whenever they arise. Instead, it features ad hoc panels, created any time it is necessary to deal with one specific dispute and dissolved once a decision is reached. Dispute settlement mechanisms were in fact a compromise, after US negotiators refused to agree on creating the common competition policy and permanent tribunals Canada and Mexico wished.[7] Additionally, those panels are a peculiar kind of tribunals, to the extent that they incorporate in their adjudication process the parts involved in the litigation.

Above all, recent experience shows that panel decisions are not being respected by the US government whenever they conflict with domestic interests. The case of Canadian exports of softwood lumber to the US clearly illustrates this point. Producers of similar products in the United States, backed by the US

---

5   Aggregate and comparative details about these two prominent cases and all claims under NAFTA's chapter 11 until Oct. 2010 are compiled in the report elaborated by Scott Sinclair, of the Canadian Centre for Policy Alternatives, available at http://www. policyalternatives.ca/sites/default/files/uploads/publications/National%20Office/2010/11/ NAFTA%20Dispute%20Table.pdf, accessed 26 January 2013.

6   See Scott Sinclair's report, 22; as well as Public Citizen/Friends of the Earth, *NAFTA's Chapter 11 Investor to State Cases: Bankrupting Democracy* (Washington: Public Citizen, 2001), 7.

7   Maxwell Cameron and Brian Tomlin, *The Making of NAFTA. How the Deal Was Done* (Ithaca: Cornell University Press, 2000), 45–46.

government, claim that those exports are subsidized, to the extent that lumber is harvested from public lands under a concession agreement to private exploiters. As a consequence, heavy anti-dumping tariffs have been imposed over Canadian exports, obviously hurting their competitiveness. The Canadian government has brought the case to arbitration on four occasions; the corresponding panels have in most instances found there is no reason for the extra tariff since there is no actual subsidy provided. However, the US government has repeatedly refused to enforce those decisions; recently claiming, without proof, that the WTO has proven them right. Eventually, in July 2006, the Canadian government proposed a settlement according to which Washington would return 75 per cent of duties retained in exchange for a voluntary cap on Canadian exports. The settlement brought temporary peace to the acrimonious dispute.

However, the settlement also underscored the vacuity of NAFTA's formal dispute resolution mechanisms, which were still unable to overcome asymmetries of market and political power. This lack of compliance clearly raises doubts on the principle of trade liberalization itself,[8] because NAFTA has not been able to put an end to US unilateralism in trade matters once and for all, which was after all one of the main objectives of the agreement in the first place.

NAFTA as a Conditioning Framework for Policy Making

NAFTA has also become a straitjacket for domestic legislatures when it comes to defining many new policies or modifying existing ones. It has obviously affected trade policy, but its influence also extends to other realms of economic policy and even public policy in general.

This straitjacket effect should not come as a surprise if we remind that it was one of the main motivations behind the agreement. The US government wished to 'lock in' market-friendly neo-liberal reforms, to prevent the return to nationalist and state-interventionist policies adopted by past governments in both Mexico and Canada.[9]

Additionally, these reforms also require to be followed by subsequent policy changes to make them mutually compatible. Quite often efficiency is not even the main engine of change, but the willingness of public officials to do as the US government does in their area of competence. Emulation of this sort, mostly

8   Greg Anderson, 'The Uncertain Politics of North American Economic Integration', in Julián Castro-Rea (ed.), *Our North America. Social and Political Issues beyond NAFTA* (Farnham: Ashgate, 2012), 51–52.

9   Ricardo Grinspun and Yasmine Shamsie, 'Canada, Free Trade, and "Deep Integration" in North America: Context, Problems and Challenges', in R. Grinspun and Y. Shamsie (eds), *Whose Canada? Continental Integration, Fortress North America and the Corporate Agenda* (Montreal: McGill-Queen's University Press, 2007), 5–6.

motivated by the policy makers' ideological convictions, is a powerful driving force along market-oriented, neo-liberal policies.[10]

Several cases of this trend could be identified: environmental policy, Indigenous policy, monetary and fiscal policies among others. In all these areas convergence is noticeable, and the US government is leading the way to follow. A couple of examples will be developed below, as an illustration of this larger trend of policy convergence.

Across North America, Indigenous policy is increasingly compatible with market imperatives. Indigenous land management is being redefined in terms of profit, above any other priority. The strategy pursued by all three North American federal governments is based on opening these lands to private investment and development. Moreover, by attempting to separate the Indigenous right to self-government from the recognition of an Indigenous territorial base, the federal governments strengthen their control over what is left of Indigenous lands, legitimizing this policy with the need to eliminate uncertainty for private investment.[11]

Another policy area where convergence is conspicuous is environmental policy, in particular regarding climate change. Not long ago, the Canadian government was a global leader in that area, notably facilitating the adoption of the so-called 'Montreal Protocol on Substances that Deplete the Ozone Layer', in force since January 1989. It was also an enthusiastic supporter and promoter of the Kyoto Protocol, an agreement adopted by the United Nations Framework Convention on Climate Change in December 1997, and implemented since February 2005. An overwhelming majority of UN members, totalling 191 sovereign states, ratified the Protocol. Canada was among them, but a notorious exception was the United States, which signed in the original version of the agreement in 1998 but never ratified it. However, in a gradual yet unexpected turn of events, Canada ended up following the example of the US in December 2011, thus becoming the only country in the world to withdraw from the Protocol after having ratified it. Pro-market disciplines imposed by NAFTA played a direct, major role in Canada's about-face regarding climate change.[12]

NAFTA thus became a useful mechanism to reorganize government functions in Mexico and Canada along market priorities, which usually converge with US interests and preferences.

---

10   For how this process unfolded in Mexico, see Sarah Babb, *Managing Mexico: Economists from Nationalism to Neoliberalism* (Princeton: Princeton University Press, 2001), 171–198.

11   Julián Castro-Rea and Isabel Altamirano-Jiménez, 'North American First Peoples: Self-Determination or Economic Development?', in Yasmeen Abu-Laban et al. (eds), *Politics in North America: Redefining Continental Relations* (Peterborough: Broadview, 2008), 225–249.

12   Elizabeth May and Sarah Dover, 'Breaking the Free Trade Addiction: An Intervention on Environmental Grounds', in Grinspun and Shamsie (eds), *Whose Canada? ...*, 424–429.

Beyond the Rules: Manipulating Dependence

NAFTA has favoured the growth of asymmetrical economic interdependence in North America. This means that, because of NAFTA, international trade and investment in Canada and Mexico have become overwhelmingly dependent on the US; a dependence that is not matched by a similar reliance of the US economy on the Canadian and Mexican markets.

Up to 80 per cent of all Canadian and Mexican foreign transactions are made with the US. In 2010, 16 years into NAFTA, the United States was still the main destination of Canadian exports, concentrating 74.9 per cent of the total, and was the origin of 50.4 per cent of imports.[13] Regarding Mexico, in 2011 34 per cent of that country's income was generated from exports, 78.6 per cent of which went to the United States, equivalent to US$274.7 billion. That same year, Mexico bought US$174.4 billion from its northern neighbour, which represented 49.7 per cent of total imports.[14] In contrast, in 2011 Canada purchased 19 per cent and Mexico 13.3 per cent of United States' total exports ($1.511 trillion), and respectively provided 14.2 per cent and around 11.8 per cent of US total imports ($2.314 trillion).[15]

The US is also, by far, the single most important source of origin of foreign direct investment for both its neighbours. Statistics Canada reports that, by 2011, the stock of US investment in Canada was CA$326.055 billion, equivalent to 53.7 per cent of total foreign direct investment in that country.[16] The stock of US foreign direct investment in Mexico was US$90.3 billion in 2010, 49.9 per cent of total foreign investment in that country. In contrast, Canadian direct investment in the United States was valued at CA$249.9 billion in 2010;[17] while the stock of Mexican FDI in the United States was US$12.6 billion that same year. Those figures respectively represent a mere 8.7 per cent and 0.4 per cent of total FDI stock in the US, amounting to US$ 2.874 trillion.[18]

---

13   Data from Canada's Department of Foreign Affairs and International Trade, available at http://www.international.gc.ca/economist-economiste/performance/state-point/state_2011_point/2011_5.aspx?lang=eng&view=d, accessed 26 December 2013.

14   Bank of Mexico data, available at http://www.economia-snci.gob.mx/sic_php/pages/bruselas/trade_links/ing/febing2012.pdf, accessed 26 December 2013.

15   Data available at http://www.ustr.gov/countries-regions/americas/mexico, and https://www.cia.gov/library/publications/the-world-factbook/geos/us.html, accessed 26 December 2013.

16   Data available at http://www.international.gc.ca/economist-economiste/assets/pdfs/Data/investments-investissements/FDI_by_Country/FDI_stocks-Inward_by_Country-ENG.pdf, accessed 26 December 2013.

17   Data from http://www.parl.gc.ca/Content/LOP/ResearchPublications/2011-06-e.htm, accessed 26 December 2013.

18   Author's calculation based on The CIA World Factbook data, available at https://www.cia.gov/library/publications/the-world-factbook/geos/us.html, accessed 26 December 2013.

In short, economic exchanges within North America are not nearly as important for the US as they are for Canada and Mexico. Put otherwise, the US can afford instability or even reductions in those markets, whereas any North American market disruption may be very costly for the Canadian and Mexican economies.

The US government understands this asymmetry perfectly well, and manipulates this dependence as a tool for applying political pressure over their neighbouring countries in other areas. In doing so, it puts into practice what analysts of international negotiations call 'issue linkage',[19] meaning that it makes use of its leverage in the economic realm to have a stronger bargaining position in other policy areas.

This manipulation is not accidental, hidden, unintended or even exceptional, it was in fact one of NAFTA's stated goals from the US perspective. Neo-conservative politician Robert B. Zoellick – at the time counsellor of the Department of State, later on US Trade Representative (USTR) from 2001 to 2005, and president of the World Bank from 2007 to 2012 – argued that NAFTA was important to his country not just from the trade policy perspective but also as:

> a rare strategic opportunity to secure, strengthen, and develop our continental base, economically and politically, in a way that will promote America's foreign policy agenda, our economic strength and leadership, and US global influence.[20]

Specifically about Mexico, John D. Negroponte – then US Ambassador to that country and subsequently Director of National Intelligence (2005–07) and Deputy Secretary of State (2007–09) – wrote in a June 1991 confidential cable to Assistant Secretary of State Bernard Aronson, leaked to the Mexican magazine *Proceso*, that NAFTA:

> would institutionalize acceptance of a North American orientation to Mexican foreign relations. Just think of how this contrasts with past behaviour ... Previously, as now, 60 or 70 percent of Mexico's business would be with the United States; but if you listened to us in the UN or debating Central America you would think we were arch-enemies.[21]

---

19   For a definition, see for instance Ernst B. Haas, 'Why Collaborate?: Issue-Linkage and International Regimes', in *World Politics*, 32 (3) (April 1980), 357–405.

20   Robert O. Zoellick, 'The North American FTA: The New World Order Takes Shape in the Western Hemisphere', in *US Department of State Dispatch*, 3 (15) (13 April 1992), 290.

21   Quoted by Michael Reid, 'Vote in US Congress May Hinder President's Attempt to Modernise the Economy', in *The Guardian* (20 May 1991). See also David Clark Scout, 'US Foresees Foreign Policy Impact of Mexican Trade Pact', in *The Christian Science Monitor* (1 August 1991).

In order to illustrate how this manipulation of dependence works, two issues deserve closer analysis: border management and foreign policy.

In the aftermath of the attacks of 11 September, 2001 the US government perceived its borders as weak links that could lead to other possible attacks. Even if it was not supported by conclusive evidence, the perception that potential terrorists or material to carry out attacks could make their way into the United States through Canada or Mexico grew in the United States.[22] Pressures to make sure Canadian and Mexican security standards would meet the challenge ensued.[23] As a result, the US government demanded Mexico and Canada to increase control over the movement of people and goods across borders. It conditioned continued inflow of goods and people on negotiation and enforcement of two separate border agreements with each one of its two neighbours.

The agreements adopted to beef up border security were the United States-Canada Smart Border Declaration of 12 December, 2001 and the United States-Mexico Border Partnership Agreement of 22 March, 2002. These agreements force Ottawa and Mexico City to fundamentally reorganize their border management policies in order to make them compatible with US increased border controls; a reorganization that has implied a considerable raise in budget allocations and higher numbers in personnel. Neither Mexico's nor Canada's government had much choice if they wanted to keep the borders open. While joint US-Mexico border management stuck to the original agreement and somewhat stalled, Washington and Ottawa went several steps further. In February 2011 the two countries concluded the 'Beyond the Border' agreement, where cooperation on border management reaches unprecedented areas and scope.[24]

These agreements clearly express how US pressure on its neighbours was successful in accommodating its new concerns; although they also represent the implicit acknowledgement by the US of the impossibility of effective unilateral action to protect its territory.

US pressures were also applied in foreign policy matters. Let us recall the way the US government put pressure on Canada and Mexico, in early 2003, to join the coalition that attacked Iraq or at least diplomatically supported the invasion.

Washington took for granted that Canada would support the US in Iraq. Not surprisingly, Prime Minister Jean Chrétien came under pressure to intervene in favour of the US position in the Security Council. In late February, he received telephone calls from George W. Bush – as well as from then British Prime Minister Tony Blair – before he left for an official visit to Mexico. Mexico was not exempt

---

22   See for instance Anonymous, 'Alleged Hizballah "Fighter" Snuck into US from Mexico', in *Human Events* (26 January 2004), 1 and Terrence P. Jeffrey, 'A Case of Selective Enforcement', in *Human Events* (14 July 2003), 8.

23   T. Jeffrey, 'A Case …', 8 and Naomi Klein, 'The Rise of the Fortress Continent', in *The Nation*, 276 (4), 10.

24   The joint declaration giving birth to the agreement is available at http://pm.gc.ca/eng/media.asp?id=3938, accessed 26 December 2013.

from pressure, especially because that year the country was a non-permanent member of UN Security Council, whose leadership and support may be crucial to secure the Council's endorsement of the invasion. When specifically questioned on the issue, Mexican President Vicente Fox denied that pressure was put over him, and dismissed speculation that Mexico's position in the Security Council was leaning toward support to the US.[25] However, President Bush himself indicated he telephoned Fox repeatedly – the first time, on 22 February, 2003 – to ask him to support the US position in the Security Council.[26]

Instead of supporting the US position, however, the Canadian mission proposed a compromise, aimed at solving the impasse within the Security Council while making room for multilateral endorsement of US plans. Canada's compromise was actively supported by Mexico. Even if immediately after its public presentation a US diplomatic source said the proposal 'was noted and was positive', it was nonetheless quickly dismissed offhand by US officials. Bush himself telephoned Jean Chrétien on 26 February, criticizing him for having floated and promoted the proposal. He reportedly complained Canada's plan only aimed at buying time for Iraq, while undermining the tough resolve behind US allies within the Security Council. After the telephone conference, when asked whether Bush found some value on the Canadian proposal, White House spokesman Ari Fleischer expressed that 'The president has offered a resolution that he thinks is the way to go ...'.[27] Also, after another telephone conference between Canada's foreign minister Bill Graham and US Secretary of State Colin Powell, Richard Boucher, spokesman to the latter, declared that the proposal 'only procrastinates on a decision we all should be prepared to take'.[28]

The decision of Mexico and Canada not to support the war against Iraq was also openly criticized by US officials. On 18 March, Richard Boucher declared the following: 'We are disappointed because some of our closest allies, including Canada, did not reach an agreement on the urgent need for action ... Regarding Mexico, we think the same'.[29] He later offered some conciliatory statements to the two countries. One week later, Paul Celucci, US Ambassador to Canada, elaborated on those comments during a speech delivered to the Economic Club of Toronto. After praising economic exchanges and recent official collaborative efforts between the two countries, he expressed that:

25   Cordon, 'Chrétien Warns ...'.

26   Copley News Service, 'Transcript of the president's comments on Mexico' at the San Diego Union Tribune website signonsandiego.printthis.clickability.com (6 March 2003), accessed 26 December 2013.

27   'US Slaps Down Canadian Compromise on Iraq', from *CTV News* at www.ctv.ca (27 February 2003).

28   'Germany Rejects Canadian Proposal on Iraq', from cnews.canoe.ca (26 February 2003).

29   Quoted in 'EU, "decepcionado" de México y Canadá', in *La Jornada* (19 March 2003). My translation.

... there is disappointment in Washington and in the United States that Canada is not supporting us fully ... There is no security threat to Canada that the United States would not be ready, willing and able to help with. There would be no debate ... no hesitation. We would be there for Canada, part of our family. That is why so many in the United States are disappointed and upset that Canada is not fully supporting us now.[30]

In other words, the US government expects that its closest trade partners will also be its diplomatic allies, even if US positions conflict with Canadian and Mexican perspectives or interests on international matters. Because of the strong dependence of their countries' economies on the US, the Canadian and Mexican cannot ignore this pressure, and will eventually try to find ways to accommodate to US positions.

Conclusions

NAFTA's experience provides ample evidence that, from a historical perspective, while discussing free trade the US does not intend to engage in horizontal trade partnerships, levelling the playing field to create the conditions for fair competition. Not only is the principle of preferential treatment for weaker partners absent from the spirit of any agreement promoted by the US government, also all rules are created in such a way that they favour US firms and government objectives. Moreover, beyond the formal rules, economic and political asymmetries are still at play, favouring the US when it comes to competing and exercising leadership and influence.

There is every reason to believe that the FTAA project was following the same pattern. Therefore, the FTAA project should not be seen as a tool for development, the way other economic integration schemes of the Americas put in practice in the past (ALADI, Andean Pact, CARICOM, MCCA, etc.) and present (UNASUR) could.[31] The FTAA project was rather a market-oriented mechanism – therefore precluding state intervention for the achievement of development objectives – that could also be used to increase the US grip on the Americas. Not only was it aimed at giving US corporations competitive advantages, it was also poised to provide enhanced political leverage to the US government over other sovereign states in the hemisphere. It was therefore an instrument for renewed US economic and political hegemony in the Americas.

To be sure, prospects for the eventual re-enactment of the FTAA seem now dimmer, due to several events. First, the election of left-wing governments in Venezuela, Bolivia, Ecuador and to some extent Brazil, which have become vocal critics of US dominance in the hemisphere, brought the voices of dissent to the

---

30   Quoted by *CBC News Online* at www.cbc.ca (28 March 2003).
31   See Chapter 1 in this volume.

free trade agenda to the very heart of the intergovernmental negotiation process. Secondly, the failure of the WTO ministerial meeting in Cancún in September 2003, and the rejection of the FTAA project in Mar del Plata two years later, cast a shadow on prospects of generalized trade liberalization in the hemisphere.

However, the failure of a comprehensive FTAA gave place to a prospect that is even more alarming from the weaker countries' perspective. The USTR office engaged from then on in negotiating trade liberalization agreements in the hemisphere on a bilateral or selective basis. Former USTR Zoellick appealed to 'the coalition of the liberalizers' – in a clear reference to the so-called 'coalition of the willing' who supported the invasion of Iraq – to join the United States in bilateral or regional trade pacts in the face of mounting opposition from Brazil and other developing nations to the US global economy agenda.[32]

In early 2003 Zoellick outlined a free trade strategy that anticipated rising opposition to Washington's liberalization agenda. Instead of committing itself to making the compromises necessary to completing another negotiating round in the WTO, the Bush administration announced that it would pursue its agenda through free trade agreements (FTAs) with single nations or subregional groupings. 'Our FTA partners are the vanguard of a new global coalition of open markets', declared Zoellick.

The recent free trade agreement with Central America and the Dominican Republic (CAFTA-DR), fully implemented since January 2009, illustrates this pattern. The new bilateral strategy puts weaker countries in an even more fragile bargaining position, from which they can be coerced to accept the terms decided in the US as a condition for reaching an agreement. This new approach opens the possibility for even less fair trade agreements from the weaker partners' perspective.[33] The Obama administration has not sent any signal that it intends to modify the approach just described to international negotiations carried out by his government's representatives.

Once a patchwork of regional agreements exists, it will be easier to call for the creation of an umbrella framework linking them all. But it would be an institutional arrangement that would be even more biased in favour of US interests than the FTAA project was; because it has been negotiated on a bilateral basis, putting less powerful partners in a weaker bargaining position. This way, 'free trade' is still indeed a tool for securing that the Lion's share in the Americas will go to the United States; just as it did in Monterroso's story.

---

32   Quoted in http://rightweb.irc-online.org/ind/zoellick/zoellick.php, accessed 12 October 2005.

33   María Eugenia Trejos París and Mario Fernández Arias (eds), *Tratado de Libre Comercio Estados Unidos-Centroamérica-República Dominicana. Estrategia de tierra arrasada* (San José: EUNED, 2006).

Chapter 5

Re-mapping Trade Relations in the Americas: The Influence of Shifting Power

Gaspare M. Genna

Introduction

This chapter[1] will focus primarily on the negotiations between the European Union (EU), Common Market of the South (MERCOSUR) and the United States but will also attempt to explain why each of these actors, while unsuccessfully negotiating agreements among themselves, are successful in completing FTAs with other members of the western hemisphere. On 23 February 2005, Robert B. Zoellick, the US Trade Representative, failed to reach an agreement with his Canadian and Latin American counterparts for the establishment of the Free Trade Area of the Americas (FTAA). Negotiations for the FTAA began in 1994 with the idea of establishing a FTA that would include all the economies of the western hemisphere, except Cuba (34 in all). The potential total market size is estimated to be 923.8 million people with a total output of $22.3 trillion in 2011, of which the US would account for about 67 per cent of the total.[2] The US already established trade agreements with the following countries of the western hemisphere:[3]

- Canada and Mexico under the North American Free Trade Agreement (NAFTA) (1994);
- Chile (2004);
- Costa Rica, the Dominican Republic, El Salvador, Guatemala, Honduras, and Nicaragua under the Central American Free Trade Agreement (CAFTA-DR) (2006);
- Peru (2009);
- Panama (2011); and
- Colombia (2012).

---

1   This chapter draws from Gaspare M. Genna, 'Economic Size and the Changing International Political Economy of Trade: The Development of the Western Hemispheric FTAs', *International Politics*, 47 (6) (2010), 638–658.

2   World Bank, 2013. World Development Indicators. http://data.worldbank.org/data-catalog/world-development-indicators, accessed 26 December 2013.

3   Years denote date of FTA implementation.

Similarly, EU Trade Commissioner, Pascal Lamy, failed to reach a FTA with his counterparts from MERCOSUR on 26 May 2005, and while negotiations are still continuing, there has been no final resolution. The MERCOSUR customs union includes Argentina, Brazil, Paraguay, Uruguay and Venezuela. The 2011 MERCOSUR market size is 276.7 million people with a total output of US$3.3 trillion, of which Brazil represents approximately 75 per cent of the total. Negotiations for the EU-MERCOSUR FTA began in earnest in 1999 after years of preliminary talks. It would represent an estimated market size of 780.4 million people with a total output of US$20.9 trillion in 2011, of which the EU would account for approximately 84 per cent of the total.[4] The EU already has a trade association agreement with Chile (2002) and Mexico (2000) as well as a preferential trade agreement with former colonies in the region. MERCOSUR countries also have association agreements with The Andean Community (Bolivia, Colombia, Ecuador and Peru), Mexico, and Chile, with Guyana and Suriname as potential future associate members. In turn all MERCOSUR members became associate members of the Andean Community to form the South American Community of Nations.

To understand the puzzle of why some negotiations ended successfully while others have not, I conducted an analysis that includes two key interacting variables: the economic size of the three actors (EU, MERCOSUR, US) and their respective preferences. FTAs are more likely to form when actors believe that there are advantages to signing than not signing. The respective advantages are the actors' preferences which reflect a desired pattern of trade depending on the actors' level of development and strength of domestic economic actors. Developing actors (like the MERCOSUR members) would prefer a trading relationship where they can ease market entry of their primary goods while hoping to shield infant industries. Developed (EU and US) actors prefer a relationship where they can maximize exports of their capital-intensive goods while protecting their agricultural sectors.

These preferences interact with the relative size of the actors. Large economic asymmetries can lead smaller actors to accept less than preferred trade patterns if being locked out of the larger market would make them worse off. But a point can be reached when the economic size differential is not large enough to accept trade patterns demanded by the larger actor(s). More specifically, both the EU and US are attempting to reorganize the global trade regime along their individual preferences through the EU-MERCOSUR FTA and FTAA, respectively. However, the members of MERCOSUR see this reorganization to their economic disadvantage. In addition, having the limited access to the EU and US markets do not have enough economic value for MERCOSUR because a rapidly growing China offers an alternative market for the MERCOSUR members to sell their exports, under more preferred conditions.

---

4   World Bank, 2013.

Explaining the Lack of Success: Relative Size and Actors' Preferences

In order to explain the EU-MERCOSUR and FTAA outcomes, a brief overview of the prior research[5] indicates that successful development of regional integration depends on the economic asymmetries and compatible preferences. Power theories stress the distribution of power among states as a central factor influencing international outcomes. Proponents of hegemonic stability theory argue that the presence of a hegemonic state is a necessary condition for liberal international commerce.[6] Others demonstrate empirically that cooperation can develop under asymmetric conditions if political and military alliances are present.[7] It is logical for allies to cooperate economically because of the intimate relationship physical security has with economic security; reciprocal enhancement of an allies' economic strength will aid in improving military readiness.

Nonetheless the claim that alliance portfolios will always trump other rationales for trade preferences can be contested. Trade policies can run counter to the ideal suggested by the alliance portfolio literature because of the consequences a potential FTA poses to domestic groups and the related implication it would have on political leadership survival.[8] The preferences of an actor would therefore also need to balance the needs of potential FTA winners and losers with a stronger emphasis on the more powerful and better organized interest groups in the society.[9]

---

5   For a complete assessment of regional integration theory, please see Yi Feng and Gaspare M. Genna, 'Regional Integration and Domestic Institutional Homogeneity: A Comparative Analysis of Regional Integration in the Americas, Pacific Asia and Western Europe', *Review of International Political Economy*, 10 (2) (2003), 278–309 and Gaspare M. Genna and Taeko Hiroi, 'Power Preponderance and Domestic Politics: Explaining Regional Economic Integration in Latin America and the Caribbean', *International Interactions*, 30 (2) (2004), 143–164.

6   Stephan Krasner, 'State Power and the Structure of International Trade', *World Politics*, 28 (1976), 317; Robert Gilpin, *The Political Economy of International Relations* (Princeton: Princeton University Press, 1987).

7   Joanne Gowa and Edward D. Mansfield, 'Power Politics and International Trade', *American Political Science Review*, 87 (1993), 408; Joanne Gowa, *Allies, Adversaries and International Trade* (Princeton: Princeton University Press, 1994); Edward D. Mansfield and Rachel Bronson, 'The Political Economy of Major Power Trade Flows', in Edward D. Mansfield and Helen V. Milner (eds), *The Political Economy of Regionalism* (New York: Columbia University Press, 1997); and Robert Gilpin, *Global Political Economy: Understanding the International Economic Order* (Princeton: Princeton University Press, 2001).

8   Gaspare M. Genna and Taeko Hiroi, 'Power Preponderance and Domestic Politics: Explaining Regional Economic Integration in Latin America and the Caribbean', *International Interactions*, 30 (2) (2004), 143–164.

9   Robert Putnam, 'Diplomacy and Domestic Policies: The Logic of Two Level Games', *International Organization*, 42 (1988), 427–460; Helen Milner, *Resisting Protectionism* (Princeton: Princeton University Press, 1988); Jeffry Frieden, *Debt, Development and Democracy: Modern Political Economy and Latin America, 1965–1985* (Princeton:

In sum, power asymmetry and a focus on domestically derived preferences, in combination, can offer an accurate picture of when FTA negotiations, and other developments of regional integration, are successful.[10] Integration develops because the larger member of the asymmetric power relationship provides incentives to smaller states by leveraging its economic size. Leverage employed can vary from offering economic assistance to discontinuing assistance. It could also include retaliatory actions such as increasing existing trade barriers. Preferences in trade patterns also matter. Compatible preferences are associated with overall trade dependence; the more trade dependent the potential partners, the more likely they will integrate formally. The preferences of a state could be fine-tuned through an extrapolation of the pattern of trade using the concept of comparative advantage. Specific groups who own relatively abundant factors that are used intensively in production would favour a FTA while those that do not would oppose.[11] (See also the Heckscher Ohlin and Stopler Samuelson theorems in Krugman and Obstfeld book.)[12] Current trade patterns would reflect the preferences of potential FTA partners. In order for all sides to be satisfied, the negotiations need to favour those economic sectors that already have a higher volume of trade than other sectors. For developing countries, these are the primary goods sectors (especially agriculture) while for developed countries this includes the manufacturing, financial, and service sectors. Therefore, a smaller member would not join a FTA if it would be worse off; but if the smaller partner is satisfied with the current relationship and would not wish to harm that relationship, it would join the FTA.

Using this theory, the strategies of the EU, MERCOSUR (particularly Brazil) and the US can be understood. It is important to first look at the logic of the EU and US strategies and then Brazil's counter-strategy. Both the EU and US follow a strategy of competitive liberalization. The central idea of competitive liberalization

---

Princeton University Press, 1991); Jeffry Frieden, 'The Euro: Who Wins? Who Loses?', *Foreign Policy*, 25 (September 1998); Ronald Rogowski, *Commerce and Coalitions: How Trade Affects Domestic Political Alignments* (Princeton: Princeton University Press, 1989); Geoffrey Garrett and Peter Lange, 'International, Institutions and Political Change', *International Organization*, 49 (1995), 627; and Andrew Moravcsik, 'Taking Preferences Seriously: A Liberal Theory of International Politics', *International Organization*, 51 (5) (1997), 513–553.

10   Brian Efird and Gaspare M. Genna, 'Structural Conditions and the Propensity for Regional Integration', *European Union Politics*, 3 (3) (2002), 267–295; and Gaspare M. Genna and Taeko Hiroi, 'Power Preponderance and Domestic Politics: Explaining Regional Economic Integration in Latin America and the Caribbean', *International Interactions*, 30 (2) (2004), 143–164.

11   Stephen P. Magee, William A. Brock and Leslie Young, *Black Hole Tariffs and Endogenous Policy Theory: Political Economy in General Equilibrium* (Cambridge: Cambridge University Press, 1989).

12   Paul R. Krugman and Maurice Obstfeld, *International Economics: Theory and Policy* (Boston: Addison Wesley, 2002).

is that nonmembers will fear a cost of being excluded from FTAs.[13] They perceive that an established FTA is a 'gold standard' for trade that incurs a cost for them in the denial of access to a large market for the non-member's products.[14] Not wanting to lose, they join the arrangement. Therefore, FTAs expand when a large economy forms a central hub of a FTA wheel and other smaller economies are the spokes. In sum the nonmember decides that it prefers to trade-off the costs of increased competition in its domestic market with the gains of access to the FTA market. The final conclusion of competitive liberalism is that a global trading system emerges from the expanding FTA and primarily along the preferences of the hub economy.

The logic of competitive liberalization is, however, problematic and as a result can explain the lack of success in the two sets of negotiations. Knowing that the larger economy has this leverage, similar sized or middle sized economies would also adopt the same strategy so that they can develop their own trading blocs. The goal would be to develop 'competitive leverage' against the dominant player that wishes to play the role of the global hub economy. It is possible for a group of economies to compete as a unit to either be that hub economy or more likely, to diminish the leveraging power of the dominant economy in its effort to reorganize the global trade regime under its preferred trading pattern. Also, the logic of competitive liberalization suggests that 'spoke' economies have no alternative but to attach themselves to a specific 'hub'. It does not include the possibility that the smaller economies have alternative markets to sell their most important exports.

Preferences therefore play a key role and interact with the asymmetric power relations for the success of regional integration. If the dominant economic power wishes to develop or expand a FTA along its preferences, the likelihood of success diminishes with the larger nonmember's economic size *and* the less satisfied it is with the dominant actor's preferences. Success will also diminish when alternative markets are available. A relatively mid-sized economic power sees that not joining the FTA would leave it better off because the dominant economy is not large enough, is dissatisfied with the dominant actor's preferences, and alternative markets are available. However, the smaller the nonmember's size, the greater the likelihood of a successfully negotiating a FTA even if preferences are not ideal because not joining the FTA would still leave the smaller economy worse off, even if alterative markets are available.

If this theory holds, then the lack of success in the trade negotiations would start to result after the small economies join the larger economies attempting to reorganize the global trade regime under their preferences. This leaves the mid-sized economies that do not have the incentive to join but do have the incentive to

---

13   Soamiely Andriamananjara, 'Competitive Liberalization or Competitive Diversion? Preferential Trade Agreements and the Multilateral Trading System' (Working Paper, US International Trade Commission, 2003).

14   Gary C. Hufbauer and Yee Wong, 'Grading Growth: The Trade Legacy of President Bush', *Harvard International Review*, 26 (2) (Summer 2004).

form their own FTAs in order to safeguard their interests in the reorganization of the global trade regime. Unless the global large economies are willing to yield to the preferences of the mid-sized economies, then FTAs will be difficult to conclude.

Re-mapping Trade Relations

The EU and US have different approaches to negotiating FTAs, but are of the same mind in certain key issues that have characterized the talks between these economically developed actors and their developing counterparts. While the US follows an explicit strategy of competitive liberalization, the EU follows an implicit one under its Common Commercial Policy (CCP). Their goal is to reorganize the global trade regime by establishing bilateral or multilateral FTAs and then use these FTAs as greater leverages inside the global trade negotiations. Each attempts to become the hub of a FTA wheel and thereby slowly developing a trade regime along their trade pattern preferences.

Demonstrating the US strategy is straightforward; a brief overview of the statements of the leading negotiators can suffice. Allen F. Johnson, Chief Agriculture Negotiator, made the following statement before a US Senate subcommittee:

> Our strategy is to incite competitive liberalization by negotiating regional and bilateral trade agreements to complement our global strategy in the WTO. If others are ready to open their markets, America will be their partner. If some are not ready, or want to complain but not lower their own barriers, the United States will proceed with countries that are ready.[15]

Echoing this view and providing greater insight is Johnson's supervisor, Robert Zoellick before a US House of Representatives committee:

> We would like to pursue FTAs with the largest markets around the world, including the European Union and Japan among others. But right now, those countries are unwilling to move forward. As a result, we are pushing for the liberalization of their markets through the WTO. At the same time, as another facet of competitive liberalization, we hope our progress on other FTAs will encourage these important markets to reconsider their stance (US House of Representatives).[16]

---

15   Allen F. Johnson, 'Statement before Senate Committee on Foreign Relations Subcommittee on Western Hemisphere, Peace Corps and Narcotics Affairs', *United States Senate* (2004).

16   Robert B. Zoellick, 'Statement of U.S. Trade Representative before the Committee on Agriculture of the United States House of Representative', 2004.

But Johnson goes deeper into the US strategy in another quote from his US Senate subcommittee testimony:

> This competition in liberalization strengthens the United States' already considerable leverage, including in the WTO ... Our bilateral and regional FTAs in the hemisphere – the U.S.-Chile FTA, the CAFTA, and the FTAA – also complement our trade objectives in the WTO. They set high standards for trade agreements and spur competitive liberalization. They provide a counterweight to the FTAs our Western Hemisphere partners have signed with other countries, including Canada, Chile, and the EU. Finally, U.S. trade pacts in the Western Hemisphere deepen our ties with individual and small groups of trading partners – alliances that could help us in the WTO (US Senate 20 May 2003).

In sum, the US strategy, under the logic of comparative liberalization, is to gather steam in the WTO by establishing FTAs with willing partners. These FTAs would begin a process of making its preferences resonate in the global trade regime by countering other FTAs and establishing greater leverage against the biggest economies, namely those of the EU and Japan.

The EU strategy is parallel to that of the US, but not as explicit. In 1996, the EU developed the Market Access Strategy (MAS). The MAS is a multifaceted policy with one simple goal, to obtain access to external markets through the use of bilateral and multilateral agreements. To this end, the EU negotiates all external trade associations under the CCP. Part of the CCP is the contractual commercial policy that gives the EU Commission the power to initiate and the exclusive right to negotiate trade agreements.[17] The Commission can use its supranational stature to negotiate with non-members not only regarding tariffs and quotas but also non-tariff barriers, without the fear that another body will amend the final trade agreement. The EU Council, however, oversees negotiations through observers and the 113 Committee.[18] Final negotiations need to be approved by the Council using qualified majority voting in an up or down vote.[19]

Given this single voice, the Commission, through its chief negotiator, can develop specific strategies to achieve the goal of market access. The EU's pattern of FTA behaviour suggests that it is following a parallel strategy vis-à-vis the US. As mentioned in the introduction, the EU has trade association agreements with Chile

---

17 Desmond Dinan, *Ever Closer Union: An Introduction to European Integration* (Boulder: Lynne Rienner, 1999); Steve Marsh and Hans Mackenstein, *The International Relations of the European Union* (Harlow: Pearson Longman, 2005).

18 The name '113 Committee' comes from Article 113 using the old numbering system of the Treaty Establishing the European Community. This is the same as Article 133 using the new numbering system (Treaty of Amsterdam); however the name '133 Committee' has not come into vogue.

19 Simon Hix, *The Political System of the European Union* (Hampshire: Palgrave, 1999).

and Mexico. In addition to the current talks with MERCOSUR members, the EU is also in beginning stages of negotiations with the Central American states and Andean Community for future FTAs. Given this pattern, the EU strategy reflects the competitive liberalization logic, and with it, a potential centre of global trade regime reorganization.

More telling of the EU and US parallel strategies is their behaviour with the smaller economies of the Caribbean basin. Small, more trade-dependent countries need agreements to remove uncertainty from their trade relations with larger economies. The US provided preferential access for Caribbean countries (including Guatemala and El Salvador but with the exception Cuba) under the Caribbean Basin Initiative (CBI), but it did so unilaterally. The CBI came into being with the signing into law of the Caribbean Basin Economic Recovery Act.[20] Other legislation was enacted to expand the types of products and conditions for further preferential trade relationships, namely through the Caribbean Basin Economic Recovery Expansion Act of 1990 and the US-Caribbean Basin Trade Partnership Act of 2000. The CBI provides tariff reductions or exemptions for products from Central America and the Caribbean region countries. CBI benefits are, however, conditional. As stated in Section 202 of the Trade Partnership Act:

(1) to offer Caribbean Basin beneficiary countries willing to prepare to become a party to the FTAA or another free trade agreement, tariff treatment essentially equivalent to that accorded to products of NAFTA countries ... and

(2) to seek the participation of Caribbean Basin beneficiary countries in the FTAA or another free trade agreement at the earliest possible date, with the goal of achieving full participation in such agreement not later than 2005.

This section sets up the precondition of signing on to the FTAA or other FTAs on terms that were yet to be specified, but giving the Caribbean countries benefits immediately. The US established a status quo that would cause these countries to be worse off by not signing on to a FTA because not doing so could lead to losing access to the US market. Singing the FTA will lock in the trade arrangements of the CBI. The result was the enactment of the CAFTA-DR and the current negotiations with the other Caribbean countries.

The EU also practices a similar relationship with Caribbean countries that were former colonies of the member states. First initiated under the Lomé Convention, the EU has a preferential trading relationship with a group of countries referred to as the African, Caribbean, Pacific group (ACP). Lomé[21] provided a development assistance package that included free access to the European market for products

---

20   The Act went into effect on 1 January 1984.
21   The Lomé Convention was actually a series of five agreements: Lomé I–IV and an amended IV.

that originated in the ACP countries as well as aid and technical assistance.[22] The ACP–EU relationship is currently evolving as a result of the Cotonou Partnership Agreement (2000). A central pillar of the agreement is the movement away from the non-reciprocal trade arrangement under Lomé to a series of negotiated economic partnership agreements (EPAs) (Articles 36 and 37 of the Cotonou Partnership Agreement). The rationale is to make the ACP economies more competitive in the global economy. However the choice for each trade-dependent state, like the case of the CBI, is to either lose access to the larger market or sign EPAs and lock-in access through a WTO recognized agreement. Again, the smaller states would opt for the free trade arrangement and diminish the uncertainty that may result from not signing.

I now turn to the Brazilian perspective in the re-mapping of trade patterns and policy in the Americas. During an interview with an Argentine journalist, Brazil's Foreign Affairs Minister Celso Amorim said, 'Even though Brazil is the largest economy in South America, it needs the company of other countries, and above all, it needs MERCOSUR. To have a true multipolar system, there must be some minimal correlation of power'.[23] These two sentences were given in the context of the EU-MERCOSUR FTA and FTAA negotiations, and provide the key component of the Brazilian strategy vis-à-vis the EU and US. By developing its own trading bloc, Brazil can credibility maximize the expression of its preferences in the global trade regime. While the size of the MERCOSUR economies is small when compared to the EU or US, the strategy has been endorsed by the Inter-American Development Bank (IDB 2002). By combining the economic weight of several Latin American countries, Brazil has the ability to reduce the economic leverage of the economic heavyweights. Therefore, Brazil's calculation for forming a FTA differs: it could be worse off by signing a FTA if the trade preferences of the larger states are very distant from its own. If it can convince other states to form a bloc with aligned trade preferences, then it is not stuck in the competitive liberalization trap because it will not be left out of a market that others access. By re-mapping the conditions, the cost of not joining is low.

However, Brazil must do what the other larger actors do, namely provide incentives for regional partners to form a trading bloc. Although Brazil does not have as large a capacity as the larger actors, it has demonstrated the ability to keep the block together even in the worst of times (Genna and Hiroi 2007). This leadership continued in December 2004 when a FTA was finalized between MERCOSUR and the Andean Community bringing about the South American Community (SAC). In a practical sense, a free trade area of the Americas has already formed with the SAC given Mexico's upcoming associate status with MERCOSUR. It is one, however, where Brazil is potentially the hub economy than the US.

---

22   Desmond Dinan, *Ever Closer Union: An Introduction to European Integration* (Boulder: Lynne Rienner, 1999).

23   Natasha Niebieskikwiat, 'Brazil's Amorim Wants Strong MERCOSUR to Negotiate with United States', *Buenos Aires Clarin* (2003).

The previous two sections laid out the trade strategies of Brazil, the EU and the US. These strategies include the desire of the larger actors to reorganize the global trade regime under their preferences and Brazil's desire to modify that reorganization. However, the central argument rests on two key variables, with relative size being only one. The other is the degree of satisfaction actors have with the reorganization of the global trade regime. This satisfaction comes out of specific preferences associated with the EU-MERCOSUR FTA and FTAA negotiations. Each of the actors wishes to maximize market access for those sectors where they have a comparative advantage while attempting to limit competition in their respective markets.

I next turn to the preferences of the EU and MERCOSUR as derived from the pattern of trade. Overall, the trade relationship is asymmetric with MERCOSUR having the greater dependence on the EU market. However, the EU-MERCOSUR trade patterns illustrate a high percentage of primary goods exports from MERCOSUR and a larger proportion of manufactures exports from the EU. This characteristic of the current trade pattern leads Brazil and MERCOSUR in general, to demand greater openness for agricultural products. The lack of success came about when the EU refused to open up their agricultural market, but made greater demands on MERCOSUR to open up those sectors that would consume manufactured products.

First, MERCOSUR is dependent on the EU for their trade. In 2004 Brazil was the EU's eleventh major trading partner but accounted for only 1.8 per cent of overall EU trade.[24] In 2011, Brazil was the bloc's ninth major trading partner and accounted for 2.3 per cent (Eurostat 2012). The remaining three members scored in the bottom of the rankings. However, the EU ranks as the number one trading partner for MERCOSUR, accounting for 22.9 per cent of its total trade.[25] This ranking still holds at 20 per cent.[26]

This story is repeated in a closer examination of the trade statistics. MERCOSUR's share of total EU trade ranged from 2.7 to 2.3 per cent during 2000–04. However, the degree of the EU's overall trade dependence on MERCOSUR is very small. The same can be said for EU exports. The largest category of products sold in the MERCOSUR market is machinery and transport equipment. In 2004, this accounted for 50.1 per cent of exports, but only 2.1 per cent of total EU exports. The next largest category is chemicals and related products, which account for 22.5 per cent of MERCOSUR trade, but only a 2.7 per cent share of total exports.[27]

---

24   Eurostat, 'EU Bilateral Trade and Trade with the World: MERCOSUR', http://trade-info.cec.eu.int/doclib/html/113488.htm, accessed 26 December 2013.

25   Ibid.

26   Eurostat 'EU Bilateral Trade and Trade with the World: MERCOSUR', http://trade.ec.europa.eu/doclib/docs/2006/september/tradoc_113488.pdf, accessed 26 December 2013.

27   Eurostat, 'EU Bilateral Trade and Trade with the World: MERCOSUR', http://trade-info.cec.eu.int/doclib/html/113488.htm, accessed 26 December 2013.

When we examine specific categories of products imported into the EU in 2004, a slightly different picture develops. The largest category is food and live animals, accounting for 37.2 per cent of imports from MERCOSUR and 20.2 per cent of total EU imports. The next category is raw goods (except fuels), accounting for 25.7 per cent of MERCOSUR imports and 17.1 per cent of all imports.[28] In total, these primary materials comprise 37.3 per cent of all EU imports. Therefore, there is some EU trade dependence on MERCOSUR, but only in the two categories of primary goods.

From 1999 to 2004, the EU's per cent share of overall trade ranges from 23.2 per cent to 26.8 per cent with an average of 24.3 per cent.[29] This is reflected in both exports and imports, which averages 22.8 per cent and 25.9 per cent respectively. However, MERCOSUR's export dependence with the EU is not as high as the EU dependence on MERCOSUR. While 25.7 per cent of the EU's imports of food and live animals is from MERCOSUR, this is only 9.9 per cent of total MERCOSUR exports but 37.2 per cent of exports to the EU in 2004.[30] In addition, 6.8 per cent of total MERCOSUR exports of raw materials (excluding fuels) go to the EU, accounting for 25.7 per cent of all exports to the EU. The two items together account for 16.8 per cent of all MERCOSUR exports but 62.9 per cent of exports to the EU. In sum, MERCOSUR's main export to the EU and the EU's main dependence is in the category of primary goods.

In the case of EU exports to MERCOSUR, we again see a small amount of value, but a large share of a specific product, namely manufactured goods. The top categories of MERCOSUR imports from the EU are machinery and transportation equipment, chemicals, and other manufactured goods. Together they are 22.4 per cent of world imports into MERCOSUR, but 89.6 per cent of EU imports.[31] However this is only 1.7 per cent of global EU exports. Again, MERCOSUR does not represent a large value of trade for EU exports, but manufactured products do overwhelm the value of trade into MERCOSUR.

The areas of negotiation are centred on the primary products and manufactured goods. Both sides wish to maximize the amount of trade in their favoured area of comparative advantage while attempting to minimize competition for domestic firms. In March 2003, MERCOSUR offered to eliminate tariffs on 83–85 per cent of the average value of EU goods over ten years with the remaining 15 per cent eliminated over a period greater than ten years .[32] The EU, however, wanted to see 90 per cent instead of 85 per cent. The EU's counteroffer was an exclusion from tariffs for 10 per cent of MERCOSUR imports, which were primarily agricultural

28   Ibid.

29   Ibid.

30   Ibid.

31   Ibid.

32   BBC Monitoring International Reports, 'MERCOSUR to Present "Ambitious" Tariff Elimination Proposal to EU', IR 5 March 2003.

goods.[33] The increase by MERCOSUR to 85 per cent was not for the proposed EU offer, but an attempt to get the EU to discuss agricultural subsidies, which the EU refuses to do bilaterally but wanted instead to hold such discussions at the Doha Round.[34] In November 2003, the EU attempted to gain greater access for their products through the liberalization of MERCOSUR members' government procurement and services sector.[35] The EU offered to increase the import quotas for agricultural goods, but this was not satisfactory for MERCOSUR that still insisted on discussing agricultural subsidies.[36] The EU offered to further increase the agricultural import quota if MERCOSUR did not request a reform of the EU agricultural subsidies in December 2003.[37] The new negotiations at the beginning of 2004 began with deep frustration on the EU side. At the commencement of the March 2004 talks, EU trade representative Karl Falkenberg questioned the integration of the MERCOSUR members when he stated that it was 'more a vision than reality' and went on to question the degree of trust among the four members.[38] This lead to a defence of MERCOSUR's integration practices by the Argentine trade representative, Martín Redrado.[39] The talks also failed due the MERCOSUR refusal to open government procurement contracts and the services sector because the EU would not allow unrestricted access for beef, cereals, poultry and other agricultural products.[40] In April 2004, the same requests were made again, but both sides refused to acquiesce.[41] MERCOSUR negotiators did budge in June 2004 and agreed to increase the percentage of manufactured goods coming in at a reduced tariff to 90 per cent, without a favourable reply from the EU side.[42] In an interesting escalation of negotiations, MERCOSUR negotiators walked out of the July Brussels discussions after the EU negotiators reduced the quota amounts

---

33   Ibid.

34   Ibid.

35   Mario Osava, 'FTAA is the Key for a MERCOSUR EU Accord' (Inter Press Service, 2003).

36   Ibid.

37   Ibid.

38   MercoPress News Agency, 'MERCOSUR "is More Vision than Reality" Claims EU' (11 March 2004), www.mercopress.com/Detalle.asp?NUM-3380, accessed 26 December 2013.

39   Ibid.

40   MercoPress News Agency, 'MERCOSUR "Surprised" by EU Uncompromising Stance' (30 March 2005), www.mercopress.com/Detalle.asp?NUM-5366, accessed 26 December 2013.

41   Todd Benson, 'EU Nears Trade Pact with Latin America', *New York Times* (21 April 2004).

42   Latin News Daily, 'Brazil: Breakthrough in MERCOSUR EU Negotiations' (14 June 2004). O Estado de São Paulo, 'MERCOSUR, European Union Unlock FTA Negotiations' (14 June 2004).

on agricultural goods by half the amount they previously promised.[43] The EU delegation returned the favour by walking out of the August Brasília negotiations over the issue of agricultural products.[44]

At the beginning of September 2004, Pascal Lamy stated that the problem with the EU-MERCOSUR negotiations is with the MERCOSUR members because they were unwilling to match the agricultural concessions the EU made with greater access to investment markets, telecommunications, maritime transport, and banking services.[45] However, the MERCOSUR negotiators (after agreeing not to talk about EU agricultural subsidies) felt that the concessions were not enough and wanted larger agricultural quotas, especially for wheat and beef, and for these quotas not to have a ten year limit.[46]

On 26 May 2005, the representatives of the EU and MERCOSUR put forth a joint communiqué reiterating their comment to finalizing a FTA in conformity with the 1995 Declaration on Political Dialogue that began the negotiation process. The publication of the communiqué signalled that the FTA would not be finalized soon. The transatlantic failure to successfully negotiate an FTA occurred because MERCOSUR members understood that they had nothing to lose from not signing the FTA. The EU already depends on their exports of primary goods, and short of switching to another set of providers, would continue to import. The large share of EU manufactured goods entering into the MERCOSUR market would threaten domestic producers leaving MERCOSUR economies worse off. Unless the EU liberalizes their agricultural sector, it would not be in the interest of MERCOSUR members to sign the FTA.

The conditions of negotiations were not different with regard to the FTAA. While the US was able to develop willing partners among the small trade dependent states of the Caribbean and its NAFTA partners, it could not develop such relations with the MERCOSUR members.

Like the EU-MERCOSUR trade relationship, MERCOSUR is more trade dependent on the US than vice versa. Total US trade with MERCOSUR has remained somewhat level during the 1997–2001 timeframe: 2.3 per cent to 1.9 per cent with an average value of 2.1 per cent (FTAA 2005). The per cent value of imports to MERCOSUR also has remained level ranging from 1.6 per cent to 1.4

43   Claudia Mancini, 'MERCOSUR Suspends Negotiations for Commercial Agreement with European Union', *Gazeta Mercantil* (22 July 2004).

44   Gisele Teixeira, 'Negotiations Between MERCOSUR and European Union are Interrupted Once Again; Impasse Continues Between EU and MERCOSUR', *Gazeta Mercantil* (13 August 2004).

45   MercoPress News Agency, 'EU Blames MERCOSUR for Stalled Trade Talks' (1 September 2004), www.mercopress.com/Detalle.asp?NUM-4191, accessed 26 December 2013.

46   Ibid.

per cent and an average value of 1.4 per cent (FTAA 2005). Furthermore, as in the EU case, US exports have declined from 3.4 per cent to 2.7 per cent.[47]

MERCOSUR's overall trade dependence on the US resembles that on the EU. Overall, the per cent share of global MERCOSUR trade ranges from 17.0 per cent to 20.7 per cent with an average of 19.3 per cent during 1997–2001.[48] US imports account for 21.0 per cent to 22.7 per cent with an average of 21.6 per cent.[49] Exports to the US account for 11.3 per cent to 19.4 per cent with an average of 16.6 per cent.[50]

A deeper look exposes the same pattern of trade between MERCOSUR and the US as in the EU-MERCOSUR case. While 28.3 per cent of the US imports from MERCOSUR is in the category of primary goods, this only accounts for 5.8 per cent of total MERCOSUR exports (FTAA 2005). Also, 83.3 per cent of the MERCOSUR imports from the US are in the category of manufactured goods, accounting for 17.4 per cent of total US exports. Therefore, primary goods sent to the US is a small portion of MERCOSUR exports but manufactured goods represent a larger share of US exports to MERCOSUR. In sum, while MERCOSUR is more dependent on trade with the US, the US also is dependent on MERCOSUR for sales of manufactured goods and acquisitions of primary products.

When examining the negotiations for the FTAA, the first item that becomes apparent is the emphasis on US preferences. Only a small fraction of the official areas of the negotiations lend themselves to liberalizing commodity markets but many do talk about the liberalization of sectors that will increase trade in manufactured goods. Like the EU, the US has been and continues to be opposed to discussing agricultural subsidies at the FTAA table. With this off the FTAA table, the vast majority of discussions involve manufactured goods.

The discussions of the meetings divided the participants in the predicted manner. Sides were drawn between the US, Canada, Mexico, and Central American countries favouring a comprehensive agreement while MERCOSUR members wished to remove subjects such as government procurement, services rules and intellectual property rights from discussions.[51] Given the ties that Canada, Mexico, and Central American countries already had with the US, they favoured the US position that included negotiation topics that would liberalize sectors and be receptive for its products. However, MERCOSUR, given the current trade pattern, would be at a disadvantage by signing an agreement

---

47 Free Trade Area of the Americas, 'Hemispheric Trade and Tariff Database' (2005), http://www.ftaa-alca.org/HGROUPS/NGMADB_E.asp, accessed 26 December 2013.

48 Ibid.

49 Ibid.

50 Ibid.

51 Christina Sevilla, 'Can the United States and Brazil Spur Free Trade in the Americas?', *The National Interest*, 3 (1) (January 2004).

that did not liberalize market sectors that would favour their products (i.e., agricultural products).

To end this impasse, Brazil suggested in May 2003 a '4+1' set of negotiations. This would produce two versions of the FTAA. One version is that the members of MERCOSUR negotiate with the US directly. The other is a parallel set of negotiations that would include the US and the remaining states.[52] The proposed arrangement would permit the process to continue at two speeds and allow Brazil to focus on issues that the US and its coalition wanted to ignore. Robert Zoellick rejected Brazil's suggestion knowing that it would be possible to get a wider FTAA by keeping the US coalition together in order to thwart Brazil's preferences. This would allow no discussions of agricultural subsidy cuts and anti-dumping rules. In addition, by keeping the coalition together, it would be more likely to get the service sector liberalized and reward the Caribbean and Central American countries with extra trade preferences.[53]

The talks became more heated after the failure of the September 2003 WTO Cancún talks. Both the EU and US requested that the MERCOSUR members forgo discussing agricultural subsidies until the Doha Round resumed. Brazil along with other members of the G-20[54] held the EU and US (as well as Japan) to their words, but without a satisfactory outcome. At the resumption of the FTAA negotiations, the MERCOSUR members reintroduced the topic of agricultural subsidies, which the US refused to discuss but pointed to the need for the liberalization of services, which the MERCOSUR members stated would be better discussed at the Doha Round.[55] This response prompted US Deputy Trade Representative Peter Allgeier to state that an FTAA can be created without Brazil.[56] This was not the only time a US trade representative mentioned that Brazil could be left out. In 2002, Zoellick stated that Brazil could trade in 'another direction … Antarctica' if it did not want to trade with the US.[57] In reaction, the MERCOSUR members formalized their unity by signing the 'Buenos Aires Consensus' outlining a common position regarding agricultural subsidies.[58]

---

52   Mario Osava, 'Trade Americas: Brazil and US Face Off in Decisive FTAA Talks', *Inter Press Service* (28 May 2003).

53   Ibid.

54   Brazil's international strategy included commercial ties with other developing nations other than MERCOSUR. To this end it helped form a negotiating alliance first with India and South Africa, call the BIAS Group, that later transformed into the G-20, which also includes China (Brazil Report 23 November 2004).

55   Marcela Valente, 'Argentina and Brazil Claim for US Reduction of Farm Subsidies; FTAA Puts Consensus to the Test', *Inter Press Agency* (24 October 2003).

56   Ibid.

57   Andrew Hay, 'America's Trade Target lost in Politics', *Reuters* (28 December 2004), http://www.citizenstrade.org/ctc/wp-content/uploads/2011/05/reuters_ftaapolitics_12282004.pdf, accessed 26 December 2013.

58   Marcela Valente, 'Argentina and Brazil Claim for US Reduction of Farm Subsidies'; FTAA.

In the hope of moving the negotiations forward, a new negotiation framework was decided ahead of the ministerial meetings in Miami in November 2003. 'FTAA lite', as it was called, would allow each country to negotiate in certain areas and not in others.[59] However this did not stop the MERCOSUR members from continuing their common strategy, which was further developed ahead of the February 2004 meetings.[60] Most of 2004 resulted in the same negotiations failure between MERCOSUR and the US regarding agricultural subsidies and liberalization of services. In the most recent attempt, Brazil and US representatives met in Washington, DC from 22–23 February 2005. The result was an insipid joint communiqué stating that both sides are committed to a FTAA in the future but without stating how this would occur.

Like the EU-MERCOSUR failed negotiations, the western hemispheric one occurred because MERCOSUR members understood that signing the FTAA would place them in a worse position. The US exports a large percentage of manufactured goods to and imports a fair percentage of primary goods from MERCOSUR members. As in the case of the EU, an increase of manufactured goods entering into the MERCOSUR market would threaten domestic producers leaving MERCOSUR economies worse off.

An added complication to the EU-MERCOSUR-US trade negotiating relations is the growing economy of China. With average annual growth rates of 8 per cent, the Chinese economy is becoming increasingly in need of food, raw materials, and energy. For example, China has been the world's largest consumer of oil since 2003. They continually need reliable sources of raw materials with a portion of them already arriving from Latin America. In 2003, Brazilian exports to China grew 79.8 per cent and MERCOSUR exports increased by 96.5 per cent from 2000 to 2003.[61] Overall trade with Latin America increased 50.4 per cent from 2002 to 2003.[62] China is also becoming an active business partner, accounting for 36.5 per cent of total foreign direct investment in Latin America in 2003.[63] Although trade with Latin America only accounted for 3.4 per cent of total Chinese trade volume in 2003, and with a growing trade deficit with Latin America, Chinese state analysts say trade is valuable if they are able to secure raw materials for their fast growing economy.[64] If China is willing to buy

---

59   Mario Osava, 'Trade Americas: Flexible New Trade Pact Welcome by Most', *Inter Press Service* (20 November 2003).

60   Invertia, 'Argentina, Brazil Agree on Common Strategy in FTAA Talks', *Latin America News Digest* (16 January 2004).

61   Mario Osava, 'Lula is Going to China, Brazil's Third Largest Market', *Inter Press Service* (18 May 2004).

62   Business Daily Update, 'Latin American Free Trade' (3 December 2004).

63   MercoPress News Agency, 'Latin America Quick to Dance to China's Tune' (11 November 2004), http://en.mercopress.com/2004/11/11/latin-america-quick-to-dance-to-china-s-tune, accessed 26 December 2013.

64   Business Daily Update, 'Latin American Free Trade' (3 December 2004).

more and more Latin American goods along favourable trade arrangements, then Brazil and its MERCOSUR partners would be able to expand the market for their products even with the EU and US failures to negotiate FTAs. In addition, pressure would be off of these countries to sign unfavourable FTAs.

The Latin American process of courting China has begun. In May 2004 Brazilian President Luiz Inácio 'Lula' da Silva visited China with a large entourage of business representatives in order to begin the process of extending commercial ties for exports such as food products, chemicals, and machinery, among others.[65] In return for officially recognizing China as a market economy within the rules of the WTO during President Hu Jintao's visit in November 2004, China signed numerous commercial agreements with Brazil.[66] One such agreement included Brazilian and Chinese state-owned oil firms (Petrobras and China Petroleum and Chemical Corporation) and China's Export and Import Bank for a US$ 1 billion Brazilian north-south natural gas pipeline construction project.[67] Another was a US$ 2 billion investment in Brazilian rail so as to improve freight transportation and lower commodity prices.[68] Overall, Hu pledged a US$ 10 billion multiyear investment in Brazil during his visit.[69]

China has wider economic plans in Latin America. After his Brazilian visit, Hu stopped in Argentina where he and Argentine President Nestor Kirchner announced a US$ 19.7 billion investment package for infrastructure improvement and hydrocarbon exploration and production over the five years.[70] Also as a result of Hu's visit, Chinese sanitary authorities later certified several Argentine beef and poultry processing plants, thereby expanding trade of these products for the Chinese market.[71] In addition, Chile and China began negotiations for a FTA in November 2004[72] with its enactment in August 2006. Finally, China wishes to join

---

65   Mario Osava, 'Lula is Going to China, Brazil's Third Largest Market', *Inter Press Service* (18 May 2004).

66   Deutsche Presse Agentur, '2nd Round Up: Brazil Recognizes China as a Market Economy' (12 November 2004).

67   MercoPress News Agency, 'Brazil Signs Lucrative Deals with China' (13 November 2004), http://en.mercopress.com/2004/11/13/brazil-signs-lucrative-deals-with-china, accessed 26 December 2013.

68   Ibid.

69   Business Daily Update, 'Latin American Free Trade' (3 December 2004).

70   MercoPress News Agency, 'China Will Finance Argentine Infrastructure' (17 November 2004), http://en.mercopress.com/2004/11/17/china-will-finance-argentine-infrastructure, accessed 26 December 2013.

71   MercoPress News Agency, 'New EU-MERCOSUR Target: Vienna May 2006' (13 July 2005), http://en.mercopress.com/2005/07/13/new-eu-mercosur-target-vienna-may-2006, accessed 26 December 2013.

72   China Daily, 'Sino-Chilean FTA Talks Launched' (26 January 2005), http://www.highbeam.com/doc/1P2-8830589.html, accessed 26 December 2013.

the Inter-American Development Bank and has garnered MERCOSUR's support, with opposition coming from the US and the Central American states.[73]

The growth of Chinese importation of Latin American primary products and investment in the region can produce possible security issues for both the EU and the US. Scholars have already recognized the future power transition between China and the US and its implication for potential conflict.[74] When China and the US achieve parity in economic and military power, and should this parity come with Chinese dissatisfaction with the US management of the global status quo, there is a good likelihood of armed conflict. This conflict will not likely see the EU on the sidelines. Should the EU and the US decide to open up the markets for agricultural goods, resources can possibly shift away from China to toward EU and US markets given their higher per capita income. In addition, it will diffuse possible military alliances that may become associated with the stronger investment and trade between China and Latin America.

Conclusions

The lack of success in the EU-MERCOSUR and MERCOSUR-US negotiations resulted from a combination of disjointed preferences and relative market size. When entering into a FTA, all potential partners prefer to sign an agreement so long as they are better off than not signing it. For a large economy the goal of signing FTAs with smaller economies does have a marginal economic advantage, but the primary goal is an evolution toward a global trade regime more favourable to its preferences. Smaller economies do look favourably on accessing larger markets, but they fear domestic market competition. If their domestic market is vulnerable, then they would be better off signing an FTA if they can take advantage of their exports. Lacking this, they would be worse off signing the FTA. Alternative markets in rapidly growing economies also lower the incentives to sign.

The EU and the US have similar goals. The idea of establishing FTAs alongside the WTO negotiations allows for a reorganization of the global trade regime along their preferences. The idea is to expand markets for their exports while protecting their more vulnerable products. If they convince states to sign FTAs along these preferences, then they have a de facto global trade regime without the WTO negotiations. As such they consolidate their status as hub economies and continue to compete with each other over a greater share of the global market.

The EU and US have developed FTAs in the western hemisphere, but with the smaller more dependent states. The Caribbean states benefited from favourable

---

73   MercoPress News Agency, 'Latin America After Closer Ties With Asia' (30 March 2005), http://en.mercopress.com/2005/04/11/latinamerica-after-closer-ties-with-asia, accessed 26 December 2013.

74   Brian Efrid, Gaspare M. Genna and Jacek Kugler, 'From War to Integration Generalizing the Dynamic of Power', *International Interactions*, 29 (4) (2003), 292–313.

trade relations established by the EU and US through their respective unilateral policies. Therefore not signing an FTA for these countries could threaten their trade dependence with the larger actors. The Andean Community will more than likely follow suit given the amount of military and other aid given to fight their domestic drug/insurgency problems (Venezuela being the exception). The MERCOSUR members, on the other hand, do not have such incentives. They primarily sell raw goods to the EU and US who shield their domestic producers with tariffs and subsidies. The larger economies wish to increase sales of manufactured goods to MERCOSUR without exposing domestic agricultural producers to competition. Although they wish to address these issues at the WTO talks, the Cancún negotiations proved otherwise. Since no incentive is present, an FTAA with MERCOSUR is not very likely during the current preferences of the US.

Adding to the calculation is the growing economy of China. They are in need of raw materials and an improved status in the WTO, both of which MERCOSUR is willing to provide. In return, China does provide incentives for MERCOSUR cooperation. The current trajectory implies greater trade relations between the larger economies of the developing world and some problems for the north-south variety of trade. Implications also spill over into the security realm as potential alliances develop among burgeoning economic partners. The growth of China on the dissatisfaction of western hemisphere can produce unwanted consequences. To improve the degree of global trade cooperation, greater incentives are needed from the EU and US. The liberalization of the agricultural sectors is an important first step towards this. Another policy suggestion is a slow opening for services and government procurement so as to improve the integration of these sectors in the international market. This will elevate the likelihood of increasing domestic stability in the smaller, poorer countries. The final policy implication is the strengthening of the Asia-Pacific Economic Cooperation (APEC) with the added membership of the MERCOSUR countries. A FTA that spans the Pacific Rim can further not only economic growth but also security. To improve APEC members' integration, the US, as the preponderant power, will need to modify its trade preferences so as to reach a common ground with MERCOSUR.

Chapter 6

CARICOM's Engagement with Latin America: The Community of Latin American and Caribbean States (CELAC), its Promise and Challenges

Mark Kirton

Introduction

The view has been advanced that, over the last five decades, Latin American and Caribbean states have been engaged separately in several initiatives to sustain their efforts at regional cooperation and integration. As Dabène posits, Latin American governments have been 'consistent with their efforts to keep their collective endeavour afloat and have found ways of reinventing their regional agendas'.[1] As he further suggests, even the widely shared disappointments concerning previous integration efforts and outcomes have 'never totally annihilated their commitment to move on with new initiatives'. Beginning in 1960 with the establishment of the Latin American Free Trade Association (LAFTA), and the Central American Common Market (CACM), followed by the formation of the Andean Group in 1969 and the Latin American Integration Association (ALADI) in 1981, the post-World War II wave of Latin American integration efforts persisted, in spite of periods of fragmentation and decline. Since the beginning of the twenty-first century, the region has witnessed significant political and economic reconfigurations and re-mapping as well as new initiatives for regional integration which now go far beyond the traditional agenda of trade and commercial facilitation.

Caribbean states, on the other hand, have also been involved in their separate efforts at regional integration, moving from the West Indies Federation in 1958, to CARIFTA in 1965, then to CARICOM in 1973 and the Organization of Eastern Caribbean states (OECS) in 1981. Eric Williams, the Prime Minister of Trinidad at the time of the establishment of CARICOM, hailed it as 'a most progressive step forward in the direction of a larger integration' and while the pace of the process of collaboration between the two sets of states has been slow since that time, the

---

1   Olivier Dabène, 'Consistency and Resilience through Cycles of Repoliticization', in Pía Riggirozzi and Diana Tussie (eds), *The Rise of Post-hegemonic Regionalism: The Case of Latin America* (New York: Springer, 2012), 41.

Caribbean region witnessed the beginning of efforts to engage its Latin neighbours since the early 1970s.

More recently, as a result of recommendations from the West Indian Commission,[2] CARICOM states led the way in the establishment of the Association of Caribbean States (ACS) in 1994 which sought to 'widen and deepen' the integration movement and brought several Latin states into new areas of engagement with CARICOM states, facilitated by the ACS. While there is clear evidence of on-going integration efforts in both Latin America and the Caribbean, since the 1960s, when one assesses the early period of CARICOM-Latin American relations, however, it is observed that these relations were very limited, and constrained traditionally by factors such as linguistic differences, varying levels of development, differences in physical and population size, natural resource endowments and the presence and influence of strong extra-regional cultural influences. Indeed, Maira suggests that there was a long period of mutual disinterest when the states of CARICOM and Latin America 'appeared to constitute two separate worlds which took no notice of each other in spite of their proximity. Separately, they organized their own national existence, having as axis, a preferential relationship with the countries that fulfilled a hegemonic function with respect to them'.[3]

In the recent past, however, common agendas, perceptions of a shared economic and political space and converging interests have been increasing as the Latin American and Caribbean states grapple with serious common contemporary issues such as poverty alleviation, climate change and security, among others. According to Girvan, the CARICOM states started to build 'a web of institutional ties with Latin America' since the 1990s and in the twenty-first century, the 'turn to the South' has developed speed and intensity.[4] The increased levels of intensity are reflected in the fact that, in the twenty first century, CARICOM states have become immersed in these new strategic regional networks, led by Latin American states, particularly Brazil and Venezuela, and are active participants in the latest efforts. One notes that Antigua and Barbuda, Dominica, and St Vincent and the Grenadines have already fully signed on to the Bolivarian Alliance of The Peoples of Our Americas (ALBA), with other member states, including St Lucia, Haiti and Suriname, moving toward greater collaboration with the grouping.

---

2   The West Indian Commission, 'Time for Action: The Report of the West Indian Commission Barbados' (1992).

3   Maira, Luis, 'Caribbean State Systems and Middle-Status Powers', in P. Henry and C. Stone (eds), *The Newer Caribbean, Democracy and Development* (Philadelphia: Institute for the Study of Human Issues, 1983), 181.

4   Norman Girvan, 'Turning to the South? CARICOM, the Southern Cone and ALBA' (2012), revised version of paper presented at Fundacion Vidanta/FUNGLODE/ CIES/UNIBE Seminar on 'Integracion, Cooperacion Y Desarrollo En El Caribe De La Globalizacion'; Santo Domingo, R.D., 10–11 November 2011.

All of the CARICOM states, except Barbados and Trinidad and Tobago, are signatories to the PETROCARIBE arrangement and most of those states are already benefitting from the special conditions attached to it. Additionally, Guyana and Suriname are full members of the Union of South American Nations (UNASUR) and in recent times, Belize, also a CARICOM member state, has increased its levels of engagement with the Central American Integration System (SICA).

It was, however, the historic first meeting of heads of states and governments of Latin America and the Caribbean in Brazil in 2008 which initiated the dialogue and set the stage for the decision taken in Mexico in 2010 to establish the Community of Latin American and Caribbean States (CELAC). As the communiqué indicated at the end of the Mexico summit, the decision was made to 'develop ties of solidarity and cooperation' in an environment conducive to generating solutions to common regional challenges. On the other hand, one can also suggest that CARICOM states have been led into this new arrangement influenced by the interests of the leading states, Brazil, Venezuela and Mexico and have entered the CELAC arrangement unprepared to satisfy the commitments required to participate effectively in its activities.

It is against this background that this chapter assesses the major factors which influenced the recent increase in collaboration between CARICOM states and Latin America, and in particular the challenges and prospects for CELAC as a sustainable and viable mechanism for Latin American and Caribbean collaboration.

New Integration Initiatives

It is significant that in the twenty-first century the integration initiatives which now bring Latin American and CARICOM states together in higher levels of cooperation are taking place in the context of 'new regionalism' which has also emerged as a framework for analysis of these new integration efforts. Hettne has argued that new regionalism has been shaped in a new multi-polar global environment and could be considered a more autonomous process than the traditional forms of regionalism, and that it now includes both state and non-state actors. Hettne also posits that new regionalism could be described as a 'multidimensional form of integration which includes economic, political, social, and cultural aspects and thus goes far beyond the goal of creating region-based free trade regimes or security alliances'.[5]

The return to regionalism has been observed globally and Fawcett and Palmer have suggested that this return was influenced by the new attitudes towards international cooperation and the decentralization of the international system

5   B. Hettne, 'Globalisation and the New Regionalism: The Second Great Trans-formation', in B. Hettne, A. Inotai and O. Sunkel (eds), *Globalism and the New Regionalism* (Basingstoke: Macmillan, 1999), 1–24.

brought about by the collapse of Communism and the end of the Cold War.[6] There has been the emergence of new actors in the integration process globally, and Soderbaum posits that new regionalism can be considered as a 'range of formal/informal mid-level 'triangular' relations among not only states but also non-state actors, notably civil societies and private companies and these are central aspects of the 'new' inter or transnational relations'.[7] It is now generally accepted that, as Soderbaum suggests, the new trends in regional cooperation are characterized by 'multidimensionality, complexity, fluidity, and non-conformity'.[8] All of these explanations of the contemporary processes of regional integration point to the convergence of interests and agendas of Latin American and Caribbean states which has served to advance the collaboration between the two sets of states. Indeed, as several analysts have observed, the new regional initiatives in Latin America such as UNASUR, ALBA and now CELAC are now seen to reflect the emergence of transformative regional politics that have been characterized as post-liberal, post-commercial or post-hegemonic regionalism.[9]

Undoubtedly, the new era of regionalism since the beginning of the twenty-first century has brought with it the re-politicization of the agenda and a shift from trade and economic issues as the central focus of the integration process to more political issues as the primary concerns[10] and this also contributed to the

---

6   Louise Fawcett, 'Regionalism in Historical Perspective', in Louise Fawcett and Andrew Hurrell (eds), *Regionalism in World Politics: Regional Organization and International Order* (Oxford and New York: Oxford University Press, 1996) and Norman D. Palmer, *The New Regionalism in Asia and the Pacific* (Lexington: Lexington Books, 1991).

7   Fredrik Soderbaum, 'Introduction: Theories of New Regionalism', in Fredrik Söderbaum and Timothy Shaw (eds), *Theories of New Regionalism. A Palgrave Reader* (Basingstoke: Palgrave, 2003), 1.

8   Ibid. (2003), 1.

9   Pía Riggirozzi, 'Region, Regionness and Regionalism in Latin America: Towards a New Synthesis' (Buenos Aires: FLACSO, 2010). Available at www.flacso.org.ar/rrii, accessed 26 December 2013; J.A. Sanahuja, 'La construcción de una región: Sudamérica y el egionalismo posliberal', in M. Cienfuegos and J.A. Sanhauja (eds), *Una región en construcción. UNASUR y la integración en América del Sur* (Barcelona: Fundación CIDOB, 2010); and Pía Riggirozzi and Diana Tussie (eds), *The Rise of Post-hegemonic Regionalism: The Case of Latin America* (Heidelberg; London; New York: Springer, 2012).

10   Andrés Serbin, Lanyedi Martinez and Haroldo Ramanzinni (eds), *El regionalismo post-liberal en América Latina y el Caribe: nuevos actores, nuevos temas, nuevos desafíos* (Buenos Aires: CRIES); Battaglino, Jorge, 'Defence in a Post-Hegemonic Regional Agenda: The Case of the South American Defence Council', in Pía Riggirozzi and Diana Tussie (eds), *The Rise of Post-hegemonic Regionalism: The Case of Latin America* (Heidelberg; London; New York: Springer, 2012), 81–100; Pía Riggirozzi and Diana Tussie (eds), *The Rise of Post-hegemonic Regionalism: The Case of Latin America* (Heidelberg; London; New York: Springer, 2012); and M. Saguier, 'Socio-Environmental Regionalism in South America: Tensions in New Development Models', in Pía Riggirozzi and Diana Tussie (eds), *The Rise of Post-hegemonic Regionalism. The Case of Latin America* (Heidelberg; London; New York: Springer, 2012), 125–145.

increased attention given to the process by political leaders in both Latin America and the Caribbean. Further, new priorities have been identified in the regional agenda, including the need for the creation of common policies and institutions, cooperation in non-trade environments and a greater emphasis on the social context and existing asymmetries as well as a focus on regional infrastructure, energy, finance and security issues.[11,12,13] One can also discern an increasing interest in South-South cooperation, both on the part of the emerging new regional architecture as well as on the part of countries of the Global South which are oriented towards a cross-regional, trans-regional and global reach, and these have also contributed to the new interest in collaboration between the Latin American and Caribbean states.

The Foundations of CELAC

It is therefore appropriate to discuss the growing levels of engagement between CARICOM states and Latin America and the establishment of the Community of Latin American and Caribbean States (CELAC/CLACS) in the context of the framework of new regionalism. In the first place, CARICOM states have no doubt recognized the growing influence and strength of Latin America in the global arena. And, in the context of the need for CARICOM to strategically reposition the region, Caribbean states have begun to look to Latin America to develop a new alliance. With both sets of states promoting economic development and South-South cooperation, CELAC could be seen as the ideal setting for CARICOM to anchor its efforts at diversification of markets and political alliances, after decades of linkages with the United States and Great Britain.

CELAC is the latest in the series of regional integration initiatives which have emerged in the hemisphere since the beginning of the twenty-first century. Indeed, CELAC's establishment can also be seen in the context of the reconfigurations in the regional political economy taking place as a result of the growing disenchantment with the neoliberal economic order and the growing recognition by regional states of the need to 'speak with one voice'. It must also be observed that, for many, the move to unite the region follows from the legacy of the nineteenth century integrationist, Simon Bolivar, who initiated the process of Latin American unity and the 'patria grande' concept, which was articulated in the twenty-first century

---

11   Pía Riggirozzi and Diana Tussie (eds), *The Rise of Post-hegemonic Regionalism: The Case of Latin America*.

12   Ricardo Carciofi, 'Cooperation for the Provision of Regional Public Goods: The IIRSA Case', in Pía Riggirozzi and Diana Tussie (eds), *The Rise of Post-hegemonic Regionalism: The Case of Latin America*, 65–80.

13   P. Trucco, 'The Rise of Monetary Agreements in South America', in Pía Riggirozzi and Diana Tussie (eds), *The Rise of Post-hegemonic Regionalism: The Case of Latin America*, 101–123.

by the late President Hugo Chavez of Venezuela, who championed the process of contemporary integration initiatives involving Latin America and the Caribbean.

The establishment of CELAC can also be seen as building on the foundation laid by the Permanent Mechanism for Consultation and Political Coordination (The Rio Group) which provided for dialogue among heads of states and governments of both Latin America and the Caribbean for more than a decade. Brazil hosted the first Latin America-Caribbean Summit on Development and Integration (CALC) in 2008 and provided the forum for the states to meet for the first time without the presence and influence of the United States and Canada. The Latin American and Caribbean Unity Summit held in Mexico in 2010 saw final agreement being reached to establish the organization, with Brazil, Mexico and Venezuela leading the process. It must also be noted that the experiences of the ALBA (The Bolivarian Alliance for Our Americas) and UNASUR (The Union of South American Nations), both of which brought together Latin American and Caribbean states in practical programmes of cooperation, also influenced the formulation of this recent initiative. One can therefore support the contention that emerging institutional arrangements and structures such as CELAC are a part of a complex set of alternative ideas and motivations being pursued to provide new economic and political space for Latin American and Caribbean states as part of the process of new regional transformation. As Riggirozzi and Tussie argue, 'the contours of the regional arena are being defined by formal and informal trans-boundary practices that denote a rich variety of forms of regionalisms that are moving beyond the issue of trade and finance, contesting the wisdom of neoliberal market-led integration and relocating the focus of regionalism'.[14]

The establishment of CELAC can also be considered as arising out of the movement towards post-hegemonic regionalism, which according to Riggirozzi and Tussie can be described as 'regional structures characterized by hybrid practices as a result of a partial displacement of dominant forms of US-led neoliberal governance in the acknowledgement of other political forms of organization and economic management of regional (common) goods'.[15] Indeed, it is posited that this new trend in regionalism is anchored in new conceptualizations of development, regional cohesion and identity formation. In considering the raison d'être for the emergence of CELAC one cannot underestimate the influence of the ideological shifts which have taken place in the region in the twenty-first century and the role of the 'new left' in Latin America in influencing and shaping the agenda for the organization.

An assessment of the emergence of CELAC indicates that the member states have agreed that the organization must be founded on 'common values' – respect for international law, the sovereign equality of states, the non-use nor the threat

---

14   Pía Riggirozzi and Diana Tussie (eds), *The Rise of Post-hegemonic Regionalism: The Case of Latin America*.

15   Pía Riggirozzi and Diana Tussie (eds), *The Rise of Post-hegemonic Regionalism: The Case of Latin America*, 12.

of use of force, democracy, respect for human rights, respect for the environment, international cooperation and permanent political dialogue, among other fundamental issues. As the Caracas Declaration at the end of the 2011 summit of the leaders of CELAC in Venezuela indicated, the member states were 'convinced that the unity, and political, social and cultural integration of Latin America and the Caribbean constitute both a fundamental aspiration of the peoples represented here, and a requirement for the region to successfully confront the challenges before us'.[16]

CELAC – Its Strengths and Prospects

A fundamental question which still arises, however, is the extent to which this new organization differs from those already in existence and whether there were new initiatives and innovations which CELAC could introduce to the region. In the first place, CELAC considers itself dedicated to the enhancement of cooperation and the construction of its own regional space, that 'consolidates and projects the Latin American and Caribbean identity based on shared principles and values; and on the ideals of unity and democracy of our peoples'.[17] CELAC was established in a significantly different political and economic environment from that of the other large hemispheric body, the Organization of American States (OAS), which was created in the post-World War II environment of the Cold War and whose agenda was largely influenced by the hemispheric major powers, the US and Canada. As the Caracas Declaration noted, CELAC was launched as 'a representative mechanism for political consultation, integration and cooperation of Latin American and Caribbean states and as common space to ensure the unity and integration of our region'.[18]

Further, in this context, it can be argued that the new organization differs from those already established in that there are 33 members, which comprise all the states of Latin America and the Caribbean, but does not include the United States of America and Canada. This in itself contrasts significantly to other regional bodies and signals a movement towards the expansion of collaboration among regional states, free from the pervasive influence of the hegemon (the United States). It can also be seen as a clear indication of the region's new self- assertion and as a move

---

16 Caracas Declaration (2011), Summit of the CELAC. Available at http://www. pnuma.org/forodeministros/19-reunion%20intersesional/documentos/CARACAS%20 DECLARATION.pdf, accessed 26 December 2013.

17 Latin American and Caribbean Unity Summit Declaration (2010). Available at http://www.europarl.europa.eu/intcoop/eurolat/key_documents/cancun_declaration_2010_ en.pdf, accessed 26 December 2013.

18 Caracas Declaration (2011), Summit of the CELAC. Available at http://www. pnuma.org/forodeministros/19-reunion%20intersesional/documentos/CARACAS%20 DECLARATION.pdf, accessed 26 December 2013.

to highlight the increasing levels of interdependence which have recently emerged. Serbin has argued on the other hand, that as the United States shifted its foreign policy attention away from the hemisphere, this 'benign neglect' resulted in the creation of new regional forums and 'instruments of action' and created space for the emergence of CELAC as a coordinating mechanism for the new regional arrangement.[19] The Montego Bay Plan of Action contemplated the 'identification of possible synergies between the various regional and sub-regional mechanisms of cooperation and integration', which clearly demonstrates the focus of CELAC as a coordinating body. Further, 'the procedures for the Organic Operation of CELAC' indicate that the organization shall be responsible for, inter alia, 'political dialogue with other intergovernmental actors, international organisations and mechanisms; coordination of common positions in multilateral forums to promote and advance the interests of the Latin American and Caribbean and Caribbean Community, vis-a-vis the new issues on the international agenda; promotion of the Latin American and Caribbean agenda in global forums' and these activities indicate the major focus on coordination to be carried out by CELAC.[20]

Challenges for CELAC

There are also issues related to the potential, prospects and challenges for CELAC and more specifically, the possible constraints and benefits to Caribbean participating states. With respect to the prospects for CELAC, one can argue that the emergence of this new trans-societal network with fresh approaches, and a focus on building new regional economic and political spaces and promoting autonomous development can serve to energize the integration process and provide a catalyst for increased trade, joint venture activity in the private sector and sustained political dialogue. Furthermore, a well-coordinated arrangement between Latin American and Caribbean states provides an enabling environment for the region to promote its interests more efficiently, and CELAC can play this role. As Latin America is no longer considered a peripheral or marginalized region, its presence on the world stage, coordinated by CELAC, can have positive outcomes, both at the political and economic levels, with potential benefits accruing to both Latin America and the CARICOM states.

In the recent past, the focus globally has been placed on the integration and development of physical infrastructure as a priority element for the strengthening of the wider integration process. Since 2000, The Initiative for the Integration of The Regional Infrastructure of South America (IIRSA) has been ongoing in the sub-region, and in 2010, UNASUR became the mechanism which has led the process.

---

19   A. Serbin, 'Regionalismo y soberanía nacional en América Latina: Los nuevosdesafíos' (Buenos Aires: CRIES, 2010), Documentos CRIES 15.

20   Montego Bay Plan of Action (2009). Available at www.itu.int/.../The%20 Montego%20Bay%20Action%20Plan.pdf, accessed 28 December 2013.

As part of this arrangement, South American states have improved connectivity through roads and bridges, reduced isolation of hinterland areas, and facilitated greater 'people contact' in the sub-region. The success of this initiative, which has also facilitated the reduction in transportation and transaction costs, promoted public-private partnerships (PPPs), trade and investments in South America, and has also begun to change the economic geography and provide for the enlargement of the economic space. As Carciofi has observed, the IIRSA project has succeeded in 'launching an agenda for physical integration'.[21] Given the need for greater connectivity in the region, CELAC, as a new multilateral space, can build on the successes of IIRSA and with efficient institutional infrastructure, develop programmes at the regional level which can offer economic and social benefits to its member states.

The issue of security has become a priority concern for the governments and citizens in both Latin America and the Caribbean. According to the UNDP Caribbean Human Development Report of 2012, 'the increase in violence and crime in Latin America and the Caribbean is an undeniable fact that erodes the very foundation of the democratic processes in the region and imposes high social, economic and cultural costs. Our region is home to 8.5 percent of the world's population, yet it concentrates some 27 percent of the world's homicides. Violence and crime are therefore perceived by a majority of Latin American and Caribbean citizens as a top pressing challenge'.[22] The security issues therefore require a regional approach and CELAC can be the coordinating mechanism for providing a multi-layered response. As the Prime Minister of Trinidad and Tobago, Kamla Persad-Bissessar noted at the 2011 CELAC Summit in Venezuela: 'What is clear is that several of the challenges which are common to the countries of CELAC are best faced together. We should confront the myriad problems associated with transnational crime standing together'.[23] A priority for CELAC, therefore, will be to bring together agencies such as CARICOM's Implementation Agency for Crime and Security (IMPACS) and other Latin American security agencies to coordinate information sharing, training and operations in a structured framework for crime reduction and citizen security.

---

21   Ricardo Carciofi, 'Cooperation for the Provision of Regional Public Goods: The IIRSA Case', in Pía Riggirozzi and Diana Tussie (eds), *The Rise of Post-hegemonic Regionalism: The Case of Latin America*, 65–80.

22   UNDP Caribbean Human Development Report, 'Human Development and the Shift to Better Citizen Security' (New York: UNDP, 2012). Available at http://www.undp.org.gy/web/documents/bk/Caribbean_HDR_Jan25_2012_3MB.pdf, accessed 28 December 2013.

23   Government of the Republic of Trinidad and Tobago, 'Statement by Prime Minister, the Honourable Kamla Persad-Bissessar at the Plenary Session of CELAC' (3 December 2011). Available at http://www.news.gov.tt/index.php?news=10132, accessed 28 December 2013.

The view has been also advanced that, given the continued global concern about the fiscal issues facing the United States, and the questions being raised about the maintenance of the standing of the US dollar as the traditional reserve currency, it gives CELAC the opportunity to consider a new financial and currency arrangement. Of significant interest is the increasing use of the sucre – the virtual currency of the ALBA – currently utilized for direct trading among participating ALBA states – which allows them to circumvent the use of US dollars and thus minimize foreign exchange risks. Trucco has argued that the region recently witnessed an increase in monetary cooperation agreements which have intensified 'in the face of the international crisis, offering an alternative to the power of the dollar as an exchange currency for intra-regional trade transactions'.[24] Indeed one notes the most recent move by Brazil and China to change the financing of trade and to use each other's currencies so that there would be no interruptions to their commercial linkages 'if a new banking crisis causes dollar trade finance to dry up'.[25] As a leading CELAC state, Brazil can provide the analysis of the intricacies of this arrangement for possible replication in the region.

For small states, like those of CARICOM, a well-defined monetary arrangement which could reduce the pressures linked to the need for dollar reserves for trade would certainly be attractive. This leaves room for comprehensive assessment of the prospects for as well as the constraints of the widening of the use of the sucre, as well as other financial cooperation initiatives among CELAC states – another potential coordinating role for CELAC.

However, the argument is advanced here that Latin America and the Caribbean have a history of establishing new regional organizations, notwithstanding the myriad of existing institutions, which either do not function or operate less than optimally. It is also argued that the linguistic, cultural, political and historical differences also complicate attempts to harmonize regional arrangements. Furthermore, as a new organization, CELAC will add to the 'spaghetti bowl' of integration activities currently underway and may duplicate effort, create overlap and add more pressure on the human and financial resources, especially in the cases of small Caribbean states. The region's states are already bogged down with multiple commitments to regional organizations and in a period of economic downturn, the less-endowed states will be especially challenged to meet their financial and other resource commitments.

One of the major challenges for CELAC will therefore be how to deal with these multiple commitments, especially when some countries may have different integration priorities. In fact, given the presence of other regional arrangements (ACS, ALBA, UNASUR, SICA) the issue of overlapping goals becomes a major challenge which must be addressed frontally by CELAC. Indeed, the diverse

---

24   P. Trucco, 'The Rise of Monetary Agreements in South America', in Pía Riggirozzi and Diana Tussie (eds), *The Rise of Post-hegemonic Regionalism: The Case of Latin America* (2012), 101–123.

25   Ibid. (2012).

policy fields and arenas and the difficulties of coordinating states with such a large number of institutions and mandates present yet another challenge for CELAC. For CARICOM states, their preoccupation and concerns about the slow pace with which CARICOM's own regional integration effort is proceeding, the implementation deficit which has brought serious strains on the movement, as well as the general reduction in the attractiveness of the CARICOM effort have all served to place questions about the meaning and basic priorities of the integration movement in the minds of the people of the Caribbean. For there to be sustained engagement by CARICOM states in this arrangement, there will have to be concrete actions and programmes led by CELAC, with visible impact, to sustain the confidence of its citizens.

One of the early challenges faced by CELAC was the issue of CARICOM's involvement in its coordination. The Caribbean group sought greater inclusiveness and equity in the coordinating structure and raised the issue in 2011 at the Caracas summit. It is interesting to observe that, beginning in February 2013 CELAC is now run by a 'quartet' of states – the immediate Chair (Chile), the current Chair (Cuba), the incoming Chair (Costa Rica) and the Caribbean Community (CARICOM) represented by Haiti, its current chairman, in what might be termed the Troika+1 approach. This development can be interpreted as a recognition of CARICOM's role as an equal partner and now allows for better coordination of CARICOM positions within CELAC and at the same time, providing the small states with an opportunity for greater participation in CELAC's decision making. Significantly also, there is no permanent secretariat so that this is a loose arrangement and it may be argued that this lack of structure can limit the effectiveness and coordination of the organization.

Another recent challenge for CELAC has been the death in March this year of President Hugo Chavez of Venezuela, considered one of the most influential leaders in support of the regional integration process and the inclusion of the CARICOM states in the new integration mechanisms. Undoubtedly, Chavez's commitment to autonomy and independence from the hegemon resonated greatly in the region and his approach and profile facilitated the emergence of bold initiatives, including the exclusion of the United States and Canada from CELAC. While the view exists that the 'Bolivarian revolution' will lose momentum in the region,[26] an important priority for CELAC will be to ensure that the pace and progress of the new regionalist arrangements, driven by Chavez, will be intensified; especially the social programmes which benefit the poor and marginalized.

Additionally, there are those who perceive the new organization CELAC as assuming the lead organizational role in the hemisphere, in the process reducing the role of the Organization of American States.[27] The OAS, established in 1948,

---

26   Andres Oppenheimer, 'Chavez "Revelountion" will Lose Steam Abroad, But Not At Home', *Stabroak News* (10 March 2013).

27   Third World Network, 'Third World Resurgence: Out of the Backyard', No 255/256 (November/December 2011), 53–55.

has been described as limited in its successes over the years and subject to the influences and dominance of the United States. A challenge therefore will be the extent to which the two organizations (CELAC and the OAS) can co-exist and collaborate on issues of common concern or the extent to which there will be competition for 'regional space' and fragmentation of the integration process.

There are also mixed signals about CELAC coming out of the United States. On one hand, the US government has indicated that it will 'continue to work through the OAS as the pre-eminent multilateral organization, speaking for the hemisphere' while at the same time signalling that the US could engage in a partnership with the new organization.[28] As the US Department of State noted, 'subregional groupings are potentially important representatives of the hemisphere and can be useful partners for the United States'.[29] Given the experiences with US commitment to genuine partnerships in the hemisphere, one is left to wonder if this will be a commitment which will be honoured in the immediate future and especially since, on assuming office, President Obama promised 'a new beginning' in inter-American relations which to-date has also not materialized.

There are several common challenges facing Latin America and the Caribbean including the need to develop trade, the critical imperative to develop joint action in relation to drug trafficking, money laundering, environmental degradation, climate change and sea level rise, among others. The effective management and coordination on these issues by CELAC can result in positive outcomes. With respect to trade, a large imbalance in favour of Latin America can be observed and apart from the trade in the energy sector (which is dominated by Trinidad), observers posit that the main economic linkage among the two sets of states (Latin American and Caribbean) is centred around the trans-shipment of illicit drugs from the producer states of the south to the consumer demand centres of the north,[30] There must therefore be renewed efforts to enhance trade and commercial relations, led by CARICOM. These must include detailed surveys of Caribbean firms exporting to other CELAC member states to determine scientifically the constraints and possibilities for the enhancement of the trade collaboration. There should also be efforts in the tourism sector to organize multi-destination tourism packages which focus on ecology, culture and education as well as joint marketing of Latin America and the Caribbean as key tourism destinations. In addition,

---

28 Timur Zolotoev, 'Latin America Unites in New Bloc, US Not Invited' (2011), available at: http://rt.com/news/latin-america-celac-bloc-975/, accessed 28 December 2013.

29 Anna Pelegri, 'New Americas Summit Aims Criticism at US', available at http://www.google.com/hostednews/afp/article/ALeqM5i6fWdANXBfHxBIyYYUYLzEXfl au w?docId=CNG.8ad710369797ec2360f737fc0ae5e858.5a1, accessed 26 December 2013.

30 Norman Girvan, 'Turning to the South? CARICOM, the Southern Cone and ALBA' (2012), revised version of paper presented at Fundacion Vidanta/FUNGLODE/ CIES/UNIBE Seminar on 'Integracion, Cooperacion Y Desarrollo En El Caribe De La Globalizacion'; Santo Domingo, R.D., 10–11 November 2011.

joint initiatives to promote music, entertainment and sport must be given priority attention in the CELAC states to add another dimension to the potential trade and cultural linkages. Additionally, support for language training should be made a priority and the curricula of schools in both sets of states should be reworked to include information on comparative history, geography, culture and business.

From a CARICOM perspective, however, the time is long overdue for an efficiently managed sustained engagement with Latin America which can yield mutual benefits. The ad hoc nature of the engagements have only served to limit the success of the interaction and as Girvan suggests, 'CARICOM's turn to the South is less effective than it could be because of a relatively inchoate series of ad hoc responses by individual member states, rather than a truly unified policy of engagement informed by a strategic perspective'.[31]

Another challenge for the new organization is the divergent views on the structure of its organizational arrangements. CELAC has not followed the traditional pattern of institutionalization and while some CELAC proponents would have preferred early institutionalization and structure to create a more coherent agenda, free from the 'ad hoc approaches' which often lack consistency, and also shows a preference for the more efficient distribution of decision making, others demonstrated a preference for flexibility and the absence of a rigid structure which, it is argued, allows for states to adapt the new integration initiatives into their national agendas, utilizing a gradualist approach. Legler posits that 'pro tempore multilateralism' in now common in Latin America and the Caribbean and he suggests that it allows for individual countries to 'demonstrate their leadership over short periods'. He also asserts that in 'pro tempore' arrangements, 'sustained leadership and institutional memory are also sacrificed'.[32] This suggests therefore that CELAC must make an informed decision with respect to its institutional structure in order to ensure the efficient conduct of its affairs.

Conclusion

Given the history of misunderstanding and mistrust that has characterized Caribbean-Latin American relations until recently, CELAC will be presented with another important challenge – i.e., to see Caribbean small states as genuine partners and not just as appendages. While the former Troika of countries which manage the affairs of the organization has now been expanded to include a Caribbean presence, there appears to be continued suspicions about the secondary role that Caribbean states will be forced to play, and this leads to questions about the equality of the small states in the wider integration movement. If not properly

---

31 Ibid., 13.

32 Thomas Legler, *Multilateralism and Regional Governance in the Americas*, in 'Latin American Multilateralism: New Directions'. Canadian Foundation for the Americas – FOCAL, 2010.

managed, these perceptions could lead to unacceptable levels of mistrust in the Community and retard the integration process.

Furthermore, there continues to be the persistence of issues such as on-going border controversies, competing political and economic agendas and ideological considerations that beset the two sub-regions. However, this latest integration arrangement also brings special significance to CARICOM states since it implies increased impetus to redefine the so-called 'Anglocentric' nature of the English-speaking Caribbean regionalism. There will have to be a serious mindset change and sustained consciousness-raising activities, so as not to limit the potential of this new effort at Caribbean-Latin American relations.

Serbin observes that a serious challenge for CELAC is the return of the State as the most prominent actor in the integration process. In the new environment in which the agenda is no longer trade-led, 'non-state actors such as civil society organizations (CSOs) and business are relegated to lesser influential positions in negotiations, which barely go beyond so-called consultation mechanisms, which do not monitor or follow up the government commitments'.[33] Much energy therefore will have to spent to ensure that non-state actors are seen as equal partners in the development of the regional integration process. Cuba has assumed the chairmanship of CELAC in January this year and with the experience of 40 years of sustained engagement with CARICOM, this can serve to create more opportunities for Caribbean collaboration with other Latin American states. Cuba's involvement with CARICOM states in areas of culture, education, health and trade can serve to move the Caribbean closer to its neighbours. As President Raul Castro noted, 'we are building the ideal of a diverse Latin American and Caribbean region united in a common space of political independence and sovereignty over our enormous natural resources to advance toward sustainable development [and] regional integration'.[34]

If one were to consider the collective strength of the CELAC, with its total GDP of approximately US$5.3 trillion (which would make it the third largest global economic power), the greatest oil reserves (approximately 338 billion barrels) the world's principal producer of food, among other positive features, then CELAC can have a strong voice in the international political economy. If one were to predict, it could be argued that in the long term, a structured, effectively coordinated and well-defined CELAC could subsume the current regional efforts such as UNASUR, MERCOSUR, ALBA, SICA, CARICOM and the ACS, among others, in a 'big tent' arrangement that would provide the region with a mega-institution that has the capacity to move the regional economic and social development at such a pace and with such dynamism to place Latin America and the Caribbean at the forefront of global affairs.

---

33   Andrés Serbin, Lanyedi Martinez and Haroldo Ramanzinni (eds), *El regionalismo post-liberal en América Latina y el Caribe: nuevos actores, nuevos temas, nuevos desafíos*.
34   Ibid. (2012).

To conclude, it is important therefore that there be a demonstration of political will on all sides to accelerate the pace and process of collaboration and move the condition from one of 'distant cousin' to reliable partner so as to respond properly to the challenges of the new global environment.

Chapter 7

Latin America in China's Peaceful Rise[1]

Joseph Y.S. Cheng

I. Introduction

Two and a half centuries ago, the French Sinologist De Giognes proposed that the New World was discovered not by Columbus, but by the Chinese. Proven contacts between China and Latin America can be dated back to the 1570s, when trade between them started to flourish across the Pacific.[2] In the eighteenth and early nineteenth century, hundreds of thousands of Chinese labourers were trafficked by Western colonialists to Latin America to serve as contracted workers (*kuli*), and their strenuous physical labour contributed to local economic development.

In the first two decades of the People's Republic of China (PRC), contacts between China and Latin America were limited to the non-governmental level. Cuba was the first country in the region to establish diplomatic relations with China in September 1960. In 1970, Chile became the first South American country to establish diplomatic relations with China. Subsequent to China's admission into the United Nations in 1971, many Latin American countries followed the examples of Cuba and Chile; by the mid-1980s, all countries in South America except Paraguay had established diplomatic relations with China.[3]

There were no close ties between China and Latin America in the 1970s and 1980s. Trade was limited, and high-level contacts were few. Trade began to pick up in the 1990s (see Tables 7.1 and 7.2). In May 1990, the then PRC President, Yang Shangkun, paid a state visit to Mexico, Brazil, Uruguay, Argentina and Chile; Yang was the first Chinese head of state to visit Latin America. In 1992, the then Chinese Premier Li Peng went to Brazil to attend the United Nations Conference

---

1   In 2004 and the first half of 2005, I visited the Chinese Academy of Social Science, Beijing University, the Central Party School, the China Institute for International Strategic Studies, and the Shanghai Institute of International Studies. I held extensive discussions with over 50 academics and research workers on Chinese foreign policy. To facilitate exchange of ideas, they will not be quoted directly. Instead, their views will be summarized and presented as those of the Chinese research community on China's foreign policy.

2   Shixue Jiang, 'Latin American Studies in China: An Overview', n.d. (a): 3, http://www.cesla.uw.edu.pl/cesla/images/stories/wydawnictwo/czasopisma/Revista/Revista_6/277-281_Debates.pdf, accessed 29 December 2013.

3   Yuqin Liu, 'Friendly and Co-operative Relations between China and Latin American and Caribbean countries & China's Foreign Policy towards Latin America', *International Understanding* (Beijing), 2 (2003), 11.

Table 7.1   China's trade with South American countries, 1991 and 2001–03 (in US$ million)

Country	1991 Exports	1991 Imports	1991 Total	2001 Exports	2001 Imports	2001 Total	2002 Exports	2002 Imports	2002 Total	2003 Imports	2003 Exports	2003 Total
Argentina	51.72	305.45	357.17	573.70	1,281.03	1,854.73	185.37	1,239.46	1,424.83	2,729.08	447.19	3,176.27
Bolivia	4.46	–	4.46	7.74	9.52	17.26	9.55	12.08	21.63	6.88	11.84	18.72
Brazil	68.03	345.81	413.84	1,350.93	2,347.23	3,698.16	1,466.38	3,003.02	4,469.40	5,842.29	2,143.26	7,985.55
Chile	94.20	106.99	201.19	814.78	1,303.46	2,118.24	998.26	1,567.10	2,565.36	2,248.16	1,283.44	3,531.60
Colombia	5.03	2.45	7.48	205.27	26.93	232.20	287.26	29.12	316.38	60.46	398.20	458.66
Ecuador	14.05	1.10	15.15	134.05	28.10	162.15	194.48	13.57	208.05	39.73	239.29	279.02
Guyana	–	–	–	12.41	2.37	14.78	13.72	4.00	17.72	0.30	18.12	18.42
Paraguay	16.72	19.82	36.54	72.10	2.83	74.93	79.03	7.87	86.90	12.74	126.19	138.93
Peru	31.31	294.41	325.72	176.52	498.02	674.54	246.64	731.61	978.25	760.01	353.74	1,113.75
Uruguay	10.51	118.13	128.64	188.95	95.53	284.48	94.95	78.07	173.02	75.75	127.62	203.37
Venezuela	32.74	6.17	38.91	443.35	145.77	589.12	332.67	144.96	477.63	542.16	199.24	741.40
Total	91.28	438.53	529.81	3,979.8	5,740.79	9,720.59	3,908.31	6,830.86	10,739.17	12,317.56	5,348.13	17,665.69
South America as a % of China's total	0.46	1.88	1.13	1.50	2.36	1.91	1.20	2.31	1.73	2.98	1.22	2.08

Source: State Statistical Bureau (comp.), *China Statistical Yearbook* (Beijing: China Statistics Press, 1993, 2003 and 2004), 1993, 2003 and 2004 issues.
Note: '–' represents that the figure is unknown, unavailable or negligible.

Table 7.2   China's trade with Central American and Caribbean countries, 1991 and 2001–03 (in US$ million)

Country	1991 Exports	1991 Imports	1991 Total	2001 Exports	2001 Imports	2001 Total	2002 Exports	2002 Imports	2002 Total	2003 Exports	2003 Imports	2003 Total
Bahamas	–	–	–	34.77	0.02	34.79	62.87	0.06	62.93	121.72	0.78	122.51
Dominica	3.93	–	3.93	87.60	0.90	88.50	45.43	0.74	46.17	33.58	0.76	34.34
Costa Rica	–	–	–	63.10	26.51	89.61	81.65	184.49	266.14	98.52	560.90	659.42
Cuba	224.40	201.65	426.05	331.44	114.05	445.49	310.66	115.69	426.35	236.30	120.51	356.81
Curacao	0.71	0.01	0.72	46.54	–	46.54	41.29	–	41.29	38.83	0.21	39.04
Dominica Republic	9.51	–	9.51	38.21	0.22	38.43	105.48	1.81	107.29	148.15	3.51	151.66
Guatemala	10.88	0.23	11.11	162.92	0.21	163.13	244.67	0.58	245.25	305.62	1.82	307.44
Haiti	–	–	–	14.45	0.03	14.48	23.47	–	23.47	26.38	0.02	26.40
Honduras	4.53	0.28	4.81	64.84	0.11	64.95	58.77	0.77	59.54	77.87	3.38	81.25
Jamaica	5.06	0.03	5.09	85.14	33.93	119.07	65.96	48.80	114.76	102.04	105.46	207.50
Mexico	86.25	148.70	234.95	1,790.22	761.28	2,551.50	2,863.66	1,114.96	3,978.62	3,267.03	1,676.74	4,943.77
Nicaragua	0.78	–	0.78	34.55	0.09	34.64	49.17	0.03	49.20	69.31	0.37	69.68
Panama	87.33	0.57	87.90	1,239.63	1.95	1,241.58	1,272.66	3.72	1,276.38	1,479.99	28.62	1,508.61
Puerto Rico	3.14	2.45	5.59	75.57	17.43	93.00	104.30	23.46	127.76	159.53	78.07	237.60
Saint Vincent and Grenadines	–	–	–	13.08	–	13.08	8.21	0.02	8.23	7.65	–	7.65
El Salvador	5.06	0.23	5.29	99.59	0.43	100.02	132.57	1.90	134.47	157.56	2.06	159.62
Surinam	2.16	–	2.16	12.64	4.08	16.72	15.15	2.57	17.72	19.77	16.09	35.86
Trinidad and Tobago	4.03	4.28	8.31	34.94	0.07	35.01	42.34	4.81	47.15	58.52	10.24	68.76
Other countries (regions) in Central America	–	–	–	1.15	0.09	1.24	1.22	0.01	1.23	0.76	–	0.76
Total	11.25	4.28	15.76	4,230.38	961.40	5,191.78	5,529.53	1,504.42	7,033.95	6,409.13	2,609.55	9,018.68
Central America as a % of China's total	0.62	0.56	0.59	1.59	0.39	1.02	1.70	0.51	1.13	1.46	0.63	1.06

Source: State Statistical Bureau (comp.), *China Statistical Yearbook* (Beijing: China Statistics Press, 1993, 2003 and 2004), 1993, 2003 and 2004 issues.

Note: '–' represents that the figure is unknown, unavailable or negligible.

on Environment and Development. In November 1993, the then President Jiang
Zemin visited Cuba and Brazil. Jiang again visited Chile, Argentina, Uruguay,
Cuba, Venezuela and Brazil in 2001. In November 2004, President Hu Jintao
too visited Brazil, Argentina, Chile and Cuba. These visits revealed China's
priorities in Latin America. Today, China enjoys strategic partnerships with Brazil,
Argentina, Venezuela and Mexico.[4]

This chapter examines the role and significance of Latin America in China's
foreign policy framework summarized as the peaceful rise strategy. It attempts
to analyse issues concerning Sino-Latin American economic relations, including
trade, the impact of the Free Trade Area of the Americas (FTAA), and investment.
Diplomatic competition with Taiwan is also considered because, in the eyes of
Beijing, this is an important aspect of Sino-Latin American relations.

Traditionally, Chinese literature divided the Americas into North America
(from Greenland to Panama) and South America (all countries south of Panama).
This division actually split Latin America. In recent years, Chinese literature in
English tends to divide the Americas into North America (the United States and
Canada), and Latin American and Caribbean countries.[5] In this article, the author
uses Latin America to cover Latin American and Caribbean countries. The focus
of the discussion is actually on South America, though Central American and
Caribbean countries are the important actors in China's diplomatic competition
with Taiwan.

II. China's Foreign Policy Framework

Chinese leaders were acutely aware of China's backwardness at the end of the
Cultural Revolution (1966–76), and they wanted to secure a peaceful international
environment to concentrate on China's modernization programme. Beginning
in 1982–83, Chinese leaders pursued what they called an independent foreign
policy of peace.[6] In his report to the Fourth Session of the Sixth National People's
Congress (NPC) on 25 March, 1986, following the Chinese leadership's usual
practice, Premier Zhao Ziyang provided a detailed account of the ten principles
guiding China's independent foreign policy line of peace.[7] Besides reaffirming the

---

4   Mingde Zhang, 'Sino-Latin American Rhythm', *Beijing Review*, 47, 48, 2
(December 2004), 12–13.

5   See, for example, the official *China's Diplomacy* yearbook series edited by the
Policy Research Office of the Ministry of Foreign Affairs and published by the Shijie Zhishi
Chubanshe in Beijing. See also the titles of the articles in *International Understanding*
and *Beijing Review* referred to above.

6   Joseph Y.S. Cheng, 'The Evolution of China's Foreign Policy in the Post-Mao Era:
From Anti-Hegemony to Modernisation Diplomacy', in Joseph Y.S. Cheng (ed.), *China:
Modernisation in the 1980s* (Hong Kong: The Chinese University Press, 1989), 161–201.

7   *Ta Kung Pao* (a Hong Kong Chinese newspaper) (14 April 1986).

general principles of defending world peace, opposing hegemonism, observing the Five Principles of Peaceful Co-existence[8] and supporting the Third World, China also reiterated its position on arms control and disarmament as well as its open-door policy and support for the United Nations.

As regards China's position of never establishing an alliance or strategic relationship with any big power, the Chinese Premier further stated that China's relations with various countries would not be determined by their social systems and ideologies, and that China's position on various international issues would be guided by the criteria of defending world peace, developing friendship and cooperation among various countries and promoting international prosperity. Premier Zhao also stressed China's emphasis on various exchanges at the people-to-people level.

After Deng Xiaoping's death in early 1997, Jiang Zemin's statements on Chinese foreign policy repeatedly emphasized continuity and peace. From an idealistic point of view, Chinese leaders' conception of peace is more than an absence of war and violence. It is related to North-South issues and the elimination of social injustice arising from the gap between the rich and poor. Peace should be based on an equality of states, while hegemonism is seen as a threat to peace.[9] The basic rationale for this continuity in Chinese foreign policy has been China's demand for a peaceful international environment to concentrate on economic development, as the Chinese leadership appreciates that the legitimacy of the Chinese Communist regime depends on its ability to improve the people's living standards. Striving for a peaceful international environment certainly involves establishing friendly relations with one's neighbours and avoiding conflicts with them. This has probably been China's most important foreign policy objectives since 1982–83, and it has been achieving satisfactory results. This means advancing China's national interests by force and the threat of force will be very costly.

In the view of China's still limited military and economic capacities, a multipolar world in the twenty-first century would provide the most favourable environment for it to exert its influence in international and regional affairs as a major power. The Chinese leadership certainly sees the predominance of the US as the sole superpower in the world as unacceptable, both from an ideological and national interest point of view. The perception that the US does not want to see a strong China and that it wants to 'contain' China has reinforced the above view. Chinese leaders therefore would like to work to facilitate the emergence and consolidation of multipolarity in the global power transfiguration in the present century.

---

8   The Five Principles of Peaceful Co-existence were jointly initiated by China, India and Burma in 1953–54; they were to apply to relations among countries with different social systems. They are: respect for territorial integrity and sovereignty, non-interference in domestic affairs, equality and mutual benefits, and mutual non-aggression and peaceful co-existence.

9   Gerald Chan, 'Chinese Perspectives on Peace and Development', *Peace Review*, 10 (1) (1998), 35.

The Chinese leadership prefers a multipolar world in which the major powers can develop friendly ties with each other and in which non-zero-sum games are the norm. Power blocs and security alliances tend to exacerbate tension and eventually limit the options of the major powers involved. Rapid economic growth is essential for China to maintain its major power status, and it is still under acute pressure to catch up with the developed countries. Diversified sources of capital, technology, management know-how, etc. as well as a broad spectrum of partners for economic cooperation constitute part of Chinese leaders' preferred scenario. Strategic partnership provides the standard mode of behaviour governing relations among major powers in a multipolar world.[10] In contrast to the Five Principles of Peaceful Co-existence, strategic partnerships imply that China looks upon itself as a major power and pursues the legitimate interests of one in a multipolar world.

In view of the Asia-Pacific financial crisis in 1997–98 and China's increasing dependence on international trade, the Chinese leadership now places considerable emphasis on China's 'economic security'. It is believed that because of the keen competition for markets and resources in the context of globalization as well as the enhancement of regionalism, the economic development of one individual country will be more vulnerable to the influence of external factors. Hence the strengthening of coordination among governments concerned will become all the more essential. This implies that Chinese leaders will attempt to further develop China's dialogue and multilateral cooperation first with the major powers, its Asian neighbours, and eventually with all countries in the world, including those in Latin America and Africa.[11] The latter are now perceived as important suppliers of resources essential to the support of China's industrialization and expansion to potential markets.

China's joining the World Trade Organization (WTO) symbolizes China's response to globalization. It appreciates that if it does not open its doors, isolation will only exacerbate its backwardness. Despite the economic and political costs, China has no alternatives but to accept world-wide competition according to the rules defined by the developed countries. China can only catch up the latter through global competition. The ultimate challenge to the Communist Party of China (CPC)'s monopoly of power is not to be under-estimated; and multilateral economic diplomacy will be more significant in China's foreign relations in the future.

---

10   Joseph Y.S. Cheng, 'The Sino-Russian Strategic Partnership in the Chinese Leadership's World View', in Peter H. Koehn and Joseph Y.S. Cheng (eds), *The Outlook for U.S.-China Security, Trade and Cultural-exchange Relations Following the 1997–1998 Summits: Chinese and U.S. Perspectives* (Hong Kong: The Chinese University Press, 1999), 85–110.

11   Zhongyuan Ma, 'Zhongguo Zuochu "Jingji Anquan" Zhanlue Juece (China Has Developed a Policy Concerning an "Economic Security" Strategy)', *The Mirror* (a Hong Kong Chinese monthly), 255 (1998), 32–34.

The idea of a 'China threat' in the post-Cold War era and the danger of separatism, including that in Taiwan, are seen as two significant sources of pressure on China. Since the early 1980s, Chinese leaders have been trying to improve relations with China's neighbours to secure a peaceful international environment and avoid any attempt to 'contain' China. While they have been successful, the challenges are yet to come. At the same time, the Taiwan question remains a serious source of friction in China's relations with many countries.

Globalization and China's deepening integration with the international economy mean that the management of its international financial and trade risks has become a much more important and difficult task. China's impressive economic growth has increased its weight in the Asia-Pacific region, and to a lesser extent, in the global economy. This implies influence as well as responsibilities. In this connection, Chinese foreign policy researchers have been engaging in discussions of interdependence in international relations as well as the relationship among interdependence, international organizations and state sovereignty since the early 1990s. Despite the Chinese leadership's upholding of the traditional notion of state sovereignty, it became aware that some adjustments had to be made. As Samuel S. Kim pointed out, in the 1980s and 1990s, the Chinese authorities' approach to international organizations was one of 'system-maintaining and system-exploiting';[12] and the organizational learning derived from China's participation in international organizations involved some elements of cognitive learning while instrumental learning dominated. In recent years, China has gradually become more active in multilateral diplomacy and in international organizations. Instead of remaining aloof as it did in the 1970s and 1980s, China has been ready to co-ordinate with other major Third World countries to push for the building of a more equitable international economic order. Major countries in South America, especially Brazil, Venezuela, etc., are important partners in this pursuit.

a) China's Peaceful Rise

Paul Kennedy discussed in his book *The Rise and Fall of the Great Powers* the emergence of China as a major power. He indicated that China was the poorest among the world's major powers and at the same time probably located in the worst strategic position. He believed that two conditions would be essential to China's rise as a major power, namely, a visionary strategy formulated by the Chinese leadership and sustainable economic growth.[13]

At the end of 2003, the new Chinese leadership began to articulate publicly the concept of China's peaceful rise. On 26 December 2003, in commemoration of the

---

12   Samuel S. Kim, 'China's International Organisational Behaviour', in Thomas W. Robinson and David Shambaugh (eds), *Chinese Foreign Policy: Theory and Practice* (Oxford: Clarendon Press, 1994), 431.

13   Paul M. Kennedy, *The Rise and Fall of the Great Powers: Economic Change and Military Conflict from 1500 to 2000* (New York: Random House, 1987), 447–457.

one hundred and tenth anniversary of Mao Zedong's birthday, Hu Jintao, General Secretary of the CPC Central Committee, stated that China had to 'insist on following the development path of a peaceful rise'.[14] About two weeks earlier, in a speech delivered at Harvard University in the US, Premier Wen Jiabao elaborated on the concepts as follows: 'In expanding our opening up to the external world, we, at the same time, have to adequately and more self-consciously rely on our own institutional innovations; rely on our developing and expanding domestic market; rely on transforming the huge savings of the residents into investment; and rely on the raising of the nation's quality and the progress of science and technology to resolve our resources and environmental problems. The gist of China's development path of a peaceful rise lies in the above'.[15]

Chinese academics in the international relations field consider China's peaceful rise to be a long-term process in motion at this stage. It focuses on the status and function of China in the international system and world market, including its adaptability, integration, influence and creativity.[16] Through active participation in the processes of economic globalization, China has captured the opportunity to rise as a major power. The contribution of China's economic growth to the world economy lies in the following areas: first, it leads to the stable improvement of the living standards of China's 1.3 billion population; second, it constitutes important momentum pushing for Asia's economic development, and in return serves as a positive factor in the global economic development; third, it facilitates the achievement of the optimal allocation of resources in the world market through China's participation in the international division of labour; and finally, it helps China assume a constructive role in the international economic mechanisms, and as a linkage between developed countries and developing countries.

The rapid increase of the weight of China's economy in the world market has generated some maladjustment between the external world and the China market, including the exchange rate of the Renminbi (RMB), China's huge trade surpluses, large-scale re-location of industries to China, global deflation, and so on. Chinese leaders have pledged to tackle these issues when China's economic structure stabilizes and when China can absorb the shock of these adjustments. They also indicate that investment outflow from China will gradually accelerate. This investment outflow is aimed at opening up markets for China's exports including the securing of access to advanced technology, management, etc. through acquisitions and the establishment of brand names, wholesale and retail networks, and so on. It is also directed at securing a stable and expanding supply of

---

14   *Renmin Ribao* (Beijing) (27 December 2003).

15   *Renmin Ribao* (Beijing) (12 December 2003).

16   Youwen Zhang, et al., 'Daolun: Heping Jueqi – Qiangguo Ding Mubiao Tuidong Shijie Gongying (Introduction: Peaceful Rise – Major Power Sets the Objective Pushing for a Global Win-Win Scenario)', in Youwen Zhang, Renwei Huang, et al., *Zhongguo Guoji Diwei Baogao (China's International Status Report)* (Beijing: Renmin Chubanshe, 2004), 1–15.

energy resources and raw materials in support of China's industrialization. Latin American countries rich in resources are expected to attract a substantial share of the latter Chinese investment.

The Chinese leadership is acutely aware of the danger of the spread of the 'China threat' perception. They understand that the rise of a new major power will probably be perceived as a challenge and threat by the existing major powers. Chinese leaders are concerned that such perception will lead to the 'containment' of China. In fact, they believe that the US has been engaging in such 'containment', which in fact is the main cause of the conflicts in Sino-American relations. Chinese academics attempt to explain that China's peaceful rise involves a re-definition of national interest and national security by the Chinese authorities as common interest and the advancement of a new concept of security.

b) China's Embrace of the New Conception of Security

According to this new concept of security, China's security is not an isolated issue; it is mutually interdependent with that of the Asia-Pacific region and indeed of the entire global community. This new concept of security involves non-traditional security and human security, and in fact can serve as the basis for cooperation between China and the other major powers. In this connection, Chinese leaders will attempt to establish a new framework for international relations, but they understand that they only have limited support. It is hoped that this new framework will expand the strategic space for China's peaceful rise. To secure another 20 to 50 years' time for China to develop its economy and to catch up with the advanced countries in the world is the most important strategic objective in accord with China's core national interest; such an objective is to facilitate China's peaceful rise. China therefore is willing to make concessions to secure this strategic space. This is probably most conspicuous in Sino-American and Sino-Japanese relations; indeed, Chinese leaders have often been criticized by the domestic intelligentsia for being weak in dealing with these two countries.

In a speech at the Institute of International Relations in Moscow on 28 May, 2003, and in another speech on the following day addressing the Moscow summit meeting of the Shanghai Co-operation Organization, Chinese President, Hu Jintao, explained China's position. Hu stated, 'China advocates the establishment of a new concept of security, building security through mutual trust, and promoting co-operation through dialogue. Military measures may win temporary victory, but will not bring long-lasting security. History and reality repeatedly demonstrate that force cannot establish peace, and power cannot ensure security. Only through the enhancement of mutual trust, consultation on the basis of equality and broad co-operation can universal and lasting security be realised'.[17]

This approach arguably is the strategy of the weak, and is in line with the Chinese leadership's objective of gaining time. Chinese leaders typically appeal

---

17   *Renmin Ribao* (Beijing) (29 and 30 December 2003).

for overcoming differences through dialogue and negotiation. As an implicit critique against US unilateralism and Samuel P. Huntington's thesis of 'the clash of civilisations',[18] the Chinese public information machinery preaches mutual respect, mutual exchange and mutual learning among various civilizations, different social systems and development paths while engaging in peaceful competition. In line with China's relative weakness, Chinese leaders have been eager to promote multipolarity as the new global power transfiguration, the democratization of international relations, the strengthening of the role of the United Nations, and respect for the diversity of development models.

Within this framework, the Chinese leadership considers that priority should go to China's neighbours, while the major powers are the key, and the developing countries are the foundation. As China's influence rises in the international community, it will seek to strengthen its foundation, and relations with Latin America and Africa will assume greater significance.

c) China's Support of Developing States and Multipolarity

Chinese leaders want to distinguish China's emergence as a major power from that of Germany before World War I and that of Japan before World War II. They emphasize the themes of peace and development, the fact that China needs a peaceful international environment for its modernization, and that China is willing to embrace globalization – symbolized by its joining the WTO in 2001. The high mobility of factors of production facilitated by globalization is perceived to have provided the strategic opportunities for China to exploit the advantage of its abundant cheap labour supply adopting an exports-oriented development strategy and emerging as 'the workshop of the world'. This development positions China as a keen competitor to many developing countries which also depend on labour-expensive exports – Mexico in Latin America is a good example. Chinese academics, however, point out that the processes of the international division of labour including the international intra-industry division of labour are controlled by multinational corporations. China is eager to move up the value-added chain in the production processes and develop more technology-intensive industries. Moreover, it also wants to establish its own brand names, its own Sony- or Samsung-type of enterprises, and its own international distribution networks. Otherwise, China's share of the profits will remain very small. The Chinese explanation is genuine; it tries to identify China with the Third World and suggest that all developing countries still have a long way to go to secure relative economic autonomy.

Similarly, the Chinese leadership is aware that developing countries perceive the attraction of foreign investment by China as benefitting at their expense.[19]

---

18   Samuel P. Huntington, *The Clash of Civilisations and the Remaking of World Order* (New York: Simon and Schuster, 1996).

19   Joseph Y.S. Cheng, 'Sino-ASEAN Relations in the Early Twenty-first Century', *Contemporary Southeast Asia*, 23 (3) (2001), 434–437.

China recognizes the contribution of foreign investment to its modernization; but at its present stage of development, it probably values more the advanced technology, management and access to the international market brought by foreign investment. At the same time, it attempts to maintain a balance between increasing foreign investment and avoiding foreign control. It is also aware that excessive competition for foreign investment among China's provinces has been counter-productive. It is obvious that China has been increasing its own investment overseas in recent years to secure supply of energy and industrial raw materials as well as to enhance its access to markets.

As economic globalization progresses and international competition intensifies, regional integration also accelerates. Since China's priority lies in the Asia-Pacific region, its cooperation with ASEAN and the ASEAN+3 framework are the most important regional integration processes to China. The development of the European Union is also perceived by the Chinese authorities in a positive light in that it promotes multipolarity. Similarly, regional integration among developing countries is supported because it enhances their bargaining power and also facilitates the emergence of multipolarity. At the WTO ministerial conference in Cancún, Mexico in September 2003, China assumed an active role in the Group of 20 in support of the leadership of Brazil, India and South Africa in fighting for the interests of the developing countries. Chinese leaders now take greater interests in narrowing the gap between the North and South as well as in South-South cooperation.

III. The Role of Latin America in China's Foreign Policy

A survey of China's media reports on Latin America in the recent two or three years would help to illustrate the Chinese leadership's perception of Latin America.[20] China's media reports tend to convey the message that the basic situation in Latin America and the Caribbean region has been stable; tensions in the hot spots have been de-escalating, but social contradictions remain serious leading to turmoil in some areas. In 2003, Brazil, Ecuador, Argentina, Paraguay, etc. experienced relatively smooth changes of government; and the new governments adopted pragmatic policies to restore domestic and international confidence. The contradictions and imbalances in the development process had been exacerbated in some countries. The lower socio-economic strata in Peru and Ecuador were engaged in series of anti-government protests; and in Bolivia in 2003, anti-government protest activities finally led to the fall of the president. Chinese media observe that many traditional political parties in Latin America cannot cope with the challenges, and their reputation and support have been in decline.

---

20   Policy Research Office, Ministry of Foreign Affairs, the People's Republic of China *Various Years, China's Diplomacy, Various Issues* (Beijing: Shijie Zhishi Chubanshe), 17–18.

Some centre-left and independent parties have strengthened themselves and won national elections. The conclusion is that the political patterns and development models in Latin America are changing and adjusting to the new situations.

The Chinese media note that the Latin American economy has been recovering, but reforms still encounter many difficulties. Most countries have adopted tight fiscal policies in order to improve the macro-economy and restore market confidence. Brazil and Argentina have been recovering from their earlier financial crises. But foreign debt in Latin America remains substantial; tight deflationary policies suppress consumption and investment. Economic growth is still low, and the room for manoeuvre in economic structural adjustments and institutional reforms is limited.

Multilateral diplomacy of the Latin American countries is perceived to be active, with Brazil playing a prominent leadership role. Regional integration has demonstrated new momentum. The Chinese media are pleased to report that on issues relating to Iraq, WTO and negotiations on the FTAA, many Latin American countries have been willing to oppose the US position. But cooperation remains the predominant aspect of US–Latin American relations; both parties accord priority to this cooperation based on self-interest. Latin American countries are seen to be interested in broadening their diplomatic horizon through developing better relations with the European Union, the Asia-Pacific region and the major countries in the developing world. Mexico, Chile and Peru actively participate in the Asia-Pacific Economic Co-operation (APEC) forum, and they also plan to reach bilateral free trade agreements with selective Asian countries. Brazil's role within the Group of 20 in WTO negotiations and the establishment of a dialogue forum at the foreign minister-level with India and South Africa are interpreted by the Chinese government as positive trends in international relations. Similarly, integration within the MERCOSUR and its negotiations with the Andean Community to form a Free Trade Area of South America, as well as the building of a single market in the Caribbean region are supported by the Chinese authorities, though they also anticipate serious difficulties ahead.

In the early years of the PRC, there was of course very limited interest in Latin America. It was said that at a meeting in the late 1950s, Chairman Mao Zedong pointed to a map of the world, and asked if there were researchers studying the two large regions of Africa and Latin America in China.[21] The Cuban revolution in 1959 naturally prompted Chinese leaders to take a new look at the revolutionary movements on the other side of the Pacific. In the early 1960s, researchers in China mainly concentrated on Latin America's revolutionary movements, agrarian reforms and US intervention in the region. Today, Chinese researchers on Latin American affairs focus on projects that include: Latin American development prospects in the twenty-first century; economic reforms in Latin America; Latin

---

21   Shixue Jiang, 'Latin American Studies in China: An Overview', n.d. (a), *Revista Del Cexla*, 6, 3, http://www.cesla.uw.edu.pl/cesla/images/stories/wydawnictwo/czasopis ma/Revista/Revista_6/277-281_Debates.pdf, accessed 29 December 2013.

America's modernization path in the twentieth century; Mexico after the fall of the Institutional Revolutionary Party (PRI); development of science and technology in Latin America; social security reforms in Latin America; and, ethnic issues in Latin America.

The only research institute in China devoted to Latin American studies is the Institute of Latin American Studies under the Chinese Academy of Social Sciences. There is also a small group of researchers studying Latin America in the Division of the Americas at the Institute of Contemporary International Relations in Beijing. Scattered researchers can be found in this field in Beijing University, Fudan University (Shanghai), Nankai University (Tianjin) and Hubei University.[22] The Chinese authorities attempt to develop Macau as China's window to the Portuguese-speaking world, and a number of international forums have been held on this theme. But the academic resources in Macau are limited.

The development experience of Latin America is of some relevance to China today because of the following consideration. The academic community in China is concerned with the country entering into a complicated and challenging stage of development. In 2003, per capita GDP in China amounted to US$1,090. Chinese academics are aware of the historical experiences of many countries in the world that after reaching the level of US$1,000 per capita GDP, a number of phenomena had emerged including the deepening of social stratification, expansion of the middle-class and its influence, the rise and development of various lines of cultural thought, exacerbation of the widening gap between the rich and poor, etc. These phenomena in turn had led to political turmoil, sharpening of social contradictions, rising tension among ethnic groups, and so on. The lessons drawn are that in this stage of development, the risks of high disharmony in society would be considerable. Chinese academics are eager to learn from the experiences of various countries in dealing with such risks.[23]

They observe that since the 1970s, economic growth in a number of countries and regions including the 'four little dragons of Asia', Malaysia and Thailand further accelerated after their per capita GDP had surpassed the US$1,000 level. But in other countries such as Brazil, Argentina, Mexico, Indonesia and the Philippines, economic development stagnated after their per capita GDP had reached the US$1,000 mark. Argentina, for example, reached the significant mark in 1961,

---

22   Shixue Jiang, 'Latin American Studies in China: An Overview', n.d. (a): 1, http://www.cesla.uw.edu.pl/cesla/images/stories/wydawnictwo/czasopisma/Revista/Revista_6/277-281_Debates.pdf, accessed 29 December 2013.

23   Guoliang Xiao and Fumin Sui, 'Chuyu Shizilukou de Zhongguo Jingji – 2005 Nian Hongguan Tiaokong Zhengce Fenxi (Chinese Economy at the Crossroads – Policy Analysis of Macro-Economic Adjustments and Control in 2005)', in *Zhongguo Gonggong Zhengce Fenxi 2005 (Analysis of Public Policies of China 2005)*, eds. Governance in Asia Research Centre, City University of Hong Kong and Centre for Public Policy Study, Chinese Academy of Social Sciences (Hong Kong: City University of Hong Kong Press, 2005), 35–39.

but its per capita GDP growth rate was only around 1.9 per cent in the following four decades and more. The situations in Brazil and Mexico were similar. They too reached the significant level in the 1970s; but subsequent economic growth has remained low, with average annual rates of about 3 per cent. The Chinese scholars are especially concerned with the expanding gap between the rich and poor. They note that after reaching the per capita GDP level of US$1,000, the respective Gini co-efficients were between 0.35 and 0.45 in Brazil, Mexico and Argentina. Then the situation further worsened, and their Gini co-efficient rose to the range of 0.45 to 0.6. Today, the Gini co-efficient in China is approaching 0.47,[24] which obviously is a very dangerous level especially in view of its claim as a socialist country. Moreover, corruption is rampant in China. Chinese scholars are therefore concerned that China should not repeat the mistakes of Latin America.

In recent years, Latin America is seen to be important to China for a number of reasons.[25] In the first place, as a developing country, China finds it ideologically and politically necessary to stand alongside Latin America in the Third World's struggle for the establishment of a new international economic and political order. Further, in order to diversify China's export markets and sources of imports, China values the development of economic relations with Latin America. China is eager to secure access to the rich natural resources in Latin America to support its rapid economic growth. In the process of moving towards the next stage of economic development, China hopes to learn from the experiences of Latin America. Finally, the Taiwan issue remains conspicuous in China's approach to Latin America. In mid-2005, Taiwan maintains formal diplomatic relations with 26 countries, and 12 of them are in Central and South America.[26]

According to the Third World struggle perspective, Chinese researchers consider that in the process of globalization, developed countries, especially the US, and international financial institutions will be able to impose constraints on the economic policy-making of several Latin American countries, thus compromising their economic sovereignty. Speculative flows of international capital will exacerbate the risks of financial crises in the region. The rapidly expanding multinational corporations will likely prevail over the national industries of

---

24   Yan Gu and Yiyong Yang, 'Shouru Fenpei Lingyu de Xin Qingkuang, Xin Tedian jiqi Duice (New Trends in Income Distribution and Related Policy Recommendations)', in Ru Xin, Lu Xueyi, Li Peilin, et al. (eds), *Shehui Lanpishu – 2005 Nian: Zhongguo Shehui Xingshi Fenxi yu Yuce (Bluebook of China's Society – Year 2005: Analysis and Forecast on China's Social Development)* (Beijing: Social Sciences Academic Press, 2004), 222.

25   Shixue Jiang, 'Sino-Latin American Relations: Perspectives on the Past and Prospects for the Future', n.d. (b), http://www.cass.net.cn/chinese/s27_lms/ESPANA/TR ABAJOS/RELACIONES%20DIPLOMATICAS/perspective.htm, accessed 28 December 2013.

26   The 12 countries are Costa Rica, Guatemala, Paraguay, St Vincent and the Grenadines, Belize, El Salvador, Haiti, Nicaragua, Dominican Republic, Honduras, Panama, and Saint Christopher and Nevis. See Ministry of Foreign Affairs, Taiwan, http://www.mofa. gov.tw/webapp/ct?xItem=11624&ctNode=123, accessed 28 December 2013.

Latin American countries. Social problems in the continent will deteriorate, and its cultures will be 'Americanized'. There is a danger that Latin America will be further marginalized and pushed to the periphery in the globalization process. Latin American countries therefore have to strengthen their solidarity and co-operation in order to protect their autonomy, and secure a more equitable way of integrating into the international economic system.

Chinese leaders want to see a reduction of Latin America's dependence on the US. In this connection, they welcome Latin America's multilateral diplomacy and trade diversification. In the twenty-first century, the European Union has become the second largest trade partner of Latin America and its largest aid donor. Central American countries have been able to send over 90 per cent of their exports to the European Union tariff free. In March 2000, Mexico and the European Union concluded the first bilateral free-trade agreement between the two countries. They both hoped to secure market access to each other according to the conditions set for the members of the FTAA. In the beginning of the post-Cold War era, Russia had 'withdrawn' from Latin America; but since 1996, the Russian government has indicated its interest to develop Russian-Latin American relations.[27]

Latin American countries noted the impressive economic growth in the Asia-Pacific region, and the latter valued the Latin American market. In this context, Mexico, Chile and Peru joined APEC in 1993, 1994 and 1998 respectively, and Colombia and Panama have also expressed an interest to participate. In September 1999, 27 East Asian and Latin American countries held their first Senior Officials Meeting of the East Asia-Latin America Forum in Singapore. In March 2001, the first foreign ministers conference of the forum was held in Santiago, Chile.

Regarding Sino-Latin American relations, Chinese researchers are very fond of the following quotations of Deng Xiaoping stated in 1988: 'People are saying that the twenty-first century will be the Pacific era. ... I firmly believe that at that time there will also be a Latin American era, and I hope the Pacific era, the Atlantic era and the Latin American era will appear at the same time'. He then went on to say: 'China's policy is to develop and maintain good relations with Latin American countries, and make Sino-Latin American relations a model of South-South co-operation'.[28]

In Sino-Latin American relations, Chinese leaders tend to emphasize more on multilateral diplomacy and relations with regional organizations. Since the establishment of a political dialogue between China and the Rio Group in 1990, over

27 Mingde Li, 'Shiji Zhijiao de Lading Meizhou he Zhongla Guanxi Gaishu (A General Summary of Latin America and Sino-Latin American Relations at the Turn of the Century)', in Mingde Li (ed.), *Lading Meizhou he Zhongla Guanxi – Xianzai yu Weilai (Latin America and Sino-Latin American Relations – Present and Future)* (Beijing: Shishi Chubanshe, 2001), 13–15.

28 Shixue Jiang, 'Sino-Latin American Relations: Perspectives on the Past and Prospects for the Future', n.d. (b), 17.

ten meetings have been held at the foreign ministry-level. The Chinese propaganda machinery often praises the important role of the Rio Group and considers it to be an important force among developing countries, as well as a reliable partner of China in international affairs. In June 1994, China became the first Asian country to join the Latin American Integration Association as an observer. In May 1997, China was admitted into the Caribbean Development Bank; and earlier in September 1993, China successfully applied to join the Inter-American Development Bank. China recognizes the MERCOSUR as an important vehicle for promoting economic integration in Latin America, and it has held a number of official talks with this group after establishing a dialogue mechanism with it.

Party-to-party diplomacy constitutes an important aspect of Sino-Latin American relations. The CPC advocates the following four principles in its relations with political parties in various countries: autonomy, full equality, mutual respect and mutual non-interference. In the first place, the CPC pursues friendly ties not only with ruling parties, but also with opposition parties. Two examples often cited by China's researchers on Latin American affairs are interesting. In Argentina, before the presidential election in 1983, most people believed that the Radical Party did not have a good chance. But the CPC nonetheless invited the party's leader, Raul Alfonsin, to visit China. After winning the presidency, Raul Alfonsin sent an important delegation to visit China. Meanwhile, the CPC continued to maintain good relations with the Peronist Party, whose leader Carlos Saul Menem won the presidential election in May 1989. In November 1989, only five months after the Tiananmen Square Incident on 4 June, President Menem sent his brother, Senate President Eduardo Menem, to visit Beijing when the Western countries were sanctioning China.[29]

Party-to-party diplomacy has been particularly important to Latin American countries without formal diplomatic relations with China. Before the PRC established formal diplomatic relations with Bolivia and Uruguay, the CPC had already cultivated good relations with the political parties in the two countries. Today, the CPC has established relations with various political parties in a majority of the Latin American countries which have no diplomatic ties with China. For example it has good contacts with the major parties in Paraguay, the only South American country which recognizes Taiwan.

IV. Sino-Latin American Economic Relations

a) Trade

Before the 1990s, Sino-Latin American trade was insignificant. In October 1952, China and Chile signed a bilateral trade agreement, the first trade agreement

---

29   Shixue Jiang, 'Sino-Latin American Relations: Perspectives on the Past and Prospects for the Future', n.d. (b), 10–11.

between China and a Latin American country. In 1955, Sino-Latin American trade was about US$7 million, which grew to over US$30 million in 1960. In 1970 and 1978, it surpassed the US$100 million and US$1 billion marks respectively. This expansion in bilateral trade in the 1970s was a result of the establishment of diplomatic relations between China and the major Latin American countries in the decade following China's entry into the United Nations in 1971 and the Nixon visit to China in February 1972.[30] In the 1970s, the annual average trade between China and Latin America amounted to US$1.028 billion; in the following decade, the average annual trade reached US$1.73 billion, with an annual average growth rate of 2.2 per cent. The 1980s was a lost decade for the Latin American economy which suffered from heavy external debt and other problems.

In the 1990s, the Latin American economy improved and China's external trade expanded in an impressive manner. As a result, China's exports to Latin America rose 5.19 times in the decade. Before 1994, China had suffered a deficit in the bilateral trade; since the mid-1990s, China has been enjoying a trade surplus until 2002. In 1998 and 1999 when China's imports from Latin America stagnated because of the Asia-Pacific financial crisis, its exports continued to grow. In the 1990s, China still maintained a trade deficit with the resource-rich Latin American countries like Brazil, Argentina, Chile and Peru. Regarding Mexico, Colombia and Panama, it secured a trade surplus with those countries. Panama served as an entrepôt; a considerable portion of its imports from China was substantially re-exported to other Latin American countries.

In the early years of the twenty-first century, China's imports from Latin America increased substantially (see Tables 7.1 and 7.2). From 2000 to 2003, China's imports from Latin America increased 80.9 per cent, 23.9 per cent, 24.4 per cent and 80.3 per cent respectively; and Latin America's share of China's imports rose from 1.8 per cent in 1999 to 2.98 per cent in 2003. In 1999, the growth rate of China's heavy industries surpassed that of its light industries for the first time in its era of economic reforms and opening to the external world, indicating the beginning of China's second phase of expansion in heavy industries.[31] Investment has been flowing to heavy industries such as coal, automobile, iron and steel, petrochemicals, machinery, etc., paving the way for the above-average growth

---

30   China established diplomatic relations with Cuba in 1960, with Chile in 1970, with Peru in 1971, with Mexico, Argentina, Guyana and Jamaica in 1972, with Trinidad and Tobago, Venezuela, and Brazil in 1974, with Surinam in 1976, with Barbados in 1977, with Ecuador and Colombia in 1980, with Antigua and Barbuda in 1983, with Bolivia, Grenada and Nicaragua in 1985, with Belize in 1987, with Uruguay in 1988, and with the Bahamas and St Lucia in 1997. Grenada, Belize and Nicaragua subsequently switched to recognize Taiwan in 1989, 1989 and 1990 respectively.

31   In the 1950s, the PRC adopted a planned economy and accorded priority to the development of heavy industries. In 1979, China under Deng Xiaoping began its economic reforms. It moved towards a market economy and gave priority to an export-orientated development strategy depending on labour-intensive consumer industries.

rates in the heavy industrial sectors. It is expected that this trend will continue for at least ten years, following the precedents of Japan and South Korea in the previous century.

As China lacks the natural resources in support of its second phase of heavy industrialization, it will have to secure their supply through approaching new sources, and resource-rich Latin America will be able to export more to China in the foreseeable future. Iron and steel, soybeans and related products, iron ore, copper, timber, fish products, sugar, etc., are the major items of China's imports from Latin America. These items will continue to have a strong demand in the China market. It is interesting to note that in recent years, China's exports to Latin America have grown at a rate below that of the expansion of China's overall exports.

China's researchers on Latin America affairs are eager to reassure Latin American countries that China will not use the bilateral trade and its investment in the continent to make unreasonable political demands, engage in economic, cultural and social infiltration, or attempt to create relations of dependency.[32] The bilateral trade is based on comparative advantage; and China probably depends on Latin America more because of its resource needs. These researchers agree that China's imports will enhance Latin America's foreign exchange earnings and improve the terms of trade regarding their exports of primary products.

In view of multinational corporations' investment in Latin America and China in the past decade and more, some manufacturing industries in both regions have been involved in such multinational corporations' global production chain and division of labour markets. For example, Germany's Volkswagen has major investment projects in Brazil and China, and many models developed by the Volkswagen joint venture in China contain technical components developed by the Volkswagen subsidiary in Brazil, including the Santana 2000 model launched by the Volkswagen plant in Shanghai in the late 1990s and the Polo model marketed by the same plant in 2003. This trend of development was expected to become more significant if the proposed FTAA had materialized at the beginning of 2006.

The development of Sino-Latin American trade encounters serious obstacles too. There is no direct air link between China and any Latin American country; and the limited maritime routes are affected by long distance, weather and other factors so that delays are very common. Exchange of market information is difficult; and differences in languages, cultures and customs have handicapped mutual understanding. There is a lack of expertise on Latin America in China, and vice versa. Moreover, the graduate students in Latin American studies in China do not often pursue careers related to their disciplines after their graduation.

The exploitation of anti-dumping measures against Chinese exports by Latin American governments has been an issue of concern. In April 1993, Mexico decided to levy anti-dumping tariffs on ten categories of imports from China. This

---

32   Wenhui Zhu, 'Quanqiuhua xia Zhongguo yu Lamei Maoyi Guanxi de Xin Qushi (New Trends in Sino-Latin American Trade Relations in the Context of Globalization)', *Lading Meizhou Yanjiu (Chinese Academy of Social Sciences)*, 26 (3) (June 2004), 13–14.

precedent was soon followed by Argentina, Brazil, Chile, Colombia, Ecuador, Venezuela, etc. Such anti-dumping measures cover a wide range of Chinese products, and the tariffs levied are very high. In some instances, the exorbitant rates (1105 per cent on Chinese shoes by Mexico in one case) amount to imports bans. There is also a tendency by countries in the Latin American region to impose tariffs before actual investigations, thus violating international norms. It is only in recent years that China has secured the recognition of its market economy status from major Latin American countries including Brazil, Argentina, Chile, Peru, Venezuela, and Antigua and Barbuda; this recognition may reduce the potential impact of anti-dumping measures on cheap Chinese imports.[33]

b) The Projected Impact of the FTAA

In anticipation of the actual operation of the FTAA in 2006, Chinese experts in Latin American affairs expected that more than 30 states would be able to share the 'trade creation effect' in the US market, while China would suffer from a greater 'trade diversion effect' than in the launch of the North American Free Trade Arrangement (NAFTA).[34] These experts indicate that China had lost its share of textile and apparel imports by the US to Mexico in the 1990s after the implementation of the NAFTA. Moreover, the export structures and the export markets of many Latin American countries are very similar to those of China. Hence, keen competition has been inevitable. According to a report released by the Inter-American Development Bank in March 1998, Asian countries' products posed a threat to 58 per cent of Latin American countries' exports to Organisation of Economic Co-operation and Development (OECD) countries; and competition was most severe in the apparel and electronics industries. There is also a concern in China that US investors would lose some interest in the Asia-Pacific region, and trade diversion from the Asia-Pacific region to Latin America would be accompanied by investment diversion in the same direction as well. Economists in China were already detecting a slight tapering off of foreign investment into China in the first half of 2005, and projected that this trend could well continue for a few years because of a mild cooling off of the Chinese economy. They did not consider this a worrying trend though because China is no longer in urgent need of foreign investment, and the trend is expected to reverse soon in view of the basic strength of the Chinese economy.

---

33   Adam Thomson, 'Granting of Market-Economy Status to China Opens Argentina's Door to Investment', *Financial Times* (London) (18 November 2004); BBC Monitoring International Reports, 'Chinese Vice President's Visit Promote Ties with Latin America' (5 February 2005).

34   Zhimin Yang, 'Challenges of FTAA and China's Responses', n.d., http://www.cass. net.cn/chinese/s27_lms/ESPANA/TRABAJOS/ECONOMIA/FTAA.htm, p. 2–3, accessed 2 June 2013.

Chinese economists expect that China will continue to upgrade its export structure and concentrate more on high value-added and high-tech products, especially information technology products. In this way, China can reduce competition with the Latin American countries in the labour-intensive industrial sectors. But this probably is a very optimistic scenario. While China's coastal provinces will upgrade their exports, its interior provinces will be eager to follow the path of the coastal provinces and engage in the exports of labour-intensive products.

South Korea concluded a bilateral free trade agreement with Chile in April 2003. This may be an example for China. Chile, Brazil and other Latin American countries have expressed an interest in concluding bilateral free trade agreements with China; and China may attempt to negotiate similar arrangements with the MERCOSUR, the Andean community and the Caribbean community. Meanwhile, China has concluded a framework agreement with ASEAN to launch a China-ASEAN Free Trade Area initially involving the five original members of ASEAN in 2010, with the participation of the other five members in 2015. Economic integration in the Asia-Pacific region was perceived as a response to the challenge of the FTAA, because it would strengthen the bargaining power of the Asian countries concerned.

c) Investment and South-South Cooperation

China's investment in Latin America is still relatively insignificant apart from that in the Cayman Islands and the British Territories (see Tables 7.3 and 7.4), but the potential is not to be under-estimated.[35] In recent years, major Chinese state-owned enterprises (SOEs) have been investing in Latin American countries to ensure China's access to the continent's natural resources. The Shougang Group's acquisition of a major Peruvian iron mine company by tender in 1992 was a classic example. Shougang Group's subsidiary in Peru now produces more than five million tons of iron ore per annum which are exported to the United States, Japan, South Korea, Mexico, etc. The company claims that in the period 1993–2003, it paid taxes and levies to the Peruvian government amounting to US$126 million. In 1997, China National Petroleum Corporation secured by tender the exploitation rights of two oilfields in Venezuela which produced 31,400 barrels of oil per day at the end of 2001. In the beginning of 2003, China National Petroleum Corporation had invested US$660 million in the oilfields; and because of the increase in production and the rise in oil prices, the SOE expected to earn back the investment in the following year. This investment also led to a number of business and technological cooperation projects between China and Venezuela.[36]

---

35   Investment in the Cayman Islands and the British Territories by Chinese corporations is obviously meant for other purposes including money laundering.

36   Delin Guo, 'Zhongguo yu Weineiruila Nengyuan Hezuo de Qianli (The Potential for Energy Co-operation Between China and Venezuela)', *Lading Meizhou Yanjiu*, 25 (2), (April 2003), 26–30.

Table 7.3   China's investment in Latin American countries (on an actually realized basis), 2003 (in US$ million)

Country	2003
Cayman Islands	807
British Territories	210
Others	23
Total	1,040
Latin America as a % of China's total	36.5%

Source: Foreign Investment Administration, Ministry of Commerce of the People's Republic of China, '2003 *niandu Zhongguo Duiwai Zhijie Touzi Tongji Gongbao* (China's Outward Foreign Direct Investment Statistics 2003)' (17 May 2005). Retrieved from http://www.fdi. gov.cn/common/info.jsp?id= ABC00000000000020810, accessed 29 December 2013.

Table 7.4   China's accumulated investment in Latin American countries (on an actually realized basis) as of 2003 (in US$ million)

Country	as of 2003
Cayman Islands	3,691
Mexico	97
Peru	126
British Territories	533
Others	173
Total	4,620
Latin America as a % of China's total	13.9%

Source: Foreign Investment Administration, Ministry of Commerce of the People's Republic of China, '2003 *niandu Zhongguo Duiwai Zhijie Touzi Tongji Gongbao* (China's Outward Foreign Direct Investment Statistics 2003)' (17 May 2005). Retrieved from http://www.fdi. gov.cn/common/info.jsp?id= ABC00000000000020810, accessed 29 December 2013.

Technological cooperation between China and Latin America has also been highlighted by the Chinese mass media to show that Sino-Latin American relations can be a model of South-South cooperation. Embraer of Brazil is the fourth largest civil aircraft manufacturer in the world, and the second largest branch-route aircraft manufacturer. In 2000, it formed a joint venture with Harbin Aircraft Industry Group [now Harbin Aviation Industry (Group) Co., Ltd. after a merger] to assemble 50 of its ERJ-145 model. The first aircraft produced by the joint venture successfully conducted its test flight in December 2003. At the governmental level, China and Brazil have been cooperating in the development of satellites for surveying the earth's resources. Two satellites were successfully launched in October 1999 and at the end of 2003 respectively; agreement has also been reached on the launch of the third and fourth satellite.

China's SOEs have also been reaching out and engaging in overseas investment in recent years to develop foreign markets, including the setting up of wholesale, retail and after-sale service networks. It is anticipated that China's investment in Latin America will increase substantially in the agriculture, forestry and fishery sectors as well as in the traditional textile, apparel and household electrical appliances industries. The Chinese government will encourage major SOEs and private enterprises to enter into Latin America; at the same time, these enterprises will try to form joint ventures with local corporations. The Chinese authorities plan to assign a major SOE to mobilize investment in a specific Latin American country, and to generate linkage effects in the form of related projects. It is hoped that such investment activities will increase Sino-Latin American trade to US$80–100 billion within three to five years, about 6–8 per cent of the total trade of either side.[37] The establishment of a China-Latin American Association of Industry and Commerce has been suggested.

Chinese President Hu Jintao's Latin American visit in November 2004 involved many investment pledges in the region in the foreseeable future. In Brazil, Hu promised that China would invest US$100 billion in Latin America in the coming decade. In Argentina alone, China indicated that it would invest US$20 billion over the next ten years. The attraction of investment from China is further enhanced by the decline in net foreign investment flows to Latin America in recent years, from US$78 billion in 2000 to US$36 billion in 2003.[38]

The investment projects highlighted in the media during President Hu's trip to Latin America included: railway, oil exploration, and construction projects in Argentina; a nickel plant in Cuba; copper mining projects in Chile; and a steel mill, railway and oil exploration projects in Brazil. These Sino-Brazilian energy projects amounted to US$10 billion; Brazil's state-owned oil company, Petrobras, and the China National Offshore Oil Corporation reportedly are studying the feasibility of joint operations in exploration, refining, and pipeline construction around the world. China is exploring energy deals in Ecuador, Bolivia, Peru and Colombia, as well as offshore projects in Argentina too. In January 2005, Venezuelan President Hugo Chavez travelled to China to sign 19 cooperation agreements, including plans for Chinese investment in oil and gas exploration. Colombian President Alvara Uribe also visited China in April 2005 to promote increase in investment in his country.[39]

Latin American countries' investment in China has been limited in scale (see Tables 7.5 and 7.6), and the potential for significant expansion is not promising.

---

37   Latin American Research Group, China Institutes of Contemporary International Relations. 2004. 'Zhongguo dui Lading Meizhou Zhengce Yanjiu Baogao (Research Report on China's Policy towards Latin America)', *Xiandai Guoji Guanxi*, 4 (2004), 5 and 11.

38   Economic Commission for Latin America and the Caribbean, 'Foreign Investment in Latin America and the Caribbean' (May 2004), 13.

39   Kerry Dumbaugh and Mark P. Sullivan, 'China's Growing Interest in Latin America', Congressional Research Service Report for Congress (20 April 2005).

It is interesting that Panama, the Cayman Islands and, to a lesser extent, the British Virgin Islands, as well as the Bahamas, have often been used to provide camouflage for investment in China from Taiwan, Southeast Asia, and even enterprises in China.

Table 7.5   South American countries' investment in China (on an actually realized basis), 1991 and 2001–03 (in US$ million)

Country	1991	2001	2002	2003
Argentina	0.16	16.38	10.30	18.89
Bolivia	0.91	0.70	6.07	2.90
Brazil	0.34	3.90	15.36	16.71
Chile	0.05	1.33	11.89	8.01
Colombia	–	12.34	–	0.47
Ecuador	–	1.36	0.27	0.53
Guyana	–	0.69	–	–
Paraguay	–	1.17	1.07	0.60
Peru	–	0.27	1.12	0.90
Uruguay	–	–	–	–
Venezuela	–	5.00	2.03	1.28
Total	1.46	43.14	48.11	50.29
South America as a % of China's total	0.012	0.087	0.087	0.090

Source: State Statistical Bureau (comp.), *China Statistical Yearbook* (Beijing: China Statistics Press, 1993, 2003 and 2004), 1993, 2003 and 2004 issues.

Note: '–' represents that the figure is unknown, unavailable or negligible.

V. Competition with Taiwan

Taiwan maintains formal diplomatic relations with 11 countries in Central America and Paraguay in South America. In terms of trade, China has obviously become a much more significant partner, than Taiwan, to the Central American and Caribbean countries. In 2003, China's trade with the Central American and Caribbean countries amounted to US$9.019 billion (see Table 7.2); while Taiwan's trade with the same region only amounted to US$2.342 billion in 2004 (see Table 7.7). Both China and Taiwan maintain a healthy trade surplus in the bilateral trade; China's trade surplus in 2003 reached US$3.8 billion, while that of Taiwan amounted to US$1.087 billion. China's trade surplus predominantly comes from Mexico and Panama, though the latter re-exports much of its imports from China to other countries in the region.

Table 7.6   Central American and Caribbean countries' investment in China (on an actually realized basis), 1991 and 2001–03 (in US$ million)

	1991	2001	2002	2003
Bahamas	–	59.60	89.90	87.87
Cayman Islands	1.50	1,066.71	1,179.54	866.04
Dominica	–	0.78	0.38	–
Costa Rica	–	1.10	5.98	–
Cuba	–	0.19	–	14.07
Curacao	–	–	–	–
Dominica Republic	–	0.01	7.48	3.07
Guatemala	–	0.78	1.47	–
Haiti	–	–	–	–
Honduras	–	1.08	1.06	0.69
Jamaica	–	1.23	–	0.10
Mexico	–	1.82	7.31	5.55
Nicaragua	–	–	–	1.20
Panama	3.56	57.85	46.46	32.83
Puerto Rico	–	–	–	0.10
Saint Vincent and Grenadines	–	0.29	–	–
El Salvador	–	0.10	–	0.34
Surinam	–	–	–	2.43
Trinidad and Tobago	–	–	–	–
Other countries (regions) in Central America	–	0.60	2.78	6.10
Total	5.06	1,192.14	1,342.36	1,020.39
Central America as a % of China's total	0.04	2.54	2.55	1.91

Source: State Statistical Bureau (comp.), *China Statistical Yearbook* (Beijing: China Statistics Press, 1993, 2003 and 2004), 1993, 2003 and 2004 issues.

Note: '–' represents that the figure is unknown, unavailable or negligible.

Taiwan's major sources of its trade surplus are the same two countries.

Taiwan's investment in the Central American and Caribbean region has been much exaggerated by its investment in the British Territories, i.e., the Cayman Islands and the British Virgin Islands, and to a lesser extent Panama (see Tables 7.8 and 7.9). Basically such investment ultimately goes to China (see Table 7.6). While the relative weight of Taiwan's trade with and investment in the Central American and Caribbean region has been in relative decline, its investment in some of the small countries such as Dominica, Costa Rica, Honduras, Nicaragua, Panama and El Salvador still contribute considerably to Taiwan's diplomatic influence in these countries. The Democratic Progressive Party of Taiwan, while in opposition, severely criticized the Kuomintang government for wasting resources

Table 7.7 Taiwan's trade with Central American and Caribbean countries, 1991 and 2001–04 (in US $million)

Country	1991			2001			2002			2003			2004		
	Exports	Imports	Total	Total	Exports	Imports	Total	Exports	Imports	Total	Exports	Imports	Total	Exports	Imports
Bahamas	1.00	0.27	1.27	61.19	61.10	0.10	49.53	49.46	0.07	52.63	52.58	0.05	2.33	2.30	0.03
Dominica	0.41	–	0.42	2.14	2.06	0.08	1.28	1.17	0.11	1.26	1.23	0.03	1.54	1.51	0.04
Costa Rica	27.17	3.69	30.87	89.03	75.75	13.28	86.87	59.00	27.86	124.66	45.09	79.56	134.61	49.71	84.90
Cuba	0.29	1.06	1.35	19.62	18.94	0.69	20.27	18.06	2.21	24.73	19.57	5.16	17.12	13.49	3.64
Dominica Republic	52.14	0.11	52.25	78.26	77.15	1.11	84.91	83.58	1.33	59.10	56.75	2.35	78.44	67.24	11.20
Guatemala	50.24	1.09	51.33	100.59	79.07	21.51	86.88	81.29	5.58	92.10	90.94	1.16	114.75	110.67	4.08
Haiti	12.79	0.01	12.80	11.10	11.09	0.01	9.49	9.42	0.07	6.75	6.70	0.05	6.33	5.20	1.13
Honduras	15.55	0.17	15.72	51.99	50.96	1.04	52.49	51.86	0.64	38.00	37.14	0.86	38.13	33.22	4.91
Jamaica	10.62	0.04	10.66	16.11	15.95	0.16	16.37	16.10	0.27	14.43	14.07	0.35	17.81	16.34	1.47
Mexico	369.14	178.34	547.49	1,437.40	1,020.09	417.31	1,300.35	941.41	358.94	1,218.05	886.53	331.52	1,392.34	978.37	413.97
Nicaragua	1.31	1.73	3.04	49.34	48.60	0.74	43.41	42.98	0.43	39.94	39.28	0.67	43.99	41.26	2.73
Panama	359.52	14.03	373.56	128.18	123.96	4.21	132.17	127.35	4.81	127.17	121.16	6.01	269.36	246.73	22.63
Puerto Rico	61.85	30.70	92.56	73.94	52.37	21.57	87.27	53.35	33.92	105.35	53.10	52.25	122.10	50.37	71.73
Saint Vincent and Grenadines	0.94	–	0.94	5.53	4.88	0.66	1.46	1.14	0.32	0.25	0.25	–	0.38	0.38	–
El Salvador	18.09	0.08	18.17	67.09	65.93	1.16	69.59	60.54	9.05	76.89	74.57	2.32	61.60	58.72	2.88
Surinam	4.29	–	4.29	2.98	2.91	0.07	3.11	2.81	0.30	3.81	3.52	0.29	4.41	4.31	0.10
Trinidad and Tobago	18.73	4.70	23.43	25.09	24.79	0.30	26.06	25.59	0.47	29.84	29.12	0.72	37.09	34.88	2.21
Other countries (regions) in Central America	6.12	1.21	7.33	–	–	–	–	–	–	–	–	–	–	–	–
Total	1010.2	237.23	1247.48	2,219.58	1,735.6	484.00	2,071.51	1625.11	446.38	2,014.96	1531.60	483.35	2,342.33	1714.70	627.65
Central America as a % of Taiwan's total	1.33	0.38	0.90	0.97	1.41	0.45	0.85	1.24	0.40	0.74	1.06	0.38	0.69	0.99	0.37

Source: Bureau of Foreign Trade, Taiwan, 'Trade Statistics'. Retrieved from http://cus93.trade.gov.tw/english/FSCE/FSC0011E.ASP on June 8 2005.

Notes: 1. '–' represents that the figure is unavailable or less than US$5,000.

2. Figures on imports and exports may not add up to the totals due to rounding up.

in maintaining Taiwan's diplomatic relations with the small Central American and Caribbean countries. But the Chen Shui-bian administration has not cut back the efforts and financial resources spent on these countries since coming to power in 2000. In that year, Chen attended the inauguration ceremony of the President of the Dominican Republic and made state visits to Nicaragua and Costa Rica. Vice-President Annette Lu followed with a second delegation one month afterwards to El Salvador, Honduras, Belize and Guatemala. These state visits also offered opportunities for Taiwanese leaders to visit the US informally in transit.

Table 7.8   **Taiwan's approved outward investment in Latin American countries, 1991 and 2001–04 (in US$ million)**

Country	1991	2001	2002	2003	2004
Mexico	–[1]	–	6.61	1.00	2.90
Panama	–	5.65	66.68	169.09	55.57
British territories	267.87	1,693.37	1,575.08	1,997.25	1,155.20
Other countries (regions) in the Americas except the US and Canada	79.05	420.15	245.20	96.53	107.86
Total	346.92	2,119.17	3,895.577	4,266.877	3,325.533
Latin America as a % of Taiwan's total[2]	20.95	48.25	56.19	57.04	39.08

Sources: Investment Commission, Ministry of Economic Affairs, Taiwan, *Statistics on Overseas Chinese & Foreign Investment, Outward Investment, Mainland Investment, The Republic of China* (published annually) (December 2004); and Investment Commission, Ministry of Economic Affairs, Taiwan, *Monthly Statistics on Overseas Chinese & Foreign Investment, Outward Investment, Mainland Investment, The Republic of China* (published monthly) (May 2005). Since there are discrepancies between the statistics in the two reports, some figures have been adjusted by the author.
Notes: 1. '–' represents that the figure is unknown, unavailable or negligible.
2. Taiwan's total in this table excludes its foreign direct investment in Mainland China.

Table 7.9   **Taiwan's accumulated investment in Central American and Caribbean countries as of 2003 (in US$ million)**

Country	as of 2003
Dominica	97.4
Costa Rica	147.0
Guatemala	31.3
Haiti	13.0
Honduras	69.2
Mexico	107.8
Nicaragua	218.3

Panama	1,045.8
El Salvador	69.0
British territories	14,456.4
Total	16,255.2
Central America as a % of Taiwan's total*	10.5

Source: Retrieved from the website of the Industrial Development and Investment Centre, Ministry of Economic Affairs, Taiwan, http://twbusiness.nat.gov.tw/invest_5.htm, accessed 9 June, 2005.
* Taiwan's total in this table excludes its foreign direct investment in Mainland China.

In August 2003, Chen Shui-bian held a summit in Taipei with the presidents from seven Central American countries. A joint communiqué was released and a free trade agreement was concluded.[40] In the following November, Chen visited Panama and participated in the centennial celebrations of the founding of the country. Chen joined the presidents from 13 Latin American countries in signing a document in commemoration of the occasion. He was able to meet the then United States Secretary of State, Colin Powell, too.[41] There are not many international occasions in which Chen can assume the formal role of a head of state. Chen believed that the Panama visit had improved his image at home and constituted a part of his preparations for the presidential re-election campaign in March 2004.

Apparently Chen Shui-bian has no intention of changing Taiwan's pattern of relations with Central America and the Caribbean. In late September 2005, Chen visited Nicaragua to participate in a summit meeting with Taiwan's Central American allies. He announced an offer of US$250 million of aid to them under a 'co-prosperity' programme. While the opposition attacked the programme as 'spending big bucks to buy foreign relations', Chen defended that his programme would be an investment scheme to create a 'win-win' situation. Chen's trip highlighted a US$27 million 'Friendship Bridge' linking the Costa Rican city of Puntarenas with the Nicoya peninsula on the Pacific Ocean; and the Instituto Technologico de las Americas, a large cyber park-cum-technical college project in the Dominican Republic.[42]

Since 1993, the Taiwan government has begun actively promoting the membership of the Republic of China in the United Nations. This campaign encounters strong resistance from the PRC and the proposal has not even succeeded in going through the United Nations General Assembly's General Committee to be included in the United Nations agenda for discussion. Further, beginning in 1997, the Taiwan government has been trying to secure observer status in the World Health Organization. The Central American and Caribbean states maintaining

---

40   *Taiwan Shin Sheng Daily News* (Taipei) (22 August 2003).
41   *Taiwan Daily News* (Taipei) (4 November 2003).
42   *South China Morning Post* (Hong Kong) (24 September, 27 September and 2 October 2005).

diplomatic relations with Taiwan have been the key supporters for these efforts of Taiwan to expand its 'international space'. The Chinese leadership was acutely concerned with the Chen Shui-bian administration's design to seek independence for Taiwan, and it worked hard to 'contain' Taiwan's diplomatic efforts. Hence the Central American and Caribbean region remained a major battle ground for the diplomatic contest across the Taiwan Straits under the DPP government. However, after 2008, the contestation between Taiwan and the mainland became less hostile after Ma Ying-Jeou, the pro-mainland China KMT candidate, won the national elections in Tawan. It has been suggested that the PRC has been interested in diplomatic relations with the Vatican because the Chinese leadership believes that they will facilitate formal diplomatic relations between the PRC and the Catholic countries in the Central American and Caribbean region.

Taiwan has also been engaging in 'informal diplomacy' with Latin American countries that have formal diplomatic relations with China. One aspect of such an endeavour has been the establishment of parliamentary cooperation and exchanges. Taiwan succeeded in establishing parliamentary friendship associations with Argentina in 1997, Brazil and Peru in 1999 and Chile in 2000. Taiwan, under the name of the Republic of China, has observer status at the Central American Parliament and the Forum of the Presidents of the Legislative Powers of Central America. In February 2000, Taiwan, under the name of the Republic of China, became an official observer with the System for the Integration of Central America, the first observer from outside the western hemisphere. The International Co-operation and Development Fund (ICDF), the foreign aid organization of the Taiwan government under the guise of an independent foundation, has been active in Latin America, especially in the Central American and Caribbean region. It has established formal working relations with the Inter-American Development Bank and the Central American Bank for Reconstruction and Development. ICDF, for example, contributed to the relief and reconstruction programmes in the Central American and Caribbean region in the aftermath of Hurricane Mitch.

In addition, more than 20 Taiwanese private international charity organizations such as the Tzu Chi Foundation, World Vision Taiwan, the Taiwan Root Medical Peace Corps and the Chinese Fund for Children and Families have been providing humanitarian assistance directly to Africa, Latin America and Oceania. Another increasingly popular form of international assistance among Taiwanese people is individual sponsorship for poor children, and a number of private organizations are working in this area. Usually these humanitarian efforts are mainly directed to countries maintaining formal diplomatic ties with Taiwan.Besides trade, investment, and official and private assistance which are naturally attractive to poor micro states with small populations, the Taiwan government apparently has some 'secret weapons' too. In May and June 2004, there were reports in Taiwan and Costa Rica that from 1986 to May 2003, the foreign ministry of Costa Rica received US$22,000 per month from the Taiwan government for the salary of its officials. It was also reported that the daughter of the president, who was working in the Costa Rican embassy in Mexico, also received her monthly salary of US$1,500 from Taiwan.[43] Earlier in August 2003, newspapers in Taiwan quoting newspapers in Costa Rica reported that two Taiwan enterprises contributed US$500,000 to President Abel Pacheco de la Espriella for his presidential campaign in the previous year. In Costa Rica, accepting campaign contributions from foreign sources is a violation of the constitution.[44] Similarly, in Panama, Mireya Moscoso, president of the republic from 1999 to 2004, was accused of receiving US$1 million from Chen Shui-bian as a birthday present.[45]

In sum, Taiwan will continue to work hard to maintain diplomatic ties with the Latin American countries. Despite the declining relative weights of its trade and investment in the region, there are ample means through which Taiwan can exercise its diplomatic influence. Hence, the Taiwan issue will continue to be an important factor in China's approach to Latin America, but it has been less a source of friction under the government of President Ma Ying-jeou.[46]

VI. Conclusion

In view of China's economic growth and rising international status, Latin American countries will accord increasing priority to their relations with the Asian giant. China's permanent seat in the United Nations Security Council is also a factor to reckon with. Today, Brazil, Argentina, Venezuela and Mexico have established strategic partnerships with China. Many Latin American countries, including Chile, have also reached a consensus with China to develop long-term cooperation in the twenty-first century. China has signed agreements on economic and technological cooperation or economic cooperation with 16 Latin American countries, agreements on encouraging and protecting investment with 11 countries in the region, and agreements on avoiding double tax imposition with five other Latin American countries. It has also established joint commissions for scientific and technological cooperation with Brazil, Mexico, Chile, Argentina and Cuba respectively.[47] All these reflect the rapid development of Sino-Latin American relations since the early 1990s largely based on expanding trade.

---

43   *Oriental Daily News* (Hong Kong) (27 May 2004); *Renmin Ribao* (Beijing) (2 June 2004).

44   *United Daily News* (Taipei) (22 August 2003).

45   Gilda González and Pablo Guerén, 'Investigan en Nicaragua y Panamá Aportes de Taiwán, una vieja historia', *Al Día* (Panama City) (21 August 2003).

46   William Wan, 'Taiwan's President Ma Ying-jeou, plans to expand relations with China,' *The Washington Post* (24 October 2013), http://www.washingtonpost.com/world/taiwans-president-ma-ying-jeou-plans-to-expand-relations-with-china/2013/10/24/0e38bb7e-3cbd-11e3-b6a9-da62c264f40e_story.html, accessed 29 December 2013.

47   Mingde Zhang, 'Sino-Latin American Rhythm', *Beijing Review*, 47, 48, 2 (December 2004), 12–13.

As indicated above, the potential for further development of trade, investment and joint ventures across the Pacific will provide a solid foundation for closer Sino-Latin American relations in the years ahead. There is a view that China's approach to Latin America is similar to Japan's 'resources diplomacy' in the years after the Yom Kippur War in 1973. But while the expansion in Sino-Latin American trade and investment activities does reflect 'resources diplomacy' considerations, Chinese leaders tend to consider that China's developing ties with Latin America demonstrate a global reach corresponding to the improvements in China's economic strength and international status. In September 2004, China sent a 'special police' peacekeeping contingent to Haiti (which maintains full diplomatic relations with Taiwan), marking Beijing's first deployment of forces ever in the western hemisphere.

The vast distance between China and Latin America generates difficulties in transportation and mutual understanding, but it also means that both parties have no serious conflicts of interest. Their Third World orientations in diplomacy contribute to an impressive 95 per cent concurrence in their votes in the United Nations.[48] These broad agreements are expected to be maintained in WTO, APEC, etc. As China is prepared to assume a more active role in Third World issues in co-operation with the leading Third World countries, there will be more diplomatic co-ordination between China and the major Latin American countries, though progress will be slow.

While the Chinese leadership wants to promote multipolarity to curb US unilateralism, it appreciates the limitations in Latin America. Actually, both China and the Latin American countries value good relations with the US, and they want to avoid any sharp deterioration in their relations with the US. Beijing understands that it should avoid forcing Latin American countries to choose between China and the US. Similarly, Chinese leaders realize that Latin America has no strategic interests in the Asia-Pacific region, and they therefore are more tolerant of the formal and informal ties between the Latin American countries and Taiwan.

In the foreseeable future, China will increase its investment in Latin America and more Sino-Latin American business joint ventures will be formed. These trends, hopefully, will reduce trade frictions such as anti-dumping measures. Distance and language barriers will continue to handicap the development of tourism, and educational and cultural exchanges. In recent years, Beijing has designated many Latin American countries as official tourism destinations for Chinese citizens; but in the near future, few Chinese citizens will be able to exploit the opportunity.

Both China and the Latin American countries hope to see increasing prosperity on the other side of the Pacific because this will mean more trade and rising demand for each other's products. There will be more participation from Latin American countries in APEC, while China will be eager to expand its multilateral diplomatic

---

48   Latin American Research Group, China Institutes of Contemporary International Relations. 2004. 'Zhongguo dui Lading Meizhou Zhengce Yanjiu Baogao (Research Report on China's Policy towards Latin America)', *Xiandai Guoji Guanxi*, 4 (2004), 5.

work in various Latin American regional organizations. Like China, major Latin American countries such as Brazil have both advanced and backward sectors in their economies, hence the scope for cooperation is broader and relations can be more balanced. A model South-South relationship can thus be achieved. It has to be recognized, however, that Sino-Latin American relations remain shallow; and the limited interactions help to maintain idealistic mutual expectations.

Postscript

The Chinese economy is about to become the second largest in the world; China exports more than any other country and is the number two trader in the global economy. Beijing held the Olympics in 2008 and Shanghai the Expo in 2010. Chinese leaders, however, do not use the term 'Beijing consensus',[49] and they certainly do not discuss its competition with the 'Washington consensus'.[50] But Chinese leaders reject the liberal democratic model advocated by the United States and the Western world as the only ideal model; and the Chinese experience of achieving impressive economic growth and social stability in the absence of democracy is perceived as an alternative to the 'Washington consensus' by many Third World countries.

In this context, Latin America has become a more important trade partner of China and destination of its investment outflow. As China's trade expands, it seeks new trade partners and their relative weights also rise. China's entry into the heavy industrialization stage means that its consumption of energy and raw materials rises substantially. Finally, in view of the decline of the Western economies especially since the financial crisis breaking out in the autumn of 2008, China's dependence on their markets has been in decline. These trends enhance the significance of China's Latin American economic crisis.

At the time of the Seventeenth Party Congress in 2007, the Chinese leadership appeared to have developed a comprehensive foreign policy framework with a harmonious world perspective as its central idea.[51] This perspective in turn is based on two important concepts: a new security concept and the democratization of international relations. Chinese leadership continue to work to maintain a peaceful international environment to allow China to concentrate on its modernization. In view of China's impressive economic growth and rising

---

49   Joshua Cooper Ramo, *The Beijing Consensus* (London: The Foreign Policy Centre, 2004), 11–13.

50   John Williamson, 'What Washington means by policy reform', in John Williamson (ed.), *Latin American Adjustment: How Much Has Happened?* (Washington, DC: Institute for International Economics, 1990), 8–19.

51   See Joseph Y.S. Cheng 'China's Foreign Policy after the Seventeenth Party Congress', in Dennis Hickey and Baogang Guo (eds), *Dancing with the Dragon – China's Emergence in the Developing World* (Lanham, Maryland: Lexington Books, 2010), 23–52.

international status, avoiding conflicts with the US and other major powers has become more challenging.

A harmonious world perspective accepts that power politics continues to exist and the democratization of international relations as yet to be realized; but dialogue, exchanges and harmonious co-existence have become the mainstream in international relations, and mutual aspect and equality among states have emerged as the consensus of the international community. These ideas are obviously influenced by constructivism. The Chinese leadership recognizes that most Third World countries adopt systems different from those of the Western world, and they would like to exert pressure on the Western countries to secure their respect for diversity and pluralism. These objectives naturally are in line with China's vital national interests.

Since China has neither territorial disputes nor serious conflicts of interest with Latin American countries, it considers that securing the latter's support in international organizations is an important foreign policy objective. In recent years, the BRICS group is perceived by Beijing as a significant vehicle to articulate Third World interests *via-a-vis* those of the developed countries in international institutions like G-20 and global climate change negotiations. These trends imply that there has emerged considerable potential for China-Latin American diplomatic cooperation. Indeed, in June 2013, China's President Xi Jinping heralded his first trip to Mexico as the dawn of a new 'golden era' for Latin America and he urged the entire region to 'hitch its economic development to China's solid growth'.[52]

---

52   'Xi Jinping heralds new "golden era" for Latin America', *South China Morning Post* (7 June 2013), http://www.scmp.com/news/china/article/1255128/xi-jinping-heralds-new-golden-era-latin-america, accessed 29 December 2013.

Chapter 8

Assessing the Developmental Potential of the FTAA and EPA for Small Developing States

Patsy Lewis

Introduction

Between 1998 and 2008, the states of the Caribbean Community (CARICOM) were involved in two major trade negotiations aimed at significantly altering their trade relations with major partners, the United States and the European Union (EU). Between 1998 and 2004 they were involved in negotiating a hemispheric free trade area, the Free Trade Area of the Americas (FTAA) with all the countries of the Americas with the exception of Cuba. The negotiations, which were to have been completed in January 2005, ended prematurely in 2004 when negotiations were suspended. Before these negotiations were over they were involved in negotiations with the European Commission (EC) for a successor agreement to the trade elements of the Cotonou Partnership Agreement (CPA). These negotiations took place in two phases. Phase I, which involved all the states of the Africa Pacific and Caribbean group (ACP) and the EC, occurred between 2002 and 2003; Phase II, which followed, was conducted with the EC and so-called regional groups and was to have concluded in 2008. CARICOM and the Dominican Republic (CARIFORUM) represented one group. Their negotiations began in 2005 and ended in 2007, with the provisional application of the agreement in January 2008.

There is an obvious case for taking a comparative approach to the Free Trade Area of the Americas (FTAA) and the CARIFORUM-EC Economic Partnership Agreement (EPA) despite the fact that the FTAA did not materialize. Both arrangements, which were premised on reciprocal trade among diverse groups of countries, hold lessons for Caribbean small states. Both sought to bring together large developed countries with a diverse mix of developing countries. The FTAA, for example, included two large developed countries – Canada and the US – large developing countries – Mexico and Brazil – alongside small, resource-poor, vulnerable states – the members of the Organization of Eastern Caribbean

States (OECS)[1] – and least developed or severely underdeveloped states – Haiti and Nicaragua. The EU represents a formidable group of wealthy European states with already deeply integrated economies, seeking reciprocal FTAs with various groupings of developing countries, including some of the world's poorest. In the Caribbean context, the EU negotiated a free trade arrangement with CARIFORUM (CARICOM[2] and the Dominican Republic), a group with some of the world's smallest and most vulnerable states, and, in the case of Haiti, a least developed state.

The EU's interest in trade agreements was not limited to its counterparts in the Africa Caribbean Pacific (ACP) group, but extended to various types of trading arrangements with countries in Latin America and the Caribbean (LAC), notably MERCOSUR. The proposed EPAs and the FTAA represented an added complexity to an already complex set of regional arrangements that existed in the LAC[3] region. In the Caribbean, these include the Caribbean Community and Common Market (CARICOM), the Caribbean Forum (CARIFORUM) group (CARICOM and the Dominican Republic), and the OECS. In the Central and South American regions, these include the Central American Common Market (CACM), the Andean Community and MERCOSUR. There was differentiation among member states within these schemes, to minimize asymmetries as in the identification of lesser developed countries (LDCs) in both CARICOM and the CACM. There was also a further complex set of trading arrangements of different levels of openness and reciprocity among groupings, between groupings and individual states, and between individual states. These included the US-Central American/Dominican Republic Free Trade Area, the CARICOM-DR FTA, a slew of bi-lateral investment treaties, and a range of partial scope trading arrangements. In addition, both the US and Canada offered one-way preferential market access to a number of LAC countries under the CARIBCAN, and CBI and CBERA initiatives, respectively. Before the EPA came into effect in January 2008 the EU offered preferential access to its markets under the Cotonou Partnership Agreement (CPA). These preferential arrangements were expected to be supplanted by Economic Partnership Agreements (EPAs) between the EU and other ACP groups. The FTAA was expected to replace existing preferential arrangements in place, while the EPA replaced the trade protocols under the CPA. The EC continued

---

1   The OECS forms a sub-group within CARICOM that groups the smallest and most vulnerable countries and which have been designated as least developed within the group. The countries within that group are Grenada, St Lucia, Dominica, Antigua and Barbuda, Montserrat, St Kitts/Nevis and St Vincent. Belize, although also classified as least developed, is not a member of this group.

2   CARICOM members are Trinidad and Tobago, Jamaica, Guyana, Belize, Haiti, Barbados, Suriname, the Bahamas and members of the OECS.

3   I use the term LAC with some degree of reservation as it can easily obscure the real differences that exist between the two groups of countries which it subsumes.

to offer grants under the CPA, although this was to end in 2020 and a successor agreement negotiated.

Despite the market access objectives of the FTAA and EPA, they were promoted as the route for developing states to achieve development. This paper assesses the treatment of development in both processes against the backdrop of debates in development, regionalism and multilateralism.

Development and Trade

Before assessing the extent to which both processes took account of development concerns, it is necessary to engage in a discussion of the meaning of development as, despite the frequent references to 'development' in the framework of the FTAA and EPA, as well as the WTO, the concept is strongly contested and it is not always clear that the term holds the same meaning for all. Development as a concept became important in the post-independence period when developing countries were contemplating ways of 'catching up' to developed countries. Development was closely associated with modernization and was viewed as a linear process which was universally applicable despite historical specificities. W.W. Rostow's stages approach which saw countries moving from primary production to industrialization best represents this.[4] As Escobar in his critique notes, this meant replicating such features as 'high levels of industrialization and urbanization, technicalization of agriculture, rapid growth of material production and living standards, and the widespread adoption of modern education and cultural values'.[5] McMichael argues that embedded in the concept were two approaches: in philosophical terms it was viewed as the improvement of humankind; and in practical terms it was viewed by political elites as the 'social engineering of emerging national societies' and the use of government policy to manage the more disruptive social effects of the strategy.[6] Development initiatives in newly independent countries took the form of large state-managed infrastructure, the establishment of education projects (schools) and other institutions to support the development project, financed and managed with the help of Western European countries and international institutions such as the United Nations (UN), the International Monetary Fund (IMF) and the World Bank (WB).[7]

There are different approaches to development, ranging from the currently dominant neo-liberal trade approach, which advocates free trade and economic

---

4   W.W. Rostow (1950; 1961).

5   Arturo Escobar, *Encountering Development: The Making and Unmaking of the Third World* (New Jersey: Princeton University Press, 1995), 4.

6   Philip McMichael, *Development and Social Change: A Global Perspective*, 3rd ed. (London; New Delhi: Pine Forge Press, 2004), 2.

7   Arturo Escobar, *Encountering Development: The Making and Unmaking of the Third World*; Philip McMichael, *Development and Social Change: A Global Perspective*.

openness as the route to prosperity, to Marxist and dependency approaches, popular in the early post-independent period, that sought the cause of underdevelopment in the unequal economic and political relations that exist between developed and developing countries. Despite important differences, however, these were all grounded in modernization theory with progress towards a 'better' way of life, measured by economic growth, at the centre. Despite modification by the UN to take account of social indicators, such as education, health, access to water, inter alia, the central approach remains the same. Differences are evident, however, in the approach adopted toward increasing growth. For neo-liberal economists, economic openness, reflected in the free access to markets, allowing countries to specialize on the basis of comparative (later competitive) advantage, was the key determinant of economic growth and, hence, success. In contrast to the neo-liberal prescription of open trade as a facilitator of development, the practice in many underdeveloped countries was for fairly high degrees of protection of infant industries and agriculture from more competitive firms in developed countries which had gained from protection.[8] This found expression in GATT Articles XVIII, XVI, XXVIII *bis*, Part IV, and the Framework Agreement on Differential and More Favourable Treatment: Reciprocity and Fuller Participation of Developing Countries. Although inspired by dependency theory, this approach was also seen to mimic the behaviour of developed countries in the early stages of their drive for industrialization. Poverty reduction is also a major concern of developmentalists of whatever persuasion, with an assumed relationship between growth and poverty.[9]

The Development paradigm has been criticized on a number of bases. These include the assumption that societies follow a natural progression from economic backwardness to progress, which ultimately leads to improved standards of living: thus, people in pre-industrialized societies were worse off than they are at present; closely associated with this assumption is the measure of poverty as reflected in the accumulation of goods.[10] Criticisms also surround the negative impact of large-scale modernization projects on the human, social and cultural fabric that knits societies together. This occurs because inherent in the modernization framework is the imposition of developmental paths pursued in seemingly successful Western

---

8   See Erick Reinert, *How Rich Countries Got Rich and Why Poor Countries Stay Poor* (New York: Public Affairs, 2007).

9   Bourguignon, the WB's chief economist, makes a clear connection between the integration of developing countries into the global economy and poverty reduction. See Global Economic Prospects, 2005: 8. WTO Director General, Pascal Lamy, in a speech to UNCTAD, projected trade as 'an engine of GDP growth and development'. See Pascal Lamy, 'Trade is a "fundamental tool" in fight against poverty', October 2005. http://www.wto.org/english/news_e/sppl-espp105_e.htm.

10   Marshall Sahlins draws on research on hunters/gatherers in pre-industrialized societies to challenge this perception of development. An abridged version of the article 'The Original Affluent Society', published in the journal, *Development: Seeds of Change* (1986), appears in Magid Mahena (ed.) with Victoria Bawtree, *The Post-Development Reader* (London: Zed Books, 2003).

economies. This is accompanied by the cultural and ideological penetration of the 'foreign' expert who brings the knowledge, practices and institutions considered necessary to facilitate this kind of progress. As Norberg-Hodge[11] and Zaoual[12] found, this can have deleterious effects on local cultures.

Concerns for its effect on the environment reflected in wildlife extinction from activities such as large-scale farming, logging, mining, damming, soil degradation from the intensive application of pesticides and herbicides, inter alia, have led to an increased awareness of the consequences of such strategies to the environment, expressed in the sustainable development approach.[13] Escobar presents a particularly damning indictment of the 'discourse and strategy of development', arguing that it produced its opposite: 'massive underdevelopment and impoverishment, untold exploitation and oppression'.[14] A greater appreciation of the negative effects of development strategies on the environment has led to attempts to make the approach more sensitive to environmental concerns, represented in the concept of 'sustainable development' which was introduced by the Bruntland report,[15] at the heart of which was a recognition of the limits of natural resources and the implications of their exhaustion for future generations.

McMichael identifies two broad approaches to development, globalization and sustainable development, which, he argues are now the two major currents of development.[16] Globalization represented a shift from modernization's focus on national development to a global process, based on the pursuit of economic growth and market openness, which made globalization and development synonymous concepts.[17] Sustainable development, in turn, was the response of 'marginalized communities' to globalization, particularly its homogenizing effects and devaluation of human experience and culture. Thus, while globalization

---

11   Helena Norberg-Hodge's insights derive from a study of the Ladakh people of the Himalayas published as *Ancient Futures: Learning from Ladakh* (San Francisco: The Sierra Club, 1991).

12   Hassan Zaoual critiques of the culture of development which accompanies the development effort, by presenting alternatives cultures in his study of the Mahgreb, Moroccan and African. An excerpt of his the article, 'The Economy and Symbolic Sites of Africa', published in the Winter issue of the journal *Interculture*, in 1994, is reproduced in Magid Mahena (ed.) with Victoria Bawtree, *The Post-Development Reader*, 30–39.

13   The term was introduced by the Bruntland report which recognized the limits of natural resources and the implications of their exhaustion for future generations. See World Commission on Environment and Development, 1987.

14   Arturo Escobar, *Encountering Development: The Making and Unmaking of the Third World* (New Jersey: Princeton University Press, 1995), 4.

15   World Commission on Environment and Development (1987).

16   Philip McMichael, *Development and Social Change: A Global Perspective*, 3rd ed. (London; New Delhi: Pine Forge Press, 2004), xxx. This does not take account of the degrowth movement which has at its centre the rejection of growth as a necessary element of development.

17   Philip McMichael, *Development and Social Change: A Global Perspective*, xxix.

sought 'to advocate a thoroughly global market to expand trade, under the aegis of powerful corporations, and spread the wealth', sustainable development strove 'to reevaluate the economic emphasis and growing global inequalities and to recover democratic and sustainable communities, at whatever scale necessary to sustain social life'.[18]

Multilateralism and Regionalism as Tools of Development

Arguably, globalization has become the dominant development paradigm. It has been defined and promulgated by international institutions and Western industrialized countries. McMichael notes the World Bank's redefinition of development from 'nationally managed growth' (used in the 1980s) to 'participation in the world market',[19] which is also at the foundation of regional initiatives such as the FTAA and EPAs. The tenets of the globalization model, captured in the prescriptions of international financial institutions such as the IMF and WB, referred to as the Washington Consensus, were liberalization of trade, reform of the state sector and its relegation to the margins of economic life in favour of a strengthened private sector, and a significant reduction in government bureaucracy. These have driven the globalization process in developing countries since the late 1970s.

Despite McMichael's assessment of sustainable development as a counter strategy to globalization, the language of sustainable development has been co-opted by international developmental institutions and neo-liberal economic processes such as the World Trade Organization (WTO), FTAA and EPAs, and seems to fit well within this paradigm. For instance, the EC and ACP agreed that the EPAs' objectives were to integrate the ACP into the global economy, address their sustainable development and poverty eradication. There is an assumption that the three goals are compatible, although the evidence of growing inequality within and among countries suggests otherwise.[20] This language is also replicated in the SOA's reference to 'free trade and increased economic integration' as 'key factors for sustainable development' (Miami Action Plan).

The globalization project, namely its liberalization prescription, has also been met with resistance at the intellectual, political and social levels. It has been criticized on very much the same grounds as the national model. These include its homogenizing intent; its privileging of Western European experience; its perpetuation of asymmetries because of its failure to take account of the real

---

18   Philip McMichael, *Development and Social Change: A Global Perspective*, xxxviii.

19   Philip McMichael, *Development and Social Change: A Global Perspective*, 116.

20   Winters et al. (2002), despite a conviction that trade liberalization was likely to reduce poverty, accept that there is no conclusive empirical evidence that this was the case.

differences that exist among countries and its embrace of regulations that favour developed countries; and its negative social implications, inter alia.[21]

In Neo-classical economic thought trade liberalization promotes competitiveness and the efficient allocation of resources among countries. Development is considered a natural outcome as all stand to benefit from expected efficiency and productivity gains which promote economic growth and employment. Liberalization, which is pursued at the multilateral level through the WTO, is central to globalization. Although unilateral liberalization by countries is considered the most desirable way to achieve liberalization, given the likely political impediments to this approach, multilateralism is perceived as the more realistic. Thus, in the multilateral context issues in development revolve around, as ECLAC has summarized it, the 'beneficial integration of developing countries into a hierarchical world economy with asymmetric risks and opportunities and, ... the features the system must have in order to ensure that liberalization and trade openness contribute to growth and development'.[22] The inclusion of SDT measures in the WTO was an attempt to recognize these challenges, but these have been limited by the focus on implementation issues, addressed largely by extended time frames and, in some cases, lower tariff reductions allowed developing, but more specifically Least Developed Countries (LDCs), and 'voluntary' and 'non-binding' commitments for developed country assistance which, ECLAC notes, have 'detracted from the effectiveness of the concept'.[23]

Challenges to liberalization as development have been directed primarily at the WTO as a result of the difficulties that developing countries have experienced in implementing WTO obligations. The development assumptions of trade liberalization have come under criticism, not least from the United Nations which argued in a 2005 report that economic growth has aggravated inequality both between and within countries, resulting in increasing levels of poverty, leaving the world more unequal than it was 10 years before.[24] The stalemate in advancing multilateral liberalization, despite the commitment of the Doha Declaration for the conclusion of a 'development round' that would take account of the concerns of developing countries, reflected in the breakdown of global talks, has reduced the legitimacy of the whole process. The global financial crisis and the prolonged recession to which it has subjected most of the world's economies, has also undermined the credibility of the liberalizing agenda.

---

21   See Mander and Goldsmith, 1996; Benn and Hall, 2000; Thomas, c. 2004; Hirst and Thompson, 1996, 1999; Rosenberg, 2000.

22   ECLAC (2004), 156.

23   ECLAC (2004), 156.

24   United Nations Press Release, 'United Nations 2005 Report on World Social Situation Finds Much of World Trapped in "Inequality Predicament": World More Unequal than 10 Years Ago' (New York: UN Department of Public Information, News Media Division, 25 August 2005), SOC/4681.

Regionalism

Regionalism, which is used loosely to refer to FTAs, is the other main avenue for promoting trade liberalization and is only nominally related to regions. The WTO notes over 400 of these of increasing complexity, marking a significant proliferation since the 1990s. These now include FTAs between developing and developed countries and between regional groups. The FTAA was an example of the first, the CARIFORUM-EC EPA an example of the second. Thus the FTAA and EPA were part of a much broader process driven primarily, though not exclusively, by developed countries.[25]

A common feature of these arrangements is the element of coercion that underlines the participation of many developing states.[26] Coercion is used loosely to refer to the limited choice most developing countries have in entering these arrangements. This does not preclude the interest some developing countries, such as South Africa and Costa Rica, have in pursuing FTAs with developed countries because of the greater market access these provide.[27] Nevertheless, it is still credible to suggest that the forms of these arrangements are guided largely by the interest of the developed 'partners', which have the option of unilaterally withdrawing preferential arrangements they have on offer. The choices available to developing countries that entered such arrangements were, in both the FTAA and EPA instances, either to participate in the reciprocal trading arrangements being negotiated or settle for a Generalized System of Preferences (GSP), which

---

25   For example, the EU has an FTA with South Africa, Chile and Mexico and is negotiating similar RTAs with the Andean group, Central America and, eventually, MERCOSUR. The process is also evident in Africa, where both the US and EU have positioned themselves to penetrate African markets. The US's African Growth and Opportunity Act (AGOA) and the EU's Everything But Arms (EBA) initiative are part of this process. Further, the EU is also negotiating EPAs with various African regional groups to replace the Cotonou agreement.

26   McMichael (2004) views coercion as also being at the heart of the role that global institutions play in ensuring compliance from developing states in accepting neoclassical economic theory. He argues that 'Coercion is necessary when liberalization is questioned or resisted' (p. 165).

27   Gaviria, OAS Director, has a different perspective. He views the FTAA as a natural offshoot of Latin American integration strategies. 'Integration and interdependence in the Americas', in José Manuel Salazar-Xirinachs and Maryse Robert (eds), *Toward Free Trade in the Americas*, Chapter 15, 310 (Washington, DC: Brookings Institution Press and the OAS, 2001). Salazar-Xirinachs also shares this perspective. He argues that 'Latin American and Caribbean (LAC) countries are interested in the Free Trade Area of the Americas (FTAA) and other free trade agreements (FTAs) because they see in it the promise of obtaining major benefits in terms of growth, development and poverty reduction'. José M. Salazar-Xirinachs, 'The FTAA and Development Strategies'.

may or may not be enhanced beyond what existed.[28] Moreover, the agenda for negotiations was determined largely by developed countries, usually based on deeper market access than was possible at the multilateral level. Regionalism, therefore, presented a means of gaining greater concessions in regional markets without the necessity to make greater concessions at the multilateral level[29] and for introducing Singapore issues currently stalled at the multilateral level. Thus, regional FTAs were a means of advancing trade liberalization at the regional level beyond what was possible at the multilateral level. This has been the main focus of theorists of international trade who tend to focus on the relations between multilateral and regional trade liberalization and to question whether the two are compatible or whether regional trade liberalization actually undermines multilateral liberalization.[30]

Another observation to be made about regional trade arrangements is that they are seldom isolated from broader political or geo-strategic goals. These include: greater control of markets by developed countries in enhancing their competitiveness vis-à-vis one another (US vs. EU); locking in gains in trade liberalization even if national politics throw up a leader who is not sanguine towards trade liberalization; and locking in 'democratic' reforms. This is reflected in the EU's insistence on the inclusion of political conditionality in the CPA, masked under terms of 'good governance' and 'democracy', which they would wish to see strengthened in EPAs. For the US, the FTAA can be viewed as part of a broader strategy for managing its relations with the region, embodied in the Summit of the Americas process.

Such arrangements hold possibilities and challenges for developing countries as they are expected to advance liberalization beyond what is feasible at the multilateral level. Thus, the WTO provides the framework for regional trading arrangements, constraining the extent to which FTAs can advance developmental goals (read concessions and exceptions). This presents some challenges to the extent that such arrangements further limit the flexibilities available within the WTO framework and undermine the legitimacy of initiatives to increase the flexibility with which developing states are treated. The specific developmental concerns in respect of the WTO which may be undermined are: extending SDT

---

28   For a discussion on the GSP as an alternative to EPAs, see Christopher Stevens, 'The GSP a Solution to the Problem of Cotonou and EPAs', *Trade Negotiations Insights*, 4 (4) (July–August, 2005), 4–5.

29   The US's reluctance to negotiate further liberalization of its agriculture within the FTAA forum, outside of the WTO, reflects this.

30   World Bank, 2005. *Global Economic Prospects*; see Alan L. Winters, 1996, 'Regionalism and Multilateralism', World Bank, International Economics Department, International Trade Division. Policy Research Working Paper 1687. http://www.unige.ch/ses/ecopo/demelo/Cdrom/RIA/Readings/Winters96.pdf; J.A. Frankel, *Regional Trading Blocs*, Institute for International Economics, Washington, DC, 1996; J.N. Bhagwati, *The World Trading System at Risk* (Harvester Wheatsheaf, Hemel, Hempstead, 1991).

measures, notably, transitional periods, and strengthening SDT commitments, especially technical and financial assistance; keeping Singapore issues off the WTO agenda, or at least stalling their progression; and advancing demands for 'policy space', a concept that recognizes the right of exceptions for developing countries on the basis of their need to promote their development as they see fit. Policy space can also be viewed more expansively to include the rolling back of commitments already undertaken. In the Cancún Ministerial, developing countries achieved some success in pursuing some of these goals, notably the removal of all Singapore issues, except for trade facilitation, from the Doha Round agenda and greater flexibility in their obligations under TRIPS to address health epidemics. They were less successful in securing enhanced policy space, including the roll-back of some of their commitments, especially under Trade Related Investment Measures (TRIMS).

For CARICOM states, the outcome of the Committee of Trade and Development's dedicated sessions to consider the more favourable integration of small and vulnerable economies into the multilateral trading system was of particular interest. This review was provided for in the Doha Declaration and was being advanced in discussions of the Negotiating Group on Rules, which included reviewing GATTS Article XXIV, especially clarifying terms such as 'substantially all trade' and 'transition' times. Thus, negotiating RTAs in advance of a successful outcome of WTO negotiations which might very well allow developing countries to roll back some of the commitments they have already made, in recognition of their weaker capacity and greater need for policy space to pursue development goals, could be undermined in FTAs which use current obligations as the means for insisting on WTO plus measures.

On the other hand RTAs offer developing countries the opportunity to pursue their particular interests with their major trading partners without making concessions to the wider WTO membership, and provided the possibility of a softer terrain for addressing development. This was certainly the case with the EPA which the CPA stated would have development as a central concern. Although there was no specific commitment to include development concerns in the FTAA, nevertheless, it was part of the broader Summit of the Americas (SOA) framework which included broad developmental goals. These are treated in more detail below.

The FTAA

Background

The objectives of FTAA negotiations were to achieve a deeper level of integration of the regional market by increasing levels of liberalization beyond that which existed at the multilateral level. Thus, the objective was for an agreement that was WTO plus, which would extend liberalization to include Singapore issues, as well as labour and the environment, which were not on the WTO agenda. Negotiations towards an FTAA began in 1999 and were expected to end in 2005. Nine negotiating groups were established on market access, agriculture, investment, services, government procurement, intellectual property rights, subsidies/antidumping/countervailing duties, competition policy, and dispute settlement. The main features of the first two draft agreements, which were common to all disciplines, were requirements of national treatment, most favoured nation (MFN) status and transparency. These provisions, with some exceptions, applied to new areas such as government procurement, where the agreement aimed at securing access to the procurement market of member states; investment, where it sought to provide protection for investors with clear rules and regulations governing investment; and competition policy, which required the development and implementation of laws and regulations and the institutions necessary to administer these. The negotiations were directed by ministers with responsibility for trade, who met every 18 months. Vice-Ministers of trade, who met twice a year, directed the work of the negotiating groups. Three draft agreements were produced before negotiations stalled in November 2003, after the Eighth Trade Ministerial meeting held in Miami. Disagreements, particularly between the United States and Brazil, led to a weakening of the negotiating commitment for the FTAA to be a single undertaking. The Miami Declaration, emerging at the end of the Miami Ministerial, provided for a common set of rights and obligations, with the possibility for plurilateral agreements with 'additional obligations and benefits' for those countries interested in deeper commitments.[31] This effectively introduced some differentiation within the group. The proposals represented a significant dilution from the original ambitious goals of a wider range of disciplines and committing all signatories to a single undertaking. Despite this attempt at a compromise, however, continued disagreement between Brazil and the US, TNC co-chairs, over the common rights and obligations to be agreed by all, led to a collapse of negotiations. Some eight years later it is fair to say that enthusiasm for the project has waned on all sides and that it was in effect dead.

The FTAA and Development

The FTAA was foremost a trade agreement. Development was not explicitly mentioned in the objectives of the draft agreements. This should not imply that there were no provisions sensitive to development goals, as SDT measures, which were discussed in negotiations, were one way to address this. The FTAA's focus was 'to generate economic growth and prosperity, contributing to the expansion of world trade', and the route by which this was to be achieved was the liberalization of trade among member states, through the removal of restrictions or barriers to trade and practices that led to trade distortion. Liberalization extended beyond trade in goods to include the removal of restrictions on the free movement of

---

31   *Ministerial Declaration* (2003).

capital and 'business persons'.[32] It can be read from this that 'development', if at all conceived within the FTAA framework, was held to be a natural off shoot of trade liberalization; with trade liberalization as the route to economic growth and prosperity, and hence, development. Nogues' analysis of the FTAA's value to LAC is premised upon the assumption that trade liberalization contributes to growth, which in turn contributes to poverty reduction.[33] He thus argues that LAC should negotiate for maximum openness in order to ensure maximum benefits from the FTAA.[34]

Given the absence of explicit references to development in the objectives of the FTAA, it is useful to look at the broader process within which the FTAA occurs; that is, the Summit of the Americas (SOA) which set out the broad framework for LAC–US relations. The FTAA was conceived of in the first SOA, held in Miami in 1994. In the Declaration of Principles 'free trade and increased economic integration' were viewed as 'key factors for raising standards of living, improving the working conditions of people in the Americas and better protecting the environment'. In the accompanying Plan of Action,[35] the FTAA was but one of a large number of initiatives intended to strengthen cooperation. Its scope covered political and economic elements as well as sustainable development. Political aspects included strengthening democracy, promoting human rights, attacking corruption and combating illegal drugs and national and international terrorism. Its trade concerns extended beyond the FTAA to include a more extensive agenda that promoted the development of hemispheric infrastructure, energy cooperation, telecommunications and information infrastructure, and cooperation in science and technology. Its social agenda spoke to reducing poverty and discrimination and included universal access to education, equitable access to basic health services, strengthening the role of women and establishing an emergency and development corps (White Helmets). It also provided for sustainable development and environmental conservation that included partnerships in sustainable energy use, biodiversity and pollution prevention. Many of these goals were elaborated upon in subsequent summits.

---

32   'Third FTAA draft' (Ch II, General Provisions, Art. 2. Objectives).

33   Julio J. Nogues, 'Reciprocity in the FTAA: The Roles of Market Access, Institutions and Negotiating Capacity' (INTAL-ITD-STA working paper-SITI-02, 2003).

34   Both Nogues and Easterly, 2002, drawing on Dollar and Kraay's studies, sought to establish a concrete relationship between growth and poverty. Dollar and Kraay suggested that a 1 per cent improvement in per capita income resulted in similar improvement in income levels of the poorest 20 per cent of the population. Cases which do not substantiate this proposition reflect either slow growth or that 'the distribution of income has to deteriorate significantly in order for poverty not to decline'. David Dollar and Aart Kraay (2001), cited in Julio J. Nogues, 'Reciprocity in the FTAA: The Roles of Market Access, Institutions and Negotiating Capacity' (INTAL-ITD-STA working paper-SITI-02, 2003).

35   'Miami Summit of the Americas Plan of Action', 1994.

The Hemispheric Cooperation Program (HCP)[36] was agreed to in 2002 at the Seventh Meeting of Ministers of Trade in Quito, Ecuador, in what can be viewed as an attempt to bridge SOA concerns with poverty, economic growth and development with the trade and liberalization centredness of the FTAA. The 2004 Declaration of Nuevo Leon, issued at the conclusion of a special summit held in Monterrey, Nuevo Leon, Mexico, sought to modify the narrow focus on trade liberalization of previous summits, to include 'economic growth with equity to reduce poverty, social development, and democratic governance'. The attempt to create a connection between growth with equity, and poverty, suggests a recognition that growth by itself does not necessarily address poverty, and that poverty and inequity go hand in hand. The HCP's origins can be located in general concerns with the high levels of inequality that characterize the LAC region as well as the struggle of FTAA small states, led by CARICOM, operating within the Consultative Group on Smaller Economies, for the inclusion of appropriate SDT to address the challenges they faced. The primary motivation for the HCP appeared to be to facilitate 'the full participation of the smaller economies and to increase their level of development', to provide for 'technical assistance' and to address the specificities of 'applying the treatment of the differences in the levels of development and size of economies'. Thus, the principles set out to guide the HCP included 'respond(ing) in an effective way to the requirements and challenges to development arising from trade liberalization, in general, and implementation of the FTAA in particular', and to 'enable countries, especially the smaller economies, to participate beneficially and equitably in the FTAA'. The HCP was thus envisaged as 'a central element of support for the FTAA'.

The specific objectives of the HCP were to address issues of limited capacity in some of the states negotiating the FTAA and to minimize its negative effects. The HCP reflected a recognition that capacity challenges extended beyond negotiations to include more intractable issues internal to economies, such as productive and innovative capacity, and the ability to respond to economic shocks. The HCP was also to include a review mechanism, although there was no indication of how extensive this was expected to be. Countries were invited to submit capacity needs for consideration under the HCP.

Despite the HCP's inclusion, the absence of the SOA goals on poverty and development from draft FTAA agreements, suggested that these were not organically connected to the trade negotiations. The trade negotiations process was thus presented as being independent of development issues. The HCP was not directed at bringing development to the forefront of the FTAA negotiating agenda, but at minimizing the negative effects of trade liberalization. The assumption was that trade will lead to development, but that some participating countries may incur initial adjustment costs before benefits were realized. The process therefore failed to put trade at the service of development. Development thus played a subordinate

---

36   'Hemispheric Cooperation Program (HCP)' (FTAA Seventh Meeting of Ministers of Trade Ministerial Declaration, Quito, Ecuador, November 2002), http://www.acla-ftaa.org.

role to trade. The Eighth Miami Ministerial attempted to create a stronger linkage between the FTAA and development goals by asserting the trade Ministers'

> commitment to a comprehensive and balanced FTAA that will most effectively foster economic growth, the reduction of poverty, development, and integration through trade liberalization. Ministers also recognize the need for flexibility to take into account the needs and sensitivities of all FTAA partners (paragraph 5).

The Ministers also accepted that 'negotiations must aim at a balanced agreement that address(ed) the issue of differences in the levels of development and size of economies of the hemisphere, through various provisions and mechanisms' (paragraph 6). Even there, though, trade liberalization remained paramount.

The CARIFORUM-EC EPA and Development

The negotiations of so-called Economic Partnership Agreements (EPAs) between the European Union and member states of the Africa Caribbean and Pacific (ACP) group, organized into five regional groupings, marked a radical transformation of their post-colonial relationship, previously accommodated within successive Lomé Conventions. The first was signed in 1975 and prevailed for some three decades before giving way, in 2000, to the Cotonou Partnership Agreement (CPA), which established a timeframe for the termination of the arrangement: 2007 for the trade protocols and 2020 for the CPA itself. The protocols were to give way to EPAs, based on reciprocal trade. The EU's insistence on negotiating EPAs with groups of countries organized along geographical lines, rather than with individual countries or the ACP as a group, significantly weakened the ACP. At the end of the negotiating period only CARIFORUM signed on to an EPA. Three years later, negotiations are still ongoing with the other regional groups, with development and financial support central concerns.[37]

The context in which the ACP–EC relationship was formalized into the Lomé Conventions ensured that development was a central issue in EPA negotiations. ACP countries feared that the aid and trade elements of the agreement, which were influenced by the post-independence development debates of the 1970s, would be sacrificed in favour of neo-liberalism, undermining their ability to achieve development outcomes.[38] Developmental concerns were at the centre

---

37 For an update of negotiations see Melissa Julian and Melissa Dalleau, 'EPA update', *Trade Negotiations Insights*, 10 (4) (June 2011).

38 The Lomé Convention was signed in 1975, at the height of the development debates, pursued through the UN. The influence of these debates can be seen in the introduction into GATT of a strengthening of norms to take account of the development concerns of developing countries. The success of developing countries in these debates was represented in the formation of the UN Conference on Trade and Development (UNCTAD) in 1964, and

of the Lomé Conventions, with aid and trade considered twin pillars for addressing these: aid was to provide FDI which could not easily be found for capital projects, and trade was the route to greater access to European markets. The main elements of the Lomé Conventions that were considered progressive, were the provision of market access to ACP countries which allowed duty-free access to all ACP industrial products and 97 per cent of all ACP exports; guaranteed financial aid, with compensatory financing to offset the effects of natural disasters and fluctuating prices provided under Stabex and Sysmin; and commodity protocols which provided guaranteed access for ACP bananas, sugar, beef and veal and rum. Even with the shift in EPAs, from non-reciprocal to reciprocal trade, there was an expectation that development goals would not fall off the agenda altogether.

This was not assured, however, in light of the evolution of the Lomé Conventions to the CPA. Lomé IV, unlike earlier conventions which covered five years, ran for 10, with a mid-term review after the first five years. Phase II of Lomé IV introduced into the relationship, for the first time, elements of conditionality. These included an emphasis on democracy as the accepted system of government and respect for human rights and the rule of law.[39] Thus Phase II of Lomé IV foreshadowed the shape of the CPA. The post-Cold War climate also enhanced the process of globalization, especially in terms of information and technology flows and the restructuring of the production process, by facilitating access to markets. The EU's inclusion of political conditionalities in its relationship with the ACP group, then, can be read as an attempt to bring the ACP in line with the new thinking, making a break, once and for all, with the more radical origins of Lomé. The emphasis on political issues such as

---

the inclusion in GATT, the following year, of Part IV, article 1, which allowed developed countries to apply the principle of non-reciprocity in their relationship with developing countries. See McQueen, C. Phillips, D. Hallan and A. Swinbank, 'ACP-EU Trade and Aid Co-operation' (paper prepared for the summit of ACP Heads of States and Governments, Libreville, Gabon, 6–7 November 1997), www.acpsec.org. The Cold War also provides an important backdrop for understanding the ACP–EU relationship, where the EEC's interest in maintaining its influence in former colonies, particularly its interest in securing raw materials supplies, undoubtedly played a role in its offer of aid and trade concessions to ACP countries. See Henri-Bernard Solignac Lecomte, *Effectiveness of Developing Country Participation in ACP-EU Negotiations* (London: Overseas Development Institute, October 2001). The dramatic modifications to Lomé IV, particularly after the mid-term review, can also be read against the backdrop of broader international movements.

39   One can argue that the inclusion of political conditionalities within the EC–ACP relationship for the first time was in response to these changes and the diminished geo-political significance of the ACP following the collapse of communism. Lomé IV was being negotiated against the backdrop of the collapse of East European political systems and at the height of the IMF's structural adjustment policy approach, which was being widely applied throughout the developing world. Martin Holland, *The European Union and the Third World* (Houndmills, Basingstoke, Hampshire: Palgrave, 2002).

human rights, democracy and the rule of law, in what was essentially a trade agreement, also reflected a particular viewpoint that saw a connection between the entrenchment of economic liberalism and the maintenance of 'democratic' governments. These same issues were reflected in the SOA process which gave birth to the FTAA.

The CPA, negotiated well after the consolidation of the WTO, strengthened the elements of conditionality that had already been established with Lomé IV. The political elements that were introduced in Lomé IV were now 'essential elements' of the agreement, with 'good governance' included as 'a principle'.[40] Other innovations included the connection between performance in the utilization of aid and the availability of funds. In other words, individual countries no longer had automatic access to allotments, which were determined on the basis of need, but were required to show efficiency in the use of aid, in order to qualify for further assistance. The agreement also introduced another potentially political element in the inclusion of the private sector and civil society (as a fundamental element of the arrangement) as eligible for participating in the political dialogue between the ACP and the EU as well as to bid directly for development assistance. This deviation from the government-to-government approach of the Lomé Conventions could conceivably be viewed as a mechanism for weakening the role of ACP governments and fit squarely within the neo-liberal agenda of a reduction in the state›s influence. The CPA also departed significantly from Lomé through its differentiation among developing countries within the ACP, and its commitment to extend preferences to non-ACP LDCs. The latter was manifested in the 'Everything But Arms' (EBA) Agreement announced shortly after the completion of the Cotonou negotiations. Differentiation among ACP countries was at the heart of the EU proposal for EPAs with ACP countries, resulting in their reorganization along regional lines.

Several reasons have been advanced to justify the shift to EPAs, primarily the CPA's incompatibility with the WTO, specifically Part IV of the GATT, as it discriminated among developing countries. Consequently, in order to maintain preferences for the ACP, the EC was required to seek waivers from the WTO's membership, something it was no longer prepared to do. The ACP's poor performance under preferential market access, which failed to significantly transform their structure of production from primary goods and raw materials to manufactures, also justified the shift. The reality was a decline in ACP shares of the EU market vis-à-vis countries not receiving preferences.[41] More overtly geo-

---

40   The EU had sought, not only to include, but to elevate to the level of an 'essential element' the principle of 'good governance'. The essential elements were principles, whose violation could ultimately lead to the suspension of aid under the agreement. In response to ACP protest, 'good governance', although included, was downgraded to 'a principle', without recourse to suspension by the EU.

41   ACP exports dropped from 6.7 per cent of the EU market in 1975 to 3 per cent in 1998; and a failure to diversify exports: ACP trade remains dominated by primary

strategic reasons were advanced: the assimilation of developing countries into the global trading system in keeping with the EU's longer-term objective of promoting global trade;[42] and competition with the US over markets in Africa.[43] Other suggestions for the failure of ACP countries to improve their trading position, despite Lomé preferences, have been offered. These include the limited capacity in some states to take advantage of preferences; limited potential in manufacturing; and the existence of barriers, especially in agriculture, to products in which ACP states were deemed to threaten EU production.[44]

Whatever the reasons for the shift from non-reciprocal to reciprocal trade between the two groups, the proposed arrangement shares some similarities with the FTAA: the adherence to strict negotiating deadlines – FTAA negotiations were to have been completed in 2005 and EPAs in 2007; the requirement of WTO compatibility; a WTO plus agenda, both in terms of deeper liberalization and IPR protection, as well as in the introduction of Singapore issues; and compatibility with GATTS Article XXIV which requires the elimination of tariffs and duties on 'substantially all trade', and relatively short transitional periods of 10 years for achieving this; as well as compatibility with GATS Article V if service is included. GATTS Article XXIV presents a difficulty for developing states participating in FTAs with developed states as it does not address the asymmetries that exist between the two groups of countries. It has been criticized on the basis of its requirement for substantially all trade to be liberalized and its short time period. These features have raised concerns about the WTO's flexibility in addressing developmental issues.

The EU, in setting out its vision for EPAs in the text of the CPA, sought to locate these in what it described as the central objective of ACP–EC cooperation, development and poverty reduction (Title 1, article 19). Regional integration was perceived as a 'key instrument' for integrating developing countries into the global economy which, in turn, facilitated sustainable development and poverty eradication (Title II, article 34). The CPA established the following guidelines for EPAs: that they must be WTO compatible (article 36 (1)); that during negotiations, described as the preparatory period (September 2002 to January 2007) the EU would address capacity building in ACP public and private sectors, including measures to enhance competitiveness and to strengthen regional integration

---

products, with 60 per cent of total exports concentrated on 10 products (Price Waterhouse; Dorothy Morrissey, 'The Cotonou Agreement ... work in progress', *The Courier*, 186 (May–June 2001), 11–12.

42   Martin Holland, *The European Union and the Third World* (Houndmills, Basingstoke, Hampshire: Palgrave, 2002).

43   Henri-Bernard Solignac Lecomte, *Effectiveness of Developing Country Participation in ACP-EU Negotiations* (London: Overseas Development Institute, October 2001).

44   Henri-Bernard Solignac Lecomte, *Effectiveness of Developing Country Participation in ACP-EU Negotiations*.

processes (article 37), and would continue to maintain non-reciprocal trade preferences (article 36 (3)); and that there would be some flexibility in negotiating (37 (7)). The CPA acknowledged that it may not be feasible for some non-LDCs to engage in EPAs, and allowed for the consideration of alternative relationships. Flexibility was to be considered in the length of the transition period, final product coverage, and the timetable for dismantling barriers.

The issues identified for negotiation under EPAs were increased market access for the ACP group via a review of rules of origins (ROOs) (37 (7)); and the inclusion of the following: services – with ACP countries adhering to GATS, information and communication technologies;[45] competition policy which commits ACP countries to 'implement national or regional rules and policies' to prevent anti-competitive practices (45); protection of intellectual property rights;[46] trade and environment;[47] and trade and labour standards.[48]

EPA Negotiations

EPA negotiations were divided into two phases. Phase one was scheduled for September 2002 to 2003, involving all ACP countries, to discuss horizontal issues of interest to all. The second phase involved the EU and various regional groupings and addressed specific commitments between the EU and each region. At the end of phase one, objectives and general principles of the EPAs were agreed upon. The parties agreed that the 'overall objectives of EPAs shall be the sustainable development of ACP countries, their smooth and gradual integration into the global economy and eradication of poverty'.[49]

There was also a commitment that EPAs would support and not undermine the regional integration processes of ACP countries, and that their first responsibility was to 'consolidate ACP markets, before fostering trade integration with the EC'.[50] EPAs were also expected to 'maintain and improve the current level of preferential

---

45   ACP were countries encouraged to accede to the protocol on Basic Telecommunications attached to GATS.

46   ACP countries were expected to adhere to TRIPS and the Convention on Biological Diversity (CBD) and accede to international conventions on IP and commercial property referred to in Part I of TRIPS (article 46).

47   They were to commit to the development of 'coherent national, regional and international policies, reinforcement of quality controls of goods and services related to the environment, the improvement of environment-friendly production methods in relevant sectors' (article 49).

48   They were to commit to ILO core labour standards, to the formulation and strengthening of national labour legislation; but with an agreement not to use labour standards for protectionist trade purposes (article 50).

49   *Joint Report on the all ACP-EC Phase of EPA Negotiations.*

50   *Joint Report on the all ACP-EC Phase of EPA Negotiations* (3).

market access into the EU for ACP exports',[51] and provide SDT 'to all ACP states, and in particular to LDCs and vulnerable small, landlocked and island countries'.[52] They also agreed to the 'principle of a continuous evaluation of the adjustment process, which EPAs would require with a view to adjusting the liberalization programme, should any serious problems occur in the ACP states'.[53]

The ACP and EU did not agree on all the issues under discussion. They disagreed over the EU's interpretation of 'substantially all trade' to mean 90 per cent coverage; the sequencing of agricultural liberalization and support for development of the agricultural sector in ACP countries; whether mode 4 access should be addressed at the all-ACP phase; on whether negotiations should occur on trade-related issues; that there was an obligation to negotiate on services; and on whether the EU should commit additional resources beyond EDF commitments, to finance ACP needs in relation to support measures and restructuring. The ACP also resisted EU attempts to include elements of the Cotonou Agreement that speak to human rights and corruption (articles 96–7) into the EPAs. There was also disagreement over the role of the regional preparatory task force (RPTF) that was agreed upon. Because of these disagreements, an all ACP-EC Technical Monitoring Committee was established to ensure transparency in EPA negotiations.

The second phase of EPA negotiations involved the EU and six regional groups: CARIFORUM; the Pacific Islands Forum; Economic and Monetary Community of Central Africa (CEMAC); the Economic Community of Western African States (ECOWAS); the Southern African Development Community (SADC); and the Common Market of East and Southern Africa (COMESA). In this phase, each region was to develop a 'roadmap' that establishes priority areas for negotiations, measures necessary to achieve competitiveness, and the adjustments required, to guide the negotiations; and establishes Technical Negotiating Groups specific to the negotiating interests of each region. The CARIFORUM group began negotiations in April 2004. Three Technical Negotiating Groups were established on services, investment, trade-related issues and rules of origins.[54]

EPA and Development

Because of the history of ACP–EU relations, development concerns played a central role in the analysis of EPAs. In other words, because the relationship had been characterized by concerns for the development of ACP countries, the EU went to great lengths to assure the ACP that these new developments would not undermine their development thrust. This was reflected in the central role accorded poverty reduction in the CPA, and EU assurances that any new arrangement would

---

51   *Joint Report on the all ACP-EC Phase of EPA Negotiations* (8).
52   *Joint Report on the all ACP-EC Phase of EPA Negotiations* (4).
53   *Joint Report on the all ACP-EC Phase of EPA Negotiations* (5).
54   Melissa Julian, *Trade Negotiations Insights (TNI)* 4 (4) (July–August 2005).

not result in a diminishing of benefits they previously enjoyed. The EU made similar assurances that the EPAs would not lead to any country being worse off than under the Lomé and Cotonou Agreements.[55]

To concretize this commitment, the EC, before the start of regional negotiations, commissioned Sustainability Impact Assessment (SIA) studies on the likely effects of the arrangement on ACP countries.[56] Despite this, developing countries were concerned that their economic objectives may not be adequately met within the EPA framework. There were a number of reasons for this: first, EPAs required ACP countries to open their markets to developed EU states; second, given the past dismal performance of ACP countries in taking advantage of access to EU markets, there were real concerns that EU market access might be an empty offer; third, EPAs, as with the FTAA, made sense only if it involved greater liberalization than was possible under the WTO which, for many ACP countries, given their challenges with meeting WTO obligations, was problematic. Finally, the challenges were compounded by the EU's commitment to include negotiations on the Singapore issues which, apart from trade facilitation, had more or less fallen off the WTO agenda. As observers have noted, despite the reluctance of ACP countries to include the Singapore issues on the negotiating agenda, as emerged from the all ACP-EU phase of negotiations, the EU had even extended the list of issues on the CPA to include government procurement, data protection and greater liberalization in services, inter alia.[57]

Notwithstanding the many commitments to development and poverty reduction, there were concerns that in EPA negotiations, trade liberalization goals might trump the development goals. Julian noted the EU's refusal to include capacity building and competitiveness concerns within the negotiating process, insisting that they be handled, instead, by the Regional Preparatory Task Force (RPTF) or other Cotonou instrument.[58] This suggested that despite the commitment to keep poverty and development as central goals of EPAs, these might be short-changed by the decision to treat trade liberalization and development goals as separate. The rigid deadline for negotiations, given the clear capacity constraints of ACP countries, also gave rise to concern. Julian noted that these could inhibit the ACP's ability to initiate proposals that ensure their developmental needs were realized, and questioned whether development assistance from EC bodies and EU

---

55   *Cape Town Declaration*, 2002; *Joint Report on all ACP-EC Phase of EPA Negotiations*.

56   For critiques of SIA studies, see Stephen Dearden, n.d., 'A Critique of the Pacific EPA Sustainability Impact Assessment', http://www.edpsg.org/Documents/DP33.doc; R. Scollay, 2002, 'An Impact Assessment of the Possible Economic Partnership Agreements with the European Union: A Report for the ACP Secretariat and the Pacific ACP States'.

57   EPA watch, 'Why the EU Approach to the EPA negotiations is bad for development' (Concord Cotonou Working Group, 23 April 2004), http://www.epawatch.net/general/text. php?itemID-166&menuID=28.

58   Melissa Julian, *Trade Negotiations Insights (TNI)* 4 (4) (July–August 2005).

member states would be delivered in time to increase their competitiveness in keeping with the urgency of the 2007 negotiating deadline.[59] Julian also noted that despite the commitment for regional integration goals to privilege development over EU market access, that in its negotiations with CARIFORUM, the EU had urged the group to 'form a customs union with a common external tariff with no differentiation among members in trade measures so that EC exporters can face a single trade regime of goods imported into CARIFORUM countries'.[60] It should be noted that trade relations between CARICOM and the DR were at a fairly rudimentary stage, involving an FTA restricted to trade in goods, although with a commitment to include services and other disciplines. While CARICOM countries were committed to implementing a CET, neither the DR nor the Bahamas were part of this process. In addition, CARICOM provided SDT to the OECS micro-states, in an effort to avoid economic polarization within the group. The EU thus appeared to be privileging its desire for uniform market access above that of the dynamics of the process within CARICOM and between CARICOM and the DR.

The United Kingdom's House of Commons Development Committee expressed doubts as to the EPAs' ability to achieve development goals. The Committee was concerned that the EU negotiating mandate for EPAs had no commitment to development and urged that poverty reduction be made the focus of trade agreements. Such a commitment to make trade subordinate to poverty goals shifted the focus from free trade, the underlying philosophical approach that guides the multilateral and regional trade agenda, to the concept of 'fair' trade, which treated trade as the basis for addressing poverty. This avoids the assumption of an automatic linkage between trade and poverty reduction but, instead, argues for a reconception of trade as a tool of development, fashioned to achieve developmental goals. Their concerns centred on the following: the absence of public scrutiny of the negotiations; the EU's limited ability to offer meaningful SDT in advance of the conclusion of the Doha Round, without which, EPAs were unlikely to be fair; the absence of EU commitment to development in EPAs, despite the development commitments implicit in the Doha Round; and the unequal character of negotiations, where negotiating outcomes were unclear to developing countries. The Committee challenged the UK government, on its assumption of the EU presidency, to 'make poverty reduction the primary goal of the EPA negotiations.[61]

Summary of EPAs and FTAA

The EPAs and FTAA thus shared a number of features. Not only did they aim to be WTO plus, but they also embraced the Singapore issues. Both processes presented

---

59   Melissa Julian, *Trade Negotiations Insights (TNI)* 4 (4) (July–August 2005).
60   *TNI*, 6.
61   International Development Committee (2005).

challenges for developing countries, particularly small economies, despite their commitment to address their concerns. The CARICOM group, with countries of the Central American Common Market and the Andean Group, working within the Consultative Group on Smaller Economies, was successful in ensuring that these concerns were acknowledged on the FTAA agenda, reflected in the commitment to SDT for developing countries and smaller economies in the second and third FTAA draft agreements and the Declaration of the Miami Ministerial.

Challenges requiring SDT can be summarized under the headings of capacity, adjustment and implementation. Capacity limitations were human and financial. They include small numbers of trade specialists, oftentimes with weak negotiating skills arising from limited experience in negotiating trade agreements; difficulties in funding attendance at meetings, including negotiations and in financing studies necessary to inform negotiating positions, particularly on the negative and/or positive effects of liberalization on specific sectors and groups. All of these had implications for their ability to adequately define their development goals and to develop the necessary strategies to achieve these.[62] These countries also faced adjustment costs in terms of revenue lost from reduced taxation, especially in the tax-dependent CARICOM states, as well as costs from sectors unable to compete, including displacement of workers. They had already felt the consequences of eroded preferences on the EU market for their bananas arising from the WTO ruling on the legality of the EU's banana regime.[63] They also faced the costs of putting in place the requisite administrative measures and institutions, and the legal and regulatory framework to implement their new commitments. Supply-side constraints, such as inadequate infrastructure, weak firm competitiveness, inter alia, also inhibited their ability to take advantage of market access opportunities.

Both the FTAA and EPA reflected a commitment to what has been described as the full integration of developing countries into the 'global' economy as a way of enhancing their prosperity. This was considered to be best achieved through FTA-type arrangements, presumably as a stepping stone to greater levels of multilateral opening. In addition, in both processes, commitments were made to take account of development, although these commitments were more central of the EPA process. Despite this, there remained legitimate concerns that the insistence on treating trade negotiations and development concerns as separate issues, in both processes, may institutionalize asymmetries and do damage to the development goals of the developing and small economies participating in these negotiations. This is particularly the case when liberalization commitments in both were legally

---

62   For a more detailed discussion of some of these challenges, see Patsy Lewis, 'Unequal Negotiations: Small States in the New Global Economy', *Journal of Eastern Caribbean Studies*, 30 (1) (March 2005), 54–107.

63   See Patsy Lewis, 'A Future for Windward Islands Bananas? Challenge and Prospect', *Journal of Commonwealth and Comparative Politics*, 38 (2) (July 2000), 51–72; 'Making a Better Banana Farmer: Restructuring the West Indian Banana Industry', *Caribbean Dialogue*, 4 (3 and 4) (July/December 1998), 1–19.

binding, while development support was non-binding. The failure to entrench direct linkages between development support and the implementation of the trade elements of the agreement maintained the subordination of developing countries that had characterized the preceding agreements. Developing countries continued to be the recipients of 'aid', with trade liberalization viewed as a neutral process.

There are similarities in how development is viewed in both processes. Development, as in the WTO, is perceived primarily in terms of capacity constraints, which is directed at helping countries 'to adjust to WTO rules and disciplines, implement obligations and exercise the rights of membership, including drawing on the benefits of an open, rules-based multilateral trading system'.[64] In the FTAA, the HCP viewed capacity as containing three elements: preparation for negotiations, implementation of trade commitments, and adjusting to integration – the latter, it must be noted, represents an improvement over the WTO which did not acknowledge adjustment challenges for developing countries. The importance of financial assistance for strengthening capacity was also recognized in both arrangements. Both the FTAA and EPA processes considered measures to address the capacity needs of their developing counterparts. In the EU, the EDF was the source of such financing. In the FTAA these were to be met under the HCP, with the support of the Tripartite Committee, which comprised the Economic Commission for Latin American and the Caribbean (ECLAC), the Inter-American Development Bank (IDB) and the Organization of American States (OAS).

In the liberalization framework, capacity is viewed in terms of human and financial resources, and, more recently, the regulatory infrastructure necessary for developing countries to be able to carry out their obligations. It is treated as a constraint which can be overcome by developing countries, once developed countries and international agencies provide the requisite assistance to overcome these shortcomings. Thus, SDT is still viewed largely in terms of transitional measures, rather than permanent derogations. Capacity building, therefore, holds the danger of continuing a pattern of development where the institutional and cultural patterns of developing countries are influenced by or are developed in line with the experiences and requirements of developed countries, which was one of the criticisms of the development project.

The HCP identified three elements of capacity: preparing for negotiations, implementing trade commitments and adjusting to integration. This would be supported by financial assistance for projects and technical assistance from the more developed members of the groups to those considered lesser developed, and involved sharing knowledge and experience, conducting studies, and so on (HCP). Addressing the capacity shortcomings of developing countries to prepare them to better participate in negotiations and to fulfil their treaty obligations suggests the limitation of this approach. In the negotiating phase, the EU was more active in seeking to target capacity needs of their developing counterparts than was the US in the FTAA. As noted before, FTAA negotiations began without any mechanism

---

64   Doha Ministerial Declaration, paragraph 38.

for providing an organic link between the liberalization goals of the FTAA and the SOA's commitment to poverty reduction and development. Thus, the HCP was a belated attempt to address challenges that emerged during the negotiations. Under the HCP, developing countries were asked to prepare trade capacity needs to be addressed so that they could better participate in the process. It is worth noting that in both the FTAA and EPA processes, the absence of an option to participate in these arrangements for the developing countries meant that the broader question of whether a country was really capable of negotiating effectively was ignored. Targeting capacity issues while negotiations were already underway ensures that asymmetries will continue to characterize these arrangements.

The capacity building needs of three FTAA countries, one, Antigua, at the lower limits of small and the other, Jamaica, at the upper limits, along with Nicaragua, one of the region's poorest countries, suggested some of the challenges that emerged. Limited human capacity, both in terms of numbers and quality, is one of the challenges that most developing countries confront in negotiating with developed countries, or even more 'advanced' developing countries, such as Brazil and Mexico. CARICOM negotiators had limited exposure to many of the new areas, such as dispute settlement, government procurement, competition policy, trade and environment being negotiated. Antigua noted that it was entering FTAA negotiations with a limited understanding of the regulations required in these new areas, limited exposure to the practice of other countries already engaged in these areas, and limited language (Spanish) expertise. Moreover, it had only two trade specialists in government service. While training courses may address some of these deficiencies, there are no capacity-building methods that can address the obvious imbalances that exist given the different levels of expertise of the participating countries. The formation of the Caribbean Regional Negotiating Machinery (CRNM), which drew from negotiators across the region and expertise from within the private sector and NGOs, and led the EPA negotiations on behalf of the CARIFORUM group, was meant to address this. This could not fully compensate, however, for imbalances in exposure and experience and the quality and abundance of expertise available to them and introduced new challenges of reconciling competing interests among the group.

Financial constraints were a main challenge for small and other developing states. The CRNM, which led CARIFORUM's negotiations with the EC, itself was heavily funded by the UK government. Both Antigua and Jamaica identified the need for financial assistance for negotiators and experts to attend FTAA meetings, as well as to address a paucity of resources that include computers (Antigua), poor data, and the need for studies upon which to base negotiation strategies. The need for finance to fund attendance at negotiations, both in FTAA and EPA processes, was of particular concern, as it suggested that without this these countries may not even get the chance to sit at the negotiating table. When they did, they were negotiations across the table from their primary benefactors. Another constraint facing developing countries, to varying degrees, was the adequacy of institutions to meet existing and future obligations. Antigua pointed to the non-existence of legal and administrative arrangements which had contributed to its failure to implement international agreements. Despite the enormity of capacity issues confronting these small states, requests for assistance centred on financial support to attend meetings, support studies and purchase equipment such as computers, leaving the underlying asymmetries that these speak to untouched.

Implementing Trade Commitments

The ability of small and developing states to meet the commitments they have made in these agreements is premised upon the requisite institutional arrangements being in place. Antigua's failure to implement WTO obligations point, in large measure, to the absence of legal and administrative arrangements, and the burden of introducing these. These weaknesses were likely to intensify in respect of the Singapore issues, in particular, government procurement and competition policy where most countries lacked the legal, institutional and administrative framework. The challenges of their embrace of competition policy have been addressed elsewhere.[65] This is an obvious area that invites capacity building measures, particularly the engagement of foreign expertise in designing and establishing these institutions and the regulatory framework within which they operate. Szepesi notes the tremendous challenges the ACP faces and queries whether,

> ... acknowledging that many ACP countries at present lack the resources, the experience and often the necessary political leadership, the question springs to mind of whether the necessary 'eruption' of institutions and capacities can occur within the relatively short timeframe that EPA negotiations pose.[66]

---

65   Only two of 14 CARICOM states have competition laws and regimes in place (Jamaica and Barbados). Up to 2004, Trinidad and Tobago was contemplating a draft competition law. No OECS country has competition regulations or regimes. Even if these were put in place to accommodate the negotiations timetable, their experience in relation to their advanced trading partners who have had longer experience in competition policy and regimes, clearly puts them at a disadvantage in the post-implementation phase. In relation to government procurement, regulations across CARICOM countries are weak, requiring an overhaul of existing regimes across the region. See chapter on 'Competition Policy and SDT in the FTAA', written by Pat Northover, in Patsy Lewis, Patricia Northover, Lucy Eugene and Don Marshall, 'The Future of Special and Differential Treatment in The Free Trade Area of the Americas', in ACS Secretariat, *Studies on Special and Differential Treatment and Evaluation of International Competitiveness* (2003); Lewis (2004); Taimoon Stewart, 'CARICOM Competition Policy Regime: Implementation Concerns', *Caribbean Dialogue*, 5 (1 and 2) (1999), 139–147; Ivor Carryl, 'Competition Policy: Implications for CARICOM Single Market and Economy', *Caribbean Dialogue*, 5 (1 and 2) (1999), 149–169.

66   S. Szepesi, 'Coercion or Engagement? Economics and Institutions in ACP-EU Negotiations' (ECDPM Discussion Paper 56, Maastricht: ECDPM, 2004).

Modernization theory emphasizes the role of institutions in the development process. When these institutions are being developed, not from the experiences and practices of states and in keeping with their own agenda and needs, but in response to an agenda that is largely determined and modelled off (and with the assistance of) developed countries, then their role becomes problematic. Szepesi notes the dangers of such a process of institution building being externally-driven without a balance of local and external input.[67] I would argue that the very process of constructing such institutions overnight is itself problematic. Rodrik also cautions against the assumption that specific institutional forms were necessary to sustain a well-functioning market.[68]

Adjustment

The implementation of liberalization measures presents particular difficulties for developing countries. These include a loss of revenue from reduced import taxes, attrition of firms and/or damage to sectors, job losses not necessarily compensated for by new employment generated by new sectors that might emerge. There are obvious implications here for increased levels of inequality and poverty. Avoiding such outcomes depends on the competitiveness of firms and the extent of asymmetries between national and foreign firms. Unlike Antigua[69] and Jamaica,[70] Nicaragua's[71] assessment of capacity needs reached beyond the challenges identified in the negotiating phases, to the competitiveness of their firms as a major constraint. This led to a request for support for infrastructural development, particularly a system of roads and ports to further the integration of Central American countries. There appeared to be increasing acknowledgement, in both the EPA and FTAA processes, that infrastructural development was an important aspect of capacity development, especially when capacity needs extended beyond the negotiating phase to include implementation and adjustment. This underpinned the AID for trade initiative embraced by the WTO.[72]

---

67   S. Szepesi, 'Coercion or Engagement? Economics and Institutions in ACP-EU Negotiations'.

68   Rodrik (2001) (quoted in Salazar and Martinez-Piva).

69   FTAA, Hemispheric Cooperation Program, 'National Strategy to Strengthen Trade-Related Capacity, Antigua and Barbuda' (October 2003b), Ftaa.sme/inf/158/Rev.

70   FTAA, Smaller Economies Group, 'Jamaica: National Strategy to Strengthen Trade-Related Capacity of FTAA Countries' (September 2003), Ftaa.sme/inf/141.

71   FTAA, Smaller Economies Group, 'Nicaragua: National Strategy to Strengthen Trade-Related Capacity of FTAA Countries' (October 2003a), Ftaa.sme/inf/159.

72   This Proposal was developed by the IMF and WB in response to G7 Finance Ministers meeting, 5 Feb. 2005, which called for IFIs to develop proposals to provide additional assistance to developing countries to enhance their capacity to take advantage of trade liberalization and to address adjustment costs. It was meant to address, in part, the Doha Round's development mandate. See IMF, WB, Development Committee (Joint

The EU has had a longer tradition of addressing adjustment needs in its relationship with the ACP group. Under the Lomé Conventions the STABEX and SYSMIN provisions, which were utilized to offset price fluctuations of agricultural and mining products, reflected a recognition that shifts in the terms of trade could undermine developing countries' economies. Since the cessation of these arrangements, the EC has provided some adjustment assistance to ACP banana and sugar sectors to compensate for changes to both regimes. This included providing financial and 'expert' assistance to address competitiveness by increasing productivity and lowering costs, and assistance to support diversification strategies for those considered unable to achieve competitiveness. FTAA states suffered from an absence of the sorts of long-term connections in respect of trade and aid that characterized the ACP–EU relationship and which were expected to be carried over into EPAs.

Development Measures in the CARIFORUM-EC EPA

The conclusion of the CARIFORUM-EC EPA did not resolve the development debate. The agreement was met with concern, despite the inclusion of certain features that were meant to address development. Sustainable development, including poverty reduction and eradication and achieving the MDGs was centrally located in the agreement's objectives and principles. Articles 7 and 8 identified specific measures that included capacity building to support EPA implementation and fiscal reform, strengthen the private sector, promote diversification of firms and economies, improve sanitary and phytosanitary and labour and environmental standards, and strengthen technological capability (article 8). These were to be supported by existing EDF allocations of €165m, contributions to a regional development fund, and aid and trade contributions from member states. In the trade elements of the agreement, development was addressed through some degree of asymmetrical treatment of CARIFORUM in terms of scope of coverage and transition.

In both the goods and services agreement the EU's liberalization commitments were greater than for CARIFORUM. In goods, this amounted of 92.7 per cent of trade for the EU to 86.9 per cent for CARIFORUM. The difference was largely accounted for by goods considered important to OECS countries. In services, the EU and the Dominican Republic committed to liberalizing 90 per cent of their services sectors, larger CARICOM countries 75 per cent, and the OECS, Guyana, Belize and Haiti, on becoming a signatory, 65 per cent. The timeframe for liberalization covered 25 years, with most measures, 82.7 per cent, introduced over 15 years. CARIFORUM countries were given a three-year moratorium on

Ministerial Committee of the Boards of Governors of the Bank and the Fund on the Transfer of Real Resources to Developing Countries), 'Doha Development Agenda and Aid for Trade', DC 2005–0016, 12 Sept. 2005.

implementation. This ended in 2012. In addition to pre-existing challenges to implementing such a wide ranging agreement, the recession has increased the challenges of implementation for CARIFORUM countries. The EU has expressed dissatisfaction with the rate of implementation of CARICOM countries.

These measures were not effective in quelling concerns, at the centre of which was whether CARIFORUM countries stood to realize substantial benefits from the agreement, which could compensate for feared losses. The most immediate challenge envisaged was the loss of revenue from trade tariffs with the elimination of customs duties, particularly for countries most dependent on revenue source. The EPA envisaged a shift to consumption taxes to address this problem which raised the prospect of increased levels of taxation on nationals without any assurance that this would address the projected revenue deficit. Since 2009, all of CARICOM's micro-states, grouped under the umbrella of the Organisation of Eastern Caribbean States (OECS), have introduced VAT as a means of increasing local tax returns in order to compensate for the loss of trade revenue. The competitiveness of firms, both in terms of their ability to survive an onslaught of competing European goods and to penetrate a highly complex European market, remain a major concern, particularly in the OECS sub-region, which asymmetrical coverage and more generous transition timelines did not alleviate. Concerns were also raised in respect of the regional integration process. These have deepened since the global financial crisis and recession. At the conclusion of the agreement, criticisms focused on its implications for the CARICOM regional integration process.[73] The fear was that rather than supporting deeper regional integration, the EPA could potentially undermine the process. The fact that the European Commission was signatory to the agreement on behalf of its members while CARICOM countries and the DR signed as individual entities, raised concerns of CARICOM's marginalization in the application of the agreement. In short, there is no organic connection between the EPA and the completion of the CSME. The global recession has underscored such concerns as CARICOM's implementation of its Single Market and Economy (CSME) has slowed as countries turn inwardly to address its effects.[74] The greater

---

73   See Norman Girvan, 'Implications of the EPA for the CSME', *Social and Economic Studies*, 58 (2) (2009), 91–128; and Norman Girvan (2008), 'CARICOM's Development Vision and the EPA: A Fork in the Road'. Public Lecture, University of the West Indies, Cave Hill, Barbados, 18 April.

74   For a discussion of the recession's effect on CARICOM see, Patsy Lewis, 'Implications of the Global Economic Crisis for Caribbean Regional Integration', *Global Development Studies*, 6 (1–2) (Winter–Spring 2010), 1–28. For a more focused assessment of the state of CSME implementation see, CARICOM Secretariat, 2009. *Report on the Appraisal of the State of Implementation of the Caribbean Single Market Arrangements Mandated by the Conference of Heads of Government of the Caribbean Community* (Draft) and Owen Arthur and Consortium (2010). 'Revised Individual Country Analytical Reports for Phase 2 of Cisp/csme/result 1.9.1.1/ser09.10 Consultancy to Support the Full Integration of Belize and the OECS in CARICOM'. Stoneman, Richard, Duke Pollard, Hugo Inniss, January 2011. 'Turning Around CARICOM: Proposals to Restructure the Secretariat'.

urgency to meet timelines for EPA liberalization schedules and the high costs of implementing both agreements,[75] also detract from CSME implementation obligations. Thus, the CSME was likely to become subordinate to Caribbean–EU relations rather than functioning as the primary mechanism for engaging with the EU.[76]

The disconnect between development and trade liberalization evident in negotiations persisted in the agreement. While the agreement itemized areas of development support, it made it clear that financing was to be addressed within the CPA framework (part 1, article 7), the development provisions of individual member states and, more pointedly, within existing EDF allocations. The latter's focus had shifted to prioritizing implementation of the EPA (part 1, article 7 (4)). The disconnect was also evident in the absence of linkages between liberalization and development outcomes. The need for such a linkage to ensure that the EPA delivered on the EC's promise of development was made before the start of regional negotiations with the proposal in the Cape Town Declaration for the development of benchmarks against which to assess development outcomes. This was not incorporated into the CARIFORUM-EC EPA. The EPA does provide for review, primarily directed at extending the scope of coverage. This includes review of the investment provisions three years after its entry into force and thereafter 'at regular intervals', 'with a view to the progressive liberalization of investment' (article 74), and the public procurement chapter every three years with a view to 'modifications of coverage'. It also provides for review by the Joint CARIFORUM-EC Council, the main implementation mechanism, on the basis of recommendations from the Parties to the agreement (article 227 (3)); as well as for an annual review of implementation.

Landell Mills Development Consultants. Prepared for CARICOM Secretariat.Draft_final_Rpt_-_turning_around_CARICOM_(in_reln_to_agenda_Item_B1(1).pdf-Adobe Reader.

75   Implementing the EPA, as detailed by Valeriano Diaz, Head EU Delegation to Barbados and the Eastern Caribbean, required 'enacting and implementing legislation, regulations and procedures in the areas of competition law, public procurement, trade and customs; enhancing the policy framework and system of support measures for improving competitiveness of agriculture and the fisheries sector and improving the regional and national capacity to assist companies to comply with international regulatory requirements'. Peter Richards, 'Caribbean struggles to make complex trade deal with EU a reality', http://ipscuba.net/index.php?option=com_k2&view=item&id=553:caribbean-struggles-to-make-complex-trade-deal-with-eu-a-reality&Itemid=7&tmpl=component&print=1.

76   It would appear that even implementation of the EPA has been slowed by the global recession. See 'An interview with Branford Isaacs, Head of CARICOM's EPA Implementation Unit and Specialist in Trade in Goods, and Ms Allyson Francis, the Unit's Trade in Services and Investment Specialist', *Trade Negotiations Insights*, 9 (10) (December 2010), http://ictsd.org/i/news/tni/97942/; and 'An Interview with H.E. Errol Humphrey, Head of the EPA Implementation Unit in Barbados', 9 (8) (October 2010), http://ictsd.org/i/news/tni/87787/. See also, David Jessop, March 2010, 'What happened to the Cariforum-EU EPA?', *Trade Negotiations Insights*, 9 (3).

The agreement does provide for the Trade and Development Committee of the EPA to monitor the agreement's effects on sustainable development, but there is no linkage of this to any of the review provisions of the agreement.

Lessons

The CARIFORUM-EC EPA experience suggests that commitment to development does not necessarily result in outcomes that favour development. Subsuming development to trade liberalization, central to which is integration in the global economy, centres trade liberalization and marginalizes goals such as poverty eradication and enhanced living standards that are at the heart of development concerns. These are expected to be a natural outcome so there is no provision for rolling back or modifying the liberalization agenda if this turns out not to be the case.

Evidence of a broader understanding of capacity building and, hence, SDT, to include challenges of implementation and adjustment still do not address the heart of the asymmetries that characterize developed and small developing countries contemplating FTAs. In fact, measures introduced to address these could very well perpetuate asymmetries. Developing countries' critique of the WTO system, especially the limited SDT offered led them to argue for more 'policy space'.[77] Inherent in policy space is greater flexibility accorded to developing countries to pursue their development goals, as they define them. The basis for this is a rejection of some of the underlying assumptions of trade theory which hold free trade to be the sine qua non for development. Instead, it looks to the experience of developed countries to show that currently outmoded strategies such as protection of infant industries and a failure to implement stiff IP protection for imported technology were essential strategies to those countries' achieving competitiveness.[78] Thus, sensitivity to a more development-friendly agenda (recognizing that this concept itself may be problematic for many) requires allowing developing countries more choice in which disciplines they choose to adhere, more scope for exceptions and exclusions, as well as an embrace of the notion, problematic for many, of a roll-back of measures already in place and commitments already made. It also suggests the inclusion of institutions to measure the extent to which various liberalization measures actually promote goals of poverty reduction and equity.[79]

---

77   Correas-Leal, 2003; ECLAC, 2002; UNDP, 2003.

78   See Erik S. Reinert, *How Rich Countries Got Rich and Why Poor Countries Stay Poor* (New York: Public Affairs, 2007) and Ha-Joon Chang, *Kicking Away the Development Ladder: Development Strategy in Historical Perspective* (London: Anthem Press, 2002).

79   Patsy Lewis, Patricia Northover, Lucy Eugene and Don Marshall, 'The Future of Special and Differential Treatment in The Free Trade Area of the Americas', in ACS Secretariat, *Studies on Special and Differential Treatment and Evaluation of International Competitiveness* (2003).

One of the ways in which a concrete linkage can be established between development and trade liberalization is through monitoring mechanisms. The Cape Town Declaration on ACP-EU negotiations, issued by the ACP-EU joint Parliamentary Assembly (2002), sought to establish 'developmental benchmarks against which to assess the conduct and outcome of the forthcoming ACP-EU trade negotiations', although it did not identify any institution with responsibility for monitoring and applying those benchmarks. The International Centre for Trade and Sustainable Development (ICTSD) and APRODEV[80] (2005), in response to what they viewed as concern by political actors and civil society groups over the development content of EPAs, made their own proposals for such a system to monitor EPA negotiations for development content, which would be based on goals of sustainable development, and competitiveness and equity reflected in various ACP and EU official texts.[81]

In the face of heavy criticism of the EPAs' weak development focus, EU Commissioner for Trade, Peter Mandelson, announced his intention to develop a review mechanism to ensure that the EPA process puts development first:

> ... I have decided to establish a mechanism to monitor the roll out of our development and trade related assistance, to check continuously whether or not it is delivering the right results to build up local economic capacity, and that the process really does constitute the true economic partnership I insist on for these agreements.[82]

It remains to be seen how the commitment to review is actualized and the extent to which it leads to any fundamental refashioning of the agreement. For any review mechanism to have meaningful effect it has to reflect a more flexible approach to trade liberalization than appeared to be the case in both EPA and FTAA negotiations. Further, it would have to be constructed to serve the life of the agreement. It would also have to be based on the acceptance of a 'roll-back' or review of agreements, once these inflict hardships. It should also be grounded in an acknowledgement that SDT measures must be constantly reviewed and that some such measures may not lend themselves to graduation. Measures that address the structural limitations of small size, for example, may need to be permanent. In addition, it must be based on an acceptance that even after graduation from SDT, the same country may need to reintroduce these if the underlying conditions they were meant to address remain unchanged.

---

80   APRODEV is an association of some 16 European faith-based organizations that seeks to influence EC development policy.

81   For a discussion of this and proposals for applying to the Caribbean, see Jessica Byron and Patsy Lewis, 'Formulating Sustainable Development Benchmarks for an EU-CARICORUM EPA: Caribbean Perspectives' (September 2007). ICTSD and APRODEV.

82   Peter Mandelson, 'Putting Development First: EU-ACP Relations, EPAs and the Doha Round' (Georgetown: Guyana, 6 January 2005), Ref: SP05–202 EN.

ECLAC goes further in calling for distributive mechanisms in such processes to ensure convergence between rich and poor countries by transferring resources from the former to the latter.[83] Such mechanisms may also be necessary to ensure that some of the benefits that accrue disproportionately to countries, sectors or companies can be transferred to those that have lost, in the interest of equity and avoiding further polarization.

In terms of the broader multilateral/RTA debates, the verdict on whether CARICOM countries have gained or lost more from negotiating at the 'regional' level is still out. On the negative side the EPA, which entrenches the EC's interpretation of substantially all trade to cover 90 per cent of all trade, may undermine efforts to reform GATTS Article XXIV in the direction of a more favourable limit in the context of FTAs between developed and developing countries. On the other hand, the EC's acceptance of a 25-year transition period for CARIFORUM to implement the EPA, was much more generous than provided for in the WTO, which could contribute to a more generous treatment in the WTO's negotiating group on rules. CARIFORUM's acceptance of MFN treatment for EC countries in arrangements between CARIFORUM and countries contributing over 1 per cent of world trade or 1.5 per cent as part of an FTA, has been particularly controversial. Brazil initially challenged this under the WTO as violating Part IV of GATT, charging further that it undermined south-south cooperation.[84] The greater access to EU services sectors was viewed as a favourable outcome for CARIFORUM, beyond what was possible in the multilateral framework. The effectiveness of this access had been questioned, however.[85]

---

83 ECLAC (2002).

84 For an argument against including MFN clause in EPAs see El Hadji Diouf, 'Why the MFN Clause should not be included in EPAs', *Trade Negotiations Insights*, 9 (8) (October 2010), http://ictsd.org/i/news/tni/87722/.

85 For assessments of the EPA see Diana Thorburn, John Rapley, Damien King, Collette Campbell (6 September 2010), 'The Economic Partnership Agreement: Towards a New Era for Caribbean Trade', Report R-10-002, Caribbean Policy Research Institute, http://www.capricaribbean.org; The Caribbean Cultural Industries Network, December 2007, 'Statement from the Caribbean Cultural Industries Network on the CARIFORUM-EU Economic Partnership Agreement'; Frederico Alberto Cuello Camilo, 13 February 2008, 'The CARIFORUM-EC EPA: the First Development Enhancing Agreement in History', Brussels: Mimeo; Havelock Brewster, April 2008, 'The Anti-Development Dimensions of the EPA', paper presented at the Commonwealth Secretariat High Level Technical Meeting: EPAs: The Way Forward for the ACP, Cape Town, South Africa, http://www.normangirvan.info/the-anti-development-dimension-of-the-european-communitys-economic-partnership-agreement-for-caribbean-havelock-brewster/; Judith Wedderburn, 'Highlights of the potential gender effects of the CARIFORUM-EU EPA', *Trade Negotiations Insights*, 10 (4) (June 2011); Clive Thomas, 'The CPA A Monumental Deception', *Stabroek News* (20 January 2008), http://www.stabroeknews.com/2008/features/sunday/01/20/guyana-and-the-wider-world-8/.

Conclusion

Despite commitments to development, the EPA experience, in particular, suggests that mere commitments are insufficient to ensure that such arrangements achieve development goals: this is because their underlying assumptions and motivations are largely in conflict with the perceived development goals of many of these states. These goals, reflected in the appeals for increased policy space which are more compatible with the national developmental framework of the earlier development project, are perceived as being incompatible with the globalizing model of development.

The promotion of regional and multilateral liberalization processes by developed countries that are bent on opening the markets of developing countries beyond trade, to include services, government procurement, and the unfettered flow of investments, and enhanced IP protection, suggests that for these developed countries development plays a subordinate role to their market access goals. The inclusion of development goals can be read as an attempt to make such arrangements appear more attractive to developing countries, particularly countries experiencing large numbers of people in extreme poverty and/or whose competitiveness is weak. The absence of real debate on the content and meaning of development and the effectiveness of liberalization/globalization to achieve these, suggests the superficiality of this approach.

Having said this, it is unlikely that developed countries would enter into trade arrangements with developing countries simply to promote the latter's development. A realistic assessment would acknowledge the interest of developed countries in enhancing the income of their firms from greater access to developing markets. What is required, therefore, are approaches that would attempt to balance these competing needs as best as possible. Developing countries are crucial to the survival prospects of globalization and trade liberalization. Their continued cooperation is essential to the WTO and FTAs with developed countries. As such, it is in the interest of developed countries to seek to accommodate their development goals within such arrangements. This cannot be done when trade negotiations are treated as apart from development, requiring separate mechanisms. The two must be integrally connected if trade is to serve development, as its proponents insist that it does. Mechanism(s) to monitor negotiations to ensure that development concerns are addressed and to monitor the implementation of agreements, with the authority to reassess and revise trade arrangements, are a necessary feature of this process.

The existence of such mechanisms and their effectiveness are a far better basis for judging the development potential of FTAs between developing and developed countries, as opposed to declarations and statements in support of development. More importantly is the need for a reopening of the debate on development as the basis for fashioning an approach that addresses some of the weaknesses evident in both the earlier national industrializing model and the more recent globalizing model. This has become more urgent since the global financial crisis and recession, and successive food and oil crises, which have emphasized the more negative consequences of increased globalization. As Sen's approach to development as freedom suggests, different perceptions of development necessarily suggest different policy approaches.[86] It may very well be that the different perspectives on development that exist are largely incompatible. This recognition, at least, should provide some check on the homogenizing tendencies of the earlier development approaches which have been intensified in the globalization/liberalization model at the heart of the FTAA and EPAs.

---

86 Amartya Sen, *Development as Freedom* (New York: Anchor Books, 1999).

Chapter 9

Whither CARICOM?

Matthew Louis Bishop

Introduction

I am far from the first person to enquire about where the Caribbean Community (CARICOM) might be headed. In the mid-1980s, just over a decade after the institution's establishment, Anthony Payne posed the very same question, noting that 'Caribbean integration seems of late to be in a state of almost permanent crisis'.[1] Furthermore, he contended, such a bleak situation had persisted for most of the post-independence era, and by the 1980s 'a critical impasse had been reached in CARICOM affairs'. More recently, commentaries and articles in many of the major regional newspapers, such as the *Jamaica Gleaner*, the *Barbados Advocate*, and the *Kaieteur News* have all asked different variants of, as the latter puts it, the 'Whither goest CARICOM?' question.[2] In fact, aside from the odd moment of progress when political will and effective leadership have come into alignment with each other, the sense is that the regional integration process has actually been in some kind of crisis for most of its history. In this regard, it would seem that expectations of forward momentum are rather misguided when stasis within CARICOM appears to be the rule rather than the exception.

If, then, some three decades after Payne first raised it for discussion, there has not materialized a satisfactory answer to this perennial conundrum, why, the reader might sensibly ask, should we be interested in tackling it again here? Before providing an answer, it is worth pausing to think about what is implied in the generalized failure to address the issue, and there are a number of salient points to make in this regard. One is that the state of crisis that endured in the 1980s continued to afflict the Caribbean integration process ceaselessly throughout the 1990s and 2000s. The impasse has become so embedded that we should, perhaps, call into question the very notion of 'integration' (which itself suggests an on-going, forward movement). Another is that, if observers are still asking where

---

1   A. Payne, 'Whither CARICOM? The performance and prospects of Caribbean integration in the 1980s', *International Journal*, 40 (2) (1985), 207–228, 207–208.

2   R.A. Shirley, 'Whither CARICOM?', *The Jamaica Gleaner* (Kingston, Jamaica, 4 July 2010); *Kaieteur News*, 'Whither goest CARICOM?' (Georgetown, Guyana, 3 July 2012); *The Barbados Advocate*, 'Whither CARICOM?' (Bridgetown, Barbados, 1 June 2011).

CARICOM is going, it suggests, first, that they care about both the institution itself and what the answer to that question entails, and second, that it really matters.

As this chapter unfolds, the reader will see that both of these assertions are unquestionably true. Yet another point is that which is implied within the question itself: on the one hand, a positive assumption that, if CARICOM should be going somewhere, the suggestion is inherently that there is a 'better' place for it to go to than where it currently finds itself; yet on the other, there is also an ominous inference which necessarily follows, which is that the very fact that nobody has discovered the map to this fabled *El Dorado* means that, perhaps, it does not actually exist.

With all of this in mind, why pose this apparently unanswerable question again, and why now? There are three main reasons. First, in contrast to the 1980s, 1990s and 2000s, the context in which Caribbean integration is operating today is discernibly different. Globally, the world is beset by an enduring crisis which, at the time of writing, potentially has many years yet to run.[3] Hemispherically, a number of interrelated shifts have latterly made themselves felt, particularly in terms of new processes of regionalization. And regionally, structural change within the Caribbean – characterized especially by political and economic fragmentation – calls into question a traditional approach to integration which is overwhelmingly centred on CARICOM and, by implication, the Caribbean Single Market and Economy (CSME) process which has dominated regional debates over the past two decades or more. Second, the clouds on the regional horizon are much darker than was the case even during the crisis years of the 1980s. Norman Girvan, for example, has questioned whether, in fact, Caribbean countries are facing truly 'existential threats' in terms of challenges to governance (particularly from drugs, guns and organized crime), climate change, food insecurity, massive debt burdens and so on.[4] Third, and in light of this, we have to pose the question first in order to illustrate that it is, today, probably the wrong thing to be asking (even though many continue to do so). What I mean by this is that the question not only implies that CARICOM can and should 'go somewhere' and that this place is necessarily 'better' than where it currently finds itself, but crucially that it is the institution itself – and the key actors which comprise it – which can chart such a course.

However, I am afraid that the analysis advanced in this chapter suggests that this is far from the case. Contemporary global, hemispheric and regional reconfigurations are such that CARICOM itself – if not the regional integration

---

3   See, *inter alia*, C. Gore, 'The global recession of 2009 in a long-term development perspective', *Journal of International Development*, 22 (6) (2010), 714–738; V.S. Peterson, 'A Long View of Globalization and Crisis', *Globalizations*, 7 (1–2) (2010), 187–202; C. Hay, 'Pathology Without Crisis? The Strange Demise of the Anglo-Liberal Growth Model', *Government and Opposition*, 46 (1) (2011), 1–31.

4   N. Girvan, 'Are Caribbean Countries Facing Existential Threats?' (2010), http://www.normangirvan.info/wp-content/uploads/2010/11/existential-threats.pdf, accessed 31 December 2013.

process as a whole – is caught in a situation in which it is unlikely to be able to generate its own forward momentum. Or, put differently, even were the requisite leadership, energy and determined agency available to advance the integration process (a questionable proposition at best), broader structural changes are today so deeply entrenched and intensifying that it would be extremely difficult to turn things around. In short, the future destiny of CARICOM is not only in question, as it has been for a long, long time, but it is also increasingly out of the organization's hands. Consequently the simple answer to the question 'whither CARICOM?' is unfortunately something along the lines of a continued – and quite possibly terminal – pattern of decline.

So if the answer to the question is apparently so straightforward, what is the purpose of this chapter? In a sense, my agenda here is an attempt to situate CARICOM within the complex processes of structural re-mapping in which it is increasingly becoming ensnared. I begin by briefly explaining how and why the organization has stagnated, and what this means for the established pattern of regional integration that has held sway in the Caribbean since the 1970s. Then, I discuss in greater detail the multifaceted processes of structural change which are calling this settlement into question, framing the analysis with reference to the global, hemispheric and regional factors hinted at above. Finally, the chapter reflects on the implications for the regional integration process in the Caribbean more broadly, before offering some concluding thoughts.

The Rise and Decline of Caribbean Integration

The story of integration in the region begins in 1958 with the establishment of the West Indies Federation, which was conceived as the vehicle through which most of the territories of the Anglophone Caribbean would be collectively decolonized. After just four years, as the bigger players (initially Jamaica, and then Barbados, Guyana and Trinidad and Tobago) withdrew from the project, the Federation collapsed and set the pattern for insularity and fragmentation that has plagued the region ever since. This episode has been discussed at length elsewhere, so does not require another attempt at revisionism here.[5]

However, there are a number of key analytical points to emphasize. One is that the collapse of the Federation, as Alleyne puts it, still 'haunts the political landscape' of the Caribbean.[6] As many of the independent territories of the region

---

5   See, for example, J. Mordecai, *Federation of the West Indies* (Evanston: North-western University Press); A. Payne (2008), *The Political History of CARICOM* (Kingston, Jamaica: Ian Randle, 1968); T.-A. Gilbert-Roberts, *The Politics of Integration: Caribbean Sovereignty Revisited* (Kingston, Jamaica: Ian Randle, 2012).

6   M.C. Alleyne, 'Governance and Caribbean Integration', Conference Paper: Paper Presented to the 8th Annual SALISES Conference, Trinidad and Tobago, 26–28 March 2007, 2.

have struggled to adapt to the postcolonial settlement and, in many cases, have experienced economic vulnerability and stagnation, the Federation remains an omnipresent reminder of what could have been. In addition, and crucially, the decolonization of the different territories as sovereign units meant that sovereignty and statehood were overwhelmingly bound up with the nation and (aside from Guyana) the island territory. This has provided clearly fixed, identifiable and highly insular boundaries that delineate where the nation begins and ends. Key political actors have, therefore, been unable to think of sovereignty in anything other than national terms, and, practically, this has made them extremely unwilling to pool it collectively in supranational regional institutions.[7] This is problematic for a number of reasons. It prevents the creation of genuinely innovative regional governance mechanisms with the power to move the integration process forward independent of, not only states in general but, their heads of government in particular. These actors are also able effectively to hold their populations to ransom by resisting any perceived dilution of their power. Moreover, there are a couple of ironies at play here. One is that, for many Caribbean states, sovereignty actually counts for very little in real-world terms. It actually buys them very little genuine autonomy of action and it is continually and relentlessly transgressed by more powerful states and other transnational forces. Another is that – arguably, but nonetheless quite plausibly – Caribbean sovereignty would actually be amplified and augmented in net terms were the countries of the region to pool it more systematically in powerful regional institutions.

Yet this has never happened in the Caribbean. The pattern of integration has consequently been stymied by the contradictions and compromises that are inherent within the settlement handed down by the collapse of the Federation in 1962. The Caribbean Free Trade Association (CARIFTA) which emerged in 1968 after the prompting of William Demas, an important Trinidadian intellectual, later merged into CARICOM which was established in 1973.[8] The remit of CARICOM was essentially threefold: the deepening of economic integration, special treatment and assistance for the smaller so-called Less-Developed Countries (LDCs), and functional cooperation to incorporate new areas of integration. However, barely a few years separated the optimistic establishment of CARICOM from the reality of pessimism and crisis that Payne diagnosed in the mid-1980s.[9]

More broadly, deeper integration has never really occurred, and when it did it came too late and with too little commitment to completion. The CSME process, which was officially instituted with the *Grand Anse Declaration* in 1989, took

---

7   M.L. Bishop and A. Payne (2010), 'Caribbean Regional Governance and the Sovereignty/Statehood Problem', Waterloo, Ontario: Centre for International Governance Innovation (CIGI) Caribbean Paper No. 8, http://www.cigionline.org, accessed 26 December 2013.

8   See W.G. Demas, *The Economics of Development in Small Countries with Special Reference to the Caribbean* (Montréal: McGill University Press, 1965).

9   Payne (1985).

until 2006 – a gap of 17 years – to come into force. The purpose of the CSME is threefold: the deepening of economic integration through the creation of a single market and, eventually, economy; the widening of CARICOM to take on new members; and the creation of new trading links with non-traditional partners. The latter two of these objectives have been less important in some ways. They have also been generally unsuccessful. CARICOM has widened to incorporate Suriname and Haiti, but the Dominican Republic has, for example, been continually – and, at times, rather rudely – rebuffed.[10] The development of new trading links, moreover, is something which has also been stubbornly difficult to engender.

It is, rather, the deepening aspect which is the central element of the CSME. This was initially supposed to take place in a number of stages and be complete by 2015. At the time of writing – early 2013 – and after significant delays in implementation, the Heads of Government have decided to officially 'pause' the process. This has been widely interpreted as, if not the death knell, at least an implicit recognition that the CSME has, for all intents and purposes, been kicked into the long grass. It is hard to see how it will ever be resuscitated: in part on account of the fiscal challenges facing many Caribbean governments; and also because, if it cannot be completed in the quarter of a century which has already passed since 1989, it is inconceivable that any amount of extra time will make any difference when – and if – the region emerges from the economic doldrums. The simple fact is that the litany of problems is just too long and too intractable. Little agreement has been reached on such relatively straightforward issues as free movement of persons (with only the highly skilled so far being allowed to migrate freely to work within the region), contingent rights and regional accreditation. Consequently the far more contentious issues, such as harmonization of legislation, a single currency, and the full acceptance of the Caribbean Court of Justice (CCJ) – to which just three member states, Barbados, Guyana and Belize, have acceded in its appellate function – seem well beyond the realms of possibility. Indeed, there is one example which illustrates and summarizes these frustrations perfectly: the so-called 'Single Domestic Space'. This was an initiative which accompanied the Cricket World Cup in 2007. It allowed for free movement around the region, a single visa for visitors, and it was underpinned by huge investments in technology, training and other infrastructure. However, rather than continue the experiment for a year or two to gauge the longer-term impact – and to permit Caribbean people to enjoy the kind of free movement that Europeans take for granted – it was wound up almost as soon as the World Cup ended. In a sense, the region took a huge and expensive step forward, and then an even bigger leap backwards.

---

10 M.L. Bishop, N. Girvan, T.M. Shaw, R.M. Kirton, M. Scobie, S. Cross-Mike, D. Mohammed and M. Anatol, 'Caribbean Regional Integration: A Report by the UWI Institute of International Relations, funded by UKaid from DFID, led by Matthew L. Bishop and Norman Girvan'. St Augustine, Trinidad and Tobago (2011), http://www.normangirvan.info/wp-content/uploads/2011/06/iir-regional-integration-report-final.pdf, accessed 26 December 2013.

Furthermore, as Norman Girvan has recently argued, the Economic Partnership Agreement (EPA) which has been signed between CARIFORUM (meaning CARICOM plus the Dominican Republic) and the European Union (EU) has, in any case, sapped much of the remaining momentum and incentive for CSME implementation.[11] Indeed, there is something of an irony in the fact that Caribbean countries have committed to liberalize 'substantially all trade' with a trading bloc of 500 million people in the EU, but have consistently resisted the incorporation of the much smaller Dominican Republic fully into the CARICOM family due to fears on the part of sectional interests in the regional business community regarding the country's competitiveness, and worries about giving the political initiative to a potential non-Anglophone hegemon. This is doubly ironic given that the country has the potential both to resurrect the integration process and drive it forward, as well as to bring the Caribbean closer to its Hispanophone neighbours (one of the major stated objectives of the CSME).

The most recent high-point of the integration process – at least rhetorically – was the Rose Hall Declaration which emerged from the CARICOM Heads of Government summit in 2003. Under the leadership of PJ Patterson, then Prime Minister of Jamaica, the leaders agreed finally to the need for institutional innovation in CARICOM and, crucially, the creation of a Commission – similar to the EU Commission – with supranational authority and the capacity to drive the implementation of key decisions. For Anthony Payne and Paul Sutton, this represented 'a momentous and potentially seminal decision'.[12] Vaughan Lewis, an eminent regional academic and former Prime Minster of St Lucia, was the man charged with developing the technical proposal for institutional innovation in the machinery of CARICOM.[13] However, by the time he reported, a number of key leaders had left office – amongst them Patterson himself – and much of the impetus had been lost, with the jealous guarding of national sovereignty being once again the order of the day. Since then, both CARICOM and the CSME process have stumbled on with little forward momentum and, as I discuss in the following section, they have done so amidst a mounting 'crisis of development' which, Payne suggests, 'is

---

11   N. Girvan, 'The Caribbean in a Turbulent World', in G. Mace, A.F. Cooper and T.M. Shaw (eds), *Inter-American Cooperation at a Crossroads* (Basingstoke: Palgrave Macmillan, 2011), 60–77. See also M.L. Bishop, T. Heron and A. Payne, 'Caribbean Development Alternatives and the CARIFORUM-European Union Economic Partnership Agreement', *Journal of International Relations and Development*, 16 (1) (2013), 82–110.

12   A. Payne and P. Sutton, 'Repositioning the Caribbean within Globalisation', Waterloo, Ontario: Centre for International Governance Innovation (CIGI) Caribbean Paper No. 1, http://www.cigionline.org (2007), 24.

13   V.A. Lewis, 'Managing Mature Regionalism: Regional Governance in the Caribbean Community', St Augustine, Trinidad (2006): Report of the Technical Working Group on Governance Appointed by CARICOM Heads of Government, http://www. caricom.org/jsp/community/twg_governance_report.pdf, accessed 31 December 2013.

perhaps the gravest [the Caribbean] has faced in the post-independence era'.[14] The 'pause' in the CSME is only the most visible aspect of this. The commitment to the regional integration process has waned markedly in recent years, and the horizons of ambition have been lowered significantly. Moreover, other related processes, such as the implementation of the EPA, have also fallen well behind track and few regional observers believe that the agreement – outside, perhaps, of those countries such as Trinidad and Tobago, Barbados or, perhaps, Guyana which have a degree of capacity – will be implemented in any meaningful way.

The Structural Challenge Facing CARICOM

The broader problem, as I suggested at the outset, is that the time is rapidly passing – or may have even passed – for purposeful Caribbean actors to be able to rectify these many deep-seated pathologies. Even were the requisite degree of inclination and capacity to move things forward in evidence, there are a number of emergent structural processes of change which, in my view, are militating against a potential solution (or, at least a solution along the lines of Caribbean integration as it has been traditionally conceived). Put another way, the time for action is drawing to a close. Action cannot change the fundamental reality that CARICOM, and with it the wider integration process, is caught between a number of global, hemispheric and regional reconfigurations which are calling the settlement of the past 40 years seriously into question. In the remainder of this section, I explore each of these in turn.

At the global level, there are myriad processes of concern, all of which are interlinked. One is the enduring economic depression in which the EU, in particular, still finds itself. At the most basic level, this is placing an unprecedented squeeze on resources, with the EU budget for 2013–20 facing a real terms cut for the first time in the institution's history. This in turn implies a reduction in the capital available for development financing in general. The more problematic issue, though, is represented by the European response to both the crisis itself and the broader structural changes which have been occurring in the global political economy since the early 2000s; notably the dramatic 'rise of the BRICS', the continued downgrading and even dismantling of many of the remaining ideological and institutional underpinnings of the post-war period of 'embedded liberalism'[15] and the consequent reinforcement of a genuinely neoliberal order.[16] In the Caribbean, this is often thought of in terms of the end of preferences and the

---

14   A. Payne, 'The Missed Opportunity: Building a CARICOM Developmental State', *Brown Journal of World Affairs*, 16 (1) (2009), 137.

15   J.G. Ruggie, 'International regimes, transactions, and change: embedded liberalism in the postwar economic order', *International Organization*, 36 (2) (1982), 379–415.

16   See P.G. Cerny, *Rethinking World Politics: A Theory of Transnational Neopluralism: A Theory of Transnational Neopluralism* (New York: Oxford University Press, 2010).

move to reciprocity, both of which, of course, are key issues. Yet the implications of these changes run far deeper and are considerably more fundamental. The EU's 'development' and 'commercial' agendas are now so intertwined that they are essentially indistinguishable.[17]

What this means is that, not only is future finance dependent on the Caribbean acquiescing fully to the reciprocity agenda, but that this will be policed aggressively by the EU, with aid only forthcoming for trade, and Caribbean countries – as well as the wider African, Caribbean and Pacific (ACP) group – will increasingly find themselves on the end of much the same assertive agenda as the bigger and more powerful developing countries whose markets the EU is attempting to open. We only have to consider the threats which have been levelled at Jamaica, for example, on account of its tardy implementation of the EPA to get a revealing glimpse of this frightening new world.

Another threat to the financing picture is that the Caribbean itself, despite pronounced levels of vulnerability, actually contains within it many countries with medium, high, and very-high levels of GDP per capita and human development.[18] Consequently, EU actors themselves – as well as other major donors – are finding it difficult to justify spending money in the Caribbean, when there exist apparently more needy places elsewhere in the world. And, to compound this, CARICOM itself is heavily dependent on donor financing for many of its initiatives and projects. Yet many donors regularly complain about their frustration with the organization's record at completing projects in a timely fashion, or seeing them followed through and implemented.[19] So, to summarize, there are a number of concurrent threats to the financial picture. European financing is likely to diminish in general, it will also be dependent on the behaviour of the Caribbean in its engagements with Brussels, and the EU is likely to take a more uncompromising and intransigent stance to perceived indiscretions in future. The Caribbean itself is no longer a prime destination for donor financing anyway, and donors themselves are generally unhappy with how much of the money they invest in regional institutions is actually being spent. With little prospect of regional governments

---

17 T. Heron, 'Asymmetric Bargaining and Development Trade-Offs in the CARIFORUM-European Union Economic Partnership Agreement', *Review of International Political Economy*, 18 (3) (2011), 328–357; G. Siles-Brügge, 'Resisting Protectionism after the Crisis: Strategic Economic Discourse and the EU–Korea Free Trade Agreement', *New Political Economy*, 16 (5) (2011), 627–653; T. Heron and G. Siles-Brügge 'Competitive Liberalization and the "Global Europe" Services and Investment Agenda: Locating the Commercial Drivers of the EU–ACP Economic Partnership Agreements', *JCMS: Journal of Common Market Studies*, 50 (2) (2012), 250–266.

18 See M.L. Bishop, 'The Political Economy of Small States: Enduring Vulnerability?', *Review of International Political Economy*, 19 (5) (2012), 942–960.

19 Bishop, Girvan, et al. (2011).

stepping up to meet the funding gap, CARICOM itself has suggested that it could face financial collapse as early as 2017.[20]

This brings us to the hemispheric *problématique*. The main issue here is that there are now an increasing number of poles of integration, all evolving at a different pace and with differences of emphasis, and all providing the potential to undermine the CARICOM process itself. This, of course, is nothing new in many ways, with the (now defunct) Free Trade Area of the Americas (FTAA) as well as the North American Free Trade Area (NAFTA) long having been cited as alternative integration pathways in the Americas. What is different today, though, is the fact that many of the newer arrangements are both attracting Caribbean members and they are potentially usurping CARICOM functions. The most recent addition to the 'spaghetti bowl' of overlapping institutions is CELAC, the Community of Latin American and Caribbean States. All of the independent members of CARICOM have joined CELAC and, since its inauguration in 2011, there has been much discussion within the region about it potentially becoming the future driver of a more intense process of hemispheric integration (for more on this, see Chapter 6 in this volume by Mark Kirton). CELAC in turn follows hard on the heels of the establishment of UNASUR (the Union of South American Nations) in 2008, which has a mandate to bring the countries of the region physically closer together through infrastructural development (and of which both Guyana and Suriname are members). And, on an even bigger scale, the US is presently negotiating the Trans-Pacific Partnership (TPP) with a diverse coalition of the willing, including Australia, Japan, Mexico, Canada, Peru, Chile, Singapore and others. If, as is expected, an agreement eventually materializes, it will create an enormous free-trade area from which the Caribbean will either be excluded or compelled to join and acquiesce to terms which are significantly WTO-plus and potentially even EPA-plus. It is, in sum, hard to overstate the structural upheaval that this could potentially presage in the wider hemisphere if the TPP becomes a reality. Finally, the organization which poses the most immediate challenge for the Caribbean specifically is the Bolivarian Alliance for the Americas (ALBA).

Since the death of President Hugo Chavez of Venezuela, there has been much debate regarding the extent to which both ALBA and the Petrocaribe initiative will outlive him. Up to now, 14 members of CARICOM have participated in Petrocaribe, such that it 'has now become the largest single source of concessionary financial assistance to CARICOM countries, exceeding the traditional bilateral and multilateral sources'.[21] Moreover, three Caribbean countries – Antigua-Barbuda, Dominica and St Vincent and the Grenadines – have forged even deeper links with the Bolivarian Republic as members of ALBA, and this has necessarily created a (limited, but nevertheless discernible) degree of ideological differentiation within CARICOM. At a more prosaic level, it has also made common CARICOM

---

20   B. Wilkinson, 'Report: CARICOM Could Collapse by 2017', *The Jamaica Gleaner* (Kingston, Jamaica, 8 March, 2012).

21   Girvan (2011), 65.

policies – for example on energy, or the creation of shared positions on foreign policy issues – more difficult to achieve. At the very least it shows that a commitment to Caribbean integration (as traditionally conceived) does not trump the perceived material needs of specific member states.

This in turn brings us to the regional aspect of the problem, which itself is characterized by four main dimensions. First, there is the perennial problem of sovereignty; Caribbean governments – or, to be more accurate, their leaders – are unprepared to, as they interpret it, dilute their sovereignty, and this has effectively neutered CARICOM.[22] The lack of institutional innovation within the organization has always been a problem. However it is today rapidly becoming clear that, not only are political elites effectively holding the Caribbean people to ransom by refusing, as P.J. Patterson put it at the Rose Hall meeting, to 'cross the Rubicon',[23] but also that their intransigence on the sovereignty question has led to CARICOM itself becoming institutionally emasculated, stunted and plunged into a state of long-term decay.

The second issue is the broader pattern of fragmentation which can be discerned in region. This manifests itself in a number of ways: developmentally, in the increasing divergence between the richer countries like Trinidad and Barbados, on the one hand, and the poorer Eastern Caribbean islands (and Haiti, and even Jamaica), on the other; geopolitically, in the sense that Guyana and Suriname have a destiny which is inexorably bringing them closer to Latin America, just as Jamaica and the Bahamas find themselves perennially under the influence of Washington; and, crucially, through intensified fragmentation *within* countries, in which certain professional groups and classes are linked into global networks through work, travel and communications, and the wider mass of people whose living standards are stagnating and for whom heightened levels of human insecurity are a daily reality. It is hardly surprising that commitment to regional integration is dwindling, if we consider that, for the former group, who are usually highly skilled, can travel the region freely and work anywhere (and often in well-remunerated employment for regional institutions), CARICOM appears to be working pretty well. Yet for the significantly larger latter group, who cannot travel as freely, who are unable to work wherever they wish, and whose traditional livelihoods in, for example, agriculture, have disappeared due to the trade agreements negotiated by the former – often leaving viable opportunities only in the grey, or even overtly criminal, economy[24] – there appears little to be gained from an integration process which has manifestly not been designed with them in mind.

---

22   Again, for more on this issue, see Bishop and Payne (2010).

23   P.J. Patterson, 'CARICOM Beyond 30: Charting New Directions', Montego Bay, Jamaica: speech given to the 24th Meeting of the CARICOM Heads of Government, 2–5 July (2003), http://www.revistainterforum.com/english/pdf_en/caricomopening2003.pdf, accessed 26 December 2013.

24   See M.L. Bishop, *The Political Economy of Caribbean Development: A Comparative Analysis* (Basingstoke: Palgrave Macmillan, 2013).

The third issue is reflected in the EPA process, which itself is already being called into question as many Caribbean states – as I have already noted – have neither the inclination nor the capacity to implement fully the agreement. In a sense, the EPA has already served its purpose from the European perspective of driving a wedge between the ACP as a whole (as well as between the member states within the different regions) and reducing its collective bargaining power.[25] This has in turn resolved – for the EU at least – the thorny nexus of problems encapsulated within its post-colonial and post-Uruguay Round settlement, consequently freeing it up to get on with the business of negotiating far more strategically important 'commercial' bilateral trade agreements with big emerging economies.[26] For the Caribbean, the EPA has in many ways superseded the CSME process, and certainly would do so were it to be implemented in full.[27] Yet the latter has now been paused, and it is actually unlikely that either will be wholly implemented; it also takes quite a leap of faith to expect huge benefits to accrue from the EPA outside of the handful of Caribbean countries with competitive goods and services to sell.

Finally, the most interesting – and potentially quite positive – regional challenge to CARICOM actually comes from the Eastern Caribbean. In June 2010, the Organization of Eastern Caribbean States (OECS), which comprises Antigua-Barbuda, Dominica, Grenada, St Lucia, St Vincent and the Grenadines, and St Kitts-Nevis – signed the Revised Treaty of Basseterre which established the OECS Economic Union.[28] Somewhat remarkably, this envisions the kind of deepening which CARICOM has been unable to achieve. The Treaty makes provision for the establishment of an OECS Commission which is blessed with supranational authority and legislative competence in five areas: the common market and customs union, monetary policy, trade policy, maritime jurisdiction and boundaries, and civil aviation. Moreover, since August 2011, *all* citizens of OECS countries, regardless of their skills and qualifications, have been able to move freely and work in other member states. It is expected that, over time, a sub-regional Assembly of Parliamentarians – comprising, initially, national politicians – will also become influential in policymaking, with decisions increasingly taken, and institutions created, at the OECS level.

25   S.R. Hurt, 'The EU–SADC Economic Partnership Agreement Negotiations: "locking in" the neoliberal development model in southern Africa?', *Third World Quarterly*, 33 (3) (2012), 495–510.

26   Heron and Siles-Brügge (2012).

27   Again, see Girvan (2011).

28   OECS 'Revised Treaty of Basseterre Establishing the Organisation of Eastern Caribbean States Economic Union', Basseterre, St Kitts-Nevis: Organisation of Eastern Caribbean States, (2010) http://www.gov.vc/foreign/images/stories/Foreign_Affairs/Article_pdf/revised%20treaty%20of%20basseterre%20.pdf, accessed 26 December 2013.

Implications for Regional Integration

The discussion so far in this chapter has, in fact, generated more questions than it has been able to answer. One of these relates to whether or not CARICOM is actually the most appropriate vehicle for Caribbean integration in the contemporary era. Or, put differently, can we straightforwardly equate the deepening and widening of CARICOM with the Caribbean integration process as a whole? Simply because one particular institution has underpinned a given process for a particular period of time, it does not necessarily follow that it will – or should – do so indefinitely. We often think of institutions of domestic, regional and global governance as static and everlasting, yet they are anything but. They rise and decline. To look beyond the Caribbean for a brief moment, this is something about which the IMF was painfully aware before the global crisis hit in 2008, with questions asked regarding its usefulness throughout the 2000s and even some calls for its abandonment. It is also, in my view, something which the WTO will soon discover – if it has not already – as it struggles to adapt intellectually to a post-crisis era which calls for new and different kinds of policymaking. Agendas shift, ideologies come in out of fashion, resources move, institutions evolve – or ossify – and structural change, whether locally or in the global political economy as a whole, continually forces them to adapt and even potentially renders them redundant.

CARICOM is no different in this regard. Resources from regional governments have been scaled back continually, and this is unlikely to change as the economic crisis intensifies. Donors, who are responsible for the lion's share of the financing of CARICOM projects, are generally unimpressed by its capacity to deliver and, in any case, are increasingly subject both to their own budget pressures and the perception that significant parts of the Caribbean, because of their generally high rankings in terms of human development and per capita GDP (certainly when compared to the poorer parts of the developing world) are no longer in need of extensive donor support. Perhaps most critically, CARICOM has been stunted in its development by a regional political class which has been either unable or unwilling to permit the kind of institutional innovation required for it to emerge as a purposeful actor in its own right, with a serious mandate and machinery with which to push forward policy agendas forcefully. It is now over a decade since the Rose Hall Declaration, when the last generation of genuinely visionary leaders – in times which, as troubling as they were, were considerably more benign than the present – came up with a plan to overcome this issue. It is difficult to envisage such an alignment of political will, leadership and institutional possibility occurring again in the near future. Consequently, there is absolutely no reason to expect CARICOM to continue to enjoy a privileged place as the driver of Caribbean integration when the reality is that its mandate has been consciously degraded over the years by a political elite which itself is hemmed in by a debilitating system of adversarial politics at the national level,[29] and it is caught in the shifting sands of dramatic regional and hemispheric change.

This in turn begs another question: is there another organization which could plausibly drive Caribbean regionalism in place of CARICOM? There is, of course, no easy answer to this, and any which is advanced is necessarily speculative. Given the intensified fragmentation which I have identified, it may be more realistic to expect that, as regional divisions are even greater than they were in 1958, the era of experimentation with Caribbean-wide integration is actually coming to a close. On this reading, Guyana and Suriname – and potentially Trinidad and Tobago, too – are increasingly likely to turn towards Latin America and engage more forcefully in the CELAC process and other hemispheric initiatives. The countries which have recently developed close ties with Venezuela under ALBA and Petrocaribe, may well find greater ideological and financial support in those programmes than they do in CARICOM, should they continue post-Chavez. Jamaica and the Bahamas may decide to orient themselves even further towards Washington than is presently the case. And the OECS, which *has* deepened its own integration process in recent years, will continue to be a critical vehicle for the closer coming together of the smaller territories of the Eastern Caribbean.

It is this process of purposeful deepening in the OECS which, in fact, offers a plausible – if, perhaps, somewhat unanticipated – alternative site for generating forward momentum in Caribbean integration in the future. There are a number of reasons why CARICOM, in contrast to the EU, has been unable successfully to deepen, widen and create supranational institutions of governance.[30] These include, but are not limited to: an evident lack of financial resources and no country willing to underwrite the project (à la Germany); an inability to comprehend the essentially diffuse and potentially positive-sum nature of sovereignty, and an unwillingness to enter into 'sovereignty bargains' in order to achieve aggregate gains in this regard; the lack of a (small) core membership early on which sets the rules and norms of the organization, which themselves imply a continual forward process (in the EU's famous notion of 'ever-closer union') and which underpin the gradual, but continual, process of widening and deepening; and a mixture of intergovernmental and supranational institutions which mediate between national and community interests. None of these conditions exist in CARICOM. However, three of them are certainly present, to some extent at least, in the OECS. It has a small core membership which has determined the rules of the organization; these have already led to the creation of an impressive array of institutions, and, crucially, an on-going and positive process of deepening which has its own forward momentum; and this has resulted in the establishment of both inter-governmental and, as discussed earlier, an OECS Commission, in which sovereignty has been

---

29   See M.L. Bishop, 'Slaying the "Westmonster" in the Caribbean? Constitutional Reform in St Vincent and the Grenadines', *British Journal of Politics and International Relations*, 13 (3) (2011), 420–437.

30   See Bishop and Payne (2010), 16–18.

pooled and which enjoys genuinely supranational powers and a mandate to take the initiative in certain progressive and distinct areas of policy.

The point, therefore, is not that the OECS is a panacea for Caribbean integration. It is rather that the foundational structures are – in my view, at least – potentially more conducive to infusing the wider regional process with new energy and impetus. The three conditions noted above which are present in both the EU and the OECS, do not, cannot or will not exist in CARICOM. Yet it would only take one major country – Barbados or Trinidad and Tobago being the most obvious candidates – to apply to join the OECS, and their importance would be immediately obvious. The new member would, firstly, be forced to join the club in its present form and on the basis of rules, norms and a community ethos which is committed to on-going integration. Secondly, it would be, by definition, part of a bargain in which some measure of sovereignty has been pooled in an integration process which has gone far deeper than CARICOM. And, thirdly, the new member would consequently have to consent to the supranational power of the OECS Commission. It barely needs saying that such an eventuality would also unleash an uncontrollable chain of events which could render the CARICOM process defunct while simultaneously intensifying the broader integration process through the framework of the OECS.

This is clearly, at present, something of a fantastical idea. And the fourth factor noted above, the necessity for the most powerful country in the region to play the 'Germany' role, is evidently lacking in both CARICOM and my imaginary future OECS scenario. There is, of course, only one country in the Anglophone Caribbean that has either the ability or potentially the will to undertake this hegemonic responsibility: Trinidad and Tobago. So this leads us to another (again, necessarily speculative) question: will it do so? The simple answer, perhaps, is that it probably will not. One thing that has always been missing from the Caribbean integration process – again, in contrast to the EU – is a shared normative commitment to the hard bargains and deployment of political and financial capital which is required to build lasting institutions, and which goes far beyond platitudinous rhetoric. The foundation of this, in the European context, is the Franco-German axis; a counterpart to which never developed in the Caribbean, in large measure because of the collapse of the Federation and persistent Jamaican reservations about the integration process in general.[31]

Nonetheless, the more complex answer is somewhat more sanguine; it recognizes, in fact, that some of the most interesting thinking about the region is actually coming out of the current Trinidad and Tobago government. The Minister of Foreign Affairs, Winston Dookeran has latterly posited the notion of 'Caribbean Convergence' as a way of overcoming the problems which have beset the integration process at this 'critical juncture' in the region's history.[32] In a sense,

31   Payne (2008).

32   W. Dookeran, 'The Case for a Caribbean Convergence Model', *Caribbean Journal of International Relations & Diplomacy*, 1 (1) (2013a), 127–131; W. Dookeran, 'Proposal

the components of Dookeran's approach to convergence are neither original nor particularly radical. They comprise: globally competitive industrial development; freer movement of capital and people; enhanced infrastructure, particularly in transport and communications; a greater leadership role for the private sector; and increased diplomatic leverage globally 'which allows us to participate effectively in designing global solutions to our problems'. Yet what is interesting – in a context of crisis where neoliberal shibboleths are increasingly being called into question globally – is that the convergence concept specifically seeks to go beyond trade being the key driver of integration (as in the CSME) and foreign policy more broadly (as in the EPA) to advocate a more holistic approach. Indeed, there are echoes of the 1970s – and, as I have argued elsewhere,[33] the huge opportunities that were missed in the Caribbean – in the notion that convergence can be pursued with the purposeful integration and transformation of the regional production structure. At this stage, the convergence idea is desperately short on specifics. There is, for example, little clear idea of which policy initiatives will be required to assuage the kind of fragmentation within the region which has provided the main focus of this chapter. Or, put another way, how can we reasonably create convergence from a fundamental structural reality of divergence? Nonetheless, the very fact that Dookeran has hinted at production integration, which itself would necessarily require a degree of interventionism, is suggestive of, at long last, the first appearance of small, yet nonetheless discernible, cracks in the edifice of the ossified, orthodox, technocratic approach to governance and development issues which has been dominant in the region for the past 30 years. There is, of course, a long way to go – and much thinking to be done – for this opening to represent anything approaching a real and fundamental transformation of the regional integration process and, it must be said, the odds are, at present, rather stacked against it.

A final question to pose here in the context of CARICOM's travails relates to whether or not it really matters if the organization is, indeed, on a long trajectory of decline. The answer, of course, is overwhelmingly 'yes'. Despite the rather pessimistic analysis that I have ventured in this chapter, the fact that the failure of CARICOM is even plausible is a tragedy. In 2011, I was the lead author – along with Norman Girvan – of a large study undertaken by the academic staff at the Institute of International Relations (IIR) at the University of the West Indies. We spoke to a hundred or more stakeholders from across the region, and came up with 20 clear recommendations for taking the regional integration process forward.[34]

These recommendations included, at the institutional level: a systematic review and root-and-branch reform of CARICOM; the granting of the legal space,

---

for a New Convergence Model for the Caribbean Sub-Region', address to the 31st Meeting of the CARICOM Council, Georgetown, Guyana, 14 January (2013b); W. Dookeran, 'The Case for a Caribbean Convergence Model', 127–131.

33   Bishop (2013).
34   Bishop, Girvan, et al. (2011).

whether through a supranational Commission or otherwise, to implement decisions taken by the Heads of Government; the pooling of sovereignty in, initially, just a single-issue area where there is a clear collective value in doing so; the creation of a single CARICOM Embassy in one location on an experimental basis to discern how limited diplomatic capacity could be leveraged by pooling it together, and so on. Our most interesting finding, though, was that there is simultaneously a huge amount of commitment to the integration process in general, and pessimism about CARICOM in particular. Or, put another way, people recognize that CARICOM is in a deep and protracted crisis, but there is a strong consensus that successful integration is critical for the development of the region. People care, but they have become extremely frustrated with the pace of change and the scale of ambition shown by many key actors. As PJ Patterson has recently argued in his own 'cri de coeur', 'as of now, some decisive steps are urgently required to rescue CARICOM, or else life support may come too late to prevent coma'.[35]

Unfortunately, though, apart from Dookeran's salvo, there is little sense of renewed ambition. A few months after the IIR report was published, CARICOM commissioned its own report from the Landell Mills development consultancy in the UK.[36] The report was narrower in scope than ours, in focusing solely on the CARICOM Secretariat, but it recognized many of the same challenges that I have discussed here: notably slow progress in implementation and the worsening financial outlook. What is striking, though, is that it was distinctly less ambitious in its recommendations. These embodied a series of consciously constrained steps which could quickly be taken: first, the determination of a limited number of priority areas for action (which, by implication, would allow non-priority commitments to be kicked into the long grass); second, strengthening some of the CARICOM organs (but also *limiting* the institution's scope in other areas which are deemed non-essential); and third, a restructuring of the Secretariat into an institution more heavily focused on implementation. This echoed our own recommendation, but crucially, the caveat was added that, outside of the priority implementation areas, CARICOM's responsibilities would dramatically narrow with the scope of its ambition circumscribed significantly.

In a sense, then, what we actually have is two competing interpretations of the purpose, function and future orientation of CARICOM. One of these – reflected in the IIR report – can be considered an optimistic yet perhaps less realistic and excessively hopeful view, which sees both CARICOM and the wider integration process that it underpins in a considerably more expansive light. The other, which

---

35   P.J. Patterson, 'A Cri de Coeur for CARICOM: Lest we Wither on the Vine', Georgetown, Guyana: speech given to the Rotary Club of Georgetown, 28 January 2013.

36   R. Stoneman, D. Pollard and H. Inniss, 'Turning Around CARICOM: Proposals to Restructure the Secretariat', Trowbridge, UK: Landell Mills Consultants Ltd. (2012), http://www.caricom.org/jsp/communications/caricom_online_pubs/Restructuring%20the%20Secretariat%20-%20Landell%20Mills%20Final%20Report.pdf, accessed 26 December 2013.

is notably more austere and pessimistic, but perhaps more pragmatic regarding the likely capacity of CARICOM to effect meaningful transformation – or even simply to survive – effectively sees the institution shrinking to take on a necessarily more narrow, but arguably more focused, portfolio of responsibilities. In sum, the former perspective still implies a degree of hope regarding CARICOM's capacity to realize its promise after 40 years of life, and sees it underpinning a considerably more ambitious, political, interventionist and transformative conception of the form and purpose of integration. The latter is predicated on a fundamentally different, narrower and more technical understanding, both of CARICOM's role and the raison d'être and substance of integration. Which of these perspectives ultimately wins out is of critical importance to the future direction of the region, particularly if abstract notions of 'convergence' are to be made a reality. It also matters because few of the region's small states are able to cope alone with the looming crises on the horizon, the most challenging of which will undeniably be represented by climate change.[37]

Conclusion

The analysis advanced in this chapter has been wholly unable to answer the question which was posed at the outset. In this, of course, it is not unusual. Many have posed exactly the same question – almost incessantly – since CARICOM's inception and none have found a convincing answer with a plausible and popular prospectus for action. There is, in short, no sunny upland to which we can realistically expect the institution to go in the near future; the pattern of steady decline which has been set over many years and decades is well established and, in my view, is unfortunately very close to becoming terminal. There have been many attempts over the years to seize the initiative at what Don Marshall once called 'conjuncturally sensitive moments'.[38] However, such moments by definition only come by rarely, and with the founding of CARICOM, the CSME process and the Rose Hall declaration already fading into memory, a combination of the rapid passage of time, stasis within the organization itself and massive structural change happening in and around the Caribbean, as well as in the wider global political economy, collectively render the likelihood of such a moment presenting itself anytime soon – let alone being glimpsed and grabbed by a coalition of purposeful regional actors – at best unlikely, and at worst fanciful.

As Payne has more recently argued, reflecting on 30 years or more of observing the integration process since he first posed the 'whither CARICOM?' question, what is not required is simply a panoply of institutions of regional governance, nor

---

37 See M.L. Bishop and A. Payne, 'Climate Change and the Future of Caribbean Development', *The Journal of Development Studies*, 48 (10) (2012), 1536–1553.

38 D. Marshall, *Caribbean Political Economy at the Crossroads: NAFTA and Regional Developmentalism* (Basingstoke: Macmillan Publishers Ltd., 1998).

even a revived and retooled Commission with a degree of supranational authority, but the considerably more ambitious creation of a 'CARICOM developmental state' which is charged with 'nothing less than charting all aspects of a region-wide development strategy capable of coming to terms with globalization'. However, the timidity and insularity which reigns within the integration process militates against such a bold and elaborate settlement, particularly during the time of crisis in which it is most desperately required: 'The Commonwealth Caribbean has missed its best recent opportunity to bring into existence what surely is the only version of a development state that a region composed of small states can hope to build. It may well not get another chance'.[39]

It is at this point that we return to the analysis which was ventured at the outset. The opportunities for Caribbean agents to take control of their own regional destiny – through the CARICOM process, at least – are rapidly slipping away. Structural change across the globe, in the Americas, and within the Caribbean itself, is posing deep, thorny and pressing questions of the regional integration process as it is presently conceived. The window in which a genuinely Caribbean response to this conundrum might be advanced is, at best, only ajar, and painfully close to slamming shut. I have been unable to give a clear and unequivocal reply to the 'whither CARICOM?' question that I posed at the beginning of this chapter. The Caribbean region has perhaps one chance left to provide a convincing response itself, otherwise global realities will answer the question for it. And they will do so forcefully and with little regard for the wellbeing of Caribbean states and the people that comprise them.

---

39   Payne (2009), 147.

PART III
Regional Security, Governance and Multilateralism

Chapter 10

The Political Economy of Post-9/11 US Security in Latin America: Has Anything Really Changed?

Greg Anderson

Introduction

In early September 2001, Mexican President, Vicente Fox, was on an official state visit to Washington, DC for meetings with President Bush. It was a meeting widely billed as emblematic of both a new and encouraging chapter in US–Mexican relations, but also as the continuation of a relatively prolonged period of increased attentiveness on the part of the United States toward Latin America more generally. The atmosphere in Washington surrounding the Fox visit was so ebullient that by the end, Fox and Bush were near agreement on one of the most contentious bilateral issues in all of US–Mexican relations, immigration.[1] Moreover, while Mexico had augmented ties to the United States, already strong by virtue of proximity, through membership in the North American Free Trade Agreement (NAFTA), Mexico had also become emblematic of the apparent widespread move toward economic openness and democratic governance throughout the western hemisphere.

Indeed, the 2000 Mexican election could be seen as a kind of capstone event in a broader set of influences in Latin America that had seemingly entrenched openness in both economics and politics in every country in the hemisphere with the exception of Cuba. In Mexico, the 2000 election ended 70 years of uninterrupted, semi-authoritarian rule by the Institutional Revolutionary Party (PRI). Similarly, during the 1990s, autocratic regimes of one form or another in Chile, Argentina, Nicaragua, Peru, and elsewhere had given way to budding economic openness and democratic governance. Along with all of these changes came a renewed interest in Latin America on the part of the United States and US policy makers. While the western hemisphere has, since at least as early as the Monroe Doctrine, been considered part of America's 'backyard', critics of American policy in the region have rightly argued that the United States has alternately meddled too forcefully where it should not have, or simply been guilty of neglect.

---

1   See White House, 'Joint Statement Between the United States of America and the United Mexican States' (6 September 2001).

Yet, starting with the Summit of the Americas in Miami in 1994, the United States appeared to have taken renewed interest in its 'backyard'. In the context of postwar US foreign policy characterized by the commitment to the linked pillars of open markets and democratic governance, Latin America seemed primed for a move away from economic stagnation and authoritarian rule. Yet, no sooner had Vicente Fox departed Washington than the terrorist attacks of 11 September 2001 dramatically altered the course of American foreign policy and, with it, US attentiveness to the Americas.

This chapter is about the post-9/11 changes in US policy and their impact on Latin America. Popular and academic analyses of the post-9/11 US policy environment have focused heavily on issues such as security and emergency preparedness in North America, and the US homeland in particular. Similarly, literature in US foreign policy is dominated by a focus on military intervention and intelligence gathering. While the impact of American policy abroad on areas of the Middle East, Asia, and even Europe has been the regular focus of foreign policy analysts, the western hemisphere is rarely mentioned in the security, emergency preparedness, or foreign policy contexts.

This chapter is organized around three simple elements. Part I will attempt to summarize the broad swath of US–Latin American relations leading up to 11 September 2001 in an effort to set the stage for what has followed since 9/11. Part II will be an analysis of some of the many changes in US foreign and domestic policy stemming from the War on Terror as they relate to Latin America. Finally, Part III will address several of the bigger questions in contemporary US relations with its hemispheric neighbours, including whether anything has really changed. It is the argument of this chapter that while the War on Terror seemingly diverted US attention away from its own backyard, evidence shows that US activities in the region suggest otherwise. The US War on Terror and the obsession with security at home have created numerous challenges for its neighbours in the western hemisphere, but the War on Terror may have actually served to augment the focus of US attention in the region.

Part I: The Pre-9/11 Environment

If one were to sketch out on the back of an envelope a history of US relations with its hemispheric neighbours, one could reasonably characterize that history with one word: sporadic. Since the Monroe Doctrine of 1823, successive US administrations have thought of Latin America and the Caribbean as part of the US sphere of influence, its foreign policy 'backyard'. Yet, the Monroe Doctrine, and the so-called Roosevelt Corollary to the Monroe Doctrine were more about Europe and the United States than Latin America. Monroe famously wanted to stay out of European wars and warned that additional European colonization efforts in the Americas would be seen as hostile acts against the United States. In 1904, Theodore Roosevelt added a corollary that reasserted US influence over the Americas vis-à-vis Europe, particularly in economic affairs, but went further in suggesting the use of US military power to ensure that influence.[2]

Roosevelt is famous for 'walking softly, and carrying a big stick'. It was a stick he used with abandon throughout the western hemisphere.[3]

Apart from periodic military interventions, US policy toward its hemispheric neighbours is best characterized as indifference. Until very recently, there were only two notable exceptions to this basic pattern – Franklin Roosevelt's 'Good Neighbor Policy', and John F. Kennedy's 'Alliance for Progress'.[4] Yet, the pattern of sporadic attention followed by inattention and neglect continued. The prevalence of despotic regimes, periodic financial crises, and problematic governance, some of which was arguably exacerbated by US interventions, made the US backyard something of an afterthought in US foreign policy.[5] In those sporadic instances in which the western hemisphere featured prominently in US policy circles, it was too often as a result of some crisis related to the Cold War (Nicaragua, Cuba, El Salvador, Grenada, Chile) or the long-running war on narcotics trafficking (Colombia, Mexico, Panama), or a crisis in immigration (Mexico, Cuba). In other words, in the context of a perennially full and complex US foreign policy agenda, the 'backyard' has historically been a complex region for the United States.

Yet, the end of the Cold War in 1989 and the Soviet Union in 1991 marked the beginning of a renewed, and seemingly sustained, interest in the western hemisphere by the United States. In the midst of discussions in the United States and elsewhere about 'peace dividends', who won the Cold War, and some bewilderment that it had ended at all, US foreign policy entered a period of considerable uncertainty.[6] The remarkable international coalition assembled by the United States to extricate Saddam Hussein from Kuwait in 1990–91 suggested that US foreign policy would be characterized by participation in a 'new world order' in international relations centred on multilateral organizations like the United Nations. Yet, in the aftermath of the humanitarian efforts in Somalia and the Balkans, sceptics, including then-

2   Thomas A. Bailey, *A Diplomatic History of the American People*, 10th ed. (Englewood Cliffs, NJ: Prentice-Hall F.S. Crofts & Co., 1980), 184–186, 548–563.

3   Ibid.

4   Richard E. Feinberg, *Summitry in the Americas: A Progress Report* (Washington, DC: Institute for International Economics, 1997), Chapter 1.

5   Ibid. See also Greg Anderson, 'Hemispheric Integration in the Post-Seattle Era: The Promise and Problems for the FTAA', *International Journal*, 56 (Spring 2001), 207–233; Rosemary Thorpe, *Progress, Poverty and Exclusion: An Economic History of Latin America in the 20th Century* (Washington, DC: Inter-American Development Bank), Chapter 7; Feinberg, *Summitry in the Americas*, 26–37.

6   Daniel Deudney and John Ikenberry, 'Who Won the Cold War', *Foreign Policy*, 87 (Summer 1992), 123–138; Stanley Sloan, 'US Perspectives on NATO's Future', *International Affairs*, 71 (2) (April 1995), 217–231; John Ruggie, 'Consolidating The European Pillar: The Key to NATO's Future', *The Washington Quarterly*, 20 (1) (Winter 1997), 109–124; Dimitri Simes, 'Losing Russia', *Foreign Affairs*, 86 (6) (November/December 2007), 36–52.

Texas Governor George W. Bush, were calling for an end to nation building as a component of US foreign policy by the end of the 1990s.[7]

More important than seizing upon particular directions for US foreign policy, the end of the Cold War seemed to signal the triumph of two pillars of post-war US foreign policy; economic openness and democratic governance. Indeed, in 1989, Francis Fukuyama argued that the end of the Cold War also represented the 'end of history' in that the great ideological struggle between the precepts of liberal capitalism and authoritarianism was won by liberal capitalism.[8] At the time, and through much of the ensuing decade, evidence supporting Fukuyama's thesis seemed to be everywhere. With the Cold War over, governance everywhere seemed to be turning solidly democratic, including in the western hemisphere where by 1994 all countries, save Cuba, had democratically elected governments. The global trading regime received a major boost in 1994 with the completion of the Uruguay Round of the General Agreement on Tariffs and Trade (GATT) and its renaming as the World Trade Organization (WTO) with the participation of more than 140 countries, and many more trying to accede, including communist China. Regionally, the 1992 Maastricht Treaty paved the way for European monetary union, and also in 1994, the North American Free Trade Agreement (NAFTA) for the first time swept away tariff barriers between economies of vastly different stages of development.

Re-mapping the Americas?

While policy makers in Washington searched for a unifying purpose for US foreign policy throughout most of the 1990s, Fukuyama's basic thesis regarding the triumph of liberal capitalism and democracy was apparently playing out, and presenting opportunities in, Latin America and the Caribbean. In February 1990, Mexican President, Carlos Salinas, formally proposed negotiations with the United States that ultimately led to the conclusion of the NAFTA. US interest in an agreement with Mexico was premised on many factors, but included a desire to support a series of economic and political reforms in Mexico that had allowed it to emerge from the effects of the debt crisis that plagued Latin America for most of the 1980s. Soon after Salinas proposed free trade with the United States, President George H.W. Bush sought to capitalize on the nascent market and political opening occurring throughout the western hemisphere when he announced a set of US initiatives toward the region labelled the Enterprise for the Americas.[9] While the Enterprise for the Americas fizzled in the last few years of the Bush presidency, renewed US interest in the western hemisphere was given additional momentum

---

7   Condoleezza Rice, 'Promoting the National Interest', *Foreign Affairs*, 79 (1) (January/February 2000), 45–62; Robert Zoellick, 'A Republican Foreign Policy', *Foreign Affairs*, 79 (1) (January/February, 2000), 63–78.

8   Francis Fukuyama, 'The End of History', *The National Interest*, 15 (Summer 1989), 3–18.

9   Feinberg, *Summitry in the Americas*, 47–49.

in the aftermath of successful completion of both the NAFTA and the Uruguay Round with the launch of the Summit of the Americas process in Miami in 1994.

The Summit of the Americas in Miami seemed to herald a new era in hemispheric relations based largely on the precepts of democratic governance and open markets. For the first time in decades, the interests of the United States and its hemispheric neighbours appeared to coalesce around a set of principles and initiatives aimed at knitting those interests ever closer together. Apart from the basic commitment to democracy, the core of the Summit process was a free trade zone stretching from Tierra del Fuego in the south to the Aleutian Islands in the north; the Free Trade Area of the Americas (FTAA). The idea was simple enough; spread the recognized economic/market benefits of open regionalism throughout the western hemisphere by knitting each of the democratically elected countries together into a single, prosperous, and peaceful trading bloc.[10] Such a process would supersede the inefficient patchwork of economic arrangements that then existed in the hemisphere, and reconcile the competing visions of hemispheric integration that the patchwork represented.[11]

Although considerable work was done on the FTAA through 2003, the Miami Summit proved to be the high-water mark of enthusiasm for deeper, multilateral integration in the western hemisphere. From the outset, a series of conflicting interests plagued the negotiations, not the least of which was the creation of the Southern Cone Common Market (MERCOSUR), a customs union, among Brazil, Uruguay, Paraguay, and Argentina established in 1995. By 2006, the economic logic of knitting together the 34 democracies of the western hemisphere remained, but the politics increasingly tenuous. Existing trade ties were weak, particularly between countries separated by long distances,[12] and patterns of regionalization

---

10   E.D. Mansfield, 'Preferential Peace: Why Preferential Trading Arrangements Inhibit Interstate Conflict', in E.D. Mansfield and B.M. Pollins (eds), *Economic Interdependence and International Conflict: New Perspectives on an Enduring Debate* (Ann Arbor: The University of Michigan Press, 2003), 222–231; E.D. Mansfield and J.C. Pevehouse, 'Trade Blocs, Trade Flows, and International Conflict', *International Organization*, 54 (4) (2000), 775–808; Patrick McDonald, 'Peace Through Trade or Free Trade?', *Journal of Conflict Resolution*, 48 (4), 547–572.

11   Stephan Haggard, 'The Political Economy of Regionalism in the Western Hemisphere', in Carol Wise (ed.), *The Post-NATA Political Economy: Mexico and the Western Hemisphere* (University Park: Pennsylvania State University Press, 1998), 312–314, 331–332.

12   See Paul Krugman, 'On the Relationship Between Trade Theory and Location Theory', *Review of International Economics*, 1 (2) (1993), 110–122; Charles Engel and John H. Rogers, 'How Wide is the Border?', *American Economic Review*, 86 (5) (December 1996), 1112–1125; John McCallum, 'National Borders Matter: Canada-U.S. Regional Trade Patterns', *American Economic Review*, 85 (3) (June 1995), 615–623; John F. Helliwell and Genevieve Verdier, 'Measuring Internal Trade Distances: A New Method Applied to Estimate Provincial Border Effects', *Canadian Journal of Economics*, 34 (4) (November 2001), 1024–1041.

were largely centred around two increasingly entrenched nodes; US dominance in the NAFTA area and Brazil's in MERCOSUR.[13]

In North America, dependence on the US market is particularly acute for Canada and Mexico where more than 80 per cent of each country's exports and 60 per cent of their imports are tied to the US market.[14] In spite of being NAFTA partners, Canada and Mexico trade very little with one another, nor is their trade significant with other parts of the western hemisphere.[15] In fact, once the NAFTA partners move beyond one another, trade volumes between the North and South within the western hemisphere fall off significantly. The MERCOSUR bloc anchored by Brazil is similar in that its members are among each other's most important trading partners.[16] For example, Paraguay's top five export partners are its immediate neighbours, Uruguay, Brazil, Argentina, and Chile. However, the further south you move geographically away from the United States, the less dependent western hemisphere countries are on US market access, and the more diverse their trading partners become.

In fact, a 1992 study by Refik Erzan and Alexander Yeats concluded that the potential for most Caribbean countries to expand their trade through a hemispheric agreement like the FTAA was more limited than is often thought. Erzan and Yeats also concluded that the rest of Latin America might only improve their aggregate export levels by about 6.6 per cent, and only then if multilateral negotiations stalled, thereby making the logic of open regionalism through the FTAA less compelling.[17] None of this is to suggest that liberalization in the hemisphere is

---

13   See Pedro da Motta Veiga, 'Brazil in Mercosur: Reciprocal Influence', in Riordan Roett (ed.), *MERCOSUR: Regional Integration, World Markets* (Boulder, Colorado: Lynne Rienner Publishers, 1999), 25–33; Greg Anderson, 'Hemispheric Integration in the Post-Seattle Era', *International Journal*, 56 (Spring 2001), 208–213.

14   Source: *CIA World Fact Book*; Statistics Canada, 'Imports, Exports and Balance of Trade on a Balance-of-Payments Basis', 2005.

15   In 2008, Canada's top export destinations were the US (77.7 per cent), Japan (2.3 per cent) and the UK (2.7 per cent) and its top import sources were the US (52.4 per cent), China (9.8 per cent) and Mexico (4.1 per cent). For Mexico, top export partners were the US (80.5 per cent), Canada (3.6 per cent) and Spain (1.4 per cent) and top sources for imports were the US (48 per cent), Germany (13.5 per cent) and Japan (4.8 per cent). Source: *CIA World Fact Book*; Statistics Canada; US Department of Commerce.

16   More broadly, the trading relationships of MERCOSUR countries are much more diverse in terms of their distribution. For instance, only Brazil has a trading relationship with the United States that approaches 20 per cent in either exports to or imports from the US.

17   Refik Erzan and Alexander Yeats, 'Free Trade Agreements With the United States: What's in it for Latin America', *Policy Research Working Paper 827* (Washington, DC: World Bank, 1992). See also Refik Erzan and Alexander Yeats, 'US-Latin American Free Trade Areas: some empirical evidence', in Sylvia Saborio (ed.), *The Premise and the Promise: Free Trade and the Americas* (Washington, DC: Overseas Development Council, 1992), 128–129.

a waste of time. In fact, the elimination of tariff barriers among just developing countries would provide an important boost to global trade flows and stimulate additional development. As EU Trade Commissioner, Peter Mandelson pointed out in 2006, 'about 70% of the tariffs paid by the poorest developing countries are paid not on their exports to Europe or the US, but to other developing countries'.[18] This is undoubtedly true in the western hemisphere as well, but the point here is that with limited existing ties between some regions, a dramatic expansion of trade patterns among far-flung would have taken some time to develop even with a successfully concluded FTAA.

Adding further to doubts about the economic efficacy of the FTAA were concerns about knitting developed and developing countries together. While the NAFTA appears to be an example of how developed and developing economies can be linked together economically, a large body of evidence suggests that those countries with economies that are most similar also attract the largest flows of trade and investment.[19] This is the kind of evidence that suggests divergent interests among hemispheric trading partners of varying degrees of development. Indeed, not only were these divergences reflected in some of the thorniest issues within the FTAA negotiations, they were largely being debated among the most powerful countries in each of the regional blocs; the United States and Brazil. In many respects, the FTAA process had effectively stalled by early 2002 due to differences between the United States and Brazil over how to handle agriculture in the FTAA negotiations. The United States insisted that agriculture first be dealt with in the context of the Doha Round of the WTO negotiations, whereas Brazil insisted it be dealt with in the FTAA. By default, the US refusal to discuss agriculture in the FTAA meant that the entire process missed the original implementation target date of 1 January 2005 while negotiators awaited the outcome of the Doha Round.[20] Doha remains deadlocked after more than a decade of talks. The Summit of the Americas process endures, with the most recent meeting having taken place in Cartagena, Colombia in 2012, but the FTAA as a major anchor of that process hasn't been mentioned since the Summit of the Americas in Mar del Plata, Argentina in 2005.

---

18   See Speech by European Union Trade Commissioner, Peter Mandelson, at the School of Economics and International Relations, Sao Paolo, Brazil, 11 September 2006; see also L. Alan Winters, 'Doha and the World Poverty Targets', World Bank Conference on Development Economics, April 2002 (Washington, DC, World Bank, 2002).

19   United Nations Conference on Trade and Development, *World Investment Report, 2004* (New York: United Nations, 2004), 33–68; see also Edward M. Graham, *Fighting the Wrong Enemy: Anti-Global Activists and Multinational Enterprises* (Washington, DC: Institute for International Economics, 2000).

20   Greg Anderson, 'The End of the Renaissance?: US Trade Policy and the Second Term of George W. Bush', in George A. MacLean (ed.), *Canada and the United States: A Relationship at a Crossroads* (Winnipeg: Centre for Defense and Security Studies, 2006), 79–93.

The Perennials

While the 1990s were a period of high optimism in hemispheric relations, there were also indicators suggesting that the more things changed, the more they remained the same. A series of perennial issues in US–Latin American relations were overshadowed during the 1990s by talk of democracy and economic integration, but nevertheless remained.

Immigration, long a major political issue in the United States, reared its head during the 1992 presidential campaign and the debate over the NAFTA. Whereas the likes of presidential candidate Ross Perot suggested the NAFTA would generate a 'giant sucking sound' as US employment went to Mexico, others, such as then-vice-presidential candidate Al Gore, dismissed such talk as fear mongering. Instead, Gore and other proponents of the NAFTA argued that approval of the Agreement would stem the flow of illegal immigration north from Mexico by fostering economic opportunities in Mexico. Opportunities in Mexico did materialize, in part, as a result of the NAFTA, but they did so unevenly and were heavily concentrated in Mexico's northern states.[21] Yet, in many ways, immigration as a political issue in the United States was quietly growing along with the size of the US economy. As the US economy expanded throughout the 1990s, so too did the United States as a magnet for workers desperate to improve their standards of living.

Moreover, political and economic instability were never far away. In Mexico alone, the signs were everywhere in 1994. In January, leftist rebels from Mexico's Chiapas state staged an armed uprising timed to coincide with the implementation of the NAFTA agreement. Additional political instability came in March when Luis Donaldo Colosio, candidate for the Mexican presidency, was assassinated. To make matters even worse, Mexico was lurching toward a financial crisis that resulted in the devaluation of the Mexican Peso in December 1994, mere months after the NAFTA, designed, supporters said, to help guard against such events, was implemented.[22] Only a hastily organized bailout package, put together by the Clinton Administration with loans and loan guarantees from the International Monetary Fund (IMF), the Bank of International Settlements (BIS), and the US Department of the Treasury's Exchange Stabilization fund, prevented the crisis from getting worse.[23] Debate still rages today over whether the NAFTA itself

---

21   Garry Clyde Hufbauer and Jeffrey J. Schott, *NAFTA Revisited: Achievements and Challenges* (Washington, DC: Institute for International Economics, 2005), 1–68, but especially 43–58; Sidney Weintraub, 'Trade, Investment, and Economic Growth', in Sidney Weintraub (ed.), *NAFTA's Impact on North America: The First Decade* (Washington, DC: Center for Strategic and International Studies, 2004), 14–16.

22   See Joseph A. Witt, Jr., 'The Mexican Peso Crisis', *Economic Review*, Federal Reserve Bank of Atlanta, January/February 1996. See also Hufbauer and Schott, *NAFTA Revisited*, 8–14.

23   Ibid., 16–17.

also contributed to stemming economic catastrophe, or possibly even made matters worse.[24]

Finally, in 1999, the US Congress approved the multi-year, multi-billion dollar assistance package known as Plan Colombia, ostensibly aimed at assisting Colombia's own efforts at combating the illegal drug trade to the United States, but also at helping to quell the drug-fuelled violence in Colombia's decades-long civil war.[25]

As many issues changed, seemingly for the better during the 1990s in US relations with its hemispheric neighbours, others such as narcotics, financial instability, and immigration remained frustratingly familiar. In spite of the challenges that lay ahead for the FTAA, and for democracy in the hemisphere, the end of the 1990s was nevertheless heralded as the first chapter in a new and refreshing story line in the western hemisphere. Then, on 11 September 2001, 19 men commandeered four jetliners and dramatically altered US foreign policy priorities away from the western hemisphere. Or did they? As the balance of this chapter will argue, the events of 9/11 may have actually augmented US attentiveness to, and engagement with, its foreign policy backyard in a way that could not have been imagined just a few years prior.

Part II: The Post-9/11 World

On the surface, 9/11 changed everything in US relations with its hemispheric neighbours as the focus of US foreign policy seemingly shifted to the Middle East and away from the consolidation of open regionalism and democratic reform in the western hemisphere and elsewhere. In other policy areas, it was business as usual, but with a bit of a twist in the context of the emerging War on Terror that actually served to focus more, not less, attention on the region.

---

24   Hufbauer and Schott, *NAFTA Revisited*, 8–14; see also Weintraub, 'Trade, Investment and Economic Growth', 14–16; Rogelio Ramierez de la O, 'Prospects for North American Monetary Cooperation in the Next Decade', in Sidney Weintraub (ed.), *NAFTA's Impact on North America: The First Decade* (Washington, DC: Center for Strategic and International Studies, 2004), 69–89; Manuel Pastor Jr., 'Pesos, Policies, and Predictions', in Carol Wise (ed.), *The Post-NAFTA Political Economy: Mexico and the Western Hemisphere* (University Park, PA: Pennsylvania State University, 1998), 119–147; see M.A. Cameron and B.W. Tomlin, *The Making of the NAFTA: How the Deal Was Done* (Ithaca, NY: Cornell University Press, 2000), 68–80, 208–236.

25   See US Department of State, Bureau of Western Hemisphere Affairs, Fact Sheet, Plan Colombia (14 March 2001); Marc Cooper, 'Plan Colombia', *The Nation* (19 March 2001).

Narco-terrorism and Terrorist Finance

Of the many policy areas targeted by the United States to combat terrorism, terrorist finance has been among the most important, and arguably the most effective, as well. The US effort to combat terrorist finance world-wide has been housed in the US Department of the Treasury's Office of Terrorism and Financial Intelligence. For many years, the US Treasury has been responsible for tracking financial transactions related to the War on Drugs. In the broader fight against terrorist finance that expertise as well as the same law enforcement tools (especially the Treasury's Office of Foreign Asset Control listing of persons whose assets had been frozen in the War on Drugs, listing many from Latin America) has been employed – bringing additional scrutiny to all forms of financial transaction emanating from Latin America. According to the US Treasury, changes alone between 11 September, 2001, and April, 2006, resulted in more than 1600 terrorist-related accounts and transactions being blocked, as well as the designation of more than 400 individuals as supporting terrorist activity and over 40 organizations posing as charities as having links to terrorism.[26]

During that time, the Inter-American Development Bank (IDB) noted concerns over potential linkages between both terrorist and narcotics financing in Latin America due to the fact, that between 2.5 and 6.3 per cent of the regional GDP in Latin America came from money laundering – an increasingly global problem which had already been linked to terrorism. Overall, financial transactions within and from Latin America have been subject of great concerns since 11 September, resulting in various agreements in several policy areas ranging from combating terrorism to facilitating development. The Organization of American States (OAS) also continued its cooperation to controvert the linkages between terrorism and the illicit trafficking in drugs and weapons.[27] Such is the concern in many quarters with terrorist financing originating in the western hemisphere that the Organization of American States recently adopted the Inter-American Convention against Terrorism in 2002,[28] and has continued its cooperation in combating the linkages between terrorism and the illicit trafficking in drugs and weapons.[29]

However, the most visible sign of activity in this area was the Merida Initiative designed to combat illicit drug trafficking and associated violence in Mexico and

---

26   See US Department of the Treasury, Office of Terrorism and Financial Intelligence, Fact Sheet, April 2006.

27   Inter-American Development Bank, 'Money Laundering: What Do We Know?', in *Unlocking Credit: The Quest for Deep and Stable Bank Lending*, IPES 2005 (Washington, DC: Inter-American Development Bank, 2005), 241–256.

28   See Organization of American States, *Inter-American Convention Against Terrorism*, AG/RES.1840 (XXXII-O/02), and adopted 3 June, 2002.

29   See Organization of American States, *Declarations and Resolutions Adopted by the General Assembly at its Thirty-Fifth Regular Session*, Fort Lauderdale, Florida, 5–7 June, 2005, AG/RES.2137 (XXXV-O/05), OEA/Ser.PAG/doc.4496/05.

Central America. Conceived of in 2007 and formalized the following year, the Merida Initiative has received more than $1.5 billion (2007–10), a large portion of which was aimed at supporting the Mexican military and judicial systems to aid efforts to combat the narco-violence that has claimed many tens of thousands of lives.[30]

Immigration

In the immediate aftermath of the 11 September attacks, there were several immediate consequences for US relations with Latin America, the most salient of which was in immigration. US President George Bush and Mexican President Vicente Fox had been making considerable progress toward 'normalizing' activity along the US-Mexican border. In fact, immigration reform was high on the agenda during Bush's first meeting with Fox at Fox's family home in San Cristobal, Mexico in February 2001 and a significant reason for selecting Mexico as the destination of Bush's first trip abroad as president. When the two leaders met for the third time in September 2001 in Washington, again in early September 2001, it seemed that 'normalization' was going to take the form of a guest-worker programme for the estimated 11–12 million unauthorized migrants in the United States, of which 57 per cent were estimated to be of Mexican origin.[31]

Yet, the gaping holes in US immigration procedures and tracking that were exposed by the 9/11 hijackers put an immediate chill on plans for liberalizing immigration with Mexico or any other country. While it is widely known that US airspace was completely closed for several days following the 9/11 attacks, it is less well known that all US land borders were also closed to both commercial and private traffic. The commercial impact of the border closures was apparent within days as supply-chains were disrupted and warehouses saw their shelves rapidly empty in the days and large-scale efforts to find ways of securing goods crossing into the United States began almost immediately.[32]

The gravity of the 9/11 attacks for the openness of borders was as immediately evident, but the solutions seemingly much more complicated. The most obvious short-term effect of the attacks was the significant increase in security procedures

---

30   See Steven Hendrix, 'The Merida Initiative for Mexico and Central America: The New Paradigm for Security Cooperation, Attacking Organized Crime, Corruption and Violence', *Loyola University of Chicago International Law Review*, 5 (2), Spring/ Summer 2008, 107–125; Sabrina Abu-Hamdeh, 'The Merida Initiative: An Effective Way of Reducing Violence in Mexico?', *Pepperdine Policy Review*, 4 (2011), article 5.

31   See White House, 'Fact Sheet on Migration' (5 September 2001); White House, 'Joint Statement between the United States of America and the United Mexican States' (6 September 2001). See also Jeffrey S. Passel, 'Unauthorized Migrants: Numbers and Characteristics' (Washington, DC: Pew Hispanic Center, June 2005), 1–44.

32   See Greg Anderson, 'North American Economic Integration and the Challenges Wrought by 9/11', *Journal of Homeland Security and Emergency Management*, 3 (2) (Summer 2006).

at all US ports of entry. However, apart from the lengthy delays stemming from more careful security procedures, US immigration authorities abroad were subjecting new applications for entry to the United States to additional scrutiny as well. A 2006 US Government Accountability Office (GAO) report on consular resource requirements found that five years after the 11 September attacks, waiting times for visa processing at US consular posts around the world were unacceptably long, owing to a combination of new statutory procedures and a lack of funding for additional staff to handle the new requirements.[33] Where prior to 9/11, consular officials had greater discretion to waive interviews for low-risk applicants, interviews are now mandatory for all applicants, as are fingerprints, and for some applicants, additional security checks.[34] According to the GAO, in 2006 US consular outposts were regularly reporting delays of between 30 and 90 days just to arrange interviews for visa applicants. Importantly for Latin America, of the nine consular outposts reporting the longest delays (90 days or more), five were in Latin America.[35]

In October 2001, the USA PATRIOT ACT (PL 107-56) significantly strengthened the range of tools available to law enforcement and intelligence gathering authorities to combat terrorist threats in the United States and around the world. Among other provisions, the PATRIOT ACT reaffirmed a previous congressional mandate (from 1996) that US immigration authorities keep better track of visa holders once inside the United States. When originally proposed, the so-called entry-exit provisions of Section 110 of the Illegal Immigration Reform and Immigrant Responsibility Act were cause for considerable concern, particularly for Canadians who until then had been able to enter the United States with little more than a driver's license.[36] However, the PATRIOT ACT again mandated that an improved system providing for greater oversight and tracking of foreigners in the United States be established.

The period since passage of the PATRIOT ACT has seen the partial implementation of Section 110 as ports of entry have been outfitted with finger-printing and digital photographic equipment and nationals of many countries are

---

33 US Government Accountability Office, 'Reassessment of Consular Resource Requirements Could Help Address Visa Delays', GAO-06-542T, 4 April 2006. See also US Government Accountability Office, 'Strengthened Visa Process Would Benefit from Improvements in Staffing and Information Sharing', GAO-05-859, September 2005.

34 See Jess T. Ford, Director, International Affairs and Trade, GAO, Testimony Before the Committee on Government Reform, House of Representatives, 4 April 2006.

35 Ibid. The five were Ciudad Juarez, Mexico (92 days), Havana, Cuba (129 days), Mexico City (134 days), Port Au Prince, Haiti (167 days), and Rio de Janeiro, Brazil (140 days).

36 Christopher Sands, 'Fading Power or Rising Power: 11 September and Lessons From the Section 110 Experience', in Normal Hillmer and Maureen Appel Molot (eds), *Canada Among Nations: A Fading Power* (Toronto: Oxford University Press, 2002), 49–73.

screened, finger-printed, and in some cases, interviewed prior to entry.[37] As of early January 2006, the US Visitor and Immigrant Status Indicator Technology (US-VISIT) programme had processed more than 45 million travellers and intercepted nearly one thousand on criminal or immigration violations.[38] Furthermore, as part of the generalized effort by authorities to overhaul the US immigration system, the 2004 Intelligence Reform and Terrorism Prevention Act mandated that the Departments of Homeland Security and State devise a plan to require passports, or other documentation, for all persons entering the United States, including US citizens, by 2008 (PL 108-458, 17 December 2004). Out of this legislation emerged the western hemisphere Travel Initiative in April 2005 (Department of State Briefing, 5 April 2005) which initially proposed to require all entrants to carry a passport with biometric identifiers embedded within. The potential impact of this initiative both for visitors to the United States from other parts of the western hemisphere and for US citizens going abroad is obvious; particularly since less than 30 per cent of US citizens actually carry passports. However, the practical hurdles to this plan more recently gave way to the introduction of driver's license-like 'passport cards' as an alternative.[39]

The effects of some of these changes to immigration rules were felt immediately at US universities and research institutions. As US anti-terrorism measures have been implemented, resulting in considerable delays in processing and approval of immigrant applications, the pace of approval for citizenship applications, student visas, and work visas fell off. According to the Department of Homeland Security, just slightly over 700,000 people became permanent US residents in 2003, down from more than 1 million the year before, and only 463,000 people actually became US citizens in 2003, a 20 per cent decline from the previous year (*Washington Post*, 23 September, 2004). So serious have these concerns become that DHS and State have been working to reduce student visa processing times, issue visas up to 12 days in advance of study, and expand the entry window for those visas from 30 to 45 days in advance of study. In the broader context of the US war on terror, security institutions affecting immigration are having a negative impact on one of America's greatest assets in winning hearts and minds: education. As Secretary of State Condoleezza Rice argued in 2006 at the US University Presidents Summit Dinner,

---

37   The US-VISIT programme continues to experience growing pains, particularly the monitoring and exit provisions of the legislation. See Government Accountability Office, 'Homeland Security: Recommendations to Improve Management of Key Border Security Program Need to Be Implemented' (February 2006), GAO-06-296.

38   See Department of Homeland Security, 'Fact Sheet: Secure Borders and Open Doors in the Information Age' (17 January 2006).

39   Ibid.

> We must actively recruit students from these new strategic countries to live and
> study in America ... we must find a way to help these students to realize their
> dreams – studying in America – because if we do not reach them, others will.[40]

Anecdotal evidence has also begun to surface that Canadian universities have
become the beneficiaries of tougher US Visa requirements on foreign student
applications whereby prospective students and researchers have elected to avoid
potential delays or problems by attending Canadian schools rather than American
universities (*Globe and Mail*, 22 February 2005).[41] If this evidence is borne out
in empirical research, the implications for the Canadian and US research and
development communities, as well as the long-term health of each country's
labour force, are obvious. For decades many of Latin America's best and brightest
students have sought advanced degrees from US universities, thereby fostering
cultural, economic, and political linkages between the US and its Latin American
neighbours. It may be some time before empirical evidence is collected, but US
immigration procedures and the ferocious debate over illegal immigration could
ultimately strengthen the tenuous linkages between Canada and Latin America
and foster a range of new ones.

Finally, what became of George Bush's guest worker programme for Mexican
nationals? In the immediate aftermath of 11 September, the issue became a non-
starter in US political circles. However, in the years since 9/11, immigration has
become an increasingly polarizing political issue in the United States because it
now mixes national security issues along the porous US-Mexican border with
the more traditional battle over the economics and law enforcement aspects of
immigration. In January 2004, President Bush again indicated his own preference
for normalization of migration along the US-Mexican frontier by proposing a
guest-worker programme that would allow those already in the United States
legally to apply without penalty and provide a path to eventual citizenship for
those that applied.[42]

In the years that have passed since the terrorist attacks of 11 September, some
of the most important institutional changes that have been made in the name of
security are now beginning to have their full effect, although some are yet to be
implemented. The US-VISIT programme, for example, has yet to be applied
completely to all Canadian citizens, and the exit provisions of the programme are

---

40   Secretary of State, Condoleezza Rice, remarks at the US University Presidents
Summit Dinner (5 January 2006).

41   This early evidence is supported by informal discussions with the registrar at my
home institution, the University of Alberta. While applications for study from abroad would
likely be increasing anyway, the number of applicants expressing a preference to study in
Canada over the United States due to challenges posed by US immigration procedures
seems to be on the rise.

42   See White House, 'Fact Sheet: Fair and Secure Immigration Reform' (7 January
2004).

still being tested in the United States. The Western Hemisphere Travel Initiative was to have been fully implemented by January 2008, but the technical and logistical problems with requiring passports from everyone entering the United States by that date gave way to proposals for both delaying the deadline for implementation and a search for alternatives to passports.[43] Throughout the course of 2005 and 2006, the debate over how to fix the problems in US immigration exposed by the 9/11 hijackers has increasingly been fused with the illegal immigration debate in the US southwest. The debate became so fractious that serious proposals in Congress for constructing a wall along much of the nearly 2000 mile US-Mexican border received more attention and support. For example, in December 2005, Republican Congressman Duncan Hunter, a long-time advocate for building a wall, received significant support for doing so when the House voted 260–159 to amend new immigration legislation to include wall construction.[44] Incredibly, and much to the frustration of people on both sides of the US-Mexican border, those proposals were implemented in 2006 with the passage of the Secure Fence Act mandating the construction of hundreds of miles of fencing.[45]

Given all of these changes to immigration in the United States, is there a danger that the western hemisphere could actually be seeing a kind of retreat by the US into more of an isolationist stance? Restrictive immigration proposals and the construction of border walls suggest just that. Yet, the flip side of this apparent turn inward by the United States was President Bush's guest-worker programme for Mexico. Supporters saw this programme as ending the decades-long inconsistency in US policy toward migrant workers from Mexico while at the same time making important steps toward securing the US frontier with Mexico by offering relatively simple, easy-to-obtain legal status to those seeking entry.[46] On the other hand, immigration reform was, and remains, an issue that bitterly divides constituencies within the Republican Party, ultimately sidelining Bush's comprehensive immigration reform proposal in 2007. On one side are 'law and order' Republicans who see the guest worker programme as rewarding

---

43   See Canada, Canada Border Services Agency, 'Western Hemisphere Travel Initiative', at http://www.cbsa.gc.ca/agency/whti-ivho/gov-gouv-e.html. See also Government Accountability Office, Letter to Loretta Sanchez, Louise M. Slaughter, and John M. McHugh, Subcommittee on Economic Security, Infrastructure Protection, and Cyber Security, Committee on Homeland Security, United States House of Representatives (25 May 2006), GAO-06-741R. By June 2009, DHS had implemented requirements for passports or 'other secure travel documents' as proof of citizenship at all land, air, and sea ports of entry.

44   See House Resolution 4437 and House Amendment 648, 109th Congress (15 December 2005). The larger immigration bill, HR4437, passed the House 239–182 and moved to the Senate for consideration in early 2006; see also *San Francisco Chronicle*, (26 February 2006).

45   Secure Fence Act of 2006, PL109-36.

46   See White House, 'Fact Sheet: Fair and Secure Immigration Reform' (7 January 2004).

those already in the United States who violated immigration law to get into the country in the first place. On the other side are those traditionally pro-business Republicans who favour regularization because of the necessary role played by migrant workers in the US economy.[47] Spread between these two factions are those concerned with securing the US southwest from use as a potential corridor for terrorist activities. Advocates argue that the guest-worker programme represents a happy compromise in that it could contribute to a considerable reduction in illegal crossings by making legal access easier while at the same time addressing the most important issue on Mexico's foreign policy agenda.[48]

After several fits and starts during his first term, President Obama has endorsed a set of immigration reform proposals in the early months of his second term remarkably similar to those put forward by Bush.[49] Throughout much of Obama's first term, many lawmakers decried proposals offering a path toward legal status for those already in the US as 'rewarding law breakers'. However, the poor showing by Republicans in the 2012 presidential elections has opened up political space for a bipartisan group in both houses of Congress to push versions of Obama's plan forward. This situation is being watched closely by Latin American countries.[50]

Trade and Democracy

Of all the significant shifts in US policy toward Latin America since 9/11, one of the most intriguing revolves around US trade policy and trade relations with the Americas. Once seen as the primary driver of both economic and political relations in the western hemisphere, the Summit of the Americas process, and the Free Trade Area of the Americas, which made up its core, were hobbled by a series of problems by early 2002, and eventually derailed. As argued above, the FTAA was beset by differences between Brazil and the United States over how to proceed on agricultural support and, while all 34 governments continued to profess interest in finding a way to move forward in the negotiations, the original target for implementation of January 2005 came and went with little prospect for a renewed effort.

---

47   See Demetrios G. Papademetriou, 'The "Regularization" Option in Managing Illegal Immigration More Effectively: A Comparative Perspective', *MPI Policy Brief No. 4* (Washington, DC: Migration Policy Institute, September 2005), 1–15.

48   See footnote 24. Mexico has made migration a major priority in its foreign policy toward the US since at least the 2000 election cycle when then-candidate Vicente Fox reached out to ex-patriot Mexicans living in the United States to participate in that year's Mexican national elections.

49   See White House, Immigration Reform, At a Glance. Four principles are outlined: 1) strengthen border security, 2) streamline legal immigration, 3) earned citizenship (path toward), and 4) crackdowns on employers hiring undocumented workers.

50   'Obama "confident" Immigration Bill could pass this summer', *Associated Press* (2 March 2013), found at http://www.foxnews.com/politics/2013/03/28/obama-says-immigration-bill-could-pass-by-summer/, accessed 30 March 2013.

In spite of the failure of the FTAA, the United States had a particularly active trade agenda during the Bush presidency, especially when contrasted with the Clinton administration.[51] And, this trend continued under the Obama administration. Moreover, the US trade agenda has been heavily focused on Latin America, in spite of the demise of the FTAA. Agreements with Chile, five Central American countries plus the Dominican Republic, as well as ongoing negotiations with Colombia and other Andean countries all point to a continuing vigour with which the Bush administration has pursued regionalism in trade liberalization. In the 2008 Democratic Primary campaign against Hillary Clinton, candidate Obama adopted a strongly anti-trade posture that created some doubt about the pending approval of free trade agreements with Colombia and Panama. But as President, Obama slowly embraced trade, pushing for approval of those agreements, and launching a National Export Initiative (NEI) in 2010 designed to double US exports, and signing onto the Trans-Pacific Partnership negotiations in 2008.

US enthusiasm for trade liberalization, even on a regional basis, should come as no surprise in the wake of 9/11 given the Bush administration's broader arguments in the global War on Terror linking the openness of markets to democracy and the reduction of extremism. Indeed, in the months following 11 September, Bush administration trade officials such as US Trade Representative, Robert Zoellick, publicly argued for a renewed emphasis on the integration of markets because of their knock-on effects on governance, development, and extremism.[52] This broad line of reasoning had its origins in the early post-war years of American foreign policy, and endured throughout most of the Cold War. The rationale then was that the re-integration of the war-torn, economically destitute countries of Europe and Asia (especially Japan), would help shore up the western alliance against encroachment by the Soviet Union. Doing so would preserve the hard-fought freedoms won during World War II, and entrench the kinds of governance structures that fostered the kind of freedom, openness, and democratic governance thought to be in the US interest.[53] Coupled with the monitoring functions of

---

51   See C. Fred Bergsten, 'A Renaissance in US Trade Policy?', *Foreign Affairs*, 81 (6) (November/December 2002), 86–99; Greg Anderson, 'The End of the Renaissance?: US Trade Policy and the Second Term of George W. Bush', in George A. MacLean (ed.), *Canada and the United States: A Relationship at a Crossroads* (Winnipeg: Centre for Defense and Security Studies, 2006), 79–93.

52   See Robert Zoellick, 'Countering Terror With Trade', *Washington Post* (20 September 2001); Robert Zoellick, 'Free Trade, Free People', *Washington Post* (11 November 2002); David Dollar and Aart Kraay, 'Spreading the Wealth', *Foreign Affairs*, 81 (1) (January/February 2002), 120–133; Bruce R. Scott, 'The Great Divide in the Global Village', *Foreign Affairs*, 80 (1) (January/February 2001), 160–177.

53   Thomas Zeiler, *Free Trade Free World: The Advent of the GATT* (Chapel Hill: University of North Carolina Press, 1999); Alfred E. Eckes, *Opening America's Market* (Chapel Hill: University of North Carolina Press, 1995); Robert A. Pollard, *Economic Security and the Origins of the Cold War, 1945–50* (New York: Cornell University Press, 1985).

the Bretton Woods institutions, the IMF, World Bank and later the GATT, the reintegration of economies would serve as a powerful check on the economic instability and competitive economic policies of the inter-years that seemingly contributed to the rise of extremism and armed conflict.[54]

This line of reasoning as applied to post-9/11 US foreign economic policy made the same basic case in favour of integrated markets, but with a twist. Open, integrated markets fostered good governance that many saw as responsible for development successes around the globe, which in turn produced economic opportunities and reduced the attractiveness of extremist ideologies, such as radical Islam. Several popular commentators, such as Thomas Friedman of the *New York Times*, have been important popularizers of this line of reasoning and have argued that many of the most underdeveloped parts of the world suffer not from too much globalization, as the opponents of globalization claim, but from too little of it.[55] Moreover, like the Cold War rationale for propping up weak or vulnerable governments economically to ensure they would remain part of the West's Cold War alliance against the Soviets, contemporary incarnations of this thinking point explicitly to the importance of economic interdependence and openness in fostering democratic governance.

It is the democratic governance aspect of US foreign economic policy that stands out as a more explicit part of the US approach to the Americas on trade. The United States has long been prepared to reward democratic governance with increased US market access.[56] The requirement that participants in the Summit of the Americas process be democracies represents just another example of this ideological bent. Good governance and democratic governance, in particular, has become a central feature of US foreign policy, including development aide, and trade policy.[57] Nothing illustrates this better than the battle within the United States to get approval from Congress for the Central American Free Trade Agreement (CAFTA).[58]

---

54   Ibid.

55   See Thomas Friedman, *The World Is Flat: A Brief History of the Twenty-First Century* (New York: Farrar, Straus and Giroux, 2005).

56   See Pollard, *Economic Security and the Origins of the Cold War*; Eckes, *Opening America's Market.*

57   See for example the criteria for funding under the US Millennium Challenge Account. Interestingly, the World Bank has adopted similar governance criteria for its loan projects as have a number of countries such as Canada. See Canada, Department of Foreign Affairs, *Canada's International Policy Statement: Development, A Role of Pride and Influence in the World*, November 2005.

58   The US-Central American Free Trade Agreement (CAFTA-DR) is comprised of Costa Rica, Dominican Republic, El Salvador, Guatemala, Honduras, and Nicaragua. See Public Law 109-53, *Dominican Republic-Central America-United States Free Trade Agreement* (2 August 2005). The US legislation implementing the CAFTA passed the Senate by a vote of 55–45, and the House by a vote of 217–215, reflecting the bitterness of the debate over the agreement and US trade policy more generally.

In the late 1990s, cracks were emerging in the flowering of democracy throughout the western hemisphere. Several countries, notably Peru and Venezuela, were democratic on the surface, but were tending toward creeping authoritarianism, prompting some observers to warn of the rise of illiberal democracy, and with it, the potential for greater political instability.[59] A significant debate has emerged among scholars over the so-called democratic peace – in other words, that stable democracies do not fight one another.[60] Coupled with the broader rationale for the openness and interdependence of markets, democratic peace theory suggests that to the degree policies could encourage the entrenching of democratic reforms; the less likely we are too see an unstable and hostile country.[61] The CAFTA was undoubtedly an important economic agreement for them in terms of increased access to the US market for their products. However, for the United States, the only way to read the agreement is to look at as a tool for 'locking in' and consolidating political and economic reforms made in each of those countries through the economic incentives of a free trade agreement.[62] For the United States, the CAFTA was virtually meaningless from an economic point of view. None of the CAFTA countries features prominently in US trade statistics, and the *combined* GDP of the five CAFTA countries amounts to less than 1 per cent of US GDP. In addition, in 2005, US imports from CAFTA country represented just 1 per cent of all US imports.[63] The really important issue in the CAFTA debate was that, each of them was a nascent democracy.[64]

---

59   Fareed Zakaria, 'The Rise of Illiberal Democracy', *Foreign Affairs*, 76 (6) (November/December 1997), 22–43.

60   Francis Fukuyama, 'The End of History', *The National Interest*, 15 (Summer 1989), 3–18; Christopher Layne, 'Kant or Cant: The Myth of the Democratic Peace', *International Security*, 19 (2) (Fall 1994), 5–49; Michael Doyle, 'The Three Pillars of the Liberal Peace', *American Political Science Review*, 99 (3) (August 2005), 463–466.

61   See *Washington Post* (27 July 2005); *New York Times* (27 July 2005); *Boston Globe* (8 June 2005); *Seattle Times* (18 May 2005); *New York Times* (9 May 2005).

62   Recall that this was also part of the rationale behind the NAFTA. The economic benefits to the United States were tangible, but one of the underlying goals was to 'lock in' many of the political and economic reforms Mexico had instituted in the decade prior to the NAFTA's implementation in 1994. See Manuel Pastor Jr. and Carol Wise, 'Mexican Style Neoliberalism: State Policy and Distributional Stress', in Carol Wise (ed.), *The Post-NATA Political Economy: Mexico and the Western Hemisphere* (University Park: Pennsylvania State University Press, 1998), 41–81. See M.A. Cameron and B.W. Tomlin, *The Making of the NAFTA: How the Deal Was Done* (Ithaca, NY: Cornell University Press, 2000), 68–80.

63   Source: USITC.

64   Venezuela was the largest source of US imports in Latin America, owing largely to petroleum shipments, but is only the 11th largest source of US imports. Brazil, the largest economy in Latin America, is just the 17th largest source, while the highest ranked CAFTA in terms of all US import partners is the Dominican Republic at 47th. Source: US International Trade Commission.

While the bitter debate over the CAFTA in the United States has cast a pall over trade policy, the debate also put into sharp relief the importance of free trade agreements for the United States from a purely political point of view. The Bush administration spent significant political capital pushing for approval of an economically insignificant, but politically important, trade deals with developing countries that fit into the larger US foreign policy agenda. In the context of the Obama Administration's foreign policy 'pivot to Asia' the Trans-Pacific Partnership appears premised on a similar logic, this time directed strategically at several of China's regional neighbours including Australia, Singapore, Malaysia, Brunei, and Vietnam. There are four countries in the western hemisphere participating (Canada, Mexico, Chile, and Peru) all of whom have existing free trade arrangements with the United States.

Security, Security, and More Security

In spite of the attention that continues to be paid by the United States to its hemispheric neighbours in the trade arena, the one set of issues that is having an indiscriminate impact on all US trading partners is security. It is indiscriminate in that US policy changes intended to protect the homeland, such as changes to immigration screening, are intended to be applicable to all countries, other kinds of measures intended to secure the flows of goods into the United States are having uneven effects.

11 September ushered in a new era in the political economy of North America when the closure of most of North America's airspace and of the two international borders separating Canada, the United States, and Mexico, effectively announced the arrival of a new nexus of security and trade. While discussions as to 'what was next' in North American integration had been taking place almost from the moment the NAFTA was implemented in 1994, 11 September permanently added security to the mixture of issues being considered. In fact, security now looms so large in this discussion that it is now the principal driver of economic integration in the North American context. In March 2005, the three NAFTA leaders announced the North American Security and Prosperity Partnership (SPP). The SPP was a grab bag of issues left over from other processes and repackaged under a new label, Prosperity. But the new, and more dynamic part of the dyad, Security, has been driving the political economy of North America ever since.

Firms engaged in cross-border economic activity now face an ever-growing barrage of security measures affecting everything from component production, through supply chains, and final assembly.[65] As the process of adding value to products advances at each stage of production, component parts in North America find themselves crossing international borders several times before ending up in a

---

65 See Greg Anderson, 'North American Economic Integration and the Challenges Wrought by 9/11', *Journal of Homeland Security and Emergency Management*, 3 (2) (Summer 2006).

finished product. At each stage, and at each crossing, firms have to be concerned about the security of their supply-chains. While some of this security is internally prudent in an age of terrorist threats, the main reason for most of it is compliance with new government mandated security measures. Programmes such as Customs Trade Partnership Against Terrorism (C-TPAT), Free and Secure Trade (FAST), the Container Security Initiative, and NEXUS, have all be implemented in an effort to facilitate the efficient movement of both goods and people across international borders more quickly than would otherwise be possible.[66]

Security Can Be Benign

On the surface at least, the range of post-9/11 security changes implemented by the United States would seem to bode ill for much of Latin America. While the relative economic importance of Latin America in overall US trade is small, and gets smaller as you move south, the United States is an important, in some cases the most important, market for Latin America. The nexus of security and economics seems to pose a significant problem for Latin America. Or does it?

In looking at the many changes that have taken place in the political economy of the United States over the past several years, one is struck by the breadth of change in many areas of domestic public policy. Most notable has been the haphazard, incomplete, and bewildering reorganization of the federal government to create the Department of Homeland Security (DHS).[67] In talking about North American integration, DHS looms large because of its jurisdiction over so many areas now comprising nexus of security and economics. Yet, once we move away from a narrow consideration of North America, one is also struck by how little things have changed as well.

One example of the absence of substantive change are the advance reporting provisions of both the US Trade Act of 2002 and the US Public Health and Bioterrorism Preparedness and Response Act of 2002 (Public Law 107-210 and 107-188 respectively). Under both laws, shippers of goods to the United States are now subject to a range of advance reporting requirements depending on the mode of transportation being used to ship them. Specifically, as of January 2005, shipping of any kind to the United States required that electronic manifests be shared with the US Customs and Border Protection Service and with advance times of as much as 24 hours in the case of ocean-going vessels, four hours if shipments are made via air, two hours by rail, down to as little as 30 minutes

---

66   Ibid. See also Greg Anderson, 'Securitization and Sovereignty in Post-9/11 North America', *Review of International Political Economy*, 19 (5) (December 2012), 711–741.

67   Stephen Flynn, 'Homeland Insecurity: Disaster at DHS', *American Interest*, 4 (5) (May/June 2009), 19–26; Donald Kettl, *System Under Stress: Homeland Security and American Politics* (Washington, DC: Congressional Quarterly Press, 2004).

for trucks participating in the FAST programme.[68] However, the Bioterrorism Act of 2002 goes even further in mandating that foreign shippers have a designated agent or representative in the United States, register with the US Food and Drug Administration (FDA), and provide advance notification of food shipments of two hours by road, four by rail or air, and eight if arriving via water.[69] Whereas all shippers to the United States are subject to these new rules, many Latin American shippers do not confront the same imperatives of time faced by those in North America due to proximity. One notable exception to this has been the advent of significant flows of fresh produce, especially fruit, from Chile to US supermarkets, in part spurred by the conclusion of the US-Chile FTA in 2004. However, even here, the imperatives of security may actually be driving unexpected efficiencies in supply chain management wherein firms are ever more cognizant of the merits of different processes.[70]

In addition, new measures such as the Container Security Initiative (CSI) are not likely to have the same impact on Latin America as in other parts of the world, primarily because Latin America's trade profile is heavily skewed toward the production of more easily securable raw materials. The Container Security Initiative aims to inspect container cargo at foreign ports before it is loaded for transport has pushed US border controls beyond US shores and into foreign ports by placing both agents and US technology in foreign countries as a kind of condition of shipping to the United States. The first countries party to the CSI came on-stream in early 2002, and currently comprises more than 40 ports, including 6 in Latin America, covering more than 80 per cent of container traffic to the United States.[71] Of the six participating Latin American ports none is a significant source of US bound container traffic, although the expansion of the Panama Canal could see that country become a significant transit point for cargo bound for many parts of the world.

---

68   US Customs and Border Protection Service, 'Frequently Asked Questions', Trade Act of 2002 Final Rule, 3 August, 2004; see also Trade Act of 2002, Title III, Section 343, Mandatory Advanced Electronic Information for Cargo and Other Improved Customs Reporting Procedures.

69   See PL 107-188, Public Health Security and Bioterrorism Preparedness and Response Act of 2002, Section 307; and FDA, Guidance for Industry, Prior Notice of Imported Food, Questions and Answers, May 2004 at http://www.cfsan.fda.gov/~pn/pnqagui2.html#require.

70   Yossi Sheffi, 'Supply Chain Management under the Threat of International Terrorism', *International Journal of Logistics Management*, 12 (2) (2001), 1–11; Hau Lee and Seungjin, 'Higher Supply Chain Security with Lower Cost: Lessons from Total Quality Management', *International Journal of Production Economics*, 96 (3) (June 2005), 289–300.

71   See Jon D. Haveman, Howard J. Shatz and Ernesto A. Vilchis, 'US Port Security Policy after 9/11: Overview and Evaluation', *Journal of Homeland Security and Emergency Management*, 2 (4) (2005).

Latin American exports are heavily oriented toward natural resource extraction. In 2005, petroleum alone represented more than 46 per cent of all exports to the United States from Latin America. And, of the top 50 export products to the United States from the region, only a small handful were high-tech, high value added products such as automobiles or aircraft.[72] Raw materials and foodstuffs tend to be shipped in bulk rather than in containers aboard ships, and are therefore more easily secured for transport than containers.

Hence, Latin America's US bound exports are often subject to less scrutiny than finished products from other parts of the world wherein concerns over terrorism rise. The obvious reasoning behind this is that Latin America, apart from the violence spawned by narcotics production, has not been a significant source of international terrorism. However, the structure of most Latin American economies and the means by which raw materials are transported may be mitigating the impact of post-9/11 security measures adopted by the United States. In fact, Latin America may be uniquely positioned to take advantage of security-driven changes in the United States. Over the past decade, high global commodity prices, coupled with US interest in preferential trade agreements with its hemispheric neighbours, and the nature of Latin America's export profile, may all be combining to make Latin America an even more important region strategically for the US than was the case nearly two decades ago when the Summit of the Americas process was hatched.

Part III: What Has Really Changed?

In many respects, 9/11 is not a good point of departure for an analysis of the political economy of US–Latin American relations. Although the past several years have witnessed so many changes in US policy both domestically and abroad, there is much about US–Latin American relations suggestive of continuity rather than change. Moreover, while the period immediately following 9/11 seemed to herald the end of what been one of the most promising eras of constructive US engagement in the region, evidence abounds to the contrary. Subscribers to the 'end of an era' thesis can point to the demise of US efforts to regularize immigration with Mexico in 2001 and again in 2007, the collapse of the FTAA process, the erosion of democracy in the region, and, of course, the dramatic expansion of the US foreign policy agenda as evidence of the cyclical return of US indifference toward Latin America.

Yet, such an interpretation is misleading. The shadow of 11 September has loomed over discussions about immigration reform, mainly because the 9/11 hijackers so obviously exploited weakness in the US immigration system to gain lawful access to the United States. Three years later, the Bush administration was again pursuing immigration reform proposals and we see both American

---

72   Source: United States International Trade Commission, Data Web, 'US Imports from Latin America and the Caribbean, 2005'.

political parties vigorously courting Latino-Americans through their positioning on immigration early in Obama's second term. Similarly, while we can accurately claim that the FTAA is either on permanent hiatus or a dead letter, the problems with knitting the entire hemisphere together under a single trade agreement were evident almost from the start and were not exacerbated in any particular way by 9/11. In fact, the demise of the FTAA was much easier to trace; a fundamental disagreement between Brazil and the United States on how or, more appropriately, where to deal with agriculture.

In addition, the demise of the FTAA process, while undoubtedly frustrating from the US point of view, does not represent a low point of US interest in knitting the region together politically and economically. Whereas the Clinton administration was frustrated throughout most of its eight years in office in terms of active trade policy, the Bush administration assumed office in early 2001 with an active trade policy agenda.[73] It was an agenda characterized by the pursuit of both multilateral negotiations within the WTO, and regionalism in the form of the FTAA and other bilateral agreements. While the FTAA floundered, the United States was in the midst one of its most historically active periods in trade policy, concluding more than 15 agreements which include 27 countries in Latin America and the Caribbean.[74] A trade sceptic in 2008, Obama has since embraced trade liberalization (export promotion in particular) with the completion of Bush-era FTAs, launch of the National Export Initiative, and a heavy emphasis on the Trans-Pacific Partnership which includes four western hemisphere countries.

Perennial issues in US–Latin American relations will continue to bedevil the relationship, not the least of which are uneven development, narcotics production and trafficking, as well as the threat of political and financial instability. Political instability and especially the rise of illiberal democracy in the region will keep the US engaged, perhaps in ways that are unwelcome. Here, the emergence of Hugo Chavez as president of oil-rich Venezuela became a real source of conflict between the US and its hemispheric neighbours as Chavez attempted to spread his Bolivarian Revolution to his neighbours and continued to reach out to US adversaries such as Iran and Syria. With the passing of Chavez, one wonders whether there will be a major political shift in Venezuela or whether President Maduro will be able to sustain the Bolivarian revolution of his predecessor.

Finally, whereas the post-9/11 nexus of economics and security is having its impact felt around the globe as many struggle to sort out how changes in the US will affect them, the effects of this post-9/11 nexus are thus far being felt most

---

73   C. Fred Bergsten, 'A Renaissance for US Trade Policy?', *Foreign Affairs*, 81 (6) (November/December 2002), 86–98.

74   Source: The Office of the United States Trade Representative. Free trade or preferences agreements the US is negotiating or has completed include: Chile (2002), Colombia (2006), Panama (2004), Peru (2006), the CAFTA-DR (Costa Rica, Dominican Republic, El Salvador, Guatemala, Honduras, and Nicaragua, 2005), and 17 Caribbean countries covered under the Caribbean Basin Initiative (2000).

acutely in North America. The provisions of US security-related legislation and the plethora of programmes to secure the transit of cargo and persons across US borders are, in many instances, felt most acutely by Canada and Mexico by virtue of proximity to the US. The adjustment process for Canadian, Mexican, and US firms whose manufactured goods cross North America's borders several times over has been costly and complicated. Although Latin American exporters have had to bring their procedures into compliance to enter the US market, compliance has been made more straightforward as a consequence of distance and the very structure of Latin America's economies.

Changes to immigration rules, apart from the proposed guest-worker programme, are in some cases causing significant delays in visa processing. More importantly, the implementation of both the US-VISIT and western hemisphere Travel Initiatives do not represent anything significantly different from existing procedures for most citizens of the region. With the exception of Canadians, few citizens of western hemisphere countries entered the United States without a passport, and most required visas that entail background checks and or interviews. In many ways, the inconveniences brought on by these procedures were felt most acutely in North America, and by Canadians simply because they were new. In fact, the main group of people who are most affected by these new rules are Canadians who enjoyed privileged access to the US for most of the post-war period.

Conclusions

It has become conventional wisdom that the course of history changed with the terrorist attacks the United States on 11 September 2001. Much changed in the aftermath of those attacks, and it will be the job of historians to sort out whether 9/11 is that pivotal moment in history upon which everything turned. However, as they cliché goes, 'the more things change, the more they stay the same'. This may be an apt description of what has happened in the western hemisphere. This chapter has attempted to assess the significance of 9/11 in US foreign policy toward the Americas and argues that while there are narrow policy areas in which 9/11 has had a significant impact on US policy that, in turn, has affected the rest of the western hemisphere, in reality the broad swath of US foreign policy toward the Americas has changed very little in the years after 9/11.

Perennial issues in US–Latin American relations such as narcotics, illegal immigration, economic development, and democratic governance continue to be major facets of the relationship, just as they were prior to 9/11. The renewed interest on the part of the United States in economic openness and democracy in Latin America, as exemplified in the Summit of the Americas process, continues apace. The FTAA may be on permanent hiatus pending resolution of differences over agriculture policy between Brazil and the United States, but the United States has maintained an active trade policy in the region, one arguably more about politics than economics. Indeed, if we mark the renewed activism in US trade policy from the conclusion of the NAFTA and the initiation of the Summit of the Americas process, we would have to conclude that the lowest point of activism in the years since then were between 1994 and 2002. If anything, the US has been more active in trade policy since 9/11, particularly so in the Americas.

Even in policy areas in which 9/11 seemingly cast a dark shadow, such as immigration, the United States has returned to the issue in an effort to regularize the migration of people with its most important Latin American partner, Mexico.

Furthermore, with the exception of Mexico, Latin America has by and large not been significantly affected by the imperatives of security in the United States. Several elements of the structure in Latin American economic relations with the United States have, in effect, offered a measure of immunity from the most restrictive provisions being felt in North America.

None of this is to suggest there are not important challenges for the United States in managing relations with countries in its 'backyard'. In fact, while the United States has been pushing an activist trade policy, we can also see that the motivations for doing so have less to do with economics and more to do with re-mapping the Americas in keeping with broader foreign policy objectives. In recent years, a significant backlash to US leadership has developed, especially in Latin America, where US leadership and US-backed economic reforms have come under attack. The most vocal critic of US policies has been the late Venezuelan President Hugo Chavez. Observing Chavez's ability to utilize his country's vast petrodollar resources to foment anti-US policies among his neighbours and around the world, we may yet conclude that 11 September did in fact mark a major change in the hemisphere – perhaps not a change initiated by the United States, but rather one that was in opposition to the United States.

Chapter 11

The Constitutional and Political Aspects of Strategic Culture in Trinidad and Tobago

Hamid Ghany

Strategic culture is defined by the United States Southern Command as follows:

> Strategic culture is the combination of internal and external influences and experiences – geographic, historical, cultural, economic, political and military – that shape and influence the way a country understands its relationship to the rest of the world ... The concept of strategic culture is a useful tool for better understanding why countries react the way they do and how they may react to specific future situations. Strategic culture describes the range of cultural, political, and military experiences that drive a country's approach to the world.[1]

In addressing the constitutional and political aspects of strategic culture in Trinidad and Tobago against the backdrop of this definition, it would be important to interrogate the political philosophy underpinnings of the strategic culture itself.

The Afro-Indian Challenge for Constitutional Development

From an historical perspective, the commentary of Major E.F.L. Wood, MP, Parliamentary Under-Secretary of State for the Colonies, in his report to the British Colonial Office may offer us a perspective of what the British Government thought of the African and Indian populations in Trinidad and Tobago. According to Major Wood (later Lord Halifax), in his report following his visit to the British West Indies in 1921–22:

> The whole history of the African population of the West Indies inevitably drives them towards representative institutions fashioned after the British model. Transplanted by the slave trade or other circumstances to foreign soil, losing in the process their social system, language and traditions, and with the exception of some relics of obeah, whatever religion they may have had, they

---

1 Jeffrey S. Lantis, 'Strategic Culture: A Multifaceted Cultural Approach to the Study of Latin America'. Paper presented at the FIU-SOUTHCOM Academic Consortium, Florida International University (May 2009), 6.

owe everything that they have now, and all that they are, to the British race that first enslaved them, and subsequently to its honour restored to them their freedom. Small wonder if they look for political growth to the only source and pattern that they know, and aspire to share in what has been the peculiarly British gift of representative institutions.[2]

Major Wood also expressed concerns about the Indian community in Trinidad and Tobago as follows:

The East Indians are an important element in the community, and it would be a great misfortune if they were encouraged to stand aside from the main current of political life instead of sharing in it and assisting to guide its course.[3]

These views expressed by Major Wood some 40 years before the first territories of the English-speaking Caribbean were granted their independence essentially argued that constitutional development in the former British West Indies emerged on the basis of filling a void of identity for the African population of the region by assimilating the British model and by appealing to the Indian population to deny separatism.

This case is argued on two fronts. Firstly, it is based on a belief of British racial supremacy and, secondly, it suggests that the African population of the British West Indies had no other choice of constitutional system but the British one, because of its superiority and the lack of knowledge about any other systems, while it challenged the Indian population to join with the African population to cooperate in building a society. With the exception of Guyana, there has not been much deviation away from the British model in the former colonies of Great Britain in the West Indies. Whether that was because of the views of Major Wood, or because of the natural evolution of representative and responsible government from the old representative system, the Crown Colony system, the new representative system, cabinet government, full internal self-government, and, independence will remain a matter of debate.

The essential undercurrent of Wood's theory is that the African population had no identity and, therefore, would accept the foundations of British institutions as part of the evolution of Caribbean societies (which included Trinidad and Tobago). At the same time, Wood felt that the presence of an Indian identity was a threat to the stability of the society if they chose to pursue the agenda of separation as was done in Trinidad by the East Indian National Congress. The challenge for the British Government was how to get the Indians in the society to identify with

---

2   Report by the Honourable E.F.L. Wood, MP (Parliamentary Under Secretary for the Colonies) on his visit to the West Indies and British Guiana, Cmnd. 1679 (London: HMSO, 1922).

3   Report by the Honourable E.F.L. Wood, MP, 24.

the insertion of British-styled political institutions that they were confident would have been accepted by the African population.

As regards economic development, Wood was very clear on the need for European domination. He expressed this as follows:

> Finally it is right to remember, that the stability and progress of the West Indies are largely dependent upon the presence of the European element ... From the political, social, commercial and imperial point of view, it is vital that this element should be maintained ... .[4]

It was precisely this viewpoint of the 1920s that would be challenged by the anti-colonialists of the 1930s, namely C.L.R. James, Eric Williams and George Padmore.

Anti-Colonial Political Thought and Caribbean Marxism

There is no doubt that the early dominant anti-colonial political thought in the West Indies, in general, and in Trinidad and Tobago in particular was dominated by two Trinidadian-born political thinkers, namely Eric Williams and C.L.R. James. To a large extent, this anti-colonial thought was based on the philosophy of Marxism. The writings of C.L.R. James bear out this strong Marxist tendency as seen in *World Revolution 1917–1936: The Rise and Fall of the Third International*[5] and *Black Jacobins: Toussaint L'Ouverture and the St. Domingue Revolution*[6] which best capture the essential strains of his political thought.

In *World Revolution*, James roundly criticized Stalin's leadership of the Soviet state while simultaneously making a case for Trotsky's leadership under a new International. With James' world view clearly espoused in *World Revolution*, three years later he published *Black Jacobins* in which he took the view that the French bourgeoisie who led the fight for the advancement of political rights in France were ambivalent about the fate of the slaves in the colony of St Domingue because of their economic interests. James had clearly established his Marxist credentials in both books and his methodology was clearly based on an appreciation of the impact of economic forces on political movements. This would prove to be a major issue of political DNA in the Caribbean which includes Trinidad and Tobago.

---

4   Report by the Honourable EFL Wood, MP (Parliamentary Under Secretary for the Colonies) on his visit to the West Indies and British Guiana, Cmnd 1679 (London: HMSO, 1922), 49.

5   C.L.R. James, *World Revolution 1917–1936: The Rise and Fall of the Third International* (London: Martin Secker and Warburg Ltd., 1935).

6   C.L.R. James, *Black Jacobins: Toussaint L'Ouverture and the St. Domingue Revolution* (London: Martin Secker and Warburg Ltd., 1938).

Eric Williams was also very strong in his anti-colonial sentiment and this was firmly expressed in his famous book *Capitalism and Slavery*[7] which was an expansion of his doctoral thesis at Oxford University. In the book, Williams challenged the view that the British Government abolished slavery and the slave trade in the nineteenth century on economic, rather than humanitarian, grounds. In making this point, he was not far away from James who established an economic connection between the French bourgeoisie and their ambivalence on the colonial question because of their economic involvement in slavery.

Williams' Contradiction

Despite his intellectual challenge to the underlying arguments against British trusteeship in the West Indies as expressed in *Capitalism and Slavery*, Williams would reveal a fundamental contradiction that would be expressed in his constitutional thought that was absolutely inconsistent with his views on the British Constitution and its suitability for Trinidad and Tobago a decade after he published *Capitalism and Slavery*. On 19 July 1955, in a speech delivered in Woodford Square, Port-of-Spain, Trinidad, Williams would say:

> The Colonial Office does not need to examine its second hand colonial constitutions. It has a constitution at hand which it can apply immediately to Trinidad and Tobago. That is the British Constitution. Ladies and Gentlemen, I suggest to you that the time has come when the British Constitution, suitably modified, can be applied to Trinidad and Tobago. After all, if the British Constitution is good enough for Great Britain, it should be good enough for Trinidad and Tobago.[8]

This point of view represented an inconsistency on the part of Williams in respect of his worldview on the influence of Great Britain on Trinidad and Tobago which was at variance with his position stated in *Capitalism and Slavery*. His rejection of the intellectual underpinnings of British trusteeship in the region could not be reconciled with his desire for constitutional mimicry.

It is important to recognize this as it explains a fundamental embrace of the Westminster-Whitehall model of constitutional design in Trinidad and Tobago against a backdrop of anti-colonial sentiment. The best expression of this today would be the absence of the political will to implement the Caribbean Court of Justice as the final court of appeal for Trinidad and Tobago despite nationalist affirmations to complete the cycle of independence by abolishing judicial appeals

---

7   Eric Williams, *Capitalism and Slavery* (Chapel Hill: University of North Carolina Press, 1944).

8   Eric Williams, Constitution Reform in Trinidad and Tobago (Trinidad: Public Affairs Pamphlet No. 2, Teachers' Educational and Cultural Association, 1955), 30.

to the Judicial Committee of the Privy Council in London as the final court of appeal for Trinidad and Tobago. When faced with the opportunity to make this constitutional change in 1976, Williams rejected the Wooding Constitution Commission Report that included such a proposal. Indeed, he refused to depart from the Westminster-Whitehall model despite the change from a monarchical to a republican system for which he had the requisite votes in the Parliament.

Westminster Foundations and Washington Desires

Trinidad and Tobago is therefore a parliamentary republic whose constitution resembles the stock of Westminster-Whitehall constitutions that are the foundation of all of the countries of the Commonwealth Caribbean with the exception of Guyana. Any reform of its constitution will be based on three possible options. These options are (i) the retention of the parliamentary monarchy; (ii) a change to a parliamentary republic; and, (iii) a change to a presidential republic. The constitutional status of Trinidad and Tobago is a product of its political history and political culture and the constitutional change that has been effected is from (i) to (ii) above.

Simultaneously, the influence of the Washington model and some of its techniques cannot be underestimated. This may present the opportunity for hybridization in some instances between parliamentary and presidential models. Some of the more popular Washington model techniques are confirmation debates for the appointment of certain public officials, the ratification of Executive appointments by the Legislature, the right of recall, term limits for certain public officials, etc.

The balance between the Westminster-Whitehall and Washington models will provide philosophical challenges in advocating reform as the attractions of the latter model are, in some instances, incompatible with the former. Trinidad and Tobago as a parliamentary republic included some Washington constitutional techniques that are reasonably compatible with the parliamentary model such as an Electoral College for the election of the President in Trinidad and Tobago, the use of the President of the Senate to act as President of the Republic (a virtual vice-president) and the use of the Speaker of the House of Representatives to act as President if the President of the Senate is unable to act.

The parliamentary system is designed to function on the basis of domination of the Parliament by the Cabinet on a natural foundation of majoritarian division (Government majority and Opposition minority) that cannot accommodate consensual techniques of divided government that would involve the Executive being controlled by one party and the Legislature by another with no harm to the political system. It was easier for Trinidad and Tobago society to absorb the effect of a change from a parliamentary monarchy to a parliamentary republic in 1976 as opposed to skipping the parliamentary republic and heading directly for a presidential republic. Nevertheless, the effect of the Washington model on the evolutionary processes of Commonwealth Caribbean constitutions in their Westminster-Whitehall attire is likely to tilt the balance in years to come as Trinidad and Tobago society becomes weary of the authoritarian tendencies of the Westminster-Whitehall model in its application in a small parliament that is just the opposite of Westminster in size.

There was considerable concern expressed in the society over the decision of former Prime Minister Patrick Manning to pursue constitutional reform in the direction of an executive presidency. As the chairman of the public consultations in 2009–10 on the working document that was a draft constitution, I was in a position to discern the diversity of views among members of the public who participated. Their manner of thinking is premised on a Westminster-Whitehall foundation, but many of their desires were for Washington techniques, namely term limits, fixed dates for elections and public scrutiny of appointments to high offices of State. There were also calls for the right of recall. These requests were made without any frame of reference of how they would fit into the Westminster-Whitehall constitutional framework.

Constitutional and Political Outlook

In writing about the issue of presidentialism, Juan Antonio Cheibub has adopted the view that uncertainties about presidentialism in many countries where such constitutional systems have encountered difficulties is based on their ability to sustain democracy rather than a systemic flaw. According to him:

> In this book I argue that intrinsic features of presidentialism are not the reason why presidential democracies are more prone to break down. On the basis of an original data set covering all democratic regimes that existed between 1946 and 2002, I show that the alleged consequences of presidential institutions are either not observed or not sufficient to account for the difference in the survival prospects of presidential and parliamentary democracies. In line with those who have advanced 'exogenous' explanations, I claim that what causes presidential democracies' brittleness is the fact that presidential institutions have been adopted in countries where any form of democracy is likely to perish.[9]

Cheibub contrasts his point of view with that of Juan Linz. According to Cheibub:

> Most (if not all) of the arguments claiming the existence of a causal relationship between presidentialism and the instability of democracy are based on the work of Juan Linz. The point of departure of Linz and his many followers is that the separation of powers that defines presidentialism implies a relationship

---

9   José Antonio Cheibub, *Presidentialism, Parliamentarism, and Democracy* (New York: Cambridge University Press, 2007), 2–3.

of 'mutual independence' between the executive and the legislature, which contrasts with the relationship of 'mutual dependence' that is presumed to characterize executive-legislative relations under parliamentarism.[10]

In other words, Linz argues that there are inherent flaws in the presidential model that make it unsuitable for developing countries. In the circumstances, he expresses a preference for the parliamentary model.

In drawing conclusions from this debate, one may argue that Trinidad and Tobago is a parliamentary model that is tending in the direction of presidentialism. The reform of the constitution in 1976 introduced some presidential features such as an Electoral College and a reduction of prime ministerial power, but essentially retained its Westminster-Whitehall foundations with some architectural alterations to the structure itself. However, the prognosis for future reform is that more presidentialism will be the direction in which the country will have to go. For the time being, there is a parliamentary-presidential hybrid that is heavily weighted in favour of parliamentarism. Further reform is likely to weight the hybrid more in the direction of presidentialism if the desire for term limits and fixed dates for elections work their way into the constitutional amendment process.

The long range prognosis for the sustenance of democracy in Trinidad and Tobago looks good as the democratic foundation is solid from a strategic culture point of view. The introduction of states of emergency have always had a response in favour of the maintenance of law and order from the wider population. The risk of Trinidad and Tobago becoming unstable as a consequence of making constitutional reforms that will incorporate more presidential techniques in the future is minimal as the reforms that are envisaged are designed to reduce personal power for the office of Prime Minister. Additionally, Cheibub's argument about presidentialism not having inherent systemic flaws, but rather being able to survive in countries where there is a good democratic tradition, can also be applied to Trinidad and Tobago.

The Relationship Between Trinidad and Tobago

The Trinidad and Tobago Act 1887[11] that provided the legal foundation for the union of the British colonies of Trinidad and of Tobago to create a single colony of Trinidad and Tobago opened the door of disadvantage for Tobago. The island was required to take a backward step by surrendering its superior legislative arrangements when compared to Trinidad to become ultimately a ward of Trinidad and Tobago by 1899.

The Act of union of 1887 was followed by an Order in Council that was made in 1888 and came into effect in 1889. Further reform was to take place in 1898

---

10   José Antonio Cheibub, *Presidentialism, Parliamentarism, and Democracy*, 7.
11   United Kingdom Statutes 50 and 51 Vict., c. 44.

that resulted in the ultimate downgrade for the island by 1899 when it became a ward. It is this act of historical disadvantage that has left a level of bitterness about the manner in which the island has been treated by officials based in Trinidad. The final act of total unification took place during the period of the governorship of Sir Hubert Jerningham who became the Governor of Trinidad and Tobago in 1897. It was he who made the case to the Colonial Office for this final legislative act of union that would come into effect in 1899.

It should be noted, however, that Tobago's Commissioner at the time, William Low, had his reservations before he yielded to Governor Jerningham's view about closer union. Writing to Jerningham on 10 December 1897, Low had this to say:

> I must candidly confess that for the first 2 or 3 years of my residence here I was not an advocate for closer union with Trinidad; and even now the fact that an essentially English island, with such a brilliant page of history, will merge its identity on being amalgamated with an island largely permeated with Franco-Spanish ideas, although a mere matter of sentiment, causes a certain amount of regret'.[12]

As far as strategic culture is concerned, there is still great relevance in what Commissioner Low had to say to Governor Jerningham in 1897. The issue of Tobago and its relationship with Trinidad has been addressed on a policy basis in 1980 and 1996 whereby a measure of internal self-government has been gradually granted. This movement is likely to continue and there have been constitutional consultations throughout the island over the last few years to discuss the issue of an enhanced degree of internal self-government. The Government is about to issue a Green Paper on its proposals for the relationship of Tobago to Trinidad.

From a strategic culture standpoint, this will continue to be a growing area of demand. The issue of independence for Tobago is unlikely to arise if matters of internal self-government and self-determination are meaningfully addressed. It is possible that a federal arrangement could be the policy endpoint unless there are substantial oil and gas finds in the waters around Tobago that may make the independence argument viable. However, it would be more realistic to conclude that the policy demands from Tobago may end at the federal option.

Coalition Politics

The advent of the People's Partnership Government has opened up new possibilities for power sharing which has changed the political process of single-party government. The introduction of a philosophy of accommodative behaviour among leaders of different parties that comprise an oversized coalition government is new to Trinidad and Tobago.

---

12   United Kingdom National Archives, CO 295/384.

The strategic culture of the country has always accepted the two-party model with the People's National Movement (PNM) being the dominant political force. However, the creation of the People's Partnership on the basis of an approach of power sharing as opposed to dominance and political hegemony is now being contrasted against the outlook of the PNM which is to stand alone, win alone and lose alone. The clarion call of the PNM is 'great is the PNM and it shall prevail!' Such a statement is inconsistent with power sharing and is based on single-party hegemony and dominance. Furthermore, the United National Congress (UNC) and the Congress of the People (COP) have both introduced direct elections from among their membership on the one person-one vote principle for choosing their national executives.

The PNM is struggling with this internal policy change which has been proposed and has met stiff internal resistance to it. The PNM is still wedded to the delegate system for the election of their national executive at conventions of the party. The PNM will have to reassess its internal and external positions on direct election and seeking a coalition partner. The strategic culture of the society will change once the PNM embraces these two phenomena. Resistance against this trend could be detrimental to the party as the wider population has come to accept the direct election approach for the national executives of political parties as well as the introduction of coalition politics.

Conclusion

The philosophical underpinnings of the strategic culture are based on an anti-colonial mentality that has been transmitted into the political rhetoric and psyche of the nation largely from Eric Williams who was influenced in aspects of his vision by C.L.R. James. Williams' reverence for British-inspired institutions, while denouncing British influence in West Indian history and politics, represents an area of confusion that is reflected in the constitutional contradictions in the society.

The main contradiction is the desire for Washington techniques and the preservation of a Westminster character. The strategic culture of Trinidad and Tobago in the constitutional and political field is changing. There are shifts in the direction of presidentialism, however, there is a strong force that seeks to retain a Westminster-Whitehall foundation for the constitution. This cross current will push the strategic culture in the direction of hybridization between the Washington and Westminster models. However, the constitutional soil is fertile enough to sustain democracy regardless of whether or not more presidential techniques are introduced.

Chapter 12

From Engagement to Influence: Civil Society Participation in the EPA Trade Negotiations and Regional Integration Processes

Annita Montoute

Introduction

Trade Agreements are instrumental in shaping regional processes, and civil society can play a role in shaping these regional processes by influencing the direction of trade negotiations. This Chapter critically examines the CARIFORUM – EU Economic Partnership Agreement (EPA), hereinafter the EPA, and the part played by civil society in its attempt at influencing the process. The EPA has played a significant role in the configuration of the Caribbean internal regional integration processes and in the broader context of the re-mapping of the Americas. The EPA negotiations have therefore provided an avenue for civil society to shape the direction of Caribbean regionalism. The critical question is whether or not civil society in the region has taken advantage of that opportunity.

  While there was some degree of civil society engagement near the conclusion of the EPA negotiations, civil society failed to affect the outcome of the negotiations and lost an opportunity to influence the direction of the regional integration processes. This chapter argues that civil society ought to have played a role beyond engagement, to actually influence the trade negotiations and, by extension, the regional integration processes. The Chapter is comprised of the following sections: first, an examination of the relationship between the EPA and Caribbean regional integration processes; second, an investigation of the neo-liberal context in which civil society attempted to influence the negotiations; third, an analysis of the Caribbean's civil society engagement in the EPA negotiations and the challenges it faced in doing so; fourth, some prescriptive suggestions on the ways in which civil society can transition from merely influencing trade agreements and, by extension, the direction of regionalism. Finally, a brief conclusion is provided.

FTAs, the EPA and Caribbean Regional Integration Processes

Global developments have had a significant impact on the evolution of Caribbean regional integration processes. More specifically, since the 1990s, the regional integration processes have been shaped in large part by the neo-liberal turn in the global economy.[1] The Caribbean's attempt to transition from the Caribbean Community (CARICOM) to the Caribbean Single Market and Economy (CSME) represented a movement away from closed regionalism towards embracing open regionalism. Open regionalism was developed as a means of reconciling Regional Trade Agreements (RTAs) with the emerging multilateral neo-liberal trade order of the 1990s. The Caribbean has therefore had to model its regional integration arrangement in accordance with the rules of the global multilateral trading system. More specifically, Preferential Trade Agreements (PTAs) have now had to fall in line with the requirements of the GATT (1994) Article XXIV of the World Trade Organization (WTO) in which all trade is to be substantially liberalized. As shown earlier in this book, the North American Free Trade Agreement (NAFTA) was the first of this new type of arrangement in the western hemisphere.

The key issue about FTAs (like NAFTA) and regional integration is whether the former promotes or detracts from the latter. This broader debate is the topic of discussion in this section, particularly as it relates to the EPA and regional integration in the Americas. The aborted Free Trade Area of the Americas (FTAA) was the Caribbean's first experience with the new generation of FTAs. But the EPA is the only such agreement to have been successfully completed in the Caribbean. The ways in which the EPA has impacted regional integration processes in the Caribbean is examined below.

The EPA and other FTA negotiations have had both positive and negative effects on Caribbean regionalism processes. The advent of the neo-liberal order and the FTAs that emerged from that order awakened the Caribbean more than ever to the importance of strengthening regional integration. The hegemonic neo-liberal agenda of North-South FTAs has ignited a counter reaction and invigorated the Caribbean's participation in alternative South-South regional processes in the hemisphere. Notable examples of this counter-hegemonic reaction are the Bolivarian Alternative to the Americas (ALBA)[2] and the Community of Latin American and Caribbean States (CLACS).[3] Although developments in the global economy in the 1990s propelled the Caribbean towards a deepening and widening of the regional integration arrangement, the Free Trade Area of the

---

1   The term 'neo-liberal turn' has been used by some including Basak Kus, 'Neoliberalism, Institutional Change and the Welfare State: The Case of Britain and France'. *International Journal of Comparative Sociology*, 47 (6) (December 2006), 488–525; Andrew Lang, *World Trade Law After Neo Liberalism Re-Imagining the Global Economic Order* (Oxford: Oxford University Press), 3.

2   Thomas Mhur refers to the ALBA as counter hegemonic in 'Venezuela and the ALBA: Counter-hegemonic regionalism and higher education for all', 2, http://www.scielo.br/pdf/ep/v36n2/en_a13v36n2.pdf, accessed 26 December 2013.

3   Alexander Brand et al., 'BRICs and US Hegemony: Theoretical Reflections on Shifting Power Patterns and Empirical Patterns from Latin America'. Mainz Papers on International and European Power Politics (Johannes Gutenberg University of Mainz, 2012), 14.

Americas (FTAA), made strengthening of regional integration even more urgent to Caribbean leaders. The EPA, in effect, highlighted very starkly the result of a weak regional integration process. But how, specifically, did the EPA affect the regional integration process? And, what role did civil society play in the EPA process?

Clearly, the EPA has had profound implications on Caribbean integration. It is important to understand whether or not civil society participation in the EPA process was an avenue for influencing the direction of the Caribbean regional integration process. First, the Caribbean Forum (CARIFORUM), comprising of CARICOM and the Dominican Republic, which the EU set up to negotiate the EPA, has introduced a new layer in the configuration of Caribbean regional processes. The Forum of the Caribbean Group of African, Caribbean and Pacific (ACP) States (CARIFORUM) is the body that comprises Caribbean ACP States for the purpose of promoting and coordinating policy dialogue, cooperation and regional integration, mainly within the framework of the Cotonou Agreement between the ACP and the European Union and also the CARIFORUM-European Community Economic Partnership Agreement (EPA). The CARIFORUM framework, has essentially integrated CARICOM with the Dominican Republic.[4] Without the EPA, CARICOM may not have gone this route, at least in the near future, principally due to concerns about the differences in the size of the Dominican Republic market compared to that of CARICOM countries.[5]

Second, the EPA is far more advanced than the CSME in terms of the degree and scope of legal commitments and implementation schedule.[6] This means that the EPA and the CSME are not compatible and the former could serve as a vehicle for speeding up the CSME. On the other hand, it means that the CSME will be driven by an external process rather than the development needs of the region.[7] In fact the EPA negotiations were not driven by the CARICOM development agenda

---

4   N. Girvan, 'Implications of the CARIFORUM – EC EPA' (2008), 18, http://www. normangirvan.info/wp-content/uploads/2008/01/girvanimplicationsepa10jan.pdf.

5   Anthony Gonzales indicated the fears among some Caribbean countries especially LDCs about competition from the Dominican Republic in the context of the CARICOM/ Dominican Republic Free Trade Agreement. This fear limited the scope of liberalization to mainly trade in goods and with CARICOM MDCs only. We argue that this fear was exacerbated in the context of a comprehensive EPA which covers more than trade in goods and with all CARICOM countries. Anthony Peter Gonzales, CARICOM Report no. 1 (Institute for the Integration of Latin America and the Caribbean Inter-American Development Bank, 2002), 53.

6   Havelock Brewster. 'The Anti-Development Dimension of the European Community's Economic Partnership Agreement for the Caribbean' (2008), http://www.nor mangirvan.info/the-anti-development-dimension-of-the-european-communitys-economic-partnership-agreement-for-caribbean-havelock-brewster/, accessed 26 December 2013.

7   N. Girvan, 'Implications of the CARIFORUM – EC EPA' (2008), 5, http://www. normangirvan.info/wp-content/uploads/2008/01/girvanimplicationsepa10jan.pdf, accessed 26 December 2013.

embodied in the Single Development Vision of 2007[8] but rather was negotiated on an EU template informed by the Global Europe Strategy. Girvan concluded that:

> (t)he most likely scenario … is one in which the CSME is melded into the EPA as an adjunct to the larger scheme of economic integration with Europe (and collaterally, with the Dominican Republic). Within 10-15 years the Caricom Common External Tariff will have largely been eliminated; market integration in goods, services and investment with much larger and more economically powerful trading partners will be far advanced; and policies in key areas will have been adapted to suit. EU and possibly DR firms may be dominating the most profitable sectors. In a sense, the logic of the EPA is to replace the Caricom Single Market and Economy with a 'Cariforum EU Single Market and Economy'.[9]

Third, by virtue of the powers given to the various EPA governance mechanisms, the EPA governance structures supersede that of the organs laid out in the Treaty of Chaguaramas (1973) which established CARICOM. The EPA gives The Joint CARIFORUM – EC Council greater legal authority than the CARICOM Heads of Government Conference, the Council for Trade and Economic Development (COTED) and other CARICOM organs. The Trade and Development Committee which is responsible for supervising EPA implementation also have authority over States.[10]

Fourth, the EPA affects Caribbean regionalism with other countries of the South in the hemisphere and with the hemisphere. The EPA contains a Most Favoured Nation (MFN) clause that provides for equal treatment to the EU as other major trading economies with which CARIFORUM enters an agreement. This has profound implications for future agreements between the Caribbean and countries in the hemisphere such as Brazil and other major developing countries. Any agreement with major Southern countries will be dictated by what has been offered to the EU in the EPA.[11]

It is clear from the above that the EPA is impacting the configuration of regional processes in the Caribbean. Unfortunately, civil society was not able to influence these processes in any meaningful way. Although, civil society has been more engaged in the CSME process, a more effective avenue to impact the movement of the CSME would have been through the EPA negotiations. The context in which civil society seeks to influence policy affects the extent to which it will

---

8   Ibid., 17.

9   Ibid., 18.

10   Ibid., 15.

11   Havelock Brewster, 'The Anti-Development Dimension of the European Community's Economic Partnership Agreement for the Caribbean' (2008), 8, http://www.nor mangirvan.info/the-anti-development-dimension-of-the-european-communitys-economic-partnership-agreement-for-caribbean-havelock-brewster/, accessed 26 December 2013.

be successful. It is important to understand that the negotiations were conducted in a framework that was settled even before the negotiations started. Therefore, the degree of influence that civil society could achieve was constrained from the outset. To expand on this point, let's examine the background of the neo-liberal paradigm within which civil society attempted to influence the negotiations.

Trade Negotiations – The Neoliberal Globalization Model

The model of trade negotiations today is a reflection of the evolution of changes in the global political economy which reflects major shifts in development thinking over the last 50 plus years.[12] From the 1950s, trade negotiations were conducted in the context of the General Agreement on Tariff and Trade (GATT) 1947. Today, trade negotiations are conducted under the umbrella of the World Trade Organization (WTO) which replaced the GATT arrangement in 1994. Under the GATT (1947), developing countries were given special consideration because they were at lower levels of development. Preferential treatment was accorded to developing countries to allow them to pursue development policies and for autonomous policy space in developing policies. In contrast, the principles of reciprocity and non-discrimination of the WTO are applied across the board with the exception of Least Developing Countries. The two distinct approaches to trade with developing countries between 1945 and 1994 and 1995 to the present coincided with the Cold War and the post-Cold War periods. The end of the Cold War gave way to the triumph of global capitalism based on profits and private capital. The Caribbean has participated in trade arrangements in both periods.

The Caribbean has participated in trade agreements under the dispensations of both developmentalism and neo-liberalism. During the Cold War era, the US and Canada signed preferential trading arrangements with the Caribbean: the Caribbean Basin Initiative (CBI) and the Caribbean-Canada Trade Agreement (CARIBCAN) respectively.[13] A preferential trade and economic system in the context of the Lomé Conventions was reached between Europe and its former colonies in the Africa, Caribbean and Pacific in 1975. A new generation of agreements (Free Trade Agreements) is now being negotiated all around the world between developed and developing countries. In 1994, the US launched a project to negotiate an FTA, the Free Trade Area of the Americas (FTAA) with the Caribbean and other countries of the western hemisphere.[14]

---

12   See, for example, David Simon, 'Development Reconsidered: New Directions in Development Thinking', *Geografiska Annaler. Series B, Human Geography*, 79 (4), Current Development Thinking (1997), 183–201.

13   Andres Serbin, 'The Caribbean: Myths and Realities for the 1990s', *Journal of Interamerican Studies and World Affairs*, 32 (2) (Summer, 1990), 121–141.

14   Organization of American States (OAS), http://www.sice.oas.org/tpd/ftaa/ftaa_e. asp, accessed 26 December 2013.

In 2008, CARICOM and the Dominican Republic (CARIFORUM) signed the Economic Partnership Agreement (EPA) with the European Union. The Agreement was to make the Caribbean's trade and economic relations with the EU WTO compatible. However the EPA encompasses commitments in the areas of investment, competition policy, government procurement and trade facilitation – also known as the Singapore Issues – which go beyond WTO requirements.

There was limited influence by civil society who mainly lobbied towards the end of the negotiations for a greater development dimension to be inserted in the Agreement. In the end, the negotiations were concluded with trade liberalization at the core. This happened despite legal provisions for civil society participation in the Cotonou Agreement for Non-State Actor Participation. Article 2 of the Cotonou Agreement defines participation as a fundamental principle of ACP-EC cooperation. One of the three main entry points for civil society in the Cotonou Agreement is trade policy, i.e., the EPAs. The Cotonou Agreement provides several avenues for civil society participation in the EPAs negotiations: in national consultations; at the negotiating table; in discussions at the regional and the ACP EU level in workshops in the DG trade initiative and the European Economic and Social Committee (EESC).[15]

Civil Society Participation and the CARIFORUM EU EPA

Research on civil society participation in the CARIFORUM-EU EPA has been conducted by Norman Girvan (2009; 2010) and me. (2009). Girvan's study examines the tactics used in the negotiation process to inform lessons for Caribbean citizen movement. Girvan (2010) argues that several tactics negatively impacted civil society participation in and influence of the EPA negotiations. Among these tactics were the use of technical language ('techification'), exaggerating the benefits of the agreement ('sweetification') and the 'incorporation of the agreement into a legally binding international treaty with muscular enforcement machinery' ('treatifycation').[16] Other factors negatively affecting participation were the inadequacies of regional governance structures and weaknesses in the citizen movement. I have examined elsewhere (2009) the degree to which civil society participation was effective in the EPA negotiations and came to the conclusion that while civil society tried to become engaged in the negotiation process through the use of specific strategies, overall, participation was inadequate, asymmetrical and ineffective.

---

15   ACP Secretariat. The Cotonou Agreement: A User's Guide for Non State Actors (2003), 56.

16   N. Girvan, 'The Caribbean EPA Affair: Lessons for the Progressive Movement' (2009), 2, http://www.normangirvan.info/wp-content/uploads/2009/08/pittsburgh-rev21.pdf, accessed 26 December 2013.

Caribbean civil society engagement in the EPA process was coordinated at the regional level by the Caribbean Policy Development Centre (CPDC). The following national regional organizations collaborated with CPDC: the Windward Islands Farmers' Association (WINFA), the Caribbean Association for Feminist Research and Action (CAFRA) and the Caribbean Congress of Labour (CCL). Also participating at the national level were groups that included the Federation of Independent Trade Unions and NGOs (FITUN) in Trinidad and Tobago, Guyana Rice Producers' Association (GRPA), the Haitian Platform for Alternative Development (PAPDA) and the National Union of Public Workers (NUPW) in Barbados.

Civil society engagement started during the preparatory stages of the negotiations, as early as 2003, when a regional consultation was hosted by the EU in partnership with the CPDC on the ACP EU Impact Assessment Study. The CPDC continued their engagement at the start of the EPA negotiations. Among the first activities was a regional rally in Barbados coinciding with the launch of the negotiations in 2004. Engagement continued outside of the official process in the form of protest action against the EPA during the third phase of the negotiations. One of these events was a public rally in St Lucia in 2005 dubbed 'Operation Get Up Stand Up'. The above events were either small in scale or involved few representatives of civil society organizations. Civil society engagement intensified and peaked towards the conclusion of the negotiations, at the initialling in 2007 and signing of the Agreement in 2008.

Between 2007 and 2009, NGOs, trade unions, joined by academics campaigned for a re-negotiation of the EPA. For example, in 2007 the attempts made by citizen groups included the following: An open letter on the EPA asked that the Draft Agreement on the EPA be made available for public discussion. In 2008, after the initialling of the EPA, the Assembly of Caribbean People, supported by groups from Latin America, in a Declaration stated that the EPA was a dangerous neo-liberal project which was not in the interest of Caribbean people and should be re-negotiated. The Caribbean Congress of Labour called for a review of the EPA and its re negotiation. The CPDC on behalf of CARIFORUM citizens launched a petition for the renegotiation of the EPA. The petition attracted 400 signatures. A group of concerned Caribbean citizens called for full and public review of the EPA. The campaign continued into 2009, when PAPDA asked the Haitian Parliament to reject the ratification of the EPA. The anti EPA campaign revealed a range of views held by various segments of civil society outlined below.

Views of Civil Society Organizations on the EPA Negotiations

Generally, critics asked for a review or re negotiation of the Agreement after its conclusion. The anti-EPA movement focused on two main areas: process and substance. In terms of the substance, the overarching criticism was for the underlying philosophical foundation of the negotiations to shift from a neo-liberal framework and for the insertion of a development dimension into the agreement. Civil Society Organizations (CSOs) therefore argued that the Agreement should be a development cooperation agreement of which trade should be only a secondary pillar. They recommended that elements of poverty reduction and sustainable development be inserted into the negotiations. More specific substantive proposals were as follows: limiting EPA obligations to the requirements of WTO compatibility; maintaining existing levels of market access to the European Union; inserting Protocols on the principal CARIFORUM productive sectors; including legally binding bilateral cooperation measures to be provided under the agreement; inserting legally binding development benchmarks to measure the socio-economic impacts of the EPA; including a provision for a mandatory review of the EPA.[17]

Concerning process, civil society called for the release of the draft EPA text for public comment and discussion. Women NGOs called for women to be represented as a separate entity at the national and regional levels in the EPA dialogue. Trade unions called for the inclusion of core labour standards to be inserted in the negotiations; greater transparency in providing information and funding; the inclusion of participation as an objective and principle of the negotiations; equity in financial support; access to meetings and information; formal processes and mechanisms for participation; creation of a website or web space to provide up to date information on the negotiations; selection of a civil society liaison officer at the OTN (formerly CRNM) and the inclusion of a clause on information disclosure.

Challenges Encountered by Civil Society During the CARIFORUM EPA Negotiations

There were many challenges encountered by civil society in the course of the negotiations. First, there was limited interest by the NGO community in the process particularly in the initial stages of the negotiations. Among the reasons for this was that some groups did not see trade as part of their mandate. Second, a lack of understanding and confusion about the participatory process e.g. the structure of the Non State Actor Panel and the role NGOs were to play in it. Third, there was a lack of confidence that CSO participation could affect the outcome of the negotiations. Some NGOs were concerned that the private sector was the preferred partner of governments in the negotiations. Fourth, there was inadequate or tardy information coming out of the process. Civil societal groups claimed that information was not reaching the relevant persons, the information was very technical and therefore difficult to understand and it was usually not received in a timely manner. This made it difficult or impossible to put forward

---

17 Caribbean Congress of Labour, 'Declaration and Plan of Action on Regional Integration and the Economic Partnership Agreement and their Social and Labour Dimensions' (June 2008), 2, http://www.ilocarib.org.tt/trade/documents/ccl-declaration-plan-of-action.pdf, accessed 26 December 2013.

positions. Fifth, some felt that the negotiations were not based on the development objectives set out in the Cotonou Agreement and in some cases the disappointment and a sense of betrayal kept some CSOs from participating. Sixth, the lack of transparency hindered participation. Participants claimed not to know if their suggestions were being taken on board. Seventh, asymmetrical participation was a source of complaint for many CSOs. There was inequity in participation in the funding as well as access to information in favour of private sector actors. Eighth, while some civil society leaders were aware and engaged in the process, the general membership and public were not engaged. Only at the conclusion of the negotiations did a larger segment of the population become aware of the process. Finally, civil society did not have the capacity to undertake necessary action or to conduct mass sensitization campaigns.

The challenges of participation were exacerbated by the general attitude of the governments towards civil society participation. It appears that the participatory structures were a mere formality to meet the requirements of the Cotonou Agreement. Therefore, while policy makers expressed willingness to engage with civil society, they acted in a contrary manner.

Although NGOs were invited to attend meetings, they were expected to bear the cost of their participation, unlike some private sectors actors who were usually sponsored. For this reason, among others, civil society participation left much to be desired. The lack of transparency which pervaded the negotiations makes it difficult to assess precisely the extent to which civil society impacted the negotiations. There is a general consensus however that civil society did not influence the outcome of the EPA negotiations in any significant way. The signing of the Agreement in December 2008, despite public outcry, is evidence that this was the case. What then are some concrete strategies CSOs can use to make an impact? A perusal of some existing literature might help provide some answers.

Critical Success Factors in Civil Society Participation – What the Literature Tells Us

Verba (1967) outlines the following as necessary for impacting the outcome of decisions: resources; the degree to which the participant is motivated; existence of structures for facilitating participation; the degree to which participation is accepted in the particular context; the degree of equity in the participatory process and the outlook of the decision-maker.

Empirical research points to concrete factors that enhance civil society influence. First, NGOs gain leverage by effectively framing the issue in a manner to capture the attention of the public and government.[18] Framing trade negotiations as a development issue rather than a technical issue has proven to be powerful.

---

18   H. Baogang, and H. Murphy, 'Global Social Justice at the WTO? The Role of NGOs in Constructing Global Social Contracts', *International Affairs*, 83 (4) (2007), 725.

Focusing on the policy implications of the negotiations proved to be a very useful strategy. NGOs have been successful when they politicized and introduced larger policy issues to the debate.[19]

In the case of the EPA negotiations in the Caribbean, it was clear that civil society made the EPA a development issue and their arguments were framed accordingly. Framing can be improved by focusing on the implications of the Agreement for development as a prerequisite for arguing for insertion of a development dimension. The need to include a development agenda becomes more convincing when both policy makers and ordinary people are able to see the development impact. Translating the development impact into language with which ordinary people can identify makes framing more potent.

The use of independent empirical research has proven to be critical for groups to influence the trade policy agenda. This was particularly useful when this type of information was not available to decision makers and the latter were dependent on groups for it.[20] In one instance, NGOs pushed for independent research to be conducted on the readiness of the country to sign the EPA and the decision made was based on the results of the research. The insertion of alternative information into the policy debate proved to be a successful strategy. NGOs used this information as a political tool by withholding it from the opposing side and to debunk mainstream information proved to be successful.[21] Research may also be used for other reasons: to establish the credibility of NGOs; to build momentum around a particular issue and to improve the effectiveness of implementation and evaluation of trade policy.[22]

The implications of this observation are many. First, civil society gains legitimacy and power when it fills in an existing information gap. With regard to regional integration, this is an issue which was limited in the negotiations. Existing studies on the impact of FTAs on regional integration in other regions would have been useful and impactful.

Second, credibility and legitimacy are attained further if the research comes from an independent source as research that comes from civil society may be perceived to be biased and ideological. Civil society therefore needs to consider who or which organization funds the study. If the sponsor is deemed to be partial

---

19   S. Trommer, 'Activists Beyond Borders: Transnational NGOs Strategies on EU West Africa Trade Relations', *Globalisations*, 8 (1) (2011), 122.

20   Ibid., 122; J. Schwartzkopff, 'Splendid Isolation: The Influence of Interest Groups on EU Trade Policy', Berlin Working Paper on European Integration, 12 (2009), 26; A. Montoute, 'Civil Society Participation in Trade Negotiations: A Caribbean Case Study' (PhD diss., The University of the West Indies, St Augustine Campus 2009), 283.

21   S. Trommer, 'Activists Beyond Borders: Transnational NGOs Strategies on EU West Africa Trade Relations', *Globalisations*, 8 (1) (2011), 122.

22   A. Pollard and J. Court, 'How Civil Society Organisations Use Evidence to Influence Trade Policy Processes: A Literature Review' (Overseas Development Institute, Working Paper 249, 2005), vi.

this could hinder the credibility of the study and its impact. NGOs may use evidence (research) to highlight the importance of a particular issue. When this is done effectively, it can lead to policy change or the opening of policy windows. One of the considerations for NGO effectiveness in this context is the communication of the evidence rather than the empirical basis. The important factor is for the ideas or concepts to have resonance with the relevant actors. Therefore in presenting research, NGOs must be as political as they are empirical. When NGOs have to compete to be part of the process, the need to be more rigorous and empirically sound is greater than those who have been asked to be part of the process. High quality research that has relevance and is effectively packaged and conveyed can play a role in the degree of impact. Research that uses familiar phraseology and is targeted is more effective. Quality research also establishes the legitimacy of CSOs providing them with increased credibility to influence policy makers. Direct communication with policy makers as well as high media coverage can help advance CSOs ability to influence.

In summary, research helps CSOs influence policy in various ways: providing them with various types of legitimacy – technical, representative, moral and legal. Legitimacy also makes CSOs work more effective. NGOs can use evidence (research) to help them assess information and improve on the impact of their work.[23] The above discussion indicates that civil society must adopt a multipronged communication strategy, i.e., one strategy for technocrats and another for constituents. Even at the level of the society there are different sectors and the language must be tailored to suit. It means therefore that various media should be used for the sector or group in question. Another implication for the observations above is that there is a need for groups that are outside of official processes (outsiders) to develop greater capacity for research. This also means that outsider groups should also seek to access official processes to increase their chance of influencing policy.

Third, the possession of information relevant to the issue helps interest groups impact trade policy. The degree of asymmetry in access to information explains why some groups have influence over others.[24] Groups that provide information to policy makers are more likely to make an impact on policy than groups that do not.[25] This means that civil society needs to continue to demand transparency and disclosure of information while at the same time seek ways to fill information gaps that may exist in the negotiations.

---

23 Ibid.

24 J. Beyers, 'Gaining and Seeking Access. The European Adaptation of Domestic Interest Associations', *Journal of Political Research*, 41 (5) (2002), 588.

25 S. Trommer, 'Activists Beyond Borders: Transnational NGOs Strategies on EU West Africa Trade Relations', *Globalisations*, 8 (1) (2011), 122; A. Montoute, 'Civil Society Participation in Trade Negotiations: A Caribbean Case Study', 283–284.

Fourth, NGOs gain greater leverage when the relevant authorities are willing to listen. For example, the EU Commission was not as receptive to NGOs positions[26] on liberalization as ACP governments in the conduct of the EPA because the Commission has generally adopted a neoliberal approach to trade. Thus, the political context in which trade negotiations take place (the existing culture of democracy and the government's position on the negotiations) will affect the degree of success NGOs have in influencing the trade policy agenda. Context is important in other ways. For example, research is more likely to impact policy if they have been invited to influence the policy process.[27] The research has less impact in contexts where NGOs have to fight to be part of the policy formulation process. The timeliness of the research, the relevance of it, and how appropriate it is, are all important considerations for influencing the policy process.[28] Civil society needs to attempt to change the culture of and the perception of policy makers towards civil society participation. This change in culture and perception comes with greater credibility and legitimacy which civil society is able to establish through research and providing critical relevant information. It may also be essential to focus primarily on influencing the overall framework and paradigm and secondarily on the micro issues of the negotiations.

Fifth, the formation of transnational alliances for solidarity and consensus is useful for influencing policy. This was found to be true for CSO influence of international trade policy for the benefit of developing countries. CSOs therefore have greater influence in multilateral negotiations where they can relate to their counterparts at other levels. These networks are weaker in bilateral negotiations making CSO influence less likely.[29] Civil society has traditionally been weaker in developing countries and therefore links with international networks are essential for developing capacity. In bilateral negotiations as in the EPA process there were fewer opportunities for international networking. Civil society can however forge alliances when issues in the bilateral negotiations are translated into larger global issues which have resonance with global social movements.

Sixth, working with national governments proved to be a useful strategy for influencing policy.[30] It is particularly important for CSOs to insert their goals in national positions in circumstances where CSOs cannot participate formally

---

26   S. Trommer, 'Activists Beyond Borders: Transnational NGOs Strategies on EU West Africa Trade Relations', *Globalisations*, 8 (1) (2011), 119, 121.

27   A. Pollard and J. Court, 'How Civil Society Organisations Use Evidence to Influence Trade Policy Processes: A Literature Review' (Overseas Development Institute, Working Paper 249, 2005), 17, 27.

28   A. Montoute, 'Civil Society Participation in Trade Negotiations: A Caribbean Case Study', 163, 288.

29   K. Kent, 'EU Trade Policy Making: What Role for Civil Society?' (Institut Européen de Hautes Etudes Internationales, 2005), 66, http://www.i.e.-ei.eu/bibliotheque/memoires/KENT.pdf.

30   H. Baogang and H. Murphy, 'Global Social Justice at the WTO? The Role of NGOs in Constructing Global Social Contracts', *International Affairs*, 83 (4) (2007), 724;

in the negotiations. This means that although it is important to be plugged into the activities of global social movements, civil society need to ensure that the issues are relevant to the national context. Case study research proved that NGOs were successful with weaker governments even with opposition from stronger governments. NGOs have successfully worked with developing countries by offering assistance to build the capacity of developing country governments to counter developing country arguments.[31]

Conclusion

Civil society participation in negotiations of trade agreements, especially those between developed and developing countries can be an indirect but effective way of influencing regional integration processes. In instances where civil society fails to influence trade negotiations they also fail to shape regional processes. The EPA highlighted the fundamental way in which regional integration can be affected by the substance and architecture of an FTA. In the Caribbean, civil society has been trying to influence the regional integration process by participating in the CSME process. Participation in the EPA offered another, and arguably a more effective avenue for influencing regional processes but the challenges of effective participation hindered their ability to do so.

Walden Bello, 'Learning from Doha: A Civil Society Perspective from the South', *Global Governance*, 8 (2002), 278.

31   H. Baogang and H. Murphy, 'Global Social Justice at the WTO? The Role of NGOs in Constructing Global Social Contracts', *International Affairs*, 83 (4) (2007), 724.

Chapter 13

Caribbean Integration: Can Cultural Production Succeed where Politics and Economics have Failed? (Confessions of a Wayward Economist)

Norman Girvan[1]

Introduction

One of the beautiful things about events like the Festival del Caribe[2] is the continual discovery that the things that unite us, as Caribbean people, are far more powerful than those that divide us. The barriers of language and political status virtually evaporate in the heat of music, dance and shared rituals. At the *desfile* held on 4 July 2013, for instance, a Jamaican would have recognized Jon Cannu and Rastafari among the Cuban groups; a Trinidadian would have recognized familiar Carnival characters like Moko Jumbies and Dame Lorraines.

At last year's Festival I had several such Epiphany moments. Allow me to share some of these with you by quoting from a commentary I made at the time:

> As scholars pondered Pan-Africanism in Cuba and Jamaica and the development of Black consciousness in Martinique and Trinidad and Tobago; Vudú and Yoruba religious ceremonies were being performed in communities adjacent to Santiago. Attending several of the cultural events, I came away with a strong sense of the power of music, dance and spiritualism as the common language of Caribbean people. Santiago's Steelband del Cobre and Trinidad's Valley Harps steel orchestra had half their audiences at Teatro Heredia jumping on the stage at the end of their respective performances. The cultural procession held in the city centre before the culture ministers of Cuba and Trinidad and Tobago and a crowd of several thousand ended with a street jump-up which to all intents and purposes was a j'ouvert – except that it was Santigueran Conga. The homage

---

1 Presentation at The Colloquium, 'The Caribbean That Unites Us', Festival del Caribe, Santiago de Cuba (5 July 2012). An earlier version of this paper was presented at the St Martin Book Fair on 31 May 2012.

2 The Festival del Caribe is a Caribbean festival of arts and culture held in the first week of July each year since 1980. It is hosted by the Casa del Caribe of that city.

to the Cimmaron (Maroon) held on a hilltop in the community of Cobre was a ceremony with powerful spiritual impact – complete with possession – which reminded me of Jamaican Kumina and, I am told, shared many elements with Trinidadian Shango. And of course the great Bob (Marley) was everywhere.[3]

The sense of the Caribbean as a 'community of culture' that one experiences on these occasions, stands in curious contrast to the difficulties that have been encountered in configuring the Caribbean as an economic and political community. Seen through a political-economic optic, the image of the Caribbean is one of extreme political fragmentation, linguistic diversity and disconnected economies. The last time I counted, there were some 38 different political jurisdictions in the Caribbean region; consisting of 16 independent states and 22 non-independent territories. We speak Spanish, French, English and Dutch and several creole languages. We trade far more with the metropolitan countries – the present and former colonial powers – than with one another. The 'view from the top' seems be out of synch with the 'view from below', so to speak.

Another example of this is the way in which Caribbean people travel from one place to another, according to where the opportunities are, to work, to trade, to make a living. When they move, the matter of language, of passport, of visa, of work permit and so on are simply obstacles to be circumvented by one means or another. They have shown, and show, incredible ingenuity in doing this. In the island of St Martin, which is half Dutch and French, a journalist once told me that his mother, who was a commercial trader, spoke at least four languages. She spoke English, because her parents were from St Kitts; Spanish, because she was born in the Dominican Republic; French, because she lived in French St Martin; and Papiamentu because she marketed her merchandise in Dutch St Marten. This lady, who had a primary school education, spoke more languages than most PhDs.

A great Caribbean thinker named George Beckford used to say, 'Caribbean people are already integrated. The only people who don't know it are the governments'. The Trinidadian calypsonian, The Black Stalin, has a calypso called 'Caribbean Man'; in which he declares that the people of the Caribbean Community (CARICOM) have discovered the secrets of integration, while the governments continue to make a mess of it. The governments should learn from the ordinary people, he says, especially from the Rastafarians, for there are Rastas in every island. In fact, our history shows us that integration from above in the Caribbean has had a very mixed record. There have been some successes, but also many failures.

In colonial times, territories were often grouped together because it was cheaper for the colonial power to administer several colonies as a single unit. In the British territories at one time or another there were federations of the Leeward Islands and the Windward Islands. The Dutch organized a federation

---

3   'Santiago's Festival of Fire: Cubans hug up their Caribbean culture', http://www. normangirvan.info/wp-content/uploads/2011/07/girvan-santiago-festival1.pdf.

of the Netherlands Antilles. For the most part, none of these colonial federations lasted. The most notable example was the West Indies Federation, of 1958 to 1962. This was a hybrid – a colonial federation on a path to decolonization. It broke up because of disagreements among the West Indian leaders over issues like how many seats each island should have in the Federal Parliament, how much power the central government should have over the island units, especially in taxation; and the extent to which people should be free to move from one island to another (freedom of movement). More recently, in 2010, there was the break-up of the five-island federation of the Netherlands Antilles.

Yet it is significant that since the break-up of the West Indies Federation, the very same territories have been engaged in schemes of economic integration and cooperation. So we have had the Caribbean Free Trade Association (CARIFTA), 1965–73; the Caribbean Community and Common Market (CARICOM), formed in 1973; and the project to establish a CARICOM Single Market and Economy (CSME), initiated in 1989. There have also been Pan-Caribbean initiatives: the Caribbean Development and Cooperation Committee (CDCC) of the UN Economic Commission for Latin America and the Caribbean; and the Association of Caribbean States (ACS), which was formed in 1994.

The political elites of the English-speaking Caribbean countries which have secured 'independence' have come to the realization that, in today's world, small countries like ours simply have no choice but to integrate, or at least cooperate. But these initiatives at regional integration have a very uneven record of success. Let us take the case of the Caribbean Community – CARICOM – (already dealt with by Matthew Bishop in Chapter 9 of this volume) which is generally recognized as the most advanced scheme of regional integration in the Caribbean. I quote from a recent report prepared by a high-level team of consultants:

CARICOM is in crisis. This is so for three reasons:

- Long-standing frustrations with the slow progress have continued to mount.
- A serious weakening in its structure and operations over the years.
- Continuing economic retrenchment since the financial crisis of 2008 and the risk of further deterioration.

The crisis is sufficiently serious as to put the very existence of CARICOM in question.[4]

The fact is that CARICOM has a long history of shortfalls in the implementation of decisions on economic integration that have been taken by the political leaders in the formal organs of the Community. The problem of lack of implementation is

---

4   Landell Mills Report, http://www.normangirvan.info/turning-around-caricom-the-landell-mills-report/, accessed 26 December 2013.

known as 'the implementation deficit'. The root of the problem is that governments are not willing to surrender any of their sovereign authority to the organs of the Community, where their sovereignty may be exercised collectively. As a result, CARICOM's economic integration project is virtually at a standstill. And without going into detail, I can say that the existence of CARICOM has not made a significant difference to the economic development of its members.

Trade within the CARICOM is just about 15 per cent of the total foreign trade of its members. The amount of investment that takes place from one country to another is small, and mostly comes from the most industrially advanced member state, Trinidad and Tobago. On the other hand, CARICOM has registered many successes in functional cooperation. This covers 12 areas, including education, health, the environment and climate change, Caribbean Sea, disaster preparedness, labour, culture, youth, sport, gender, drugs, ICTs, tourism, and fisheries. CARICOM also plays a useful role as an interlocutor with extra-regional powers. But there is an important lesson, it seems to me, in the fact that top-down integration initiatives have a mixed record, while our people are busy 'doing their own thing'. I firmly believe that true integration can never be purely or even primarily a matter of economics; one that is driven by the calculus of costs and benefits. (That is why the subtitle of this chapter is 'Confessions of a Wayward Economist'.)

Economics must play its part, of course. But the bedrock of integration must be a sense, not so much of common identity – because we do not have identical identities – but what could be called a 'community of identities'; identities fashioned in response to a very special historical experience; an experience that we all share in one way or another.

The establishment of a community of identities, it seems to me, is the result of a process of mutual self-discovery of ourselves as a Caribbean people; the discovery of our historical commonalities; discovering, and learning to appreciate, the diversity of creative responses. The late, great Rex Nettleford invented a word that he called 'smaddification'.[5] This is derived from the Jamaican word for 'somebody' (Jamaican: 'smaddy'). So 'smaddification' might be loosely translated as 'to become *somebody*'; if you like, the affirmation of *personhood*. Aimé Césaire also invented a word: 'thingification'; which for him defines 'colonization'.[6] Thus, colonized peoples became 'things' – chattels to be bought and sold, natives to be exploited or eliminated.

It occurs to me that Nettleford's 'smaddification' is the dialectical opposite of Césaire's 'thingification'. In the one, personhood is denied; in the other, it is realized; the object becomes the subject, the agent of its own liberation. If thingification is thesis, smaddification is antithesis. Further, smaddification is

---

5   For an appreciation, see Honor Ford-Smith, 'A Tribute to Rex Nettleford', http://www.bahamasuncensored.com/NettlefordTribute.html, accessed 14 July 2012.

6   Aimé Césaire, *Discourse on Colonialism*, trans. Joan Pinkham (New York: Monthly Review, 1972), 42.

not only about resistance, it is about creation. And it is not only individual, but collective – movements of the people.

Caribbean peoples have created languages, have created music, have created great works of art, of literature, of poetry, of drama; have accomplished great feats in the world of sport; they have made great revolutions; each one responding to the specificities of local experience; each enriching the collective Caribbean experience. But our people, by and large, are deprived of this knowledge, of this consciousness, of this sense of who we are, of where we are coming from, of what we have accomplished; separately and collectively. And so, our people are being deprived of that most precious resource of all – the self-knowledge that instills self-respect, respect for one other, a sense of certainty, of the necessity and the capacity to chart our own future.

It is a resource that the ordinary American, or European, or Chinese or Indian – simply takes for granted. It is something that he or she begins to acquire from infancy; becoming part of their deeply embedded consciousness of self. This sense of Caribbean self is a work in progress; in constant struggle with the legacy of our respective colonial inheritances and with the seductive distractions of so-called globalization.

Our writers, artists, musicians – those who labour in the world of cultural production – have been the torchbearers in this wonderful endeavour. And my own personal debt to them, in my self-discovery as a Caribbean person, is beyond measure. And that, for me, is the real value of events such as the Festival de Caribe; and of the many other cultural events and processes that are taking place across the Caribbean space.

I get the feeling that something is stirring in the Caribbean. Cultural festivals of diverse expressions seem to be bursting out all over the place – literary, film, music, dance, art, food. And what seems to me significant is that, even when they are initiated as 'national' festivals, they end up acquiring a *Caribbean* dimension. It is almost as if organizers come to the realization that the national melds seamlessly into the Caribbean. The one complements, and extends, the other.

Last month I was at the St Martin Book Fair. This book fair is the work of two organizations, the Conscious Lyrics Foundation and the House of Nehesi Publishers. The founder of Nehesi, whose name is Lasana Sekou, is a rather extraordinary individual: he is a poet, a writer of fiction, a historian, a newspaper editor, an essayist, a cultural activist, a former political activist, an entrepreneur. Actually, this is not necessarily extraordinary in the Caribbean; the small size of our societies and the absence of a critical mass of individuals representing a wide range of interests and capabilities, often require people like Sekou to play multiple roles. In other ways he is also very Caribbean. Sekou was born in Aruba of St Martin parentage, and, after studying in the United States, made St Martin his home. As Editor of House of Nehesi Publishers, he has eschewed an insular nationalistic policy. Nehesi publishes texts from the Pan-Caribbean; it has indeed dared to publish bilingual editions of creative writing and literary criticism; like the recently released *Haiti and the Trans-Caribbean Literary Identity/Haití y la*

transcaribeñidad literaria by Emilio Jorge Rodriguez,[7] the Cuban literary critic.
A review of this extraordinary little book, by Dr Myriam Chancy, who is herself a
writer and of Haitian descent, shows us that:

> ... Rodriguez traces with detailed attention the movements between Haiti and
> specifically the Latin Caribbean, especially since the 1940s, underscoring
> the importance of visits to Haiti by Nicolás Guillén and Alejo Carpentier and
> exchanges in person between Guillén and Jacques Stephen Alexis, between
> Alejo Carpentier and the Kreyol poet Felix Morisseau-Leroy. In this context,
> Jorge Rodriguez's bilingual collection of essays is of strategic importance
> because it uncovers key exchanges, some textual, some actual between Haitian
> and Cuban writers primarily and shows how the writers came to know, interpret,
> and, in ways, translate their works through linguistic and cultural divides, to find
> common ground.[8]

The reciprocal influences between the Cuban and the Haitian writers so revealingly
brought to light by Emilio Jorge Rodriguez and Myriam Chancy appear to me be
a kind of trans-Caribbean work in progress; or if you prefer, of organic Caribbean
integration at a cultural level, and one that has no equivalent so far in the formal
structures of economics and politics. Once I began to think about it in this way, I
began to see expressions of 'trans-Caribbeanity' almost everywhere. For example,
in the introduction to *Corazon de Pelicano/Pelican Heart*, a book of Lasana
Sekou's own poetry; I read where Emilio Jorge Rodriguez says:

> In Poems like *Nativity* ... we find an aesthetic, ethic and ideological construction,
> which transmits the desire to encompass the dissimilar roots that integrate and
> merge with Caribbean culture. More than a national chat, as some may be
> tempted to catalogue it, the poem becomes a deep reflection that transcends the
> ambit of the islands and becomes an extensive text with regional roots, drawing
> together historical and cultural experiences that have had an impact on the
> formation and development of Caribbean peoples and their intelligentsia, thirsty
> for definitions of identity. Therefore, it is also a proposal which salvages the
> honour of Caribbean beings in their ancestral diversity, as well as the various
> elements that converge in their culture and history.[9]

---

7   Trans. Maria Teresa Ortega. Published by House of Nehesi, 2011.
8   Myriam J.A. Chancy, Meditation for a Forgotten Past: Translating and Remembering
Haiti's Intellectual Legacy, http://www.normangirvan.info/wp-content/uploads/2012/06/cha
ncy-stmartin-rodriguez-intro.pdf, 2–3.
9   Emilio Jorge Rodriguez, 'Introduction and Notes', in *Corazon de Pelicano/Pelican
Heart: An Anthology of Poems by Lasana M. Sekou*, trans. Maria Teresa Ortega (St Martin:
House of Nehesi Publishers, 2010), 222.

So that in spite of (or because of?) political fragmentation, economic crisis and social problems of various kinds; we see many signs of cultural intercourse and cultural creativity, in several expressions, and across the barriers of language and polity, in the regional space.

Is there a way to bring this process into the mainstream of official intercourse, into the world and the work of governments; where the discourse on integration seems to be dominated by matters of trade and investment and administrative structures? I question why Jamaica was not at this year's Festival del Caribe? Why was Guyana not there? We had over 100 cultural representatives from Argentina; we had probably less than one-tenth of that number from the whole of the English-speaking Caribbean. And this is not the fault of the Casa del Caribe; not for want of invitation. Is it just because our governments don't have the money to send cultural delegations? Or does it speak to a failure of imagination; of appreciation, of what culture is, of what it can be as a force for integration?

I believe that a documentary film is being made of the Festival's experience. I expect that people from different part of the region will be interviewed to talk about its personal impact on them. It is the kind of film that should be shown, not only to ministers of culture; but even more importantly to prime ministers, presidents, ministers of trade and investment, educators, and students. Would this not help to motivate them, to give new life and dynamism to the formal processes of integration? Can cultural production succeed in driving integration, where economics and politics have failed? Let me leave with you a reflection by George Lamming:

> I do not think there has been anything in human history quite like the meeting of Africa, Asia, and Europe in this American archipelago we call the Caribbean. But it is so recent since we assumed responsibility for our own destiny, that the antagonistic weight of the past is felt as an inhibiting menace. And that is the most urgent task and the greatest intellectual challenge: How to control the burden of this history and incorporate it into our collective sense of the future.[10]

---

10   George Lamming, *Coming, Coming, Coming Home: Conversations II* (St Martin: House of Nehesi Publishers, 1995), 25.

Chapter 14

Liberalization of Fair Trade or Globalization of Human (In)security? Protecting Public Goods in the Emerging Economic Integration of the Americas

Obijiofor Aginam

Integrative tendencies in international life, combined with the widely imagined future of a cyber world, ensure that a global civilization in some form will take shape early in the twenty-first century. But this probable world is a civilization only in a technical sense of being bound together by a high rate of interaction and real time awareness, with reduced relevance being attached to distance, boundaries, and the territorial features of the domains being administered by sovereign states. ... The current ideological climate, with its neo-liberal dogma ... suggest that the sort of global civilization that is taking shape will be widely perceived, not as fulfillment of a vision of unity and harmony, but as a dysutopian result of globalism-from-above that is mainly constituted by economistic ideas and pressures.

Richard Falk[1]

By expediting economic growth, creating jobs and raising incomes, globalization has the potential to advance human development around the world. But globalization has also increased vulnerability and insecurity.

Kamal Malhotra et al.[2]

Introduction: The Crux of the Argument

The above grave charge by Richard Falk, albeit an indictment of economic globalization, nonetheless implicitly challenges the globalized neo-liberal dogma of free trade to be more protective of public goods and the capacity of the 'sovereign state' to facilitate the delivery of these goods to vulnerable populations. Falk's charge presents complex challenges for the emerging economic integration

---

1   'The Coming Global Civilization: Neo-Liberal or Humanist', in A. Anghie and G. Sturgess (eds), *Legal Visions of the 21st Century: Essays in Honour of Judge Christopher Weeramantry* (The Hague: Kluwer, 1998), 15.

2   *Making Global Trade Work for the Poor* (London: Earthscan, 2003), 1.

and free trade in the Americas because of the inequalities and disparities between the countries in the region. The well-founded observation by Malhotra et al. above is a microcosm of the tension between trade liberalization, and the humanistic imperative of the provision of public goods in the multilateral context of emerging trade norms that seem to constrain the capacity of 'sovereign' (developing and under-developed) nation-states to effectively develop national environmental, labour, human rights, and public health policies. In the emergent jurisprudence of the World Trade Organization (WTO), this chapter explores the perceived or real marginalization of national public health policies by the regime of free trade.

This chapter problematizes the challenges of '*humanization*' of free trade to reflect the emerging 'norms' of human security and global public goods in the Americas, a region characterized by socio-economic disparities between the two most industrialized countries in the region; USA and Canada and the poorer Latin American and the Caribbean countries. As observed by Carlyle Guerra de Macedo, past Director of the Pan-American Health Organization (PAHO),

> an understanding of the impact of regulations and institutions on the health sector in the Americas must necessarily be viewed in light of the problems the region faces – problems which differ in accordance with each society's level of development – and the challenge those problems pose. Because of the many differences and for the purpose of simplification, it is important to distinguish between the situation prevailing in the Hemisphere's two most developed countries: Canada and the United States of America, and in the developing countries of Latin America and the Caribbean.[3]

It is now widely accepted that we live in an age of globalization, and one important dimension of this phenomenon is the speed with which goods, ideas, images, people and services permeate national boundaries, and travel transcontinental distances in a 'borderless' world. There is no doubt that international trade could be, or has been an engine of economic growth within the phenomena that Falk refers to as the 'integrative tendencies in international life'. The real question, nonetheless, is whether trade liberalization in the context of the glaring asymmetry between the countries of the Americas could maximize potentials for sustainable human development. Can the economic integration of the Americas genuinely liberalize 'fair trade' or accelerate vulnerability to human insecurity? The search for answers to these questions has become imperative, especially with the emergence, in 1995, of the rules-based global trading system anchored on the governance architecture of the World Trade Organization (WTO).

---

3 'Introduction', H.L Fuenzalida and S.S Connor (eds), *The Right to Health in the Americas: A Comparative Constitutional Study* (Washington, DC: The Pan American Health Organization, 1989), v.

In just ten years of the emergence of the WTO, immutable trade norms and rules have crystallized through its adjudicatory dispute settlement mechanisms with unprecedented speed unparalleled in the history of inter-governmental multilateral institutions. With the WTO as a 'norm-generating institution', these norms and rules not only form the bulk of international trade laws; they also significantly influence negotiations for free trade and economic integration agreements across the globe. Also, the establishment of the WTO witnessed an expansion of global trade and its regulation from goods to areas such as services, and intellectual property. As observed by Malhotra et al.,

> The transformation of the General Agreement on Tariffs and Trade (GATT) into the WTO in 1995 marked a paradigm shift, resulting in significant differences between the two regimes. The GATT system was primarily about negotiating market access for traded goods. But the WTO's extension into new substantive areas, intrusiveness into domestic policy-making, 'single undertaking' mandate, explicit linkage of trade with the protection of investment and intellectual property rights, and strict enforcement of disputes and cross-retaliation have extended its authority into areas of domestic regulation, legislation, governance and policy-making central to the development process. Recent agreements under the trade regime commit members not just to liberalizing trade in goods but also to making specific policy choices on services, investment and intellectual property. These choices can affect human development through their effects on employment, education, public health, movements of capital and labour and ownership of and access to technology.[4]

The monumental influence of the WTO in global economic relations between countries, albeit supported by many leading scholars, has become the subject of scathing critiques by leading international scholars. It is now perceived that economic globalization (which the WTO is part of) either constrains the capacity of the state to finance social safety nets (public goods)[5] or contributes in very complex ways to 'democratic deficit'.[6]

---

4   *Making Global Trade Work for the Poor*, 3.

5   See generally: D. Rodrik, 'How Far Will International Economic Integration Go?', *Journal of Economic Perspectives*, 14 (Winter 2000), 177–186; D. Rodrik 'Governance of Economic Globalization', in J.S Nye and J.D. Donahue (eds), *Governance in a Globalizing World* (Washington, DC: Brookings Institution, 2000), 347; John Hilary, *The Wrong Model: GATS, Trade Liberalisation and Children's Right to Health* (London: Save the Children, 2001); Robert Howse and Makau Mutua, *Protecting Human Rights in a Global Economy: Challenges for the World Trade Organization* (Montreal: Rights and Democracy, 2000).

6   Robert Howse, 'How to Begin to Think About the "Democratic Deficit" at the WTO', available online at: http://faculty.law.umich.edu/howse/, accessed 27 September 2005.

The Concept of Public Goods

The meaning, scope and parameters of public goods have been intensely debated since the writings of political philosophers and economists like David Hume and Adam Smith in the eighteenth century. In two recent volumes published for the United Nations Development Programme (UNDP), the contributors strive to develop and apply the concept to a range of transnational, regional and global interdependence between peoples and states.[7] How, queried the editors of the UNDP's *Global Public Goods*, does the expansion of economic activity across national borders affect the demand for public goods? Kaul, Grunberg and Stern argue that,

> Global public goods must meet two criteria. The first is that their benefits have strong qualities of publicness – that is, they are marked by nonrivalry in consumption and nonexcludability. These features place them in the general category of public goods. The second criterion is that their benefits are quasi universal in terms of countries (covering more than one group of countries), people (accruing to several, preferably all, population groups, and generations (extending to both current and future generations, or at least meeting the needs of current generations without foreclosing development options for future generations). This property makes humanity as a whole the *publicum*, or beneficiary of global public goods.[8]

Following these criteria, it is important to explore how socio-economic disparities in the Americas could either facilitate or impede the national/sovereign capacity of the 'underdeveloped', and 'developing' countries in the region to promote, protect, and provide public goods (public health) to their vulnerable populations.[9] Can regional free trade and economic integration effectively and harmoniously co-exist with, and be supportive of, weak national institutions in the underdeveloped and developing countries of the Americas towards the provision of public goods to the poor? Could economic integration in the region promote the inclusion or exclusion of the developing/underdeveloped countries, or vulnerable populations within such countries from the benefits of public goods?

---

7   Inge Kaul et al. (eds), *Global Public Goods: International Cooperation in the 21st Century* (New York: Oxford University Press/UNDP, 1999); Inge Kaul et al. (eds), *Providing Global Public Goods: Managing Globalization* (New York: Oxford University Press/UNDP, 2003).

8   'Defining Global Public Goods', in I. Kaul, I. Grunberg and M. Stern (eds), *Global Public Goods: International Cooperation in the 21st Century*, 2–3.

9   For a discussion of global public goods and their application in the public health context, see Richard Smith et al., *Global Public Goods for Health: Health, Economic and Public Health Perspectives* (Oxford University Press/World Health Organization, 2003).

Human Security as Freedom from Want and Freedom from Fear

The concept of human security is as contested as the concept of public goods. In a multiplicity of contexts in which the term has been used since the UNDP's *Human Development Report* 1994,[10] it generally refers to two fundamental freedoms: 'freedom from want' and 'freedom from fear'.[11] In 2003, a more concise definition of the term emerged from the Report of the Commission on Human Security as the protection of 'the vital core of all human lives in ways that enhance human freedoms and human fulfillment'.[12] The Commission identified ten policy conclusions for human security, the fifth focusing on encouraging '*fair trade and markets to benefit the poor*', and the seventh pertaining explicitly to '*according high priority to universal access to basic health care*'.[13] On encouraging fair trade, the Commission argued that, 'the central issue from a human security perspective is not whether to use markets – it is how to support a set of diverse and complimentary institutions to ensure that markets benefit the extreme poor and enhance people's human security, freedom and rights'.[14] Can neo-liberal driven international trade liberalization accord a high priority to universal access to basic health care in the developing and underdeveloped countries in the Americas?

Trade and Health in International Trade Jurisprudence: Two Levels of Inquiry

The rules-based international trade architecture, firmly anchored on the institutional pillars of the WTO, is founded on two immutable principles: National Treatment, and Most Favoured Nation (MFN). There is a certain level of agreement between

---

10 United Nations Development Programme (UNDP), *Human Development Report 1994: New Dimensions of Human Security* (New York: Oxford University Press, 1994).

11 See the insights and perspectives on human security by 22 international scholars in 'Special Section on what is Human Security', *Security Dialogue*, 35 (3) (2004), 347–387.

12 Commission on Human Security, *Human Security Now: Protecting and Empowering People* (New York: Commission on Human Security, 2003), 4. There was a dense and illuminating human security-related literature before the work of the Commission. See for example F. Osler Hampson, *Madness in the Multitude: Human Security and World Disorder* (Toronto: Oxford University Press, 2001); R. McRae and D. Hubert (eds), *Human Security and the New Diplomacy: Protecting People, Promoting Peace* (Montreal: McGill-Queen's University Press, 2001); B. Ramcharan, *Human Rights and Human Security* (The Hague: Martinus Nijhoff, 2002); Caroline Thomas, *Global Governance, Development and Human Security* (London: Pluto Press, 2002); and J. Nef, *Human Security and Mutual Vulnerability: The Global Political Economy of Development and Underdevelopment* (Ottawa: IDRC, 1999).

13 Ibid., 133–141.

14 Ibid., 137.

proponents and critics of trade liberalization that international trade is necessary; what divides the two schools is the degree of responsiveness of free trade to the imperatives of human dignity: human rights, environmental protection, and public health (public goods). How best would the tension between these immutable trade principles and public goods be reconciled? Since the General Agreement on Tariffs and Trade (GATT) 1947, international trade governance frameworks have grappled with the task of reconciling trade liberalization and national protection of public health and other public goods. Article XX (b) of GATT[15] provides,

> Subject to the requirement that such measures are not applied in a manner which would constitute a means of arbitrary or unjustifiable discrimination between countries where the same conditions prevail, or a disguised restriction on international trade, nothing in this Agreement shall be construed to prevent the adoption or enforcement by any contracting party of measures: necessary to protect human, animal or plant life or health.

This delicate balance, albeit provided in similar but different language in other trade Agreements,[16] raises some serious conundrum in interpretation. To make use of the health exceptions, WTO Agreements generally require that the health measures adopted by a country be no more restrictive than necessary. Relying on the WTO Appellate Panel decision in the *Asbestos Case*,[17] the WTO and WHO secretariats, in a joint study, observed that human health has been recognized by the WTO as being important in the highest degree.[18] However, going by the precedents of GATT and WTO jurisprudence, national measures adopted by countries to protect public health are subjected to very strict scrutiny against immutable trade principles like the MFN, National Treatment and Elimination of Quantitative Restrictions to determine if they are 'necessary', and if non-trade restrictive alternative measures could be used to achieve the public health purpose. In this interpretive paradigm, trade therefore takes precedence over national public health measures. I use two cases to explain the subordination of domestic measures aimed at promoting public goods to the rules of free trade.

---

15   Part of GATT 1947 became GATT 1994 at the end of Uruguay Round of trade negotiations that led to the establishment of the WTO.

16   See Article XIV General Agreement on Trade in Services (GATS) 1994.

17   *Measures Affecting Asbestos and Asbestos-Containing Products*, Report of the Appellate Body, 12 March 2001 (Canada v European Communities/France).

18   WHO and WTO, *WTO Agreements and Public Health: A Joint Study by the WHO and the WTO Secretariat* (Geneva: WTO/WHO, 2002), 31.

First Level of Inquiry: *The Thai Cigarette Case* (United States v. Thailand)

Under the 1966 Tobacco Act, Thailand prohibited the importation of cigarettes and other tobacco products, but authorized the sale of domestic cigarettes. The United States challenged the ban on imports of cigarettes into Thailand as a violation of General Elimination of Quantitative Restrictions in Article XI of the GATT. Thailand defended the ban as a measure under Article XX(b) 'necessary' for the protection of public health. While no comparable ban existed on domestic Thai cigarettes, Thailand argued that American cigarettes were more likely to induce women and young persons to smoke because of sophisticated advertising directed at these groups. Thailand also argued that American cigarettes were more addictive or more likely to be consumed in larger quantities than comparable Thai cigarettes due to their higher nicotine and chemical contents. The GATT panel ruled that an import ban would only be necessary for public health reasons within Article XX(b) exceptions if alternative non-trade restricting measures could not be used to achieve the public health objectives in question. The panel found that import restrictions were not 'necessary' because other less trade-restrictive tobacco control measures could be used to protect public health on a non-discriminatory basis to both domestic and imported cigarettes.

Second Level of Inquiry: *Beef Hormones Case* (USA/Canada v European Community)

Although this dispute does not involve the health exceptions in Article XX(b) of the GATT, it nonetheless raised serious questions on the tension between domestic food safety measures and international trade. The case arose out of concerns by European consumer groups over the use of growth promotion hormones in livestock. The WHO-FAO Joint Expert Committee examined the use of these hormones and their health implications. On the basis of recommendations of the expert committee, the Codex Alimentarius Commission adopted standards for five of the growth-promoting hormones. The standards specified the maximum level of hormone residues in foods that are safe for human consumption.

The European Union, following concerns raised by consumer groups on continued use of illegal hormonal substances, imposed a complete ban on the use of growth-promoting hormones in 1988. In January 1996, the US (followed by Canada in June 1996) challenged the EU ban as a violation of the WTO's Sanitary and Phyto-sanitary Measures (SPS) Agreement. In 1988, the Appellate Body of the WTO ruled that the EU's ban violated the SPS Agreement. Since the international Codex standards existed for five out of the six hormones at issue, the Appellate Body ruled that the EU ban violated the SPS Agreement because it was not based on risk assessment. Although the Appellate Body confirmed the rights of WTO Members to have a level of health protection they want, even above international standards, this decision subjects such national measures to scientific evidence and risk assessment, and these would likely impose onerous burdens, especially on developing countries.

The task of protecting and promoting human health through domestic measures in an era of global economic integration is well illustrated in the *Thai Cigarette* and the *Beef Hormones* cases. Even in the *Asbestos Case* (Canada v. European Community/France), and the *Reformulated Gasoline Case* (Brazil and Venezuela v. United States) where the WTO Appellate Bodies upheld Article XX(b) health measures, the dispute settlement bodies did so after subjecting those measures to rigorous scrutiny against immutable trade principles. Had the Panels found those measures discriminatory or trade-restrictive, they would have ruled that they either violated National Treatment or inconsistent with the requirements of the chapeau of Article XX.

Can Free Trade Promote Human Security and Public Goods?: A Postscript on Fair Trade for the Americas

It is now widely perceived that international trade liberalization driven by WTO's compulsory settlement of disputes is either going, or has simply has gone too far.[19] Finding a willing ally in economic globalization and other 'integrative tendencies in international life' that are fast opening national boundaries to markets in developing countries, the emergent trading architecture now has a questionable grasp on issues within the domestic domain. As Malhotra et al. rightly observed,

> Recent agreements under the trade regime commit members not just to liberalizing trade in goods but also to making specific policy choices on services, investment and intellectual property. These choices can affect human development through their effects on employment, education, public health, movements of capital and labour and ownership of and access to technology.[20]

The weak institutions in most developing countries coupled with the shrinking normative and policy space for the incubation, promotion and distribution of public goods as a result of the globalization of markets, and the socio-economic inequalities between countries has, according to Rodrik, led the dilemma of globalized markets built on largely local institutions.[21] If, as Mendoza has correctly observed, that both critics and supporters of international trade do not see trade itself as a problem, because they all agree that trade has the potential to

---

19   Susan Esserman and Robert Howse, 'The WTO on Trial', *Foreign Affairs* (January/February 2003), 130.

20   *Making Global Trade Work for the Poor* (supra note 2), 3.

21   Dani Rodrik, 'Governance of Economic Globalization', in Joseph S. Nye and John D. Donahue (eds), *Governance in a Globalizing World* (Washington, DC: Brookings Institution, 2000), 348.

benefit developing countries; they only disagree on the structure and arrangements for multilateral trade,[22] how then would the '*democratic deficit*' within national jurisdictions occasioned by accelerating economic globalization be addressed? While this chapter does not have all, or even any of the answers, it is important to recall Rodrik's *global-local dilemma* as humanity enters the twenty-first century: markets are striving to become global while their supportive institutions are largely national. This implies that the existence of the nation-state restricts economic integration while the quest to globalize by producers and investors weakens the institutional base of national economies.[23] Ultimately, politics, according to Rodrik, has to become as global as economics with the emergence of a world of global federalism and a mixed economy reconstructed at the global level. But because of the continued existence of nation states, 'sound intermediate architecture has to combine international harmonization and standard setting with generalized exit schemes, opt-outs and escape clauses. This allows most of the efficiency gains from integration to be reaped while still leaving room for a range of divergent national practices'.[24]

It is therefore not as simplistic as saying that globalization and economic integration are inherently bad or innately good, especially given the divergent national policies on public health as well as the disparities between countries. What is needed first is a policy space to enable weaker nation-states (especially the developing countries) to strengthen their institutional capacity to generate and promote public goods given each country's present specific social and economic conditions. The extent to which this would likely occur largely depends on effective proposal for quality control as free trade continues to erode national capacity for the protection of public goods. Lessons from GATT/WTO jurisprudence, as exemplified by the *Thai Cigarette* and *Beef Hormone* cases, suggest that economic globalization is becoming predatory in nature, and that free trade will continue to trump public goods in national jurisdictions with the speed of a hurricane and the force of a tsunami.

---

22   Ronald U. Mendoza, 'The Multilateral Trade Regime: A Global Public Good for All', in Inge Kaul et al. (eds), *Providing Global Public Goods: Managing Globalization* (New York: Oxford University Press/UNDP, 2003), 455.

23   Dani Rodrik, supra, 'Governance of Economic Globalization', 348.

24   Ibid.

Chapter 15

The Dynamics, Limits and Potential of Formal Liberal Democracy in Latin America

Fred Judson

Introduction

For me, change does not necessarily imply progress. In fact, I choose to use the term 'transit' in reference to the changes that are occurring in the world today. I also choose – in fact I can't help myself but – to see change and transit from a historical, structural and critical perspective. It is a perspective from which I seek to understand the complexities of human social, economic and political phenomena. There is no claim here to objectivity; it's a normative stance. I would characterize the perspective an embedded context for talking about the dynamics and limits of democracy in Latin America.[1]

Combination and hybridity, boundary-crossing and layering, contestation and contradiction, domination and subjection are the conditions, it is often argued, of post-modernity.[2] From the perspective I take, they are equally the conditions of modernity. This stance combines the social science traditions indicated by both Max Weber[3] and Karl Marx,[4] the historical-structural sensibilities of Karl Polanyi[5] and Fernand Braudel[6] and those of Antonio Gramsci and Robert Cox

---

1   For an elaboration of this perspective see Fred Judson, 'For an Eclectic and Critical Political Economy Perspective on Canadian Foreign Economic Policy', *Studies in Political Economy*, 71/72 (Autumn 2003/Winter 2004), 109–132.

2   Pauline Rosenau, *Post-Modernism and the Social Sciences: Insights, Inroads and Intrusions* (Princeton: Princeton University Press, 1992); David Harvey, *The Condition of Post-Modernity: An Enquiry into the Origins of Cultural Change* (Oxford: Oxford University Press, 1990).

3   Edward A. Shils and Henry A. Finch (eds), *Max Weber on the Methodology of the Social Sciences* (Glencoe: Free Press, 1949).

4   Karl Marx, 'Economic and Philosophic Manuscripts of 1844: Selections', in Robert C. Tucker (ed.), *The Marx-Engels Reader* (New York: Norton, 1972).

5   Karl Polanyi, *The Great Transformation: The Political and Economic Origins of Our Time* (Boston: Beacon Press, 2001); Marguerite Mendel and Daniel Salée (eds), *The Legacy of Karl Polanyi. Market, State and Society at the End of the Twentieth Century* (London: Macmillan, 1991).

6   Fernand Braudel, *On History*, trans. Sarah Matthew (Chicago: University of Chicago Press, 1980); Eric Helleiner, 'Braudelian Reflections on Economic Globalisation:

(though it is not necessary to cite and name theoretical authorities to make use of the perspective).[7] The stance combines the desires for justice and liberation with the requisites of governability. It seeks to accept the open horizons of human – maybe even 'species-being' – material capacities while keeping present a global ecological consciousness. Perforce the perspective is eclectic and incomplete; it offers parameters and contexts, rather than models or fixed measures and goals; it's an analytical pathway, one which *se hace al andar y no quiere parar de andar* ('is made in the walking, and doesn't want to stop walking').

I submit that what used to be called by some 'the current conjuncture' presents three closely interacting matrices: a regime of globalizing capitalist accumulation; a regime of hegemonic global and globalizing security; and a hegemonizing ideological and discursive regime of formal liberal democracy.

These matrices I take to be dynamic historical structures in which the agency of actors – social forces and states, conceived as 'social formations' as much as 'sovereign nation-states' – takes place.

We have first the set of dynamics which by now virtually 'everyone' identifies as **globalization**. If it is evident that national economies and economic policies of countries have not ceased to exist,[8] it is also evident that the dominant and most profitable dynamics of accumulation within economic activity are those which are transnational. Some processes of production, marketing and distribution of commodities are more fully globalizing than others; many are regionalizing or continentalizing as well, as in North America NAFTA, South America CELA or Europe the EU for example. And the most globalized are the dynamics of capital markets and finance.[9] But all are liberalizing, in the neo-classical economics' meaning of the word, i.e. the social hegemony of capital and the resulting marketization of more dimensions of social life, i.e. commodification. Usually the term 'neo-liberal' is applied. In these dynamics of economic globalization, what some see as the shrinking of the inefficient and wasteful state, others see as the expanded appropriation of surplus value by capital in its organic fever to capture all within 'market principles'.[10] And we have seen that states have been accomplices in

---

The Historian as Pioneer', in Stephen Gill and James H. Mittelman (eds), *Innovation and Transformation in International Studies* (Cambridge: Cambridge University Press, 1997).

7   See Antonio Gramsci, *Selections from the Prison Notebooks*, Quentin Hoare and G. Nowell Smith (eds and trans.) (New York: International Publishers, 1971); Robert W. Cox (with Michael G. Schechter), *The Political Economy of a Plural World: Critical Reflections on Power, Morals and Civilization* (London: Routledge, 2002); Robert W. Cox, 'Political Economy and World Order: Problems of Power and Knowledge at the Turn of the Milennium', in Richard Stubbs and Jeffrey Underhill (eds), *Political Economy and the Changing Global Order*, 2nd ed. (Don Mills: Oxford University Press, 2000).

8   Eric Helleiner and Andreas Pickel (eds), *Economic Nationalism in a Globalizing World* (Ithaca: Cornell University Press, 2005).

9   Susanne Soederberg, *The Politics of the New International Financial Architecture: Re-imposing Neo-liberal Domination in the Global South* (London: Zed Books, 2004).

10   Robert McMurtry, *The Cancer Stage of Capitalism* (London: Pluto Press, 1999).

this transfer of social wealth formerly regulated and deployed in the public sphere.[11] States have advanced the programmes of privatization, have 'divested' in the form of massive public sector firings, deregulations, off-loading of public service provisions to lower and local levels, and tax cuts for wealthier income sectors and corporations.[12]

When this neoliberal agenda of states is institutionalized, for example in NAFTA, it can be considered the 'new constitutionalism of capital' by analysts such as Stephen Gill.[13] It's as if there was a 'declaration of independence' by capital from its former ties to civil society. Capital is globalizing; it is free to move where and as it wishes. It's a global 'first movement' of unregulated capital accumulation, as understood by Karl Polanyi in his writing about the 'double movement' of an earlier regime of capital accumulation in the nineteenth century.[14] Then civil society imposed regulation upon that unrestricted process, developing the modern state and eventually the welfare state. Presently, civil society at the national level is left to clean up the wreckage of the public sector, the welfare state, de-railed/abandoned/and flawed programmes of Import Substitution Industrializations, and post-debt crisis, structural adjustment deterioration of social services. The state is there, but seemingly ever less to represent civil society than to privilege capital's boundless needs.

The processes of globalization and the agency of transnational social forces with the power to direct large amounts of capital take various forms. But together they contest the notion of 'the Canadian economy' or 'the Chilean economy'. We have all seen the limited menu of economic policy choices for states: the famous 'market discipline', especially of the financial markets, punishes the use of social wealth for public purposes and encourages the transfer of wealth to private firms.[15] It discourages 'national industrial strategy', much less the redistributive directions of the former 'welfare state'. At national, regional and global levels, the regime of accumulation creates profound socio-economic polarization while it generates (at least in number measures) more wealth. Neoliberal globalization also tends, contradictorily perhaps, to regionalization. New centres or nodes of accumulation

---

11   Leo Panitch, 'Globalization and the State', in *Socialist Register 1994* (London: Merlin Press, 1994); Robert Boyer and Daniel Drache (eds), *States Against Markets: The Limits of Globalization* (New York: Routledge, 1996).

12   Duncan Green, *Silent Revolution: The Rise of Market Economics in Latin America* (London: Latin American Bureau, 1995); Sandor Halebsky and Richard Harris (eds), *Capital, Power and Inequality in Latin America* (Boulder: Westview Press, 1995).

13   Stephen Gill, *Power and Resistance in the New World Order* (London: Palgrave Macmillan, 2002).

14   Karl Polanyi, *The Great Transformation: The Political and Economic Origins of Our Time* (Boston: Beacon Press, 2001); Steven Topik, 'Karl Polanyi and the Creation of the "Market Society"', in Miguel Angel Centeno and Fernando López-Alves (eds), *The Other Mirror: Grand Theory through the Lens of Latin America* (Princeton: Princeton University Press, 2001).

15   Susanne Soederberg, George Menz and Philip Cerny (eds), *Internalizing Globalization: The Rise of Neo-liberalism and the Decline of National Varieties of Capitalism* (New York: Palgrave Macmillan, 2005).

with their own hybridizations of the market economy culture indicate an emerging multipolarity:[16] Europe, China with the potential for hegemony or condominium with Japan over East Asia, India in its subcontinent, with great swathes of Africa ever more marginalized. Many analysts see the FTAA/ALCA initiatives as the efforts of neoliberal states, essentially representative of large capital conscious of competition from and within other regions. They want to 'constitutionalize' their prerogatives of accumulation at the hemispheric level.

Two generations ago, President Eisenhower warned of the 'military-industrial complex' and its inordinate power in the US; some economic historians saw the distorting expenses of the Vietnam/Indochina Wars as the root cause of the global recession in the 1970s; others called the Cold War defence spending, particularly in the 1980s under President Reagan, a 'military Keynesianism'. And now Nobel Prize economists[17] in the US sign public declarations in the New York Times that the Bush administration's deficits endanger economic fundamentals: 'imperial fiscal over-reach', they call it. Here we witness an irony: an administration which preaches the reduction of public sector expenditures has created record deficits. It achieves salvation through the 'privatization of security': taxes buy global and homeland security, and you contract private companies to provide that 'public good'. That firms close to members of government get those contracts without a transparent and competitive bidding process and with astronomical profits does not enter the calculus.[18]

This is where the second matrix, that of a hegemonizing global security regime,[19] is highlighted. From a historico-structural and critical point of view – for example that of Noam Chomsky,[20] James Petras[21] or William Robinson[22] –

---

16   Samir Amin, *Beyond US Hegemony? Assessing the Prospects for a Multipolar World*, trans. Patrick Camiller (London: Zed Books, 2006).

17   See Joseph Stiglitz (with Linda Bilmes), *The Three Trillion Dollar War: The True Cost of the Iraq Conflict* (New York: W.W. Norton, 2008); Joseph Stiglitz, *Globalization and its Discontents* (New York: W.W. Norton, 2002).

18   See US Government Accountability Office, Testimony Before the Committee on Appropriations. United States Senate. *Stabilizing and Rebuilding Iraq. Actions Needed to Address Inadequate Accountability Over US Efforts and Investments. Statement of David M. Walker, Comptroller General of the United States* (GAO, Washington, DC, 11 March 2008). Document Number GAO 08 568T http://www.gao.gov/new.items/d08568t.pdf, accessed 26 December 2013.

19   Fred Judson, 'Components of the Emergent Global Security Regime', *Review of Constitutional Studies*, 10 (1 and 2) (2005), 21–43.

20   Noam Chomsky, *Hegemony or Survival: America's Quest for Global Dominance* (New York: Henry Holt, 2004); Noam Chomsky, *Imperial Ambitions: Conversations on the Post-9/11 World; Interviews with David Barsamian* (New York: Metropolitan Books, 2005).

21   James Petras, *Empire with Imperialism: The Globalizing Dynamics of Neo-liberal Capitalism* (London: Zed Books, 2005); James Petras and Henry Veltmeyer, *Globalization Unmasked: Imperialism in the 21st Century* (Halifax: Fernwood, 2001).

22   William I. Robinson, *Promoting Polyarchy: Globalization, Intervention and US Hegemony* (Cambridge: Cambridge University Press, 1996); William I. Robinson, *A Theory*

all long-time theorists of US imperialism – state the US has pursued hegemony throughout the twentieth century, first in its 'backyard', but after World War II in Europe, the fringes of East Asia and in the whole of 'the Global South', i.e. the 'Third World'. The Cold War had a structural content in the sense that the Soviet Union possessed sufficient arms and political will for there to be an asymmetric bipolarity. International relations scholars termed it 'deterrence' or 'balance of terror'.[23] Today there appears to be no counter-weight, though there is the capacity or potential in Europe and China. The logic of proliferation of nuclear science continues to gather force and not only states are in a position to develop nuclear weapons; 'non-state actors' may acquire them. Security right now is defined rather unilaterally, a key element in the hegemonization of a global security regime. One state alone demands 'full-spectrum dominance' and accepts no challenge to this claim of planetary dominance. Of course, that state deploys the rhetoric of 'multilateralism', collective security and 'shared values' to construct a 'coalition of the willing' which will confront 'threats' that it has the sole right to name. One state alone defines the 'enemy' and seeks to constitutionalize 'preventive' and interventionist war. There are popular theorists of formal liberal democracy (Tony Blair, the Canadian at Harvard Michael Ignatieff) who celebrate the new era of liberal imperialism. They believe that 'free markets' create 'free peoples' and that the projection of military force to create that 'dual space of economic and political freedom' is the full integration of global security.

The projection of force almost around the entire globe has been declared the legitimate option of and by a single state, reflecting this historical structural tendency to hegemony in the states system, but of course without a global state. In the structure of economic globalization we can't say there is a similar hegemony of a state, but rather of capital in general, notwithstanding the skewed distribution of capital in the world. In the 'security structure', even with hegemony, the hegemon prefers cooperation and participation. While its governance elites may well believe the discourses of 'terrorist threat' and 'global war on terror', it also usefully deploys the discourses to gain cooperation and legitimacy. It deploys them for multiple and ubiquitous disciplinary purposes, as in other moments (and not yet ended) the discourses of 'communist threat' and 'communist' had their external and domestic disciplinary function. I certainly do not wish to discard or minimize the horror, fear and pain suffered in the 9/11 events. But in linking them to the discursive, strategic and economic mobilizations of the current global security regime, it is useful to recall the famous 'security dilemma' of international relations textbooks written during the Cold War: if I increase my security, you feel less secure; when you respond with an increase in your security, I feel less secure; hence – more security produces more *in*security. When a hegemon insists that its

---

of Global Capitalism: Production, Class and State in a Transnational World (Baltimore: Johns Hopkins University Press, 2004).

23   Lawrence Freedman, *The Evolution of Nuclear Strategy* (New York: St Martin's Press, 1983).

security, and thus its security regime, must be global, even its allies feel rather uncomfortable, because they are the more vulnerable partners in the enterprise.

The third matrix is both discursive and behavioural, like the first two. There is a hegemonic, if not universal, ideology of liberal democracy, and practices/ processes of liberal democratization. They are dynamically linked to the global regimes of security and neoliberal accumulation. The supposed goal, the motivation, the impulse for the first two historical structures which the 'global Latino South' and apparently the entire planet, is now experiencing, is the supreme ideological construct of hegemonic modernity, democracy. The constitution or imposition – which word is used depends upon point of view – of a global security regime is justified by the expressed desire to expand the sphere of democracy. To set aside international law, to defy the United Nations and allies, is justified as 'bringing democracy and freedom to the world'. To violate sovereignty and human rights is permitted in the pursuit of democracy, just as it is permitted in the pursuit of security. Harsh critics would say it is permitted in the pursuit of global market capitalism, too. But democracy, in the hegemonic discourse, has rather defined characteristics: it is formal, electoral, representative and liberal. 'Manipulated, delegated, bought, frightened, commercialized, commodified and demogogic' are also its characteristics, even within the hegemon's own political regime of democracy.

Direct or participatory democracy is not contemplated, much less socialist democracy, and not even social democracy, is permitted much discursive presence, because it impedes the freedom of property and commerce, expands the public sector and seeks to reappropriate some of the surplus value (social wealth) transferred to 'market forces'. There is simply 'no alternative' contemplated in the hegemonic discourse of liberal democracy, just as 'no alternative' to unlimited marketization of modernity was/is contemplated in the neoliberal policy discourse. Dissent will be disciplined, by the security regime ultimately in the first instance, and by 'market discipline' in the second.

It is difficult to enter a dialogue with the hegemon about the character of globalizing and neoliberal capitalism. And the hegemony of the idea of the 'market' as the rightful determinant of all public policy leaves little discursive space for concepts like regulation or redistribution. You're referred to 'civil society' and even 'faith-based initiatives' if you look for solutions to poverty or the dynamics of socio-economic polarization. At times liberal democratic practice, from the hegemon to the 'global Latino South' suggests that social disintegration and degradation are either acceptable (because it's the 'inevitable result of the failure of the individual to improve themselves and to take advantage of opportunities provided by the market') or is a policing question.[24] Some 'realist' neoliberal public intellectuals will say 'it's a world of winners and losers; it's your freedom to choose which you will be, and no concern of society's. After all, society is a

---

24   Eduardo Galeano, *The World Upside Down: A Primer for the Looking-Glass World*, trans. Mark Fried (New York: Metropolitan Books, 2000).

suspect concept'. As Margaret Thatcher famously said, 'there is no such thing as society'; it's individuals, families, interests and the market.

To express a lack of faith in the capacity of the actual regime of neoliberal capitalist accumulation to respect the limits of the planetary ecological 'carrying capacity' and natural resources[25] is normally rejected as if it were asylum poetry or graffiti. To propose that the model and the agency of unlimited accumulation and consumption cannot endure is not taken seriously, either, in a kind of discursive 'tragedy of the commons'.[26] Economy and ecology are considered practically incompatible, or there is discursive recourse to a blind faith in technology and the Two Commandments, the laws of supply and demand. The disjunctures will be solved, all of them, and on time, too.

Karl Polanyi, no Marxist, understood the same basic tendencies of capital accumulation that Marx identified as contradictions within his conception of dialectical and historical materialism.[27] Simply, these are competition and monopoly, class conflict, and socio-economic polarization resulting from capital's tendency to increase its 'share' of surplus value, driven both by competition and monopoly. Polanyi saw the historical opportunity of even bourgeois liberal democracy to be the vehicle of the 'second movement', i.e. society's hegemony over capitalism. Through democracy the social interests of the majority could be sheltered and expanded via the state, which would also balance (as in Keynesian economic theory) the cyclical tendency of capitalism to recession and depression. Like Weber before him, and Keynes as well, Polanyi wanted to avoid both socialist revolution and authoritarian capitalism (i.e. European fascism or Latin American dictatorships).

In Latin America, the historical development of democracy has been both restricted and distorted. Oligarchic democracies of the nineteenth century's agro- and mineral-export economies were extremely limited and frequently fell victim to caudillo rule. Developmentalist dictatorships, such as that of Porfiriot Díaz in México, had barely any tropes of democratic discourse. A late nineteenth–early twentieth-century 'free-trade' global economic expansion, with a modernization of Latin America's 'insertion in the world system', generated new social forces. In their turn, newer bourgeois and proletarian classes and sectors pushed for political inclusion, via expansion of liberal democracy, formation of political parties and articulation within populist political projects. Some of those projects combined

---

25   Neil Smith, 'Nature as Accumulation Strategy', in Leo Panitch and Colin Leys (eds), *Coming to Terms with Nature. Socialist Register 2007* (London: Merlin Press, 2006), 16–36.

26   Costas Panayotakis, 'Working More, Selling More, Consuming More: Capitalism's "Third Contradiction"', in Leo Panitch and Colin Leys (eds), *Coming to Terms with Nature. Socialist Register 2007* (London: Merlin Press, 2006), 254–272; Ronald Wright, *A Short History of Progress* (Toronto: Anansi, 2004).

27   Karl Polanyi, *The Great Transformation: The Political and Economic Origins of Our Time* (Boston: Beacon Press, 2001).

caudillismo, corporatist inclusion and import substitution industrialization (e.g. Argentina under Perón, Brazil under Vargas and Mexico under Cárdenas). Certain 'natural' oligarchic rejections of both populism and expanded democracy contributed to the shifts to personalist and military authoritarianisms of the 1950s–1980s. Cold War anti-communism, US hegemonic impulses and some capitalist sectors' practical option for anti-democratic regimes contributed.

Nicos Poulantzas,[28] the Greco-French '60s Marxist theorist of the capitalist state, retrieved Marx's two observations about liberal democracy in the expression 'exceptional capitalist states'. Marx, as we know, saw the state under capitalism as 'the executive committee of the bourgeoisie'; at the same time he saw that the bourgeoisie privileged accumulation over democracy. Hence, as the saying goes, 'democracy if necessary, but not necessarily democracy' can be used as a mantra in order to maintain conditions of expanded reproduction, i.e. functioning of a capitalist economy. It was the way in which Poulantzas sought understand classic fascism of the 1920s–1940s, the Franco state, that of the Greek colonels in the 1960s and 70s, and the military authoritarian regimes of Latin America. Chomsky had a similar understanding of the 'chain of sub-fascist client states' of the American Cold War hegemony in most of the Global South. He extended his critique of that hegemonic and imperialist practice with the concept of 'demonstration elections' (Chomsky and his co-author Edward Herman), where elections, under no matter what human rights, repression or restricted circumstances, served the purposes of legitimation, particularly for US domestic consumption.[29] Examples that stood out were electoral regimes in post-invasion Dominican Republic and those in the conditions of civil war, repression and human rights violations in Central America (outside of Nicaragua) in the 1980s.

While Chomsky, Petras and many others questioned both the post-dictatorship democratizations as restricted or managed, Fukuyama[30] and Huntington[31] represent those who celebrated them as 'the third wave' of democratization and the triumph over communism. Critics with a political economy and neo-Gramscian orientation (Robert Cox, Stephen Gill) point to the 'transnationalization' of capitalist state functions under the orthodoxies of neoliberalism and transferences of power to international financial institutions, as well as to capital markets and corporations. They see structural hindrances to democracy, at least in the Polanyian sense that democracy lets civil society reassert authority over un-regulated capital accumulation, in the 'global constitutionalism of capital'. David Held for example, critically examining democracy as a trend within globalization, points

---

28   Nicos Poulantzas, *Fascism and Dictatorship. The Third International and the Problem of Fascism* (London: New Left Books, 1974).

29   Noam Chomsky and Edward S. Herman, *The Political Economy of Human Rights* (Montreal: Black Rose, 1979).

30   Francis Fukuyama, *The End of History and the Last Man* (New York: Avon, 1993).

31   Samuel Huntington, *The Third Wave. Democratization in the Late Twentieth Century* (Norman: University of Oklahoma Press, 1993).

to the contradiction of a polarizing neoliberal regime of accumulation set against a discourse of democratic political empowerment of those whose concrete social empowerment would actually require the erosion or reversal of that neoliberal economic regime.[32]

Marx, it can be argued, was somewhat equivocal over the possibilities of democratic paths to socialism, but certainly recognized the potential of civil society, as we would term it today, to expand the agency of labour vis-à-vis capital through unions and political parties. Certainly, John Stuart Mill[33] and other reformist liberal democratic theorists were convinced, as even Adam Smith[34] was, that liberal representative democracy and some degree of state intervention in the market was the best vehicle for the socio-economic pluralism of capitalist society and for the redistributive improvement of material conditions for working classes.

Most of the available evidence (UN, OAS, ECLA and other authoritative collections of statistical economic and quality of life information) shows that the socio-economic structural profiles of Latin American social formations have either remained the same, in terms of income distribution and degrees of poverty, or have worsened, over the past 25 years. So if it could be said, very generally, that ISI 'didn't work', then neither has the structurally-adjusted neoliberal model. Of course, both worked perfectly well as instances of a national, international and now global regime of accumulation which privileges capital over labour, and generally over the broader interests of that nebulous human reality, society.

Over some 40–50 years we had the authoritarianism of the Latin American political regimes which undemocratically represented the interests of domestic and international capital or we had varieties of those 'modern oligarchic democratic regimes' which primarily represented the same interests. In contrast, we now have a constellation of liberal democratic experiences with more potential to 'fill in' economic democracy, thus 'representing' the historic interests of working classes and the 'losers' in the dynamics of market economies. But with state downsizing and 'capital's new transnational constitutionalism', i.e., with the consolidation and embedding of the great wealth transfer to capital, the space for social forces to use the state for a 'second movement' appears to be limited.

Nonetheless, in the attitudinal, ideological and cultural dimensions of Latin America's social formations, the panorama has been broadened. Ostensible political coalitions of the democratic left and centre-left are more prominent than at any time since the election of the Popular Unity government of Salvador Allende in Chile in 1970. This is the case in Brazil, Uruguay, and Bolivia, with possibilities in Argentina. There is the unique case of democracy-supported reform and nationalist populism of Chávez in Venezuela, and even the disappointments

---

32   See David Held and Anthony McGrew (eds), *The Global Transformations Reader: An Introduction to the Globalization Debate*, 2nd ed. (Cambridge: Polity Press, 2003).

33   John Stuart Mill, *On Liberty*, eds. David Bromwich and George Kateb (New Haven: Yale University Press, 2003).

34   Adam Smith, *The Wealth of Nations* (Buffalo: Prometheus, 1991).

of popular movements in Ecuador with Lucio Gutiérrez do not mean the end of possibilities there. Much has been made of 'new social movements' over the past 15 years or so in the literature assessing democracy and democratization in Latin America: the appearance, cultural articulation and agency of non-class identities (African-American populations, indigenous peoples, in particular) and hybrid class identities (informal sector, working poor, migrant labour) and transnationalized Latino populations (gone to Spain, gone to the US, but connected socially, culturally, economically and politically to their home societies) … all this has opened the panorama. Religious identities are not missing, either, as syncretic mass religious movements in Brazil, fundamentalist Protestants and different strands of political Catholicism continue to make their presence felt. NSMs oriented to ecology, local participatory democracy and to anti-corporate and anti-neoliberal globalization also broaden the range of actors and agency.

And many of these named social forces contest the orthodox and contradictory dual ideological and cultural hegemony of formal liberal democracy and neoliberal market capitalism. In the democratic discourse, democracy equals multi-party elections and representation is a matter of 'choice'. Choice in politics is discursively equated with choice in consumption, i.e., you get what amounts to a limited range of choices (if you have the money, or the political capital). You get to 'choose' from a relatively limited range of political choices. You're implicitly asked not to be historical in your understanding how those choices came to be, and you're not supposed to 'look back' at ferocious repression, human rights violations, exile, state terror and elimination of political forces of left and even centre.

Your choice at election time is a momentary consumer experience. You choose, you consume a candidate or a party. You may not be satisfied with your purchase, but you celebrate your purchase power. You have some immediate gratification, but you move on to the next consumption moment, whether you've digested what you bought or not, whether the guarantee on the defective or non-performing product is respected or not. Your desire for 'democratic consumption' is the fundamental operating principle. Politics resembles the consumer universe. We aren't supposed to pay attention, really, to processes of production, to relations of production, or to distribution of income, either in the economic nor the political spheres. In effect, in both our market engagements as citizens we are constructed as consumers, not producers: we are useful as buyers and consumers of commodities, and we are culturally constructed as such in the hegemonic discourses. We engage with the globalizing accumulation regime in that manner, and we engage with the globalizing liberal democratic regime in that manner. In fact, we engage with the global security regime like that, too. We have security and its discourses sold to us, and we're to be content as consumers of that 'public good'.

For a particularly trenchant and poetic cultural representation of this distortion of citizenship, Eduardo Galeano's 'The World Upside Down' is highly recommended.[35] He links the local to the national to the global, and gives the term 'global village' a refreshingly subversive twist: global village (for those with consumption access) mediated by 'gated communities' and privatized/industrialized security and prison complex, over-determined by the thrust for political and military global hegemony, and socially structured by neoliberal economic accumulation. The cultural and legitimating discourse of this 'civilization' (as understood by Ronald Wright in his recent Massey Lecture publication *A Short History of Progress*) is that of formal liberal democracy.[36]

What Latin America's universe of 'paroxysms of modernity' show us is the irrepressible drive of social forces, particularly the majority, to exercise their agency in the pursuit of their interests. Economic development with equity, i.e., greater economic democracy; democracy that both represents and engages their citizenship, and recognizes and respects their difference and identities; and security which is not a security dilemma and does not create enemies constitute those interests. They are prepared, for the time being, to pursue those interests through formal liberal democracy, while they continue to strain against and push its limits.

35 Eduardo Galeano, *The World Upside Down: A Primer for the Looking-Glass World*, trans. Mark Fried (New York: Metropolitan Books, 2000).

36 Ronald Wright, *A Short History of Progress* (Toronto: Anansi Press, 2004).

Chapter 16

Why Democracy and the Free Market are Good for *Caudillos*: The Nicaragua Case

Kalowatie Deonandan

I: Introduction

The democratization wave that has engulfed Latin America since the late 1990s has been followed in its wake by another popular tide, that of free trade. This drive to re-map the Americas through bilateral and multilateral arrangements which link many of the countries of the region to each other and to partners around the globe, has been facilitated and legitimized by the democratic transition which ended military dictatorships and socialist experiments in the continent and firmly implanted the free market.

This re-mapping, however, confronts many serious challenges with one of the most serious being the corruption pandemic inundating the region. Almost daily citizens across the hemisphere are bombarded with reports of official misdeeds. Some of the more high profile scandals of the recent past include: Brazil's President Lula da Silva's party members being charged with orchestrating a cash-for-vote scheme; Costa Rica's former President Miguel Angel Rodriguez being sentenced to prison for kickbacks he received in the awarding of a contract to a French telecom company, Alcatel; Ecuador's President, Lucio Gutiérrez being ousted for his manipulation of state institutions to concentrate power in the executive; Guatemala's former President Alfonso Portillo being charged with embezzlement of funds from his nation's treasury; and Nicaragua's former President Arnoldo Alemán being imprisoned for pillaging the public coffers. In many instances, the very structures that are designed to ensure democratic protections have been corrupted to serve the self-interest of rulers and their cronies.

State-level corruption is an issue that has skyrocketed to the forefront of the international agenda since the end of the Cold War. This is not particularly surprising. As dictatorships waned and democracies rose, globalization, privatization and liberalization became the mantras of the new millennium's economic agenda. The rise of official corruption, however, imperils this programme for economic prosperity; it endangers the benefits that businesses and governments in developed states expected to reap from the wave of democratic transitions and the open markets that followed. The consequences of corruption were highlighted by the United Nations' (UN) anti-corruption initiative, the Global

Compact[1] which notes that: 'The impact on the private sector is ... considerable – it impedes economic growth, distorts competition and represents serious legal and reputational risks. Corruption is also very costly for business, with the extra financial burden estimated to add 10% or more to the costs of doing business in many parts of the world'.

Ironically, it is the market liberalization stemming from the process of democratization and advocated by these same investors that set in motion the conditions conducive to the rise of corruption. Blake and Morris[2] concur noting, 'Democracy creates new means of acquiring and exercising power ... [and concomitantly] new opportunities for corruption. For example, schemes to buy legislative votes or to influence illegally the votes of citizens in general elections are more tempting in a democracy'. Susan Hawley of the British non-governmental organization (NGO) Corner House, makes a similar claim: 'If corruption is growing throughout the world, it is largely a result of the rapid privatisation (and associated practices of contracting-out and concessions) of public enterprises worldwide. This process has been pushed by Western creditors and governments ...' This outcome is very much the antithesis of the claims by the advocates of neoliberalism, such as the international financial institutions (IFIs), which postulate that an open economy and a minimal state provide the foundation for transparency, good governance and democratic development. The World Bank's[3] *Development Report* asserts:

> In general, any reform that increases the competitiveness of the economy will reduce incentives for corrupt behavior. Thus policies that lower controls on foreign trade, remove entry barriers to private industry, and privatize state firms in a way that ensures competition will all support the fight. If the state has no authority to restrict exports or to license businesses, there will be no opportunities to pay bribes in those areas. If a subsidy program is eliminated, any bribes that accompanied it will disappear as well.

Using a case study approach, this chapter explains the corruption epidemic by linking it to the emphasis on market-oriented democratization. Focusing on Nicaragua under Presidents Arnoldo Alemán (1996–2001) and Daniel Ortega

---

1   United Nations Global Compact. 'Transparency and Anti-corruption' (2004), available at http://www.unglobalcompact.org/AboutTheGC/TheTenPrinciples/anti-corrupt ion.html, accessed 2 August 2012.

2   Charles Blake and Stephen D. Morris, 'Introduction: Political and Analytical Challenges of Corruption in Latin America', in Charles H. Blake and Stephen D. Morris (eds), *Corruption and Democracy in Latin America* (Pittsburgh, PA: University of Pittsburgh Press, 2009), 3.

3   World Bank, *World Development Report* (1997) [Online], available at http://www-wds.worldbank.org/external/default/WDSContentServer/IW3P/IB/1997/06/01/000009265 _3980217141148/Rendered/PDF/multi0page.pdf, accessed 14 August 2012.

(2007–present) primarily, the analysis contends that the nature of the democratic transition with its emphasis on competition, liberalization and privatization set in motion processes that gave rise to mismanagement, exploitation, and outright corruption by those in positions of political power.

The claim here is not that corruption is new but rather that the very democratization processes that are supposed to preclude it are in fact facilitating its spread. It is also not the intent here to suggest that corruption is a necessary outcome of liberalization. However, in societies where oversight structures are weak, unscrupulous political leaders have greater incentives to exploit the openings offered by the free-market to loot the public treasury for private gain. Relatedly, the calls for political pluralism, a necessary accompaniment to economic liberalization, present opportunities for power-hungry politicians to manipulate the political process and reconfigure laws and institutions to cement their control and dominance. And, while international institutions focus on the cost of corruption for investors and the damage corruption inflicts on market operations, arguably, the group most harmed by it is civil society, especially its most vulnerable sectors. It is not only denied its rightful share of state resources but it too can become infected with the corruption plague.

The chapter is organized into seven sections. The first is the introduction which presents the thesis. The second discusses terms and definitions. The third is a brief look at Nicaraguan history with highlights on those aspects relevant to the argument, in particular the transition from state to market led development. The fourth examines political corruption under democratization and focuses on the pact between Alemán and Ortega. The fifth looks at corruption in the economic sphere and shows the link between it and the privatization process. The sixth draws attention to the impact of corruption on civil society. The seventh, the final section, is the conclusion which briefly discusses how the agenda of international institutions contribute to the corruption wave in the global South.

II: Definition

According to Transparency International's (TI) (n.d.) definition, corruption is 'the abuse of entrusted power for private gain'. It can vary in breadth as well as in depth, 'from the minor use of influence to institutionalized bribery', and it can be both financial and non-financial in nature. TI goes further and delineates categories of corruption, two of which are of relevance here: grand corruption and political corruption. The former encompasses 'acts committed at a high level of government that distort policies or the central functioning of the state, enabling leaders to benefit at the expense of the public good', and the latter refers to the 'manipulation of policies, institutions and rules of procedure … by political decision makers, who abuse their position to sustain their power, status and wealth' (TI n.d.).

In their work on *State Crime*, Penny Green and Tony Ward[4] offer another classification structure, one that overlaps with TI's, but which has two categories of corruption, 'individual deviance' and 'organizational deviance'. The first refers to acts committed by individuals against the state and relies on TI's definition of corruption (that is, 'the abuse of public office for private gain'). This is corruption of a political and administrative nature and it is sometimes referred to as 'political white collar crime'. The second, 'organizational deviance,' is where the authors locate state corruption which they view as encompassing three types of crimes. Firstly, there are those perpetrated as 'a *means* [emphasis added] to an organisational goal', such as in the case of state agents becoming involved in illicit activities to serve the state's objective (as with Iran-Contra); secondly, there are malfeasances that serve organizational goals; that is, they benefit the organization and are thus tolerated. This is evident in some states where public servants' wages are so low that the latter are frequently driven to participate in illicit activities such as bribery or extortion to supplement their incomes. Their actions are tolerated because they inadvertently relieve the state of its obligations to pay a living wage. Finally, there are those crimes which are pursued as an organizational goal, that is, 'where the pursuit of profit determines the agency's decisions'.[5] This is the case, for example, with kickbacks to state officials for the awarding of contracts, a practice prevalent in privatization schemes.

In this analysis of the Nicaraguan context, corruption in both its individual and organizational domains are investigated. What the chapter demonstrates is that political pluralism and the free market, contrary to the claims of their defenders, have not promoted democracy and development in Nicaragua. Instead, they have given rise to corruption and clientelism, distorted the market, undermined democracy, and entrenched *caudillo* rule. Presidents Arnoldo Alemán and Daniel Ortega, despite their opposing political ideologies, have each manipulated the system to enrich themselves and their supporters, and to ensure their access to power. Largely due to their legacies, Nicaragua is today ranked 134 out of 183 on the Corruption Perception Index (CPI) and has a score of 2.5 out of 10 where '0' is highly corrupt and 10 is very clean.[6]

III: From State to Market

For four decades prior to 1979, Nicaragua was under the tyrannical rule of the Somoza dynasty until the regime's ousting by a popular social revolution led by

---

4   Penny Green and Tony Ward, *State Crime: Governments, Violence and Corruption* (London and Sterling, VA: Pluto Press 2004), 11.

5   Penny Green and Tony Ward, *State Crime: Governments, Violence and Corruption* (London and Sterling, VA: Pluto Press 2004), 11–16.

6   TI (Transparency International), Corruption Perceptions Index: Nicaragua [Online] (2011), available at http://cpi.transparency.org/cpi2011/results/, accessed 10 August 2012.

Daniel Ortega and the Sandinista National Liberation Front (Frente Sandinista Liberación Naciónal – FSLN). A Marxist inspired guerrilla movement that emerged in the 1960s, the FSLN's goal was to defeat the dictatorship and construct a society modelled on the principles of socialism.

During their reign, the dynastic Somozas had subordinated all the apparatuses of the state to their dominance. Institutions such as the judiciary, the police, the electoral system and the bureaucracy were all under their control. The right to vote was often manipulated, suspended or denied altogether. So too were legal rights and due process. For those suspected of or charged with being communists or guerrilla sympathizers, imprisonment, torture and even death awaited them. The FSLN's military defeat of the dictatorship brought an end to this brutality, however, it did not bring peace.

Almost immediately after the Sandinistas assumed power, at the start of the 1980s, a decade-long war against the US-funded and trained Contra army ensued. The conflict paralyzed the Nicaraguan economy, demoralized the population and eventually forced the FSLN into a negotiated peace. This effectively ended the socialist project and inaugurated the era of liberal democratic politics that made Nicaragua part of the so-called third wave democracies. Confirming its status in this club is the fact that the country has successfully held regular competitive elections to select its leader. Thus far, there have been five such national elections, 1990, 1996, 2001, 2006 and 2011. In the first three, the FSLN went down to defeat, first to Violeta Barrios de Chamorro of the National Opposition Union (Unión Nacional Opositora – UNO), then to Arnoldo Alemán, and finally to Enrique Bolaños both of the Liberal Constitutionalist Party (Partido Liberal Constitucionalista – PLC). In the latter two, however, the FSLN prevailed under its leader Daniel Ortega.

With the victory of Violeta Barrios de Chamorro began the process of transformation of the Nicaraguan economy, the reversing of Sandinista policies that had been aimed at strengthening the public sector. On assuming power in 1979, the FSLN had followed a mixed-economy strategy in their drive to build socialist state. As such, their economic programme allowed for some free market operations mixed with state control of huge sectors of the economy. The latter component of their agenda involved the nationalization of the enormous holdings of the Somoza family, as well as banks and other enterprises, and the introduction of price controls. Between 1978–80, GDP generated by state enterprises had risen from 15 per cent to 41 per cent.[7]

---

7   Bertelsmann Transformation Index (BTI), Country Report, Nicaragua. *Shaping Change: Strategies for Development and Transformation* [Online] (2006), available at http://bti2006.bertelsmann-transformation-index.de/fileadmin/pdf/en/2006/LatinAmerica AndTheCaribbean/Nicaragua.pdf, 5, accessed 2 August 2012.

However, by 1988, the economy was in a free fall. Hyperinflation stood at 33,000 per cent.[8] The foreign debt was reportedly 700 per cent of GDP.[9] Other figures show that by 1989, per capita debt was 33 times the value of the nation's exports.[10] The government's response was to implement a harsh austerity programme that, according to Dye and Close,[11] 'choked whatever life there was left in the economy, and by the end of the Sandinista's tenure, GDP *per capita* had fallen to 60% of its pre-revolutionary level'.

While the FSLN's economic strategy may have been partly responsible for the precipitous economic decline, it must be remembered that the regime was facing a national crisis stemming largely from the Contra war which consumed the lion's share of the national income, and which severely distorted the results of its economic programme. In light of the severity of the economic crisis, it is not surprising that competitive elections resulted in the defeat of the FSLN and the victory of the UNO coalition under Chamorro. The generally accepted rationale for the rejection of the FSLN was that Nicaraguans hoped that a US-backed regime would bring with it the end of the Contra conflict, the US embargo, and the general misery and deprivation inflicted on the population as a result of the FSLN's war-time economic measures.

The Chamorro administration campaigned on a platform of abolishing the FSLN's state-led development strategy and of implementing a free market, export-oriented model. UNO's preferences were very much in accordance with those of its international supporters, the US government and the international financial institutions (IFIs) such as the World Bank and the International Monetary Fund (IMF). The logic of this strategy is that since the market is seen as the engine of growth, as stimulating investments, efficiency, productivity and entrepreneurialism, it is important that the market be able to function without impediments. Furthermore, when it comes to corruption, the prevailing belief of free-market adherents is that the less state involvement there is in the economy, the less likelihood there is of corruption. The Nicaraguan case has not borne this out as corruption has become endemic since the return to a more liberalized economy,

----

8   David Dye and David Close, 'Patrimonialism and Economic Policy in the Alemán Administration', in David Close and Kalowatie Deonandan (eds), *Undoing Democracy: The Politics of Electoral Caudillismo* (Lanham, MD: Lexington Books, 2004), 119–142.

9   Bertelsmann Transformation Index (BTI), Country Report, Nicaragua. *Shaping Change: Strategies for Development and Transformation* [Online] (2006), available at http://bti2006.bertelsmann-transformation-index.de/fileadmin/pdf/en/2006/LatinAmerica AndTheCaribbean/Nicaragua.pdf, 5, accessed 2 August 2012.

10   Andrés Pérez Baltodano, 'Political Culture', in David Close, Salvador Marti í Puig and Shelley McConnell (eds), *The Sandinistas and Nicaragua Since 1979* (Boulder, CO: Lynne Rienner, 2012), 68.

11   David Dye and David Close, 'Patrimonialism and Economic Policy in the Alemán Administration', in David Close and Kalowatie Deonandan (eds), *Undoing Democracy: The Politics of Electoral Caudillismo* (Lanham, MD: Lexington Books, 2004), 121.

especially since the administration of Arnoldo Alemán which succeeded that of Chamorro.

Soon after assuming office, the Chamorro government committed itself to adhering to the IMF's programme to open up the Nicaraguan economy and to reduce its massive debt burden. It began by signing the Enhanced Structural Adjustment Facility (ESAF 1) in 1994. ESAF included the standard package of structural adjustment measures (SAPs): devaluation of the currency, elimination of price controls, privatization of national enterprises, encouragement of national and foreign investments, and a reduction of the budget deficit through cuts in the public sector. Under Chamorro, 346 of 351 state-owned enterprises in the industrial and agricultural sectors were either privatized or liquidated between 1990–95.[12] Concomitantly, unemployment skyrocketed, public sector jobs were reduced from 290,000 in 1990 to 107,000 in 1993, to under 80,000 in 1999.[13]

This developmental model was continued under the successor administration of Arnoldo Alemán which signed ESAF II in 1998 and which consented to all the IMF's dictates 'without a word of protest' in the drive to reduce the debt.[14] The sweep of ESAF II was extensive; it involved gutting social programmes and nationalizing public utilities, the negative impact of which would be strongly felt by the most vulnerable populations. As Marti[15] explains, the goals of the programme were to be achieved by reducing the public sector by another 10,000 workers, privatizing public utilities, and increasing electricity, water and gasoline prices by 18 per cent annually. While rising utility prices rendered this sector attractive to private investors, they imposed a severe burden on an already over-burdened population. In 2001, per capital GDP stood at US$2,450, national poverty rates at 45.8 per cent, and extreme poverty at 15.1 per cent.[16] The situation was even harsher in rural areas where 64.3 per cent of the population were living in poverty, and 24.7 per cent in extreme poverty; the latter group was surviving on less than US$1 per day.[17]

---

12   Multinational Monitor, 'Bearing the Burden of IMF and World Bank Policies: Downsizing, Privatization, Labor Flexibility, Wage Cuts – Selected Summaries of IMF/ World Bank Country Policies', *Multinational Monitor*, 22 (9) (September 2001). Available at: http://multinationalmonitor.org/mm2001/01september/sep01corp1s.html, accessed 6 August 2012.

13   Ibid.

14   Salvador Martí i Puig, 'The External Debt of Nicaragua and the Alemán Liberal Administration: Images and Realities', in David Close and Kalowatie Deonandan (eds), *Undoing Democracy: The Politics of Electoral Caudillismo* (Lanham, MD: Lexington Books, 2004), 153.

15   Ibid., 155.

16   World Bank, Nicaragua Poverty Assessment (2004) [Online], available at http://web.worldbank.org/WBSITE/EXTERNAL/COUNTRIES/LACEXT/0,contentMDK:2040 5857~pagePK:146736~piPK:146830~theSitePK:258554,00.html, accessed 8 August 2012.

17   World Bank, Nicaragua Poverty Assessment (2004) [Online], available at http://web.worldbank.org/WBSITE/EXTERNAL/COUNTRIES/LACEXT/0,contentMDK:2040 5857~pagePK:146736~piPK:146830~theSitePK:258554,00.html, accessed 8 August 2012.

Against this misery was contrasted the situation of Nicaragua's elite. A World Bank study revealed that just 695 top officials in the country received 0.86 per cent of the nation's GDP.[18] Another study, this by the private accounting firm Price Waterhouse, found that the country's leading political officials (including the President, Vice-President, ministers and members of Congress) were the highest paid in Central America, far surpassing those of Costa Rica, one of the wealthier states in the region.[19] One public figure, Luis Durán, the head of the Secretariat of the Presidency and also the individual 'in charge of designing the country's new Poverty Reduction Strategy, earned $23,500 a month, far more than the income of most of the country's municipalities'.[20]

What greatly enabled the enrichment of the political bosses was the level of executive control of many state institutions (made possible by the Pact as discussed below) such as the Office of the Comptroller General, the Supreme Court and the National Assembly. President Alemán, for example, ensured that these institutions would function to his advantage by staffing them with individuals loyal to him and who were willing to ignore or manipulate the rules at his behest. He bought their allegiance through a host of irregular and illegal schemes such as making direct financial payments to them or giving them perks in the form of tax-free imported vehicles.[21] The following sections of the chapter examine in greater depth how Nicaragua's political leaders reorganized the country's political system and its economy to serve their private interests and the legacy of this.

IV: Liberalization, Corruption and the Political System

Economic liberalization has as its attendant corollary political pluralism, that is, competitive political parties and elections. In theory, this enhances democracy. What is often neglected in this interpretation, however, is that competition can also facilitate corruption. This was made starkly clear in the Nicaraguan context where former arch enemies, the revolutionary Sandinista leader Daniel Ortega brokered a deal with his former arch-enemy Arnoldo Alemán, to subvert the political process for their mutual gain. Faced with challengers from within their respective political factions and parties, the two men exploited the opportunities

---

18   Envío, 'Nicaragua Briefs: The Mega-Salary Scandal Fueled by World Bank Study', *Revista Envío*, 291 (October 2005) [Online], available at http://www.envio.org.ni/articulo/3074, accessed 9 August 2012.

19   José Luis Rocha, 'Micro-salaries and Mega-salaries: Mega-inequality and Micro-development', *Revista Envío*, 248 (March 2002) [Online], available at http://www.envio.org.ni/articulo/1566, accessed 28 July 2012.

20   Ibid.

21   León Núñez, 'Alemán Still Controls the PLC and Will Hand Ortega the Victory', *Envio*, 292 (November 2005) [Online], available at http://www.envio.org.ni/articulo/3111, accessed 10 August 2012.

that political democracy offered and forged a notorious power-sharing alliance, famously labelled *El Pacto*, to ensure their grip on power. In so doing, they joined a very long list of Latin American strongmen and led some observers to proclaim that the country was 'in the hands of two Mafia gangs'.[22] For Ortega supporters, the Pact was a shocking betrayal given the ideals of the FSLN and even Ortega's own revolutionary credentials. An extreme form of legislative cooperation, the deal maintained the process of democracy – the electoral and party systems, the legislature, the courts, etc. – but profoundly corrupted democracy's substance to the detriment of the electorate whom the deal-makers purport to represent.

Almost 15 years have passed since the unveiling of the Pact in 1999, yet it still casts a long shadow over Nicaraguan democracy. Commenting on its legacy, Maureen Meyer[23] of the Washington Office on Latin America (WOLA) observes that: 'There are disturbing shifts in the system of checks and balances, with a growing consolidation of power in the executive branch, and the weakening of the autonomy of state institutions like the Supreme Court. Underlying these trends is the continuation of a political alliance, or "Pact", which preserves the façade of political party competition in the National Assembly while concentrating power in two party leaders'.

El Pacto entailed a series of 18 amendments to the articles of the Nicaraguan constitution.[24] Amongst the most important were: the guarantee that the outgoing President and Vice-President automatically receive a seat in the National Assembly; the requirement that the voting criteria for removing presidential immunity be two-thirds rather than the previous qualified majority; and the adjustments in the types of requirements a presidential candidate must meet in order to preclude a second run-off election. Additionally, the Pact increased the number of high ranking positions in several offices such as the Supreme Electoral Council (Consejo Supremo Electoral – CSE), the Supreme Court of Justice (Corte Suprema de Justicia – CSJ), the Office of Comptroller General of the Republic (Contralor General de la República – CGR), the Appeals Court, the Public Prosecutor's Office, and the Human Rights Defence Attorney's office.

These amendments were all designed to enhance the protections and powers of the Pact's signatories. For example, by granting parliamentary seats to the executive after they have left office, the Pact secured Alemán's and Ortega's

---

22 Mónica Baltodano, 'Nicaragua: From Sandinismo to "Danielismo"', *International Socialist Review*, 50 (November–December 2006) [Online], available at http://www. isreview.org/issues/50/nicaragua.shtml, accessed 1 August 2012.

23 Maureen Meyer, Elections in Nicaragua, *Washington Office on Latin America (WOLA)* (1 November 2011) [Online], available at http://www.wola.org/commentary/elections_in_nicaragua, accessed 29 July 2012.

24 For a detailed discussion of the Pact see Katherine Hoyt, 'Parties and Pacts in Contemporary Nicaragua', in David Close and Kalowatie Deonandan (eds), *Undoing Democracy: The Politics of Electoral Caudillismo* (Lanham, MD: Lexington Books, 2004), 17–42.

continued access to power. By reinforcing the immunity shield it protected them against future prosecution. Further, the new positions created in various strategic government offices were filled by appointees loyal to the pact-makers themselves. Illustrative of the significance of this particular amendment is the office of the Comptroller General. Previously a one-person entity, it was expanded under the Pact into a five-person office and was staffed by Presidential appointees. This is the same office which is empowered to investigate financial and other types of wrongdoing by government officials, including the President.

For analysts, the Pact represents a text book case of clientelistic politics. Clientelism denotes a situation whereby the patron grants to subordinates certain privileges or favours in return for loyalty and support. In this instance, access to high ranking jobs in state institutions, and guarantees of massive salary increases were the gifts distributed by patrons who in turn were protected by the 'clients' now in said institutions. This freed the patron/executive to implement policies favourable to itself without fear of being checked by the operations of the 'democratic' state institutions, institutions which are theoretically accountable to the people.[25]

The clientelistic politics of the Pact and the collusion between the leaders of the PLC and the FSLN signified for some a return to the politics of *caudillismo*, to the era of *Somocismo*, with Ortega and Alemán as the new strong men of Nicaraguan politics.[26] They manipulated the very mechanisms of the state, the electoral system and the constitution that are meant to preclude corruption to institutionalize their corrupt practices. Prohibited by the rules of the electoral process from single-handedly and unilaterally reorganizing state institutions for his own ends, Alemán schemed with his one-time nemesis to exploit the very rules of democracy to subvert democracy to their mutual advantage. He collaborated with the opposition (Ortega), all legal acts, to restructure state institutions in such a way that they were accountable to him rather than the converse. The legacy of the Pact on Nicaragua's democracy has been widespread; it has left 'heinous prints' which include 'all manner of arbitrariness, corruption and mafia-like murky deals'.[27] As a matter of fact, some analysts argue, '[m]aking pacts has metamorphosed into a method and a philosophy in Nicaragua; the country has moved from pacts to "pactism" as a normal way of engaging in politics'.[28]

----

25   David Close, 'President Bolanos Runs a Reverse: Or How Arnoldo Alemán Wound Up in Prison', in David Close and Kalowatie Deonandan (eds), *Undoing Democracy: The Politics of Electoral Caudillismo* (Lanham, MD: Lexington Books, 2004), 170.

26   David Close and Kalowatie Deonandan (eds), *Undoing Democracy: The Politics of Electoral Caudillismo* (Lanham, MD: Lexington Books, 2004).

27   Nitlapán – Envío, 'The Hands that Rock ... Just About Everything', *Revista Envío*, 292 (November 2005) [Online], available at http://www.envio.org.ni/articulo/3109, accessed 10 August 2012.

28   Nitlapán – Envío, 'The Hands that Rock ... Just About Everything', *Revista Envío*, 292 (November 2005) [Online], available at http://www.envio.org.ni/articulo/3109, accessed 10 August 2012.

These 'heinous footprints' of the pact were evident in the 2011 elections which saw Ortega rewrite the terms of the constitution to legitimize his run for the Presidency. Until this point, the Nicaraguan constitution had limited Presidents to two non-consecutive terms and further stipulated that an incumbent President cannot stand for re-election. Ortega, having won the 2006 elections, was thus ruled out. However, in 2009, he began the process of removing this hurdle when he mounted a legal challenge and petitioned the Supreme Court to annul those articles of the constitution that precluded his candidacy claiming that they violated his constitutional right (along with that of over 100 mayoral candidates facing similar restrictions). In a verdict that appalled Ortega's opponents, but perhaps did not shock them given the new Court structure put in place by the Pact, the justices ruled in his favour. With his way cleared, Ortega subsequently ran in the 2011 campaign and easily prevailed. With over 70 per cent voter turnout, he garnered just over 62.5 per cent of the vote (a massive majority from the 38 per cent plurality he claimed in 2006) and his party won 62 of the 92 seats in the legislature.[29]

Ortega's successful petition to the Court is a glaring example of how democracy can be undermined by legal manipulation and exposes the weaknesses of procedural democracy. He did not secure office by a coup, a revolution or any obviously illegal means. He followed one of the fundamental tenets of democracy – abide by the rule of law. The rule of law, however, was created by him to serve his will. Reflecting on the Court's verdict, Victor Tinoco,[30] a former FSLN member who is now part of the dissident faction, the Sandinista Renovation Movement (Movimiento de Renovación Sandinista – MRS), states that: 'His [Ortega's] presidential candidacy [was] an inevitable reality, just like a gang in a barrio. Like it or not, the gang is there, has power and runs the neighbourhood'. Sergio Ramírez, former Ortega Vice-President during the period of the '80s, concurs, asserting prior to Ortega's inauguration in 2012 that, 'no one in Nicaragua's history has ever had so much power in his hands'.[31]

The Supreme Court's decision that permitted Ortega's candidacy in 2011 can be traced directly to the legacy of the Pact. For critics, the verdict was based not on sound legal arguments but on the influence of the *El Pacto* in politicizing the

---

29   CIA World Factbook. Nicaragua [Online], available at https://www.cia.gov/library/publications/the-world-factbook/geos/nu.html, accessed 10 August 2012; Fox News Latino, 'Ortega Sweeps Nicaragua's Presidential Election', (7 November 2011) [Online], available at http://latino.foxnews.com/latino/politics/2011/11/07/ortega-sweeps-nicaraguas-presidential-election/, accessed 14 August 2012.

30   Victor Hugo Tinoco, 'Corruption is the Most Important Serious Aspect of the Ortega-Chávez Relationship', *Revista Envío*, 338 (September 2009) [Online], available at http://www.envio.org.ni/articulo/4061, accessed 28 July 2012.

31   *Envío*, 'Nicaragua: A Rerun with Contradictions Inside and Out', *Revista Envío*, 366 (January 2012) [Online], available at http://www.envio.org.ni/articulo/4478, accessed 9 August 2012.

judiciary. This assessment is borne out by Elena Martínez Barahona's[32] detailed study of the Court in which she reported finding a staggering level of politicization and partisanship in the institution. As she notes, as of 2009, every one of the '16 members of the Supreme Court had been deputies in National Assembly [prior] or owed some political loyalty to Daniel Ortega or Arnoldo Alemán'. Appointments to the bench are based not on merit but rather on how well the candidate can serve the interests of one or the other of the dominant parties.[33] Equally disturbing are claims made regarding back room deals in the Court that allowed for the Ortega victory. The Constitutional Court, the body that issued the Ortega decision, is in essence a chamber of the Supreme Court as it is composed of six of the members of the latter Court. Three of the justices of the Constitutional Court were known to be PLC loyalists and three FSLN supporters.[34] To win the pro-Ortega verdict, convenient absences and substitutions were orchestrated to ensure that the right composition of magistrates were present for the vote. Meyer[35] reports that 'on the day this decision was made, all six judges were aligned with the FSLN. One PLC justice was out of the country while the other two allege that they were not called in time to vote. As a result, three FSLN-oriented substitutes took their place'. These machinations led Martínez Barahona[36] to the blunt conclusion that the Court, 'is a captive of the executive'.

Why would the PLC justices cooperate in a process that facilitated an FSLN victory? According to *Envío*, a publication critical of both the FSLN and the PLC, the explanation lies in the waning power of one *caudillo*, Alemán, due to his imprisonment, and the rise of another, Ortega:

> With each new negotiation of the pact, Ortega has come out increasingly the winner. In the case of the CSE, its structures have quietly and progressively shifted from being bi-party to mainly defending Daniel Ortega's interests ... . And it happened before the very eyes of the PLC magistrates, who found themselves in the bind of being unable to renounce either the perks of the job or their loyalty to the pro-Ortega orientations of their own leader, former President Arnoldo Alemán, who since his conviction in 2002 for embezzling and money

---

32   Elena Martínez Barahona, 'A Politicized Judiciary', in David Close, Salvador Marti í Puig and Shelley McConnell (eds), *The Sandinistas and Nicaragua Since 1979* (Boulder, CO: Lynne Rienner), 108.

33   Ibid., 110.

34   Maureen Meyer, 'Elections in Nicaragua', *Washington Office on Latin America (WOLA)* (1 November 2011) [Online], available at http://www.wola.org/commentary/elections_in_nicaragua, accessed 29 July 2012.

35   Ibid.

36   Elena Martínez Barahona, 'A Politicized Judiciary', in David Close, Salvador Marti í Puig and Shelley McConnell (eds), *The Sandinistas and Nicaragua Since 1979* (Boulder, CO: Lynne Rienner), 91.

laundering has given away more and more of the store through the pact to keep himself out of prison.

Aside from the alleged chicaneries in the Court, there were also charges of electoral irregularities in 2011 such as anti-FSLN voters not receiving ID cards on time and some electoral observers not granted standing. Even the election results were challenged by some as being fraudulent. However, it must be noted that none of the allegations were ever proven and according to CID-Gallup, the results were in line with what they had predicted.[37]

What accounts for Ortega's win at the polls despite the Pact and the many accusations of corruption and *caudillo* politics? Part of the explanation undoubtedly lies in the improved economic conditions Nicaragua experienced under his administration. According to the CIA Factbook,[38] between 2009–11, macroeconomic growth was steady; real GDP which was −1.5 per cent in 2009, climbed to 4.5 per cent in 2010, and then rose slightly again to 4.7 per cent in 2011. GDP *per capita* also saw modest increases during this same period, rising from $3,000 to $3,100, and then to $3,200 respectively.[39] Much of this growth has been fuelled by increases in foreign direct investments, especially in the free trade zones, and by rising exports to the US, all facilitated by the Central America Free Trade Agreement (CAFTA).[40] In addition, Nicaraguan workers received an increase in the minimum wage under Ortega.[41] One of the President's supporters summarized the infrastructural and social developments Nicaraguans witnessed under the FSLN:

> [T]he Sandinista government has built more than 1,800 kilometers of paved roads in the countryside, provided schools for all the children, who were unable to attend classes under the previous governments; built hundreds of free health clinics throughout the country, provided a pregnant cow or sow to some 100,000 head-of-household women in the countryside, made interest-free loans available to the same group; given out nearly a million corrugated steel roofing sheets

---

37   Fred Morris, 'Nicaragua: The Other Side', *Council of Hemispheric Affairs (COHA)* (22 December 2011) [Online], available at http://www.coha.org/nicaragua-the-other-side, accessed 29 July 2012.

38   Central Intelligence Agency, USA. The World Fact Book, available at https://www.cia.gov/library/publications/the-world-factbook/geos/nu.html, accessed 29 December 2013.

39   Ibid.

40   Tim Rogers, 'Nicaragua Sets Pace for Region Under CAFTA' (11 May 2012) [Online], available at http://www.ticotimes.net/Region/Nicaragua-sets-pace-for-region-under-CAFTA_Friday-May-11-2012, accessed 28 December 2013.

41   Central Intelligence Agency, USA. The World Fact Book, available at https://www.cia.gov/library/publications/the-world-factbook/geos/nu.html, accessed 29 December 2013.

to poor families, and, at the same time, enabled the business sector to be more profitable than at any time in the country's history.[42]

Even some of Ortega's critics, such as WOLA's Meyer,[43] have conceded that his administration has been able 'to reduce poverty and illiteracy rates, [and] increase citizens' access to social services'.

Nevertheless, others have denounced the programmes as another manifestation of clientelism. In the view of Rafael Aragón,[44] a Dominican priest and liberation theologian activist, programmes such as giving roofing material to the poor are not geared towards popular conscientization but rather towards winning Ortega re-election. Aragón further objects to these initiatives on the grounds they make the poor into 'objects of charity' and not 'subjects of their own history'.[45]

Additionally, the programmes were criticized on the basis that they were not really a result of the success of any of Ortega's policies as they were in fact underwritten by Venezuela in the form of oil funds channelled through ALBANISA (or ALBA de Nicaragua, S.A), a semi-private company jointly owned by Nicaragua and Venezuela.[46] Concerns have been expressed too about the lack of transparency in the company's operations since ALBANISA is privately managed, not subject to government oversight and has as its President the Treasurer of the FSLN.

Economics are only one part of the story of the Ortega victory. Control of the media is another as it allowed Ortega to project a positive image of himself and his message and to simultaneously discredit his opponents. During the economic privatization process, the Ortega family became media magnates acquiring almost half the country's television stations including Multinoticias, and Channels 8 and 13. Additionally, the state-owned Channel 6 is effectively under Ortega's and the FSLN's control, as are a number of radio stations including Ya, Sandino, Nicaragua and la Primerísima. This media dominance is further extended by the

---

42   Fred Morris, 'Nicaragua: The Other Side', *Council of Hemispheric Affairs (COHA)* (22 December 2011) [Online], available at http://www.coha.org/nicaragua-the-other-side, accessed 29 July 2012.

43   Maureen Meyer, 'Elections in Nicaragua', *Washington Office on Latin America (WOLA)* (1 November 2011) [Online], available at http://www.wola.org/commentary/elections_in_nicaragua, accessed 29 July 2012.

44   Rafael Aragón, 'Is Ortega's Project Christian? And What is the Church's Project?', *Revista Envío,* 357 (April 2011), available at http://www.envio.org.ni/articulo/4328, accessed 28 December 2013.

45   Rafael Aragón, 'Is Ortega's Project Christian? And What is the Church's Project?', *Revista Envío,* 357 (April 2011), available at http://www.envio.org.ni/articulo/4328, accessed 28 December 2013.

46   *Envío,* 'The Dependence on Chavez', *Revista Envío,* 368 (March) [Online], available at http://www.envio.org.ni/articulo/4294, accessed 10 August 2012; NSC (Nicaragua Solidarity Network), Elections in Nicaragua (2011) [Online], available at http://www.nicaraguasc.org.uk/elections%202011/index.htm, accessed 16 August 2012.

President's ability to restrict opposing outlets by denying them public support in the form of advertising or by imposing restrictions in the form of import taxes on necessities such as ink, paper and printing materials. The impact of this according to Arturo Cruz,[47] Nicaragua's Ambassador to Washington during Ortega's second term, is that, 'There was a fundamental shift in Ortega's image over five years, and one could argue that among [sic] contributing factors is his greater presence in the media'. Undoubtedly, his resounding electoral win was due in no small measure to his ability to control the medium and the message.

V: Corruption and Economic Liberalization

What enabled Daniel Ortega to acquire a media empire, which in turn helped with his electoral victory, was the economic liberalization that Nicaragua promoted through SAPs in the form of ESAF I and II. These polices are premised on the foundation that opening up the economy to global markets and international investors will enhance growth and development, promote democracy and prevent corruption. Perversely, however, the liberalization process provided opportunities for unscrupulous political leaders to exploit for personal gain. It bears repeating that such conduct is not a *necessary outcome* of liberalization. Rather when privatization is imposed on societies where the mechanisms of accountability and transparency are weak, and when this is combined with the presence of greedy office holders, the outcome is likely to be antithetical to the public good.

Under Arnoldo Alemán, one of the more questionable aspects of privatization was the manner in which the income generated from the sale of public enterprises was spent. It was standard practice, though an ethically suspect one, for members of the National Assembly to receive funds of over $2 million without much oversight for development projects in their districts.[48] According to one estimate, in 2001 these grants were equivalent 'to 37% of that allotted to the country's 151 municipalities'[49] In 2002, legislators received an additional $21,000 bringing their bounty for that year to almost $50,000 each with the increases coming from the sale of the state owned telecommunications company ENITEL.[50] Thus, each

---

47   Blake Schmidt, 'Nicaragua's President Rules Airwaves to Control Image', *New York Times* (28 November 2011) [Online], available at http://www.nytimes.com/2011/11/29/world/americas/daniel-ortega-extends-control-to-nicaraguas-airwaves.html?_r=1, accessed 9 August 2012.

48   José Luis Rocha, 'Micro-salaries and Mega-salaries: Mega-inequality and Micro-development', *Revista Envío*, 248 (March 2002) [Online], available at http://www.envio.org.ni/articulo/1566, accessed 28 July 2012.

49   Ibid.

50   José Luis Rocha, 'Micro-salaries and Mega-salaries: Mega-inequality and Micro-development', *Revista Envío*, 248 (March 2002) [Online], available at http://www.envio.org.ni/articulo/1566, accessed 28 July 2012.

elected official was administering 'nearly $50,000 with no controls or reports or accountability'.[51] Questioning the motivations behind the fund disbursement, one tax expert and lawyer Julio Francisco Báez asked: 'If the essence of democracy lies in local power, the municipality, why not allocate these funds to the municipal governments and let the legislative representatives devote themselves to the task for which they were elected ...'.

An even more scandalous attempt to exploit the privatization process involved an apparent bid by former President Alemán and his close associates to purchase a new cell phone frequency in Nicaragua. However, as David Close[52] details, it was a strategy to line the pockets of the deal makers and it revealed how the major players exploited their insider knowledge regarding the industries scheduled for privatization in order to gain control of public enterprises. What they did was to concoct a scheme to profit from the call to globalize the economy by manufacturing a phony foreign investment bid. This is what Green and Ward[53] would classify as 'individual deviance' or as 'political white collar crime'.

The story, explained in detail by Close,[54] began in 2001 with two companies putting forth tenders. The bid was won by the Mexican telephone company, PCS de Mexico (which claimed to be acting on behalf of Azteca Holding, the parent company of Mexican media conglomerate TV Azteca). Its tender included $8 million up front with approximately another $29 million for later work. Meanwhile the competing bid was $7.15 million to begin, with $42 million later. What is interesting to note is that the PCS bid had behind it several of Alemán's associates. Prominent amongst them were Ricardo Galán, one of the main lobbyists for PCS and someone who had also served as the Mexican Ambassador to Nicaragua, and Alejandro Lopez Toledo, a member of the committee evaluating the offers. Reportedly, as a committee member he was influential in altering the criteria for selection in PCS' favour.[55]

Shockingly, the deal was later revealed to be fraudulent. TV Azteca claimed it had never heard of PCS – the company making the bid under its auspices. What the courts concluded was that the objective of the fraud was to purchase the frequency cheaply then sell it for a much higher rate later on. It seems PCS was a shell established to gain control of the frequency so that the co-conspirators

---

51   Ibid.

52   David Close, 'President Bolanos Runs a Reverse: Or How Arnoldo Alemán Wound Up in Prison', in David Close and Kalowatie Deonandan (eds), *Undoing Democracy: The Politics of Electoral Caudillismo* (Lanham, MD: Lexington Books, 2004), 174–175.

53   Penny Green and Tony Ward, *State Crime: Governments, Violence and Corruption* (London and Sterling, VA: Pluto Press, 2004).

54   David Close, 'President Bolanos Runs a Reverse: Or How Arnoldo Alemán Wound Up in Prison', in David Close and Kalowatie Deonandan (eds), *Undoing Democracy: The Politics of Electoral Caudillismo* (Lanham, MD: Lexington Books, 2004), 174–175.

55   David Close, 'President Bolanos Runs a Reverse: Or How Arnoldo Alemán Wound Up in Prison', in David Close and Kalowatie Deonandan (eds), *Undoing Democracy: The Politics of Electoral Caudillismo* (Lanham, MD: Lexington Books, 2004), 175.

could assure themselves a hefty profit later on. This interpretation was given validity when PCS could not make the monthly payments after winning its bid despite its claims to being a branch of the massive TV Azteca empire. This lack of funds reportedly led to other illegal acts involving many state agencies, including Channel 6 (the country's last publicly owned TV station), the Airport Authority (EAAI), the tourism institute (INTUR), the post office, the communications department (TELCOR), the phone company (ENITEL) and the finance department. These agencies were all used as pawns to divert funds to PCS so it could make its payments.

The PCS and other cases involving illegal acts and state agencies represent what Green and Ward[56] have identified as a form of state crime whereby corruption becomes the organizational goal in itself, or as they noted earlier, 'the pursuit of profit determines the agency's decisions'. In addition, these cases show the ease with which clientelistic politics can be practiced within a theoretically democratic framework. What they highlight too is that an emphasis on the market oriented approach does little to ensure transparency and accountability. As a matter of fact, it can often have the opposite effect, especially where state structures are weak and elites dominant. Eventually, Alemán was subject to criminal prosecution and conviction but this did not represent a victory for Nicaraguan democracy. Rather it was a testimony to the enduring legacy of the Pact and of clientelism and *caudillismo*. Alemán only faced prosecution because of more deal making by *caudillos*, in this instance Ortega and Nicaragua's next leader, Alemán's successor.

In 2002, Nicaraguans elected a new President, Enrique Bolaños of the PLC, the former Vice-President under Alemán. The two men soon became entangled in a power struggle for control of the Party. To cement his position, Bolaños used the power of his office and embarked on an anti-corruption crusade against his former boss. However, because Alemán still wielded immense power over PLC members in the National Assembly, the rivalry frequently brought the legislature to a standstill. Seizing on the dissension in the opposing camp, Ortega used the occasion to advance his own position rather than, as former FSLN guerrilla commander and now fervent FSLN critic Mónica Baltodano[57] suggests, helping to advance the struggle against corruption. Ortega's strategy was again a resort to *caudillo* politics whereby he orchestrated a deal that granted him control of the legislature in return for assisting Bolaños in the latter's campaign against Alemán. Explains Baltodano:[58] 'It was not until Ortega reached an agreement with Bolaños

---

56   Penny Green and Tony Ward, *State Crime: Governments, Violence and Corruption.* (London and Sterling, VA: Pluto Press, 2004), 16.

57   Mónica Baltodano, 'Nicaragua: From Sandinismo to "Danielismo"', *International Socialist Review*, 50 (November–December 2006) [Online], available at http://www.isreview.org/issues/50/nicaragua.shtml, accessed 1 August 2012.

58   Mónica Baltodano, 'Nicaragua: From Sandinismo to "Danielismo"', *International Socialist Review*, 50 (November–December 2006) [Online], available at http://www.isreview.org/issues/50/nicaragua.shtml, accessed 1 August 2012.

for control of parliament and other perks that "Danielismo" – it must be called that, and not Sandinismo – voted to suspend Alemán's immunity from prosecution. It wasn't until then that Ortega gave the order to a Sandinista judge to hand down an indictment against Alemán'. It was not democracy and the rule of law that held Alemán accountable, but the back room deals of the *caudillos*.

The Ortega–Bolaños agreement, however, did not mean that the Ortega–Alemán Pact was terminated. Because the former PLC leader still controlled his power base in the Assembly, he was successful in negotiating more power sharing arrangements with the FSLN leader.[59] The fact that he served just over five years of his 20-year sentence, and much of that was under house arrest at his personal estate, is evidence of his ongoing deals with Ortega.[60] His debt to Ortega was likely paid by the latter's definitive 2011 electoral victory and the Supreme Court ruling that made it possible.

VI: Corruption and Civil Society

Corruption not only deleteriously affects the functioning of the state but it is also, as the UN's Global Compact[61] notes, 'corrosive on the very fabric of society'. The same processes of liberalization that promote corruption above also encourage it below. Yet, a strong civil society is fundamental to an effective democracy, and many international organizations including the United Nations see civil society as an key weapon in their anti-corruption campaigns.

Theoretically, political democratization and economic liberalization should increase transparency and accountability. However, the focus on privatization and the reduction of the public sector that is inherent in the liberalization process have resulted in the contrary in Nicaragua. The increases in the cost of living that come from privatization of many basic services (utilities, health care, education, etc.) and the rising unemployment due to cuts across the economic spectrum, especially in the public sector, have meant that people have to find alternative means of subsistence. Lacking such options, many turn to gangs, drugs and other crimes. In Managua alone, there are over 100 youth gangs spread out in the different barrios.[62] The lack of viable options for this group due in no small measure to declining state spending on job creation programmes, recreational facilities and educational opportunities have meant that drugs and gang membership have

---

59   Ibid.
60   Ibid.
61   United Nations Global Compact. 'Transparency and Anti-corruption' (2004), available at http://www.unglobalcompact.org/AboutTheGC/TheTenPrinciples/anti-corrupt ion.html, accessed 2 August 2012.
62   José Luis Rocha, 'Traido: A Key to Youth Gang Continuity', *Revista Envío*, 288 (July 2005) [Online], available at http://www.envio.org.ni/articulo/2990, accessed 10 August 2012.

become viable alternatives.[63] It has been suggested that the behaviour of street gangs reflect that of the political *caudillos* or the political gangs; each group looks out for its own interests and a strong sense of 'us' versus 'them' is the dominant principle governing relationships. The demise of the revolutionary project has led to new forms of competition, all very much in keeping with the competitiveness embedded in the liberalization agenda.

Corruption, combined with deteriorating economic conditions also promotes political apathy and undermines the functioning of civil society. According to one poll conducted on the corruption question during the Alemán period, 77 per cent of Nicaraguans questioned Alemán's integrity[64] while 85.6 per cent expressed the belief that corruption has affected them.[65] One of the effects noted is a high level of 'disaffection' or withdrawal from political activism. According to Grigsby Vado,[66] despite the 'many social tragedies' in Nicaragua, there is a significant degree of 'apathy and social demobilization' and a noticeable lack of motivation 'to fight against a socio-economic system that batters them on a daily basis ...'. He writes:

> Violeta Chamorro's government liquidated almost all of the state-run industrial and agricultural companies, even selling off the railway system's trains and tracks for scrap metal, paying people to rip up the rails. Arnoldo Alemán's government sold off the state electricity and telephone companies at derisory prices and pillaged the public coffers. And Enrique Bolaños' government's budgetary priority is to pay local bankers usurious interest on the treasury bonds issued to cover the enormous fraud perpetrated by the owners of five bankrupt banks ... . The rich don't pay taxes. And ministers and magistrates, legislators and top public officials from all state branches earn the kind of salaries more associated with developed countries. Yet while all of this has been going on – and it still is – the three governments have enjoyed relative social stability.[67]

Nicaraguans even approved CAFTA without any major protests or uprisings despite the agreement's potentially deleterious impact on them.[68] Such indifference is particularly striking in a country once highly mobilized in a revolutionary struggle.

---

63   Ibid.

64   Infopress Central America, *Central America Report* (14 May 1999).

65   Infopress Central America, *Central America Report* (12 May 2000).

66   William Grigsby Vado, 'Why So Little Social Mobilization', *Revista Envío*, 288 (July 2005) [Online], available at http://www.envio.org.ni/articulo/2988, accessed 9 August 2012.

67   Ibid.

68   Nitlapán – Envío, 'The Hands that Rock ... Just About Everything', *Revista Envío*, 292 (November 2005) [Online], available at http://www.envio.org.ni/articulo/3109, accessed 10 August 2012.

Baltodano[69] links this apathy directly to the legacy of the Alemán–Ortega deal in noting that: 'The most damaging thing about the FSLN–PLC pact was Ortega's pledge to demobilize social forces and to neutralize any popular struggle. With the deal, all resistance to privatization, to the policies of the IMF, the World Bank, and the various structural adjustment plans, ended'. In fact, the ease with which Nicaragua assented to CAFTA is attributed largely to the now seemingly entrenched strategy of pact-making; this time it was between Ortega and President Enrique Bolaños, Alemán's. Political observers noted that during the National Assembly debates on the agreement, Ortega had a seven-hour private meeting with Bolaños. Soon after, the ratification of the agreement was announced without any of the mass demonstrations the FSLN had threatened or any of the protective legislation it had promised.[70] In Grigsby Vado's summation,[71] the pact with Bolaños represents Ortega's surrender to neoliberalism in exchange for power. Others suggest that what Ortega obtained from the negotiations was that 'he bought legitimacy, presenting himself to the international community as the person who can ensure a truce'[72] who can control political mobilization.

It can be argued too that the social apathy evident in the CAFTA process is also a symptom of the wider malady of the clientelism, which Aragón[73] suggests is what drives Ortega's pro-poor initiatives (Zero Hunger, Zero Usury and Roofs for the People). He sees them as forms of charity and paternalism masquerading as sound public policy. He contends that the manner in which the programmes are implemented promotes dependency on Ortega, reifies him as the provider and reduces opposition to him. This is his observation from watching FSLN news reports of the programmes:

> [W]e see the ideological expression of those who feel helped ... [They become] thankful for favors, in a relationship of dependence that has mythical-religious nuances: 'We thank the *comandante*; no one has helped us before, only him' ... One doesn't perceive the creation of citizens' consciousness but

---

69   Mónica Baltodano, 'Nicaragua: From Sandinismo to "Danielismo"', *International Socialist Review*, 50 (November–December 2006) [Online], available at http://www.isreview.org/issues/50/nicaragua.shtml, accessed 1 August 2012.

70   Nitlapán – Envío, 'The Hands that Rock ... Just About Everything', *Revista Envío*, 292 (November 2005) [Online], available at http://www.envio.org.ni/articulo/3109, accessed 10 August 2012.

71   William Grigsby Vado, 'Why So Little Social Mobilization', *Revista Envío*, 288 (July 2005) [Online], available at http://www.envio.org.ni/articulo/2988, accessed 9 August 2012.

72   Nitlapán – Envío, 'The Hands that Rock ... Just About Everything', *Revista Envío*, 292 (November 2005) [Online], available at http://www.envio.org.ni/articulo/3109, accessed 10 August 2012.

73   Rafael Aragón, 'Is Ortega's Project Christian? And What is the Church's Project?', *Revista Envio*, 357 (April 2011), available at http://www.envio.org.ni/articulo/4328, accessed 28 December 2013.

rather people's dependence on a party. Based on this, we can judge the logic of these social programs as paternalism and people's quasi-religious dependence on charity.[74]

Complementing this is the growing religious conservatism which further undermines social activism. Nicaragua has witnessed an explosion in the growth of evangelical protestantism, specifically in denominations such as Pentecostalism and the Assembly of God. Initially, these groups were promoted as part of the US sponsored counter revolutionary campaign in the 1980s to stem the tide of religious progressivism embodied in liberation theology. According to one estimate, prior to the revolution, there were 20 Pentecostal religious organizations and by 2011 there were 1,200.[75] In explaining the growing preference for such religious conservatism, Grigsby Vado[76] writes that 'tens of thousands of Nicaraguans of all social classes are currently taking refuge in mystic cults, adopting the philosophy of "God will provide" or "God knows what He is doing" as a defense against the constant aggression of the market system and society, renouncing their own capacity to think, organize and fight to change the situation in which they are living'. Inadvertently, the FSLN has helped to legitimize this process as several of its members have also converted to Protestant evangelicalism. This, suggests Baltodano,[77] produces a 'confused mix of political militancy and religious magic, in which crimes are transmuted into sins'. Since accountability for sins are matters of the afterlife and not the concerns of human institutions, social inaction is the righteous path in the face of it; judgement will come in the hereafter, a position that serves well the interest of ambitious and unscrupulous state leaders.

VII: Conclusion

Efforts to combat corruption have led to a proliferation of international declarations, conventions and agreements since the late 1990s. Amongst them are: the Anti-Bribery Convention (1999) of the OECD; the Anti-Corruption Principle adopted by the UN Global Compact Leaders Summit (2004); The World Bank Group's Annual Integrity Report; and of course the well-known Corruptions Perception Index

---

74   Rafael Aragón, 'Is Ortega's Project Christian? And What is the Church's Project?', *Revista Envio*, 357 (April 2011), available at http://www.envio.org.ni/articulo/4328, accessed 28 December 2013.

75   Ibid.

76   William Grigsby Vado, 'Why So Little Social Mobilization', *Revista Envío*, 288 (July 2005) [Online], available at http://www.envio.org.ni/articulo/2988, accessed 9 August 2012.

77   Mónica Baltodano, 'Nicaragua: From Sandinismo to "Danielismo"', *International Socialist Review*, 50 (November–December 2006) [Online], available at http://www.isreview.org/issues/50/nicaragua.shtml, accessed 1 August 2012.

compiled by TI which tracks state malfeasance. A common theme amongst all these international promulgations is the importance accorded to 'good governance'.

However, when it comes to the global south and countries like Nicaragua, the call for 'good governance' by many of these global institutions is really a call for social demobilization, for the establishment of conditions conducive to the smooth functioning of the market for the benefit of private investors, and more specifically international private investors. In essence, the global anti-corruption fight is a struggle on behalf of the private businesses in the industrialized North and it reflects the neoliberal focus of the Washington consensus. Corner House's Susan Hawley[78] explains why: 'Every year Western businesses pay huge amounts of money in bribes to win friends, influence and contracts. These bribes are conservatively estimated to run to US\$80 billion a year – roughly the amount that the UN believes is needed to eradicate global poverty'. Less than five years later, the UN's Global Compact[79] estimated this figure at US\$1 trillion.

While these declarations and agreements do speak of corruption's corrosive impact on the poor and on civil society generally, the policies stemming from them in the form of IMF imposed SAPs promoted under the ESAF, and now its new incarnation, the Poverty Reduction Strategies (PRSPs) which are being advanced under the Poverty Reduction and Growth Facility (PRGF), encourage the very processes that exacerbate corruption and poverty. They weaken the state's oversight capacity and eliminate the social net on which the poor relies. According to Hawley:[80] 'Donor governments and multilateral agencies such as the World Bank and International Monetary Fund frequently put forward anti-poverty and "good governance" agendas, but their other actions send a different signal about where their priorities lie'. To fight corruption effectively, she believes, demands a shift away from marketization policies. For example, she suggested, the 'focus [should not be] on symptoms such as missing resources, [but on] … causes such as deregulation of state enterprises'.[81] Unless a re-examination of the Anti-Corruption agenda is undertaken, governments such as those in Nicaragua will continue to adopt *ad hoc*, piecemeal programmes and sign international conventions that placate international institutions but which in fact do little to address the real problems.

---

78   Susan Hawley, 'Exporting Corruption: Privatisation, Multinationals and Bribery', *Corner House Briefing*, 19 (June 30 2000) [Online], available at http://www.thecorner house.org.uk/resource/exporting-corruption-0, accessed 8 August 2012.

79   United Nations Global Compact. 'Transparency and Anti-corruption' (2004), available at http://www.unglobalcompact.org/AboutTheGC/TheTenPrinciples/anti-corrupt ion.html, accessed 2 August 2012.

80   Susan Hawley, 'Exporting Corruption: Privatisation, Multinationals and Bribery', *Corner House Briefing*, 19 (June 30 2000) [Online], available at http://www.thecorner house.org.uk/resource/exporting-corruption-0, accessed 8 August 2012.

81   Susan Hawley, 'Exporting Corruption: Privatisation, Multinationals and Bribery', *Corner House Briefing*, 19 (June 30 2000) [Online], available at http://www.thecorner house.org.uk/resource/exporting-corruption-0, accessed 8 August 2012.

Conclusions

W. Andy Knight, Julián Castro-Rea and Hamid Ghany

Introduction

We note that the revitalization of regionalism has been occurring alongside the intensification in the phenomenon of globalization. Both processes represent, in fact, alternative principles of order in a world that calls into question the Westphalian notion of a global order that has been based upon the prevalence of independent and autonomous states.

As readers would have noticed from the chapters in this book, regionalism and regionalization are in full sway in the Americas. During this process of regional re-mapping over the past few decades, many changes have altered the trade relationships in the western hemisphere. Latin America has opened up and North America has taken a greater interest in increasing commerce with South America and the Caribbean. 'Countries in the Americas are trading more intensively with one another – of the $1.5 trillion exported in 1997 by the countries of the Western Hemisphere, over 55 per cent was sold within the Americas'.[1] Starting in the late 1980s, existing regional integration arrangements were rejuvenated to fit new economic conditions.

New Trends in Regionalism in the Americas

As explained earlier in this volume, historically, the United States has considered the Americas as its natural sphere of influence in global politics. Over time, a broad range of policy options has been put into practice that demonstrated this influence, spanning from overt military intervention to soft power measures and gentle everyday diplomacy.[2] Recently, the preferred policy tool has been trade liberalization. Initially, the opportunity to trade with and receive investment from the United States was offered on an indiscriminating basis, the best expression of which was the attempt to champion the Free Trade Area of the Americas (FTAA)

---

1   Gary C. Hufbauer and Barbara Kotschwar, 'The Future of Regional Trading Arrangements in the Western Hemisphere', paper for Michigan State University 10th anniversary conference – The US/Canada Free Trade Agreement (11–12 September 1998), http://ctrc.sice.oas.org/geograph/papers/iie/hufbauer0998.asp, accessed 31 December 2013.

2   For US policy in the Caribbean, see Ivelaw L. Griffith (ed.), *Caribbean Security in the Age of Terror. Challenge and Change* (Kingston: Ian Randle, 2004).

between 1994 and 2005. However, once generalized economic liberalization throughout the Americas proved elusive, Washington resorted to an alternative strategy: viz, proliferation of bilateral trade liberalization agreements throughout the Americas, linking the United States with specific countries in the hemisphere.[3] This proliferation is partly a result of the failure of the September 2003 WTO Ministerial Conference held in Cancún, Mexico. That conference ended with a failure to reach consensus, among country representatives, on the further promotion of global trade and investment, competition policy, and transparency in government procurement.[4] Of course, the FTAA's failure less than two years later also provided as an additional reason to pursue bilateral trade liberalization.

The first wave of US-promoted agreements was launched by Robert Zoellik, then US Trade Representative and future President of the World Bank. When free trade talks broke down in Cancún, Zoellick declared that the 'won't do' countries had won the day over the 'can do' countries. Referring to the developing country coalitions that had come together to block the agenda of Washington and the EU, Zoellick issued a veiled threat to the multilateral process: 'We're going to keep opening markets one way or another', he warned.[5]

Clearly inspired by the term 'the coalition of the willing' used by the US government to designate the international forces that invaded Iraq in March 2003, Zoellick coined the phrase 'the coalition of the liberalizers' in reference to the group of countries that have joined the United States in establishing bilateral or regional trade pacts. 'Our FTA partners are the vanguard of a new global coalition of open markets', declared Zoellick. In the face of mounting opposition from Brazil and other developing countries, to the US global economic agenda, Zoellick began forging a 'coalition' of trade partners who would agree to open up their markets and protect US investment to ensure coveted access to the huge US market.[6]

In a 2003 speech at the Institute for International Economics, Zoellick similarly prioritized trade in his vision of US foreign policy interests, arguing:

> The United States seeks cooperation – or better – on foreign policy and security. Given that the United States has international interests beyond trade, why not try to urge people to support our overall policies? Negotiating a free trade agreement with the United States is not something one has a right to do – it's a privilege.[7]

---

3   The full list of bilateral trade agreements involving the US is available at http://www.ustr.gov/trade-agreements/free-trade-agreements, accessed 31 December 2013.

4   http://www.wto.org/english/thewto_e/minist_e/min03_e/min03_14sept_e.htm, accessed 31 December 2013.

5   Quoted in http://www.rightweb.irc-online.org/profile/Zoellick_Robert, accessed 31 December 2013.

6   Anonymous, 'Coalition Forces Advance', *IRC Americas Program Policy Brief* (24 July 2004).

7   Quoted in http://www.rightweb.irc-online.org/profile/Zoellick_Robert, accessed 31 December 2013.

Zoellick termed his free trade strategy one of 'competitive liberalization'. By establishing numerous bilateral and regional agreements outside the WTO, the United States hoped to undermine opposition to its aggressive liberalizing agenda and to weaken developing country demands for US market access, subsidy reduction, and special treatment in the WTO. In a 10 July 2003 op-ed in the *Wall Street Journal*, the trade czar articulated the US global trade and investment strategy. Zoellick explained that under WTO consensus procedures, 'one nation can block progress' in extending economic liberalization to new areas. Explaining that Washington can pursue its liberalization agenda outside the WTO, Zoellick warned: 'It would be a grave mistake to permit any one country to veto America's drive for global free trade'.[8]

Having been the first among bilateral agreements in the hemisphere, the Canada-US Free Trade agreement (CUSFTA) became the template for subsequent market expansion deals involving the United States. So far, Washington has implemented the North American Free Trade Agreement (NAFTA, in force since 1994), expanding CUSFTA with the inclusion of Mexico, the United States-Chile Free Trade Agreement (2004), the Dominican Republic-Central America-United States Free Trade Agreement (CAFTA-DR, 2004), and the United States-Peru Trade Promotion Agreement (PTPA, effective since 2009). Other similar deals now completed are: the United States-Colombia Trade Promotion Agreement signed in November 2006 and now in force, and the United States – Panama Trade Promotion Agreement, approved by Panama in July 2007 which was entered into force on 31 October 2012. These trade agreements are not exclusive to the Americas. They are, in fact, a key component of a US global strategy. Trade liberalization agreements are a tool in the US economic strategy aimed at acquiring and preserving a competitive edge in the confrontation with other global economic centres, notably Europe and South East Asia.

Aside from trade liberalization, the other axis of US activity in the Americas in the early 2000s was drug enforcement. In a similar way that trade liberalization plays a convenient cover for broader US foreign policy issues – articulated eloquently by Zoellick – drug enforcement has become a useful way for the US government to encourage security and military cooperation in the hemisphere. The pattern, originating with the Caribbean Basin Initiative (CBI) in the 1980s, acquired full force with the launch of Plan Colombia in 2000. The Plan is an approximately US$1.6 billion foreign aid package provided by Washington to the Colombian government to assist that government with drug enforcement, increased military capabilities and counter insurgency measures. The accent has consistently been on the military side, with at least 75 per cent of total funding being spent on it every year.

Although the Clinton administration launched Plan Colombia, the George W. Bush administration willingly carried it on, for understandable reasons.

---

8   Quoted in http://www.rightweb.irc-online.org/profile/Zoellick_Robert, accessed 31 December 2013.

Indeed, both the goals and the strategy of the Plan bode well with the security oriented, militaristic agenda which the Bush administration pursued in its global relations. Moreover, Plan Colombia became the template for a similar programme with Mexico. Titled the Mérida Initiative, after the Mexican city where the programme was announced in October 2007, this programme provides up to USD$1.6 billion of in-kind support to Mexico and Central America, to assist these countries in curbing illegal drugs being smuggled into the United States. The strong similarities between the Initiative and the Plan have prompted critics to call the new programme 'Plan México', thus alerting us to the risks of increased militarization and integration with the US security apparatus that is supported by this Initiative. Aside from trade liberalization and drug enforcement, the Americas did not appear to be among the Bush administration's foreign policy priorities. The net result of eight years of official American government neglect was the emergence of a new geopolitical configuration of the hemisphere, where US leadership was no longer the defining factor, as shown in several chapters in this volume.

Aware of the ground lost over a number of decades by his country, President Barack Obama set in motion a new approach to US–Latin America relations. This approach carries the potential for a review of US policy in the region. In April 2009, Obama and his new US Trade Representative, Ron Kirk, participated in the fifth Summit of the Americas in Port of Spain, Trinidad. The Summit was attended by nearly all of the state leaders in the western hemisphere. In his speech delivered at that meeting, President Obama announced a new approach to his country's engagement in the Americas, in general, and 'a new beginning' to relations with Cuba more specifically. Obama reiterated areas of opportunity for new partnerships, from stimulating the economy throughout the hemisphere, to alleviating poverty, and using the hemisphere's vast resources as a means of revolutionizing energy use as we know it.[9]

However, the President's statements were followed by very little concrete action or policies – something that seemed bitterly familiar to many observers in Latin America and the Caribbean. First, there was Washington's ambiguous reaction to the military coup that ousted Honduran president Manuel Zelaya in June 2009. The US government hesitated between defending democracy unconditionally and grasping the coup as an opportunity to get rid of a hemispheric rival, allied to Venezuela's Hugo Chávez. Then, there was the continuation of militarized approaches (securitization) to existing issues with Latin America: drug trade and violence in Colombia and Mexico and unauthorized migration across the US southern border.[10] In August 2009, the US government concluded a defence cooperation agreement with Colombia that expanded the goals of Plan Colombia

---

9   Michael D. Barnes, 'Time is ripe for new approach with Cuba', *Progreso Weekly* (6 March 2013), found at http://progreso-weekly.com/ini/index.php/home/in-the-united-states/3799-time-is-ripe-for-new-approach-with-cuba, accessed 25 May 2013.

10   NACLA, Casas-Zamora, Kevin, 'Obama and Latin America: As Time Goes By' in *Brookings Institution Blog*, posted 20 May 2010.

and allowed the long-term presence of the US military at seven Colombian military bases. The agreement raised the ire of most South American countries' governments. In a publicly televised meeting, the presidents of Argentina, Brazil, Venezuela, Ecuador and Chile jointly condemned the agreement, stating that no foreign military force should be allowed to threaten the sovereignty of a South American country.[11] Rafael Correa, president of Ecuador, stated that the US was treating the region like a colony, because the agreement could set the stage for military intervention in neighbour countries.

While there have been some cosmetic changes to relations with Cuba, inertia is still the name of the game.[12] In fact, both Canada and the US wanted to block Cuba's participation in future Summits of the Americas, while all of the other countries in the region supported the notion of Cuban involvement in those future Summits.[13]

Note that the fifth Summit of the Americas, held in Trinidad and Tobago, was largely procedural because it came at the very beginning of President Obama's first term of office. At the sixth Summit in Cartagena, which was marred by a number of missteps, including a scandal involving bodyguards in the US Secret Service and local prostitutes was notable by the fact that the Latin American and Caribbean countries were united against the US over its position on Cuba and over the nature of the war on drugs. In fact, the US policy with respect to the war on drugs is widely view in the region as an utter failure. Why? It is clear that the policy which has centred on the prohibition of drugs over the past four decades or so has not actually impeded the production, trafficking, or consumption of drugs. Instead, this policy has helped to increase violence and instability in the region. Drug traffickers are now looking for new routes and trans-shipment points for their drugs, which has caused instability and internal violence in places like Trinidad and Tobago. Indeed, countries in the region, with the exception of Mexico and Chile, now seem unwilling to continue following the US's lead.

In sum, those who were expecting that President Obama would adopt a new US–Latin America/Caribbean paradigm in the hemisphere have so far been disappointed. What became clear at the Sixth Summit of the Americas is that the US hegemonic influence in the region is on the wane. At the moment of writing, the US is not driving any major emerging trend in the Americas. In fact, the vacuum of US influence in the region has opened up space for emerging powers like Brazil, Russia, India and China (the BRICs) to play a major role in the hemisphere in a number of sectors.

---

11   Juan Forero, 'South American Leaders Assail US Access to Colombian Military Bases', *The Washington Post* (29 August 2009).

12   Casas-Zamora, 'Obama and Latin America ...'

13   See CBC News, 'Canada, U.S. scuttle Summit of the Americas Statement' (15 April 2012).

Alternatives to the Washington Consensus

Close to a decade of relative neglect of the Americas by the US has had a predictable, yet unprecedented, consequence: the countries in the hemisphere are actively looking for alternatives to Washington Consensus-led regionalism. Some of the alternatives proposed are actually remarkably original.

The search for alternatives has often implied taking some distance from the 'Washington consensus'.[14] Rejection of this policy paradigm not only came about as a result of the inadequacies of US policy in the region but also because of the disappointing results that orthodox economic policy prescriptions have delivered in Latin America and the Caribbean. Admittedly, this rejection is uneven across the region, as some countries (e.g. Venezuela and Bolivia) took radical turns to the left, radically contesting the hegemony of that model, while some (e.g. Mexico and Colombia) remained attached to the classic tenets of neo-liberalism and to their support of the US, and still others (e.g. Brazil and Argentina) have attempted to create alternative models that attempt to reconcile capitalist globalization with social goals ('globalization with a human face'). Some alternatives also took the form of new alliances built through the Americas, viz., a new political re-mapping.

Traditional, all-inclusive clubs often led by the United States, such as the OAS and the potential FTAA, are now giving way to more selective and plurilateral alliances, led by regional powers. South America, more often than not, has tended to be at the centre of this transformative trend. To provide a snapshot of the emerging geopolitical landscape in the Americas, let's take a look at the following: a) the emergence of Brazil as a world power; b) the creation of UNASUR; the establishment of ALBA; and the formation of CELAC.

The Emergence of Brazil as a World Power

Brazil is the largest and most populated country in Latin America, with 186 million people and a land mass of 8,514,215 million square kilometres.[15] It shares 15,735 kilometres (about 8,000 miles) of its border with all of the South American countries with the exception of Ecuador and Chile. This places Brazil in a very influential position vis-à-vis the other countries on the continent.

During the Second World War, Brazil was viewed by the US as strategically and politically important because of Brazil's geographical position – immediately south of the equator and the mouth of the Amazon River, and stretching deep into South America as well as having its easterly extensions in proximity to Africa. After the War, Brazil remained relatively close to the US, although its leadership resented what was seen as a snub from the US when the emerging hegemon at the

---

14   Williamson, 'What Washington Means …', op. cit.
15   See http://www.odci.gov/cia/publications/factbook/rankorder/2119rank.html, accessed 2 August 2010.

time gave economic aid, through the Marshall Plan, to the defeated enemies of the allies – Germany, Italy and Japan – and did not find it necessary to advance aid to Brazil which was undergoing a process of early industrialization.

During the Cold War, the US was much more concerned with ensuring that Brazil did not go the way of Cuba than with democratizing Brazil or improving its economy.[16] During President Ernesto Geisel term in office (1973–79), tension arose between Brazil and the US over the former's recognition of the leftist revolutionary governments of Angola, Mozambique, and Guinea-Bissau, its signing of a nuclear agreement with the Federal Republic of Germany, and its abrogation of a military agreement with the US over the American approach to human rights and nuclear issues. This show of independence from Washington was cemented with the creation of MERCOSUR and with Brazil's leadership in developing this sub-regional arrangement.

Over the past 25 years or so, we have witnessed a Brazil that wants to assert a prominent place in the hierarchy of the international system's power structure. Thus, we see Brazil shifting away from its alliance with the US, its refusal to accept passively US dominance in the region, and its attempts at improving its ties with other South American countries as a means of increasing its bargaining power vis-à-vis the US.[17]

Today, according to the criterion of purchasing power parity (PPP) used by the World Bank (IBRD), Brazil's economy is the ninth largest market-based centre of production in the globe, with US$1,580 trillion, a gross domestic product (GDP) of over three times that of Argentina's US$537 billion, and larger than those of Russia at US$1,535 billion, Canada at US$1,077 trillion, Mexico at US$1,066 trillion, and Spain at US$1,014 trillion. Brazil's GDP is only slightly smaller than that of Italy (US$1,645 trillion), France (US$1,816 trillion) and the United Kingdom (US$1,867 trillion).[18] The country is part of the BRICs (Brazil, Russia, India and China) – a group of nations that symbolizes what seems to be a shift in global economic power away from the Group of 7/8 economies towards populous developing world economies, that are challenging the existing North Atlantic global hegemony. These four countries encompass 25 per cent of the global land mass and have 40 per cent of the global population within their borders. It is estimated that their economies will be the most globally dominant by 2050. Brazil, like the other members of the BRICs, has expressed the view that a multipolar world order would be best for humanity in the twenty-first

---

16   Luiz Alberto Bandeira, 'Brazil as a regional power and its relations with the United States', *Latin American Perspectives*, 33 (3) (May 2006), 16.

17   Bandeira, 'Brazil as a regional power …', 12–27.

18   All figures at 2005 estimates. See http://www.odci.gov/cia/publications/factbook/rankorder/2001rank.html, accessed 2 August 2010.

century.[19] Brazil has also expressed interest in becoming a permanent member of the UN Security Council.[20]

In 2008, to demonstrate its rise to prominence as a major global economic power, during the global economic crisis, in 2008, Brazil offered to lend the IMF the sum of $10 billion 'to help improve the availability of credit' to developing countries. This was the first time that a South American country had ever offered such a loan to a major global financial institution. This offer was part of the BRICs's attempt to boost global financial stability. China also offered $50 billion and Russia $10 billion for this purpose.[21]

Brazil's rise to prominence as a major global economic actor has no doubt had an impact on its relationship with the US. Some policy makers in Washington perceive that Brazil's approach of strengthening trade within MERCOSUR runs at odds with their understanding of global free trade. Under the Presidency of George H.W. Bush, the US had attempted to draw Brazil into its neoliberal ideological orbit, but not with total success. It is true that President Fernando Henrique Cardoso, who ruled over Brazil from 1995 to 2002, was considered a strong ally of the George W. Bush administration and that he accepted the original FTAA idea. Despite going along initially with the FTAA negotiations, the Brazilian government resisted the US-style trade liberalization approach that would underlie this free trade arrangement. Instead, Brazil preferred a policy of trade diversification as a way to reduce its dependency on the US market. It is this clash of approaches to market liberalization that contributed, in part, to the eventual death of the FTAA.[22]

Most analysts in Brazil had come to the conclusion that the FTAA could have a profoundly negative impact on the country's economy. Some Brazilian trade experts even went so far as to suggest that implementing the FTAA would be suicidal for Brazil and for MERCOSUR.[23] Such sentiments were shared by labour unions, non-governmental organizations and leftist parties in Brazil which joined in vociferous protests against the FTAA at the Summit of the Americas in Quebec City (April 2001). There is no doubt that if the FTAA had been established, the manufacturing exports of Brazil to other South American countries would have been in jeopardy. Inácio 'Lula' da Silva, who was at the time the leftist opposition leader in the country and who later became President of Brazil, warned that FTAA

---

19   See Simon Tisdall, 'Can the Brics create a new world order?', *The Guardian* (29 March 2012).

20   'Brazil has credentials for a permanent seat at the United Nations Security Council, Ambassador says', *Portal de Noticias* (30 November 2012).

21   Gary Duffy, 'Brazil to make $10 bn loan to IMF', *BBC News* (11 June 2009), found at http://news.bbc.co.uk/2/hi/business/8094402.stm, accessed 2 August 2010.

22   See Jeffrey Carson, 'Resisting Free Trade: Brazil and the FTAA', unpublished paper presented at the 48th annual meeting of the International Studies Association (ISA), Hilton, Chicago, Illinois (February 28 2007).

23   Third World Network, 'Latin America: FTAA divides nations and trade blocs', (2001), found at www.twnside.org.sg/title/blocs.htm, accessed 26 May 2013.

was not really a free trade pact but rather a policy of annexation of Latin America by the US. Once Lula da Silva won the Brazilian election and became President, the FTAA was, for all intents and purposes, dead. The economic integration of South America was a much higher priority to the Brazilian president.[24]

Moreover, Brazil is no longer content with its already uncontested role as regional leader both in South America and the hemisphere; it is now going global. Starting with President Cardoso, and supported by its highly professional foreign service. Brazil is established its reputation as a respected multilateralist, an advocate for the respect of state sovereignty and for the peaceful resolution of conflicts. Moreover, as mentioned previously, Brazil has joined the informal group of countries known as the BRICs. From that position, Brazil has been promoting cooperation between developing countries (a South-South strategy) as a key strategy for addressing their international issues.[25]

Brazil is thus flexing its international muscles. For example, Brasilia signed a defence cooperation agreement with the United States in April 2010, creating an unprecedented horizontal, true partnership, framework of collaboration between these two countries. Within this framework, Brazil is no longer a subordinate recipient of US aid, as used to be the case in the post-war years. The agreement is rather about two signatory states that have committed themselves to joint defence-related research and development (R&D), reciprocal supply of defence equipment (including aircraft), and joint military exercises.[26]

One month after signing that agreement with the US, Brazil acted as mediator and broker, jointly with Turkey, in a high stakes international dispute outside the Americas. In May 2010, the South American country nailed down an agreement between Iran and Turkey, whereby Ankara accepted to supply Tehran with nuclear fuel rods, to be used for medical purposes, in exchange for 1,200 kg of low enriched uranium, which could have potentially been used by Iran for nuclear weapons. In essence, the agreement effectively indicated that Tehran was willing to abandon its nuclear programme if there was a de-escalation in the UN Security Council sanctions against Iran. The US rebuffed the deal as a side-show and revealed that it had secured the agreement of the five UN Security Council permanent members (P5) for sanctions against Iran.

Brazil's move was precisely meant to offer an alternative to Washington's punitive approach to dealing with Iran – an approach largely supported by the US Western allies, and reluctantly accepted by China and Russia. Brasilia attempted to defend the agreement from an international legal perspective, arguing that it

---

24   Peter Hakim, 'The Reluctant Partner', *Foreign Affairs*, 83 (1) (2004), 117.

25   Raveendran, Manasi, 'Are Brazil and Lula Out of Their Depth on Iran?', Council on Hemispheric Affairs website, http://www.coha.org/are-brazil-and-lula-out-of-their-depth-in-iran/, posted 4 June 2010, accessed 31 December 2013.

26   Cárdenas, Mauricio and João Augusto de Castro Neve, 'Brazil and the United States: A New Beginning?', Brookings Upfront Blog, 19 April 2010, available at http://www.brookings.edu/opinions/2010/0419_us_brazil_cardenas.aspx, accessed 31 December 2013.

follows a suggestion made by the Vienna Group in 2009, it was presented to the International Atomic Energy Agency (IAEA) for approval, it builds on previous Brazil-Iran nuclear exchanges dating back to 1992, and it promises to put an end to an enduring source of tension in the Middle East. Bottom line, the Brazilian leadership wanted to show that their country is now in a position to play an important role as an independent actor on major international issues.[27] Finally, Brazil has also set its eyes on a permanent seat in the UN Security Council, making the case based on its regional strength, its population of close to 200 million people, and its military, technological and financial capabilities.

The Establishment of CSN and UNASUR

Other than its global ambitions, Brazil is also championing regional initiatives. In December 2004, that country presided over the creation of the South American Community of Nations (*Comunidad Sudamericana de Naciones*, CSN), an integration project renamed UNASUR (*Unión de Naciones Suramericanas*, Union of South American Nations) in April 2007. Involving 12 South American countries, UNASUR wants to merge MERCOSUR with the Andean Community, while going beyond merely commercial objectives. Explicitly citing the European Union as its model, UNASUR hopes to evolve into a customs union, on the way to adopting a common currency, parliament and passport by 2019. It aims at coordinating domestic and foreign policies, adopting commonly-funded development projects for the regions in most need of support and supporting regional cooperation in defence matters. Eventually, the members of UNASUR also contemplate some degree of political union. In doing so, this integration process conforms to the terms of other existing schemes, such as MERCOSUR, the Andean Community and LAIA/ALADI.

UNASUR is already delivering on some of those objectives. It has created a South American Defence Council (SADC), a mechanism for coordinated regional security similar to NATO.[28] It has launched a regional infrastructure programme (IIRSA), pooling resources for transportation, telecommunications and energy projects. The goal is to create an integrated network of highways, maritime routes, river ways, hydroelectric dams and telecommunications infrastructure through the sub-continent; starting with an Atlantic-Pacific highway whose Brazil-Peru leg is already completed.[29] In May 2005, Brazil, Argentina and Venezuela laid the basis for the creation of *Petrosur*, an international agency that aims at coordinating

---

27   Raveendran, 'Are Brazil and Lula ...', op. cit.

28   Alex Sánchez, 'The South American Defense Council, UNASUR, the Latin American Military and the Region's Political Process', Council on Hemispheric Affairs website, posted 1 October 2008.

29   Lyra Spang, 'IIRSA Projects: Some Facts about the Inter-Oceanic Highway', *Bank Information Center*, July 2005, available at www.bicusa.org/en/article.2226.aspx, accessed 31 December 2013.

member countries' energy policies, and aspires to become hemispheric with the creation of *Petroamérica*.[30] UNASUR also created a Bank of the South that funds development programmes, with offices in Caracas, Buenos Aires and La Paz.

The South American organization has also taken joint stances on international matters, such as providing US$100 million in aid to Haiti and rejecting Arizona's Bill 1070, an anti-immigration piece of legislation that carries the potential for justifying discrimination against Latin Americans living in that US state. In May 2010, the former president of Argentina – and husband of that country's current president Néstor Kirchner, was elected unanimously as UNASUR's first Secretary-General. In short, South America seems to be losing its patience with outmoded US hegemonic schemes. Under Brazil's leadership, and its increasingly assertive posture, the Southern part of the western hemisphere is breaking new ground in international cooperation and regional re-mapping.

The Emergence of ALBA

For instance, we witnessed the emergence of *Alianza Bolivariana para los pueblos de nuestra América* (Bolivarian Alliance for the Peoples of Our Americas, or ALBA) in December 2004[31] – a subregional bloc in Latin America and the Caribbean that is radically opposing neoliberal globalization and US hegemony in the hemisphere. It originated from a partnership between Venezuela and Cuba, the two countries that more openly contested the FTAA.[32] In due time, ALBA grew to include six more partners: Bolivia, Ecuador, Nicaragua, Antigua and Barbuda, Dominica, and Saint Vincent. All member countries have in common lively social movements and either leftist or social democratic governments, and are critical, to different degrees, of orthodox economic policies.

ALBA defines itself as 'a people's trade agreement', that is, an integration model that places development and social objectives at the forefront. State involvement in the definition of priorities and their management is strong, as opposed to trade liberalization agreements focused on the market where corporations play the major role. Trade among member countries is focused on what is beneficial to their economies or social needs, allowing for in-kind exchanges rather than monetary transactions – a barter system, in fact – and taking into account existing asymmetries among member countries. Joint initiatives of 'economic complementarity' in mining, infrastructure and maritime transport are

---

30   Paul Kellogg, 'Regional Integration in Latin America: Dawn of an Alternative to Neoliberalism?', *New Political Science*, 19 (2) (June 2007), 193.

31   The word *alba* means 'dawn' in Spanish, a meaning that the creators of the organization also wished to convey, as they claim the organization represents a new dawn for the peoples of the Americas.

32   Paul Kellogg, 'Regional Integration in Latin America: Dawn of an Alternative to Neoliberalism?', 188; Max Azicri, 'The Castro-Chávez Alliance', *Latin American Perspectives*, 36 (1) (January 2009), 99–110.

foreseen. The agreement also allows for the mutual provision of services to address the existing needs of its members. For instance, Cuba is supporting Venezuela's social programmes by providing instructors to fight illiteracy, offering university scholarships to Venezuelan students, and sending 15,000 medical personnel to Venezuela to create clinics and collaborate with health care programmes.[33] In exchange, Venezuela provides Cuba with oil, charging a very low interest rate on unpaid balances (1 per cent over 17 to 25 years). Oil debt can also be paid with goods or services.

Other initiatives that ALBA has put on the table include the creation of a multinational television network called TVSUR, the creation of *Petrocaribe* as a counterpart of UNASUR's *Petrosur*, with similar and converging objectives, and the founding of an ALBA Bank in 2008 that aims at becoming a financing-for-development alternative to the commercial, 'Washington consensus'-controlled banks. More recently, ALBA has adopted more controversial measures. In January 2008 it announced the creation of a military alliance for mutual defence, in reaction to the agreements to intensify the presence of the US military in Colombian bases mentioned earlier. In October 2009, during the ALBA leaders' summit in Cochabamba, Bolivia, the organization agreed on the creation of a new common regional currency, called *sucre*, which is intended to replace the US dollar in all electronic international transactions among ALBA members.[34]

In sum, whereas UNASUR represents the reassertion of South American countries' sovereignties in the face of past US hegemony, and has a broader appeal virtually encompassing the whole subregion, ALBA goes beyond those objectives. ALBA aims to create parallel channels to global markets and, because of its more radical nature it has only been able to attract a handful of countries as members.

The Advent of CELAC

The Community of Latin American and Caribbean States (*Comunidad de Estados Latinoamericanos y del Caribe*, CELAC) is the most recent iteration of re-mapping in the Americas. It is also the most comprehensive. CELAC emerged on 23 February 2010 at a summit in Cancún, Mexico, to which every Latin American and Caribbean government was invited, with the exception of the *de facto* government of Honduras. Thirty-one governments were represented at the summit. Because the meeting was convened by the government of Mexico, it is possible to interpret the initiative as Mexico's attempt at not being left totally behind in the movement toward the development of new alternative integration schemes that has been sweeping through the Americas.

The summit's final declaration employed language rarely seen in OAS documents: 'the need to carry out efforts to advance towards ... political,

---

33   Paul Kellogg, 'Regional Integration in Latin America: Dawn of an Alternative to Neoliberalism?', 200–202.

34   That is, no legal tender (bills or coins) in *sucres* is planned to be issued.

economic, social and cultural integration'; 'we reaffirm our commitment to the defence of sovereignty and the right of each state to constitute its own political system, free of threats, aggressions and unilateral coercive measures'; 'the need for a distinct regional space that consolidates and protects the Latin American and Caribbean identity'. The statement also reiterated calls to 'solidarity', 'social inclusion', 'complementarity'; leaving aside the 'Washington consensus' mantras of 'free trade' and 'open markets'.[35] Furthermore, CELAC members condemned the US economic and financial blockade of Cuba.

The governments of Chile and Venezuela were mandated to draft CELAC's charter and organizational structure and they were assisted by Mexico, Brazil, and Jamaica. The composition of this commission reflects the ideologically plural nature of the emerging organization, putting together at its head a Christian Democrat and a socialist government, supported by three sub-regional state leaders with contrasting approaches to regionalism. CELAC held a ministerial summit in Caracas, Venezuela, in early July 2010.

The creation of CELAC was, in part, a reaction to: the disappointment with orthodox economic policies; the failure of the FTAA; and the ambiguity of US policies in the Americas. Clearly, this regional body is viewed as an alternative to the Washington-dominated Organization of American States (OAS). It is not surprising therefore that the US and Canada were not invited to attend the summits or to join this nascent hemispheric organization. In contrast, CELAC members gave a strong embrace to Cuba, sending a signal to the OAS which had suspended Cuba's membership in that body in 1962. When Cuba was invited in 2009 to rejoin the OAS, it flatly rejected the invitation, showing instead its preference for the alternative to OAS – namely CELAC.[36]

If CELAC is successful, it may well mesh with other alternative organizational initiatives such as UNASUR or ALBA and even displace the OAS as a forum for hemispheric dialogue and regional cooperation and for addressing critical issues and disputes between member states in the Americas. So far, the US State Department has minimized the importance of the initiative, perhaps hoping that it is too ambitious to succeed, or perhaps counting on entrenched regional loyalties and a divide-and-conquer strategy that has been implicitly applied to this region by successive hegemons. A potential Mexico-Brazil rivalry for leadership also has the potential of scuttling this nascent organization's future.

---

35   Alex Main, 'Latin America and Caribbean: CELAC Steams Ahead', in http:// mrzine.monthlyreview.org/2010/main180710.html, posted 18 July 2010, accessed 31 December 2013.

36   BBC, 'Cuba rejects OAS readmission', found at http://www.bbc.co.uk/Caribb ean/news/story/2009/06/090608_cubaaosupdate.shtml, accessed 26 May 2013.

The Evolution of Regionalism in the Caribbean

The Caribbean region has had its own experiments with regionalism. Attempts at regional integration in the Caribbean were evident as early as the seventeenth century. The earliest attempts by the British were aimed at rationalizing the administrative costs of running its colonial possessions in the West Indies. However, most of these efforts ended in failure in the sense that they did not meet the goals that were set out by Great Britain.

The earliest experimentation with a regional federal system in the West Indies was in 1626 when Barbados and the Leeward Islands were integrated under one governor, the Earl of Carlisle. Between 1833 and 1855 the Windward Islands and Barbados were united under a central government of which Trinidad was a part for at least two years. In 1871, the Leeward Islands federation gave way to the idea of a federation for the entire British Caribbean. A Royal Commission from Britain was sent to the region in 1882–83 to ascertain ways of rationalizing the economic administration of the Leeward and Windward Islands, along with Jamaica. This Commission recommended the notion of a closer union, a federal scheme that would make the management and governance of these territories more efficient and reduce the cost of administering them. The Commission felt strongly that all of the islands in the British Antilles could be placed under a single governor-general.

Another Royal Commission in 1896–97 made the recommendation that Barbados merge with the Windward Islands, again to make the management and administration of the British territories more management and efficient. Major E.F. Wood, and later Lord Halifax, actually toured the region in 1922 to see if conditions were ripe for the establishment of a federation. The Wood Report issued after the tour indicated that public opinion really did not support a federation in the Anglophone Caribbean territories. In addition, the local opposition that emerged to that idea in places like Barbados pretty much stalled any momentum towards federation.[37] However, by the 1930s, the idea again emerged of integrating the West Indian territories as a Caribbean community under one federal system of government and a number of meetings were held in the UK to explore this possibility.

The West Indies Federation came into being on 3 January 1958 and was comprised of ten territories in the Anglophone West Indies (Jamaica, Antigua, Barbados, Trinidad and Tobago, Grenada, Montserrat, St Kitts/Nevis/Anguilla, Dominica, St Lucia and St Vincent). British Guiana and British Honduras, two of the largest territories, did not join the federation but became associated territories. This federation however, did not last long. By 1961, Jamaica, after a referendum in which people were asked to vote whether or not to let Jamaica remain in the federation, to which the people of Jamaica responded 'No', officially withdrew.

---

37   Report by the Hon. E.F.L. Wood, MP, cited in Elisabeth Wallace, *The British Caribbean: From Decline of Colonialism to the End of Federation* (Toronto, 1977).

Dr Eric Williams of Trinidad and Tobago stated after Jamaica's withdrawal that 'ten minus one equals nothing', which meant that Jamaica's withdrawal would make it impossible to bring about a strong and unified federation, so he declared Trinidad and Tobago would also withdraw. In 1961, the federation was dissolved.[38]

It is important to understand why the idea of a federated British West Indies was in the cards to begin with. From the point of view of the British, it was generally felt that a federal government in the British West Indies would make administrative decisions easier. Instead of dealing with several disparate entities, the British government would be able to deal with one federal government that, in turn, would be answerable to the metro pole. As alluded to earlier, there was a general view that a single federal government in this region would also allow for more efficient and cheaper governance. Furthermore, with British hegemony on the wane, and with the devastating economic depression of the 1930s, some pragmatic British politicians began to realize that an overly costly Empire and imperial overstretch would do irreparable harm to Great Britain.

Growing radical and nationalist movements of the 1920s in some of the islands of the British West Indies were calling for constitutional self-government. Many West Indians were dissatisfied with the unresponsiveness or slowness of the British government to tackle a variety of socio-economic and political problems that were facing the colonies around that time. Issues of poverty, poor working conditions, racial and class discrimination and limited access to political power were catalysts for the nationalist movements.

Several of the leaders within the Anglophone West Indies felt that they could govern their respective countries without help from Britain. Many were emboldened by the teachings of Marcus Garvey who urged blacks to take charge of their own governments. Colonialism, itself, came under attack as a constitutional and ideological form of governance. For Garvey and other nationalists, colonialism was viewed as both outdated and backward. However, many of the individuals in these movements were also federalists because they realized that the individual colonies might not be viable as independent entities due to their smallness of size and economic vulnerabilities. This is why many of them pushed for a federation as a means of achieving eventual self-government. And the idea of a federation was also supported by such groups as the Barbados Chamber of Commerce, the Trinidad Chamber of Commerce, the Jamaican Imperial Association, and the Associated West Indian Chambers.

Evolving Caribbean Regionalism

Despite the failure of West Indian Federation, and the fits and starts of regional integration efforts in the Caribbean, relations across borders among non-state

---

38   See Hugh Springer, *Reflections on the Failure of the First West Indian Federation* (Harvard, 1962).

actors in the Americas have been on the increase. This interaction not only tends to ignore the priorities defined in government agendas, but it may even subvert the hierarchical relations among states, which generally place the United States at the top of the Inter-American system.[39] These relations are manifest in the continuous flows of peopleworkers, migrants, refugees, touristsmedia messages, financial transactions, technologies, values on public matters such as democracy, human rights development and the environment. These flows are asymmetrical and irregular, yet they are constant and increasing with time. This speaks to the multidimensional and pluralistic character of new forms of global regionalism.

There has therefore been an informal integration of the state/society complexes of the Caribbean Basin, in regards to the insertion of these complexes into globalization. The Caribbean basin is that region that comprises the large area spanning from southern United States to the north shore of South America, comprising the eastern coasts of Mexico and Central America, as well as all Caribbean countries. This area is labelled 'the Hurricane Basin'; since the entire region has in common the regular impact of these meteorological events. The Hurricane Basin comprises a broad array of networks – local, national and transnational – that connect its communities, production centres and markets, both materially and symbolically.[40] The purpose of these networks may be either: economic (i.e., formal or informal market transactions, labour opportunities, investment); political (e.g., refugee protection, joint activism, solidarity); criminal (viz., drug and gun smuggling, money laundering, human trafficking, etc.); familial; and, educational or even cultural (i.e., maintaining identities in a diasporic situation, promoting religions, fashions, hobbies or lifestyles). Quite often, different objectives overlap within a single network, making these regional interactions more complex and giving an increased sense to considering the Hurricane Basin as an informally-integrated sub-region within the Americas.

Most Commonwealth Caribbean states have embraced a technocratic, neo-liberal model of development, which aims at repositioning the sub-region in the global economy through three key policy strategies: competitiveness, diplomacy and governance.[41] Their progress has been limited, however, requiring some rethinking along the lines of development strategies practiced in South East Asia, where decisive state intervention has paved the way for more meaningful, sustained development.

---

39   Francis Pisani, Natalia Saltalamacchia, Arlene Tickner and Nielan Barnes (eds), *Redes transnacionales en la Cuenca de los huracanes: Un aporte a los studios interamericanos* (Mexico City: Instituto Tecnológico Autónomo de México, 2007), 7.

40   Francis Pisani, Natalia Saltalamacchia, Arlene Tickner and Nielan Barnes (eds), *Redes transnacionales en la Cuenca de los huracanes: Un aporte a los studios interamericanos*, 9.

41   Anthony Payne and Paul Sutton, 'Repositioning the Caribbean within Globalization', *The Caribbean Papers – a project on Caribbean Economic Governance*, The Centre for International Governance Innovation, Caribbean Paper No. 1 (June 2007).

The Role of Non-State Actors in Region-making

The development of regional integration has typically been conceptually driven by elites in the region, particularly by state actors. This view is supported by regional experts, such as Jean Grugel, who state that '... regionalist governance in the Americas is undemocratic, elitist and closed. Consultation is limited and the views of social actors rarely count'.[42] While this remains a valid observation, there are emerging trends which indicate that non-state actors are playing an increasingly active role in the re-mapping of the Americas. The new forms of regionalism have opened up space for organized non-state actors to play an important role in regional re-mapping. Gerda van Roozendaal, for instance, differentiates between 'old regionalism' – which is linked to hegemonic, state-driven patterns of international relations during the Cold War and its bipolar system – and 'new regionalism', in which a multipolar environment creates an opening for the participation of non-state actors who are increasingly involved in the processes of regionalization.[43] The influence of these actors can be mostly seen within the negotiation processes that produce regional agreements, mostly related to trade. For instance, mass-movements, NGOs, and civil society resistance to hegemonic trade agreements such as the FTAA has widely been cited as a reason for the agreement's demise. Moreover, multi-national enterprises (MNE) and other corporate/industry actors are playing an important role in both the development of regional trade agreements and with respect to opposing treaties viewed as unfavourable to particular business interests.

An examination of the failed FTAA reveals the extent to which it was a corporate-driven process. Among the de-regulatory propositions contained within the FTAA were the expansion of foreign direct investment (FDI) to include a variety of previously public industries, resources and services (such as forestry, water, petroleum industries and health care); privatization of state industries developed under earlier policies of import substitution industrialization (ISI); and the liberalization or 'protection' of intellectual property rights.[44] As argued by Ruiz, agreements such as the FTAA are, 'an example of strategic regionalism, which is the result of an alliance between multinational enterprises (MNEs) and the US government. This explains the nature of the FTAA's policy agenda, the main pillar of which is the promotion of free trade and "trade related issues"'.[45]

---

42   Jean Grugel, 'Regionalist governance and transnational collective action in Latin America', *Economy and Society*, 35 (2) (2006), 226–227.

43   Gerda van Roozendaal, 'Regional policy in the Americas: The EU experience as a guide for north-south integration?', *Intereconomics*, 41 (3) (2006), 159.

44   Gary Prevost, 'Contesting free trade: the development of the anti-FTAA movement in the streets and in the corridors of state power', *Journal of Developing Societies*, 21 (3–4) (2005), 369–387.

45   Jose Briceno Ruiz, 'Strategic regionalism and regional social policy in the FTAA process', *Global Social Policy*, 7 (3) (2007), 296.

By the 1980s, the US government was working closely with MNEs in the development of regional integration initiatives – the key thrust of these initiatives being trade de-regulation and liberalization aimed at promoting a more favourable international trade environment for US corporations. As Latin America had long been considered the United States' 'backyard', there was a considerable push to develop these trade arrangements commencing with the FTA, NAFTA, bilateral trade agreements and then the failed FTAA.

However, to view industry influence on regional trade negotiations as a one-sided enterprise, in which US players were the only relevant actors, would be incorrect and misleading. Non-US industries have also played key roles in, for instance, opposing agreements such as the FTAA. An example of this opposition was the key role played by the agricultural sector, especially in Brazil, in de-railing FTAA negotiations. In general, much of the Brazilian business community was opposed to the FTAA, most notably this opposition centred on US farm subsidies and antidumping/countervailing duty polices which laced barriers on Brazilian exporters.[46] With this oppositional stance towards the FTAA in mind, Latin American business interests supported alternative regional arrangements, such as MERCOSUR, which were viewed as being more supportive of local manufacturing, agricultural, chemical and pharmaceutical industries.[47] Additionally, some key industrial sectors have been increasingly looking to external hemispheric trading possibilities. The expansion of Brazil's oil industry, particularly the state owned company Petrobras, together with other regional natural resources industries have been stimulated by the increasing demands of emerging powers such as China.[48] In sum, corporate actors have played important roles in constructing, influencing and opposing both regional and international trade agreements – in this way they play a key role in re-mapping the Americas.

While MNEs and various business interests have had a long-standing role in regional integration, the part played by other non-state actors, such as mass movements, NGOs, trade unions and other civil society actors, has more recently been seen as a key driver in recent regional integration initiatives. The large alliances that emerged within the last few decades between NGOs, various civil society organizations representing environmental and Indigenous groups, together with mass protest groups such as the anti-globalization movement, have mobilized into an increasingly formidable and relevant network actor in regional affairs. As previously noted, much of the resistance to proposed regional trade agreements, such as the FTAA has come from elites; however, as noted by numerous observers, including several of the authors in this volume, there has also been considerable resistance coming from the bottom-up in the form of civil society organizations and mass protest movements. While corporate opposition to the FTAA focused on concerns over competitiveness with more established/developed US industries, the

46   Hakim, 'The Reluctant ...', 117.
47   Ruiz, 'Strategic Regionalism ...'.
48   Kellogg, 'Regional Integration ...'.

chief concern among civil society groups was a lack of social policy protections within agreements such as the FTAA. The prevailing view among these actors was that corporate-driven treaties flowed from a neo-liberal policy aimed at furthering US influence in the region, rather than at improving the lot of the region as a whole.

According to Prevost, the largest and most critical civil society umbrella group to help derail the FTAA was the Continental Social Alliance.[49] Formed in 1999, this umbrella organization consisted of a variety of actors, including labour unions, human rights groups, environmental activists, indigenous peoples and peasant movements. As Prevost notes, the Third Summit of the Americas, held in Quebec in 2001, became a focal point for these civil society groups and inadvertently helped to spur the transformation of a wide range of disparate organizations into a more coherent anti-FTAA movement. Indeed, state leaders in the hemisphere succumbed to the pressure of these groups to make the deliberations and communiqués coming out of that Summit more readily open to the public than had been during previous Summits. Other notable umbrella civil society organizations such as the Hemispheric Social Alliance (HSA) also played an important oppositional role to the FTAA. According to Saguier, this alliance aimed to

> make the FTAA project a means of advancing equitable, democratic and sustainable development in the region rather than strictly trade liberalization. Its broad base of support covers social organizations working on issues of labour and human rights, environment, indigenous rights, gender issues, rural and faith organizations from across the continent.[50]

As the FTAA was largely the result of the strategic alliance between MNEs and the US government, civil society actors rightly felt that their concerns were excluded from negotiating processes.

Buoyed by successful opposition to the FTAA, and re-organized under larger umbrella organizations, civil society actors became increasingly active in alternative regional integration initiatives. According to Kellogg, the Bolivarian Alliance for the Americas (ALBA), discussed earlier, represents the most distinct alternative to prior neo-liberal regional arrangements and is most closely associated with left-leaning mass movements, unions and other actors that emerged as new important players in Latin American integration attempts.[51] However, as previously noted, sub-regional initiatives such as MERCOSUR and UNASUR have been touted by state leaders in the region as likely alternatives to the omnibus FTAA. In general, this reflects the reality that despite the emergence of civil society groups as important oppositional actors against trade agreements,

---

49 Prevost, 'Contesting Free Trade …'.

50 Marcelo I. Saguier, 'The Hemispheric Social Alliance and the Free Trade Area of the Americas process: the challenges and opportunities of transnational coalitions against neo-liberalism', *Globalizations*, 4 (2) (2007), 252.

51 Kellogg, 'Regional Integration …'.

state and large corporate actors continue to play a central role both in constructing regional integration initiatives and in opposing them. Clearly, non-state actors, such as mass-protest movements and civil society groups are playing a more active role in regionalization, in general and in re-mapping the Americas, in particular.

Regionalism remains, to a large degree, an elite driven enterprise. But the empirical evidence within the western hemisphere demonstrates that the distinction between regionalism and regionalization is not as stark as Ann Capling and Kim Richard Nossal claim. In fact, non-state actors are influencing both regionalism and regionalization in our hemisphere and thus contributing to the re-mapping that is taking place in the Americas.

Other non-state actors have also had an impact on the ways the Americas are being re-mapped. Perhaps the most salient among these actors are the communities of migrants. Diaspora communities across the Americas have grown in importance over recent years, and are poised to increase their salience. Diaspora communities now carry considerable demographic, economic and cultural weight which is nonetheless not matched by political influence simply because of the very transnational character of these communities, i.e., most of their members are non-citizens of the countries in which they live and they are diverse sociologically. The hemispheric diaspora now number several million people, distributed in virtually all 35 countries in the Americas. Their economic importance is usually measured in the amount of money they are able to send back to their home countries – so-called remittances – which grew from USD 20 billion in 2000 to over USD 65 billion by 2008.[52] Remittances can have important impacts on the receiving societies, spanning from maintaining the country's macroeconomic balance. For instance, in Haiti, remittances accounted for 24.8 per cent of that country's GDP in 2003, and they funded development projects or were used for the subsistence of poor families. The cultural impact of remittances is conspicuous in the creation of new artistic hybrid expressions that blend elements of the home countries with components from the host societies, the musical genre *reggaetón* being a recent example of this.[53]

Extra Regional Power, Policies and Actions

The re-mapping of the Americas is also in evidence as the sub-regions of Central America, South America, Latin America and the Caribbean have all undergone a major process of diversification in their foreign and trade relations. No longer are

---

52   World Bank data, available at http://siteresources.worldbank.org/INTPROSPECTS /Resources/334934-1110315015165/RemittancesData_Inflows_Apr10(Public).xls, accessed September 2010.

53   James Lull, 'Our North America: A Continent of Cultural Change', in Julián Castro-Rea (ed.), *Our North America: From Turtle Island to the Security and Prosperity Partnership* (Farnham: Ashgate, 2012).

these sub-regions in our hemisphere totally dependent on the region's hegemon – the United States. In fact, there is a sense that sub-regional and trans-regional activity may be an indication that the developing countries in the western hemisphere are actors in their own right; capable of making strategic and tactical choices in order to give themselves more freedom of movement and independence with respect to their decision making. The traditional ties of dependency on the metropole that have strangled developing countries of this hemisphere are being rent asunder as important new trade and economic linkages as well as strategic partnerships, are being undertaken with Europe, China, India, and other parts of the globe. There is definitely a re-mapping going on in the western hemisphere. However, the final map has not yet been fully drawn.[54] The European Union, for instance, is increasingly present in Latin America, in the face of US drift away from the region. There are several different ways in which the EU has been able to contribute to the process of re-mapping the western hemisphere.

Trends in Re-mapping: The EU in Latin America and the Caribbean

The European Union (EU) is Latin America's second most important trading partner. It is also the number one trading partner of MERCOSUR and Chile. The EU has been steadily strengthening its economic and trade links with Latin America and the Caribbean over the past few decades. Trade figures between the EU and Latin America and the Caribbean doubled between 1999 and 2008. EU imports from Latin America and the Caribbean increased from €42.5 to €102.4 billion, and its exports to the region rose from €52.2 to €86.4 billion over the same period.

In May 2010, the Sixth EU, Latin America and the Caribbean Summit was held in Madrid. This summit, gathering the 27 leaders of the EU and 33 leaders representing the same number of countries in Latin America and the Caribbean (LAC), turned out to be a watershed in European-Latin American-Caribbean relations. A brief account of the massive amount of agreements reached in the Madrid summit is offered below.

EU-LAC Foundation

First, at the Madrid Summit the leaders decided to act on an idea that had been discussed two years earlier, i.e. the creation of a EU-LAC Foundation. The foundation's mandate is to strengthen the relationship between the regions. Led by an executive director who will serve a four-year term, the foundation will provide seminars, lectures, classes, presentations and the coordination of events

---

54 See Celestino del Arenal, 'Relations between the EU and Latin America: Abandoning Regionalism in Favour of a New Bilateral Strategy?, working paper 36/2009 (Madrid: Real Instituto Elcano, 2009), 30 pp.

that engage civil society. The primary goal of this engagement is to foster new networking opportunities among civil society actors. The European Commission has contributed €3 million up to the year 2013 to cover the cost of running this foundation.[55] The EU also announced the creation of a development project for Latin America, totalling € 125 million over three years, which may also generate up to €3 billion in fresh investment in the region.[56]

Madrid Declaration and Action Plan

At the Madrid Summit, a Declaration and Action Plan was also concluded and adopted. Among some of the issues covered in that Declaration and Plan was the acknowledgment that gender issues need to be integrated into all aspects of the international agenda. This document also recognized the need for the EU and LAC to combine forces to improve energy efficiency, reduce and limit greenhouse gas (GHG) emissions, and address the challenge of climate change. The Madrid Action Plan 2010–12 conceives of transnational, or bi-regional, cooperation programmes and initiatives that will actively deal with issues related to science and technology, research and development, sustainable development, the environment, climate change, biodiversity and energy.[57]

EU-Central American Agreement

Moreover, a comprehensive EU-Central America agreement was also announced in Madrid. This agreement, linking the 27 EU members to the six Central American republics, provides for the full liberalization of industrial products in both regions, tariff reduction for food imports, and the opening up of the Central American market to European car imports. The free trade agreement will remove more tariff barriers among the European members and the Central American bloc of countries. Central American countries will now have fewer tariffs on their beef, rice and plantains, while European countries will be given free access to the automotive market for 10 years. This agreement will also promote cooperation and political dialogue among the two regions.[58]

The EU and Central America agreement, according to the former Spanish Prime Minister José Luis Rodriguez Zapatero, will 'politically, economically and

---

55   See http://ec.europa.eu/external_relations/lac/index_en.htm (18 May 2010), accessed 23 August 2010.

56   Oncenoticias, online service of Mexico City's Canal Once TV channel, http://oncetv-ipn.net/noticias/index.php, accessed 18 May 2010.

57   http://climate-l.org/2010/05/20/eu-latin-america-and-caribbean-summit-adopts-madrid-declaration-and-action-plan/ (12/10/05), accessed 23 August 2010.

58   These Central American states are Costa Rica, El Salvador, Guatemala, Honduras, Nicaragua and Panama. Oncenoticias, online service of Mexico City's Canal Once TV channel, http://oncetv-ipn.net/noticias/index.php, accessed 18 May 2010.

socially [strengthen] Central America and the European Union'. It will certainly link a market of 40 million Central Americans to 500 million European consumers. It is expected that this agreement will result in an increase of about €2.6 billion in annual Central American exports and approximately €2.4 billion in the opposite direction. The agreement could very well bring the economies as well as the peoples of the two regions closer together and create prosperity while alleviating poverty in Central America. Further, as Herman van Rompuy, the President of the European Council, hopes, the agreement could also help promote integration within the Central American region. Central American political leaders are hopeful that one of the side benefits of this association agreement will be increased trans-regional cooperation on security matters and on the fight against drug trafficking. On the latter issue, it has been recognized by both sides that the Central American region is 'the first frontier where a large part of the drugs consumed in Europe is produced, and we need to have more effective security, cooperation and much more technology, so that we can fight this curse together'.[59]

The CARIFORUM-EU Joint Council and EPAs

Beyond Central America, the EU and CARIFORUM states also held in Madrid the inaugural meeting of their joint council, in conjunction with the EU-Latin America and Caribbean Summit. CARIFORUM states comprise of the 14 members of the Caribbean Community (CARICOM).[60] The meeting built on the Economic Partnership Agreements (EPAs) that the EU had promoted with many former colonies, turned independent countries, in Africa, the Caribbean and the Pacific (ACP). The incentive for developing this special relationship stems from the belief that the twenty-first century would offer up new challenges as well as opportunities, as old political and economic certainties give way to new patterns of trade, development and governance. The belief held by many policy makers in the EU and the ACP countries was that the world is about to become even more integrated and complex and therefore it is better to address certain problems through collaboration between the two regions. The EPAs thus pay special attention to individual ACP countries' geography and structure – particularly those that are landlocked or those that are small islands; those ACP countries that take ownership of their development and design their own strategies for achieving economic growth and prosperity; the involvement of civil society and business organization during the negotiations that result in the EPAs; and the least developed countries.

---

59 This quote was attributed to the Panamanian President, Ricardo Martinelli in European Union-Latin America and the Caribbean Summit, 'EU signs with Central America its first region-to-region association agreement' (19 May 2010), found at http://eu2010.biz/en/cumbre_ue-alc/noticias/may19centroamerica.html, accessed 21 August 2010.

60 Antigua and Barbuda, the Bahamas, Barbados, Belize, Dominica, Grenada, Guyana, Haiti, Jamaica, St Lucia, St Vincent and the Grenadines, St Kitts and Nevis, Surinam, and Trinidad and Tobago.

The EU has established an EPA with all Caribbean countries that are members of CARIFORUM, save one, since January 2008. However, Haiti, the remaining country, joined that EPA in 2009. The EU also included the Dominican Republic in that EPA, even though it is not a member of CARICOM. Through this EPA, Caribbean countries exports to the EU include fuel (gas, oil), chemicals, iron and steel, corundum, and agricultural products (such as mangoes, bananas, rice, rum, and sugar). Caribbean countries import from the EU mostly mechanical and electrical machinery products. The EPA has resulted in greater predictability in market access for the countries of both regions; duty-free/quota-free (DFQF) market access into the EU for CARIFORUM products; a commitment that EU exports will be liberalized over a period of 25 years, with a longer phase-in period (or exclusion) for some 'sensitive' products; improvements in the rules of origin in select areas such as garments of knit and non-knit fabric (which can now be produced from non-originating material); the opening of markets beyond WTO commitments in the service sector, including creative and entertainment industries; firms being able to establish a commercial presence in the EU; and the permission for Caribbean sales staff, investors and graduate trainees to make short-term business trips and temporary travel throughout Europe.[61] The overall intent of this EPA is to help make the Caribbean more competitive in world markets and to help Caribbean exporters meet EU and international standards.

As mentioned earlier, during the Madrid meeting Haiti formally signed on to the EPA, although implementation of this country's commitments has been delayed due to the massive earthquake that struck the country in January 2010. In Madrid too, the joint CARIFORUM-EU council explored ways of making the EPA fully operational and of making sure that this trade and development instrument becomes a tool for the sustainable development of the Caribbean region. It should be noted that the CARIFORUM-EU EPA covers more than just trade in goods. It also covers trade in services, investment, social and labour standards, competition policy and transparency in government procurement. It is the first such comprehensive EPA to be implemented in the ACP regions.

EU-Andean Community Summit

Similar types of issues were discussed between the EU and the four Andean countries (Ecuador, Bolivia, Colombia and Peru) at the Madrid summit. This was the sixth EU-Andean Community Summit and it tackled such agenda items as drug trafficking, the environment, climate change, migration, the global economic crisis and regional integration. The drug trafficking issue was addressed deliberately at the Heads of State level in order to demonstrate the importance that this issue, and related ones such as money laundering, holds for the leaders of both regions.

---

61   See http://ec.europa.eu/trade/wider-agenda/development/economic-partnerships/negotiations-and-agreements/#caribbean, accessed 21 August 2010.

The European Commission provided substantial financial support to the Andean countries to assist them in their fight against the drug trafficking problem.

Also discussed at some length during this EU-Andean Community Summit was the climate change issue, particularly in light of the upcoming Cancún conference on climate change, as well as the global financial crisis. On the latter agenda item, the President of Peru, Alan García, noted that the global financial crisis of 2008 only served to demonstrate the importance of moving towards sub-regional economic integration to create employment, to attract investment and to promote economic growth. In stating this, it would seem that García touts sub-regionalism as a buffer against the onslaught of the negative aspect of globalization.

EU Trade Deal with Peru and Colombia

At the conclusion of this summit, the EU signed a trade with Peru and Colombia. The aim of that agreement is to free up trade in certain sectors, such as industrial products, agriculture, fishing, and services and investment. But the agreement also included the desire for trans-regional collaboration around the issue of human rights. In some sense, this trade agreement was devised as a carrot to encourage both Peru and Colombia to continue progress on reforming their respective societies and developing greater social protection within their communities. This type of multi-party, and plurilateral, trade arrangement allows other countries in the Andean community to join at a point in time that they consider to be appropriate to their own circumstances.[62]

EU-MERCOSUR Trade Talks

A new round of negotiations between the EU and MERCOSUR for the achievement of a trade agreement was also launched at the Madrid summit. The trade talks between the EU and MERCOSUR, which had been stalled for several years, seemed back on track. A brief recount of previous EU-MERCOSUR contacts is in order here.

In 1992, the European Commission and MERCOSUR had signed an inter-institutional cooperation agreement to establish technical cooperation and dialogue between the two regions. This was followed in 1995 with the signing of a joint declaration of inter-regional economic cooperation between MERCOSUR and the EU, whose objective was to pursue a bi-regional political association and advance trade liberalization between the two regional blocs.[63] Once Bolivia and Peru joined MERCOSUR as associate members, in 1996 and 2003 respectively,

---

62   See http://www.eu2010.es/en/cumbre_ue-alc/noticias/may19_andinos.html (19/05/ 2010), accessed 23 August 2010.

63   For an expanded account see Paulo Roberto de Almeida, *Effects of EU Activities and Cooperation with MERCOSUR on Regional Democracy Building* (Stockholm: International Institute for Democracy and Electoral Assistance, 2009), 4–6.

it looked as though the vision of sub-regional integration along the lines of what occurred in Europe might be possible. However, the Mexican financial crisis of 1994, followed by the Asian financial crises in 1997 and 1998, coupled with the Russian Long term Capital Management crash of 1998, had a major negative impact on MERCOSUR. Brazil, in particular, was saddled with huge imbalances in its current accounts, and Argentina suffered its own financial crisis between 1999 and 2002. Furthermore, MERCOSUR has been further impeded by the protectionist tendencies of both its leading members – Argentina and Brazil.

Nevertheless, the EU kept trying to conclude a trade liberalization and association agreement with MERCOSUR. A bi-regional Free Trade Agreement between MERCOSUR and the EU was, however, derailed in 2005 when the proposed Free Trade Area of the Americas (FTAA) was stopped in its tracks by Argentina, Brazil and Venezuela. According to de Almeida, the sabotage of the EU-MERCOSUR free trade arrangement likely occurred for the same reasons that the FTAA was derailed: 'divergences among the partners in connection with European farm protectionism, and resistance from MERCOSUR countries in industrial services and intellectual property matters'.[64] Despite this derailment in EU-MERCOSUR trade relations, there was some optimism that the bi-regional trade negotiations could get back on track.[65] If the round of negotiations launched in Madrid is successful, the EU-MERCOSUR trading bloc will become the largest free trade zone in the globerepresenting 750 million people with annual commerce worth nearly €100 billion ($123 billion USD).[66]

EU-LAC Cooperation in Civil Aviation

Trade is only one among many elements of the relationship that has recently developed between the EU, Latin America and the Caribbean. Cooperation around such issues as civil aviation is now part of the agenda of these two regions. Air transport is vital for EU-LAC relations because it facilitates trade and the movement of people. EU-LAC air travel has grown exponentially in recent years, with the doubling of passengers both ways between 1997 and 2008. It is forecasted that the Latin American air transport market will be the fastest growing aviation

---

64   Ibid., 5–6.

65   France 24, 'EU and Mercosur attempt to revive deadlocked trade talks', found at http://www.france24.com/en/20100517-eu-mercosur-trade-talks-zapatero-business-ame ricas-europe (17/05/2010), accessed 23 August 2010.

66   Note that EU farmers are not very happy with the re-launch of these trade talks. See EurActive, 'Farmers oppose relaunch of EU-Mercosur Trade Talks', 18 May 2010, found at http://www.euractiv.com/en/cap/farmers-oppose-relaunch-eu-mercosur-trade-tal ks-news-494278, accessed 23 August 2010.

market in the world over the next 20 years. In excess of 20 million passengers are travelling each year on direct flights between the EU and Latin America.[67]

At a civil aviation summit held in Rio de Janeiro on 25 and 26 May 2010, the European Commission, the National Civil Aviation Agency of Brazil, and the Latin American Civil Aviation Commission jointly agreed to enhance political, technical, and industrial cooperation between Latin America and the EU in the aviation sector. This agenda item demonstrates the strategic importance of Latin America to the EU. The main areas addressed at that joint meeting included: the removal of barriers to air transport in the EU and Latin America; recent developments in the airline industry in Latin America and the EU; safety and security challenges and the potential for cooperation in this area; air traffic management and the emergence of new technologies; environmental implication for air transport; airport infrastructure and airport policy of the two regions; the economic and social dimensions of aviation; and future EU-Latin American cooperation in civil aviation, including technical assistance and industrial cooperation.[68]

China's Expansion into Latin America

China's explicit strategy of expanding its relations with countries outside of its own region has had an important impact on the re-mapping of the Americas as noted by Joseph Cheng earlier in this volume. But this strategy has also been facilitated by the open regionalism being embraced by countries in Latin America and the Caribbean. The desire of many leaders in the Americas to find alternatives to the North American market, and specifically to get from under the stranglehold of the US hegemonic tentacles, has opened up the prospects for further intrusion in this hemisphere by China – much to the chagrin of some in the US government. Today, the PRC has relations with countries of the Southern Cone (Argentina, Brazil, Chile, Paraguay and Uruguay), with countries in the Andean region (Bolivia, Colombia, Ecuador, Peru and Venezuela), and with Mexico as well as countries in Central American and the Caribbean; without, for that matter, neglecting the US and Canada.

China's largest trading partner in Latin America is Brazil. Bilateral trade between these two countries reached $14.8 billion by 2005.[69] China has had a strategic partnership with Brazil since 1993. After signing a free trade agreement with Chile in 2005, China has now become Chile's second largest trading partner

---

67 See Europa, Press Release Rapid, 'Vice President Kallas leads high-level delegation to the EU-Latin America civil aviation summit' (21 May 2010), found at http://europa.eu/rapid/pressReleasesAction.do?reference=IP/10/591&type=HTML, accessed 21 August 2010.

68 Ibid.

69 See figures from Chinese Embassy in Brazil, at http://br.china-embassy.org/chn/zbgxgs/t239731.htm, accessed 21 July 2010.

(after the United States). Mexico is one of the fastest growing markets for China in the western hemisphere. In 2003, China replaced Japan as Mexico's second largest import partner. Mexican imports from China reached $14.4 billion in 2005.[70]

The reasons for China's expansion into the Americas are multiple. The region is viewed as a good source for primary products that China needs in order to sustain its rapid economic growth and to meet the demands of its large and growing population, especially its growing middle class. China's economy has quadrupled over the past 40 years or so. By 1993, China had been transformed from a petroleum exporter to an importer of this primary product. By the turn of the century, China's dependency on foreign oil jumped some 40 per cent.[71] Today China consumes more than 7.5 million barrels of oil per day,[72] making this country the top energy consumer in the world. By 2020, China's economy could quadruple, thus requiring even more resources to sustain this growth.

This has led China to search out new sources of energy, including in Latin America – a region traditionally considered in the backyard of the United States. China has penetrated into the Latin American region in significant ways, so much so that its engagement 'has created winners and losers at both national and sectoral levels'.[73] Exports from the PRC to Latin America have expanded exponentially over the past few decades to include products from a broad range of sectors, spanning from labour intensive, low-end manufacturing product (toys, textiles, footwear) to more sophisticated products such as motorcycles, automobiles, telephone, computers, etc. Latin American countries have also expanded their exports to China significantly – particularly in the area of primary products like petroleum, metals, mineral, fisheries, and agricultural products. As the Chinese middle class grows, Latin American exports are expected to rise particularly in consumer goods that cater to the increasingly cosmopolitan tastes of China's rising middle class. It seems that most Latin American countries are in fact preparing for this increase in economic interaction with China. One can see this in the growing number of China-oriented businesses, Chinese-language institutes, and the increasing number of trade fairs and service companies that are giving opportunities for Latin American producers to place their products in the Chinese market.

China is also investing heavily in Latin America. In 2004, some 49 per cent of China's total foreign investment went to Latin America.[74] One can see this

---

70 Latin Business Chronicle, 'US-Latin Trade Boom' (March 2006), at http://www. latinbusinesschronicle.com/reports/reports/0306/trade.htm#chi, accessed 21 July 2010.

71 Wenran Jiang, 'China and India come to Latin America for Energy', found at http://www.china.ualberta.ca/publication.cfm, accessed 15 June 2010.

72 See http://www.nationmaster.com/graph/ene_oil_con-energy-oil-consumption, accessed 21 July 2010.

73 R. Evan Ellis, *China in Latin America: The Whats & Wherefores* (Boulder: Lynne Rienner Publishers, 2009), 2.

74 See Tim Johnson, 'The Chinese Boom', *Knight Ridder News Service* (10 July 2005).

development in the number of Chinese corporations, banks, and enterprises that are investing significant quantities of capital in the region. The primary purpose of this investment is to ensure that China can gain access to a steady supply of primary products which Latin American countries produce. China needs these primary products in order to sustain its economic growth and meet the demands of its large population. Some of these investments come in the form of acquisitions and joint ventures, particularly in the petroleum and mining sectors. But China has also been investing heavily in infrastructure throughout the Latin American region to facilitate the imports and exports between itself and Latin America. It is noteworthy to mention that much of this investment is taking place in countries that have become disillusioned with the US and its foreign policy in the region, e.g., in countries like Venezuela and Ecuador.

Some of China's investment is also a blatant attempt to force countries in the region to change their diplomatic posture with respect to Taiwan. Clearly, China believes that it can thwart any attempt by Taiwan to gain international recognition of that island's claim to sovereignty if it can get countries that currently recognize Taiwan as a state to retract their position. As it has done in other world regions, China uses the promise of infrastructural and other investments as a means of getting some of the states in the Latin American region to change their diplomatic posture with respect to Taiwan. Costa Rica has been one of the latest countries in the hemisphere to shift its diplomatic loyalties from Taiwan to mainland China because of the PRC's promise of increased investment in that Central American country.

Venezuela-China bilateral trade was $2.14 billion by 2005. China's largest energy company, China National Petroleum Corporation (CNPC) has acquired access to develop oil and gas fields in Venezuela. In return, Venezuela promised to increase its export of oil to China to about 100,000 barrels per day.[75] President Chávez stated openly in 2005: 'We have been producing and exporting oil for more than 100 years, but they have been years of dependence on the United States. Now we are free and we make our resources available to the great country of China'.[76] The expansion in ties between Latin America and China is not limited to economic activity. Over the past decade, about 74 Latin American heads of state have visited China. Similarly, Chinese leaders have gone on trips to at least 19 different Latin American states.[77] For instance, in 2001, Chinese President Jiang Zemin went on

---

75 Buenos Aires, 'China and Latin America: Magic or Realism?', *The Economist* (29 December 2005).

76 See quote in Gal Luft, 'In search of crude China goes to the Americas', Institute for the Analysis of Global Security, *Energy Security* (18 January 2005), at www.iags.org/n0118041.htm, accessed 21 July 2010.

77 Shixue Jiang, 'Three Factors in Recent Development of Sino-Latin American Relations', in Cynthia Aranson, Mark Mohr and Riordan Roett (eds), *Enter the Dragon? China's Presence in Latin America* (Washington, DC: Woodrow Wilson International Centre for Scholars, 2008), 43.

a Latin American tour that included Venezuela, Cuba, Chile, Argentina, Uruguay, and Brazil. During the visit to Venezuela, President Zemin engaged in talks on energy cooperation with President Hugo Chávez. In 2003, Chinese Premier Wen Jiabao visited Mexico. This was followed by his participation in the Twelfth Asia-Pacific Economic Cooperation meeting in Chile and a 13-day tour of Brazil, Argentina, Chile, and Cuba. In 2004, Chinese Vice president Zeng Qinghong led a delegation to Mexico, Peru, Venezuela, Trinidad and Tobago, and Jamaica.

These political exchanges go beyond the heads of state realm. They include trips by parliamentarians, party delegations, military officers, representatives of language institutes, and the establishment of cultural programmes, the construction of Confucius institutes and the creation of sister-cities. China has also been increasing its influence in regional institutions in Latin America and the Caribbean – such as the Inter-American Development Bank (IDB), the Caribbean Development Bank (CDB), the Organization of American States (OAS), and the *Corporación Andina de Fomento*. It is also involved in other trans-regional organizations and dialogues, such as the China-Latin America Forum, the China-South American Common Market Dialogue, and the China-Andean Community consultations.

Such engagement of countries in our hemisphere with China has had profound impacts on the performance and structure of the economies of those countries. We have witnessed a commodity-led export boom that has affected almost all the countries of the region as a result of the so-called China surge.[78] This boom led to unprecedented GDP growth in the region despite the market crash of late 2008. China's economic and investment expansion in the Andean region, for instance, helped off-set the withdrawal of US and European companies from that sub-region. In some cases, Chinese manufactured goods are increasingly gaining market share in certain Latin American countries and 'displacing Latin American producers from their traditional export markets'.[79] This is not necessarily a good thing. In fact, the end result for some Latin American countries has been a movement away from manufacturing industries back to an overdependence on export-oriented primary product sectors.[80] This structural shift towards 'deindustrialization'[81] can

---

78   See for instance, Carol Wise and Cinthia Quiliconi, 'China's Surge in Latin American Markets: Policy Challenges and Responses', *Politics and Policy*, 1 (2007), 410–438.

79   Ellis, 3.

80   Richard Feinberg, 'Latin American and the Caribbean's Response to the Growth of China and India: Overview of Research Findings and Policy Implications; Angel or Devil? China's Trade Impact on Latin American Emerging Markets', *Foreign Affairs* (January/ February 2007).

81   See Francisco E. González, 'Latin America in the Economic Equation – Winners and Losers: What Can Losers Do?', in Riordan Roett and Guadalupe Paz (eds), *China's Expansion into the Western Hemisphere* (Washington, DC: Brookings Institute Press, 2008), 148–169; and Kevin P. Gallagher and Roberto Porzecanski, *The Dragon in the Room. China and the Future of Latin American Industrialization* (Stanford: Stanford University Press, 2010).

have long-term, and possibly negative, implications for development and political stability throughout our hemisphere. But it is certainly a representation of the re-mapping that is going on in the region.

India and Latin America

While China's trade with countries in the western hemisphere has been growing at an exponential rate, India's trade with these countries has also been growing steadily, but at a much slower rate. One of the reasons for this difference is the high reciprocal tariffs placed on goods coming from both areas. India's average tariff on Latin American agriculture goods is 65 per cent, more than five times that of China's. Latin American tariffs on Indian goods reach as high as 9.8 per cent for manufactured products, well above the range of 4 per cent to 6 per cent imposed on Indian trade by developed nations in the Organization for Economic Cooperation and Development (OECD). Another reason has to do with the fact that, at the moment, India has no direct shipping service to Latin American countries. As a result, Indian goods headed for Latin America are usually shipped through Singapore or through Europe, a triangulation that adds cost to the final price of the merchandise.[82]

However, there are signs that this situation has begun to change as the Indian government, diplomats and businesses begin to pay more attention to the western hemisphere as a place to do business, and as Latin America and the Caribbean recognize the strategic importance of catering to a country whose market is almost as large as that of China's. The Indian population is 1.1 billion and the country has a scarcity of natural resources relative to other continent-size nations. Thus, the potential for India to be a major purchaser of agriculture, energy and mineral products stemming from the Latin American and Caribbean region is huge.

In the future, India could become a major trade partner, along with China, in the LAC region, if governments can cut trade barriers and find a way to lower shipping costs. Certainly, India devotes more of its GDP to consumption than does China.[83] So Latin American and Caribbean countries might find an even more hospitable market for their goods in India than they would in China. The Indian Preferential Trade Agreement (PTA) with MERCOSUR, which became operational in June 2009, acknowledges that potential. The PTA now covers 450 items on both sides, and that amount is expected to increase to 1,600 items on MERCOSUR's list and 3,200 items on India's list. It is expected that over the next five years, the combined trade between India and South America, as a result

82   Sandrine Rastello, 'India, Latin America have "massive" trade potential, IDB says', *Bloomberg Business Week* (1 August 2010), found at http://www.businessweek. com/news/2010-07-27/india-latin-america-have-massive-trade-potential-idb-says.html, accessed 2 August 2010.

83   R. Evan Ellis, *China in Latin America: The Whats and Wherefores*, 25.

of the PTA, will be over $10 billion.[84] The PTA will reduce the tariffs on selected items between the partners, and the scope of those items can expand over time upon agreement of the partners. India's major trade items to MERCOSUR include drugs, pharmaceuticals and fine chemicals, while major imports from the South American trade bloc comprise of edible oils (primarily soya bean), metal scrap and non-electrical machinery.

In April 2010, a number of Indian, Latin American and Caribbean firms met in New Delhi at the fourth annual India-Latin America and Caribbean Conclave to discuss business proposals worth $10.4 billion, covering a wide array of business sectors. Sectors included agriculture, food processing, machinery, sugar production, ethanol, contract farming, floriculture, and textiles. Delegates at the Conclave came from Argentina, Brazil, Chile, Colombia, Costa Rica, Cuba, the Dominican Republic, Ecuador, El Salvador, Mexico, Peru, Trinidad and Tobago, and Uruguay. While many of these countries in the western hemisphere are relatively small, collectively the Latin American and Caribbean (LAC) market may be quite substantial for India. Already by 2008–09, trade between India and the LAC region had risen four-fold since 2004–05 (from $4.2 billion to $16.1 billion). According to a statement made by the Confederation of Indian Industry (CII), 'Indian businesses are ... looking at larger footprints in specific regional blocs spread across the South American continent and the Caribbean region on the basis of the success achieved by these trade blocs in promoting trade among the member countries'.[85]

Sometimes it simply takes the initiative of individual actors or firms to help shape trans-regional relationships. Rengaraj Viswanathan, the Indian Ambassador to Argentina, Uruguay and Paraguay, is one such individual actor. He has done a lot to educate the people of the Southern Cone about the advantages of doing business with India, while at the same time extolling Latin American values and the regional market when advising Indian enterprises on possibilities of doing business with that region.[86] One such firm is the Tata Group, India's largest business group and multinational company, which already has consultancy services in Peru, Chile and Ecuador, and it also has offices in Mexico, Uruguay, Argentina, Brazil, and Colombia.

---

84   'Post-PTA, India-Mercosur trade to touch $10 bn', *Business Standard Reporter*, New Delhi (4 June 2009), found at http://www.business-standard.com/india/news/post-pta-india-mercosur-trade-to-touch-10-bn/360072/, accessed 2 August 2010.

85   Indo-Asian News Service, 'India-Latin America meet to consider $10.39 billion deals', *Hindustantimes* (27 April 2010), found at http://www.hindustantimes.com/Story Page/Print/536373.aspx, accessed 2 August 2010.

86   See Joachim Bamrud, 'India's Latin America Booster', found at http://www.businesswithlatinamerica.blogspot.com, accessed 2 August 2010.

Bibliography

Abu-Hamdeh, Sabrina. 2011. 'The Merida Initiative: An Effective Way of Reducing Violence in Mexico?', *Perpperdine Policy Review*, 4, article 5: 37–54.

ACP Secretariat. 2003. The Cotonou Agreement: A User's Guide for Non State Actors.

ACP-EU Joint Parliamentary Assembly. March 2002. 'Cape Town Declaration on Future ACP-EU negotiations for new trading arrangements', http://eur-lex. europa.eu/LexUriServ/LexUriServ.do?uri=CELEX:22002P0927(20):EN:HT ML [accessed: 29 December 2013].

Alleyne, M.C. 2007. 'Governance and Caribbean Integration', Conference Paper: Paper Presented to the 8th Annual SALISES Conference, Trinidad and Tobago, 26th–28th March 2007.

de Almeida, Paulo Roberto. 2009. *Effects of EU Activities and Cooperation with MERCOSUR on Regional Democracy Building*. Stockholm: International Institute for Democracy and Electoral Assistance.

Almeida, Paulo Roberto. 2009. 'Lula's Foreign Policy: Regional and Global Strategies', in Joseph Love and Werner Baer (eds), *Brazil under Lula: Economy, Politics, and Society under the Worker-President*. New York: Palgrave-Macmillan.

Amin, Samir. 2006. *Beyond US Hegemony? Assessing the Prospects for a Multipolar World*, trans. Patrick Camiller. London: Zed Books.

Anderson, Greg. 2001. 'Hemispheric Integration in the Post-Seattle Era: The Promise and Problems for the FTAA', *International Journal*, 56 (Spring): 205–233.

Anderson, Greg. 2006. 'The End of the Renaissance?: U.S. Trade Policy and the Second Term of George W. Bush', in George A. MacLean (ed.), *Canada and the United States: A Relationship at a Crossroads*. Winnipeg: Centre for Defense and Security Studies.

Anderson, Greg. 2006. 'North American Economic Integration and the Challenges Wrought by 9/11', *Journal of Homeland Security and Emergency Management*, 3 (2) (Summer): 1–30.

Anderson, Greg. 2012. 'Securitization and Sovereignty in Post-9/11 North America', *Review of International Political Economy*, 19 (5) (December): 711–741.

Anderson, Greg. 2012. 'The Uncertain Politics of North American Economic Integration', in Julián Castro-Rea (ed.), *Our North America. Social and Political Issues beyond NAFTA*. Farnham: Ashgate.

Andriamananjara, Soamiely. 2003. 'Competitive Liberalization or Competitive Diversion? Preferential Trade Agreements and the Multilateral Trading System', working paper, US International Trade Commission.

Anonymous. 2004. 'Alleged Hezbollah "Fighter" Snuck into US from Mexico', *Human Events* (26 January 2004).

Anonymous. 2004. 'Coalition Forces Advance', *IRC Americas Program Policy Brief*, 24 July.

Aragón, Rafael. 2011. 'Is Ortega's Project Christian? And What is the Church's Project?', *Revista Envio*, 357, http://www.envio.org.ni/articulo/4328 [accessed: 8 August 2012].

del Arenal, Celestino. 2009. 'Relations between the EU and Latin America: Abandoning Regionalism in Favour of a New Bilateral Strategy?', Working Paper 36. Madrid: Real Instituto Elcano.

Arthur, Owen and Consortium. 2010. 'Revised Individual Country Analytical Reports for Phase 2 of Cisp/csme/result 1.9.1.1/ser09.10 Consultancy to Support the Full Integration of Belize and the OECS in CARICOM'.

Associated Press. 2 March 2013. 'Obama "confident" Immigration Bill could pass this summer', http://www.foxnews.com/politics/2013/03/28/obama-says-im migration-bill-could-pass-by-summer/ [accessed: 30 March 2013].

Azicri, Max. 2009. 'The Castro-Chávez Alliance', *Latin American Perspectives*, 36 (1), January: 99–110.

Babb, Sarah. 2001. *Managing Mexico: Economists from Nationalism to Neo-liberalism.* Princeton: Princeton University Press.

Bailey, Thomas A. 1980. *A Diplomatic History of the American People*, 10th ed. Englewood Cliffs, NJ: Prentice-Hall F.S. Crofts & Co.

Baltodano, Mónica. 2006. 'Nicaragua: From Sandinismo to "Danielismo"', *International Socialist Review*, 50 (November–December) [Online]. Available at: http://www.isreview.org/issues/50/nicaragua.shtml [accessed: 1 August 2012].

Bamrud, Joachim. 'India's Latin America Booster', www.businesswithlatinam erica.blogspot.com [accessed: 2 August 2010].

Bandeira, Luiz Alberto. 2006. 'Brazil as a regional power and its relations with the United States', *Latin American Perspectives*, 33 (3) (May): 12–27.

Baogang, H. and H. Murphy. 2007. 'Global Social Justice at the WTO? The Role of NGOs in Constructing Global Social Contracts', *International Affairs*, 83 (4): 707–727.

The Barbados Advocate. 2011. 'Whither CARICOM?' (Bridgetown, Barbados, 1 June).

Barnes, Michael D. 2013. 'Time is ripe for new approach with Cuba', *Progreso Weekly* (6 March 2013), http://progreso-weekly.com/ini/index.php/home/in-the-united-states/3799-time-is-ripe-for-new-approach-with-cuba [accessed: 25 May 2013].

Barry, Tom. 2004. 'On the Economic Front: Coalition Forces Advance,' Americas Program Silver City, NM: Interhemispheric Resource Centre, July 24, http://www.bilaterals.org/IMG/pdf/0407econ.pdf [accessed: 30 December 2013].

Battaglino, Jorge. 2012. 'Defence in a Post-Hegemonic Regional Agenda: The Case of the South American Defence Council', in Riggirozzi, Pía and Diana Tussie (eds), *The Rise of Post-Hegemonic Regionalism. The Case of Latin America.* Heidelberg; London; New York: Springer, pp. 81–100.

BBC. 2009. 'Cuba rejects OAS readmission', www.bbc.co.uk/Caribbean/news/story/2009/06/090608_cubaaosupdate.shtml [accessed: 26 May 2013].

BBC Monitoring International Reports. IR 5 March 2003. 'Mercosur to Present "Ambitious" Tariff-Elimination Proposal to EU'.

BBC Monitoring International Reports. 2005. 'Chinese Vice President's Visit Promote Ties with Latin America'. 5 February.

Bello, Walden. 2002. 'Learning from Doha: A Civil Society Perspective from the South', *Global Governance*, 8: 273–279.

Benson, Todd. 21 April 2004. 'EU Nears Trade Pact with Latin America', *New York Times*.

Bergsten, C. Fred. 1997. 'Open Regionalism', Working Paper 97–3, Peterson Institute for International Economics.

Bergsten, C. Fred. 2002. 'A Renaissance for U.S. Trade Policy?', *Foreign Affairs*, 81 (6): 86–98.

Bertelsmann Transformation Index (BTI). 2006. Country Report, Nicaragua. *Shaping Change: Strategies for Development and Transformation* [Online]. Available at: http://bti2006.bertelsmann-transformation-index.de/fileadmin/pdf/en/2006/LatinAmericaAndTheCaribbean/Nicaragua.pdf [accessed: 2 August 2012].

Beyers, J. 2002. 'Gaining and Seeking Access. The European Adaptation of Domestic Interest Associations', *Journal of Political Research*, 41 (5): 585–612.

Bhagwati, Jagdish 1991. *The World Trading System at Risk.* Harvester Wheatsheaf, Hemel, Hempstead.

Bishop, M.L. 2011. 'Slaying the "Westmonster" in the Caribbean? Constitutional Reform in St Vincent and the Grenadines', *British Journal of Politics and International Relations*, 13 (3): 420–437.

Bishop, M.L. 2012. 'The Political Economy of Small States: Enduring Vulnerability?', *Review of International Political Economy*, 19 (5): 942–960.

Bishop, M.L. 2013. *The Political Economy of Caribbean Development: A Comparative Analysis.* Basingstoke: Palgrave Macmillan.

Bishop, M.L. and A. Payne. 2010. 'Caribbean Regional Governance and the Sovereignty/Statehood Problem', Waterloo, Ontario: Centre for International Governance Innovation (CIGI) Caribbean Paper No. 8, http://www.cigionline.org/sites/default/files/Caribbean_Paper_8.pdf [accessed 26 December 2013].

Bishop, M.L. and A. Payne. 2012. 'Climate Change and the Future of Caribbean Development', *The Journal of Development Studies*, 48 (10): 1536–1553.

Bishop, M.L., N. Girvan, T.M. Shaw, R.M. Kirton, M. Scobie, S. Cross-Mike, D. Mohammed and M. Anatol. 2011. 'Caribbean Regional Integration: A Report by the UWI Institute of International Relations, funded by UKaid from

DFID, led by Matthew L. Bishop and Norman Girvan', St Augustine, Trinidad and Tobago, http://www.normangirvan.info/wp-content/uploads/2011/06/iir-regional-integration-report-final.pdf [accessed 28 December 2013].

Bishop, M.L., T. Heron and A. Payne. 2013. 'Caribbean Development Alternatives and the CARIFORUM-European Union Economic Partnership Agreement', *Journal of International Relations and Development*, 16 (1): 82–110.

Blake, Charles and Stephen D. Morris. 2009. *Corruption and Democracy in Latin America*. Pittsburgh, PA: University of Pittsburgh Press.

Blake, Charles and Stephen D. Morris. 2009. 'Introduction: Political and Analytical Challenges of Corruption in Latin America', in Charles H. Blake and Stephen D. Morris (eds), *Corruption and Democracy in Latin America*. Pittsburgh, PA: University of Pittsburgh Press, 1–24.

Boyer, Robert and Daniel Drache (eds). 1996. *States Against Markets: The Limits of Globalization*. New York: Routledge.

Brand, A., S. Mc Ewen-Fial, W. Muno and A.R. Hoffmann. 2012. 'BRICs and US Hegemony: Theoretical Reflections on Shifting Power Patterns and Empirical Patterns from Latin America', Mainz Papers on International and European Power Politics (Johannes Gutenberg University of Mainz).

Braudel, Fernand. 1980. *On History*, trans. Sarah Matthew. Chicago: University of Chicago Press.

Brazil Report. 23 November 2004. 'Brazil Seals Partnership with Asia and Russia'.

Brewster, H. 2008. 'The Anti-Development Dimension of the European Community's Economic Partnership Agreement for the Caribbean', http://www.normangirvan.info/the-anti-development-dimension-of-the-european-communitys-economic-partnership-agreement-for-caribbean-havelock-brewster/ [accessed 26 December 2013].

Buenos Aires. 2005. 'China and Latin America: Magic or Realism?', *The Economist*, 29 December.

Bumiller, Elisabeth and Larry Rohter. 2005. 'Bush's Troubles Follow Him to Summit in Argentina', *The New York Times*, 4 November.

Business Daily Update. 2004. 'Latin American Free Trade', 3 December

Business Standard. 2009. 'Post-PTA, India-Mercosur trade to touch $10 bn', Business Standard Reporter, New Delhi. 4 June 2009. http://www.business-standard.com/india/news/post-pta-india-mercosur-trade-to-touch-10-bn/360072/ [accessed: 2 August 2010].

Byron, Jessica and Patsy Lewis. 2007. 'Formulating Sustainable Development Benchmarks for an EU-CARICORUM EPA: Caribbean Perspectives'. ICTSD and APRODEV, September.

Cameron, M.A. and B.W. Tomlin. 2000. *The Making of the NAFTA: How the Deal Was Done*. Ithaca, NY: Cornell University Press.

Camilo, Frederico Alberto Cuello. 2008. 'The CARIFORUM-EC EPA: the First Development Enhancing Agreement in History'. 13 February, Brussels: Mimeo.

Campaign for Labour Rights. 2003. 'Civil Society Comments on FTAA', http://www.iadb.org/intal/intalcdi/PE/2007/00394.pdf [accessed 19 May 2013].

Canada, Canada Border Services Agency. 'Western Hemisphere Travel Initiative'.

Canada, Department of Foreign Affairs. 2005. 'Canada's International Policy Statement: Development, A Role of Pride and Influence in the World', November.

Canada, Department of Foreign Affairs. 2011. 'Canada's State of Trade: Trade and Investment Update 2011', http://www.international.gc.ca/economist-econo miste/performance/state-point/state_2011_point/2011_5.aspx?lang=eng &view=d [accessed 26 December 2013].

Cape Town Declaration. 2002. Joint Report on all ACP-EC Phase of EPA Negotiations.

Capling, Ann, and Kim Richard Nossal. 2009. 'The contradictions of regionalism in North America', *Review of International Studies*, 35, February: 147–167.

Caracas Declaration. 2011. Summit of the CELAC, http://www.pnuma.org/for odeministros/19-reunion%20intersesional/documentos/CARACAS%20DE CLARATION.pdf [accessed 26 December 2013].

Carciofi, Ricardo. 2012. 'Cooperation for the Provision of Regional Public Goods: The IIRSA Case', in Riggirozzi, Pía and Diana Tussie (eds), *The Rise of Post-hegemonic Regionalism. The Case of Latin America*. Heidelberg; London; New York: Springer, pp. 65–80.

Cárdenas, Mauricio and João Augusto de Castro Neve. 2010. 'Brazil and the United States: A New Beginning?', in Brookings Upfront Blog, 19 April, 2010, http://www.brookings.edu/blogs/up-front/posts/2010/04/19-us-brazil-cardenas.

Caribbean Community Secretariat, http://www.caricom.org/jsp/single_market/sin gle_market_index.jsp?menu=csme [accessed 29 December 2013].

Caribbean Congress of Labour Declaration and Plan of Action on Regional Integration and the Economic Partnership Agreement and their Social and Labour Dimensions. Barbados 23–25 June 2008, http://www.ilocarib.org.tt/ trade/documents/ccl-declaration-plan-of-action.pdf [accessed 26 December 2013].

The Caribbean Cultural Industries Network. 2007. 'Statement from the Caribbean Cultural Industries Network on the CARIFORUM-EU Economic Partnership Agreement', December.

Caribbean Journal. 2013. 'CARICOM to Suspend Consideration of Dominican Republic's Bid For Membership', *Caribbean Journal*, 26 November, http://www.caribjournal.com/2013/11/26/caricom-to-suspend-consideration-of-dominican-republics-bid-for-membership/ [accessed 29 December 2013].

Caribbean Tourist Organisation, 'Caribbean Response to the UK Government's Consultation on Reform of the Air Passenger Duty' (June 2011), http://www.onecaribbean.org/content/files/CaribbeanResponseAPDBriefingDocJune 2011.pdf [accessed 29 December 2013].

CARICOM Secretariat. 2009. *Report on the Appraisal of the State of Implementation of the Caribbean Single Market Arrangements Mandated by the Conference of Heads of Government of the Caribbean Community* (Draft).

Carranza, Mario E. 2004. 'Mercosur and the end game of the FTAA negotiations: challenges and prospects after the Argentine crisis', *Third World Quarterly*, 25 (2): 319–337.

Carryl, Ivor. 1999. 'Competition Policy: Implications for CARICOM Single Market and Economy', *Caribbean Dialogue*, 5 (1 and 2): 149–169.

Carson, Jeffrey. 2007. 'Resisting Free Trade: Brazil and the FTAA', unpublished paper presented at the 48th annual meeting of the International Studies Association (ISA), Hilton, Chicago, Illinois. 28 February, 2007.

Casas-Zamora, Kevin. 2010. 'Obama and Latin America: As Time Goes By', in *Brookings Institution Blog*, posted 20 May, 2010.

Castells, Manuel. 1996. *The Rise of the Network Society, Vol. I: The Information Age: Economy, Society, and Culture*. Oxford: Blackwell.

Castro-Rea, Julián. 1993. 'Du pessimisme chronique à l'optimisme témeraire. L'intégration latino-américaine et l'Initiative pour les Amériques', *Continentalisation*, 93–3, Montreal: UQAM, May.

Castro-Rea, Julián and Isabel Altamirano-Jiménez. 2008. 'North American First Peoples: Self-Determination or Economic Development?', in Yasmeen Abu-Laban, et al. (eds), *Politics in North America: Redefining Continental Relations*. Peterborough: Broadview.

CBC News. 2012. 'Canada, U.S. scuttle Summit of the Americas Statement', 15 April, http://www.cbc.ca/news/world/canada-u-s-scuttle-summit-of-the-americas-statement-1.1135363 [accessed 30 December 2013].

Cellucci, Paul. 2003. 'We are Family', *Policy Options*, 24 (5) (May): 13, http://www.irpp.org/assets/po/canada-and-the-iraq-war/cellucci.pdf [accessed 30 December 2013].

Central Intelligence Agency, U.S.A. The World Fact Book, https://www.cia.gov/library/publications/the-world-factbook/geos/nu.html [accessed 26 December 2013].

Central Intelligence Agency, U.S.A. 2013. 'The World Factbook, "Brazil"', https://www.cia.gov/library/publications/the-world-factbook/geos/br.html [accessed 30 December 2013].

Cerny, P.G. 2010. *Rethinking World Politics: A Theory of Transnational Neopluralism*. New York: Oxford University Press.

Césaire, Aimé. 1972. *Discourse on Colonialism*. Trans. Joan Pinkham. New York: Monthly Review.

Chan, Gerald. 1998. 'Chinese Perspectives on Peace and Development', *Peace Review*, 10 (1): 35–41.

Chancy, Myriam J.A. 2012. 'Meditation for a Forgotten Past: Translating and Remembering Haiti's Intellectual Legacy', http://www.normangirvan.info/wp-content/uploads/2012/06/chancy-stmartin-rodriguez-intro.pdf [accessed 29 December 2013].

Chang, Ha-Joon. 2002. *Kicking Away the Development Ladder: Development Strategy in Historical Perspective*. London: Anthem Press.

Cheibub, José Antonio. 2007. *Presidentialism, Parliamentarism, and Democracy*. New York: Cambridge University Press.

Cheng, Joseph Y.S. 1989. 'The Evolution of China's Foreign Policy in the Post-Mao Era: From Anti-Hegemony to Modernisation Diplomacy', in Joseph Y.S. Cheng (ed.), *China: Modernisation in the 1980s*. Hong Kong: The Chinese University Press, 161–201.

Cheng, Joseph Y.S. 1999. 'The Sino-Russian Strategic Partnership in the Chinese Leadership's World View', in Peter H. Koehn and Joseph Y.S. Cheng (eds), *The Outlook for U.S.-China Security, Trade and Cultural-exchange Relations Following the 1997–1998 Summits: Chinese and U.S. Perspectives*. Hong Kong: The Chinese University Press, 85–110.

Cheng, Joseph Y.S. 2001. 'Sino-ASEAN Relations in the Early Twenty-first Century', *Contemporary Southeast Asia*, 23 (3): 434–437.

Cheng, Joseph Y.S. 2010. 'China's Foreign Policy after the Seventeenth Party Congress', in Dennis Hickey and Baogang Guo (eds), *Dancing with the Dragon: China's Emergence in the Developing World*. Lanham, Maryland Lexington Books, 23–52.

China Daily. 26 January 2005. 'Sino-Chilean FTA Talks Launched', http://www.highbeam.com/doc/1P2-8830589.html [accessed: 26 December 2013].

China's Embassy in Brazil. 2006. Bilateral Relations. 16 February 2006. http://br.china-embassy.org/chn/zbgxgs/t239731.htm [accessed: 21 July 2010].

Chomsky, Noam. 2004. *Hegemony or Survival: America's Quest for Global Dominance*. New York: Henry Holt.

Chomsky, Noam. 2005. *Imperial Ambitions: Conversations on the Post-9/11 World; Interviews with David Barsamian*. New York: Metropolitan Books.

Chomsky, Noam and Edward S. Herman. 1979. *The Political Economy of Human Rights*. Montreal: Black Rose.

CIA World Fact Book; Statistics Canada. 2005. 'Imports, Exports and Balance of Trade on a Balance-of-Payments Basis'.

CIA World Factbook. 2012. Nicaragua [Online]. Available at: https://www.cia.gov/library/publications/the-world-factbook/geos/nu.html [accessed: 10 August 2012].

Close, David. 2004. 'President Bolanos Runs a Reverse: Or How Arnoldo Alemán Wound Up in Prison', in *Undoing Democracy: The Politics of Electoral Caudillismo*, edited by David Close and Kalowatie Deonandan. Lanham, MD: Lexington Books, 167–182.

Close, David and Kalowatie Deonandan. 2004. *Undoing Democracy: The Politics of Electoral Caudillismo*. Lanham, MD: Lexington Books.

CNews. 26 February 2003. 'Germany Rejects Canadian Proposal on Iraq', cnews.canoe.ca [accessed 29 December 2013].

Commission on Human Security. 2003. *Human Security Now: Protecting and Empowering People*. New York: Commission on Human Security.

Cooper, Marc. 2001. 'Plan Colombia', *The Nation*, 19 March, 2001, http://www. thenation.com/article/plan-colombia# [accessed 30 December 2013].

Copley News Service. 6 March 2003. 'Transcript of the president's comments on Mexico', The San Diego Union Tribune website, http://legacy.utsandiego. com/news/mexico/20030306-9999_1n6trans.html [accessed 29 December 2013].

Cordon, Sandra. February 27 2003. 'Chrétien Warns War against Iraq Could Seriously Harm UN', cnews.canoe.ca [accessed 8 July 2004].

Correa, Carlos M. 2000. *Intellectual Property Rights, The WTO and Developing Countries*. London, New York: Zed Books; Penang, Malaysia: Third World Network.

Cotonou Partnership Agreement. 2000, http://www.europarl.europa.eu/intcoop/ acp/03_01/pdf/cotonou_2006_en.pdf [accessed December 30 2013].

Cox, Robert W. 2000. 'Political Economy and World Order: Problems of Power and Knowledge at the Turn of the Milennium', in Stubbs, Richard and Jeffrey Underhill (eds), *Political Economy and the Changing Global Order*, 2nd edn. Don Mills: Oxford University Press.

Cox Robert W. (with Michael G. Schechter). 2002. *The Political Economy of a Plural World: Critical Reflections on Power, Morals and Civilization.* London: Routledge.

CTV News. 27 February 2013. 'US Slaps Down Canadian Compromise on Iraq', www.ctv.ca [accessed 30 December 2013].

Dabene, Oliver. 2012. 'Consistency and Resilience through Cycles of Re-politicization', in Riggirozzi, Pía and Diana Tussie (eds), *The Rise of Post-hegemonic Regionalism: The Case of Latin America.* New York: Springer, 41–64.

Dearden, Stephen. n.d. 'A Critique of the Pacific EPA Sustainability Impact Assessment', www.edpsg.org/Documents/DP33.doc [accessed 30 December 2013].

Demas, W.G. 1965. *The Economics of Development in Small Countries with Special Reference to the Caribbean.* Montréal: McGill University Press.

Deonandan, Kalowatie. 1991. *Religion and the Struggle for Hegemony.* Ph.D. Dissertation. Kingston, Ont.: Queen's University, 1991.

Deudney, Daniel and John Ikenberry. 1992. 'Who Won the Cold War', *Foreign Policy*, 87 (Summer): 123–138.

Deutsche Presse-Agentur. 12 November 2004. '2nd Roundup: Brazil Recognizes China as Market Economy'.

Dinan, Desmond. 1999. *Ever Closer Union: An Introduction to European Integration*, 2nd edn. Boulder, CO: Lynne Rienner.

Diouf, El Hadji. October 2010. 'Why the MFN Clause should not be included in EPAs', *Trade Negotiations Insights*, 9 (8), http://ictsd.org/i/news/tni/87722/ [accessed 30 December 2013].

Dollar, David and Aart Kraay. 2001. Cited in Julio J. Nogues, 'Reciprocity in the FTAA: The Roles of Market Access, Institutions and Negotiating Capacity'. INTAL – ITDD – STA working paper, SITI-02, 2003.

Dollar, David and Aart Kraay. 2002. 'Spreading the Wealth', *Foreign Affairs*, 81 (1) (January/February 2002): 120–133.

Dookeran, W. 2013a. 'The Case for a Caribbean Convergence Model', *Caribbean Journal of International Relations & Diplomacy*, 1 (1): 127–131.

Dookeran, W. 2013b. 'Proposal for a New Convergence Model for the Caribbean Sub-Region'. Address to the 31st Meeting of the CARICOM Council, Georgetown, Guyana 14 January.

Doyle, Michael. 2005. 'The Three Pillars of the Liberal Peace', *American Political Science Review*, 99 (3) (August): 463–466.

Duffy, Gary. 2009. 'Brazil to make $10 bn loan to IMF', BBC News, 11 June, http://news.bbc.co.uk/2/hi/business/8094402.stm [accessed: 2 August 2010].

Dumbaugh, Kerry and Mark P. Sullivan. 2005. 'China's Growing Interest in Latin America', Congressional Research Service Report for Congress, 20 April.

Dur, A. 2008. 'Bringing Economic Interest Back into the Study of EU Trade Policy Making', *British Journal of Politics and International Relations*, 10: 27–45.

Dye, David and David Close. 2004. 'Patrimonialism and Economic Policy in the Alemán Administration', in David Close and Kalowatie Deonandan (eds), *Undoing Democracy: The Politics of Electoral Caudillismo*. Lanham, MD: Lexington Books, 119–142.

Easterly, William. 2002. *The Elusive Quest for Growth: Economists' Adventures and Misadventures in the Tropics*. Cambridge, MA; London, England: The MIT Press.

EC Directorate General for Trade. 'Invitation to tender related to a framework contract to provide Sustainability Impact Assessments (SIA) of the negotiations of the ACP – EC Economic Partnership Agreements', http://trade.ec.europa.eu/doclib/docs/2003/april/tradoc_112097.pdf [accessed 30 December 2013].

Eckes, Alfred E. 1995. 'Opening America's Market'. Chapel Hill: University of North Carolina Press.

Economic Commission for Latin America and the Caribbean. 2004. 'Foreign Investment in Latin America and the Caribbean'. May.

Economic Commission for Latin America and the Caribbean (ECLAC). 2010. 'Opportunities for Convergence and Regional Cooperation'. High-Level Summit of Latin America and the Caribbean. Cancún, Mexico, 21–23 February, http://www.eclac.org/publicaciones/xml/5/38525/Opportunities_convergence_regional_cooperation_proposals.pdf [accessed: 18 July 2013].

Economic Commission for Latin America and the Caribbean (ECLAC). 2012. 'Social panorama of Latin America 2012', http://www.eclac.cl/cgi-bin/getProd.asp?xml=/prensa/noticias/comunicados/9/48459/P48459.xml&xsl=/prensa/tpl-i/p6f.xsl&base=/washington/tpl-i/top-bottom.xsl [accessed: 16 July 2013].

Economic Commission for Latin America and the Caribbean (ECLAC). 2012. http://www.eclac.org/cgi-bin/getProd.asp?xml=/publicaciones/xml/2/46722/P46722.xml&xsl=/mexico/tpl/p9f.xsl&base=/mexico/tpl/top-bottom.xslt [accessed: 18 July 2013].

Efird, Brian and Gaspare M. Genna. 2002. 'Structural Conditions and the Propensity for Regional Integration', *European Union Politics*, 3 (3): 267–295.

Efird, Brian, Gaspare M. Genna and Jacek Kugler. 2003. 'From War to Integration: Generalizing the Dynamic of Power', *International Interactions*, 29 (4): 293–313.

Ellis, R. Evan. 2009. *China in Latin America: The Whats & Wherefores.* Boulder: Lynne Rienner Publishers.

Engel, Charles and John H. Rogers. 1996. 'How Wide is the Border?', *American Economic Review*, 86 (5) (December): 1112–1125.

Envío. 2005. 'Nicaragua Briefs: The Mega-Salary Scandal Fueled by World Bank Study'. *Revista Envío*, 291. October [Online]. Available at: http://www.envio.org.ni/articulo/3074 [accessed: 9 August 2012].

Envío. 2011. 'Nicaragua Briefs: Ortega's Illegal Candidacy'. *Revista Envío*, 354. January. Available at: http://www.envio.org.ni/articulo/4297 [accessed: 28 July 2012].

Envío. 2012a. 'Nicaragua: A Rerun with Contradictions Inside and Out'. *Revista Envío*, 366. January [Online]. Available at: http://www.envio.org.ni/articulo/4478 [accessed: 9 August 2012].

Envío. 2012b. 'The Dependence on Chávez', *Revista Envío*, 368. March [Online]. Available at: http://www.envio.org.ni/articulo/4294 [accessed: 10 August 2012].

EPA Watch. 2004. 'Why the EU approach to the EPA negotiations is bad for development', Concord Cotonou Working Group, 23 April, 2004. www.epawatch.net/general/text.php?itemID-166&menuID=28.

Erzan, Refik and Alexander Yeats. 1992. 'Free Trade Agreements with the United States: What's in it for Latin America', *Policy Research Working Paper 827.* Washington, DC: World Bank.

Erzan, Refik and Alexander Yeats. 1992. 'U.S.-Latin American Free Trade Areas: some empirical evidence', in Sylvia Saborio (ed.), *The Premise and the Promise: Free Trade and the Americas.* Washington, DC: Overseas Development Council.

Escobar, Arturo. 1995. *Encountering Development: The Making and Unmaking of the Third World.* New Jersey: Princeton University Press.

Esserman, Susan and Robert Howse. 2003. 'The WTO on Trial', *Foreign Affairs*, January/February 2003: 130–140.

EurActive. 2010. 'Farmers oppose relaunch of EU-Mercosur Trade Talks'. 18 May, http://www.euractiv.com/en/cap/farmers-oppose-relaunch-eu-mercosur-trade-talks-news-494278 [accessed: 23 August 2010].

Europa, Press Release Rapid. 2010. 'Vice President Kallas leads high-level delegation to the EU-Latin America civil aviation summit', 21 May, http://

europa.eu/rapid/pressReleasesAction.do?reference=IP/10/591&type=HTML [accessed: 21 August 2010].

European Commission. 2010. EU-LAC Madrid Summit, 18 May 2010, http://ec.europa.eu/external_relations/lac/index_en.htm [accessed: 23 August 2010].

European Commission. Trade Policy Regions, http://ec.europa.eu/trade/wider-agenda/development/economic-partnerships/negotiations-and-agreements/#caribbean [accessed: 21 August 2010].

Eurostat. 2005. 'EU Bilateral Trade and Trade with the World: MERCOSUR', http://trade-info.cec.eu.int/doclib/html/113488.htm [accessed 26 December 2013].

Falk, Richard. 1998. 'The Coming Global Civilization: Neo-Liberal or Humanist', in A. Anghie and G. Sturgess (eds), *Legal Visions of the 21st Century: Essays in Honour of Judge Christopher Weeramantry*. The Hague: Kluwer.

Fawcett, Louise. 1996. 'Regionalism in Historical Perspective', in Louise Fawcett and Andrew Hurrell (eds), *Regionalism in World Politics: Regional Organization and International Order*. Oxford; New York: Oxford University Press.

Feinberg, Richard E. 1997. *Summitry in the Americas: A Progress Report*. Washington, DC: Institute for International Economics.

Feinberg, Richard. 2007. 'Latin American and the Caribbean's Response to the Growth of China and India: Overview of Research Findings and Policy Implications; Angel or Devil? China's Trade Impact on Latin American Emerging Markets', *Foreign Affairs*, January/February: 167–168.

Feng, Yi and Gaspare M. Genna. 2003. 'Regional Integration and Domestic Institutional Homogeneity: A Comparative Analysis of Regional Integration in the Americas, Pacific Asia, and Western Europe', *Review of International Political Economy*, 10 (2): 278–309.

Flynn, Stephen. 2009. 'Homeland Insecurity: Disaster at DHS', *American Interest*, 4 (5), May/June: 19–26.

Ford, Jess T. 2006. Director, International Affairs and Trade, GAO, Testimony Before the Committee on Government Reform, House of Representatives, 4 April, 2006.

Ford-Smith, Honor. 2012. 'A Tribute to Rex Nettleford', http://www.bahamasun censored.com/NettlefordTribute.html [accessed: 14 July 2012].

Foreign Investment Administration, Ministry of Commerce of the People's Republic of China. 2003. 2003 Niandu Zhongguo, Duiwai Zhije, Touzi Tongii Gongbao, China's Outward Foreign Direct Investment Statistics. 17 May, 2005, http://www.fdi.gov.cn/common/info.jsp?id=ABC00000000000020810 [accessed 30 December 2013].

Forero, Juan. 2009. 'South American Leaders Assail US Access to Colombian Military Bases', *The Washington Post*, 29 August.

Foster, J. 2010. 'Obama, Canada and Civil Society South and North', in *Canada-Watch (Ottawa)*, Fall 2010, 1–6.

Fox News Latino. 2011. Ortega Sweeps Nicaragua's Presidential Election. 7 November [Online]. Available at: http://latino.foxnews.com/latino/politics/2011/11/07/ortega-sweeps-nicaraguas-presidential-election/ [accessed: 14 August 2012].

France 24. 2010. 'EU and Mercosur attempt to revive deadlocked trade talks'. 17 May 2010, http://www.france24.com/en/20100517-eu-mercosur-trade-talks-zapatero-business-americas-europe [accessed: 23 August 2010].

Frankel, J.A. 1996. *Regional Trading Blocs*, Institute for International Economics, Washington, DC.

Free Trade Area of the Americas (FTAA). 2003. 'Third Draft FTAA Agreement', http://www.ftaa-alca.org/FTAADraft03/Index_e.asp [accessed 26 December 2013].

Free Trade Area of the Americas (FTAA). 2005. 'Hemispheric Trade and Tariff Database', www.ftaa-alca.org/NGROUPS/NGMADB_E.asp [accessed 30 December 2013].

Freedman, Lawrence. 1983. *The Evolution of Nuclear Strategy.* New York: St Martin's Press.

Frey M. and G. Friesen. 2005. In Lothar Honnighausen, et al. (eds), *Regionalism in the Age of Globalism. Vol. I Concepts of Regionalism*. Madison, Wisconsin: University of Wisconsin Press.

Frieden, Jeffry A. 1991. *Debt, Development, and Democracy: Modern Political Economy and Latin America, 1965–1985*. Princeton: Princeton University Press.

Frieden, Jeffry A. 1998. 'The Euro: Who Wins? Who Loses?', *Foreign Policy*, Fall, 25–40.

Friedman, Thomas. 2005. *The World Is Flat: A Brief History of the Twenty-First Century*. New York: Farrar, Straus and Giroux.

FTAA, Hemispheric Cooperation Programme. November 2002. 'FTAA Seventh Meeting of Ministers of Trade Ministerial Declaration, Quito, Ecuador', http://www.ftaa-alca.org/ministerials/quito/quito_e.asp [accessed 31 December 2013].

FTAA, Smaller Economies Group. September 2003. 'Jamaica: National Strategy to Strengthen Trade-Related Capacity of FTAA Countries', http://www.ftaa-alca.org/TAssistance_e.asp [accessed 31 December 2013].

FTAA, Smaller Economies Group. October 2003a. 'Nicaragua: National Strategy to Strengthen Trade-Related Capacity of FTAA Countries', http://www.iadb.org/intal/intalcdi/PE/2007/00964.pdf [accessed 31 December 2013].

FTAA, Hemispheric Cooperation Programme. October 2003b. 'National Strategy to Strengthen Trade-Related Capacity, Antigua and Barbuda', http://www.ftaa-alca.org/TAssistance_e.asp [accessed 30 December 2013].

Fukuyama, Francis. 1989. 'The End of History', *The National Interest*, 15 (Summer): 3–18.

Fukuyama, Francis. 1993. *The End of History and the Last Man*. New York: Avon.

Galeano, Eduardo. 2000. *The World Upside Down: A Primer for the Looking-Glass World*, trans. Mark Fried. New York: Metropolitan Books.

Gallagher, Kevin P. and Roberto Porzecanski. 2010. *The Dragon in the Room. China and the Future of Latin American Industrialization.* Stanford: Stanford University Press.

Garrett, Geoffrey and Peter Lange. 1995. 'Internationalization, Institutions, and Political Change', *International Organization*, 49: 627–655.

Gauthier, Alexandre and Raphael Guevin-Nicoloff. 2011. 'Canada Trade and Investment Activity, Canada-US,' http://www.parl.gc.ca/Content/LOP/ResearchPublications/2011-06-e.htm [accessed 26 December 2013].

Gaviria, César, 'Integration and Interdependence in the Americas', Chapter 15, p. 310, http://www.sedi.oas.org/DTTC/TRADE/Pub/Books/Free_Trade/ftch 15_e.pdf [accessed 29 December 2013].

Genna, Gaspare M. 2010. 'Economic Size and the Changing International Political Economy of Trade: The Development of the Western Hemispheric FTAs', *International Politics*, 47 (6) (2010): 638–658.

Genna, Gaspare M. and Taeko Hiroi. 2004. 'Power Preponderance and Domestic Politics: Explaining Regional Economic Integration in Latin America and the Caribbean, 1960–1997', *International Interactions*, 30 (2): 143–164.

Genna, Gaspare M. and Taeko Hiroi. Forthcoming. 'Brazilian Regional Power in the Development of Mercosul', *Latin American Perspectives*.

Gilbert-Roberts, T.-A. 2012. *The Politics of Integration: Caribbean Sovereignty Revisited*. Kingston, Jamaica: Ian Randle.

Gill, Stephen. 2002. *Power and Resistance in the New World Order.* London: Palgrave Macmillan.

Gilpin, Robert. 1987. *The Political Economy of International Relations*. Princeton: Princeton University Press.

Gilpin, Robert. 2001. *Global Political Economy: Understanding the International Economic Order*. Princeton: Princeton University Press.

Girvan, Norman, 2008. 'CARICOM's Development Vision and the EPA: A Fork in the Road'. Public Lecture, The University of the West Indies, Cave Hill, Barbados, April 18.

Girvan, Norman. 2008. 'The Cariforum-ECEPA – A Critical Evaluation'.

Girvan, Norman. 2008. 'Implications of the CARIFORUM – EC EPA', http://www.normangirvan.info/wp-content/uploads/2008/01/girvanimplications epa10jan.pdf [accessed 30 December 2013].

Girvan, Norman. 2009. 'The Caribbean EPA Affair: Lessons for the Progressive Movement', http://www.normangirvan.info/wp-content/uploads/2009/08/pitts burgh-rev21.pdf [accessed 26 December 2013].

Girvan, Norman. 2009. 'Implications of the EPA for the CSME', *Social and Economic Studies*, 58 (2): 91–128.

Girvan, Norman. 2010. 'Are Caribbean Countries Facing Existential Threats?', http://www.normangirvan.info/wp-content/uploads/2010/11/existential-threats.pdf [accessed 31 December 2013].

Girvan, Norman. 2010. 'Technification, Sweetification, and Treatyfication: Politics of the Caribbean EU EPA', *Interventions: International Journal of Post-Colonial Studies*, 12 (1): 100–111.

Girvan, Norman. 2011. 'The Caribbean in a Turbulent World', in G. Mace, A.F. Cooper and T.M. Shaw (eds), *Inter-American Cooperation at a Crossroads*. Basingstoke: Palgrave Macmillan, 60–77.

Girvan, Norman. 2011. 'Santiago's Festival of Fire: Cubans hug up their Caribbean culture', http://www.normangirvan.info/wp-content/uploads/2011/0 7/girvan-santiago-festival1.pdf [accessed 30 December 2013].

Girvan, Norman. 2011. 'Turning to the South? CARICOM, the Southern Cone and ALBA'. Revised version of paper presented at Fundacion Vidanta/FUNGLODE/ CIES/UNIBE Seminar on 'Integracion, Cooperacion Y Desarrollo En El Caribe De La Globalizacion'; Santo Domingo, R.D., 10–11 November, 2011.

Gonsalves, Ralph. 2013. 'An Outrageous Ruling', *Trinidad Express*, 21 October, http://www.trinidadexpress.com/commentaries/An-outrageous-ruling-22870 2751.html [accessed 29 December 2013].

Gonzales, A.P. 2002. CARICOM Report no. 1, Institute for the Integration of Latin America and the Caribbean Inter-American Development Bank.

González, Francisco E. 2008. 'Latin America in the Economic Equation – Winners and Losers: What Can Losers do?', in Riordan Roett and Guadalupe Paz (eds), *China's Expansion into the Western Hemisphere*. Washington, DC: Brookings Institute Press.

González, Gilda and Pablo Guerén. 2003. 'Investigan en Nicaragua y Panamá Aportes de Taiwán, una vieja historia', Al Día (Panama City), 21 August.

Gore, C. 2010. 'The global recession of 2009 in a long-term development perspective', *Journal of International Development*, 22 (6): 714–738.

Government Information Office. 'Foreign Relations', The Republic of China Yearbook, Taipei: Government Information Office, various issues.

Government of Canada, Foreign Affairs and International Trade. 'Foreign Direct Investment (stocks) in Canada', http://www.international.gc.ca/economist-economiste/assets/pdfs/Data/investments-investissements/FDI_by_Country/ FDI_stocks-Inward_by_Country-ENG.pdf.

Government of Canada, Foreign Affairs and International Trade. 2011. 'Canada's State of Trade: Trade and Investment update 2011', http://www.international. gc.ca/economist-economiste/performance/statepoint/state_2011_point/2011_ 5.aspx?lang=eng&view=d.

Government of Canada: Foreign Affairs and International Trade Canada. 'Canada-Caribbean Community (CARICOM) Trade Agreement Negotiations', www. international/gc/trade-agrements-accords-commerciaux/agro-acc/caricom/ index.aspx.

Government of the Republic of Trinidad and Tobago. 2011. 'Statement by Prime Minister, the Honourable Kamla Persad-Bissessar at the Plenary Session of CELAC', 3 December, 2011. http://www.news.gov.tt/archive/index.php?news =10132 [accessed 28 December 2013].

Government of Taiwan, Bureau of Foreign Trade. 'Trade Statistics'. Retrieved.

Gowa, Joanne. 1994. *Allies, Adversaries, and International Trade.* Princeton: Princeton University Press.

Gowa, Joanne and Edward D. Mansfield. 1993. 'Power Politics and International Trade', *American Political Science Review,* 87: 408–420.

The Graduate Institute, Centre for Trade and Economic Integration. 2009. 'The MFN Provision Contained in the CARIFORUM EC Economic Partnership Agreement and its Consistency with WTO Law', http://graduateinstitute. ch/webdav/site/ctei/shared/CTEI/Research%20Projects/Trade%20Law%20 Clinic/The%20MFN%20Provision%20Contained%20in%20the%20 CARIFORUM-EC%20Economic%20Partnership%20Agreement%20 and%20its%20consistency%20with%20WTO%20Law,%202009.pdf [accessed 30 December 2013].

Graham, Edward M. 2000. *Fighting the Wrong Enemy: Anti-Global Activists and Multinational Enterprises.* Washington, DC: Institute for International Economics.

Gramsci, Antonio. 1971. *Selections from the Prison Notebooks,* Quentin Hoare and G. Nowell Smith (eds. and trans.). New York: International Publishers.

Green, Duncan. 1995. *Silent Revolution: The Rise of Market Economics in Latin America.* London: Latin American Bureau.

Green, Penny and Tony Ward. 2004. *State Crime: Governments, Violence and Corruption.* London and Sterling, VA: Pluto Press.

Grieco, Joseph M. 1988. 'Anarchy and the Limits of Cooperation: A Realist Critique of the Newest Liberal Institutionalism', *International Organization,* 42: 485–507.

Griffith, Ivelaw L. (ed.) 2004. *Caribbean Security in the Age of Terror. Challenge and Change.* Kingston: Ian Randle.

Grigsby Vado, William. 2005. 'Why So Little Social Mobilization', *Revista Envío,* 288 (July) [Online]. Available at: http://www.envio.org.ni/articulo/29 88 [accessed: 9 August 2012].

Grinspun, Ricardo and Yasmine Shamsie. 2007. 'Canada, Free Trade, and "Deep Integration" in North America: Context, Problems and Challenges', in R. Grinspun and Y. Shamsie (eds), *Whose Canada? Continental Integration, Fortress North America and the Corporate Agenda.* Montreal: McGill-Queen's University Press.

Grugel, Jean. 2006. 'Regionalist governance and transnational collective action in Latin America', *Economy and Society,* 35 (2) (May): 209–231.

Gu, Yan and Yiyong Yang. 2004. 'Shouru Fenpei Lingyu de Xin Qingkuang, Xin Tedian jiqi Duice (New Trends in Income Distribution and Related Policy Recommendations)', in Ru Xin, Lu Xueyi, Li Peilin et al. (eds), *Shehui Lanpishu – 2005 Nian: Zhongguo Shehui Xingshi Fenxi yu Yuce (Bluebook of China's Society – Year 2005: Analysis and Forecast on China's Social Development).* Beijing: Social Sciences Academic Press, 222.

Gudynas, Eduardo. 2005. '"Open Regionalism" or Alternative Regional Integration?', *Hemispheric Watch*, 26 October.

Guerra de Macedo, Carlyle. 1989. 'Introduction', in H.L Fuenzalida and S.S Connor (eds), *The Right to Health in the Americas: A Comparative Constitutional Study*. Washington, DC: The Pan American Health Organization.

Guo, Delin. 2003. 'Zhongguo yu Weineiruila Nengyuan Hezuo de Qianli (The Potential for Energy Co-operation Between China and Venezuela)', Lading Meizhou Yanjiu, 25, 2, April, 26–30.

Haas, Ernst B. 1980. 'Why Collaborate?: Issue-Linkage and International Regimes', *World Politics* 32 (3) (April), 357–405.

Haggard, Stephan. 1998. 'The Political Economy of Regionalism in the Western Hemisphere', in Carol Wise (ed.), *The Post-NAFTA Political Economy: Mexico and the Western Hemisphere*. University Park: Pennsylvania State University Press.

Hakim, Peter. 2004. 'The Reluctant Partner', *Foreign Affairs*, 83 (1): 114–123.

Halebsky, Sandor and Richard Harris (eds). 1995. *Capital, Power and Inequality in Latin America*. Boulder: Westview Press.

Hampson, F. Osler. 2001. *Madness in the Multitude: Human Security and World Disorder*. Toronto: Oxford University Press.

Harper, Stephen (Prime Minister of Canada). 2011. 'Beyond the Border: a shared vision for perimeter security and economic competitiveness. A declaration by the PM of Canada and the President of USA'. http://pm.gc.ca/eng/media. asp?id=3938 [accessed 26 December 2013].

Harvey, David. 1990. *The Condition of Post-Modernity: An Enquiry into the Origins of Cultural Change*. Oxford: Oxford University Press.

Haveman, Jon D., Howard J. Shatz and Ernesto A. Vilchis. 2005. 'U.S. Port Security Policy after 9/11: Overview and Evaluation', *Journal of Homeland Security and Emergency Management*, 2 (4): 1–24.

Hawley, Susan. 2000. 'Exporting Corruption: Privatisation, Multinationals and Bribery'. Corner House Briefing 19 [Online]. Available at: http://www. thecornerhouse.org.uk/resource/exporting-corruption-0 [accessed: 8 August 2012].

Hay, Andrew. 2013. 'America's Trade Target Lost in Politics', *Reuters*, 28 December 2004 http://www.citizenstrade.org/ctc/wp-content/uploads/2011/05/ reuters_ftaapolitics_12282004.pdf [accessed 26 December 2013].

Hay, C. 2011. 'Pathology Without Crisis? The Strange Demise of the Anglo-Liberal Growth Model', *Government and Opposition*, 46 (1): 1–31.

He, B. and H. Murphy. 2007. 'Global Social Justice at the WTO? The Role of NGOs in Constructing Global Social Contracts', *International Affairs*, 83 (4): 707–727.

Held, David and Anthony McGrew (eds). 2003. *The Global Transformations Reader: An Introduction to the Globalization Debate*, 2nd ed. Cambridge: Polity Press.

Helleiner, Eric. 1997. 'Braudelian Reflections on Economic Globalisation: The Historian as Pioneer', in Stephen Gill and James H. Mittelman (eds), *Innovation and Transformation in International Studies*. Cambridge: Cambridge University Press.

Helleiner, Eric and Andreas Pickel (eds). 2005. *Economic Nationalism in a Globalizing World*. Ithaca: Cornell University Press.

Helliwell, John F. and Genevieve Verdier. 2001. 'Measuring Internal Trade Distances: A New Method Applied to Estimate Provincial Border Effects', *Canadian Journal of Economics*, 34 (4) (November): 1024–1041.

Hendrix, Steven. 2008. 'The Merida Initiative for Mexico and Central America: The New Paradigm for Security Cooperation, Attacking Organized Crime, Corruption and Violence', *Loyola University of Chicago International Law Review*, 5 (2), Spring/Summer 2008, 107–125.

Heron, T. 2011. 'Asymmetric Bargaining and Development Trade-Offs in the CARIFORUM-European Union Economic Partnership Agreement', *Review of International Political Economy*, 18 (3): 328–357.

Heron, T. and G. Siles-Brügge. 2012. 'Competitive Liberalization and the "Global Europe" Services and Investment Agenda: Locating the Commercial Drivers of the EU–ACP Economic Partnership Agreements', *JCMS: Journal of Common Market Studies*, 50 (2): 250–266.

Hettne, B. 1999. 'Globalisation and the New Regionalism: The Second Great Transformation', in B. Hettne, A. Inotai and O. Sunkel (eds), *Globalism and the New Regionalism*. Basingstoke: Macmillan, 1–24.

Hettne, Björn and Andras Inotai. 1994. *The New Regionalism: Implications for Global Development and International Security*. Helsinki: UNU/WIDER.

Hilary, John. 2001. *The Wrong Model: GATS, Trade Liberalisation and Children's Right to Health*. London: Save the Children.

Hix, Simon. 1999. *The Political System of the European Union*. Hampshire, UK: Palgrave.

Holland, Martin. 2002. *The European Union and the Third World*. Houndmills, Basingstoke, Hampshire: Palgrave.

Honnighausen, Lothar et al. (eds). 2005. *Regionalism in the Age of Globalism. Vol. 1: Concepts of Regionalism*. Madison, Wisconsin: University of Wisconsin Press.

Howse, Robert. 2005. 'How to Begin to Think About the "Democratic Deficit" at the WTO', http://faculty.law.umich.edu/howse/ [accessed: 27 September 2005].

Howse, Robert and Makau Mutua. 2000. *Protecting Human Rights in a Global Economy: Challenges for the World Trade Organization*. Montreal: Rights and Democracy.

Hoyt, Katherine. 2004. 'Parties and Pacts in Contemporary Nicaragua', in David Close and Kalowatie Deonandan (eds), *Undoing Democracy: The Politics of Electoral Caudillismo*. Lanham, MD: Lexington Books, 17–42.

Hufbauer, Gary Clyde and Barbara Kotschwar. 1998. 'The Future of Regional Trading Arrangements in the Western Hemisphere,' paper for Michigan State University 10th Anniversary Conference – The US/Canada Free Trade Agreement, 11–12 September, http://ctrc.sice.oas.org/geograph/papers/iie/huf bauer0998.asp [accessed 31 December 2013].

Hufbauer, Gary Clyde and Jeffrey J. Schott. 2002. *North American Free Trade: Issues and Recommendations*. Washington: Institute for International Economics.

Hufbauer, Gary Clyde and Jeffrey J. Schott. 2005. *NAFTA Revisited: Achievements and Challenges*. Washington, DC: Institute for International Economics.

Hufbauer, Gary Clyde and Yee Wong. 2004. 'Grading Growth: The Trade Legacy of President Bush', *Harvard International Review*, 26 (2) (Summer): 72–76.

Huntington, Samuel. 1993. *The Third Wave. Democratization in the Late Twentieth Century*. Norman: University of Oklahoma Press.

Huntington, Samuel P. 1996. *The Clash of Civilisations and the Remaking of World Order*. New York: Simon and Schuster.

Hurrell, Andrew and Louise Fawcett. 1995. *Regionalism in World Politics: Regional Organization and International Order*. New York: Oxford University Press.

Hurt, S.R. 2012. 'The EU–SADC Economic Partnership Agreement Negotiations: "locking in" the neoliberal development model in southern Africa?', *Third World Quarterly*, 33 (3): 495–510.

ICTSD and APRODEV. 2005. 'Benchmark for a Pro-Development Monitoring of EPA Negotiations', *Trade Negotiations Insight*, 4 (4), July–August: 1–3.

Indo-Asian News Service. 2010. 'India-Latin America meet to consider $10.39 billion deals', *Hindustantimes*, 27 April, http://www.hindustantimes.com/ StoryPage/Print/536373.aspx [accessed: 2 August 2010].

Infopress Central America. 1999. *Central America Report*, 14 May.

Infopress Central America. 2000. *Central America Report*, 12 May.

Institute for Policy Studies, Right Web. 2012. 'Profile of Robert Zoellick', 13 September, http://www.rightweb.irc-online.org/profile/Zoellick_Robert [accessed 31 December 2013].

Inter-American Development Bank. 2002. *Beyond Borders: The New Regionalism in Latin America*. Washington, DC: Inter-American Development Bank.

Inter-American Development Bank. 2005. 'Money Laundering: What Do We Know?', in *Unlocking Credit: The Quest for Deep and Stable Bank Lending*, IPES. Washington, DC: Inter-American Development Bank.

International Centre for Trade and Sustainable Development. 2010. 'An Interview with Branford Isaacs, Head of CARICOM's EPA Implementation Unit and Specialist in Trade in Goods, and Ms Allyson Francis, the Unit's Trade in Services and Investment Specialist', *Trade Negotiations Insights*, 9 (10), December, http://ictsd.org/i/news/tni/97942/ [accessed 30 December 2013].

International Centre for Trade and Sustainable Development. 2010. 'An Interview with H.E. Errol Humphrey, Head of the EPA Implementation Unit in

Barbados', 9 (8), October, http://ictsd.org/i/news/tni/87787/ [accessed 30 December 2013].

International Institute for Sustainable Development. 2010. 'EU-Latin America and Caribben Summit Adopts Madrid Declaration and Action Plan'. 18 May, http://climate-l.org/2010/05/20/eu-latin-america-and-caribbean-summit-adopts-madrid-declaration-and-action-plan/ [accessed: 23 August 2010].

Invertia. 2004. 'Argentina, Brazil Agree on Common Strategy in FTAA Talks', *Latin America News Digest*, 16 January.

Investment Commission, Ministry of Economic Affairs, Taiwan. Statistics on Overseas Chinese and Foreign Investment, Outward Investment, Mainland Investment, The Republic of China. December 2004, May 2005.

Isbester, Katherine. 2001. 'Nicaragua 1996–2001: Sex, Corruption, and Other Natural Disasters', *International Journal*, 56 (4), 632–648.

James, C.L.R. 1935. *World Revolution 1917–1936: The Rise and Fall of the Third International*. London: Martin Secker and Warburg Ltd.

James, C.L.R. 1938. *Black Jacobins: Toussaint L'Ouverture and the St. Domingue Revolution*. London: Martin Secker and Warburg Ltd.

Jasper, William F. 2003. 'Welcome Mat for Terrorists', *The New America*, 29 December 2003, http://www.stoptheftaa.org/artman/publish/article_89.shtml [accessed: 16 October 2005].

Jeffrey, Terrence P. 2003. 'A Case of Selective Enforcement', *Human Events* (14 July).

Jessop, David. 2010. 'What happened to the Cariforum-EU EPA?', *Trade Negotiations Insights*, 9 (3), March: 1&3.

Jiang, Shixue. 2008. 'Three Factors in recent development of Sino-Latin American Relations', in Cynthia Aranson, Mark Mohr, and Riordan Roett (eds), *Enter the Dragon? China's Presence in Latin America*. Washington, DC: Woodrow Wilson International Centre for Scholars.

Jiang, Shixue. n.d.(a). 'Latin American Studies in China: An Overview', http://www.cesla.uw.edu.pl/cesla/images/stories/wydawnictwo/czasopisma/Revista/Revista_6/277-281_Debates.pdf [accessed 29 December 2013].

Jiang, Shixue. n.d.(b). 'Sino-Latin American Relations: Perspectives on the Past and Prospects for the Future', http://www.cass.net.cn/chinese/s27_lms/ESPANA/TRABAJOS/RELACIONES%20DIPLOMATICAS/perspective.htm.

Jiang, Wenran. 'China and India come to Latin America for Energy', http://www.china.ualberta.ca/publication.cfm [accessed: 15 June 2010].

Johnson, Allen F. 2003. 'Statement before Senate Committee on Foreign Relations, Subcommittee on Western Hemisphere, Peace Corps, and Narcotics Affairs'. United States Senate. 20 May.

Johnson, Tim. 2005. 'The Chinese Boom', *Knight Ridder News Service*. 10 July.

Judson, Fred. 2003. 'For an Eclectic and Critical Political Economy Perspective on Canadian Foreign Economic Policy', *Studies in Political Economy*, 71/72 Autumn 2003/Winter 2004: 109–132.

Judson, Fred. 2005. 'Components of the Emergent Global Security Regime', *Review of Constitutional Studies*, 10 (1 and 2) (2005): 21–43.

Julian, Melissa. 2005. 'EPA Negotiations Update', *Trade Negotiations Insights*. July–August, 4 (4): 6–7.

Julian, Melissa and Melissa Dalleau. 2011. 'EPA Update', *Trade Negotiations Insights*, 10 (4), June: 14–15.

Julio J. Nogues. 2003. 'Reciprocity in the FTAA: The Roles of Market Access, Institutions and Negotiating Capacity' (INTAL-ITD-STA working paper-SITI-02, 2003).

Kacowicz, Arie M. 1998. *Regionalisation, Globalisation and Nationalism: Converging, Diverging or Overlapping?* Notre Dame: The Helen Kellogg Institute for International Studies.

Kaieteur News. 2012. 'Whither goest CARICOM?', Georgetown, Guyana, 3 July.

Katzenstein, Peter J. 2005. *A World of Regions: Asia and Europe in the American Imperium*. Ithaca: Cornell University Press.

Kaul, Inge et al. 2003. *Providing Global Public Goods: Managing Globalization.* New York: Oxford University Press/UNDP.

Kaul, Inge, I. Grunberg and M. Stern. 1999. 'Defining Global Public Goods', in I. Kaul, I. Grunberg and M. Stern (eds), *Global Public Goods: International Cooperation in the 21st Century*. New York: Oxford University Press/UNDP.

Kellogg, Paul. 2007. 'Regional Integration in Latin America: Dawn of an Alternative to Neoliberalism?', *New Political Science*, 29 (2), June: 187–209.

Kennedy, Paul M. 1987. *The Rise and Fall of the Great Powers: Economic Change and Military Conflict from 1500 to 2000*. New York: Random House, 447–457.

Kent, K. 2005. EU Trade Policy Making: What Role for Civil Society? Institut Europeen de Hautes Etudes Internationales, http://www.ie-ei.eu/IE-EI/Res sources/file/memoires/2005/KENT.pdf [accessed 30 December 2013].

Kettl, Donald. 2004. *System Under Stress: Homeland Security and American Politics*. Washington, DC, Congressional Quarterly Press.

Kim, Samuel S. 1994. 'China's International Organisational Behaviour', in Thomas W. Robinson and David Shambaugh (eds), *Chinese Foreign Policy: Theory and Practice*. Oxford: Clarendon Press, 431.

Kim, Samuel. 2004. 'Regionalisation and Regionalism in East Asia', *Journal of East Asian Studies*, 4: 39–67.

Klein, Naomi. 2003. 'The Rise of the Fortress Continent', *The Nation*, 276 (4), January 16.

Knight, W. Andy. 1996. 'Towards a Subsidiarity Model for Peacemaking and Preventive Diplomacy: Making Chapter VIII of the UN Charter Operational', *Third World Quarterly*, 17 (1), March: 31–52.

Krasner, Stephan. 1976. 'State Power and the structure of International Trade', *World Politics*, 28: 317–347.

Krugman, Paul. 1993. 'On the Relationship Between Trade Theory and Location Theory', *Review of International Economics*, 1 (2): 110–122.

Krugman, Paul R. and Maurice Obstfeld. 2002. *International Economics: Theory and Policy*, 6th edn. Boston: Addison Wesley.

Kus, Basak. 2006. 'Neoliberalism, Institutional Change and the Welfare State: The Case of Britain and France', *International Journal of Comparative Sociology*, 47 (6) (December): 488–525.

La Jornada. 19 March 2003. 'EU, "decepcionado" de México y Canadá', *La Jornada*.

Lamming, George. 1995. *Coming, Coming, Coming Home: Conversations II*. St Martin: House of Nehesi Publishers.

Lamy, Pascal. 2005. 'Trade is "fundamental tool" in fight against poverty', October, http://www.wto.org/english/news_e/sppl_e/sppl05_e.htm [accessed 30 December 2013].

Lang, Andrew. 2011. *World Trade Law After Neo Liberalism: Re-Imagining the Global Economic Order*. Oxford: Oxford University Press.

Lantis, Jeffrey S. 2009. 'Strategic Culture: A Multifaceted Cultural Approach to the Study of Latin America'. Paper presented to the FIU-SOUTHCOM Academic Consortium, Florida International University.

Larner, Wendy and William Walters. 2002. 'The Political Rationality of "New Regionalism". Toward a Genealogy of Region', in *Theory and Society*, 31: 391–432.

Latin American and Caribbean Unity Summit Declaration. 2010. http://www.europarl.europa.eu/intcoop/eurolat/key_documents/cancun_declaration_2010_en.pdf [accessed 26 December 2013].

Latin American Integration Association (Aladi) Handbook. 2007. International Business Publications.

Latin American Research Group, China Institutes of Contemporary International Relations. 2004. 'Zhongguo dui Lading Meizhou Zhengce Yanjiu Baogao (Research Report on China's Policy towards Latin America)', Xiandai Guoji Guanxi, 4, p. 5 and 11.

Latin Business Chronicle. 2006. 'US-Latin Trade Boom', March, www.latinbusinesschronicle.com/reports/reports/0306/trade.htm#chi [accessed: 21 July 2010].

Latin News Daily. 14 June 2004. 'Brazil: Breakthrough in Mercosur-EU Negotiations'.

Layne, Christopher. 1994. 'Kant or Cant: The Myth of the Democratic Peace', *International Security*, 19 (2) (Fall): 5–49.

Lecomte, Henri-Bernard Solignac. October 2001. 'Effectiveness of Developing Country Participation in ACP-EU Negotiatons'. London: Overseas Development Institute.

Lee, Hau and Seungjin Whang. 2005. 'Higher Supply Chain Security with Lower Cost: Lessons from Total Quality Management', *International Journal of Production Economics*, 96 (3) (June): 289–300.

Legler, Thomas. 2010. Multilateralism and Regional Governance in the Americas in 'Latin American Multilateralism: New Directions'. Canadian Foundation for the Americas – FOCAL.

Lemke, Douglas. 1996. 'Small States and War', in Jacek Kulger and Douglas Lemke (eds), *Parity and War*. Ann Arbor, MI: University of Michigan Press.

Lewis, Patsy. 1998. 'Making a Better Banana Farmer: Restructuring the Windward Islands Banana Industry', *Caribbean Dialogue*, 4 (3 and 4), July/December: 1–19.

Lewis, Patsy. 2000. 'A Future for Windward Islands Bananas? Challenge and Prospect', *Journal of Commonwealth and Comparative Politics*, 38 (2) (July): 51–72.

Lewis, Patsy. 2005. 'Unequal Negotiations: Small States in the New Global Economy', *Journal of Eastern Caribbean States*, 30 (1): 54–107.

Lewis, Patsy. 2010. 'Implications of the Global Crisis for Caribbean Regional Integration', *Global Development Studies*, 6 (1–2), Winter–Spring: 1–28.

Lewis, Patsy, Patricia Northover, Lucy Eugene and Don Marshall. 2003. 'The Future of Special and Differential Treatment in The Free Trade Area of the Americas', in ACS Secretariat, *Studies on Special and Differential Treatment and Evaluation of International Competitiveness.*

Lewis, V.A. 2006. 'Managing Mature Regionalism: Regional Governance in the Caribbean Community'. St Augustine, Trinidad: Report of the Technical Working Group on Governance Appointed by CARICOM Heads of Government. http://www.caricom.org/jsp/community/twg_governance_report.pdf [accessed 30 December 2013].

Li, Mingde. 2001. 'Shiji Zhijiao de Lading Meizhou he Zhongla Guanxi Gaishu (A General Summary of Latin America and Sino-Latin American Relations at the Turn of the Century)', in Mingde Li (ed.), *Lading Meizhou he Zhongla Guanxi – Xianzai yu Weilai (Latin America and Sino-Latin American Relations – Present and Future)*. Beijing: Shishi Chubanshe, 13–15.

Liu, Yuqin. 2003. 'Friendly and Co-operative Relations between China and Latin American and Caribbean countries & China's Foreign Policy towards Latin America', International Understanding (Beijing), 2, 11–16.

Lloyd, Vincent and Robert Weissman, 'Against the Workers: How IMF and World Bank Policies Undermine Labor Power and Rights,' 22 (9) (September 2001), http://www.multinationalmonitor.org/mm2001/092001/lloyd.html [accessed 29 December 2013].

Luft, Gal. 2005. 'In search of crude China goes to the Americas', Institute for the Analysis of Global Security, *Energy Security*, 18 January, www.iags.org/n0118041.htm [accessed: 21 July 2010].

Luis Rocha, José. 2002. 'Micro-salaries and Mega-salaries: Mega-inequality and Micro-development'. *Revista Envío*, 248 (March) [Online]. Available at: http://www.envio.org.ni/articulo/1566 [accessed: 28 July 2012].

Luis Rocha, José. 2005. 'Traido: A Key to Youth Gang Continuity', *Revista Envío*, 288 (July) [Online]. Available at: http://www.envio.org.ni/articulo/2990 [accessed: 10 August 2012].

Lull, James. 2012. 'Our North America: A Continent of Cultural Change', in Castro-Rea, Julián (ed.), *Our North America: From Turtle Island to the Security and Prosperity Partnership.* Farnham: Ashgate.

Ma, Zhongyuan. 1998. 'Zhongguo Zuochu "Jingji Anquan" Zhanlue Juece (China Has Developed a Policy Concerning an "Economic Security" Strategy)', *The Mirror* (a Hong Kong Chinese monthly), 255, 32–34.

McCallum, John. 1995. 'National Borders Matter: Canada-U.S. Regional Trade Patterns', *American Economic Review*, 85 (3) (June): 615–623.

McDonald, Patrick. 2004. 'Peace Through Trade or Free Trade?', *Journal of Conflict Resolution*, August, 48 (4): 547–572.

McMichael, Philip. 2004. *Development and Social Change: A Global Perspective*, 3rd ed. London; New Delhi: Pine Forge Press.

McMurtry, Robert. 1999. *The Cancer Stage of Capitalism.* London: Pluto Press.

McQueen, M, C. Phillips, D. Hallan and A. Swinbank. 1997. 'ACP-EU Trade and Aid Co-operation', paper prepared for the summit of ACP Heads of States and Governments, Libreville, Gabon, 6–7 November. www.acpsec.org [accessed 30 December 2013].

McRae, R. and D. Hubert. 2001. *Human Security and the New Diplomacy: Protecting People, Promoting Peace.* Montreal: McGill-Queen's University Press.

Magalhães, Marcos. 2012. 'Brazil has credentials for a permanent seat at the United Nations Security Council, Ambassador says', *Portal de Noticias*, 30 November.

Magee, Stephen P., William A. Brock and Leslie Young. 1989. *Black Hole Tariffs and Endogenous Policy Theory: Political Economy in General Equilibrium.* Cambridge: Cambridge University Press.

Main, Alex. 2010. 'Latin America and Caribbean: CELAC Steams Ahead', 18 July, *MRZine*, 18 July, http://mrzine.monthlyreview.org/2010/main180710.html [accessed 31 December 2013].

Maira, Luis. 1983. 'Caribbean State Systems and Middle-Status Powers', in P. Henry and C. Stone (eds), *The Newer Caribbean, Democracy and Development.* Philadelphia: Institute for the Study of Human Issues, 181.

Malhotra, Kamal. 2003. *Making Global Trade Work for the Poor.* London: Earthscan.

Mancini, Claudia. 22 July 2004. 'Mercosur Suspends Negotiations for Commercial Agreement with European Union'. *Gazeta Mercantil.*

Mandelson, Peter. 6 January, 2005. 'Putting Development first: EU-ACP relations, EPAs and the Doha Round'. Georgetown, Guyana. Ref: SP05-202 EN.

Mandelson, Peter. 2006. Speech by European Union Trade Commissioner at the School of Economics and International Relations, Sao Paolo, Brazil, 11 September, 2006.

Mansfield, Edward D. 2003. 'Preferential Peace: Why Preferential Trading Arrangements Inhibit Interstate Conflict', in E.D. Mansfield and B.M. Pollins (eds), *Economic Interdependence and International Conflict: New*

Perspectives on an Enduring Debate. Ann Arbor: The University of Michigan Press.

Mansfield, Edward D. and Rachel Bronson. 1997. 'The Political Economy of Major-Power Trade Flows', in Edward D. Mansfield and Helen V. Milner (eds), *The Political Economy of Regionalism*. New York: Columbia University Press.

Mansfield, Edward D. and J.C. Pevehouse. 2000. 'Trade Blocs, Trade Flows, and International Conflict', *International Organization*, 54 (4): 775–808.

Marguerite Mendel and Daniel Salée (eds). 1991. *The Legacy of Karl Polanyi: Market, State and Society at the End of the Twentieth Century*. London: Macmillan.

Marsh, Steve and Hans Mackenstein. 2005. *The International Relations of the European Union*. Harlow, UK: Pearson Longman.

Marshall, D. 1998. *Caribbean Political Economy at the Crossroads: NAFTA and Regional Developmentalism*. Basingstoke: Macmillan Publishers Ltd.

Martí i Puig, Salvador. 2004. 'The External Debt of Nicaragua and the Alemán Liberal Administration: Images and Realities', in David Close and Kalowatie Deonandan (eds), *Undoing Democracy: The Politics of Electoral Caudillismo*. Lanham, MD: Lexington Books, 143–166.

Martinelli, Ricardo. 2010. European Union-Latin America and the Caribbean Summit, 'EU signs with Central America its first region-to-region association agreement', 19 May, http://eu2010.biz/en/cumbre_ue-alc/noticias/may19cen troamerica.html [accessed: 21 August 2010].

Martínez Barahona, Elena. 2012. A Politicized Judiciary, in David Close, Salvador Marti í Puig and Shelley McConnell (eds), *The Sandinistas and Nicaragua Since 1979*. Boulder, CO: Lynne Rienner, 91–120.

Marx, Karl. 1972. 'Economic and Philosophic Manuscripts of 1844: Selections', in Robert C. Tucker (ed.), *The Marx-Engels Reader*. New York: Norton.

May, Elizabeth and Sarah Dover. 2007. 'Breaking the Free Trade Addiction: An Intervention on Environmental Grounds', in R. Grinspun, and Y. Shamsie (eds), *Whose Canada? Continental Integration, Fortress North America and the Corporate Agenda*. Montreal: McGill-Queen's University Press.

Meisler, Stanley. 1996. 'From Hope to Scapegoat', *The Washington Monthly*, July–August.

Mendoza, Ronald U. 2003. 'The Multilateral Trade Regime: A Global Public Good for All', in Inge Kaul et al. (eds), *Providing Global Public Goods: Managing Globalization*. New York: Oxford University Press/UNDP.

MercoPress News Agency. 11 March 2004. 'Mercosur "is more vision than reality" claims EU', http://en.mercopress.com/2004/03/11/mercosur-is-more-vision-than-reality-claims-eu [accessed 30 December 2013].

MercoPress News Agency. 1 September 2004. 'EU blames Mercosur for stalled trade talks', http://en.mercopress.com/2004/09/01/eu-blames-mercosur-for-stalled-trade-talks [accessed 30 December 2013].

MercoPress News Agency. 11 November 2004. 'Latin America Quick to Dance to China's Tune', http://en.mercopress.com/2004/11/11/latin-america-quick-to-dance-to-china-s-tune [accessed 26 December 2013].

MercoPress News Agency. 13 November 2004. 'Brazil Signs Lucrative Deals with China', http://en.mercopress.com/2004/11/13/brazil-signs-lucrative-deals-with-china [accessed on 26 December 2013].

MercoPress News Agency. 17 November 2004. 'China Will Finance Argentine Infrastructure', http://en.mercopress.com/2004/11/17/china-will-finance-argentine-infrastructure [accessed 26 December 2013].

MercoPress News Agency. 11 April 2005. 'Latin America after closer ties with Asia', http://en.mercopress.com/2005/04/11/latinamerica-after-closer-ties-with-asia [accessed 30 December 2013].

MercoPress News Agency. 13 July 2005. 'New EU-MERCOSUR Target: Vienna May 2006', http://en.mercopress.com/2005/07/13/new-eu-mercosur-target-vienna-may-2006 [accessed 26 December 2013].

Mexican Mission to the EU, Representative Office of the Ministry of the Economy. 2012. 'Mexico's Foreign Trade Strengthens Even in World Crisis', *Mexico-EU Trade Links*, Year 12, 2 (February), http://www.economia-snci.gob.mx/sic_php/pages/bruselas/trade_links/ing/febing2012.pdf [accessed 26 December 2013].

Meyer, Maureen. 2011. Elections in Nicaragua. *Washington Office on Latin America (WOLA)*. [Online] http://www.wola.org/commentary/elections_in_nicaragua [accessed 29 July 2012].

Mhur, Thomas. 2010. 'Venezuela and the ALBA: Counter-hegemonic regionalism and higher education for all', http://www.scielo.br/pdf/ep/v36n2/en_a13v36n2.pdf [accessed 26 December 2013].

Miami Summit of the Americas Plan of Action, 1994. http://www.state.gov/p/wha/rls/59683.htm [accessed 30 December 2013].

Mill, John Stuart. 2003. *On Liberty*, David Bromwich and George Kateb (eds). New Haven: Yale University Press.

Milner, Helen. 1988. *Resisting Protectionism*. Princeton: Princeton University Press.

Milner, Helen. 1997. 'Industries, Governments, and the Creation of Regional Trade Blocs', in Edward D. Mansfield and Helen V. Milner (eds), *The Political Economy of Regionalism*. New York: Columbia University Press.

Minister of Sustainable Development, Government of St. Lucia (5 December 2012).

Montego Bay Plan of Action. 2009, http://www.itu.int/ITU-D/finance/work-cost-tariffs/events/tariff-seminars/jamaica-00/The%20Montego%20Bay%20Action%20Plan.pdf [accessed 28 December 2013].

Monterroso, Augusto. 1969. *La oveja negra y demás fábulas*. Mexico City: Joaquín Mortiz.

Montoute, A. 2009. 'Civil Society Participation in Trade Negotiations: A Caribbean Case Study', unpublished Ph.D. thesis, The University of the West Indies, St Augustine Campus.

Moravcsik, Andrew. 1997. 'Taking Preferences Seriously: A Liberal Theory of International Politics', *International Organization*, 51 (5): 513–553.

Mordecai, J. 1968. *Federation of the West Indies*. Evanston: Northwestern University Press.

Morris, Fred. 2011. Nicaragua: The Other Side. *Council of Hemispheric Affairs (COHA)*, 22 December [Online]. Available at: http://www.coha.org/nicara gua-the-other-side/ [accessed: 29 July 2012].

Morrissey, Dorothy. 2001. 'The Cotonou Agreement … Work in Progress', in *The Courier*, 186 (May–June).

da Motta Veiga, Pedro. 1999. 'Brazil in Mercosur: Reciprocal Influence', in Riordan Roett (ed.), *MERCOSUR: Regional Integration, World Markets*. Boulder, Colorado: Lynne Rienner Publishers.

Multinational Monitor. 2001. 'Bearing the Burden of IMF and World Bank Policies: Downsizing, Privatization, Labor Flexibility, Wage Cuts – Selected Summaries of IMF/World Bank Country Policies', *Multinational Monitor*, 22 (9), September. Available at: http://multinationalmonitor.org/mm2001/01sep tember/sep01corp1s.html [accessed: 6 August 2012].

NationMaster. Energy Statistics Oil Consumption (most recent) by country, http://www.nationmaster.com/graph/ene_oil_con-energy-oil-consumption [accessed: 21 July 2010].

Nef, J. 1999. *Human Security and Mutual Vulnerability: The Global Political Economy of Development and Underdevelopment*. Ottawa: IDRC.

The New York Times. 1936. 'League of Nations in Americas urged by 3 Latin states', *The New York Times*, 13 April.

The New York Times. 1936. 'Americas adopt neutrality pact', *The New York Times*, 20 December.

Niebieskikwiat, Natasha. 5 February 2003. 'Brazil's Amorim Wants Strong Mercosur to Negotiate with United States'. *Buenos Aires Clarin*.

Nitlapán – Envío. 2005. 'The Hands that Rock … Just About Everything'. *Revista Envío*, 292. November [Online]. Available at: http://www.envio.org.ni/ articulo/3109 [accessed: 10 August 2012].

Nogues, Julio, J. 2003. 'Reciprocity in the FTAA: The Roles of Market Access, Institutions and Negotiating Capacity', INTAL-ITD-STA Working Paper-SITI-02.

Norberg-Hodge, Helena. 2009. *Ancient Futures: Learning from Ladakh for a Globalizing World*. San Francisco: Sierra Club Books.

NSC (Nicaragua Solidarity Network). 2011. Elections in Nicaragua [Online]. Available at: http://www.nicaraguasc.org.uk/elections%202011/index.htm [accessed: 16 August 2012].

Núñez, León. 2005. 'Alemán Still Controls the PLC and Will Hand Ortega the Victory', *Envio*, 292. November [Online]. Available at: http://www.envio.org.ni/articulo/3111 [accessed: 10 August 2012].

O Estado de São Paulo. 14 June 2004. 'Mercosur, European Union Unlock FTA Negotiations'.

OECS. 2010. 'Revised Treaty of Basseterre Establishing the Organisation of Eastern Caribbean States Economic Union'. Basseterre, St Kitts-Nevis: Organisation of Eastern Caribbean States, http://www.gov.vc/foreign/images/stories/Foreign_Affairs/Article_pdf/revised%20treaty%20of%20basseterre%20.pdf [accessed 26 December 2013].

Office of the United States Trade Representative, Executive Office of the Preident. Free Trade Agreements. 'Mexico', http://www.ustr.gov/countries-regions/americas/mexico [accessed 26 December 2013].

Oncenoticias. 2010. Online service of Mexico City's Canal Once TV channel, http://oncetv-ipn.net/noticias/index.php [accessed: 18 May 2010].

Oppenheimer, Andres. 2013. 'Chávez "revolution" will lose steam abroad, but not at home', *Stabroek News* (10 March).

Organization of American States. 2002. *Inter-American Convention Against Terrorism*, AG/RES.1840 (XXXII-O/02), and adopted 3 June, 2002.

Organization of American States. 2005. *Declarations and Resolutions Adopted by the General Assembly at its Thirty-Fifth Regular Session*, Fort Lauderdale, Florida, 5–7 June, 2005, AG/RES.2137 (XXXV-O/05), OEA/Ser.PAG/doc. 4496/05.

Organization of American States Summit of the Americas Secretariat. http://www.summit-americas.org/previous_summits.html [accessed 26 December 2013].

Organski, A.F.K. 1958. *World Politics*, 1st edn. New York: Alfred A. Knopf.

Organski, A.F.K. 1968. *World Politics*, 2nd edn. New York: Alfred A. Knopf.

Organski, A.F.K. and Jacek Kugler. 1977. 'The Costs of Major Wars: The Phoenix Factor', *American Political Science Review*, 71: 1347–1366.

Oriental Daily News (Hong Kong). 27 May 2004.

Osava, Mario. 28 May 2003. 'Trade-Americas: Brazil and US Face Off in Decisive FTAA Talks', Inter Press Service.

Osava, Mario. 3 November 2003. 'FTAA is the Key for a Mercosur-EU Accord', Inter Press Service.

Osava, Mario. 20 November 2003. 'Trade-Americas: Flexible New Trade Pact Welcome by Most', Inter Press Service.

Osava, Mario. 18 May 2004. 'Lula is going to china, Brazil's Third-Largest Market', Inter Press Service.

Palmer, Norman D. 1991. 'The New Regionalism in Asia and the Pacific'. Lexington: Lexington Books.

Panayotakis, Costas. 2006. 'Working More, Selling More, Consuming More: Capitalism's "Third Contradiction"', in Leo Panitch and Colin Leys (eds), *Coming to Terms with Nature. Socialist Register 2007*. London: Merlin Press.

Panitch, Leo. 1994. 'Globalization and the State', in *Socialist Register 1994*. London: Merlin Press.

Papademetriou, Demetrios G. 2005. 'The "Regularization" Option in Managing Illegal Immigration More Effectively: A Comparative Perspective', *MPI Policy Brief No. 4*. Washington, DC: Migration Policy Institute, September.

Passel, Jeffrey S. 2005. 'Unauthorized Migrants: Numbers and Characteristics'. Washington, DC: Pew Hispanic Center, June.

Pastor Jr., Manuel. 1998. 'Pesos, Policies, and Predictions', in Carol Wise (ed.), *The Post-NAFTA Political Economy: Mexico and the Western Hemisphere*. University Park, PA: Pennsylvania State University.

Pastor Jr., Manuel and Carol Wise. 1998. 'Mexican Style Neoliberalism: State Policy and Distributional Stress', in Carol Wise (ed.), *The Post-NAFTA Political Economy: Mexico and the Western Hemisphere*. University Park: Pennsylvania State University Press.

Patterson, P.J. 2003. 'CARICOM Beyond 30: Charting New Directions'. Montego Bay, Jamaica: Speech given to the 24th Meeting of the CARICOM Heads of Government, 2–5 July. http://www.revistainterforum.com/english/pdf_en/cari comopening2003.pdf [accessed 26 December 2013].

Patterson, P.J. 2013. 'A Cri de Coeur for CARICOM: Lest we Wither on the Vine'. Georgetown, Guyana: Speech Given to the Rotary Club of Georgetown, 28 January.

Payne, Anthony. 1985. 'Whither CARICOM? The performance and prospects of Caribbean integration in the 1980s', *International Journal*, 40 (2): 207–228.

Payne, Anthony. 1999. 'The Remapping of the Americas', review essay, *Review of International Studies*, 25 (3), July: 507–514.

Payne, Anthony. 2008. *The Political History of CARICOM*. Kingston, Jamaica: Ian Randle.

Payne, Anthony. 2009. 'The Missed Opportunity: Building a CARICOM Developmental State', *Brown Journal of World Affairs*, 16 (1): 137–149.

Payne, Anthony and Paul Sutton. 2007. 'Repositioning the Caribbean within Globalization', *The Caribbean Papers – a project on Caribbean Economic Governance*, The Centre for International Governance Innovation, Caribbean Paper No. 1, June.

Pelegri, Anna. 2011. 'New Americas Summit Aims Criticism at US', http://www. google.com/hostednews/afp/article/ALeqM5i6fWdANXBfHxBIyYYUYLzE Xf1auw?docId=CNG.8ad710369797ec2360f737fc0ae5e858.5a1 [accessed 26 December 2013].

People's Daily Online. 14 January 2013. 'Unleash 'China energy' in global governance'.

Pérez Baltodano, Andrés. 2012. 'Political Culture', in David Close, Salvador Marti í Puig and Shelley McConnell (eds), *The Sandinistas and Nicaragua Since 1979*. Boulder, CO: Lynne Rienner, 65–90.

Peterson, V.S. 2010. 'A Long View of Globalization and Crisis', *Globalizations*, 7 (1–2): 187–202.

Petras, James. 2005. *Empire with Imperialism: The Globalizing Dynamics of Neo-liberal Capitalism.* London: Zed Books.

Petras, James and Henry Veltmeyer. 2001. *Globalization Unmasked: Imperialism in the 21st Century.* Halifax: Fernwood.

Phillips, Nicola. 2003a. 'Hemispheric integration and subregionalism in the Americas', *International Affairs*, 79 (2): 327–349.

Phillips, Nicola. 2003b. 'The rise and fall of open regionalism? Comparative reflections on regional governance in the Southern Cone of Latin America', *Third World Quarterly*, 24 (2): 217–234.

Pisani, Francis, Natalia Saltalamacchia, Arlene Tickner and Nielan Barnes (eds). 2007. *Redes transnacionales en la Cuenca de los huracanes: Un aporte a los studios interamericanos.* Mexico City: Instituto Tecnológico Autónomo de México.

Polanyi, Karl. 2001. *The Great Transformation: The Political and Economic Origins of Our Time.* Boston: Beacon Press.

Policy Research Office, Ministry of Foreign Affairs, the People's Republic of China (ed.). 2004. 'The International Situation in 2003', Zhongguo Waijiao 2004 (China's Foreign Affairs 2004). Beijing: Shijie Zhishi Chubanshe, 17–18.

Policy Research Office, Ministry of Foreign Affairs, the People's Republic of China (ed.). Various years. China's Diplomacy, various issues. Beijing: Shijie Zhishi Chubanshe.

Pollard, A. and J. Court. 2005. 'How Civil Society Organisations Use Evidence to Influence Trade Policy Processes: A Literature Review', Overseas Development Institute. Working Paper 249.

Pollard, Robert A. 1985. *Economic Security and the Origins of the Cold War, 1945–50.* New York: Cornell University Press.

Port of Spain Climate Change Consensus: The Commonwealth Climate Change Declaration (November 2009), found at http://secretariat.thecommonwealth.org/press/34580/34582/217482/281109climatechange.htm [accessed 30 December 2013].

Poulantzas, Nicos. 1974. *Fascism and Dictatorship. The Third International and the Problem of Fascism.* London: New Left Books.

Prevost, Gary. 2005. 'Contesting free trade: the development of the anti-FTAA movement in the streets and in the corridors of state power', *Journal of Developing Societies*, 21 (3–4): 369–387.

Public Citizen/Friends of the Earth. 2001. *NAFTA's Chapter 11 Investor to State Cases: Bankrupting Democracy.* Washington: Public Citizen.

Putnam, Robert D. 1988. 'Diplomacy and Domestic Politics: The Logic of Two-Level Games', *International Organization*, 42: 427–460.

Ramcharan, B. 2002. *Human Rights and Human Security.* The Hague: Martinus Nijhoff.

Ramírez de la O, Rogelio. 2004. 'Prospects for North American Monetary Cooperation in the Next Decade', in Sidney Weintraub (ed.), *NAFTA's Impact on North America: The First Decade*. Washington, DC: Center for Strategic and International Studies.

Ramo, Joshua Cooper. 2004. 'The Beijing Consensus'. London: The Foreign Policy Center, 11–13.

Rastello, Sandrine. 2010. 'India, Latin America have "massive" trade potential, IDB says', Bloomberg Business Week, 1 August, http://www.businessweek.com/news/2010–07–27/india-latin-america-have-massive-trade-potential-idb-says.html [accessed: 2 August 2010].

Raveendran, Manasi. 2010. 'Are Brazil and Lula Out of Their Depth on Iran?', Council on Hemispheric Affairs, posted 4 June 2010, http://www.coha.org/are-brazil-and-lula-out-of-their-depth-in-iran/ [accessed 31 December 2013].

Reid, Michael. 1991. 'Vote in US Congress May Hinder President's Attempt to Modernise the Economy', *The Guardian*, 20 May.

Reinert, Erik S. 2007. *How Rich Countries Got Rich and Why Poor Countries Stay Poor*. Public Affairs: New York.

Renmin Ribao (Beijing). 27, 29 and 30 December 2003, and 2 June 2004.

Renmin Ribao (overseas edition). 12 December 2003.

Report of the Appellate Body. 2001. *Measures Affecting Asbestos and Asbestos-Containing Products*. 12 March.

Rice, Condoleezza. 2000. 'Promoting the National Interest', *Foreign Affairs*, 79 (1) (January/February 2000): 45–62.

Richards, Peter. 2011. 'Caribbean struggles to make complex trade deal with EU a reality', 12 May, http://ipscuba.net/index.php?option=com_k2&view=item&id=553:caribbean-struggles-to-make-complex-trade-deal-with-eu-a-reality&Itemid=7&tmpl=component&print=1 [accessed 30 December 2013].

Richards, Peter. 2013. 'Venezuela and Dominican Republic come calling at CARICOM', *Inter Press Service News Agency*, 8 July, http://www.ipsnews.net/2013/07/venezuela-and-dominican-republic-come-calling-at-caricom/ [accessed 29 December 2013].

Riggirozzi, Pía. 2010. 'Region, Regionness and Regionalism in Latin America: Towards a New Synthesis', Latin American Trade Network, Working Paper, April, no. 130, http://www.redlatn.org/wp-content/uploads/2013/03/WP130.pdf [accessed 26 December 2013].

Riggirozzi, Pía and Diana Tussie (eds). 2012. *The Rise of Post-hegemonic Regionalism: The Case of Latin America*. Heidelberg; London; New York: Springer.

RNM, RNM Update 0513, 'Special Issue: WTO, FTAA, EPA Negotiations – Status and Prospects', 9 September 2005.

Robertson, Roland. 2012. 'Globalisation or Glocalisation?', *The Journal of International Communication*, 18 (2): 191–208.

Robinson, William I. 1996. *Promoting Polyarchy: Globalization, Intervention and US Hegemony*. Cambridge: Cambridge University Press.

Robinson, William I. 2004. *A Theory of Global Capitalism: Production, Class and State in a Transnational World*. Baltimore: Johns Hopkins University Press.

Rodriguez, Emilio Jorge. 2010. 'Introduction and Notes', in *Corazon de Pelicano/ Pelican Heart: An Anthology of Poems by Lasana M. Sekou*. Trans. Maria Teresa Ortega. St Martin: House of Nehesi Publishers.

Rodrik, Dani. 2000. 'Governance of Economic Globalization', in Joseph S. Nye and John D. Donahue (eds), *Governance in a Globalizing World*. Washington, DC: Brookings Institution.

Rodrik, Dani. 2000. 'How Far Will International Economic Integration Go?', *Journal of Economic Perspectives*, 14 (Winter 2000): 177–186.

Rogers, Tim. 2012. Nicaragua Sets Pace for Region Under CAFTA. 11 May [Online]. Available at: http://www.ticotimes.net/Region/Nicaragua-sets-pace-for-region-under-CAFTA_Friday-May-11-2012 [accessed 28 December 2013].

Rogowski, Ronald. 1989. *Commerce and Coalitions: How Trade Affects Domestic Political Alignments*. Princeton, NJ: Princeton University Press.

van Roozendaal, Gerda. 2006. 'Regional policy in the Americas: The EU experience as a guide for north-South integration?' *Intereconomics*, 41 (3): 159–168.

Rosenau, James N. 1994. 'New Dimensions of Security: the interaction of globalizing and localizing dynamics', *Security Dialogue*, 25 (3): 255–281.

Rosenau, Pauline. 1992. *Post-Modernism and the Social Sciences: Insights, Inroads and Intrusions*. Princeton: Princeton University Press.

Rostow, Walt W. 1950. 'The Terms of Trade in Theory and Practice', *The Economic History Review* Second Series, III (1): 1–20.

Rozman, Gilbert. 2005. 'Korea at the Center: The Growing Quest for Regionalism in Northeast Asia', in Armstrong, Charles et al. (eds), *Korea at the Center: The Search for Regionalism in Northeast Asia*. New York: M.E. Sharpe.

Ruggie, J.G. 1982. 'International regimes, transactions, and change: embedded liberalism in the postwar economic order', *International Organization*, 36 (2): 379–415.

Ruggie, John. 1997. 'Consolidating The European Pillar: The Key to NATO's Future', *The Washington Quarterly*, 20 (1) (Winter): 109–124.

Ruiz, Jose Briceno. 2007. 'Strategic regionalism and regional social policy in the FTAA process', *Global Social Policy*, 7 (3): 294–315.

Russell, James W. 2009. *Class and Race Formation in North America*. Toronto: University of Toronto Press.

Saguier, Marcelo. 2007. 'The Hemispheric Social Alliance and the Free Trade Area of the Americas process: the challenges and opportunities of transnational coalitions against neo-liberalism', *Globalizations*, 4 (2): 251–265.

Saguier, Marcelo. 2012. 'Socio-Environmental Regionalism in South America: Tensions in New Development Models', in Pía Riggirozzi and Diana Tussie (eds), *The Rise of Post-hegemonic Regionalism. The Case of Latin America*. Heidelberg; London; New York: Springer.

Sahlins, Marshall. 2003. 'The Original Affluent Society', in Raknema, Majid (ed.) and Victoria Bawtree, *The Post Development Reader*. London; New Jersey: Zed Books.

Salazar-Xirnachs, Jose L. 2004. 'The FTAA and Development Strategies in Latin America and the Caribbean'. Organization of the American States Trade Unit.

Salazar-Xirnachs, Jose L. and Jorge Mario Martinez-Piva. 2002. 'Trade, Labour Standards and Global Governance: A Perspective from the Americas', http://www.ggt.uqam.ca/IMG/pdf/jmsx04_salazar_martinez.pdf [accessed 30 December 2013].

Sanahuja, J.A. 2010. 'La construcción de una región: Sudamérica y el regionalismo posliberal', in Cienfuegos, M. and J.A. Sanhauja (eds), Una región en construcción. UNASUR y la integración en América del Sur. Barcelona: Fundación CIDOB.

Sánchez, Alex. 2008. 'The South American Defense Council, UNASUR, the Latin American Military and the Region's Political Process', in Council on Hemispheric Affairs website, 1 October, http://www.coha.org/the-south-american-defense-council-unasur-the-latin-american-military-and-the-region%E2%80%99s-political-process/ [accessed 30 December 2013].

Sands, Christopher. 2002. 'Fading Power or Rising Power: 11 September and Lessons From the Section 110 Experience', in Normal Hillmer and Maureen Appel Molot (eds), *Canada Among Nations: A Fading Power*. Toronto: Oxford University Press.

Scheman, L. Ronald (ed.). 1988. *The Alliance for Progress: A Retrospective*. New York: Praeger.

Schmidt, Blake. 2011. 'Nicaragua's President Rules Airwaves to Control Image'. *New York Times*. 28 November [Online]. Available at: http://www.nytimes.com/2011/11/29/world/americas/daniel-ortega-extends-control-to-nicaraguas-airwaves.html?_r=1 [accessed: 9 August 2012].

Schulz, Michael et al. 2001. *Regionalization in a Globalizing World*. London: Zed Books.

Schwartzkopff, J. 2009. 'Splendid Isolation: The Influence of Interest Groups on EU Trade Policy', Berlin Working Paper on European Integration, no. 12.

Scollay, R. 2002. 'An Impact Assessment of the Possible Economic Partnership Agreements with the European Union: A Report for the ACP Secretariat and the Pacific ACP States'.

Scott, Bruce R. 2001. 'The Great Divide in the Global Village', *Foreign Affairs*, 80 (1), January/February: 160–177.

Scout, David Clark. 1991. 'US Foresees Foreign Policy Impact of Mexican Trade Pact', *The Christian Science Monitor*, 1 August.

Sen, Amartya. 1999. *Development as Freedom*. New York: Anchor Books.

Serbin, Andrés. 1990. 'The Caribbean: Myths and Realities for the 1990s', *Journal of Interamerican Studies and World Affairs*, 32 (2) (Summer): 121–141.

Serbin, Andrés. 2010. 'Regionalismo y soberanía nacional en América Latina: Los nuevosdesafíos', Buenos Aires: CRIES, Documentos CRIES 15.

Serbin, Andrés, Lanyedi Martinez and Haroldo Ramanzinni (eds). 2012. El regionalismo post-liberal en América Latina y el Caribe: nuevos actores, nuevos temas, nuevos desafíos. Buenos Aires: CRIES.

Sevilla, Christina R. 2004. 'Can the United States and Brazil Spur Free Trade in the Americas?', *The National Interest*, http://nationalinterest.org/article/can-the-united-states-and-brazil-spur-free-trade-in-the-americas-2529?page=show (accessed 16 February 2014).

Shadrina, Elena. 2006. 'Regionalization and Regionalism: Featuring Northeast Asia', *Gendai Shakai Bunka Kenkyu*, 37, December: 403–436.

Shaw, Timothy. 'New Regionalisms at the Start of the Second Decade of 21st Century: Lessons from/for the South?', paper presented at the Institute of International Relations, The University of the West Indies, St Augustine, Trinidad.

Sheffi, Yossi. 2001. 'Supply Chain Management under the Threat of International Terrorism', *International Journal of Logistics Management*, 12 (2): 1–11.

Shepherd, Andrew. 1998. *Sustainable Rural Development*. New York: St. Martin's Press, Inc.; Houndmills, Basingstoke, Hampshire: Macmillan Publishers Ltd.

Shils, Edward A. and Henry A. Finch (eds). 1949. *Max Weber on the Methodology of the Social Sciences*. Glencoe: Free Press.

Shirley, R.A. 2010. 'Whither CARICOM?', *The Jamaica Gleaner* (Kingston, Jamaica, 4 July).

Siles-Brügge, G. 2011. 'Resisting Protectionism after the Crisis: Strategic Economic Discourse and the EU–Korea Free Trade Agreement', *New Political Economy*, 16 (5): 627–653.

Simes, Dimitri. 2007. 'Losing Russia: The Costs of Renewed Confrontation', *Foreign Affairs*, 86 (6) (November/December): 36–48, 50–52.

Simon, D. 1997. 'Development Reconsidered: New Directions in Development Thinking', *Geografiska Annaler. Series B, Human Geography*, 79 (4): 183–201.

Sinclair, Scott. 2010. NAFTA Chapter 11 Investor- State Disputes, http://www.policyalternatives.ca/sites/default/files/uploads/publications/National%20Office/2010/11/NAFTA%20Dispute%20Table.pdf [accessed 26 December 2013].

Sloan, Stanley. 1995. 'US Perspectives on NATO's Future', *International Affairs*, 71 (2) (April): 217–231.

Smith, Adam. 1991. *The Wealth of Nations*. Buffalo: Prometheus.

Smith, E. Timothy. 2004. 'From Miami to Quebec and beyond: Opposition to the Free Trade Area of the Americas', *Peace & Change*, 29 (2) (April): 221–249.

Smith, Neil. 2006. 'Nature as Accumulation Strategy', in Leo Panitch and Colin Leys (eds), *Coming to Terms with Nature. Socialist Register 2007*. London: Merlin Press.

Smith, Richard et al. 2003. *Global Public Goods for Health: Health, Economic and Public Health Perspectives*. USA: Oxford University Press/World Health Organization.

Soderbaum, Fredrik. 2003. 'Introduction: Theories of New Regionalism', in Fredrik Söderbaum and Timothy Shaw (eds), *Theories of New Regionalism: A Palgrave Reader*. Basingstoke: Palgrave, 1–21.

Soederberg, Susanne. 2004. *The Politics of the New International Financial Architecture: Re-imposing Neo-liberal Domination in the Global South.* London: Zed Books.

Soederberg, Susanne, George Menz and Philip Cerny (eds). 2005. *Internalizing Globalization: The Rise of Neo-liberalism and the Decline of National Varieties of Capitalism.* New York: Palgrave Macmillan.

South China Morning Post (Hong Kong). 24 September, 27 September and 2 October 2005.

Spalding, Rose. 2012. 'Poverty Politics', in David Close, Salvador Marti í Puig and Shelley McConnell (eds), *The Sandinistas and Nicaragua Since 1979.* Boulder, CO: Lynne Rienner, 215–244.

Spang, Lyra. 2005. 'IIRSA Projects: Some Facts about the Inter-Oceanic Highway', in Bank Information Center, July, www.bicusa.org/en/article.2226.aspx [accessed 31 December 2013].

'Special Section on what is Human Security'. 2004. *Security Dialogue*, 35 (3): 347–387.

Springer, Hugh. 1973. *Reflections on the Failure of the first West Indian Federation.* New York: AMS Press.

State Statistical Bureau (comp.). *China's Statistical Yearbook.* Beijing: China Statistics Press, 1993, 2003 and 2004.

Stevens, Christopher. 2005. 'The GSP a Solution to the Problem of Cotonou and EPAs', *Trade Negotiations Insights*, 4 (4), July–August: 4–5.

Stewart, Taimoon. 1999. 'CARICOM Competition Policy Regime: Implementation Concerns', *Caribbean Dialogue*, 5 (1 and 2): 139–147.

Stewart, Taimoon. 2004. 'Competition Issues in Selected CARICOM Countries: An Empirical Examination'. Trinidad: Sir Arthur Lewis Institute for Social and Economic Studies, University of the West Indies.

Stiglitz, Joseph. 2002. *Globalization and its Discontents.* New York: W.W. Norton.

Stiglitz, Joseph (with Linda Bilmes). 2008. *The Three Trillion Dollar War: The True Cost of the Iraq Conflict.* New York: W.W. Norton.

Stoneman, Richard, Justice Duke Pollard and Hugo Inniss. 2012. 'Turning Around CARICOM: Proposals to restructure the secretariat', http://www.caricom.org/jsp/communications/caricom_online_pubs/Restructuring%20the%20Secretariat%20-%20Landell%20Mills%20Final%20Report.pdf [accessed 26 December 2013].

Stop the FTAA. http://www.stoptheftaa.org/faq/faq1.html#answer [accessed: 21 August 2010].

Szepesi, S. 2004. 'Coercion or Engagement? Economics and Institutions in ACP-EU Negotiations'. ECDPM Discussion Paper 56, Maastricht: ECDPM.

Ta Kung Pao (a Hong Kong Chinese newspaper). 14 April 1986.

Taiwan Daily News (Taipei). 4 November 2003.

Taiwan Shin Sheng Daily News (Taipei). 22 August 2003.

Talakai, Malia. 2013. 'Climate conversations – small island states need action on climate loss and damage', *Alert Net* (15 January).

Teixeira, Gisele. 13 August 2004. 'Negotiations Between Mercosur and European Union are Interrupted Once Again; Impasse Continues Between EU and Mercosur', *Gazeta Mercantil*.

Theory Talk #37. 2010. 'Robert Cox on World Orders, Historical Change, and the Purpose of Theory in International Relations', www.theory-talks.org/2010/03/theory-talk-37.html, posted 12 March [accessed 16 August 2010].

Third World Network. 2001. 'Latin America: FTAA divides nations and trade blocs', www.twnside.org.sg/title/blocs.htm [accessed: 26 May 2013].

Third World Network. 2011. 'Third World Resurgence: out of the backyard'. 255/256, November/December.

Thomas, Caroline. 2002. *Global Governance, Development and Human Security*. London: Pluto Press.

Thomas, Clive. 2008. 'The CPA A Monumental Deception', *Stabroek News*, January 20, http://www.stabroeknews.com/2008/features/sunday/01/20/guyana-and-the-wider-world-8/.

Thomson, Adam. 2004. 'Granting of Market-Economy Status to China Opens Argentina's Door to Investment', *Financial Times* (London), 18 November.

Thorburn, Diana, John Rapley, Damien King and Collette Campbell. 6 September 2010. 'The Economic Partnership Agreement: towards a New Era for Caribbean Trade'. Report R-10-002. Caribbean Policy Research Institute. www.capricaribbean.com [accessed 30 December 2013].

Thorp, Rosemary. 1998. 'Progress, Poverty and Exclusion: An Economic History of Latin America in the 20th Century'. Washington, DC: Inter-American Development Bank.

TI (Transparency International). 2011. Corruption Perceptions Index: Nicaragua [Online]. Available at: http://cpi.transparency.org/cpi2011/results/ [accessed: 10 August 2012].

Tinoco, Victor Hugo. 2009. 'Corruption is the Most Important Serious Aspect of the Ortega-Chávez Relationship'. *Revista Envío*, 338 (September) [Online]. Available at: http://www.envio.org.ni/articulo/4061 [accessed: 28 July 2012].

Tisdall, Simon. 2012. 'Can the BRICS create a new world order?', *The Guardian*, 29 March.

Topik, Steven. 2001. 'Karl Polanyi and the Creation of the "Market Society", in Miguel Angel Centeno and Fernando López-Alves (eds), *The Other Mirror: Grand Theory through the Lens of Latin America*. Princeton: Princeton University Press.

Transparency International. http://www.transparency.org/whatwedo [accessed 29 December 2013].

Trejos París, María Eugenia and Mario Fernández Arias (eds). 2006. *Tratado de Libre Comercio Estados Unidos-Centroamérica-República Dominicana. Estrategia de tierra arrasada*. San José: EUNED.

Trommer, S. 2011. 'Activists Beyond Borders: Transnational NGOs Strategies on EU West Africa Trade Relations', *Globalisations*, 8 (1): 113–126.

Trucco, Pablo. 2012. 'The Rise of Monetary Agreements in South America', in Pía Riggirozzi, and Diana Tussie (eds), *The Rise of Post-hegemonic Regionalism. The Case of Latin America*. Heidelberg; London; New York: Springer, 101–123.

UN (United Nations) Global Compact. 2004. Transparency and Anti-corruption [Online]. Available at: http://www.unglobalcompact.org/AboutTheGC/The TenPrinciples/anti-corruption.html [accessed: 2 August 2012].

UN Report of the World Social Situation. 2005. The Inequality Predicament, United Kingdom House of Commons International Development Committee, 'Fair Trade? The European Union's trade agreements with African, Caribbean and Pacific Countries'. Sixth Report of Session 2004–05, April.

UNDP Caribbean Human Development Report. 2012. 'Human Development and the Shift to Better Citizen Security'. New York: UNDP. Available at: http://www.undp.org.gy/web/documents/bk/Caribbean_HDR_Jan25_2012_3MB.pdf [accessed 28 December 2013].

UNECLAC. 2002. Globalization and Development. UN Economic Commission for Latin America and the Caribbean.

United Daily News (Taipei). 22 August 2003.

United Kingdom National Archives, CO 295/384.

United Nations Conference on Trade and Development. 2004. *World Investment Report*. New York: United Nations.

United Nations Development Programme (UNDP). 1994. *Human Development Report 1994: New Dimensions of Human Security*. New York: Oxford University Press.

United Nations Development Programme. 2005. 'Human Development Reports'. http://hdr.undp.org/en/data [accessed 30 December 2013].

United Nations Press Release, SOC/4681. 2005. 'United Nations 2005 Report on World Social Situation Finds Much of World Trapped in "Inequality Predicament": World More Unequal than 10 Years Ago'. New York: UN Department of Public Information, News Media Division, 25 August.

U.S. Customs and Border Protection Service. 2002. Trade Act of 2002, Title III, Section 343, Mandatory Advanced Electronic Information for Cargo and Other Improved Customs Reporting Procedures.

U.S. Customs and Border Protection Service. 2004. 'Frequently Asked Questions', Trade Act of 2002 Final Rule, 3 August.

U.S. Department of Homeland Security. 2006. 'Fact Sheet: Secure Borders and Open Doors in the Information Age', 17 January.

U.S. Department of State, Bureau of Western Hemisphere Affairs. 2001. 'Fact Sheet, Plan Colombia', 14 March, http://2001-2009.state.gov/p/wha/rls/fs/2001/1042.htm [accessed 30 December 2013].

U.S. Department of the Treasury, Office of Terrorism and Financial Intelligence. 2006. 'Fact Sheet', April.

U.S. Government Accountability Office. 2005. 'Strengthened Visa Process Would Benefit from Improvements in Staffing and Information Sharing', GAO-05-859, September.

U.S. Government Accountability Office. 2006. 'Homeland Security: Recommendations to Improve Management of Key Border Security Program Need to Be Implemented', February, GAO-06-296.

U.S. Government Accountability Office. 2006. 'Reassessment of Consular Resource Requirements Could Help Address Visa Delays', GAO-06-542T, 4 April.

U.S. Government Accountability Office. 2006. Letter to Loretta Sanchez, Louise M. Slaughter, and John M. McHugh, Subcommittee on Economic Security, Infrastructure Protection, and Cyber Security, Committee on Homeland Security, United States House of Representatives, 25 May, GAO-06-741R.

U.S. Government Accountability Office. 2008. Testimony Before the Committee on Appropriations. United States Senate. *Stabilizing and Rebuilding Iraq. Actions Needed to Address Inadequate Accountability Over US Efforts and Investments. Statement of David M. Walker, Comptroller General of the United States.* GAO, Washington, DC, 11 March. Document Number GAO 08 568T http://www.gao.gov/new.items/d08568t.pdf [accessed 26 December 2013].

Valente, Marcela. 24 October 2003. 'Argentina and Brazil Claim for US Reduction of Farm Subsidies; FTAA Puts Consensus to the Test'. Inter Press Service.

Van Genderen-Naar, Joyce. 2012. 'The Cariforum-EUEPA- Five Years After', Presentation to the ACP-EU Joint Parliamentary Assembly (JPA), Paramaribo, Suriname (27 November).

Väyrynen, Raimo. 2003. 'Regionalism: Old and New', *International Studies Review*, 5: 25–51.

Verba, S. 1967. 'Democratic Participation', *Annals of the American Academy of Political and Social Science* (2): 53–78.

Waltz, Kenneth N. 1979. *Theory of International Politics.* New York: McGraw-Hill Publishing Company.

Wedderburn, Judith. 2011. 'Highlights of the potential gender effects of the CARIFORUM-EU EPA'. *Trade Negotiations Insights*, 10 (4), June: 8–9.

Weintraub, Sidney. 2004. 'Trade, Investment, and Economic Growth', in Sidney Weintraub (ed.), *NAFTA's Impact on North America: The First Decade.* Washington, DC: Center for Strategic and International Studies.

The West Indian Commission. 1992. 'Time for Action: The Report of the West Indian Commission Barbados'.

White House. 2001. 'Fact Sheet on Migration', 5 September.

White House. 2001. 'Joint Statement between the United States of America and the United Mexican States', 6 September.

White House. 2004. 'Fact Sheet: Fair and Secure Immigration Reform', 7 January.

WHO and WTO. 2002. *WTO Agreements and Public Health: A Joint Study by the WHO and the WTO Secretariat.* Geneva: WTO/WHO.

Wilkinson, B. 2012. 'Report: CARICOM Could Collapse by 2017', *The Jamaica Gleaner*, Kingston, Jamaica, 8 March.

Williams, Eric. 1944. *Capitalism and Slavery*. Chapel Hill: University of North Carolina Press.

Williams, Eric. 1955. Constitution Reform in Trinidad and Tobago. Trinidad: Public Affairs Pamphlet No. 2, Teachers' Educational and Cultural Association, 1955.

Williamson, John. 1990. 'What Washington means by policy reform', in John Williamson (ed.), *Latin American Adjustment: How Much has Happened?* Washington, DC: Institute for International Economics.

Winters, Alan L. 1996. 'Regionalism and Multilateralism', World Bank, International Economics Department, International Trade Division. Policy Research Working Paper 1687. http://www.unige.ch/ses/ecopo/demelo/Cd rom/RIA/Readings/Winters96.pdf [accessed 30 December 2013].

Winters, L. Alan. 2002. 'Doha and the World Poverty Targets', World Bank Conference on Development Economics, April. Washington, DC, World Bank.

Wise, Carol and Cinthia Quiliconi. 2007. 'China's Surge in Latin American Markets: Policy Challenges and Responses', *Politics and Policy*, 1: 410–438.

Witt Jr., Joseph A. 1996. 'The Mexican Peso Crisis', *Economic Review*, Federal Reserve Bank of Atlanta, January/February 1996.

Wood, E.F.L. 1922. Report by Honorable MP (Parliamentary Under Secretary for the Colonies) on his visit to the West Indies and British Guiana, Cmnd. 1679. London: HMSO.

Wood, Hon. E.F.L. MP. 1977. Report cited in Elisabeth Wallace, *The British Caribbean: From Decline of Colonialism to the end of Federation.* Toronto: 1977.

World Bank. 1997. *World Development Report* [Online]. Available at: http://www-wds.worldbank.org/external/default/WDSContentServer/IW3P/IB/1997/06/01/000009265_3980217141148/Rendered/PDF/multi0page.pdf [accessed 14 August 2012].

World Bank. 2004. Nicaragua Poverty Assessment [Online]. Available at: http://web.worldbank.org/WBSITE/EXTERNAL/COUNTRIES/LACEXT/0,content tMDK:20405857~pagePK:146736~piPK:146830~theSitePK:258554,00.html [accessed: 8 August 2012].

World Bank. 2010. http://siteresources.worldbank.org/INTPROSPECTS/Resour ces/334934-1110315015165/RemittancesData_Inflows_Apr10(Public).xls [accessed: September 2010].

World Bank. 2011. Nicaragua [Online]. Available at: http://data.worldbank.org/country/nicaragua#cp_wdi [accessed: 2 August 2012].

World Bank. 2013. *World Development Indicators*. http://data.worldbank.org/data-catalog/world-development-indicators [accessed December 26 2013].

World Bank. 'Poverty Analysis', http://web.worldbank.org/WBSITE/EXTER NAL/TOPICS/EXTPOVERTY/EXTPA/0,contentMDK:20040961~menuPK :435040~pagePK:148956~piPK:216618~theSitePK:430367~isCURL:Y,00. html [accessed 16 July 2013].

World Trade Organization. 2002. 'WTO Trade Policy Reviews: European Union'. Washington, DC: World Trade Organization.

World Trade Organization. 2003. 'Day 5: Conference ends without consensus', 14 September, http://www.wto.org/english/thewto_e/minist_e/min03_e/min03 _14sept_e.htm [accessed 31 December 2013].

Wright, Ronald. 2004. *A Short History of Progress*. Toronto: Anansi.

www.trade.gov.tw.

Xiao, Guoliang and Fumin Sui. 2005. 'Chuyu Shizilukou de Zhongguo Jingji – 2005 Nian Hongguan Tiaokong Zhengce Fenxi (Chinese Economy at the Crossroads – Policy Analysis of Macro-Economic Adjustments and Control in 2005)', in Governance in Asia Research Centre, City University of Hong Kong and Centre for Public Policy Study, Chinese Academy of Social Sciences (eds), Zhongguo Gonggong Zhengce Fenxi 2005 (Analysis of Public Policies of China 2005), Hong Kong: City University of Hong Kong Press, pp. 35–39.

Yang, Zhi-min. n.d. 'Challenges of FTAA and China's Responses', http://www. cass.net.cn/chinese/s27_lms/ESPANA/TRABAJOS/ECONOMIA/FTAA.htm, p. 2–3.

Zakaria, Fareed. 1997. 'The Rise of Illiberal Democracy', *Foreign Affairs*, 76 (6), November/December 1997: 22–43.

Zaoual, Hassan. 1994. 'The Economy and Symbolic Sites of Africa', *Interculture*, Winter: 30–39, excerpts in Raknema, Majid (ed.) and Victoria Bawtree, 2003, *The Post Development Reader*. London; New Jersey: Zed Books.

Zeiler, Thomas. 1999. *Free Trade Free World: The Advent of the GATT.* Chapel Hill: University of North Carolina Press.

Zhang, Mingde. 2004. 'Sino-Latin American Rhythm', *Beijing Review*, 47, 48, 2 December: 12–13.

Zhang, Youwen et al. 2004. 'Daolun: Heping Jueqi – Qiangguo Ding Mubiao Tuidong Shijie Gongying (Introduction: Peaceful Rise – Major Power Sets the Objective Pushing for a Global Win-Win Scenario)', in Youwen Zhang, Renwei Huang et al., Zhongguo Guoji Diwei Baogao (China's International Status Report 2004). Beijing: Renmin Chubanshe, pp. 1–15.

Zhu, Wenhui. 2004. 'Quanqiuhua xia Zhongguo yu Lamei Maoyi Guanxi de Xin Qushi (New Trends in Sino-Latin American Trade Relations in the Context of Globalisation)', Lading Meizhou Yanjiu (Chinese Academy of Social Sciences), 26, 3, June, pp. 13–14.

Zoellick, Robert. 1992. 'The North American FTA: The New World Order Takes Shape in the Western Hemisphere', *US Department of State Dispatch*, 3 (15), 13 April.

Zoellick, Robert. 2000. 'A Republican Foreign Policy', *Foreign Affairs*, 79 (1) (January/February): 63–78.

Zoellick, Robert. 2001. 'Countering Terror with Trade', *Washington Post*, 20 September.

Zoellick, Robert. 2002. 'Free Trade, Free People', *Washington Post*, 11 November, 2002.

Zoellick, Robert. 2004. 'Statement of U.S. Trade Representative before the Committee on Agriculture of the United States House of Representatives', 28 April.

Zolotoev, Timur. 2011. 'Latin America unites in new bloc, US not invited', http://rt.com/news/latin-america-celac-bloc-975/ [accessed 28 December 2013].

Index

THE INTERNATIONAL POLITICAL ECONOMY OF NEW REGIONALISMS SERIES

Other titles in the series

www.ingramcontent.com/pod-product-compliance
Ingram Content Group UK Ltd.
Pitfield, Milton Keynes, MK11 3LW, UK
UKHW020402010325
455677UK00021B/590

9 781138 269828